Gabriele Münter
1877–1962

Painting to the Point

Edited by Isabelle Jansen for
the Gabriele Münter- und
Johannes Eichner-Stiftung and
Matthias Mühling for the
Städtische Galerie im Lenbachhaus
und Kunstbau München

Gabriele Münter
1877–1962

Painting to the Point

Isabelle Jansen

LENBACHHAUS
Munich

GABRIELE MÜNTER- UND
JOHANNES EICHNER-STIFTUNG
Munich

PRESTEL
Munich · London · New York

Intro

Plates Section, with Introductions by Isabelle Jansen

Appendix

Preface to the New Edition of the Exhibition Catalogue—*Gabriele Münter (1877–1962): Painting to the Point*

January 2019 marked the end of the touring exhibition *Gabriele Münter (1877–1962): Painting to the Point,* with its last stop at the Museum Ludwig in Cologne. The exhibition had begun at the Städtische Galerie im Lenbachhaus in October 2017 and was on view during the summer of 2018 in Humlebæk, near Copenhagen, at the Louisiana Museum of Modern Art. When we first conceived this exhibition in Munich, we did so with the wish of bringing Gabriele Münter's work closer to the European public outside the German-speaking world. And indeed, this aspiration was fulfilled faster than we had originally hoped. The exhibition was met with great international acclaim, and cooperations between the Lenbachhaus and the Gabriele Münter- und Johannes Eichner-Stiftung with foreign museums began to take shape—due to COVID-19, however, with a partial delay. Thus, in 2022, the Zentrum Paul Klee in Bern hosted the exhibition *Gabriele Münter: Pioneer of Modern Art.* A documentary of the same name by French director Florence Mauro and commissioned by the European television station ARTE accompanied the project.

The Lenbachhaus devoted 2020 to the artist's early studies with the exhibition *Under the Open Sky: Traveling with Wassily Kandinsky and Gabriele Münter.*

Further collaborations with the Museo Nacional Thyssen-Bornemisza in Madrid and the Musée d'Art moderne de Paris are in preparation for 2024 and 2025.

Other institutions have concurrently developed their own projects around Münter's oeuvre. In spring 2023, the Bucerius Kunst Forum in Hamburg will hold the first exhibition dedicated to Münter's portraiture. The Pavillon Populaire in Montpellier, a public gallery dedicated to photography, will devote itself to Münter's photographs from the United States in spring 2024. A selection of these works will be juxtaposed with photographs by the American writer Eudora Welty. Both women captured life in the Southern United States in their photographs, and both began their artistic careers with the use of a camera before turning to a different medium.

For the lasting and broad dissemination of an artist's oeuvre, however, the acquisition of works by museums is crucial. Here, too, we have seen advances. Many museums that house a collection of Expressionist works are finding that they do not own anything by Münter and have begun trying to fill that gap. In 2019, the Museum Ludwig in Cologne acquired the expressive *Head of a Young Boy (Willi Blab)* of 1908. Cat. 90 Also in 2019, the Van Gogh Museum in Amsterdam became the owner of a 1909 landscape, *House in the Winter Sun.* The Musée national d'art moderne at the Centre Pompidou in Paris added two drawings from the 1920s to its holdings of paintings by Münter; already in 2015, thanks to the Société Kandinsky, two paintings by Münter had entered its collection, the first of a French museum. New York's Museum of Modern Art (MoMA) was also interested in this hitherto little-known period in Münter's oeuvre and, thanks to the generosity of Marie-Josée and Henry R. Kravis, has been able to exhibit the 1928 large-format painting *Woman in Thought II* since 2019. Cat. 180

After such intensely productive six years, it was obvious that a revised and updated edition of this 2017 exhibition catalogue was called for. And so we hope that the interest in the art of Gabriele Münter, which still remains far too little known, will continue to grow.

Matthias Mühling

Chairman of the Foundation Board of the Gabriele Münter- und Johannes Eichner-Stiftung, Munich

Director of the Städtische Galerie im Lenbachhaus und Kunstbau München, Munich

Isabelle Jansen

Curator and Chief Executive of the Gabriele Münter- und Johannes Eichner-Stiftung, Munich

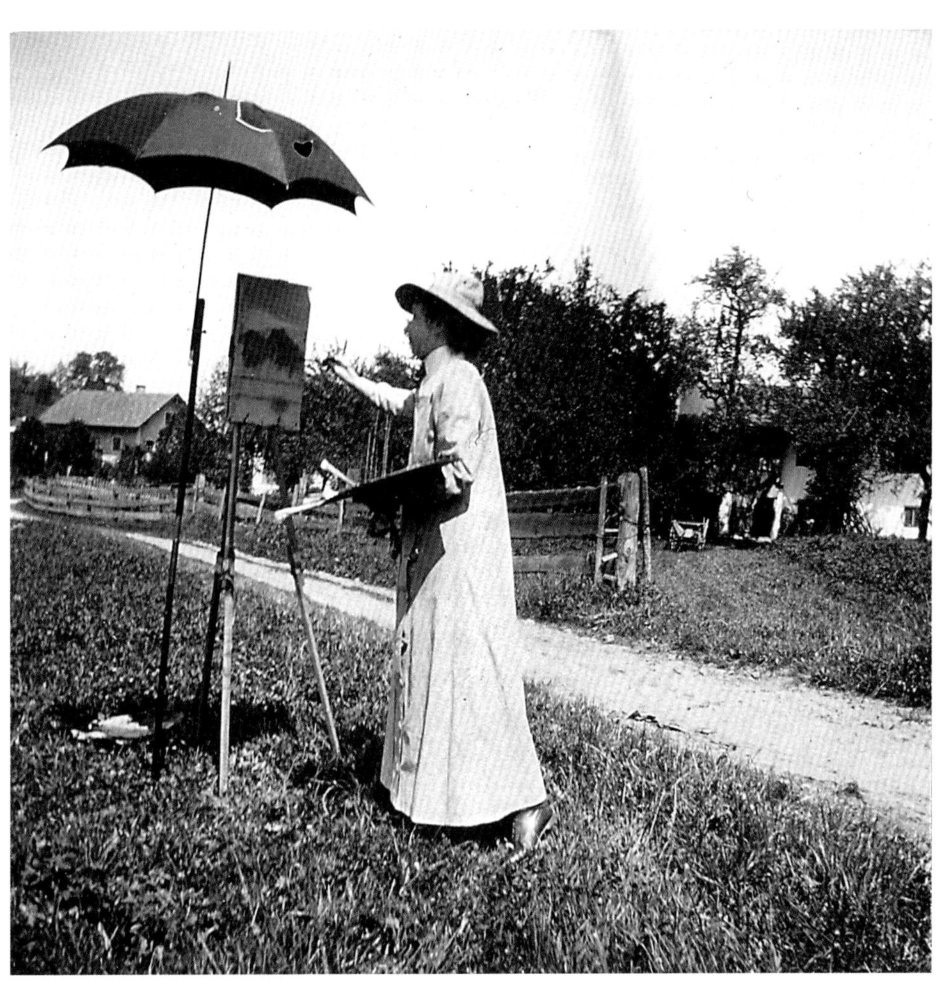

WASSILY KANDINSKY
Münter painting at the easel
en plein air, Kochel, 1902
Photograph | Gabriele Münter- und Johannes Eichner-Stiftung, Munich, inv. no. 2391

Acknowledgments

This publication is based on the exhibition *Gabriele Münter (1877–1962): Painting to the Point* which took place between 2017 and 2019 at the Städtische Galerie im Lenbachhaus und Kunstbau München, the Louisiana Museum of Modern Art, Humlebæk, and the Museum Ludwig, Cologne.

A project of this magnitude could only be realized with the support of many individuals and institutions. We wish to express our sincerest thanks to them all.

The Foundation Board of the Gabriele Münter- und Johannes Eichner-Stiftung, Munich
Matthias Mühling (Chairman), Hans-Werner Hürholz (Deputy Chairman), Beatrix Burkhardt (Representative of the City Council), Alexander Farenholtz

The Münter House in Murnau
Michael Rueß, Ingrid Blank, Angelika George, Hildegard Götz, Kathrin Manusch, Christian Schied

Former Staff Members:
Robert Drexler, Sus Eid, Hanna Glück, Helga Pintsch, Ulrich Ufer †

In addition, we particularly wish to thank the following people:
Frauke Berchtig, Anja Besserer, Andrea Firmenich, Rita Forbes, Helmut Friedel, Dorothee Gutzeit, Katharina Haderer, Sabine Helms, Annegret Hoberg, Micaela Kapitzky, Rupert Keim, Thomas Keller, Robert Ketterer, Cilly Klotz, Ralph Netzer, Tanja Pirsig-Marshall, Brigitte Salmen, Bronwen Saunders, Marieke Schroeder, Bernd Schultz, John Southard, James C. Steward, Katrin Stoll, Sandra Uhrig, and Doris Würgert.

Gabriele Münter (1877–1962) Painting to the Point

"I extract the most expressive aspects of reality and depict them simply, to the point, with no frills. Thus the entirety of the natural manifestation is left unconsidered; the forms gather in outlines, the colors become fields, and contours—images—of the world emerge."[1]

This quote from Gabriele Münter inspired the title of the exhibition: *Painting to the Point*. With these words, the artist reveals her conception of painterly creativity, which is about rendering the essence of a motif as directly as possible. Her paintings capture the world in works of art whose seemingly plain formal language and catchy quality stand in contrast to their complex meaning. Münter's talent for quickly capturing scenes she found interesting—and imbuing them with expressive clarity—solidified into the cliché of the spontaneous, intuitive painter. She gladly accepted this interpretation and made use of its effective power, for the cliché corresponded to the ideals of a European modernism that attributed greater authority to the immediate, the naïve, and the unsophisticated than to the academic and intellectual arabesque. And she used it as a signet for her painting.

Painting "to the point" is above all a concept. "No frills" painting embodies a confident and carefully considered principle of aesthetic design. The former exhibition sought, and the present publication seeks, to emphasize precisely this aspect of conceptual ambiguity—the simplicity of the manifest image versus the complexity of meaning—in Gabriele Münter's oeuvre.

Münter's art is much more complex than it appears at first glance. In order to present this abundant richness, we decided in favor of a thematic organization in which biographical information is used for the purpose of complementing, rather than interpreting, her oeuvre. To this day, her work has been interpreted primarily with reference to the circumstances of her life—a pitfall frequently encountered in the context of research on the work of women artists. This approach is particularly unsatisfying in Münter's case since the artist rarely referred to her personal life in her paintings, even though she often depicted her immediate surroundings. Furthermore, a structure based on a chronological concept would have represented a linear approach to Münter's oeuvre—an approach that implies the principle of development, and thus of progress, which can easily lead to an overly simplistic assessment of an artist's creative process. In our view, a narrative approach to the work of this artist, based on a linear progression, is no longer appropriate; her paintings themselves defy such an approach. Münter often used different visual languages in parallel, which makes it difficult to identify consistent phases in her oeuvre. For her, the expressive aspect of an artwork, and not its form, was critical, and she believed that the resources of painting should be employed accordingly: "I am not committed to a single, sustained mood, and I refuse to cloak the world in preconceived notions."[2]

Paintings from different periods are presented here in ten sections devoted to various themes. This structure emphasizes the production

1
Translated from undated manuscript, MES.

2
Translated from Münter 1948, p. 25.

process and reveals both the diversity and the continuity of Münter's oeuvre. Each section features a specific aspect of her art which, in combination with the others, reflects the complexity of her oeuvre. The different sections should be viewed as aids to an understanding of her art, whereby a given painting could be assigned to several groups at once. In this way, the tension between what appears to have been painted spontaneously and the more profound artistic issues it embodies becomes visible. Münter's fellow artists in the Blue Rider group found this paradox especially intriguing, and it remains a source of great fascination for those who view her works today. This effect is further heightened by the mysterious quality of many of her compositions.

The focus of the 2017–19 exhibition *Gabriele Münter: Painting to the Point* was on painting. Yet Münter's paintings were presented for the first time together with a large number of her photographs from turn-of-the-century North America. It is important to realize that before Münter began painting, she trained her eye on the basis of photographic techniques. She was also a frequent moviegoer, and the new medium had a lasting impact on her perception of the world. Excerpts from a selection of the films she is known to have seen were presented in the exhibition as evidence of this previously unrecognized interest.

In realizing this exhibition, we relied for the most part on the artist's estate, which is managed by the Gabriele Münter- und Johannes Eichner-Stiftung. About 90 of the 132 paintings exhibited were provided on loan by this foundation. Most of these had either never been presented to the public before or were last exhibited during the artist's lifetime. The primary mission of the Gabriele Münter- und Johannes Eichner-Stiftung is to make the works of Gabriele Münter accessible to the general public as a means of promoting the study of her art. One could hardly imagine more fitting museums in support of the exhibition than our partners, the Louisiana Museum of Modern Art in Humlebæk and the Museum Ludwig in Cologne: after growing up in the Rhineland, Münter presented her first solo exhibition in Cologne in 1908 and her first major solo exhibition in Copenhagen in 1918. This catalogue is also meant to serve as a reminder that throughout her lifetime Münter was constantly in search of new personal and artistic points of departure. She lived and worked in many European countries. In addition to her native language, she spoke English, French, Danish, and Swedish. She maintained ties with the leading artists of her time, traveled to many of the art centers of the world, was acquainted with the most important currents of each period, and exhibited frequently from 1907 until the end of her life. In 1950, at the age of seventy-three, she showed three works at the 25th Venice Biennale, and five years later she was represented at Arnold Bode's legendary documenta 1 exhibition.

The goal of the 2017–19 exhibition and this publication is to present Gabriele Münter's oeuvre as a whole in all of its many facets.

Matthias Mühling and Isabelle Jansen

“Visual delight”[1]

Pre-Painting:
Münter’s Early Work

Pre-Painting: Münter's Early Work

Gabriele Münter became famous primarily for her impressive handling of color. Rather less well known is that she discovered the medium of painting almost by chance. Her earliest painting dates from 1902, a full five years after she began studying art. She had taken her first drawing lessons as a private pupil of the portrait and genre painter Ernst Bosch (1834–1917) in Düsseldorf in 1897, but the death of her mother in November of that year led her to abandon her studies. This loss was also the main motivation behind her decision to embark on an extended tour of America that was to have a decisive influence on her future career. Although she did briefly resume her studies at a school for ladies run by Willy Spatz (1861–1931) in Düsseldorf, she and her sister Emmy, who was eight years her senior, set off in September 1898 to visit their late mother's family in North America.[2]

This two-year journey, which would take the sisters from New York to Texas, with stops in Missouri and Arkansas, marks the true beginning of Münter's development as an artist. At some point in 1899 Emmy gave her a camera, a Kodak Bull's Eye No. 2,[3] which she henceforth used so liberally that she did rather less drawing. By the time she returned to Germany in October 1900 she had taken some four hundred photographs, whose artistic quality is all the more astonishing when we bear in mind that Münter had not so much as held a camera, let alone used one, prior to her trip.[4] Thus it can indeed be asserted that the technique of photography helped school her eye: Münter developed a photographic gaze that had an enduring impact on her painting as well. Our exhibition therefore opened with a selection of her photographs of North America, which had never before been shown on such a scale alongside her paintings. As befits the formative role that they played in her development, they were presented as an integral part of her oeuvre and treated as works on a par with her paintings, prints, and drawings.[5] Some of the motifs of the photographs, and even the way the artist approached them, are reflected in the paintings. This kind of continuity is typical of Münter's way of working.

Most of the photographs belong to one of two groups, showing either Münter's family members (indoors or out) or—an even larger group—the American landscape. These two themes would later inform many of her paintings; landscape, in fact, is the genre in which Münter was at her most prolific. But she was also interested in what her relatives actually did and liked to capture them going about their work. Especially worth mentioning here are the images of people working in the fields, whose composition and sheer poetry recalls many a nineteenth-century painting. Cat. 19; 20 The painterly aspect infuses other photographs, too, among them *Woman with a Parasol on the Levee of the Mississippi* and *Woman in Profile, Reading*. Cat. 25; 18

The practice of repeating a specific motif, a creative principle which Münter would uphold her whole life long, is already in evidence in the American photos. *"Jane Lee's 'shanty' in snow while the peaches were blooming," Guion, Texas*, for example, comprises two views of her cousin's log cabin, both shot from the same angle, but one closer to the subject than the other. Cat. 5; 6 Applying the same method of repetition, she photographed the courthouses of the various towns that she visited and so produced a small typological series.

Some scenes, such as the two girls acting out a theater sketch, were photographed in a series of pictures taken just a few seconds apart in order to capture each stage in a sequence of movements. Cat. 8–12 The idea of using consecutive images to reproduce moving subjects recalls the recent invention of cinematography—and Münter did, in fact, become an enthusiastic moviegoer. Her first visit to a film screening is thought to have taken place in Cologne as early as 1900.[6]

Some snapshots, such as *Little Girl in Her Sunday Best Standing on a Street, Back View*, show the same sense of humor that also shines through in paintings like *Listening (Potrait of Jawlensky)*. Cat. 15; 100

1
Gabriele Münter: "Later there was often talk of my affinity with Munch, but it was not about influences, rather about occasional similarities in mood. It is important not to forget that other pictures by me were born simply of unadulterated visual delight, and some have comical traits, too. I am not tied to any one mood and I do not try to make the world fit any preconceived worldview." Translated from Münter 1948, p. 25.

2
Exh. cat. Munich 2006/07, pp. 222–23.

3
On the difficulty of ascertaining exactly when Gabriele Münter came into possession of the camera, see Annegret Hoberg, "Gabriele Münter in Amerika," in exh. cat. Munich 2006/07, pp. 24–26.

4
Isabelle Jansen, "Die Bilderwelt der Amerika-Photos von Gabriele Münter," in exh. cat. Munich 2006/07, pp. 179–87.

5
The photographs were not intended for public consumption, and Münter herself never exhibited them. On the role of photography in her creative process and for an appraisal of this medium as an artistic technique, see Isabelle Jansen, "Fotografieren oder Malen? Das Wechselspiel zwischen Fotografie und Malerei im Frühwerk von Gabriele Münter," in exh. cat. Kochel am See 2015, pp. 151ff.

6
In her diary entry of November 9, 1939, she remarked, "I never cease to be astonished at what has become of the 'cinematograph' of 1899—when I laughed myself silly over those rascals in Cologne." Since she was still in the United States in 1899, the scene described presumably took place a little later.

Münter's photographs of North America are remarkable for the outstanding quality of their compositions. This is even more noteworthy when we recall that cameras in those days had to be held at chest height and hence were not easy for a beginner to handle.[7] Fig. A The lightness of touch with which Münter took to the new medium is typical of her. As an example, her first still life, created in the painting class of Wassily Kandinsky (1866–1944) at the Phalanx School in 1902, is said to have attracted notice all round.[8] Writing retrospectively in 1952, she herself explained that she came to "master color as naturally and effortlessly as the line."[9] This ability, coupled with her capacity to instantly form a mental picture of any scene that she happened to find interesting, meant that Münter never had to go off in search of a motif. As advantageous as these skills were to her work as an artist, they proved problematic when it came to her work's reception, since they reinforced the clichéd view of the gifted woman artist who works intuitively and spontaneously, without any real mental effort—which is a judgment that certainly does not do justice to Münter.[10] Although finding a motif did not pose any real difficulty for her, she still had to work very hard on translating her ideas into paint to produce a result that met her own exacting standards.[11] Significantly, spontaneity and intuition were to become the highly intellectualized principles not only of the Blue Rider group but of modernism generally, whose exponents sought to appropriate the visual language of children, for example. They wanted their paintings to at least look spontaneous, even if they were anything but.[12] This interplay of (illusory) spontaneity and careful planning was a remarkable, indeed a unique, aspect of Münter's work. It was also one that her fellow Blue Rider artists found fascinating.

In April 1901, after returning from North America, Münter decided to move to Munich to continue her study of art, or rather to begin it in earnest. Uninspired by the drawing lessons provided at the Ladies' Academy of the Künstlerinnen-Verein (Association of Women Artists), she tried her hand at the woodcut, a printing technique that was very popular at the time. She learned the technique at a teaching studio run by the famous printmakers Heinrich Wolff (1875–1940) and Ernst Neumann (1871–1954), and it was probably there that she cut her first woodblock, showing a larger than life-size female face. Fig. B This was the only block that she made there.[13]

In the winter of the same year, acting on the suggestion of a fellow lodger at her boarding house in the district of Schwabing, Münter attended an exhibition of an artists' group called Phalanx. There she saw works by the sculptor Wilhelm Hüsgen (1877–1962), which so thrilled her that she decided to learn the

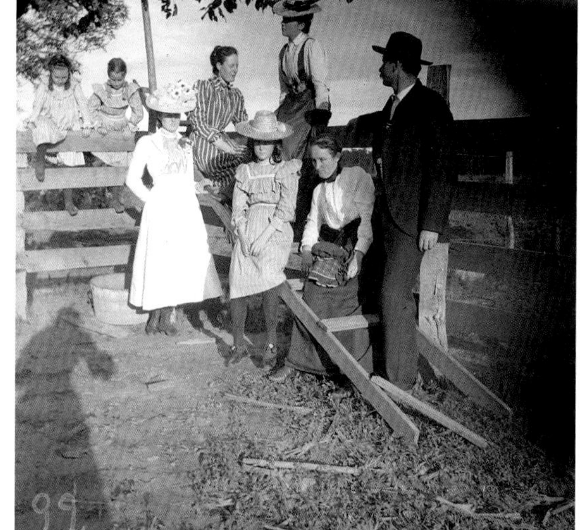

A **Family Group at a Wooden Fence, Marshall, Texas, 1899/1900**
Photograph by Gabriele Münter | Gabriele Münter- und Johannes Eichner-Stiftung, Munich, inv. no. 3607

7
On Gabriele Münter's handling of the camera, see Daniel Oggenfuss, "Kamera- und Verfahrenstechnik der Amerika-Photographien Gabriele Münters," in exh. cat. Munich 2006/07, p. 191. On the Kodak Bull's Eye No. 2 as a camera, see Ulrich Pohlmann, "Die Fragilität des Augenblicks. Gabriele Münters Photographien der USA-Reise im Spiegel der zeitgenössischen (Moment)Photographie," also in exh. cat. Munich 2006/07, pp. 205–6.

8
Eichner 1957, p. 39.

9
Translated from Münter 1952a, n.p.

10
Curiously, Münter herself helped spread this myth. For example, she once claimed, "My pictures are all moments of my life, I mean instantaneous visual experiences, generally noted very rapidly and spontaneously." Quoted in Roditi 1960, p. 148. See also Windecker 1991, pp. 70–71.

11
See the chapter "Repetitions and Variations," pp. 188–89.

12
See the chapter "Primitivism," p. 136.

13
Exh. cat. Munich/Bonn/Murnau 2000/01, no. 1.

art of sculpting. The Phalanx group, which had been founded by Kandinsky and others in 1901, also ran its own private art school, whose teachers included Hüsgen. Münter enrolled in his sculpture class and before long was molding her first female nudes, Fig. C having previously made herself a plaster-cast mask of a smiling old woman.[14] As part of the sculpting course, she also had to attend the life drawing and painting classes taught by Kandinsky, and it was there that she began experimenting with painting techniques. Münter's intensive engagement with color, in other words, began only with her participation in Kandinsky's painting class at the Phalanx School, in the spring of 1902. Painting itself does not seem to have posed

B **Female Head [Weiblicher Kopf], ca.1902**

Woodcut on Japan paper, approx. 30.5 × 21 cm | Städtische Galerie im Lenbachhaus und Kunstbau München, inv. no. GMS 820

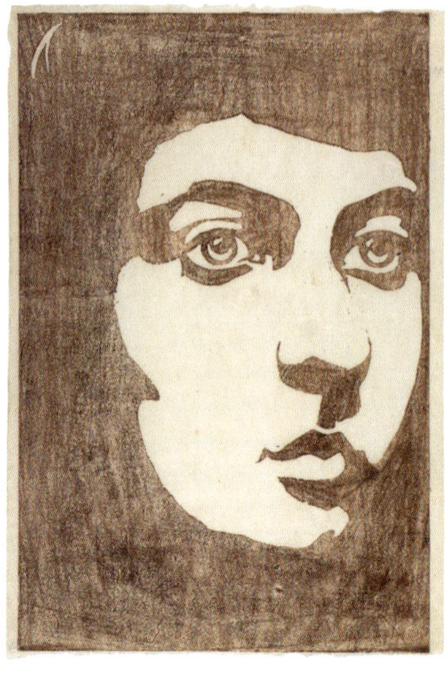

C **Two clay models (the one on the left by G. Münter), Wilhelm Hüsgen's sculpture class, Phalanx School, Munich, 1902**

Photograph by Gabriele Münter | Gabriele Münter- und Johannes Eichner-Stiftung, Munich, inv. no. 2116

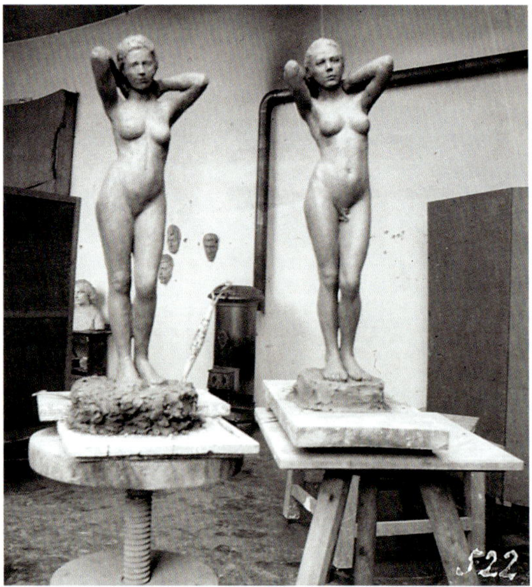

D **Bavarian Landscape [Bayerische Landschaft], 1902**

Oil on canvas, 17 × 24.7 cm | Private collection, Germany

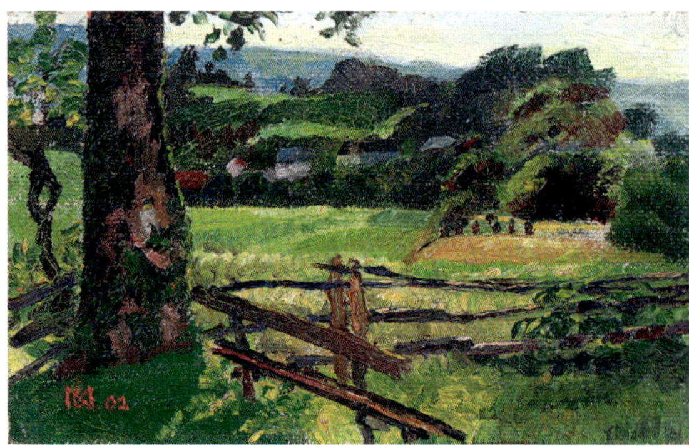

14
Eichner 1957, p. 37, illustrated in exh. cat. Munich 1977, no. 112.

any great difficulty for her, although we can certainly imagine what a fundamental adjustment working in color instead of black and white, with only light and dark contrasts, must have entailed.

Kandinsky's curriculum included painting *en plein air,* for which purpose he liked to take his class on painting expeditions into the countryside. In the summer of 1902, the class went to Kochel, and it was there that Münter's earliest known painting was produced. Fig. D Especially striking here is the way the composition is structured: the tree trunk and the fence form a kind of frame for the landscape in the background. This rather bold composition, with the tree cut off by the edge of the canvas, could well have been influenced by photography. The echoes of the photograph *View of the Landscape Over a Fence* Cat. 7 may be faint, but they are audible.

Landscapes, portraits, interiors, work and technology, the repetition of a motif, the sequence—all these themes, which first manifested themselves in Münter's photographs of North America, were to become equally important aspects of her painted oeuvre. Münter must have been aware of photography's potential for the rest of her work. Her linking of photography and painting put her far ahead of her time, and as an approach it was without parallel in the Blue Rider group.

General notes:
– Digitized original negatives or original prints were used as masters for the printed reproductions of photographs in the catalogue.
– The term "Stillleben" (still life) is written with two l's (i.e., *Stilleben*) in work titles that have been handed down with this spelling irregularity by the artist herself.
– The Gabriele Münter- und Johannes Eichner-Stiftung, Munich, is abbreviated as "MES" in the footnotes.

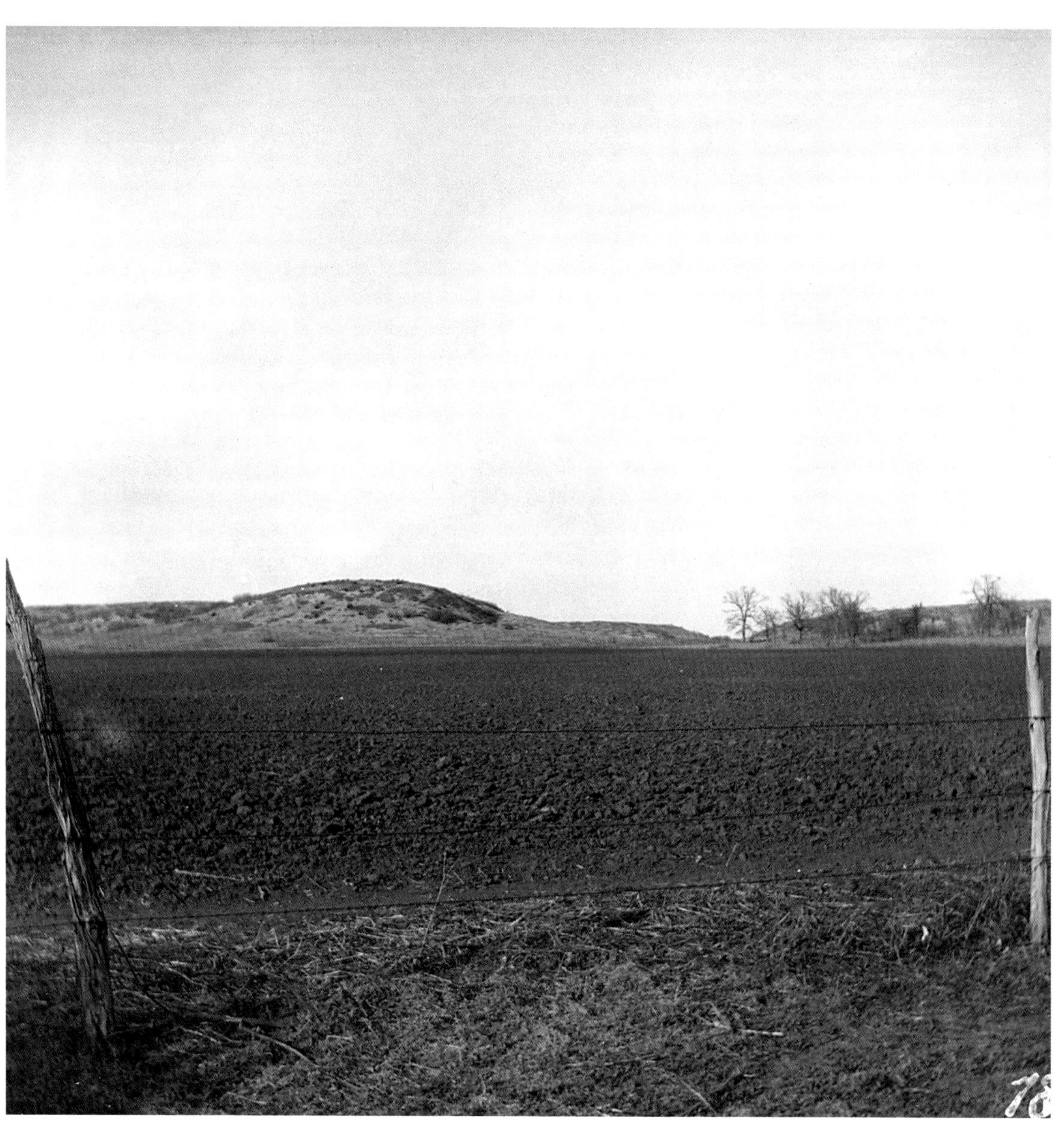

Cat. 1
Landscape near Guion, Texas, March 9, 1900
Photograph | Gabriele Münter- und Johannes Eichner-Stiftung, Munich, inv. no. 3532

Cat. 2
House on the Prairie near Guion, Texas, March 9, 1900
Photograph | Gabriele Münter- und Johannes Eichner-Stiftung, Munich, inv. no. 3533

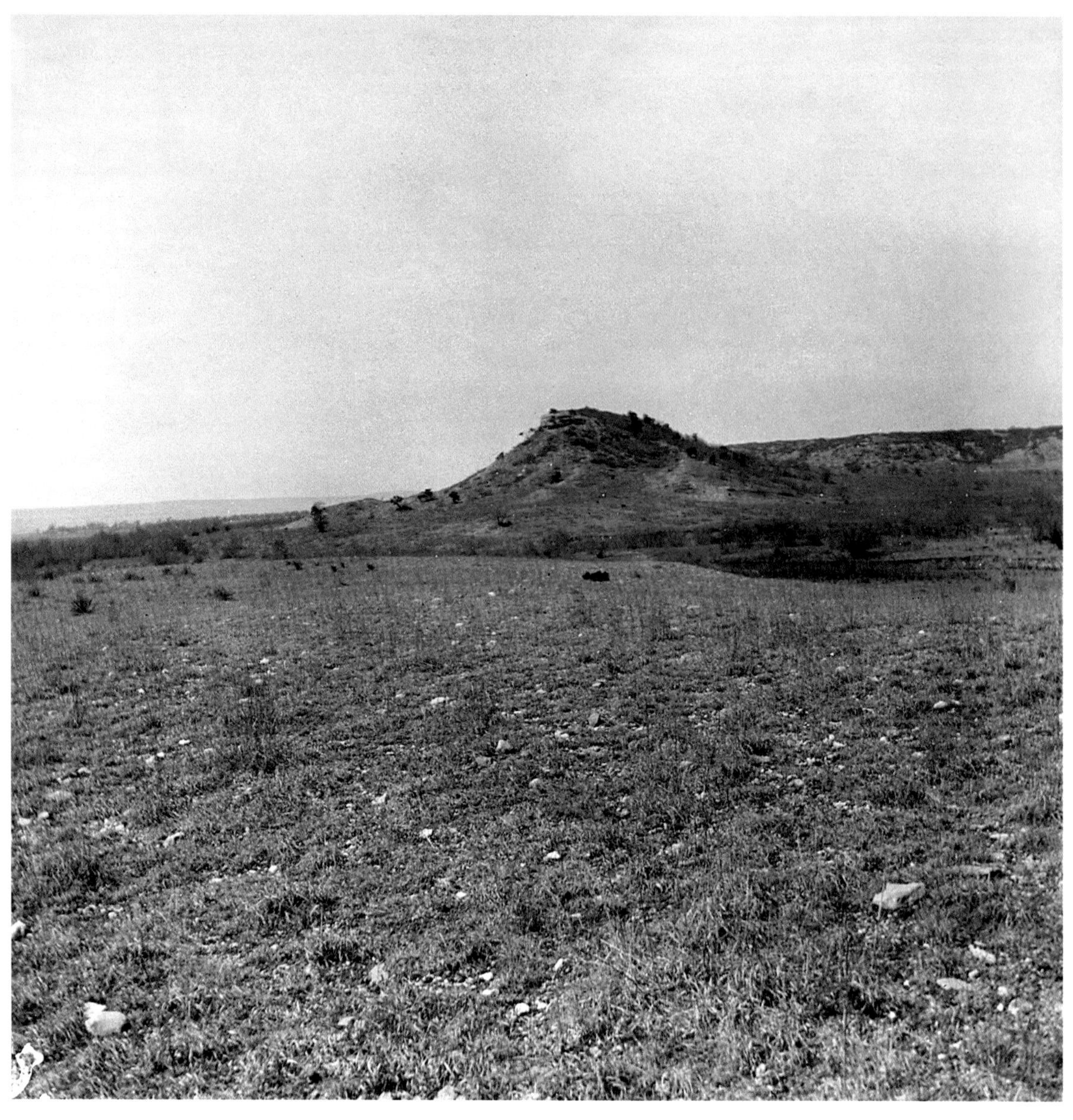

Cat. 3
"Steamboat Mountain, East," near Guion, Texas, March 13, 1900
Photograph | Gabriele Münter- und Johannes Eichner-Stiftung, Munich, inv. no. 3539

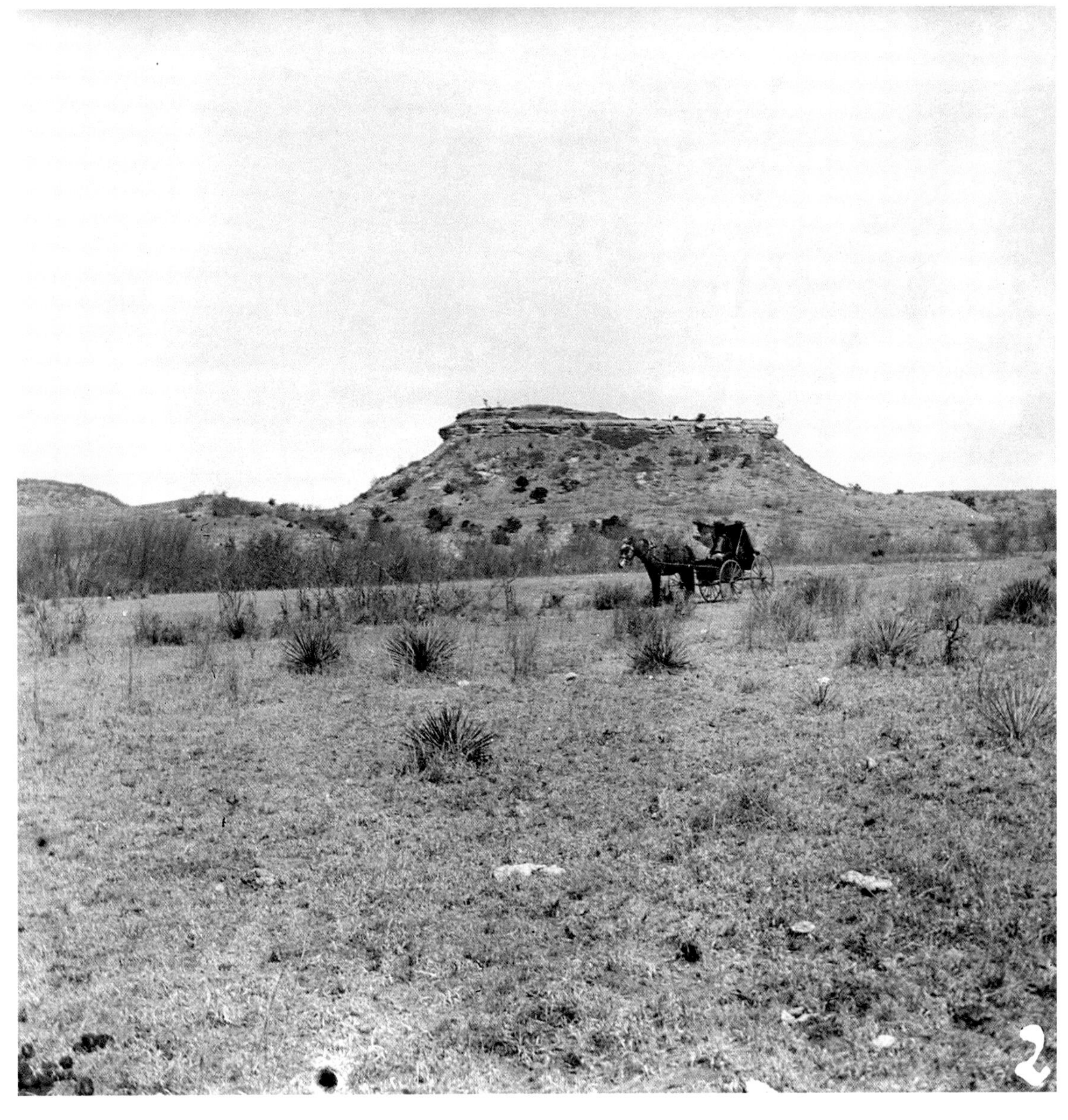

Cat. 4
“Steamboat Mountain, South,” near Guion, Texas, March 13, 1900
Photograph | Gabriele Münter- und Johannes Eichner-Stiftung, Munich, inv. no. 3540

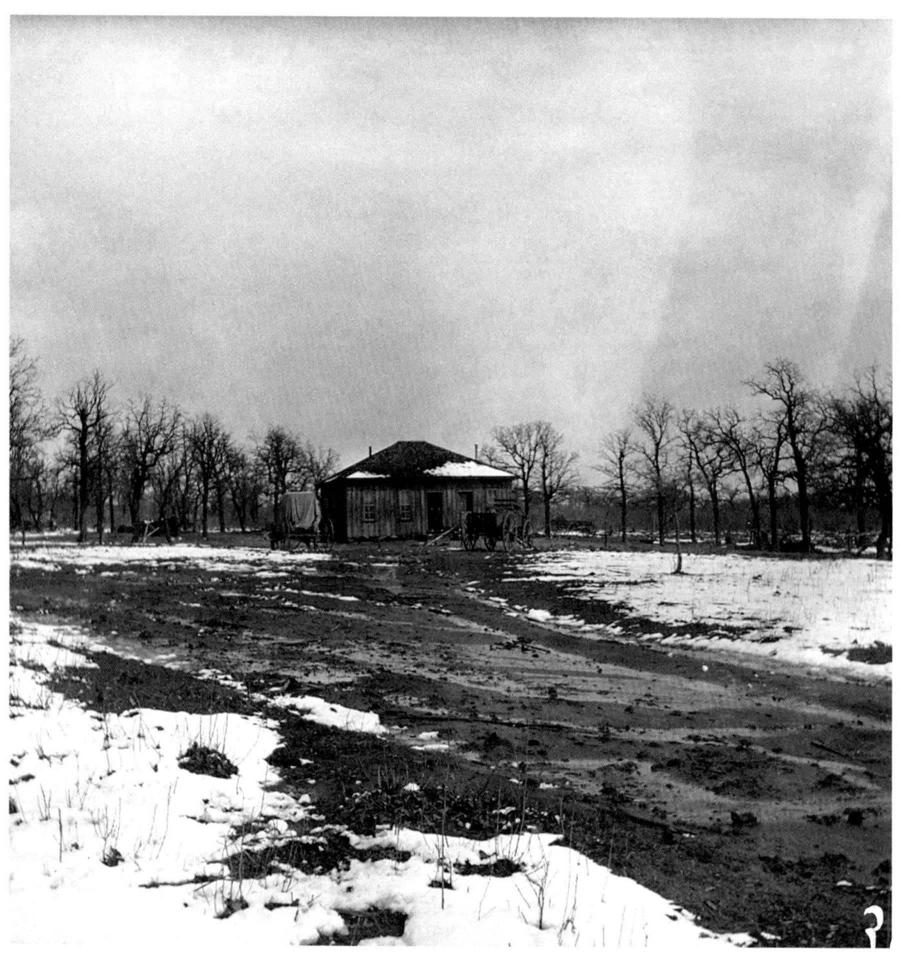

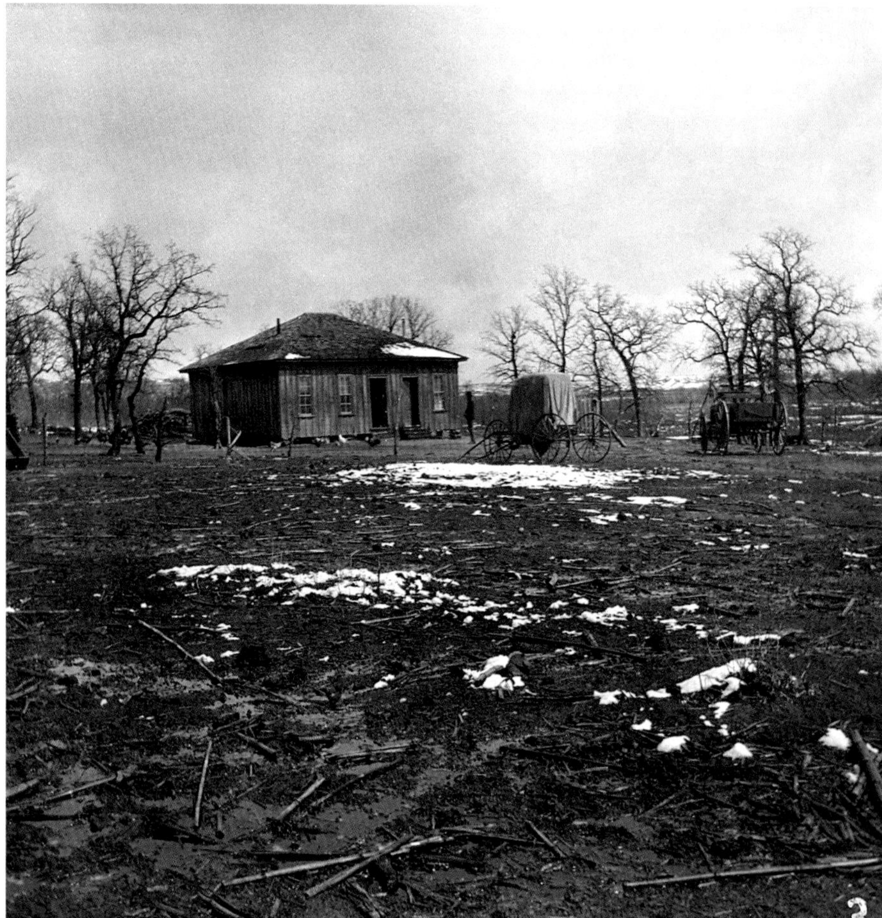

Cat. 5
"Jane Lee's 'shanty' in snow while the peaches were blooming," Guion, Texas, March 15, 1900
Photograph | Gabriele Münter- und Johannes Eichner-Stiftung, Munich, inv. no. 3545

Cat. 6
"Jane Lee's 'shanty' in snow while the peaches were blooming," Guion, Texas, March 15, 1900
Photograph | Gabriele Münter- und Johannes Eichner-Stiftung, Munich, inv. no. 3547

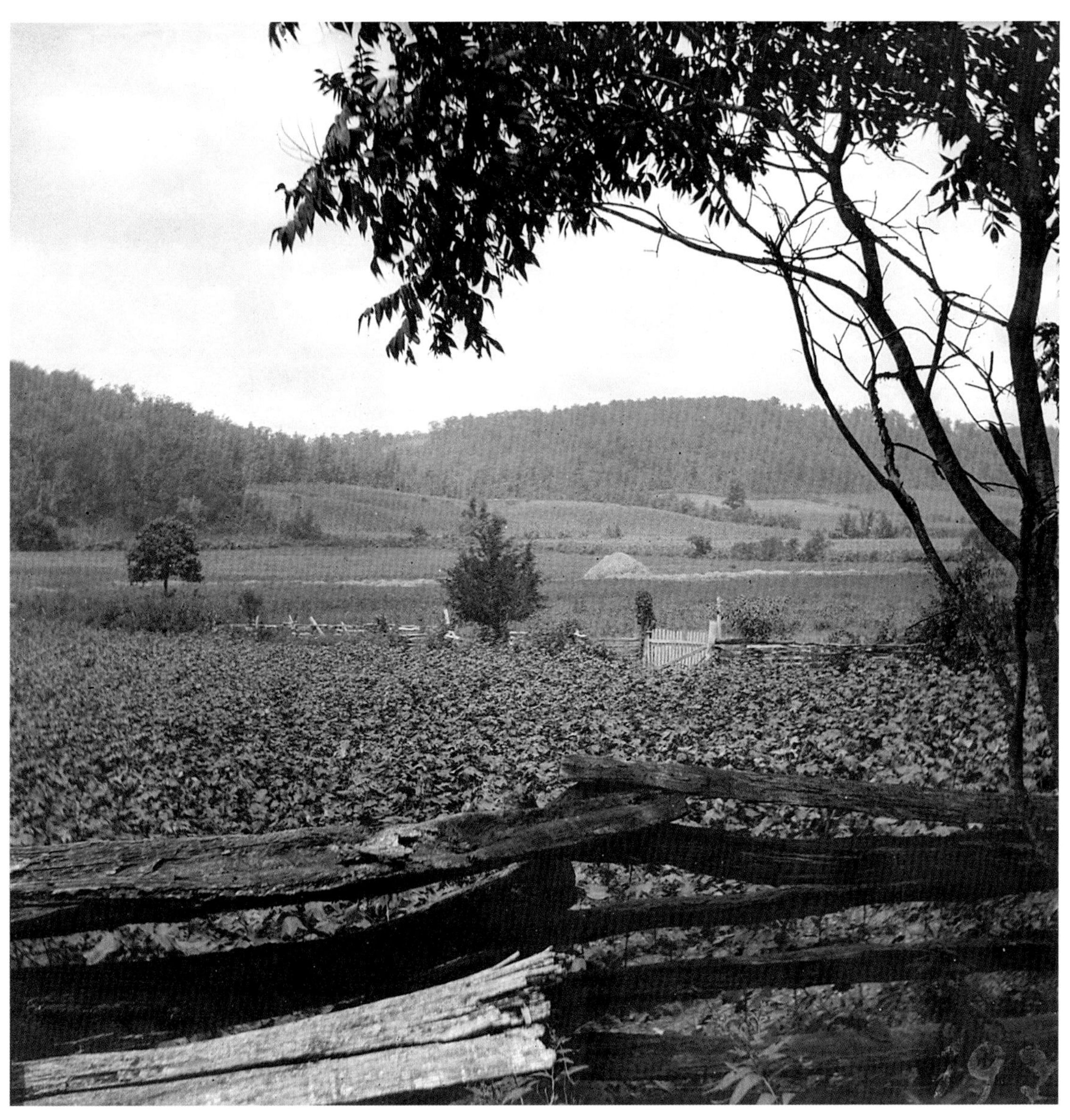

Cat. 7
View of the Landscape Over a Fence, Moorefield, Arkansas, 1899/1900
Photograph | Gabriele Münter- und Johannes Eichner-Stiftung, Munich, inv. no. 3710

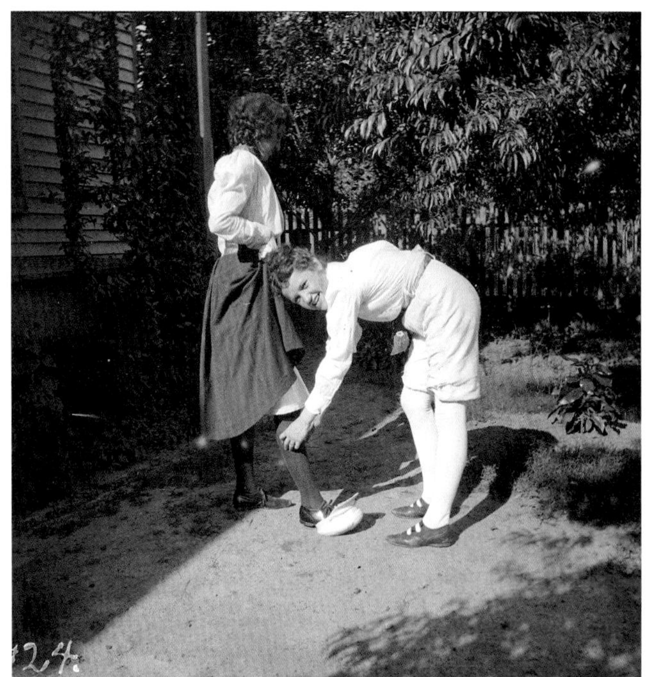

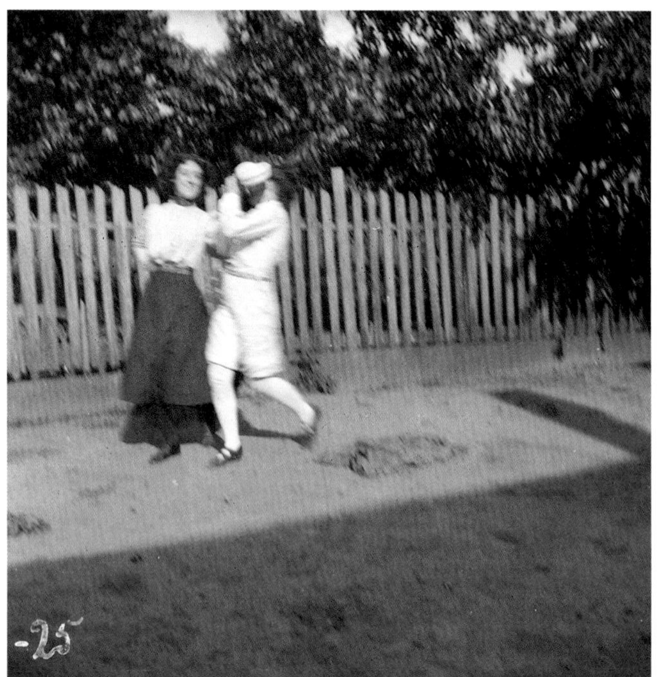

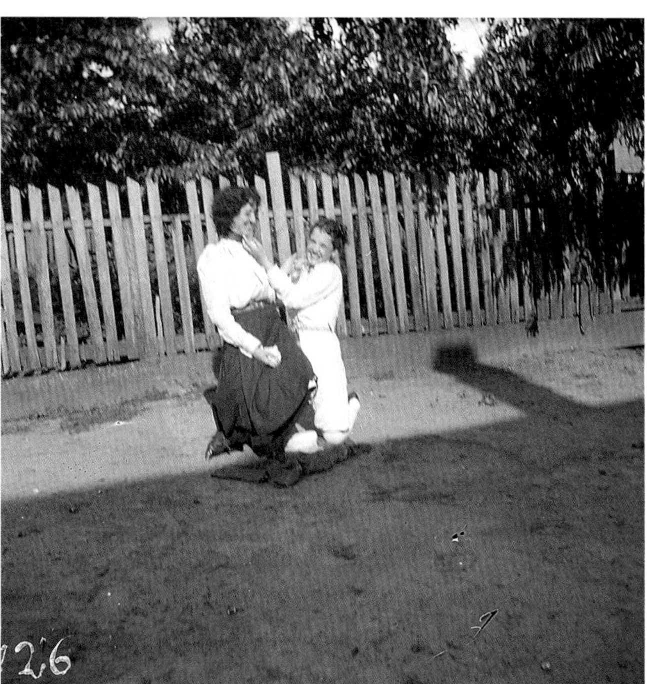

Cat. 8
Two Young Women Acting Out a Parody of a Theater Scene: A Bow, Marshall, Texas, 1899/1900
Photograph | Gabriele Münter- und Johannes Eichner-Stiftung, Munich, inv. no. 3630

Cat. 9
Theatrical Parody: A Stroll, Marshall, Texas, 1899/1900
Photograph | Gabriele Münter- und Johannes Eichner-Stiftung, Munich, inv. no. 3631

Cat. 10
Theatrical Parody: Genuflection, Marshall, Texas, 1899/1900
Photograph | Gabriele Münter- und Johannes Eichner-Stiftung, Munich, inv. no. 3632

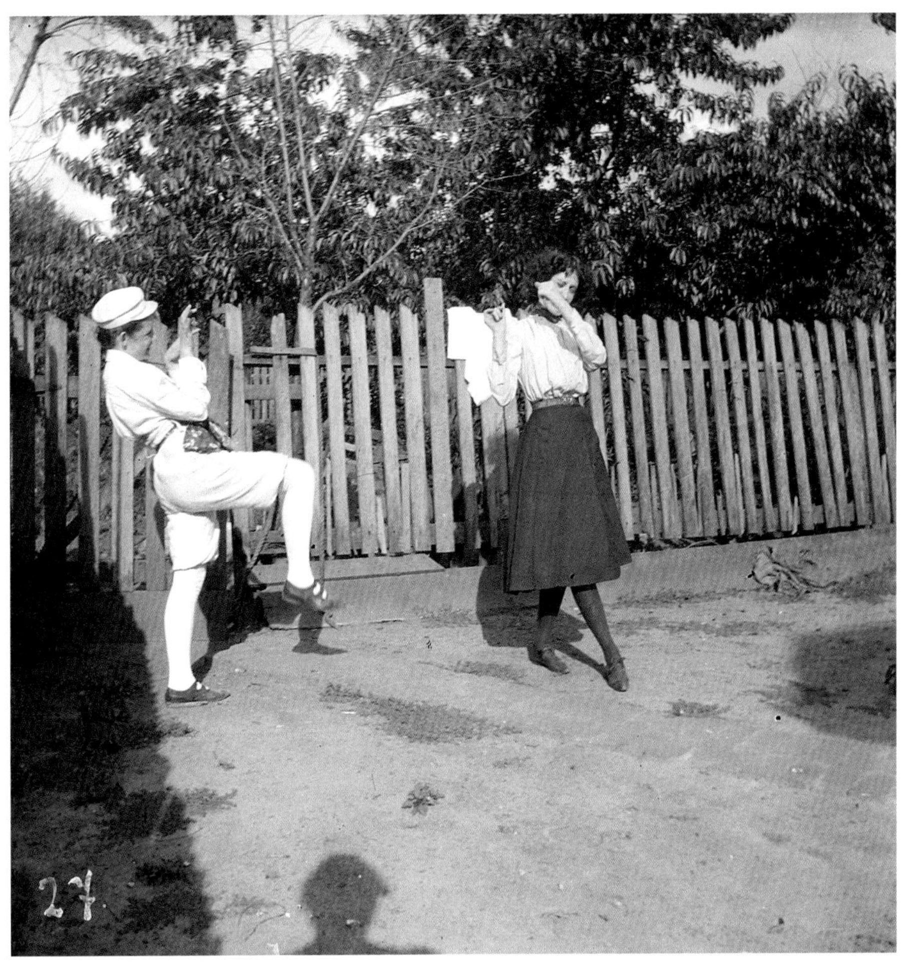

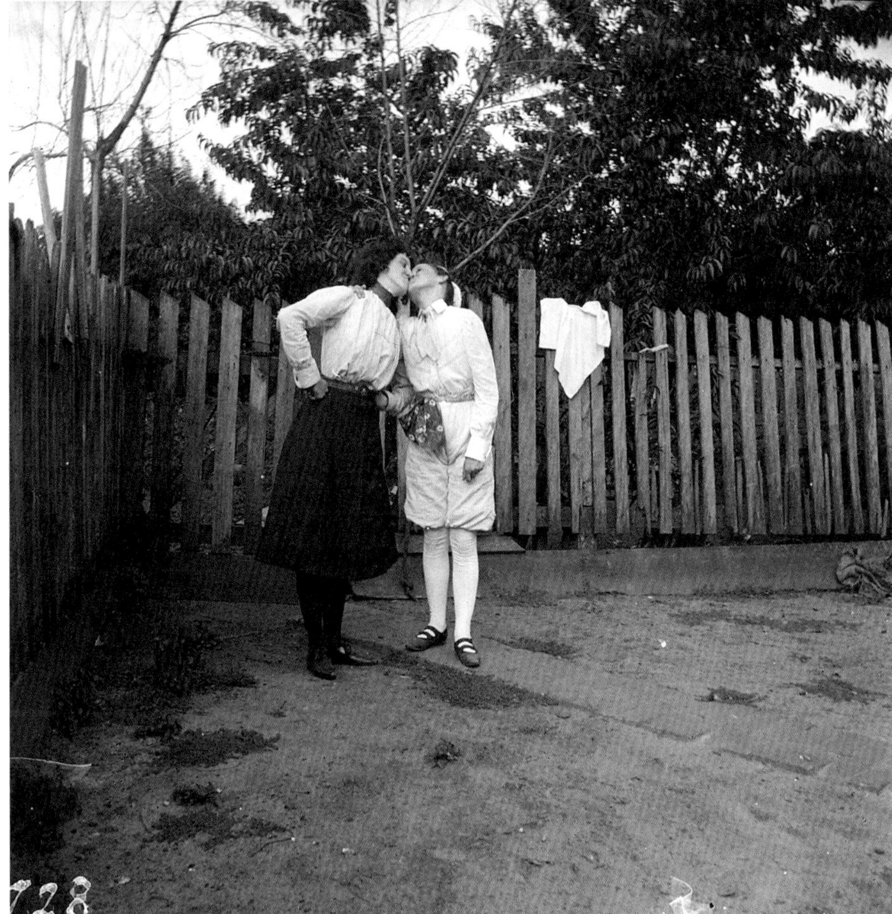

Cat. 11
Theatrical Parody: A Dance, Marshall, Texas, 1899/1900
Photograph | Gabriele Münter- und Johannes Eichner-Stiftung, Munich, inv. no. 3633

Cat. 12
Theatrical Parody: A Kiss, Marshall, Texas, 1899/1900
Photograph | Gabriele Münter- und Johannes Eichner-Stiftung, Munich, inv. no. 3634

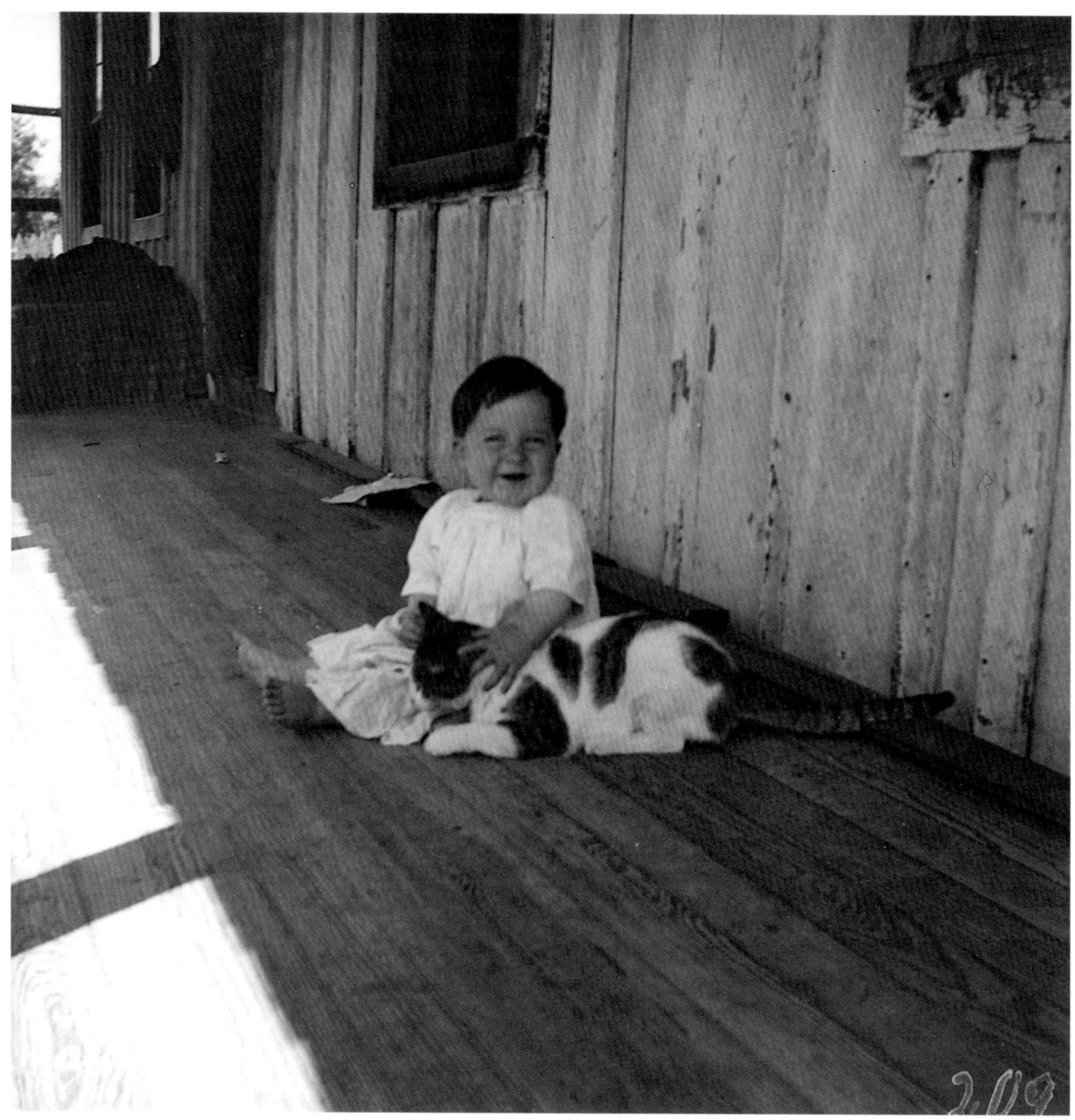

Cat. 13
Paul Leroy Wade with Cat, Schreiber Hill, near Moorefield, Arkansas, July 1900
Photograph | Gabriele Münter- und Johannes Eichner-Stiftung, Munich, inv. no. 3721

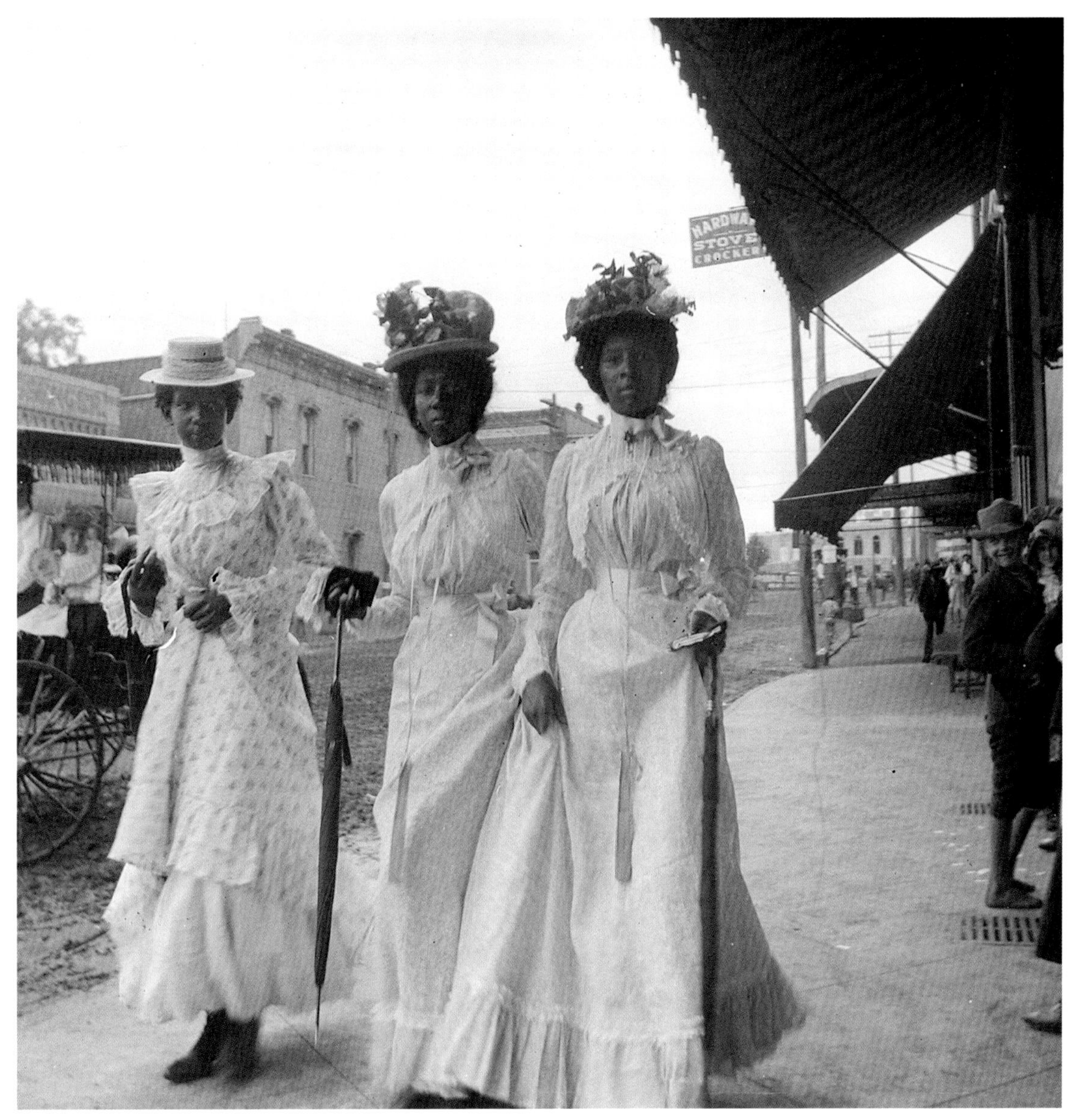

Cat. 14
Three Women in Their Sunday Best, Marshall, Texas, 1899/1900
Photograph | Gabriele Münter- und Johannes Eichner-Stiftung, Munich, inv. no. 3635

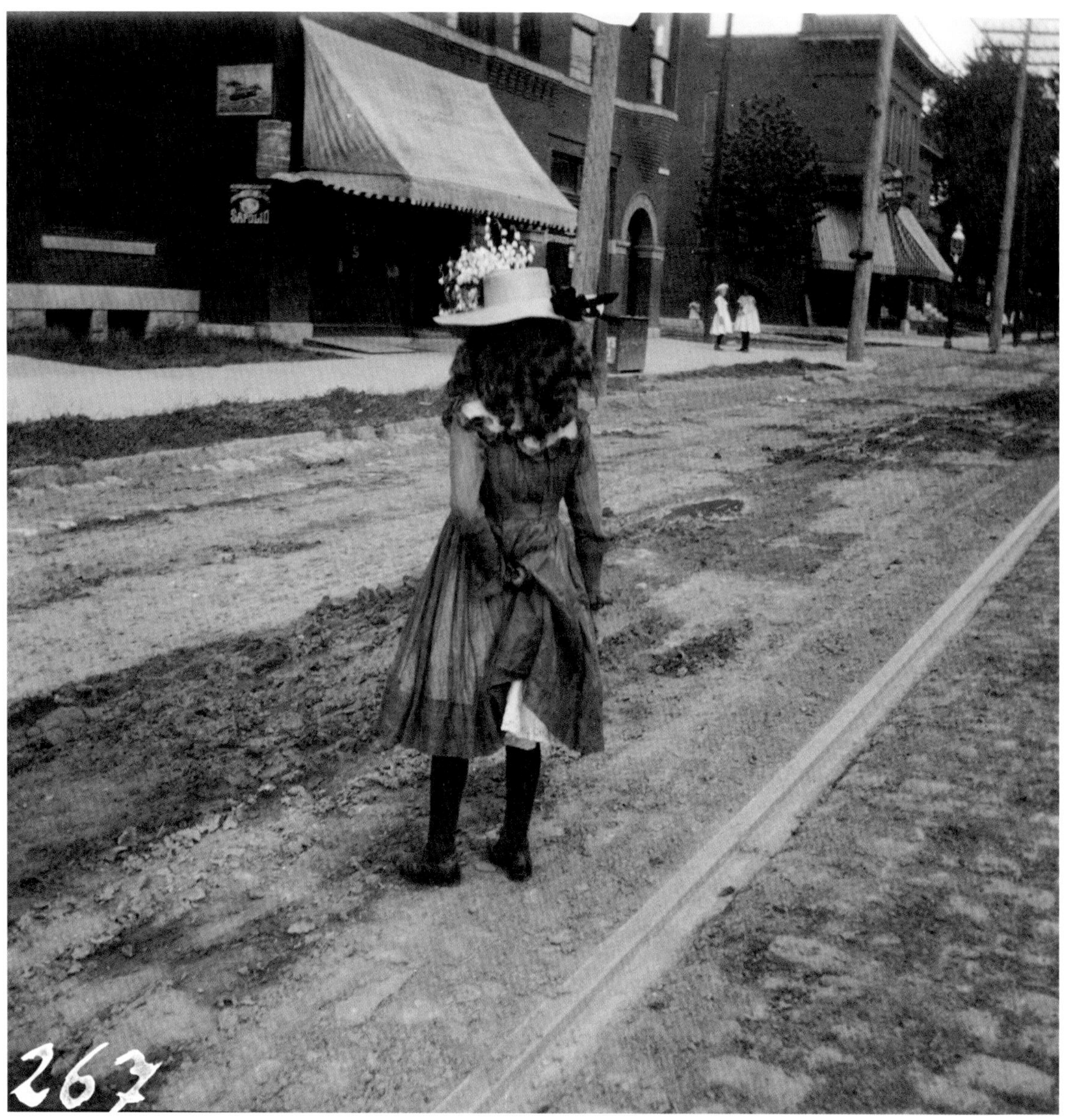

Cat. 15
Little Girl in Her Sunday Best Standing on a Street, Back View, Saint Louis, Missouri, 1900
Photograph | Gabriele Münter- und Johannes Eichner-Stiftung, Munich, inv. no. 3800

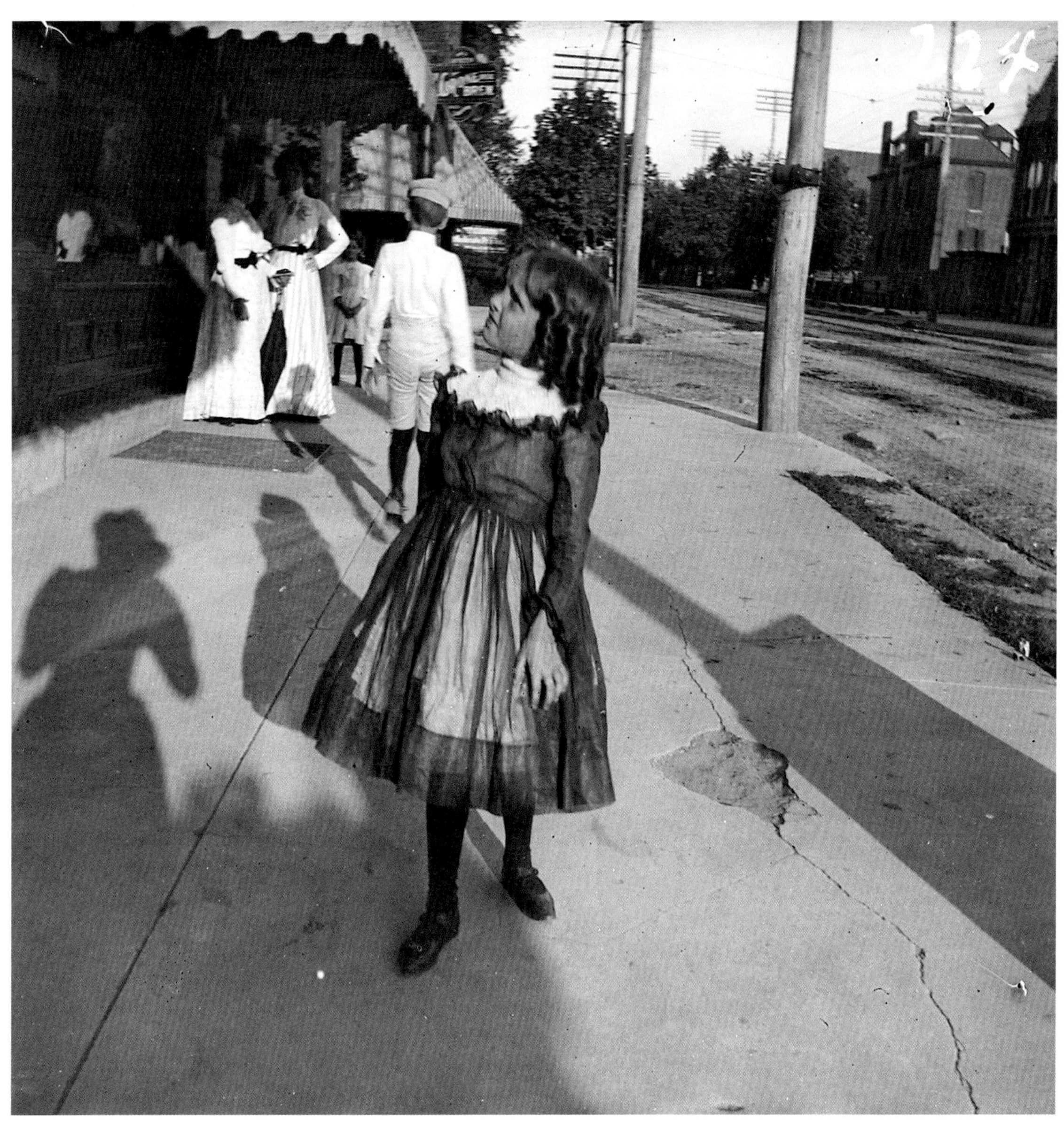

Cat. 16
Little Girl Standing at the Side of a Street, Saint Louis, Missouri, 1900
Photograph | Gabriele Münter- und Johannes Eichner-Stiftung, Munich, inv. no. 3757

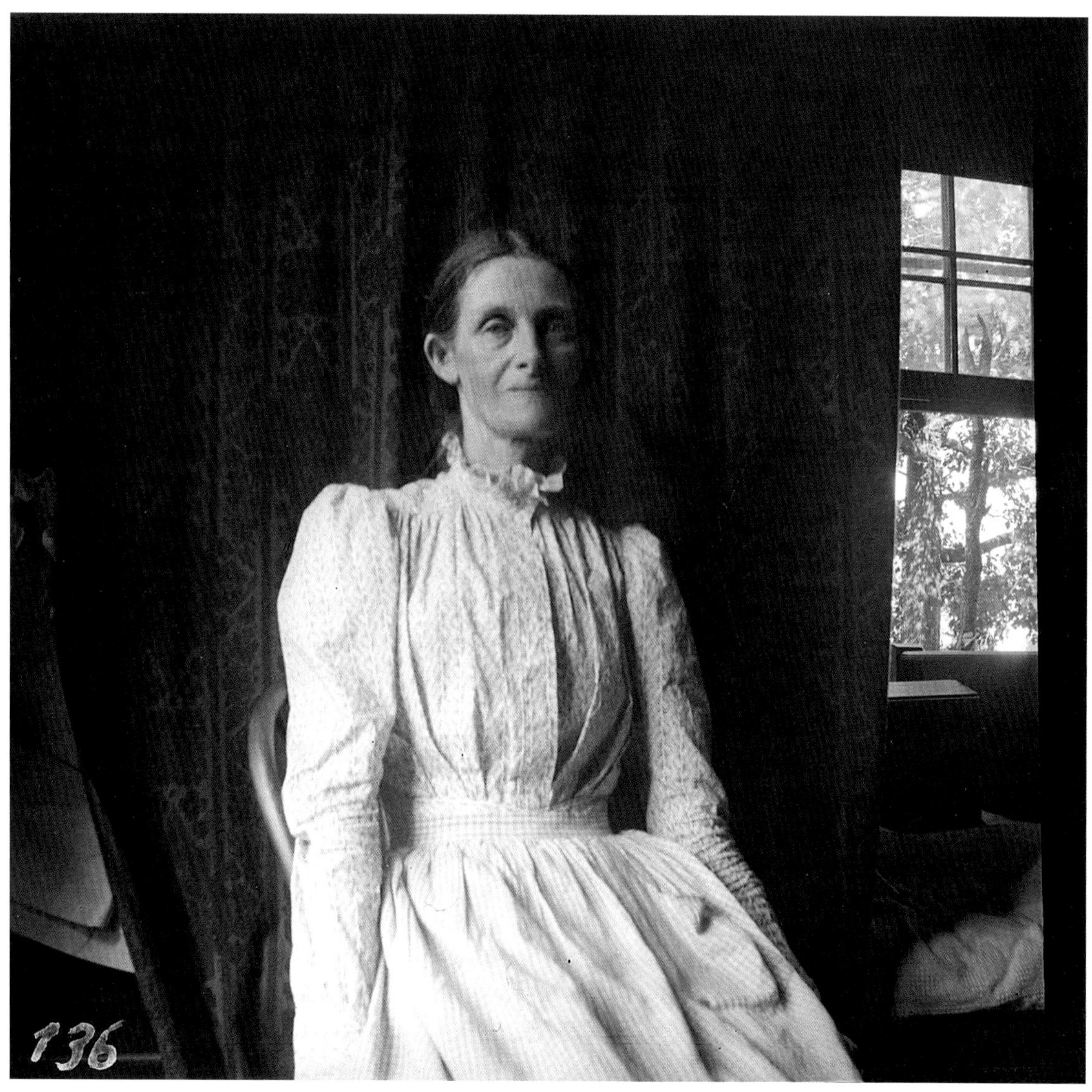

Cat. 17
Mrs. Allen in Her Living Room, Marshall, Texas, 1899/1900
Photograph | Gabriele Münter- und Johannes Eichner-Stiftung, Munich, inv. no. 3651

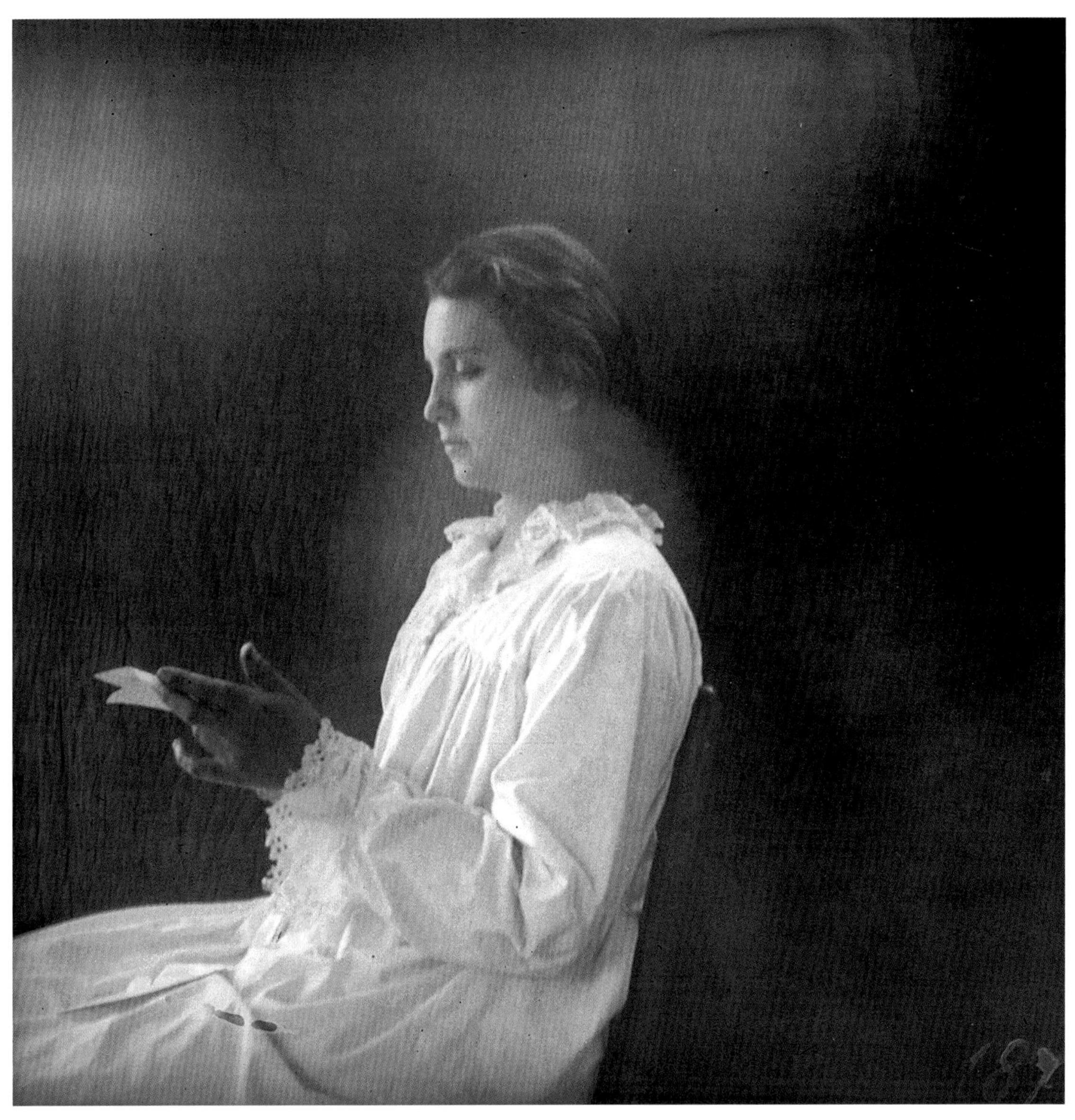

Cat. 18
Woman in Profile, Reading, Moorefield, Arkansas, 1899/1900
Photograph | Gabriele Münter- und Johannes Eichner-Stiftung, Munich, inv. no. 3702

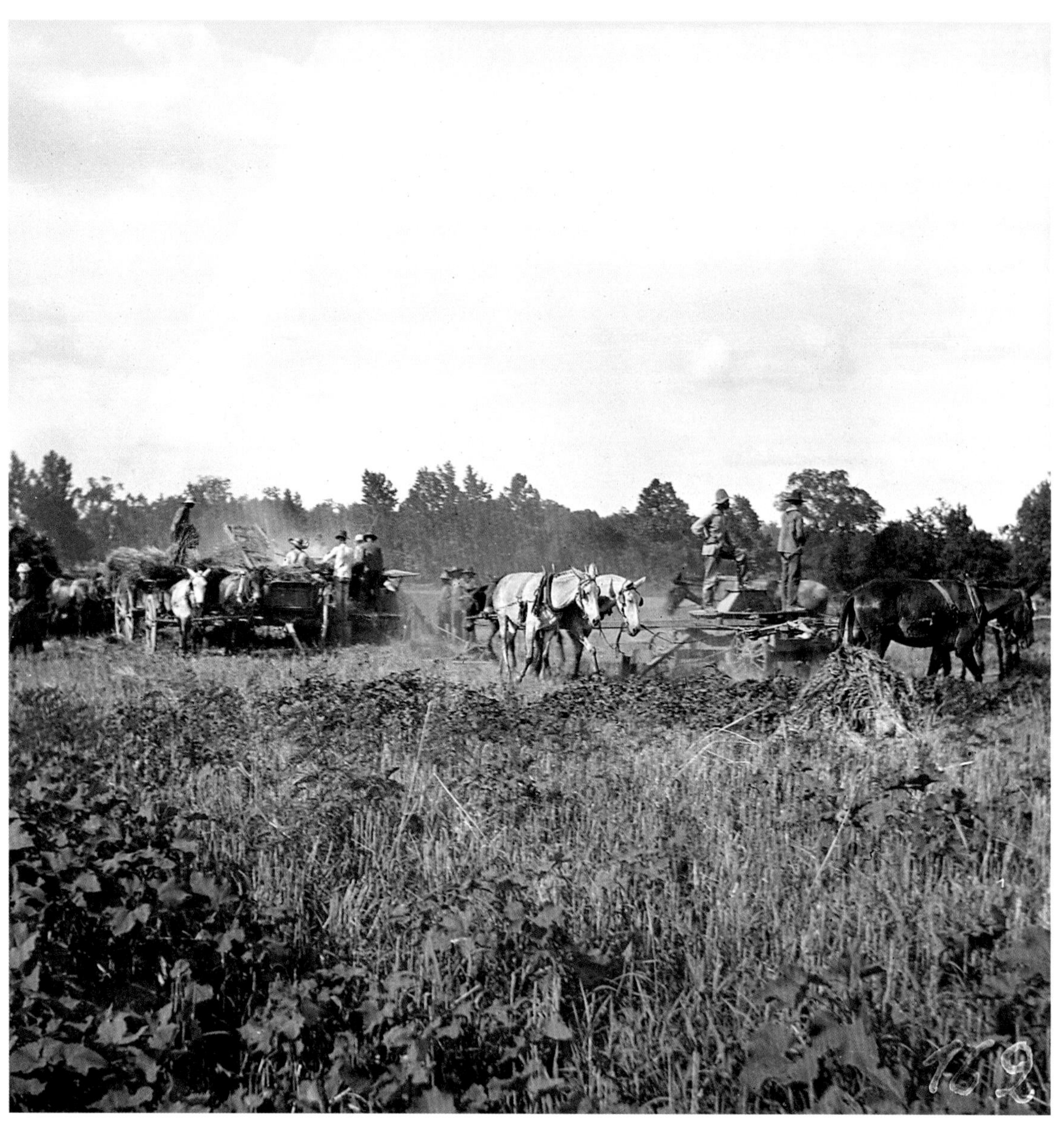

Cat. 19
Hay Harvest, Moorefield, Arkansas, 1899/1900
Photograph | Gabriele Münter- und Johannes Eichner-Stiftung, Munich, inv. no. 3681

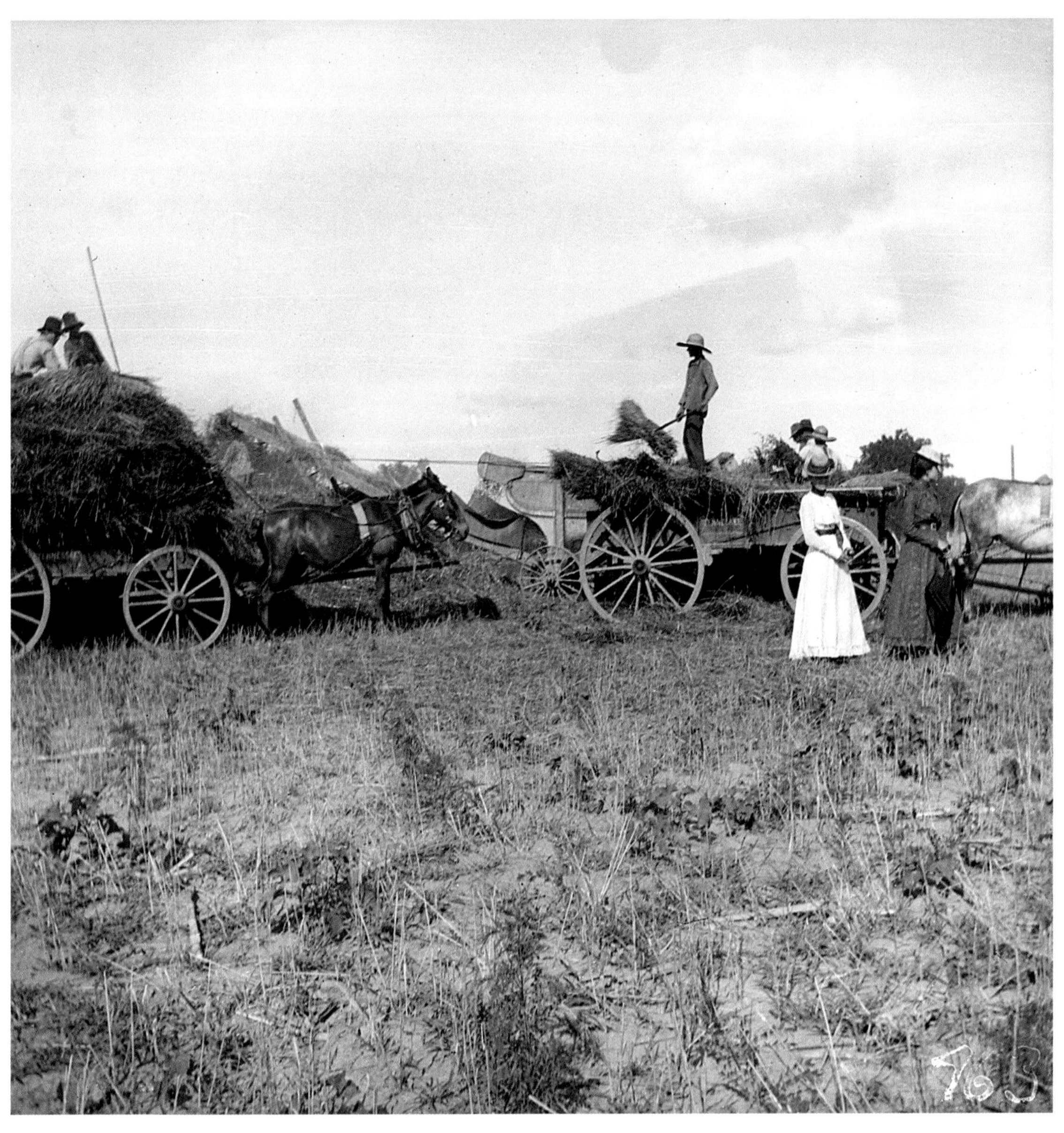

Cat. 20
Hay Harvest, Moorefield, Arkansas, 1899/1900
Photograph | Gabriele Münter- und Johannes Eichner-Stiftung, Munich, inv. no. 3682

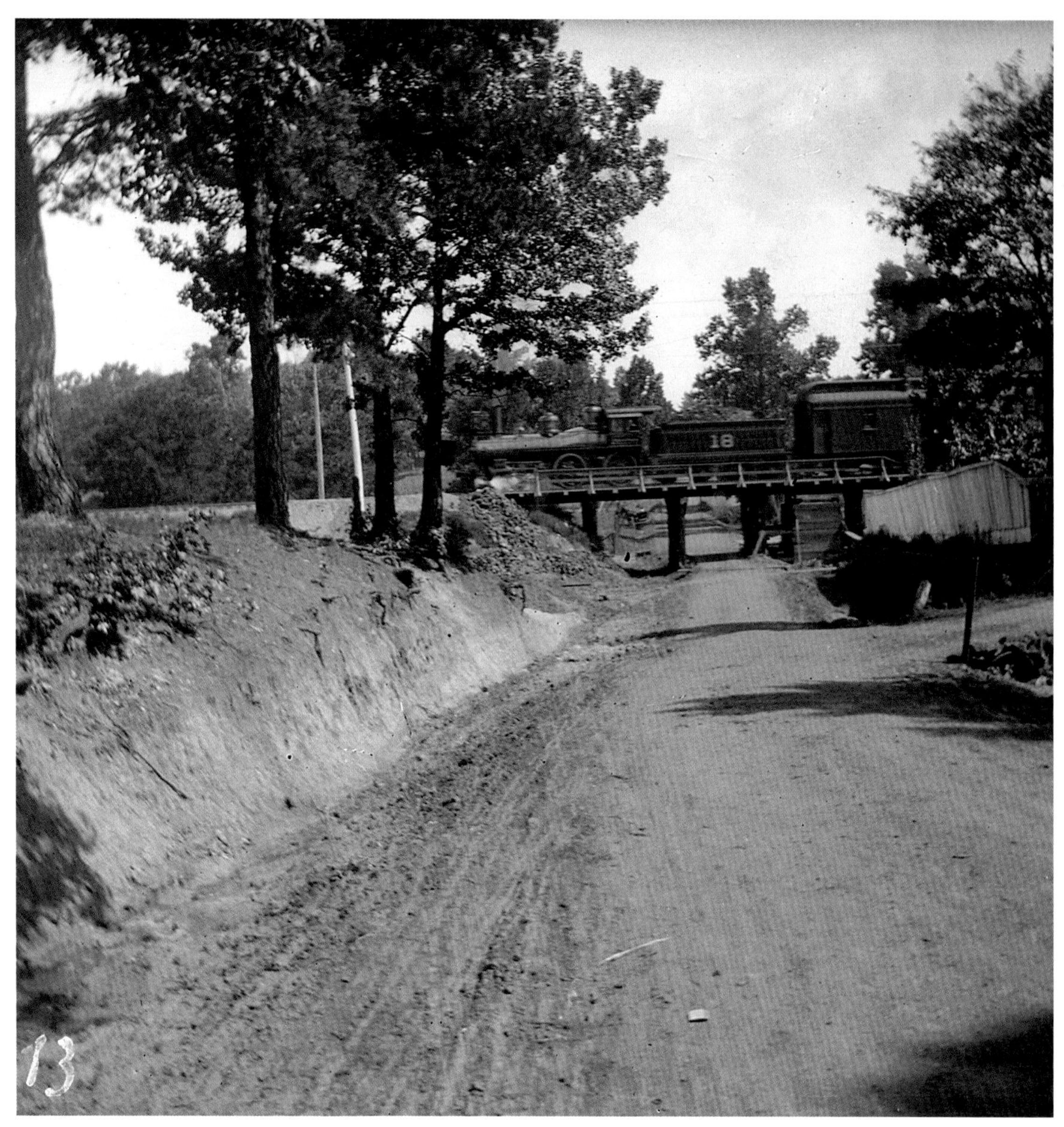

Cat. 21
Steam-Powered Train on a Bridge, Arkansas or Texas, 1899/1900
Photograph | Gabriele Münter- und Johannes Eichner-Stiftung, Munich, inv. no. 3619

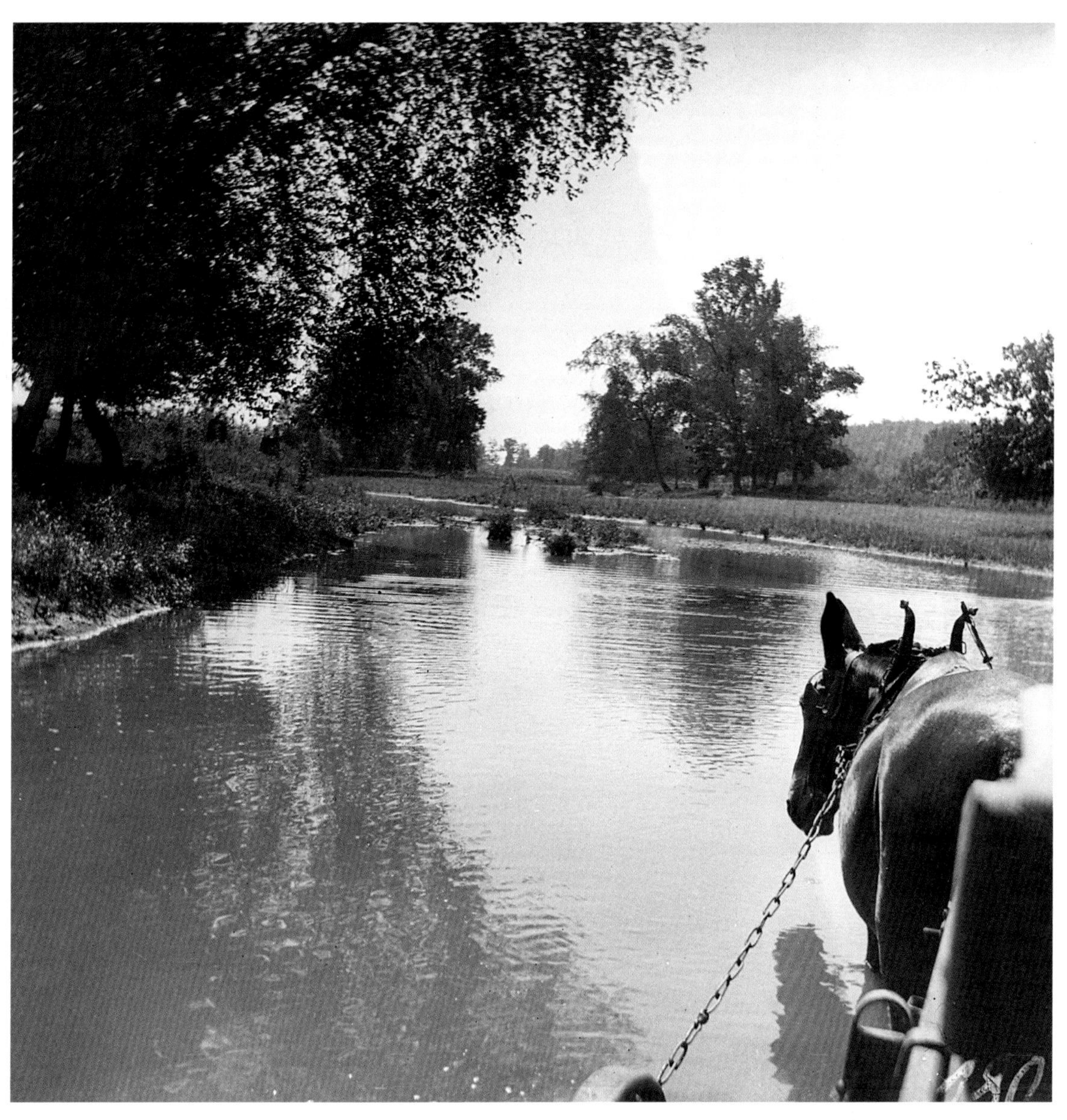

Cat. 22
Coach Ride across a River, Moorefield, Arkansas, 1899/1900
Photograph | Gabriele Münter- und Johannes Eichner-Stiftung, Munich, inv. no. 3696

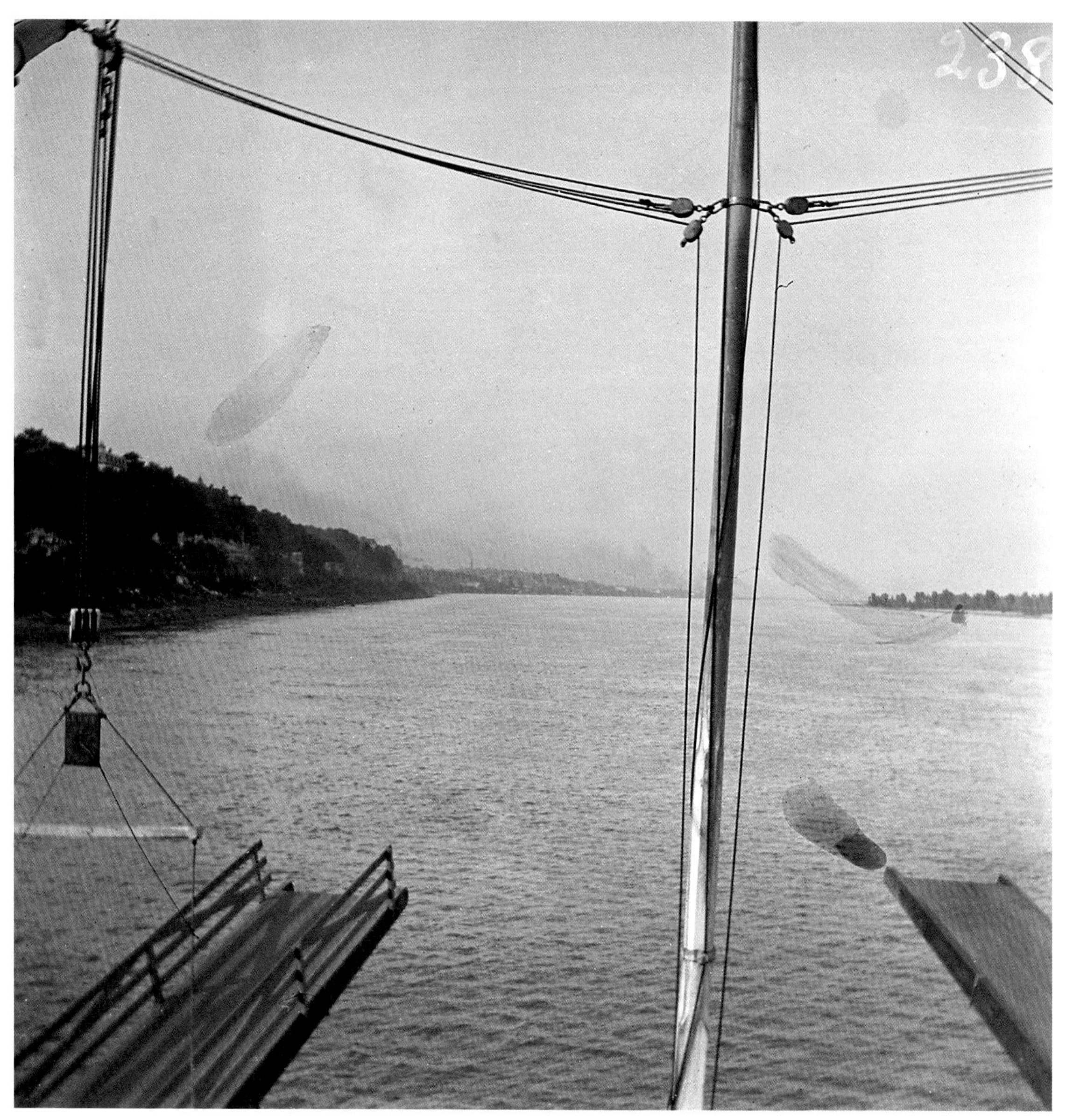

Cat. 23
View over the Outriggers of a Ship on the Mississippi, near Saint Louis, Missouri, 1900
Photograph | Gabriele Münter- und Johannes Eichner-Stiftung, Munich, inv. no. 3770

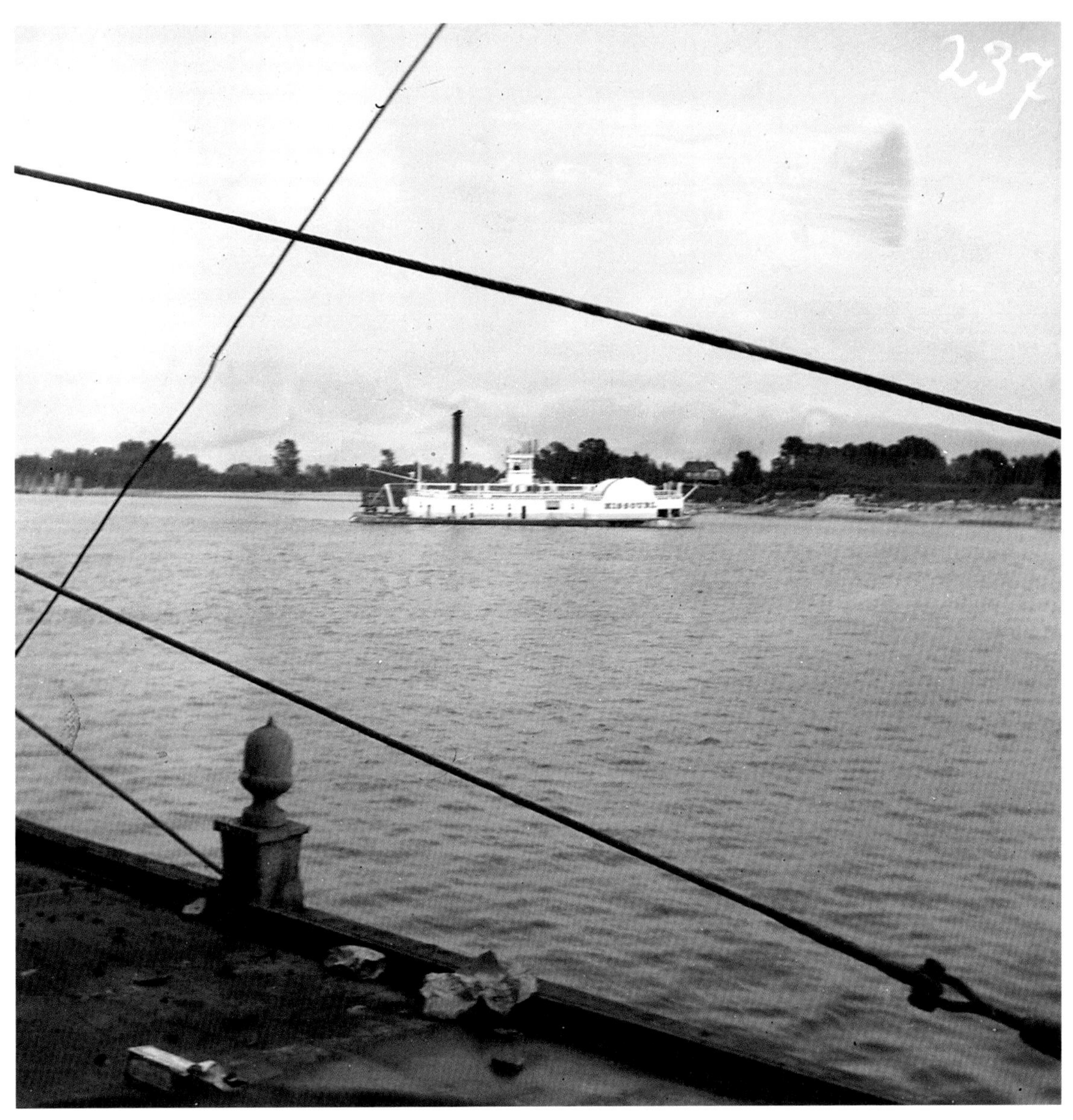

Cat. 24
Paddle Steamer on the Mississippi, near Saint Louis, Missouri, 1900
Photograph | Gabriele Münter- und Johannes Eichner-Stiftung, Munich, inv. no. 3769

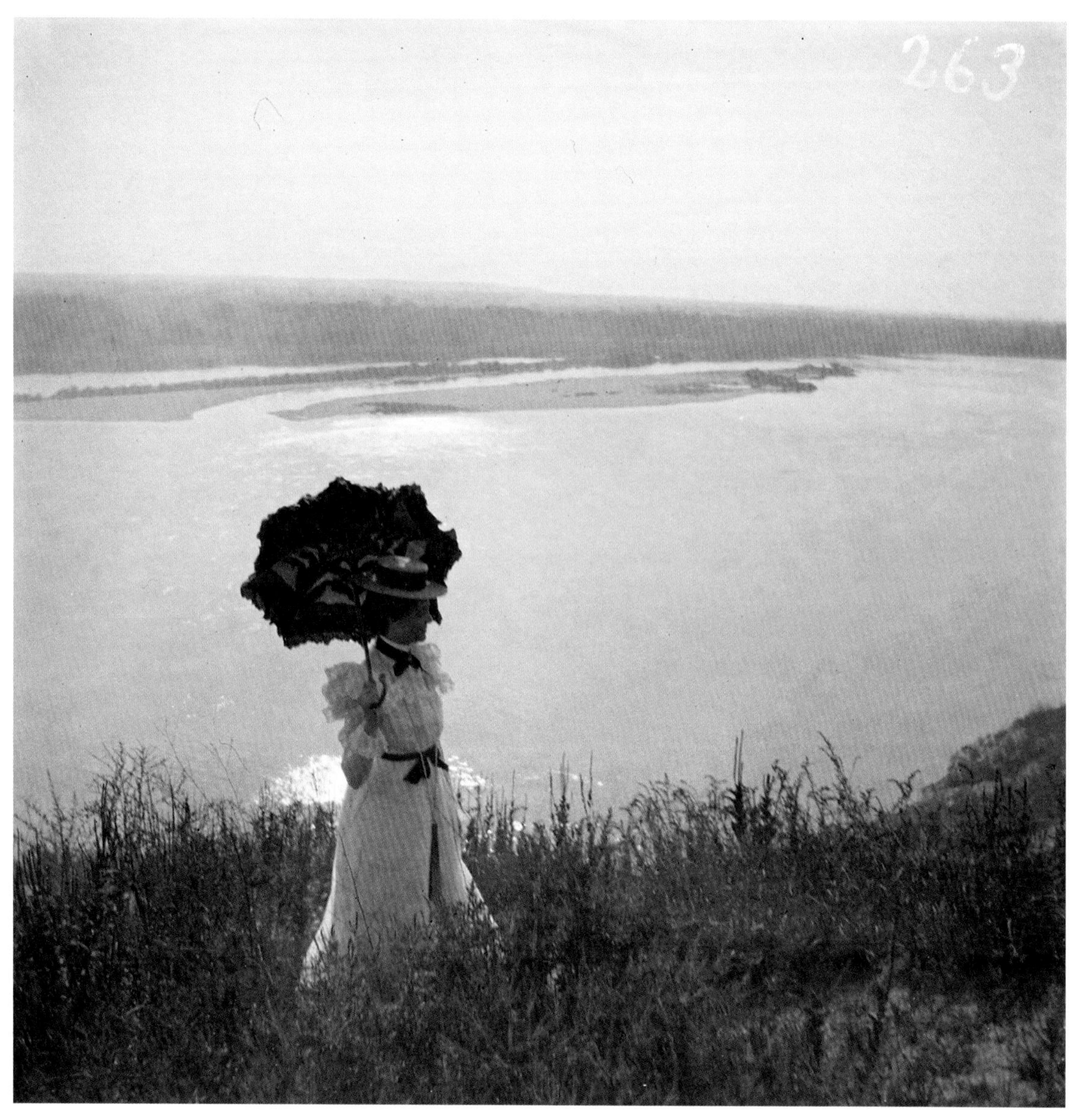

Cat. 25
Woman with a Parasol on the Levee of the Mississippi, near Saint Louis, Missouri, 1900
Photograph | Gabriele Münter- und Johannes Eichner-Stiftung, Munich, inv. no. 3797

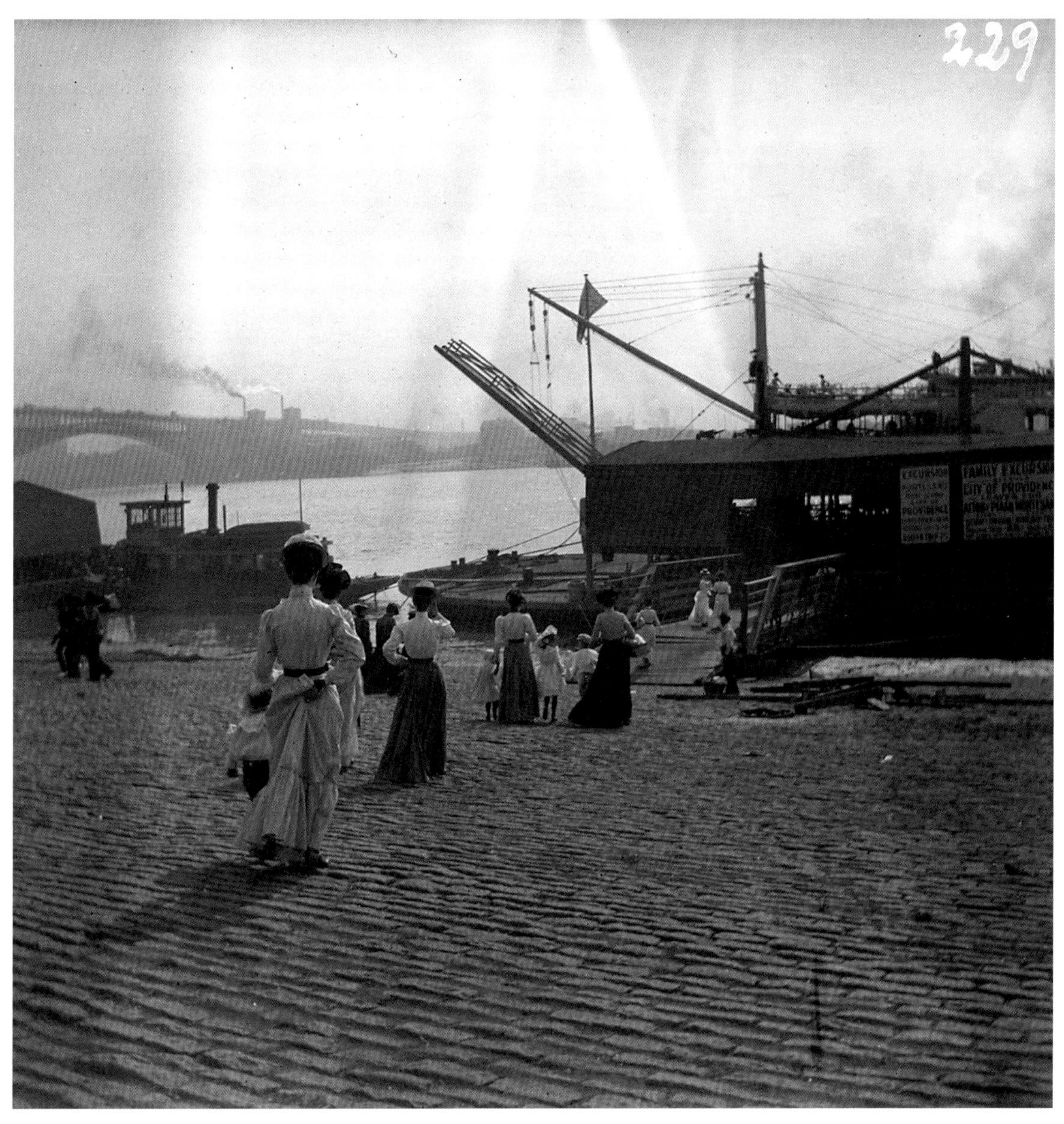

Cat. 26

On the Way to a Steamboat for an Excursion on the Mississippi, Saint Louis, Missouri, 1900

Photograph | Gabriele Münter- und Johannes Eichner-Stiftung, Munich, inv. no. 3761

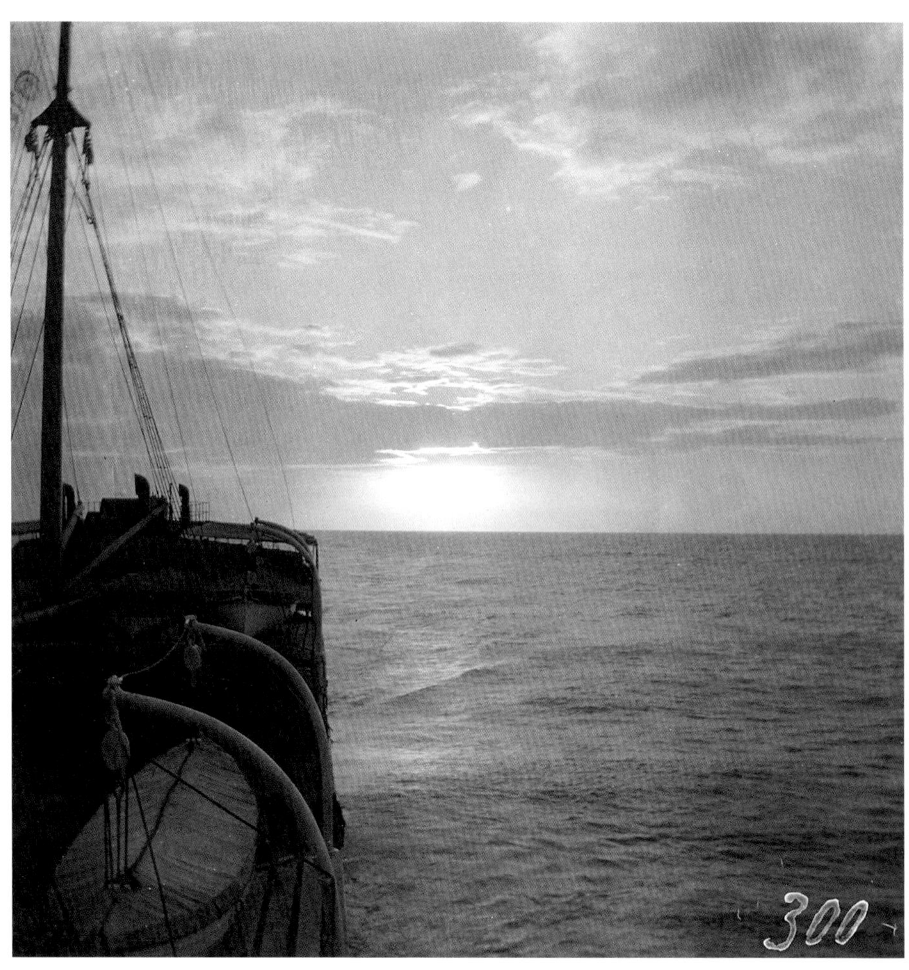

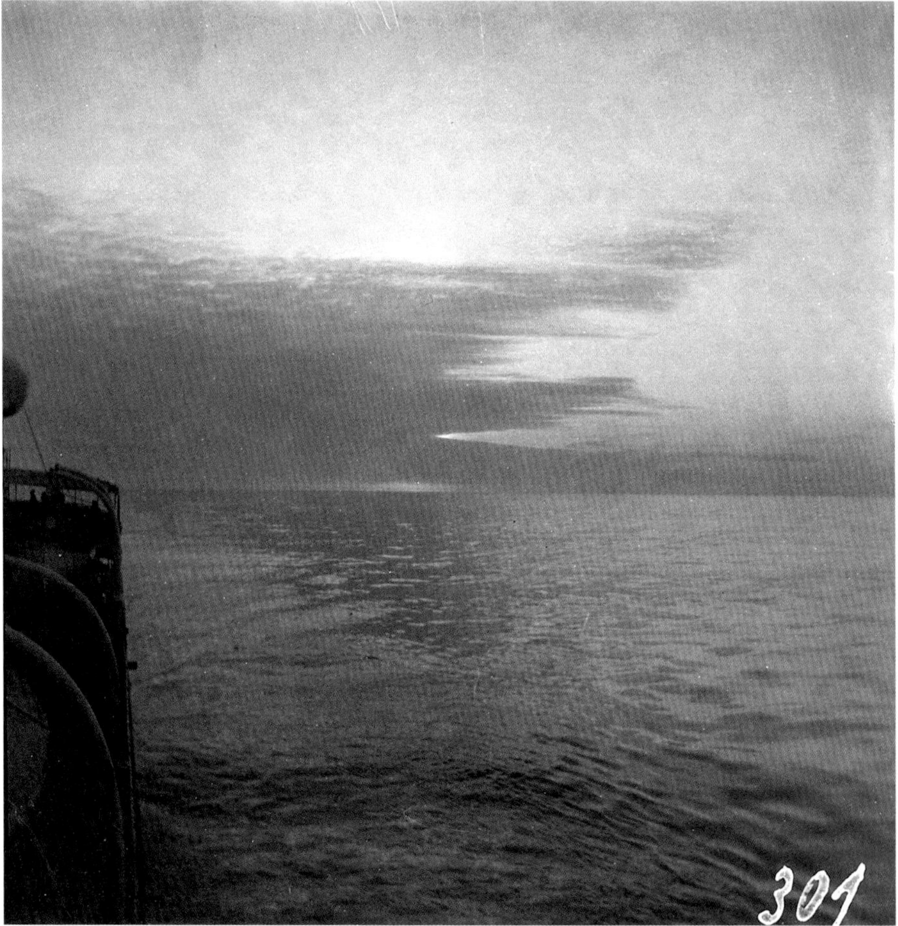

Cat. 27 and 28
Sunset during the Return Journey from the USA, Steamship "Pennsylvania," October 1900
Photograph | Gabriele Münter- und Johannes Eichner-Stiftung, Munich, inv. nos. 3834, 3835

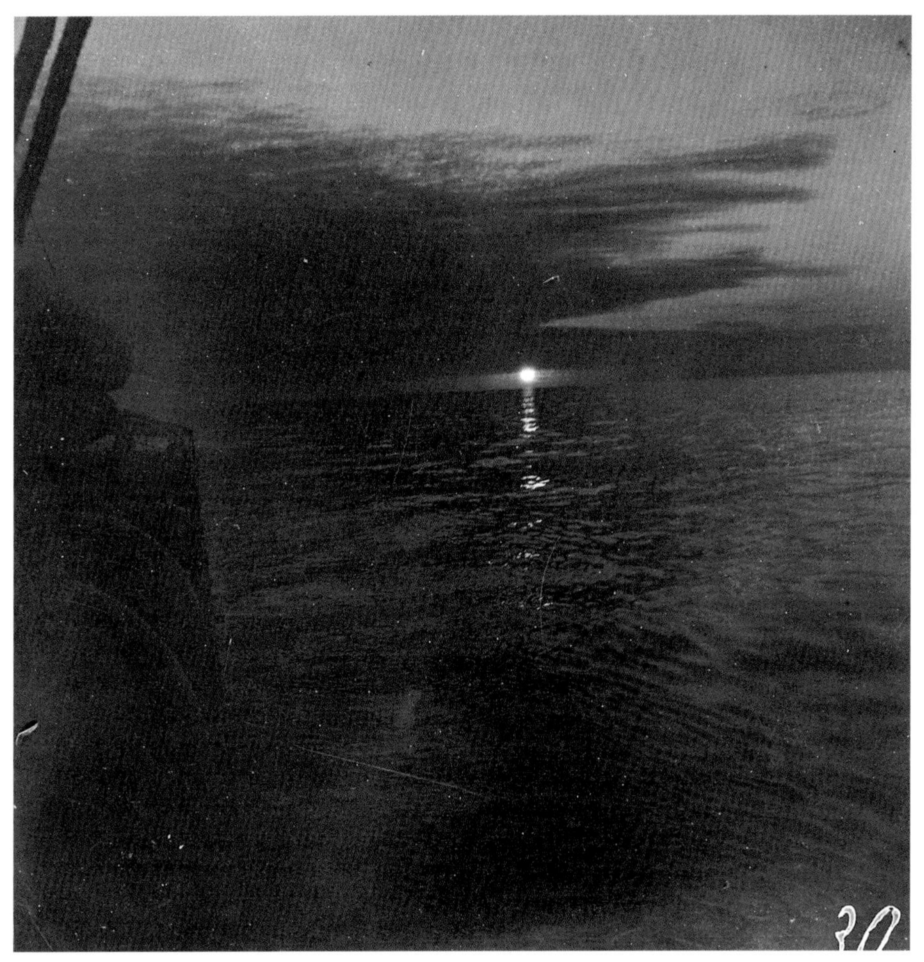

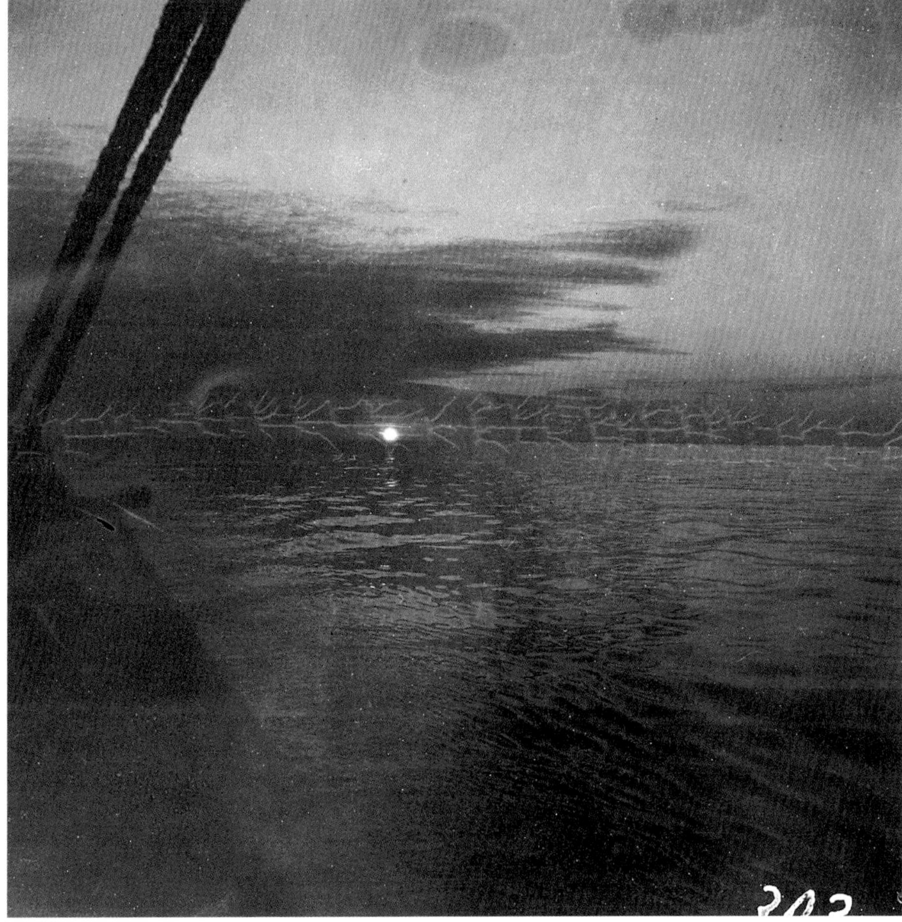

Cat. 29 and 30
Sunset during the Return Journey from the USA, Steamship "Pennsylvania," October 1900
Photograph | Gabriele Münter- und Johannes Eichner-Stiftung, Munich, inv. nos. 3836, 3837

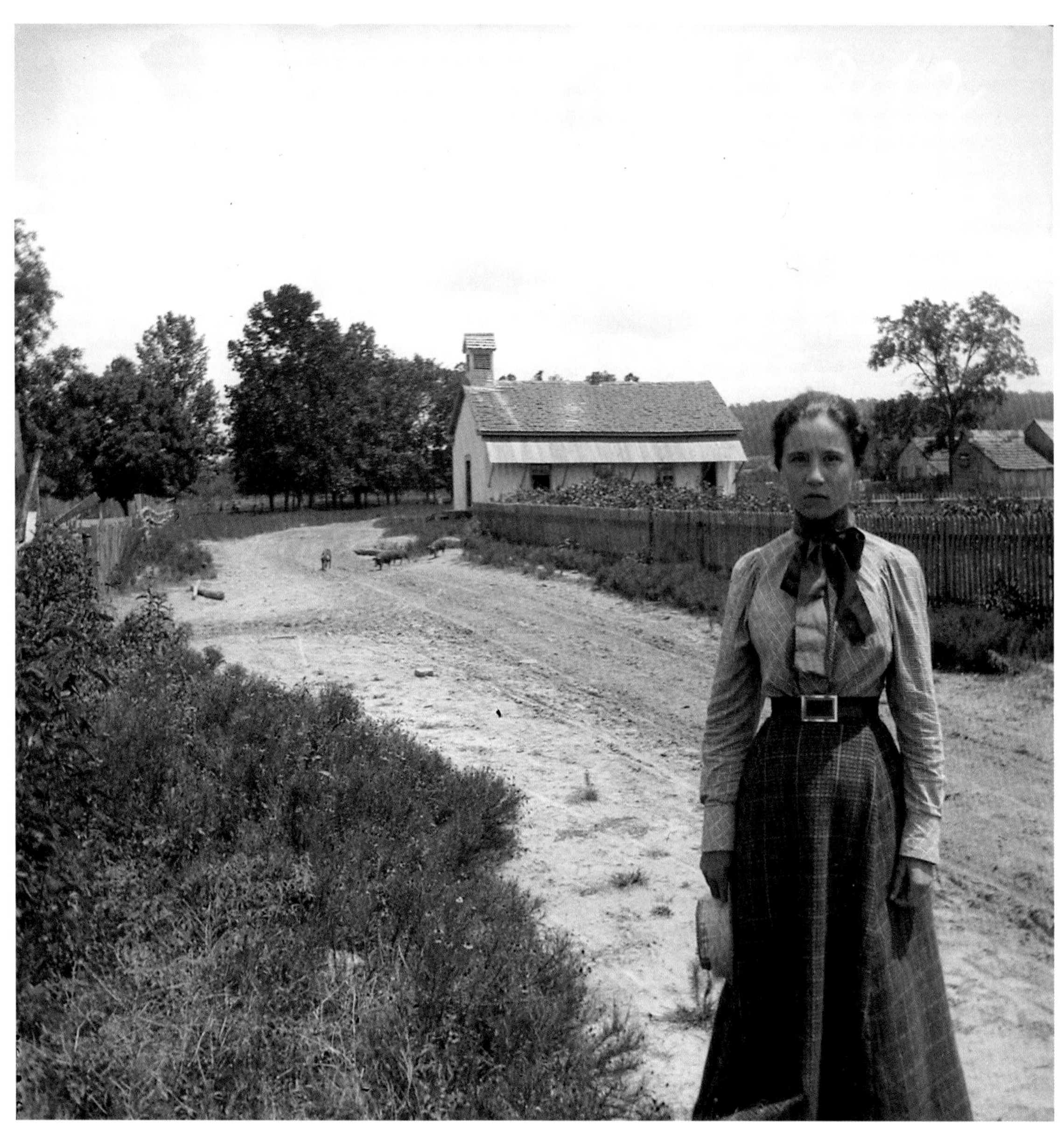

Cat. 31
Young Woman near Moorefield, Arkansas, 1899/1900
Photograph | Gabriele Münter- und Johannes Eichner-Stiftung, Munich, inv. no. 3724

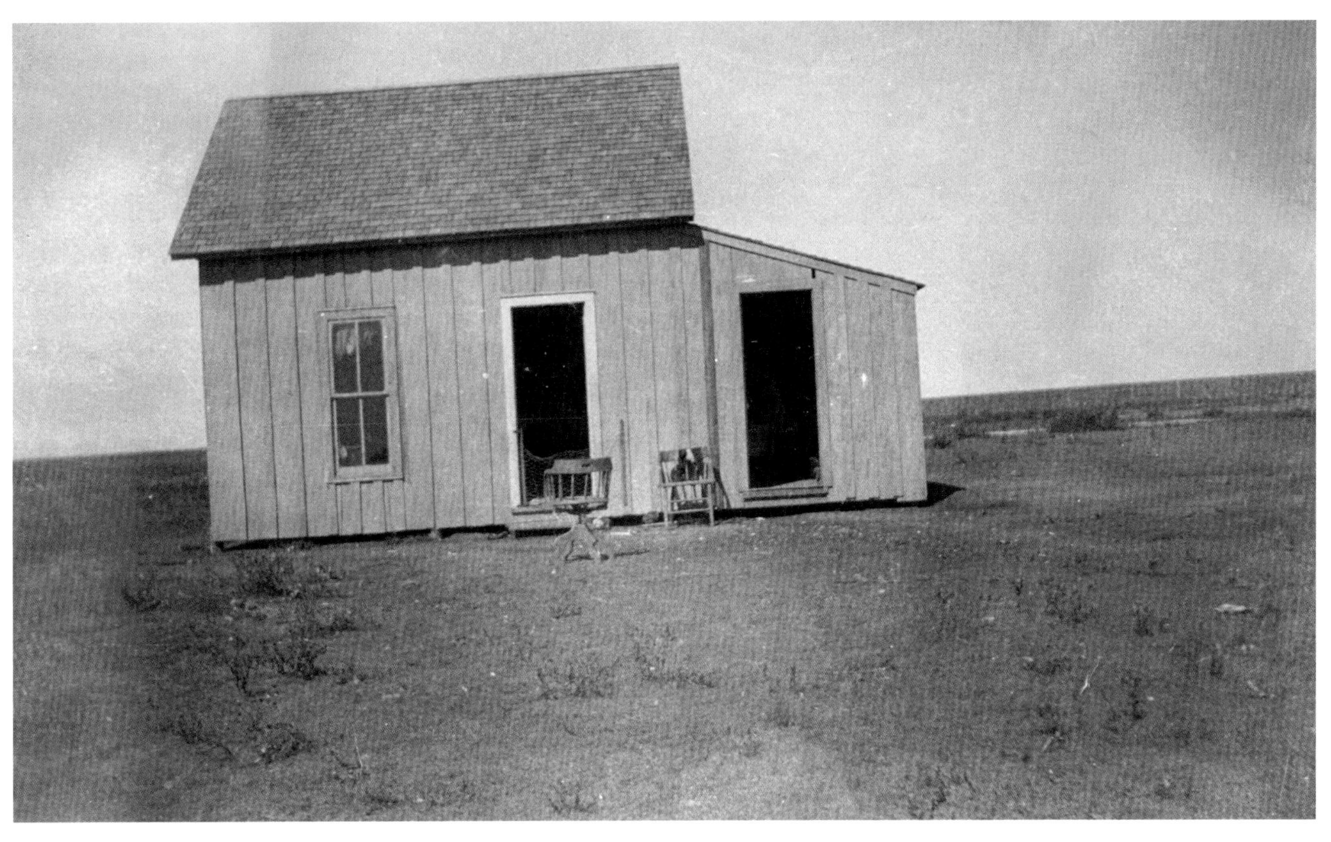

Cat. 32
"Home sweet home at aunt Annie's," Plainview, Texas, 1899
Photograph | Gabriele Münter- und Johannes Eichner-Stiftung, Munich, inv. no. 3919

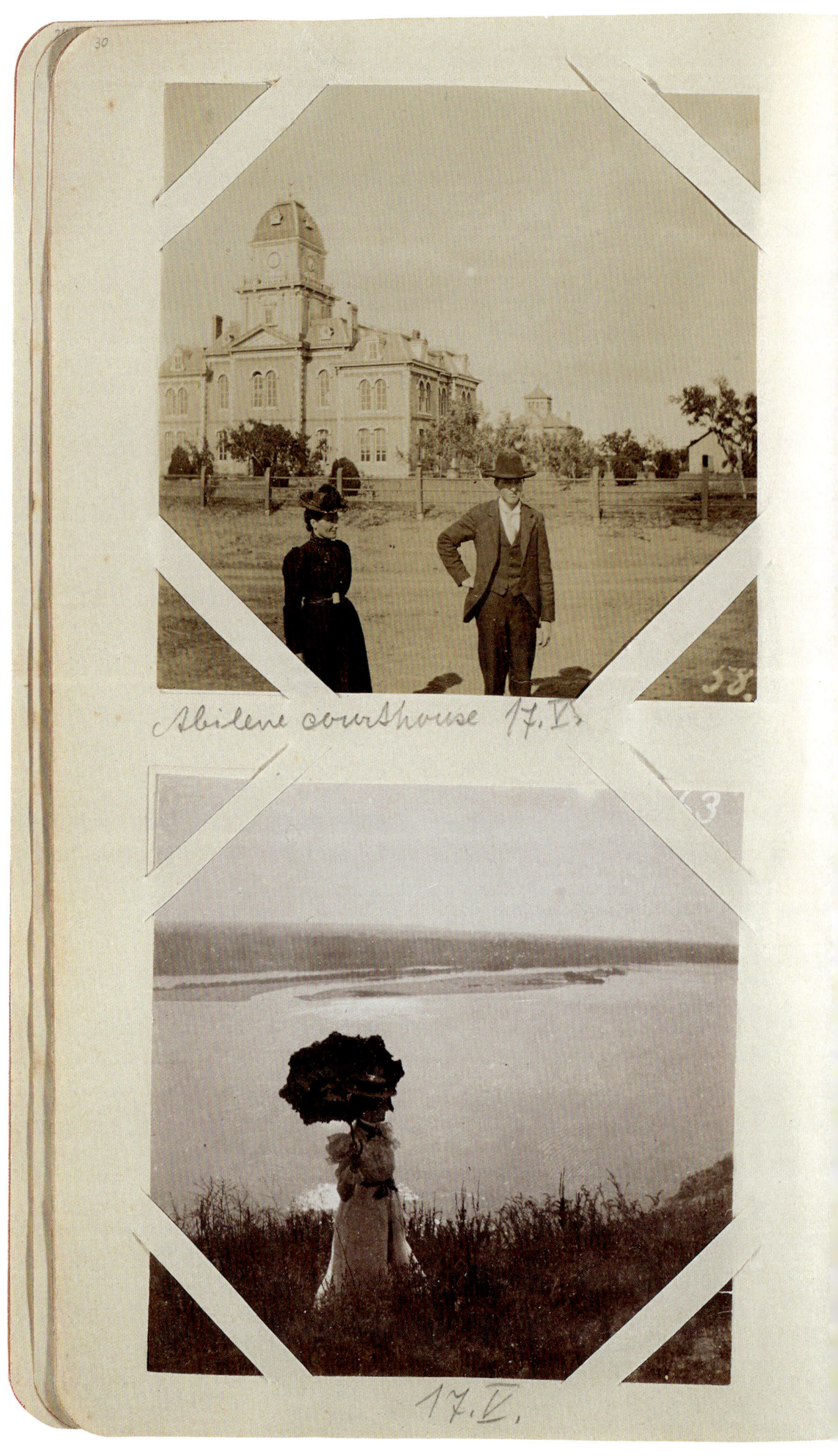

Cat. 33
Double-page spread from Gabriele Münter's photo album from her travels in North America, ca. 1900
Gabriele Münter- und Johannes Eichner-Stiftung, Munich

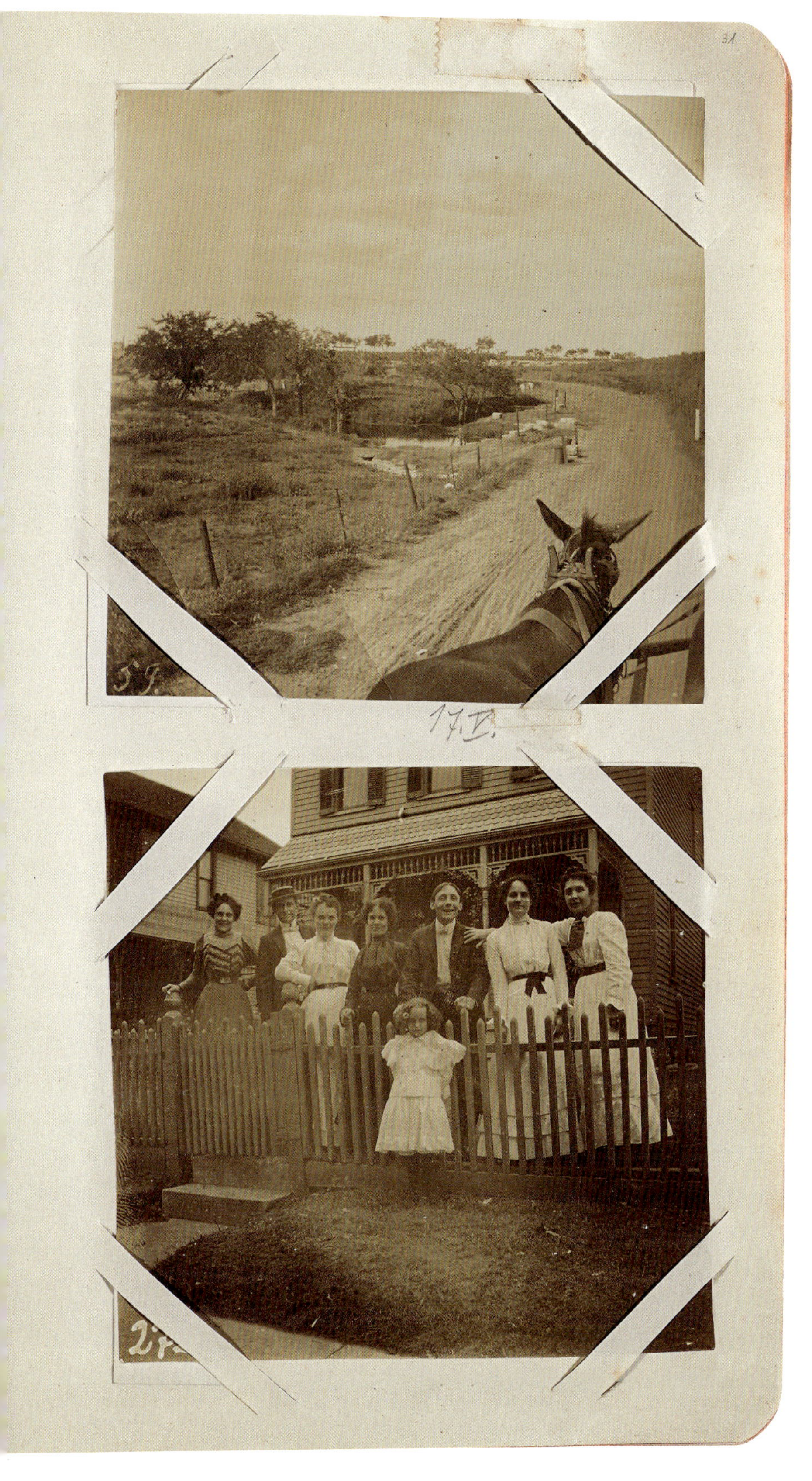

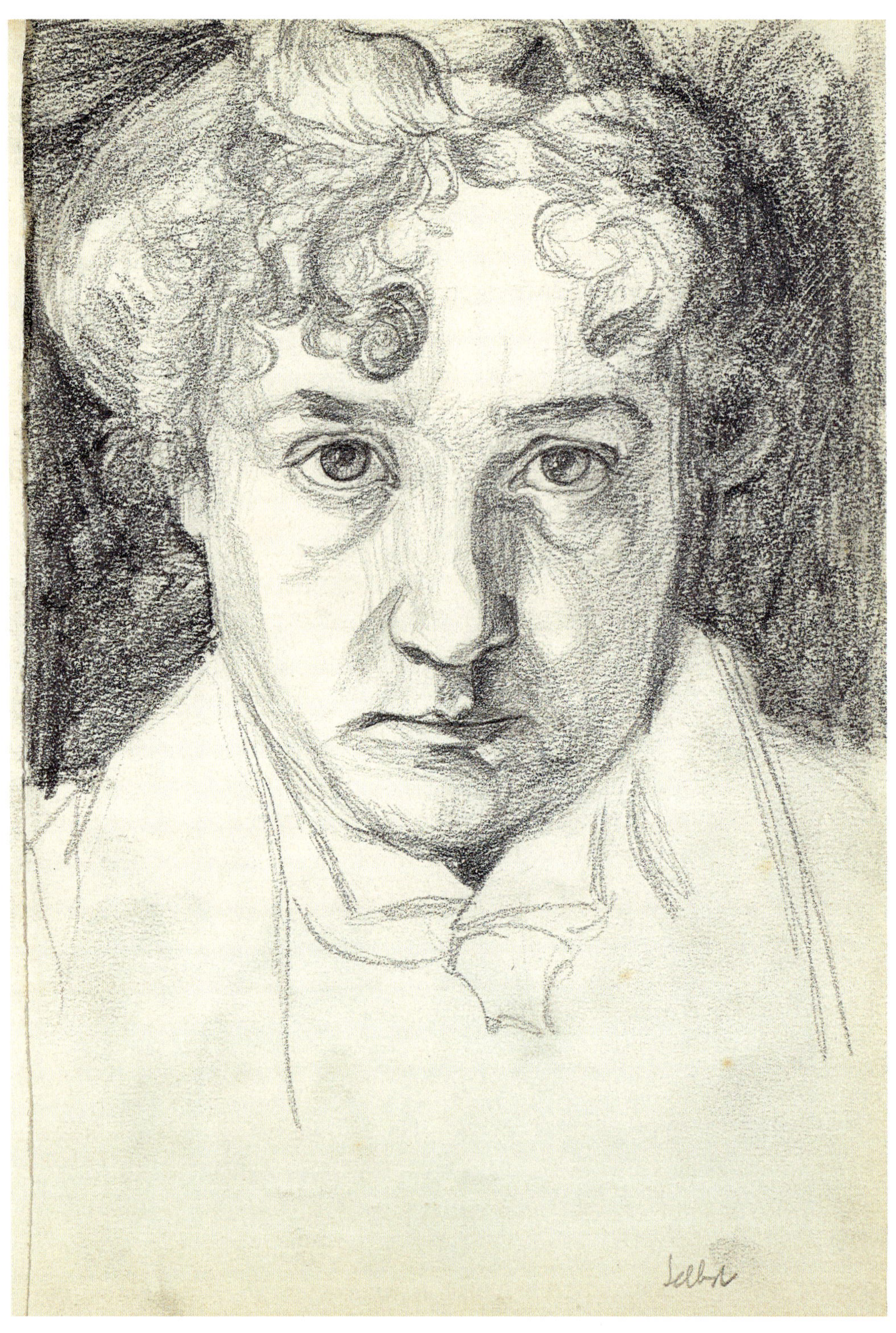

Cat. 34
“Self” [“Selbst”], 1902
Pencil, 19.5 × 13.7 cm | Gabriele Münter- und Johannes Eichner-Stiftung, Munich, sketchbook, inv. no. Kon. 46/6, p. 33

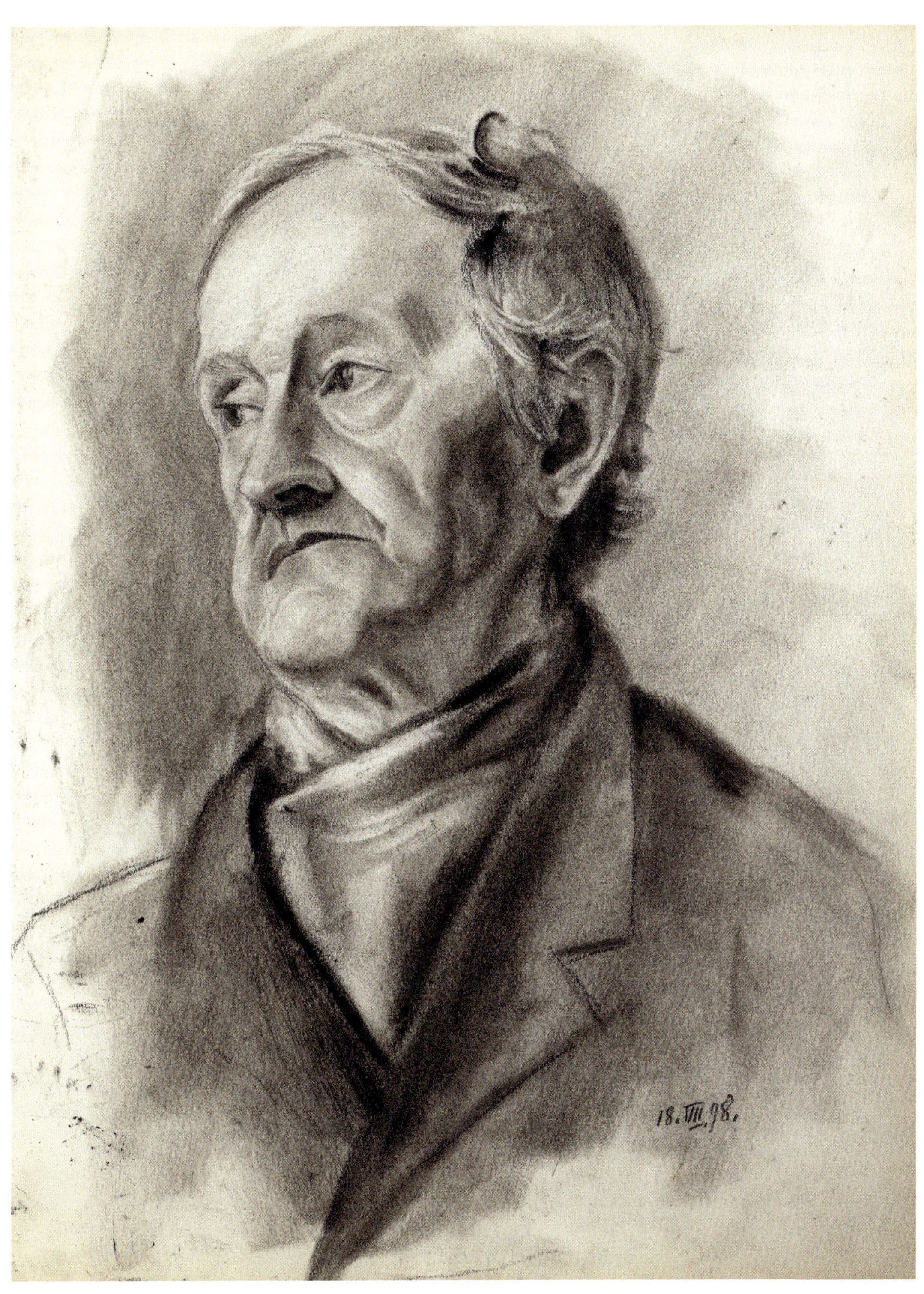

Cat. 35
Portrait of a Man
[Porträt eines Mannes], 1898
Black chalk, 31 × 23.5 cm | Gabriele Münter- und Johannes Eichner-Stiftung, Munich, sketchbook, inv. no. Kon. 38/4, p. 25

“You have probably understood that I had always been mainly a plein-air painter . . .”[1]

Out and About:
Landscapes and Outdoor Scenes

Out and About: Landscapes and Outdoor Scenes

"The language of nature is different from the language of art. Only by translating, not by copying, can you get from one language to the other. In addition to literal and loose translation, rewriting is also a legitimate form."[2] As can be inferred from this programmatic quote, Gabriele Münter's own concern as an artist was always to find a fitting artistic transcription of nature.[3]

Landscapes and outdoor scenes occupied an important place in her painted oeuvre from the very start. Even early on, they predominated over all other subjects and apparently so inspired Münter that they account for the majority of her paintings.

Her earliest dated painting is a landscape. Titled *Bavarian Landscape*, it was painted in the summer of 1902 during a visit to Kochel with Kandinsky's painting class from the Phalanx School.[4] The class spent the following summer in Kallmünz in the Upper Palatinate, where Münter painted for the most part small, atmospheric reproductions of the countryside. Cat. 36 The love affair that by then was developing between her and Kandinsky was complicated by the fact that Kandinsky had already married his cousin, Anja Shemiakina, who had accompanied him to Munich. In May 1904, therefore, anxious to flee this fraught situation, the artists embarked on a series of journeys that would last four years. They first spent four weeks in Holland, where Münter did more drawing than painting. The few paintings with Dutch motifs she did produce were in fact executed in her studio back in Germany after sketches made in situ. Cat. 39; 40 Münter did not paint much in Tunisia either: although the couple was there from December 25, 1904, to April 5, 1905, she produced only some twenty-five paintings—compared with numerous photographs (about 180 of which have survived) and sketches.[5] Alongside coastal landscapes and views of vast plains dotted with isolated houses, Münter also liked to paint and photograph the narrow lanes and stone arches of Tunisia's cities.

The artists' next extended stay was in Rapallo, a little town on the Ligurian coast where they took lodgings in late 1905. There Münter created some twenty paintings of the coast, the beach with boats, and the harbors of Rapallo and neighboring villages. By May 1906 she and Kandinsky were on the road again, this time headed for Paris, where they remained for a whole year. While Kandinsky lived as a recluse in the suburb of Sèvres, Münter rented a room in the bohemian quarter of Montparnasse and there attended a drawing course at the Académie de la Grande Chaumière.[6] Engaging with printmaking was especially important to her during this period, Fig. A although she did do some painting as well. We know of some seventy paintings showing the park of Saint-Cloud at various times of the year, as well as countless street scenes of Sèvres and the neighboring suburb of Bellevue with its bourgeois villas.

The painting *In Sèvres (Street in Bellevue)* is a harmonious composition of just a few colors—brown, gray, yellow, green, and blue—which between them convey the soft light of Paris most effectively. Cat. 51 The park of Saint-Cloud was also the subject of some of the photographs—few in number—that Münter took during her stay in the French capital. The motif of one of them recurs in the oil painting *Park of Saint-Cloud (Étude n°3)*: a view of Paris from the park of Saint-Cloud with the Eiffel Tower just visible in the background. Figs. B; C This raises the question of whether Münter perhaps painted it after the photograph. But since the photograph is black and white, and thus would have provided no information about colors, this seems unlikely. It is possible that the artist frequently went for walks in the park of Saint-Cloud—which is very close to Sèvres—and that she chose this motif for both photographs and paintings produced on various days. We know that she had adopted a similar working method during her stay in Kallmünz in 1903.[7]

The Paris paintings are the first to feature the deliberate and extensive use of little dabs of ultramarine, a color that was very important to Münter and

1
Roditi 1960, p. 148.

2
Translated from Gabriele Münter, undated note, MES.

3
Münter sometimes used the term "nature" to mean not just the world of nature but also reality itself.

4
See the chapter "Pre-Painting: Münter's Early Work," fig. D, p. 18.

5
A selection of these was exhibited and published in exh. cat. Munich 2007.

6
Isabelle Jansen, "Gabriele Münter in Paris 1906 bis 1907," in exh. cat. Munich/Bonn/Murnau 2000/01, pp. 39–47.

7
Isabelle Jansen, "Fotografieren oder Malen? Das Wechselspiel zwischen Fotografie und Malerei im Frühwerk von Gabriele Münter," in exh. cat. Kochel am See 2015, p. 150.

8
Our exhibition featured two of these paintings: *The Park of Saint-Cloud (Étude n°3)* and *View from the Window in Sèvres,* Cat. 50; 52.

9
Translated from "Murnau und ich," handwritten manuscript by Gabriele Münter, Schlossmuseum Murnau, inv. no. 10462.

would henceforth be present in all her paintings. She must have been satisfied with the results of her work, since she decided to submit six paintings to the Salon des Indépendants in the spring of 1907.[8] This event meant a great deal to her, as it was the first time that she had presented her works in public at all.

The paintings that Münter created while traveling, starting with the landscapes from Kallmünz, are stylistically similar: all are impastos done in Late Impressionist style, while the canvases themselves are generally small (the format of 16 × 25 centimeters being especially common) and often mounted on cardboard by the artist herself.

The year 1908 marked the end of Kandinsky's and Münter's wanderings. They decided to settle down permanently, and it was during their search for a suitable place that they chanced upon the little market town of Murnau on the Staffelsee Lake. While Kandinsky had been there before, in 1904, it was Münter's first visit. Much later, in 1957, she described how captivated she had been right from the start: "I first set foot [in Murnau] during a three-day excursion from Munich to Lake Starnberg and the Staffelsee Lake in June 1908, and was instantly enchanted. The preceding years had taken me to Holland, Tunisia, Saxony, Belgium, the French Riviera, Paris, Switzerland, Berlin, and the Merano region. But nowhere had I seen such an abundance of fine views all in the one place as here in Murnau, between lake and highlands, between rolling hills and moor."[9]

Münter and Kandinsky visited Murnau again in August 1908, spending several weeks there together with Alexej von Jawlensky (1864–1941) and

A **Parc Saint-Cloud, 1907**

Presumably a colored linoleum cut on Japan paper, approx. 12.2 × 26.3 cm | Städtische Galerie im Lenbachhaus und Kunstbau München, inv. no. GMS 828

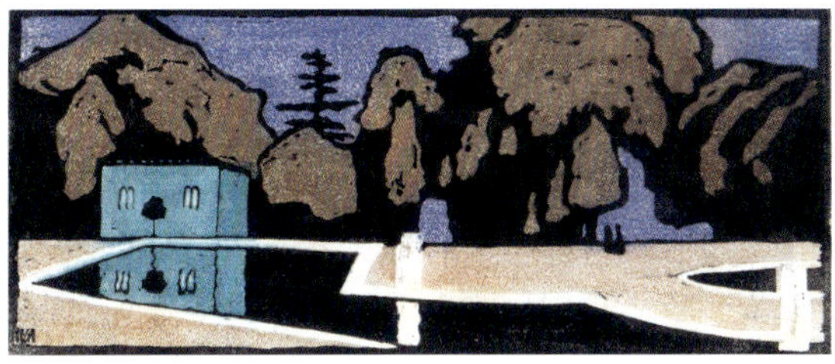

B **Park Terrace of Saint-Cloud, View of Paris, ca. 1906**

Photograph by Gabriele Münter | Gabriele Münter- und Johannes Eichner-Stiftung, Munich, inv. no. 2822

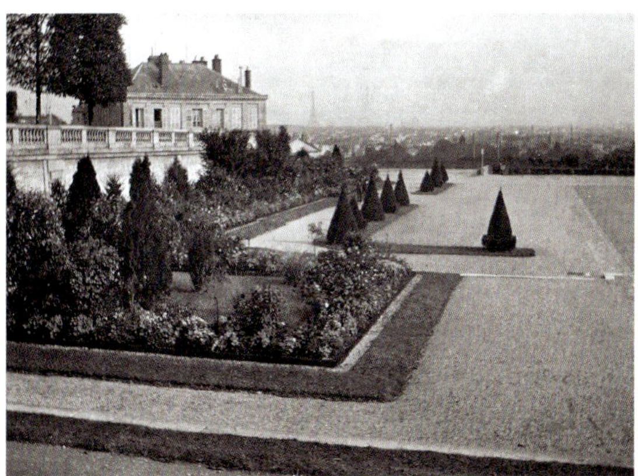

C **Park of Saint-Cloud (Étude n°3) [Park von Saint-Cloud (Étude n°3)], 1906**

Oil on canvas, mounted on cardboard, 22.2 × 34 cm | Private collection

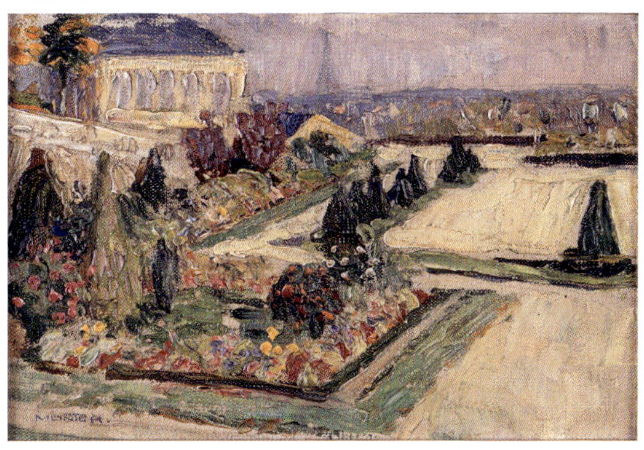

Marianne von Werefkin (1860–1938). The two couples took rooms at the Gasthof Griesbräu am Obermarkt and did a lot of painting together. The importance of that painting vacation to Münter's development as an artist is well known. As she herself later recalled, "I'd reached for the palette knife because I couldn't produce anything clear or pleasing with the brush. But I wanted to paint with brushes, and in somewhat larger formats than the studies of 1903–6. Then suddenly it came to me—I was standing dejectedly at the window of the Griesbräu—when all at once it 'clicked' and I felt liberated. From then on I took my 6 f painting box (K had a longer one, the 8 p) and went out into the countryside; my eyes had been opened—I saw and I painted."[10] This experience is the subject of two paintings: *View from the Griesbräu Window* and *From the Griesbräu Window*. Cat. 56; 55 Although the canvases are the same size, they differ both in format—one is landscape, the other portrait format—and in the handling of the motif. Whereas the roofs of Murnau are a prominent, close-up feature of the portrait-format painting, the angle selected for the other work required the houses to be positioned further away. Their colored façades are therefore clearly visible, and the line of the street can at least be inferred. The Alps in the background also look rather less schematic. A small study of the same subject presumably predates the paintings. The technique is the same as that of the paintings produced during Münter's nomadic period; the canvas is small and mounted on cardboard, and the paint seems to have been thickly applied.[11]

As anecdotal as the above-quoted lines about Münter's epiphany at the Griesbräu may sound, they do enable us to make sense of her sudden and radical change of style. For it is indeed astonishing how swiftly and seamlessly the artist transitioned from a Late Impressionist style, combining thickly applied paint and tiny brushstrokes, to a new visual idiom characterized by simplified forms and large expanses of bold colors brushed onto the cardboard in liquid paint. The opportunity to work alongside Jawlensky during their painting vacation in Murnau was undoubtedly a crucial factor in this development.[12] The Russian painter had at this point already switched to a flatter style of painting and was able to share what he had learned with Münter. While there are signs of an impending change of style in some of the portraits that Münter painted in Berlin earlier in 1908, as well as in some of the views of the Etsch Valley as seen from Lana near Merano, painted from April to June 1908,[13] Cat. 53; 54 it was not until the visit to Murnau that she at last made the definitive breakthrough to a simpler, more two-dimensional style. Inspired by the mental leap made at the Griesbräu, Münter began roaming the countryside and painting whatever took her fancy. In the course of those few weeks, she produced numerous landscapes on cardboard in what was for her the standard format of 33 × 41 centimeters.

Münter did not apply her newly acquired visual language to the exclusion of all others, however; on the contrary, she applied different styles simultaneously, depending on the kind of painting she was working on.[14] While the layer of paint in *Landscape with Hut at Sunset* (1908) is thick and compact, the brushwork in *Woodcutter (Pfarrgasse with Woodcutter)* (1909) is much looser, so that the cardboard actually shines through in places. Cat. 60; 65 This gives rise to a certain unrest that amplifies the sense of menace emanating from the dark cumulus clouds. The mood in *Landscape with Hut at Sunset*, in contrast, is calm; the painting radiates serenity. The impact made by *House in Schwabing* (1911) Cat. 68 is very different. This remarkably large—by Münter's standards—painting was executed after a small study that she had already produced of the same motif. Fig. D The palette is subdued and the composition unusual: occupying the foreground in the lower half of the work is a road and an area of raised ground, both of which verge on the abstract, while the background shows a house standing in front of a rather vague, unidentifiable shape.

These examples are typical of Münter's perception of nature, since what they show is a domesticated nature in which traces of a human presence are

10
Translated from Gabriele Münter, undated note, MES. 6 f and 8 p are canvas formats in France. 6 f stands for "6 figure" and is equivalent to the format 41 × 33 cm; 8 p stands for "8 paysage" and is equivalent to the format 46 × 33 cm. On Münter's change of style, see also the chapter "Primitivism," p. 142.

11
Murnau from the Griesbräu, 1908, textile support mounted on cardboard, 17.8 × 26 cm, whereabouts unknown.

12
On the role played by Jawlensky, see the chapter "Primitivism," p. 142.

13
See the chapter "Portraits," p. 100; see also Helena Pereña, "'In bester Stimmung auf unserer Tour . . .' Münter (1908), Kandinsky (1908, 1914) und Marc (1913) in Südtirol," in exh. cat. Innsbruck 2014, pp. 139–44, here p. 140.

14
See the chapter "Portraits," p. 100.

15
Exh. cat. Milwaukee/Columbus/Richmond/San Antonio 1997–99, pp. 146ff.

16
Mühling/Jansen 2014.

17
Most commentators attribute the slump in her output of paintings during this period to the separation from Kandinsky, but the difficulty of adjusting to life in Germany again after a five-year absence must have compounded both the separation and her inability to settle down. She was now utterly alone, both personally and professionally. Furthermore, during her years in Berlin, she only sporadically had her own studio, whereas before the war, and even while in Scandinavia, she had generally been surrounded by fellow artists.

clearly visible, whether in the form of buildings—houses, churches, castles—or as actual figures.[15] This is especially clear in the Scandinavian landscapes, in which the subject of the individual carries even more weight. Indeed, human figures frequently play a key role in her compositions, as is evident in the beach scenes painted in Denmark in the summer of 1919. Cat. 82; 83

In 1909 Münter bought a house in Murnau where she and Kandinsky could enjoy long breaks together, especially during the summer months.[16] The garden there was important to both of them, yet she selected it as a motif surprisingly rarely. The painting *In the Garden in Murnau*, which shows her holding a bucket amid luxuriant flowerbeds, is a rather lovely exception from the prewar period. Cat. 67 When she revisited the theme in 1931, the subject was Johannes Eichner (1886–1958), her life partner from 1928, busy at work in the garden. Fig. E

The outbreak of World War I marked a momentous turning point for both Münter and Kandinsky. As a citizen of what was now an "enemy power," Kandinsky had to leave Germany and so set off for Switzerland together with Münter. In November 1914, however, he returned to Russia alone, where three years later he married Nina Andreevskaia. In early 1915 Münter also left Switzerland, and that same summer, after a few months back in Munich, she traveled on to Scandinavia, where she would remain for nearly five years. On returning to Germany in February 1920 she at first lived alternately in Munich, in Murnau, at Schloss Elmau, and in Cologne, but in 1925 she moved to Berlin, where she reconnected with the art world and even attended a painting school run by Arthur Segal (1875–1944).

Not least owing to her frequent changes of abode, Münter painted very little in the 1920s and tended to prefer drawing as the less complicated undertaking.[17] Yet she still painted some landscapes even during this period. Most are views of Murnau and the surrounding region, while others were painted during her travels, among them the work called *Landscape in Lauenstein with Red Children*

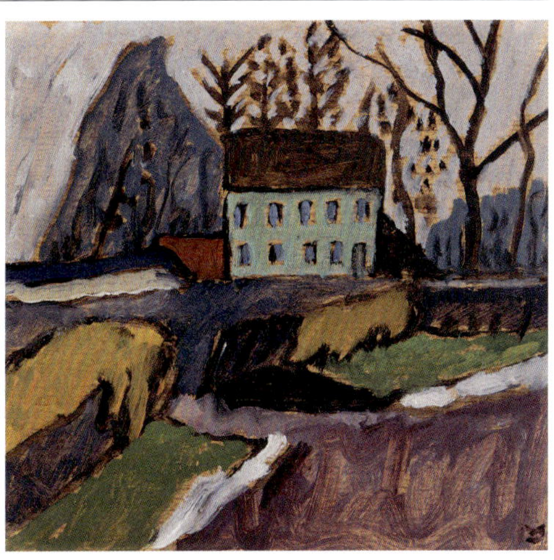

D **House in Schwabing [Haus in Schwabing], ca. 1911**
Oil on cardboard, 25.3 × 27.8 cm | Private collection, London

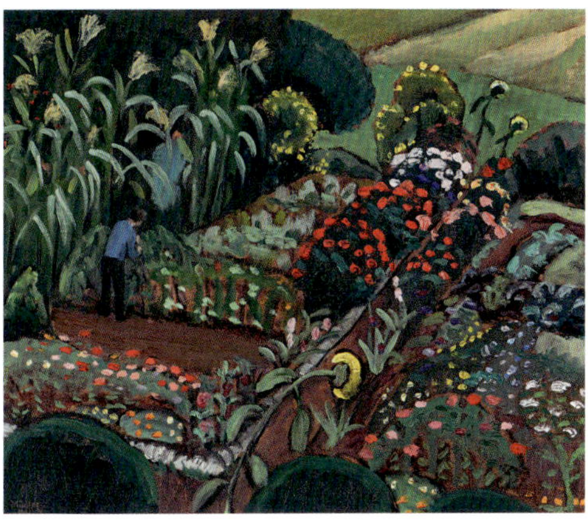

E **My Garden [Mein Garten], 1931**
Oil on canvas, 46 × 55 cm | Private collection

of 1928; its naïve style makes for a stark contrast with *Little Church in Ramsach* also of 1928, whose composition seems conventional by comparison. Cat. 71; 72

The dawn of the new decade saw a sharp rise in Münter's artistic output, starting during an extended stay in Paris from October 1929 to September 1930. From Paris, she and her new partner, Johannes Eichner, set off for the south of France, to Sanary-sur-Mer, which for over two decades had been a popular haunt of writers and artists from all over Europe, including the painter Hans Purrmann (1880–1966), whom Münter frequently encountered there. It was there, and in the surrounding countryside, that she painted some of her large-format landscapes, including *At the Wall (Bandol)*, showing a motif from the nearby port of Bandol. Cat. 85

Münter at last made the house in Murnau her permanent home in 1931. Once installed there, she again began painting prolifically and was able to maintain the pace that she had set herself in Paris the previous year. The town and its environs would henceforth be at the heart of her work, for as she herself wrote: "There are motifs that move you, and, in turn, you want to get hold of them—and there are motifs that inspire you to make something out of them, that are not complete as they are. I would like to eat it all up again just as it is, bright and clean—to bring order into the chaos. Synthesis. The play of variations."[18] This diary entry pinpoints two hallmarks of Münter's work that are in fact interconnected, namely the relish she took both in repeating herself and in working doggedly at a motif until the results satisfied her own high standards. Another characteristic of her working method that can be inferred from this quotation is that Münter apparently never felt the need to go off in search of subjects. On the contrary, she found them effortlessly, usually right in front of her, wherever she happened to be.[19]

18
Diary entry of September 20, 1941, in exh. cat. Milwaukee/Columbus/Richmond/San Antonio 1997–99, p. 147.

19
See the chapter "Pre-Painting: Münter's Early Work," p. 17.

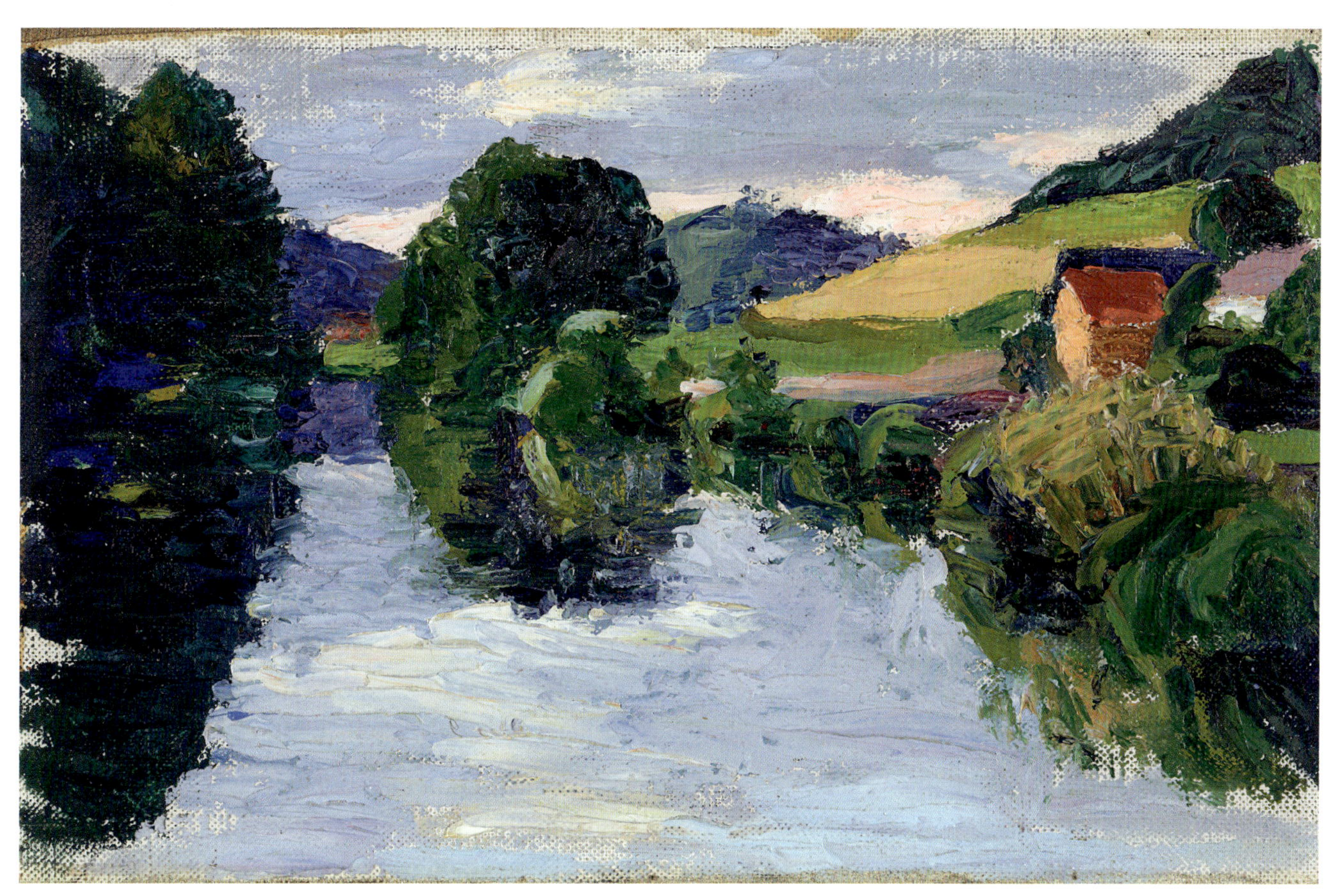

Cat. 36
Summer Day [Sommertag], 1903
Oil on canvas, 18.5 × 29 cm |
Private collection, Württemberg

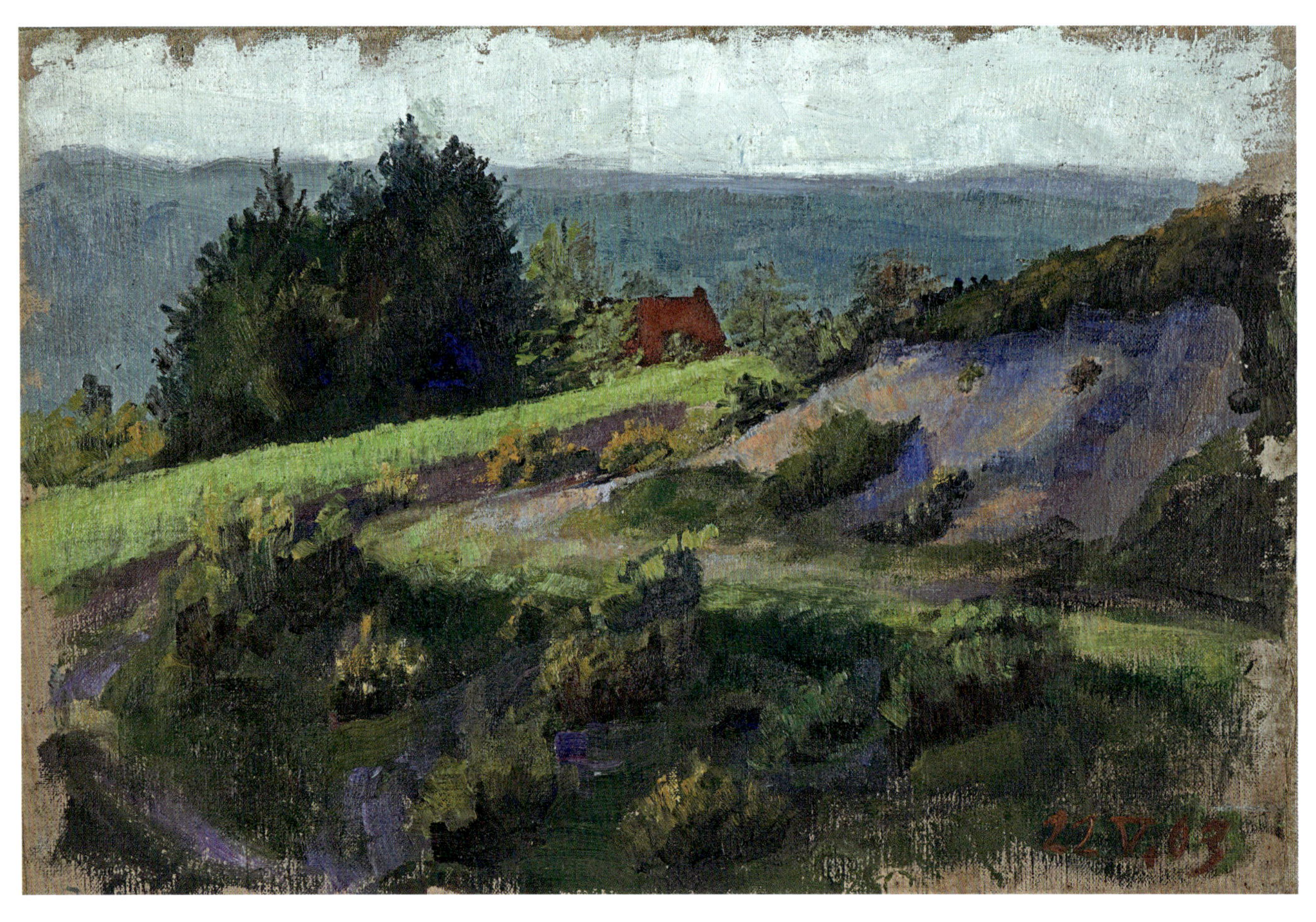

Cat. 37
Landscape in Westphalia with a Red House [Westfälische Landschaft mit rotem Haus], 1903
Textile support, approx. 31.5 × 47.2 cm | Gabriele Münter- und Johannes Eichner-Stiftung, Munich, inv. no. L 660

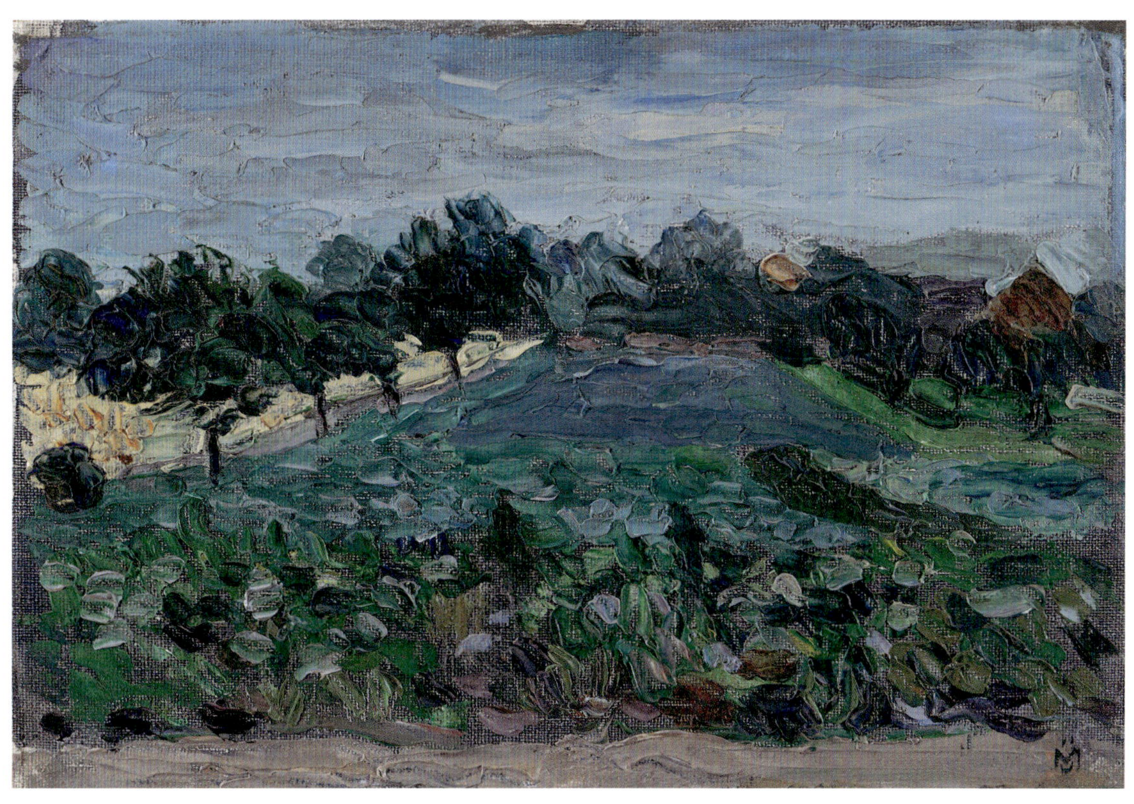

Cat. 38
Landscape in Saxony [Landschaft in Sachsen], 1905
Oil on canvas, 18.2 × 26.2 cm | On permanent loan to the Schloßmuseum Murnau from a private collection

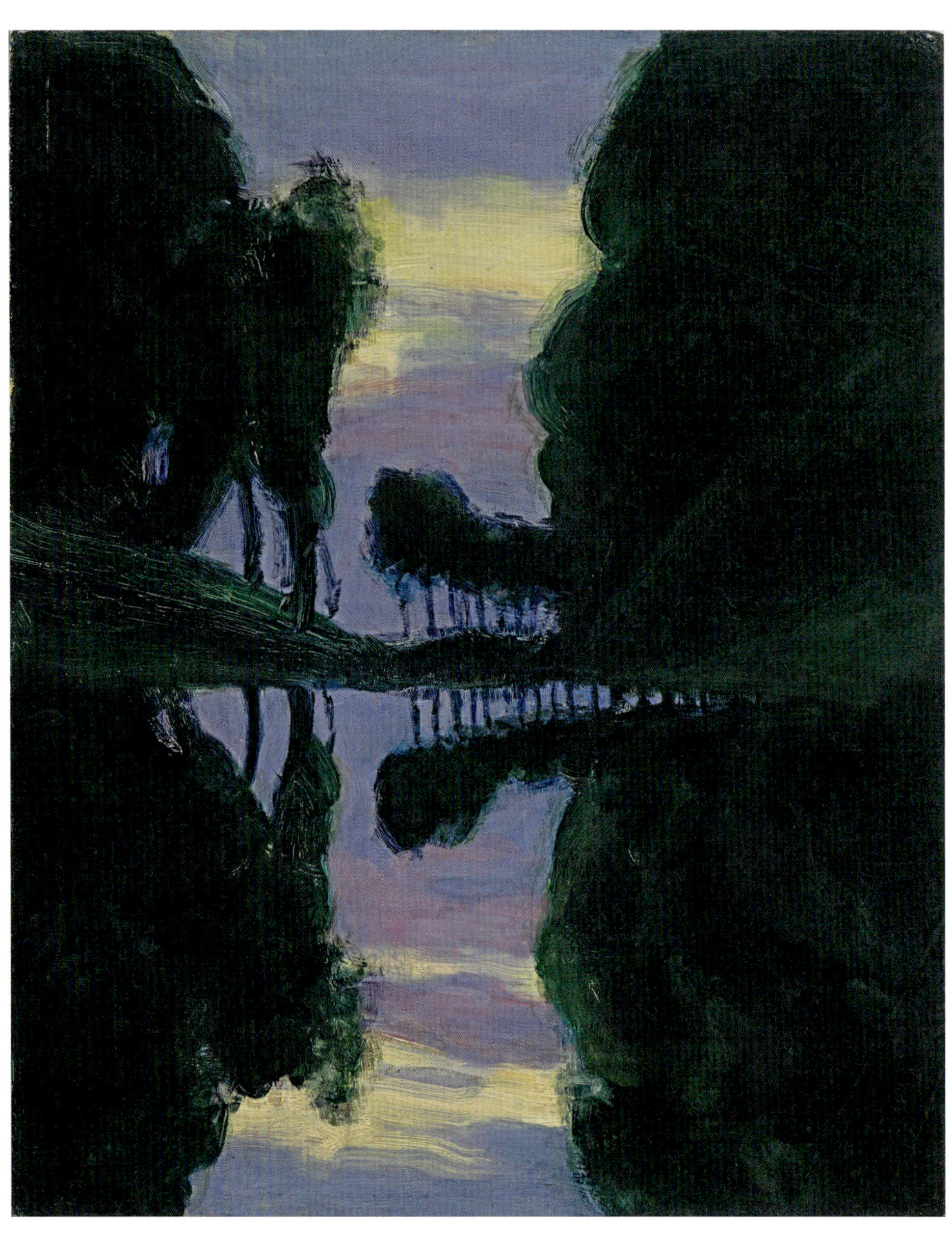

Cat. 39
Holland (Edam), 1904
Cardboard, 27 × 22 cm |
Gabriele Münter- und Johannes Eichner-Stiftung, Munich, inv. no. L 440

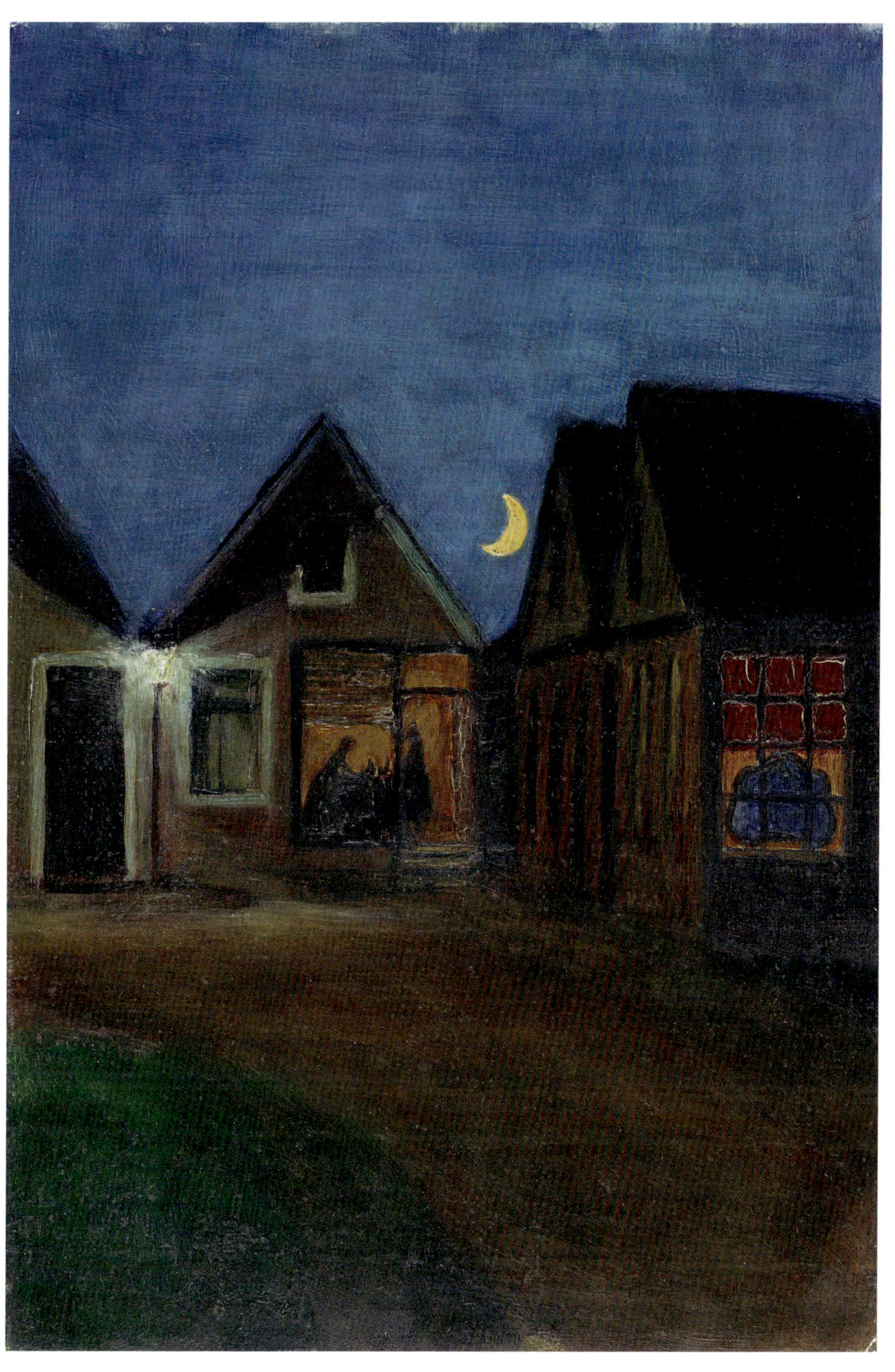

Cat. 40
Holland, 1904
Cardboard, 26.2 × 17.7 cm |
Gabriele Münter- und Johannes Eichner-Stiftung, Munich, inv. no. L 444

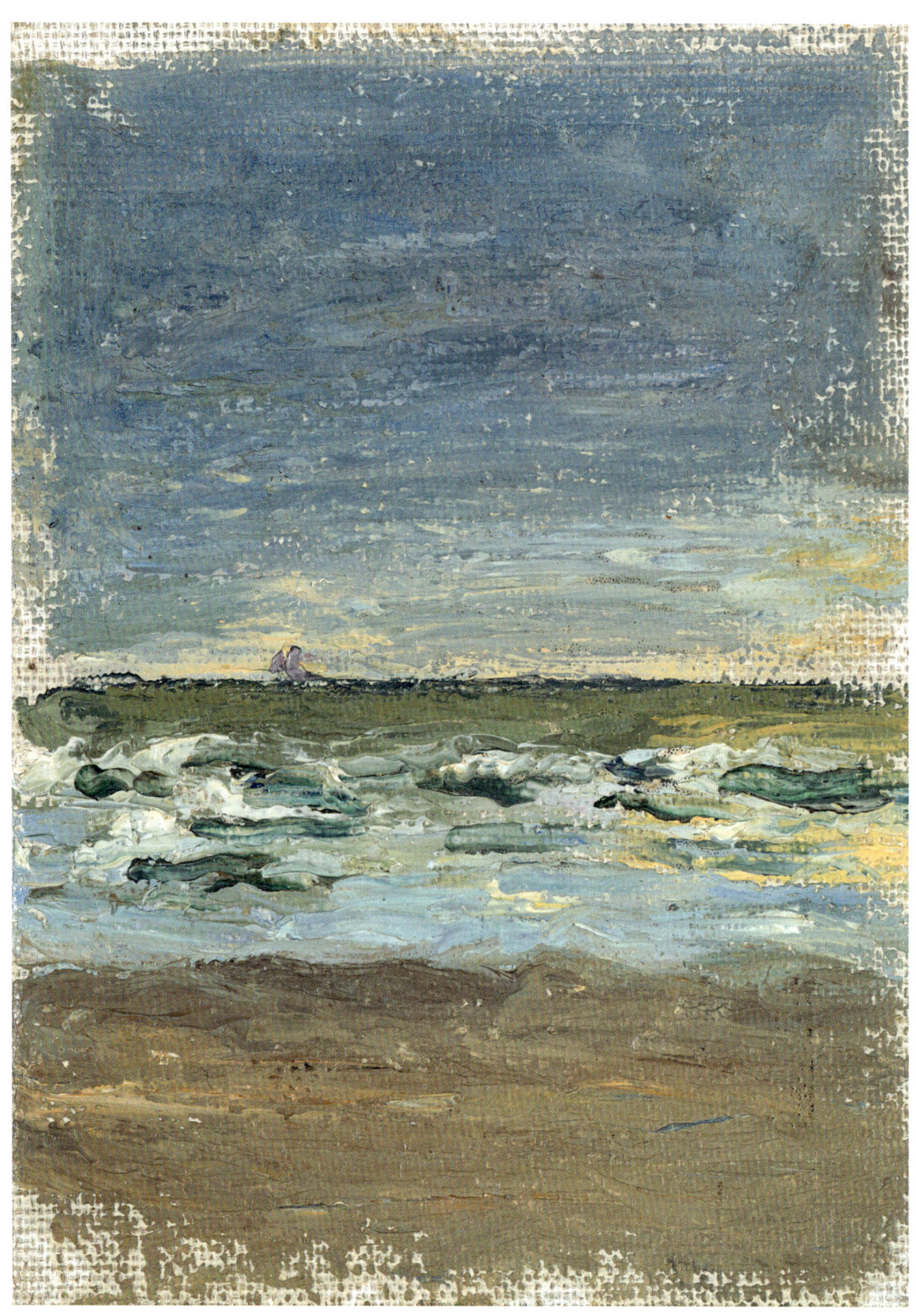

Cat. 41
Surf at the Seashore [Meeresbrandung], ca. 1904
Textile support on cardboard, 23.4 × 17 cm | Gabriele Münter- und Johannes Eichner-Stiftung, Munich, inv. no. L 592

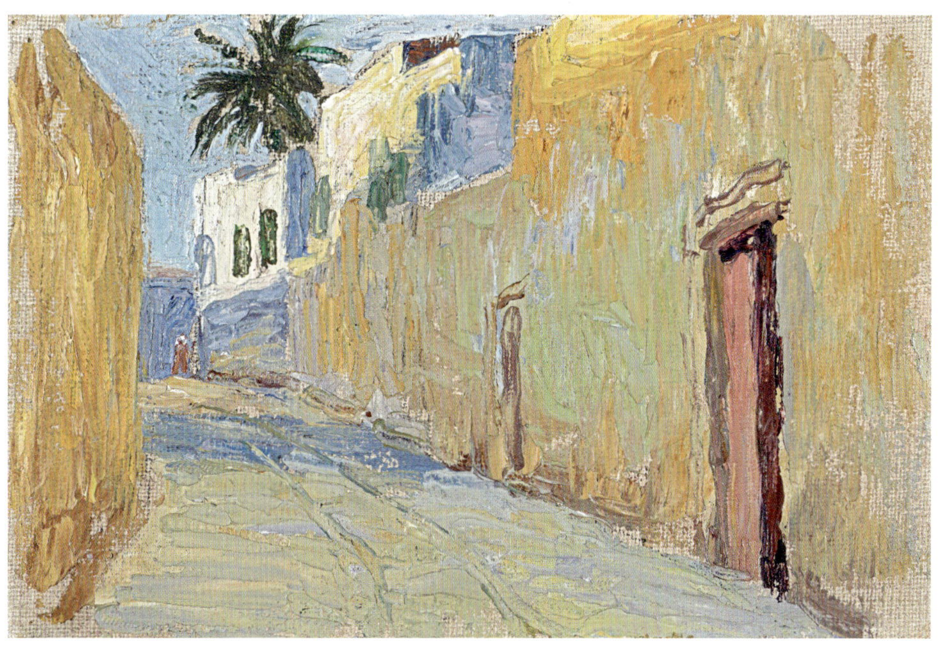

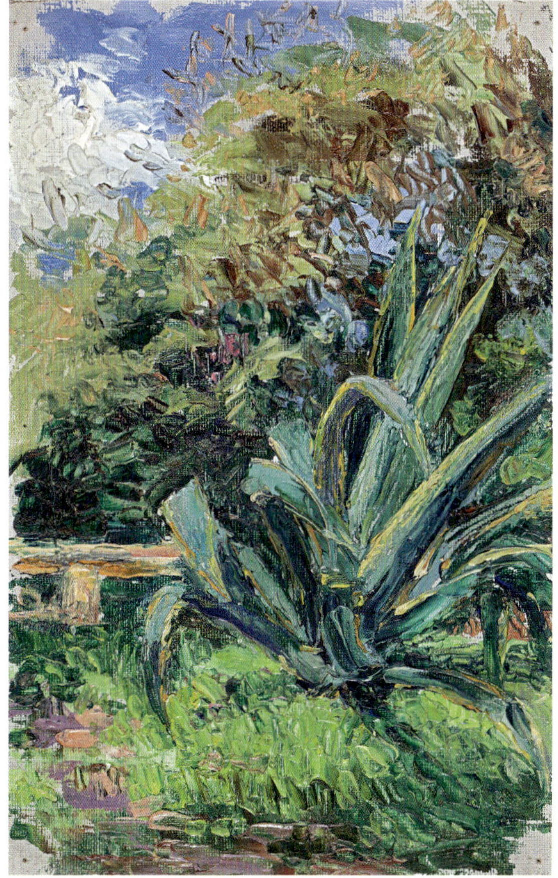

Cat. 42
Lane in Tunis
[Gasse in Tunis], 1905
Textile support, 16.3 × 24.5 cm |
Gabriele Münter- und Johannes Eichner-Stiftung, Munich, inv. no. L 573

Cat. 43
Aloe, 1905
Textile support, 25.8 × 16.8 cm |
Gabriele Münter- und Johannes Eichner-Stiftung, Munich, inv. no. L 354

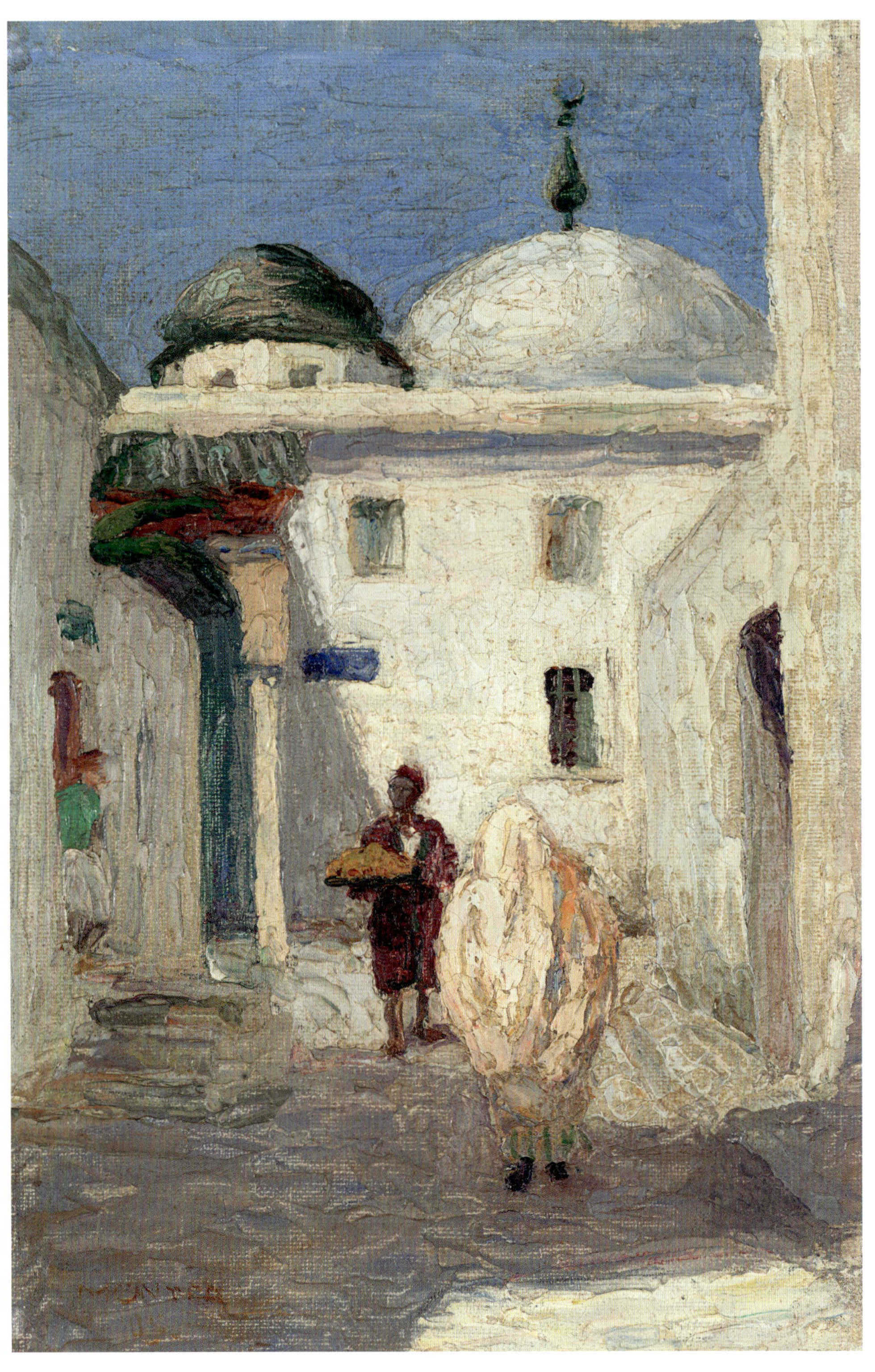

Cat. 44
Street in Tunis
[Straße in Tunis], 1905
Oil on canvas, mounted on cardboard, 25.4 × 17.2 cm | Private collection

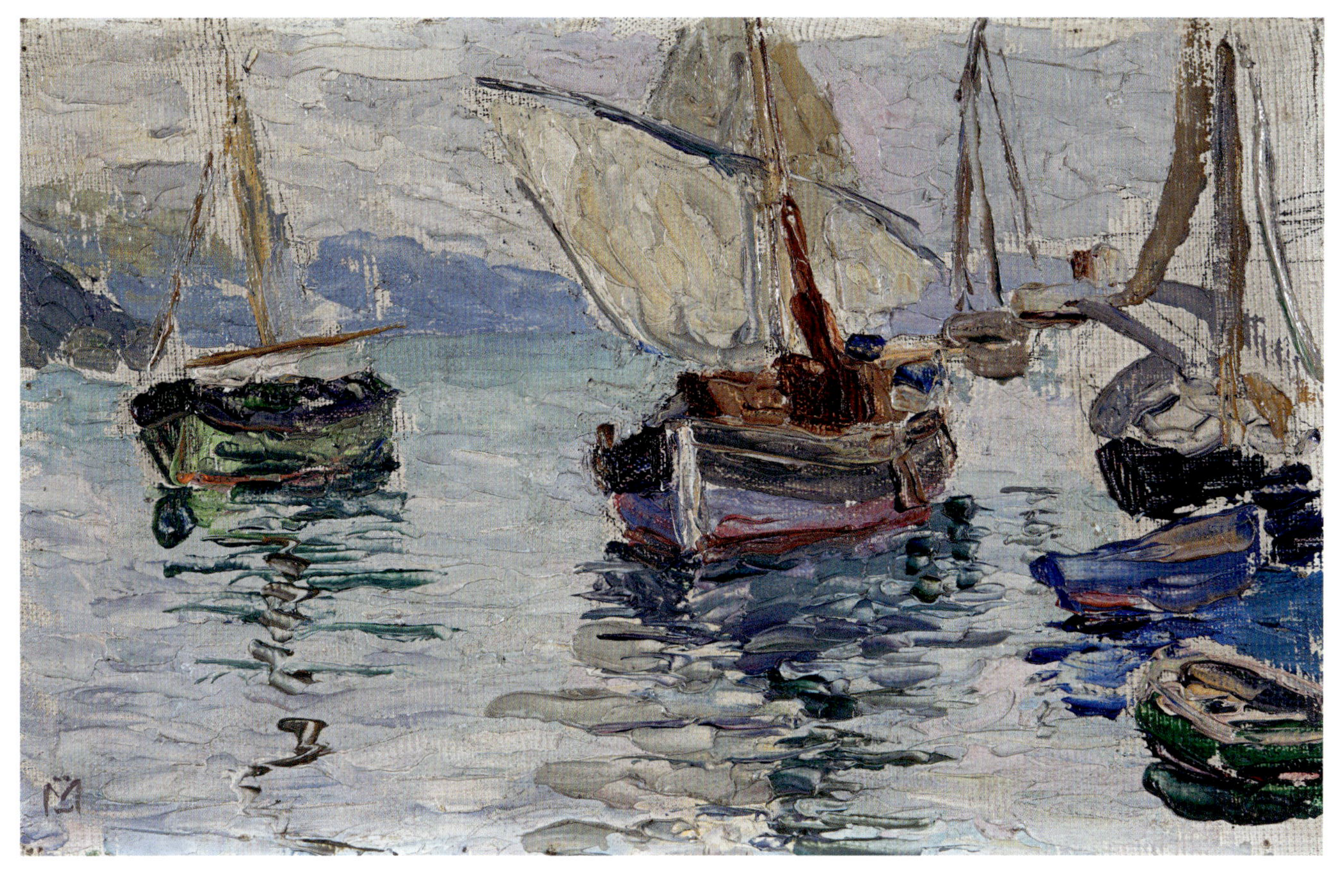

Cat. 45
Sailboats on the Water [Segelboote im Wasser], 1906
Oil and pencil on canvas,
17 × 26 cm | On loan from the PSM Privatstiftung Schloßmuseum Murnau as a loan from the Sammlung Deutsche Bank, inv. no. PSM 68/12672

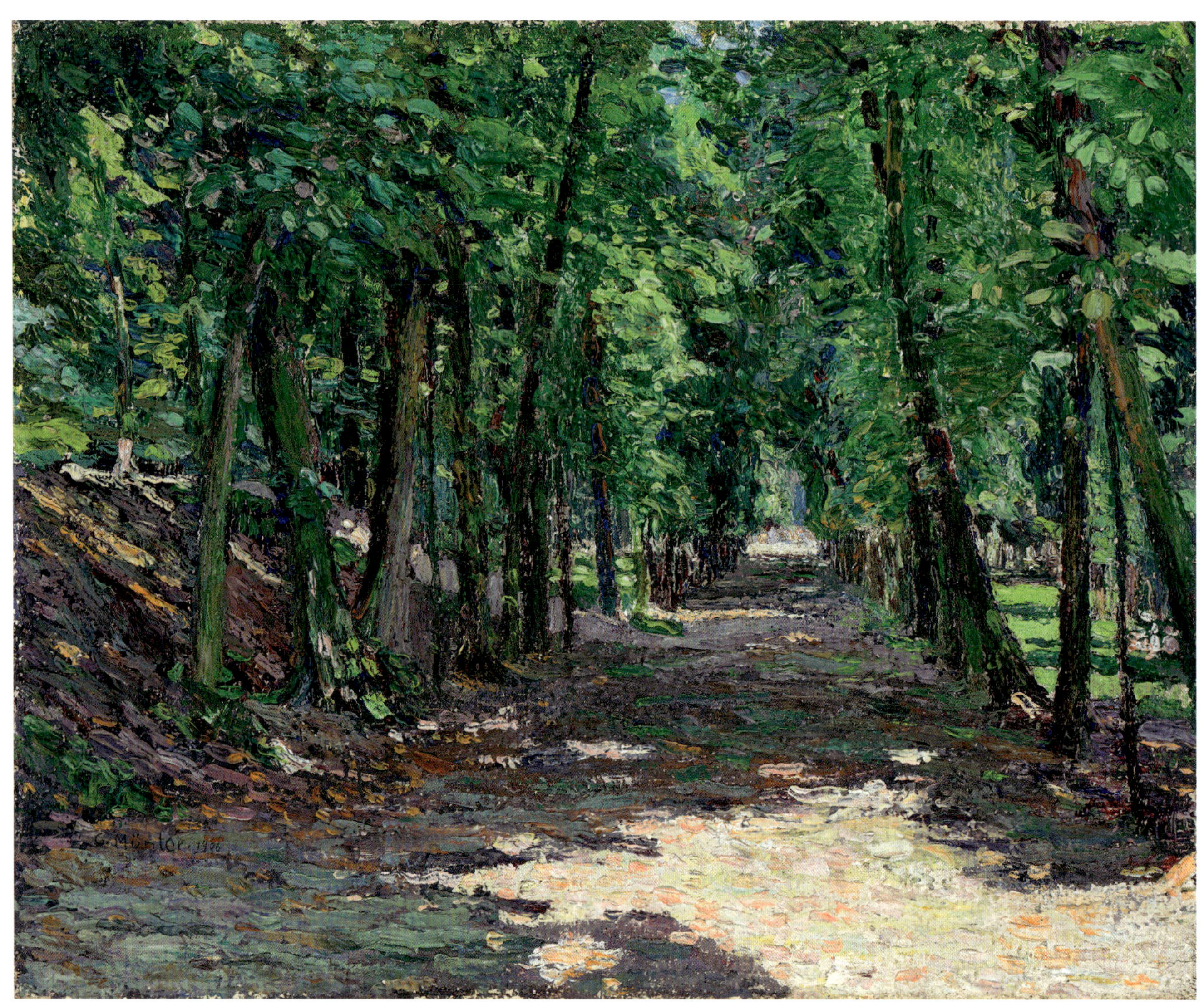

Cat. 46
Avenue in the Park of Saint-Cloud [Allee im Park von Saint-Cloud], 1906
Textile support, 40.5 × 50.5 cm | Städtische Galerie im Lenbachhaus und Kunstbau München, inv. no. GMS 651

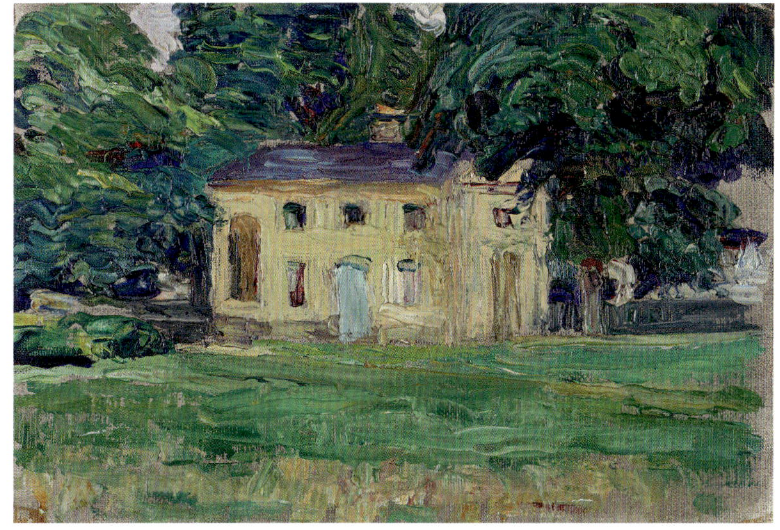

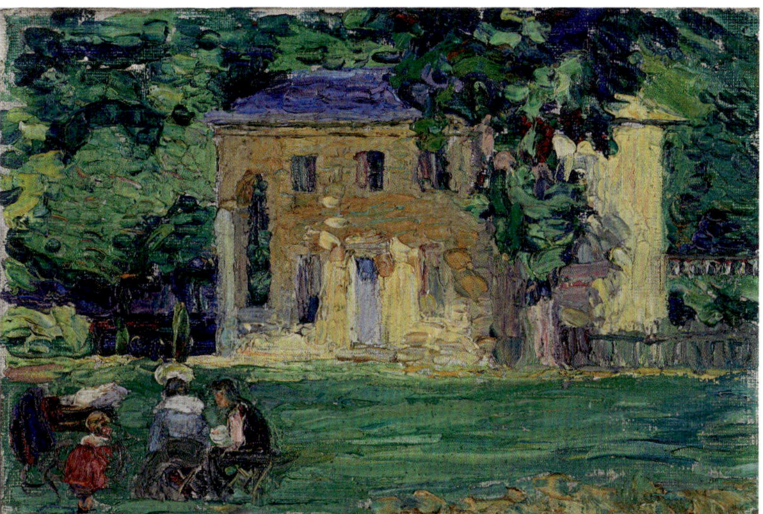

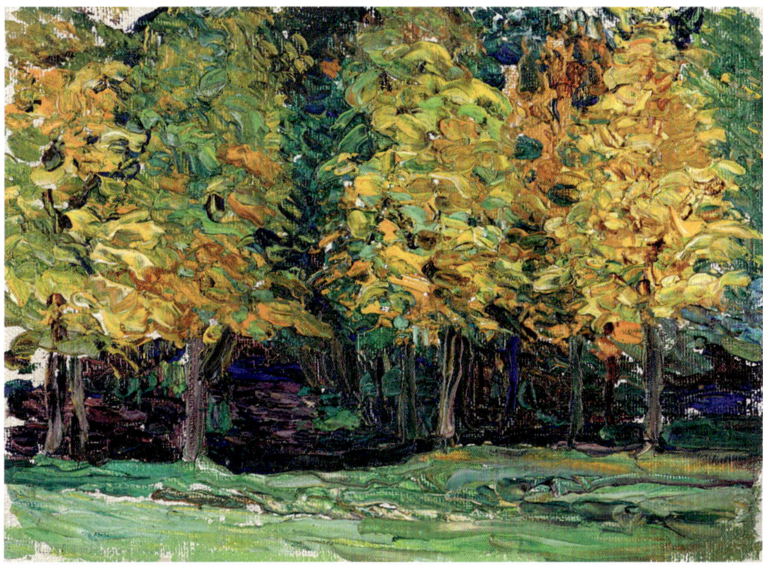

Cat. 47
House in the Park, Sèvres [Haus im Park, Sèvres], 1906/07
Oil on canvas, 16.6 × 25 cm | Collectio Artium, Augsburg

Cat. 48
Family in the Park of Saint-Cloud [Familie im Park von Saint-Cloud], 1906/07
Oil on canvas, 16.2 × 23 cm | Collectio Artium, Augsburg

Cat. 49
Park in Autumn [Park im Herbst], 1906/07
Canvas, mounted on cardboard, 16.2 × 23.1 cm | Gabriele Münter- und Johannes Eichner-Stiftung, Munich, inv. no. L 578

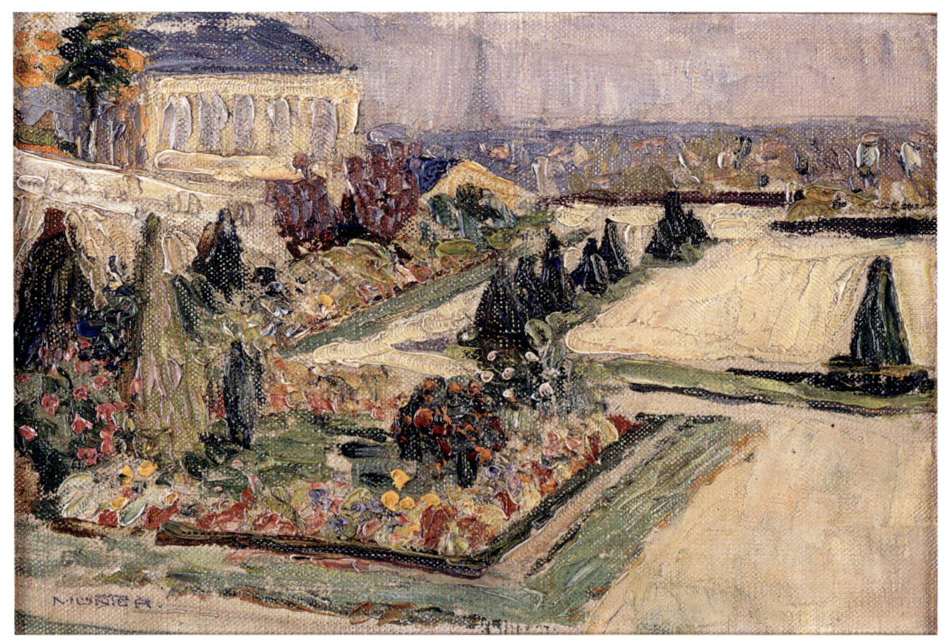

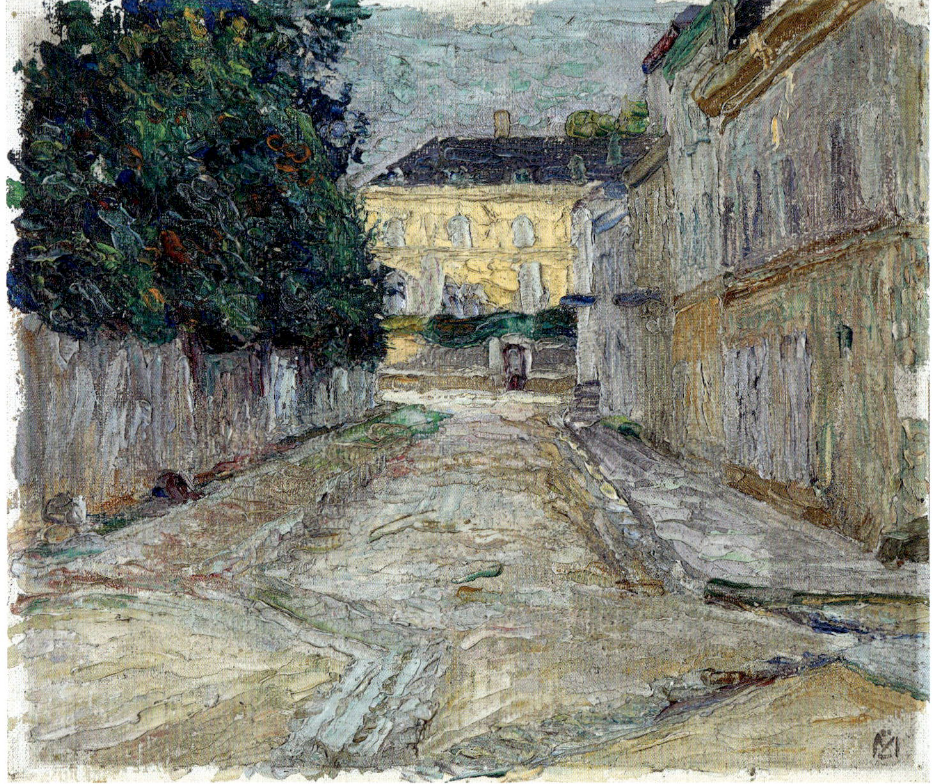

Cat. 50
Park of Saint-Cloud (Étude n°3) [Park von Saint-Cloud (Étude n°3)], 1906
Oil on canvas, mounted on cardboard, 22.2 × 34 cm | Private collection

Cat. 51
In Sèvres (Street in Bellevue) [In Sèvres (Straße in Bellevue)], 1906
Oil on canvas, mounted on cardboard, 22.3 × 27 cm | Kunstsammlungen Chemnitz – Museum Gunzenhauser, property of the Stiftung Gunzenhauser, inv. no. GUN-M-0001

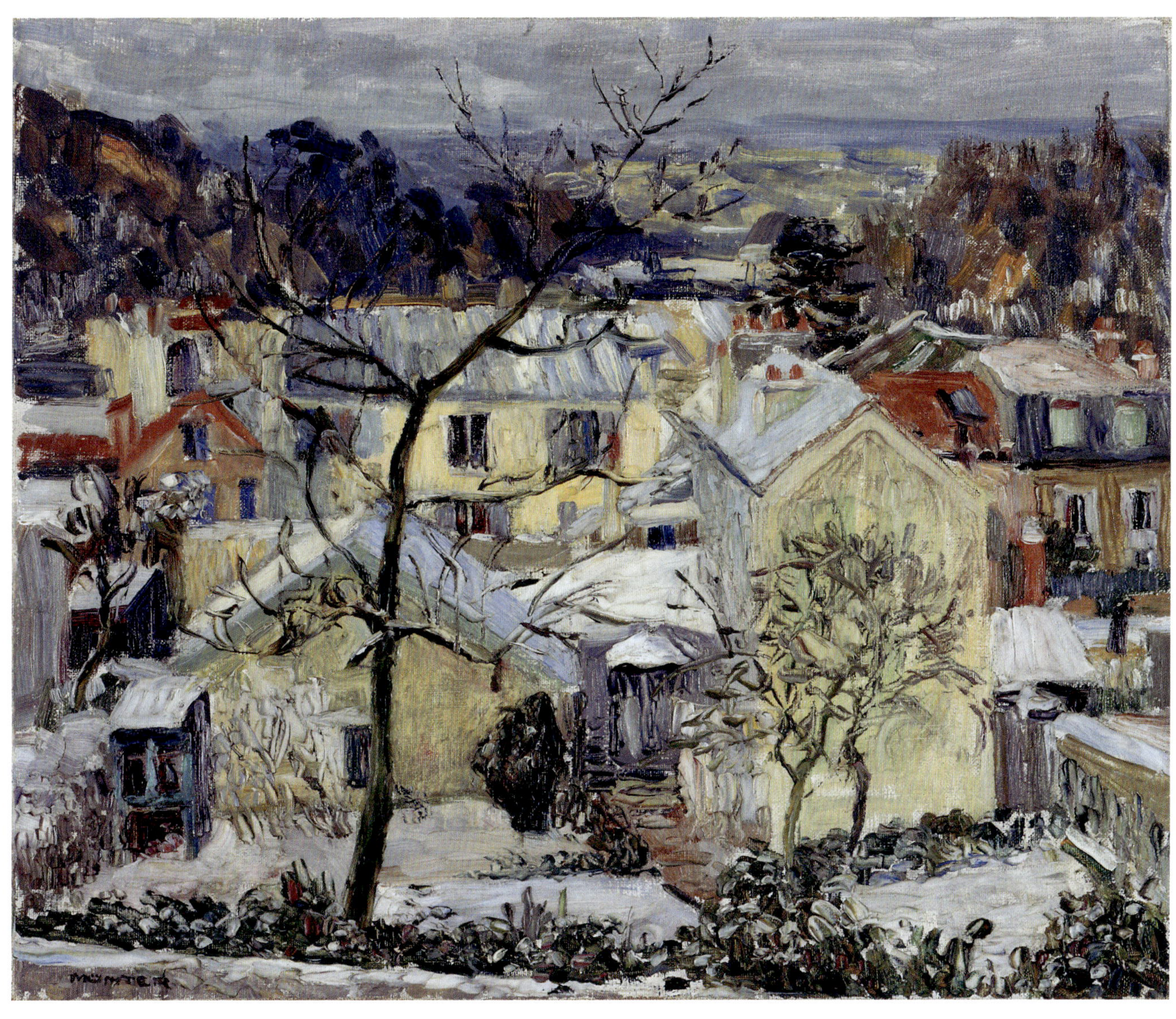

Cat. 52
View from the Window in Sèvres [Blick aus dem Fenster in Sèvres], 1906
Textile support, 38 × 46 cm | Städtische Galerie im Lenbachhaus und Kunstbau München, inv. no. G 11770

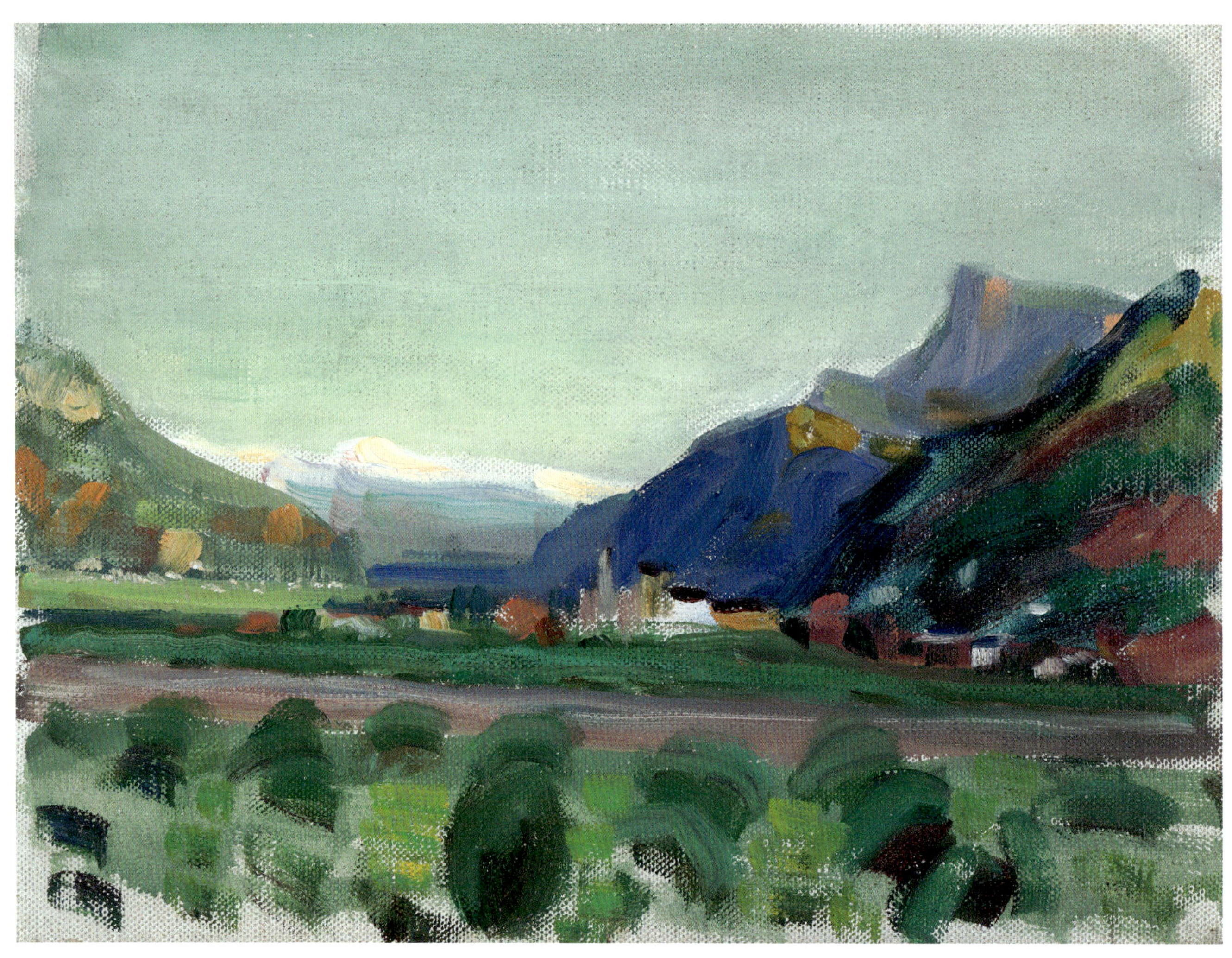

Cat. 53
Before Lana [Vor Lana], 1908
Textile support, 28.4 × 38.2 cm |
Gabriele Münter- und Johannes Eichner-Stiftung, Munich, inv. no. L 351

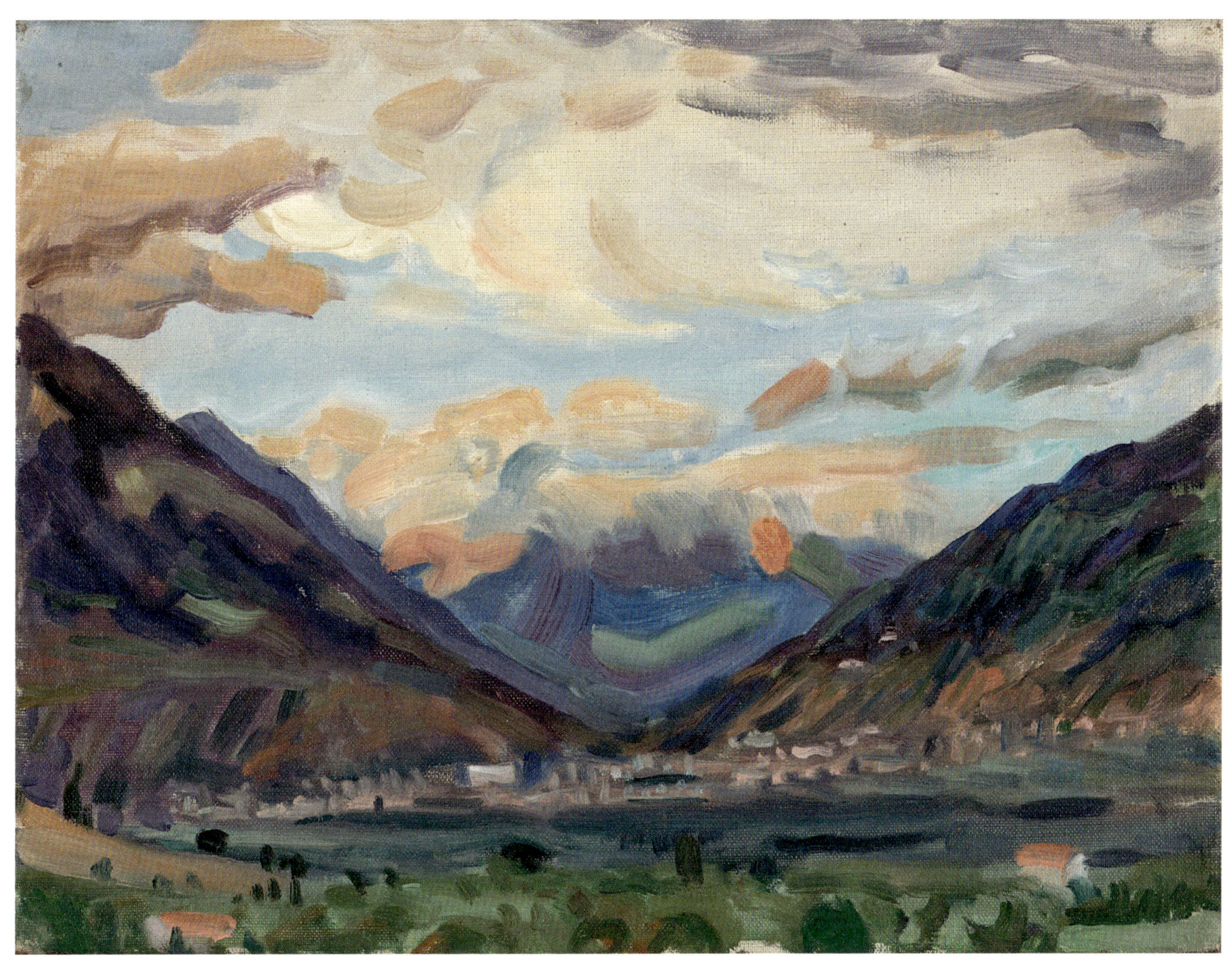

Cat. 54
Before Lana [Vor Lana], 1908
Textile support, 29.6 × 39.6 cm |
Gabriele Münter- und Johannes Eichner-Stiftung, Munich, inv. no. L 350

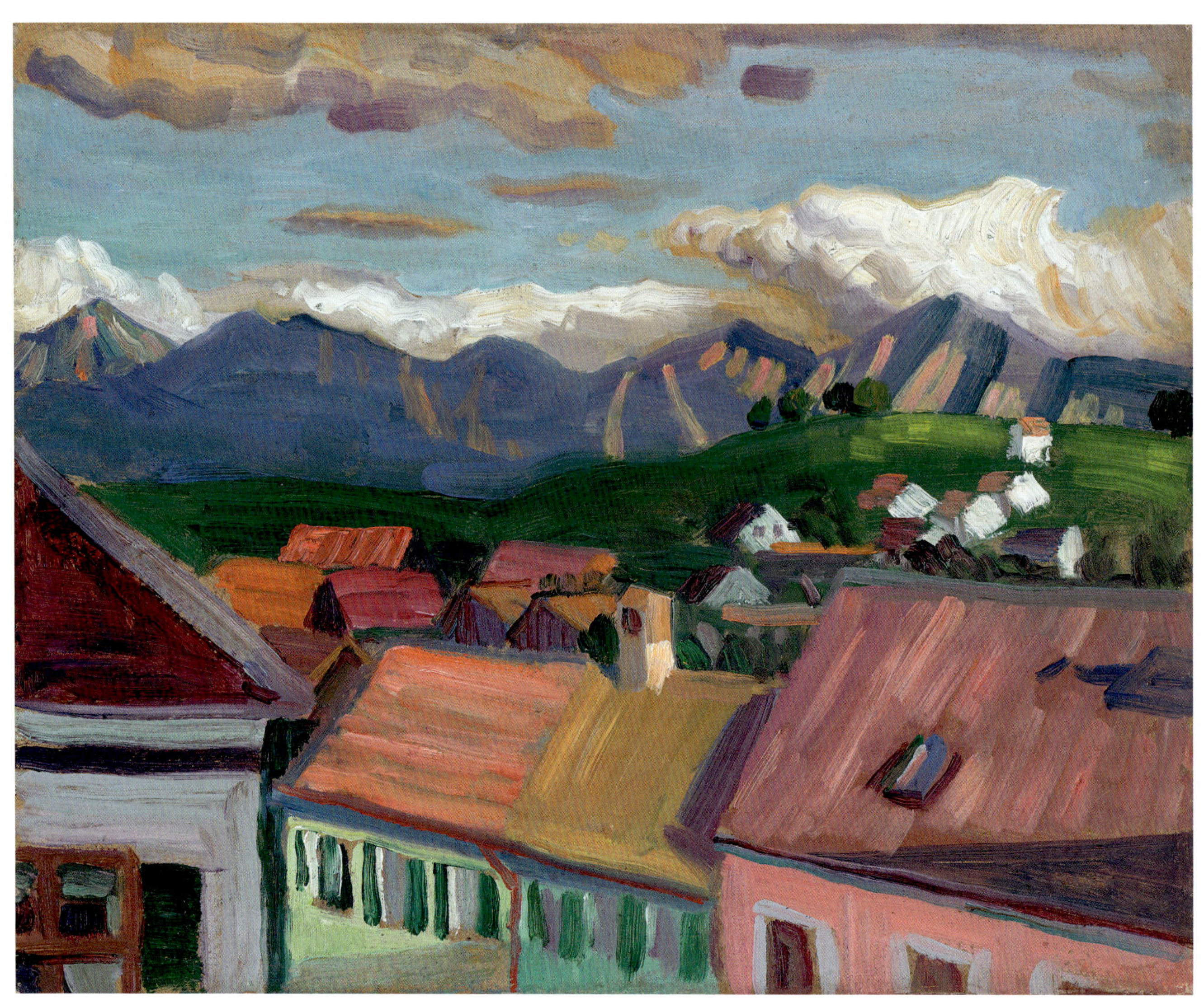

Cat. 55
From the Griesbräu Window [Vom Griesbräu-Fenster], 1908
Cardboard, 33 × 40.1 cm |
Gabriele Münter- und Johannes Eichner-Stiftung, Munich, inv. no. L 142

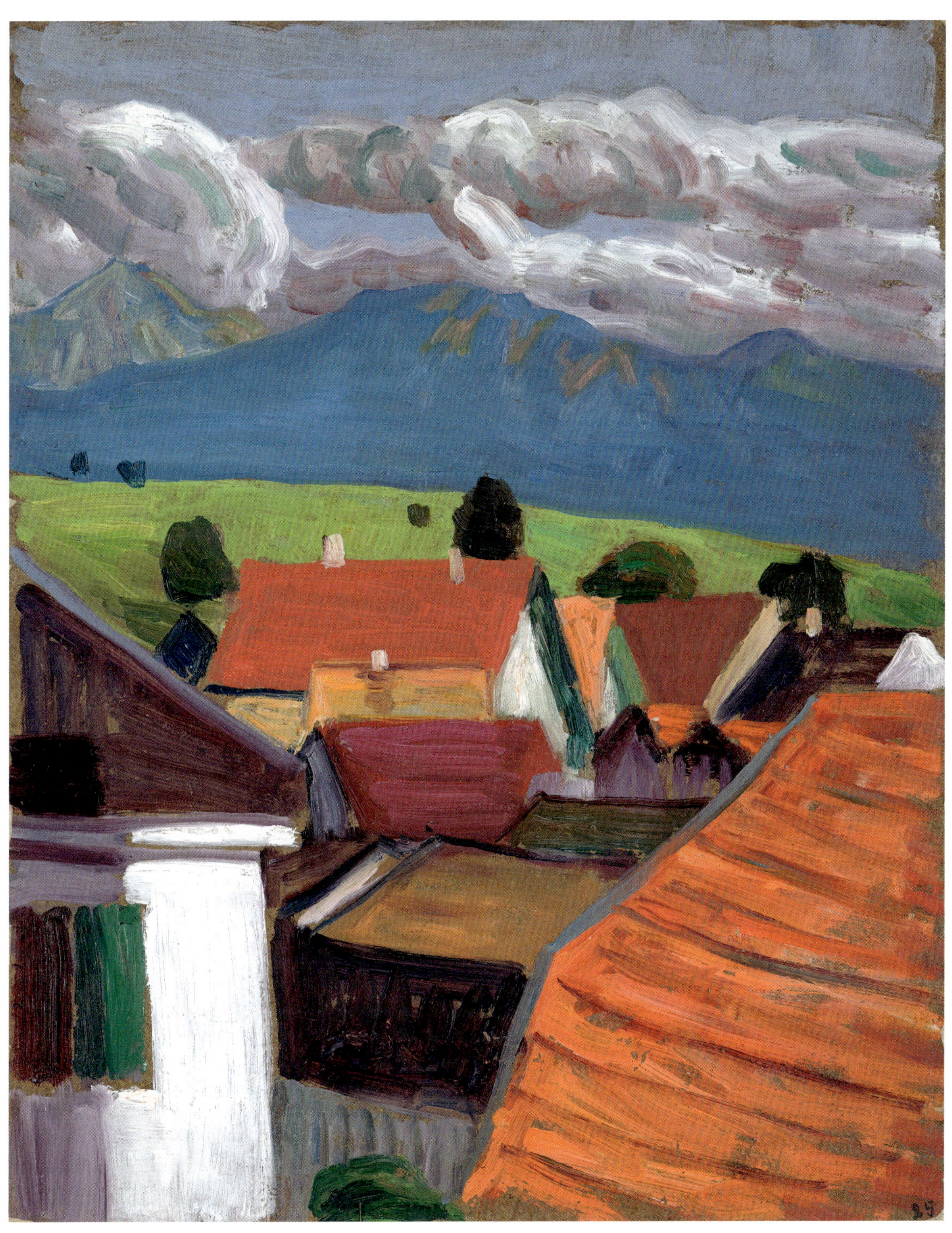

Cat. 56
View from the Griesbräu Window [Aussicht vom Griesbräu-Fenster], 1908
Cardboard, 41 × 33 cm |
Gabriele Münter- und Johannes Eichner-Stiftung, Munich, inv. no. P 78Rs

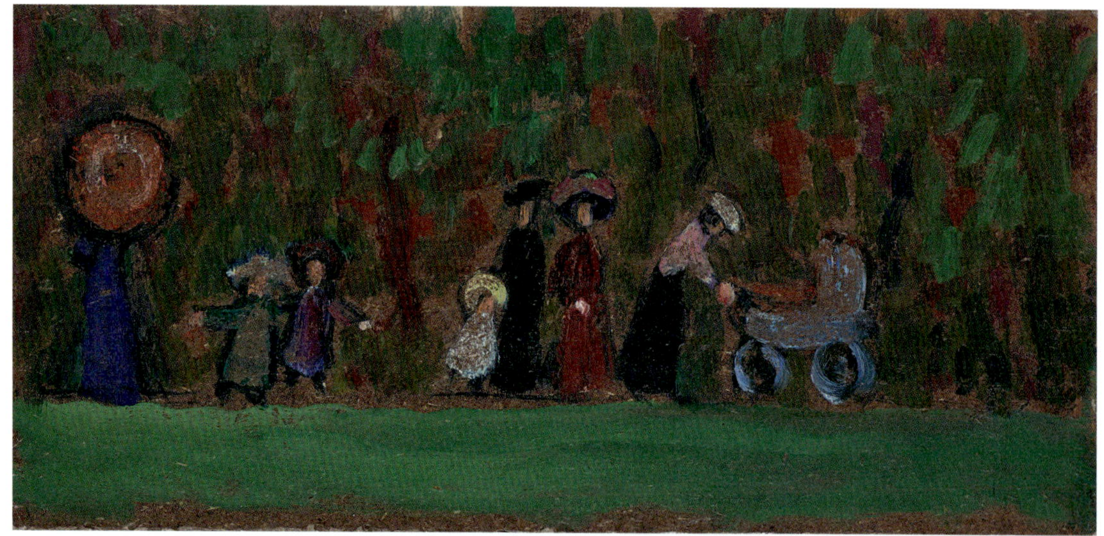

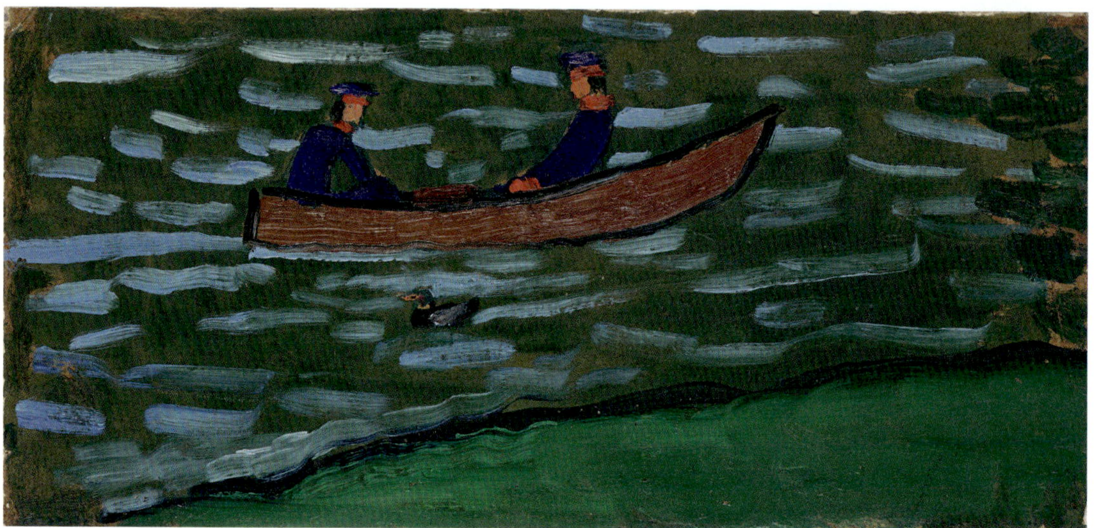

Cat. 57
Nannies in the Park [Kindermädchen im Park], 1909

Cardboard, 15.4 × 32.5 cm | Gabriele Münter- und Johannes Eichner-Stiftung, Munich, inv. no. V 66

Cat. 58
Two Soldiers in a Boat [Zwei Soldaten im Boot], 1909

Cardboard, 15.3 × 32.6 cm | Gabriele Münter- und Johannes Eichner-Stiftung, Munich, inv. no. V 65

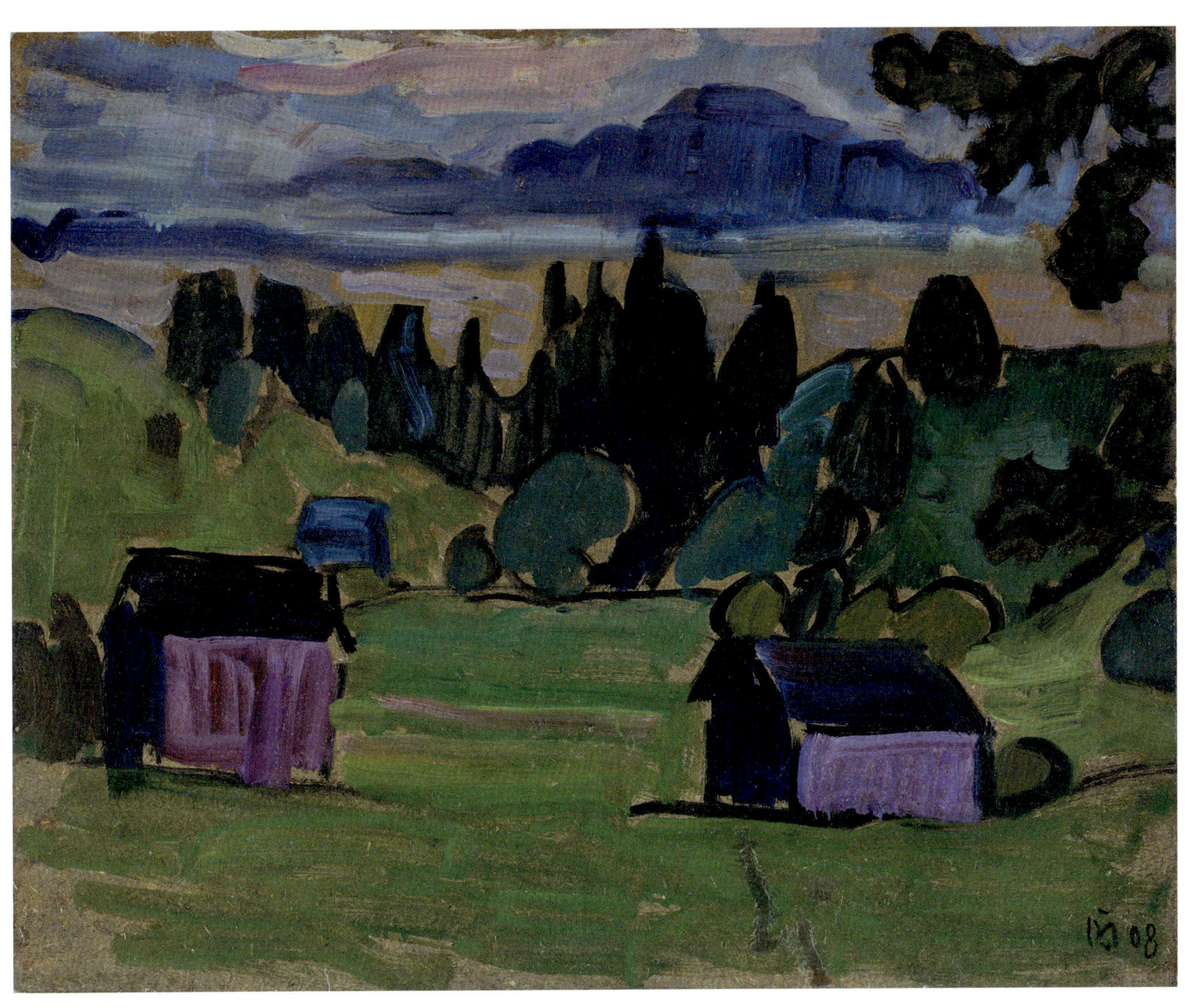

Cat. 59

View of the Murnauer Moos [Blick aufs Murnauer Moos], 1908

Cardboard, 32.7 × 40.5 cm | Städtische Galerie im Lenbachhaus und Kunstbau München, inv. no. GMS 654

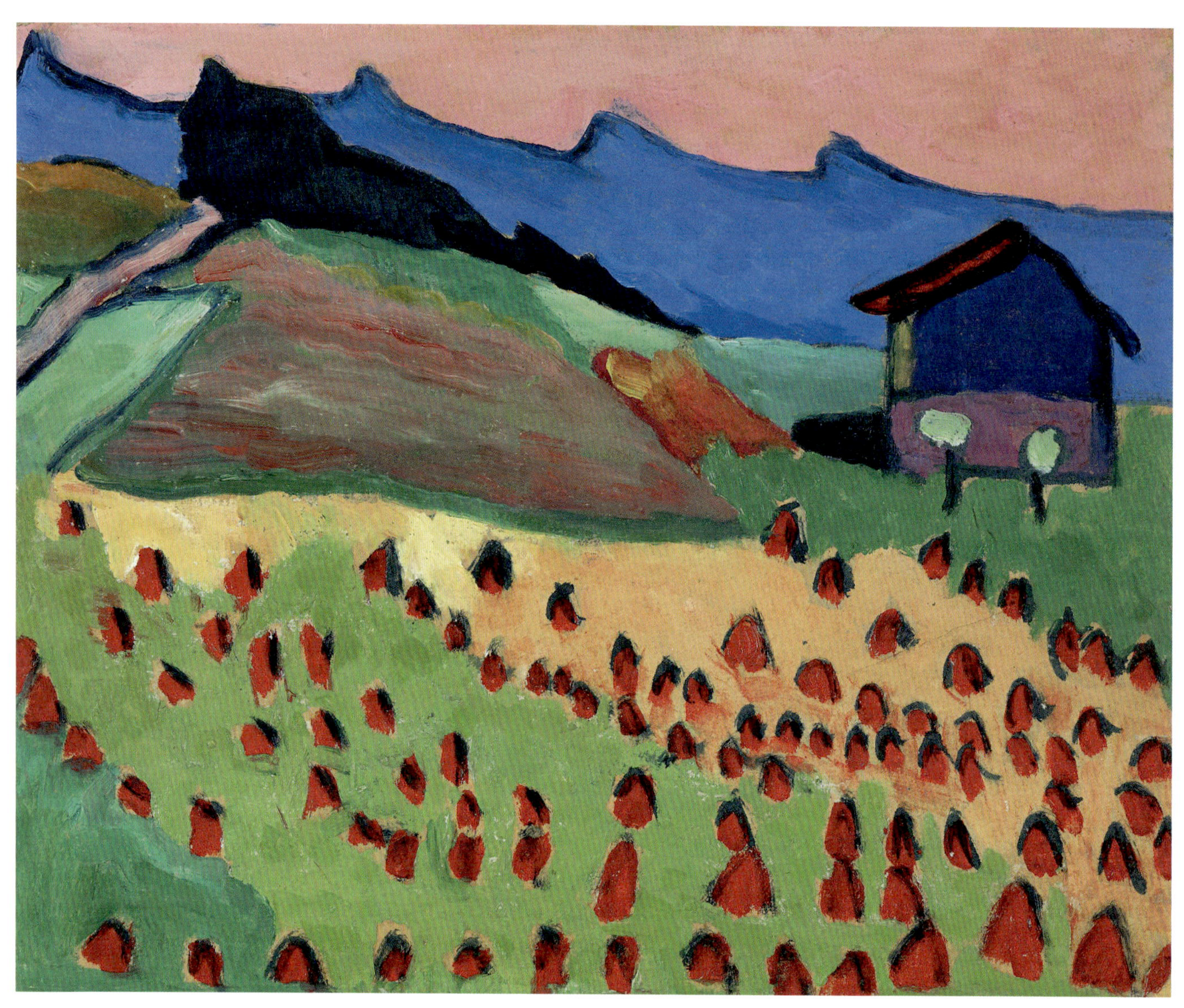

Cat. 60

Landscape with Hut at Sunset [Landschaft mit Hütte im Abendrot], 1908

Oil on cardboard, 33 × 40.8 cm | Kunstsammlungen Chemnitz – Museum Gunzenhauser, Property of the Stiftung Gunzenhauser, inv. no. GUN-M-0003

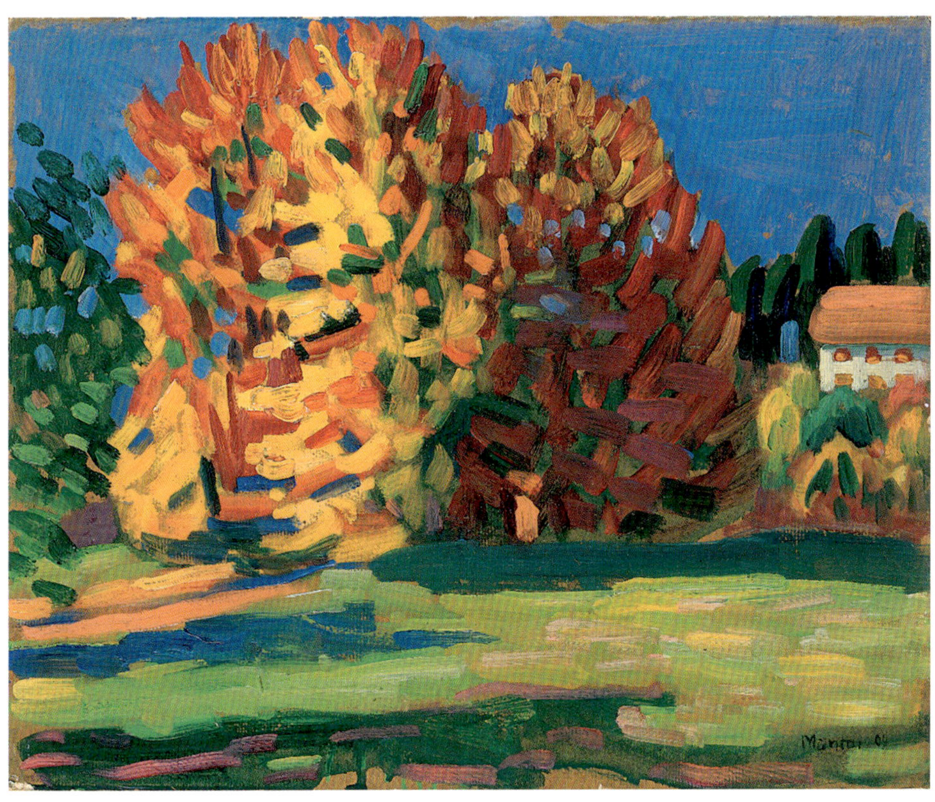

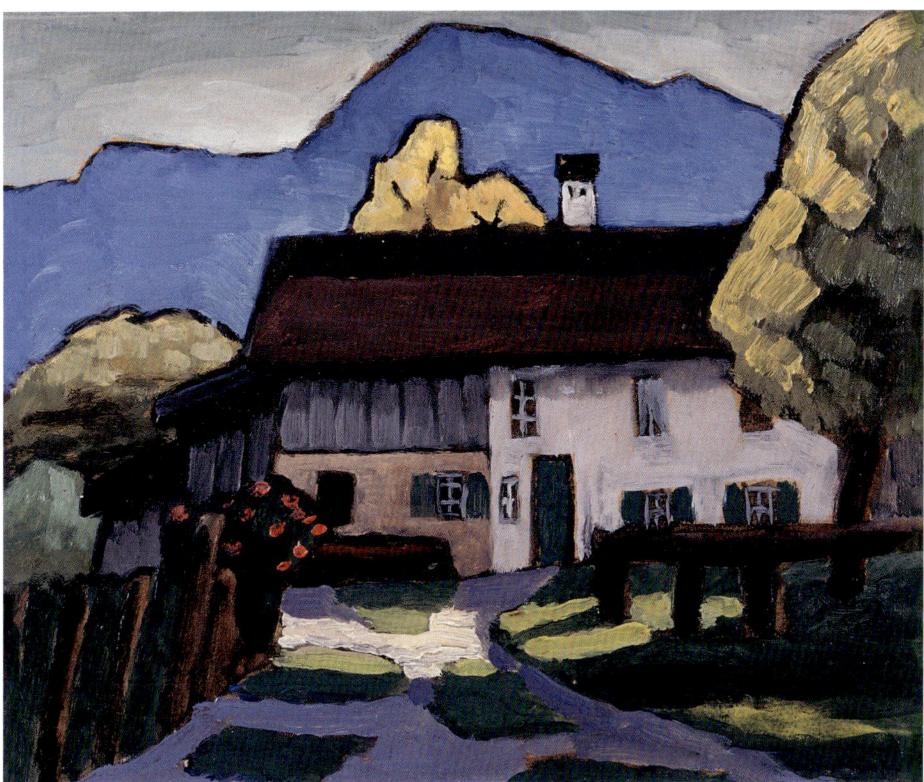

Cat. 61
Trees in Autumn near Tutzing [Herbstbäume bei Tutzing], 1908
Oil on cardboard, 32.8 × 40.5 cm | Kunsthalle Emden – Stiftung Henri und Eske Nannen und Schenkung Otto van de Loo, inv. no. 1986/61

Cat. 62
Country House near Murnau [Landhaus bei Murnau], 1908
Oil on cardboard, 33 × 41 cm | Private collection

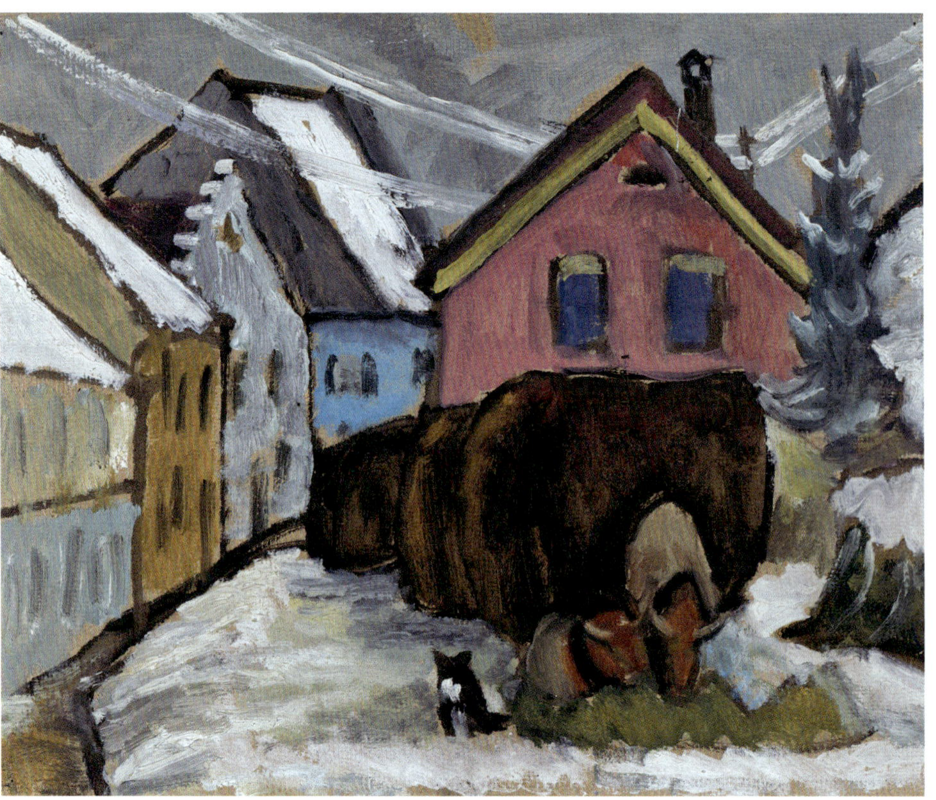

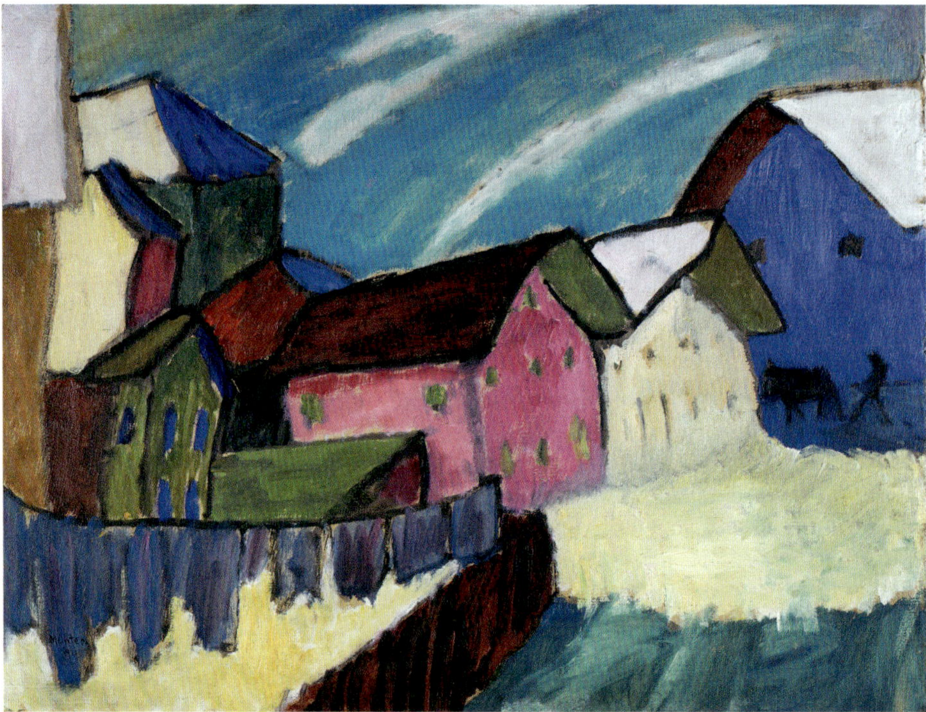

Cat. 63
Wagon Loads of Chaff [Spreufuhren], 1910/11
Cardboard, 30.9 × 40.8 cm | Städtische Galerie im Lenbachhaus und Kunstbau München, inv. no. GMS 648

Cat. 64
Village Street in Winter [Dorfstraße im Winter], 1911
Cardboard mounted on wood, 52.4 × 69 cm | Städtische Galerie im Lenbachhaus und Kunstbau München, inv. no. GMS 664

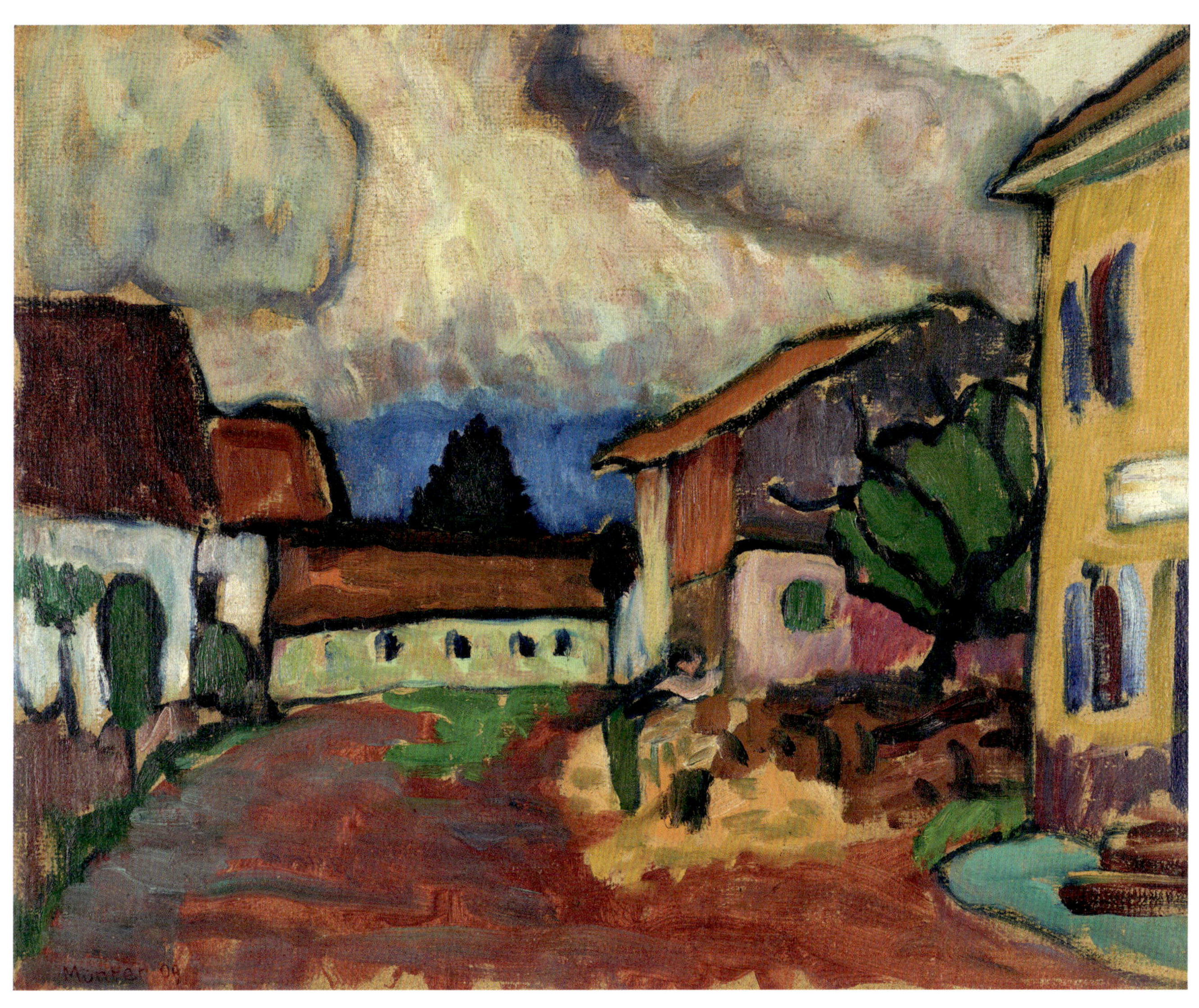

Cat. 65
Woodcutter (Pfarrgasse with Woodcutter) [Holzhauer (Pfarrgasse mit Holzhacker)], 1909
Oil on cardboard, 33 × 40.7 cm |
Private collection, Southern Germany

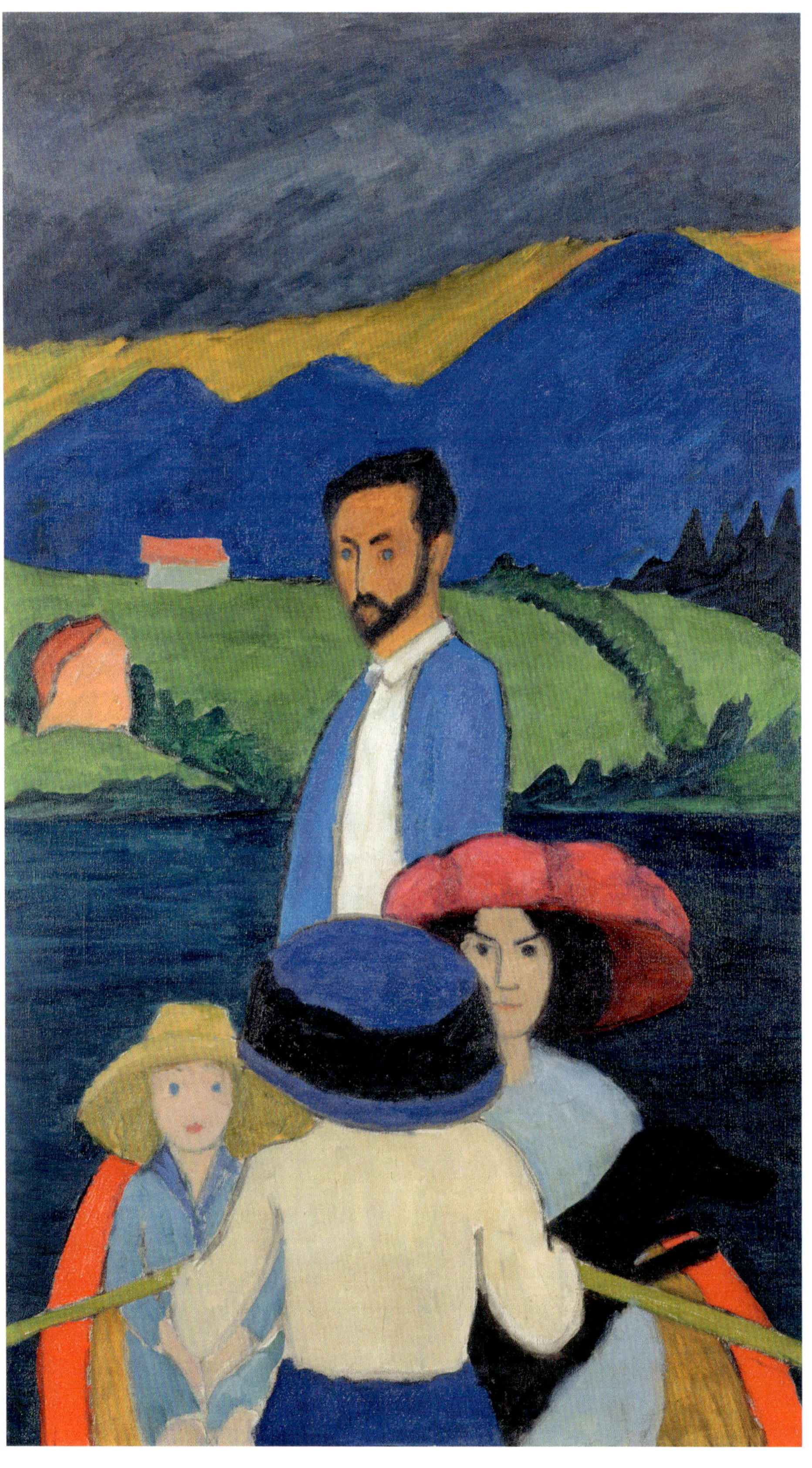

Cat. 66
Boating [Kahnfahrt], 1910
Oil on canvas, 125.1 × 73.6 cm |
Milwaukee Art Museum,
Gift of Mrs. Harry Lynde Bradley,
inv. no. M1977.128

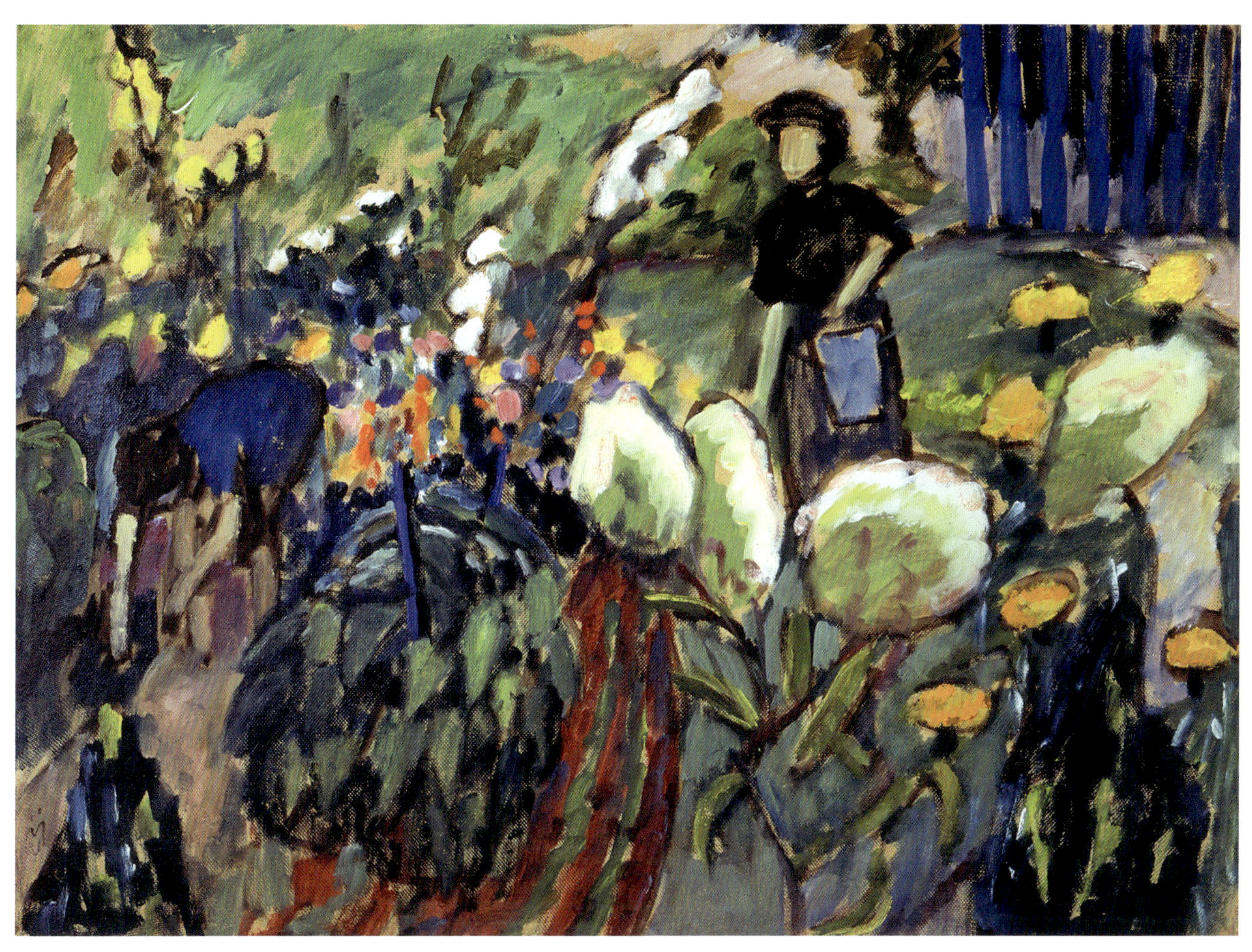

Cat. 67
In the Garden in Murnau [Im Garten in Murnau], 1911
Oil on cardboard, 50.5 × 69.3 cm | Neue Galerie New York. This work is part of the collection of Estée Lauder and was made available through the generosity of Estée Lauder, inv. no. EL.51

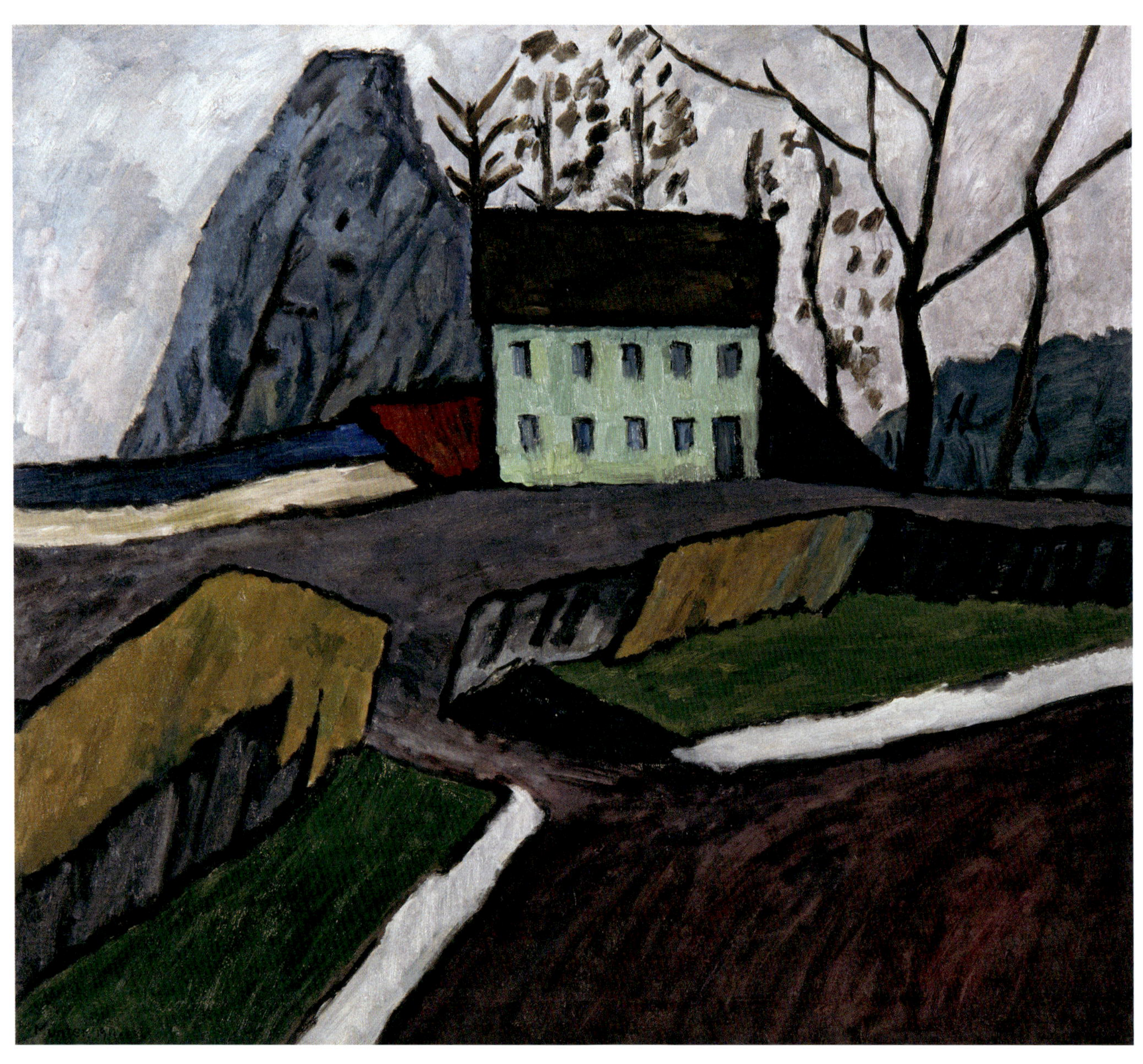

Cat. 68
House in Schwabing
[Haus in Schwabing], 1911
Oil on canvas, 88.3 × 100.3 cm | Milwaukee Art Museum, Gift of Mrs. Harry Lynde Bradley, inv. no. M1975.127

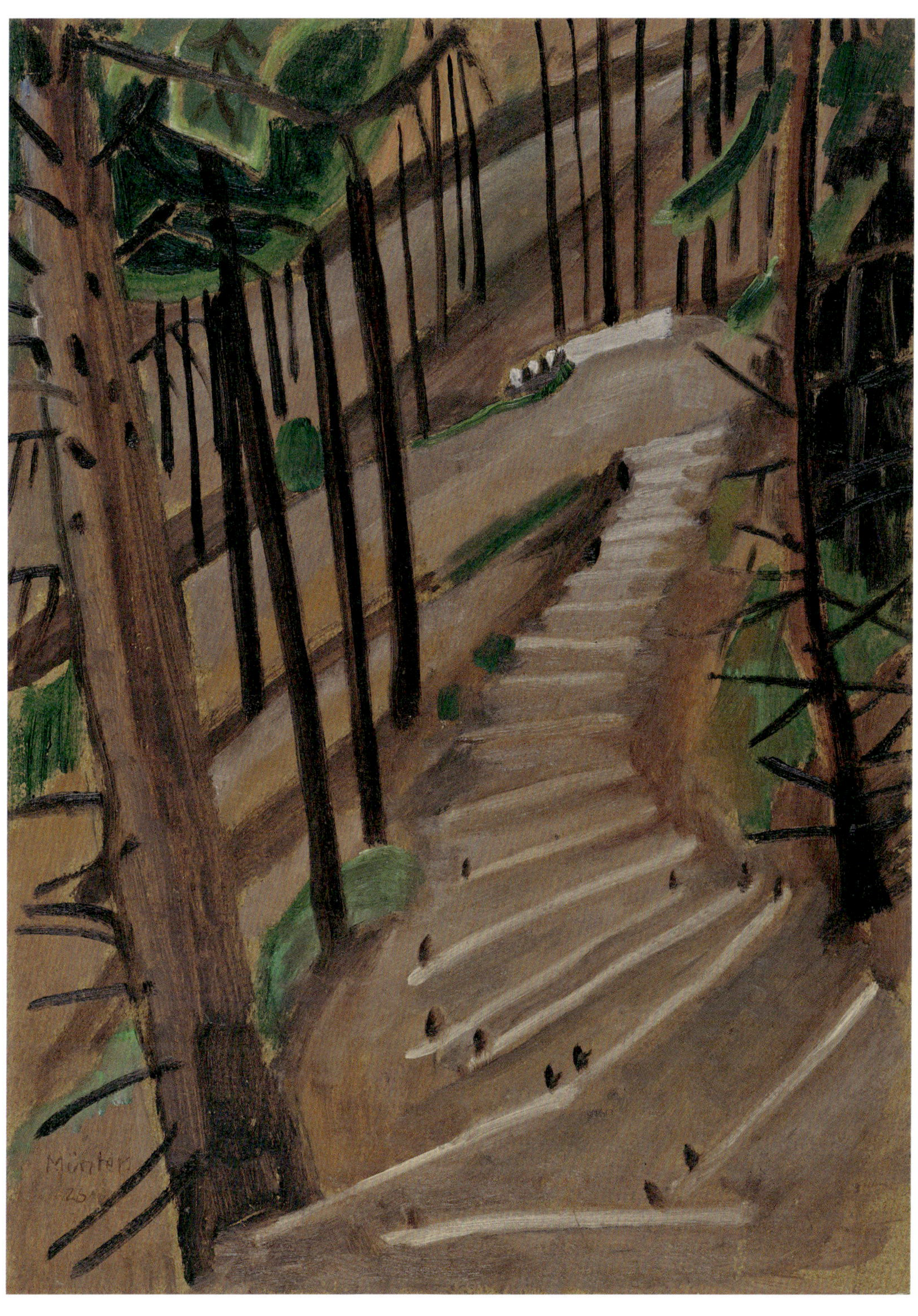

Cat. 69
In the Forest III
[Im Wald III], 1926

Cardboard, 45.3 × 33.2 cm |
Gabriele Münter- und Johannes Eichner-Stiftung, Munich, inv. no. L 267

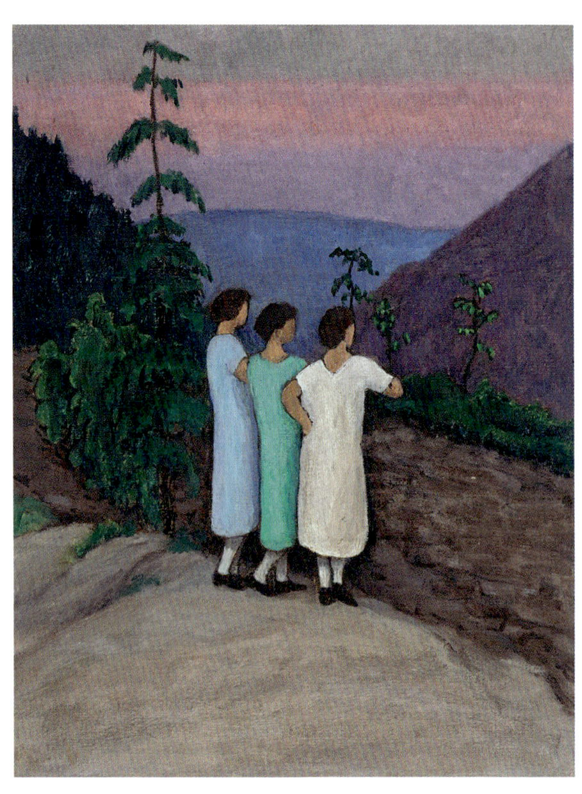

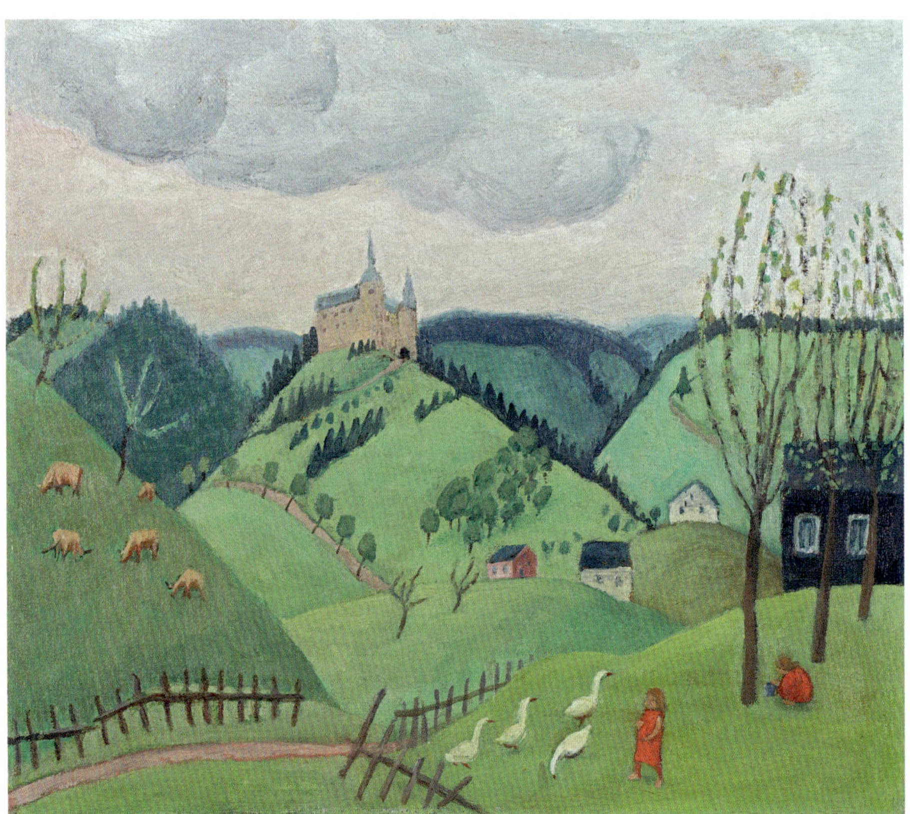

Cat. 70
Midnight Sun [Mitternachts-sonne], ca. 1925
Cardboard mounted on textile support, 39.7 × 24.3 cm | Gabriele Münter- und Johannes Eichner-Stiftung, Munich, inv. no. V 95

Cat. 71
Landscape in Lauenstein with Red Children [Lauensteiner Landschaft mit roten Kindern], 1928
Textile support, 26.3 × 30.7 cm | Gabriele Münter- und Johannes Eichner-Stiftung, Munich, inv. no. L 91

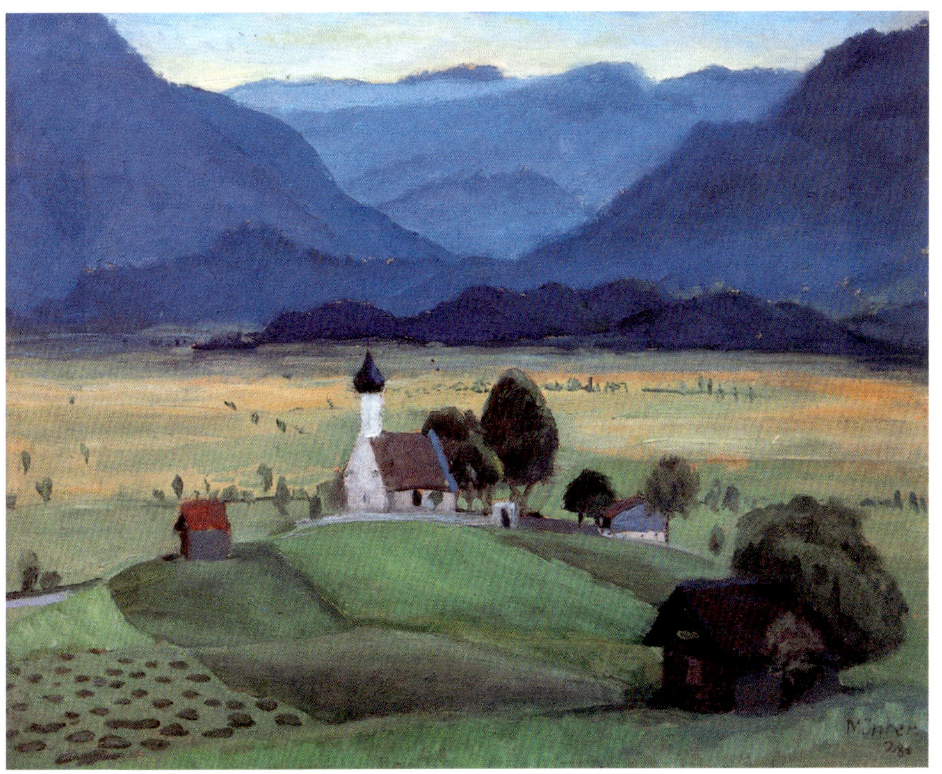

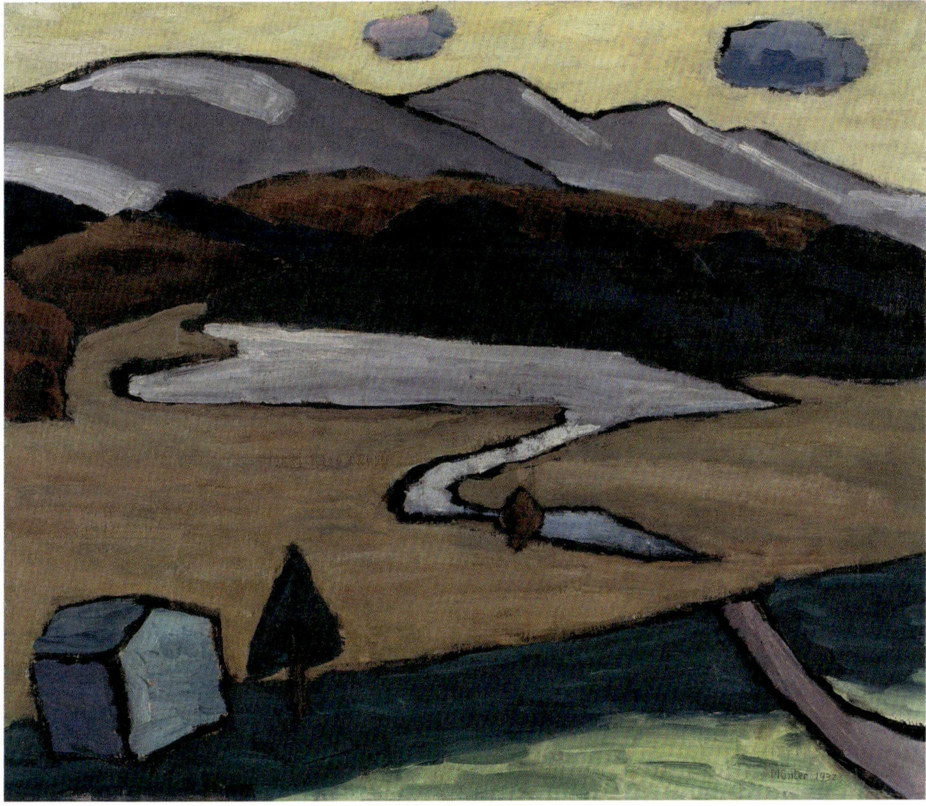

Cat. 72
Little Church in Ramsach [Ramsach Kirchlein], 1928
Oil on canvas, 33 × 41 cm | Private collection

Cat. 73
The Gray Lake [Der graue See], 1932
Textile support, 54.8 × 65.7 cm | Städtische Galerie im Lenbachhaus und Kunstbau München, inv. no. GMS 670

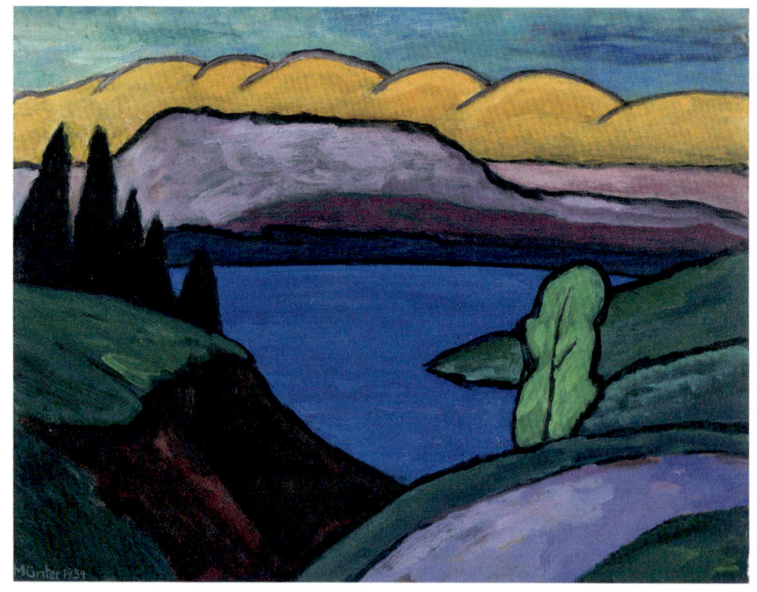

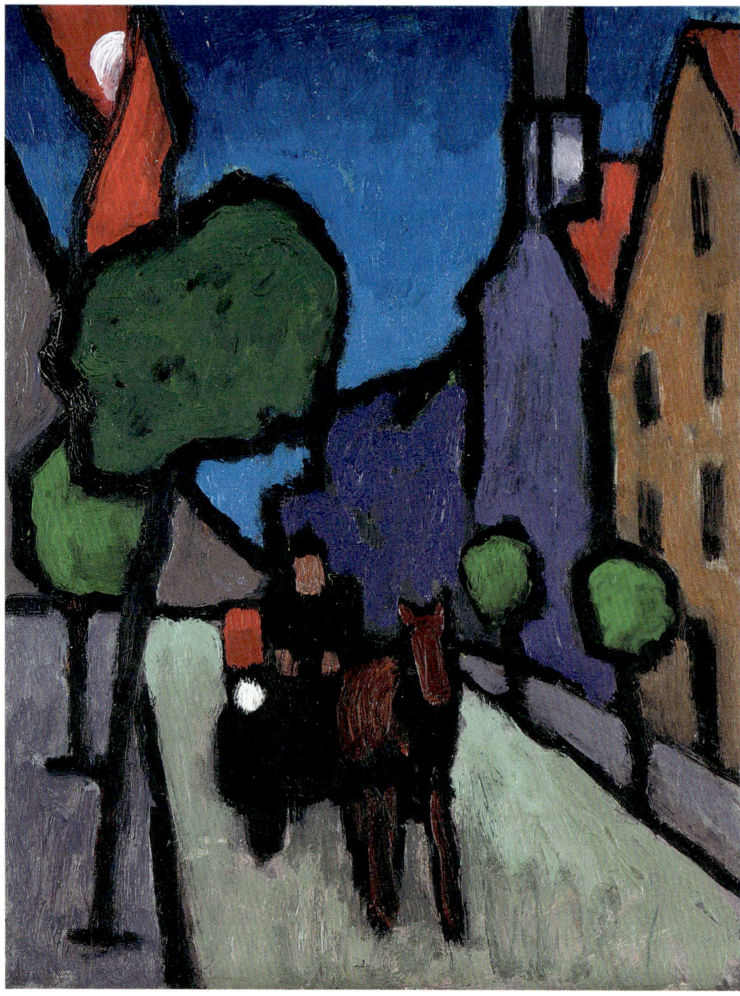

Cat. 74
The Blue Lake [Der blaue See], 1954
Oil on canvas, 50 × 65 cm | LENTOS Kunstmuseum Linz, inv. no. 211

Cat. 75
Main Street in Murnau with Horse and Cart [Murnauer Hauptstraße mit Pferdegespann], 1933
Oil on wood, 35.5 × 27.5 cm | Private collection, Southern Germany

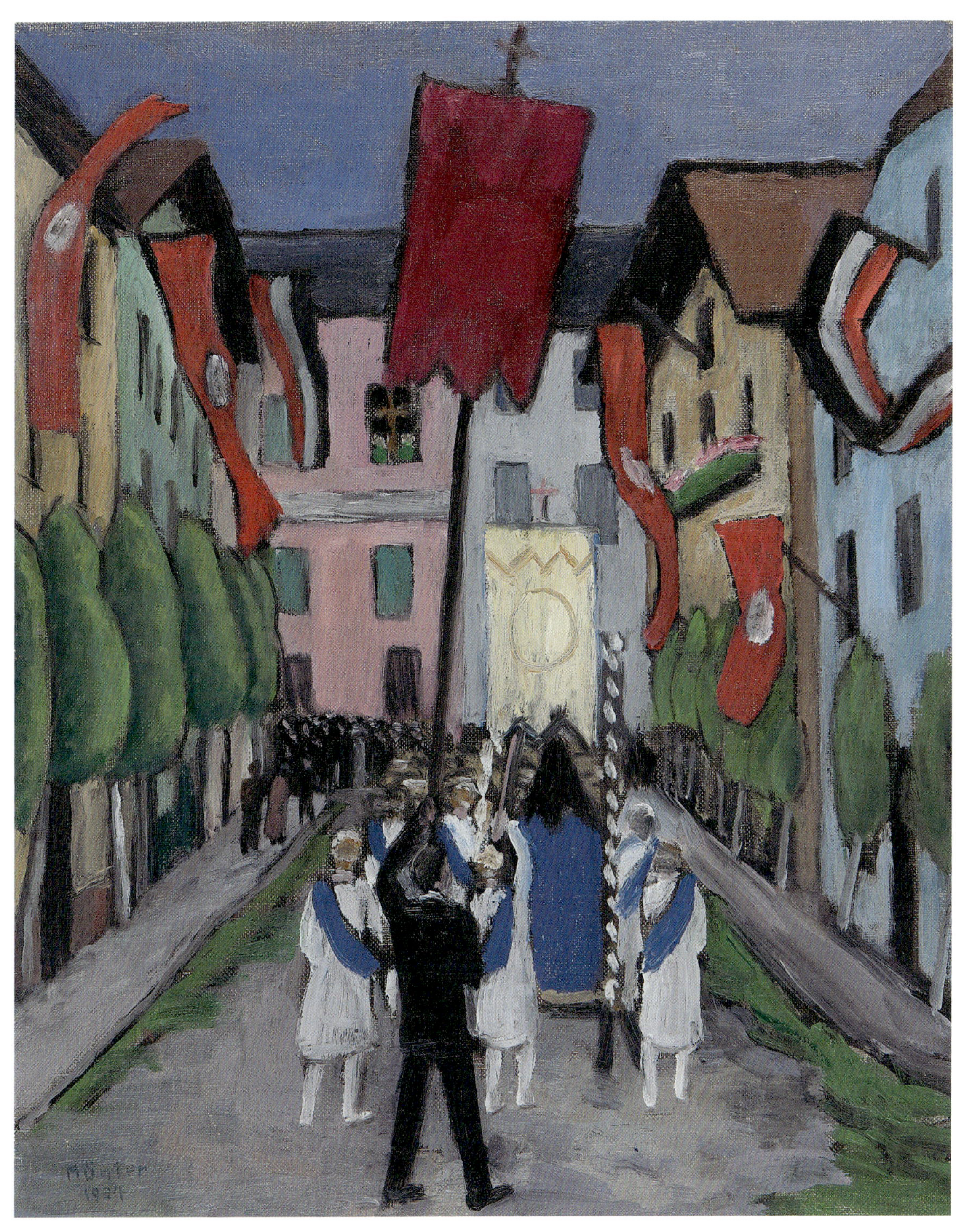

Cat. 76
Procession in Murnau
[Prozession in Murnau], 1934
Oil on canvas, 46.6 × 38.3 cm |
Private collection

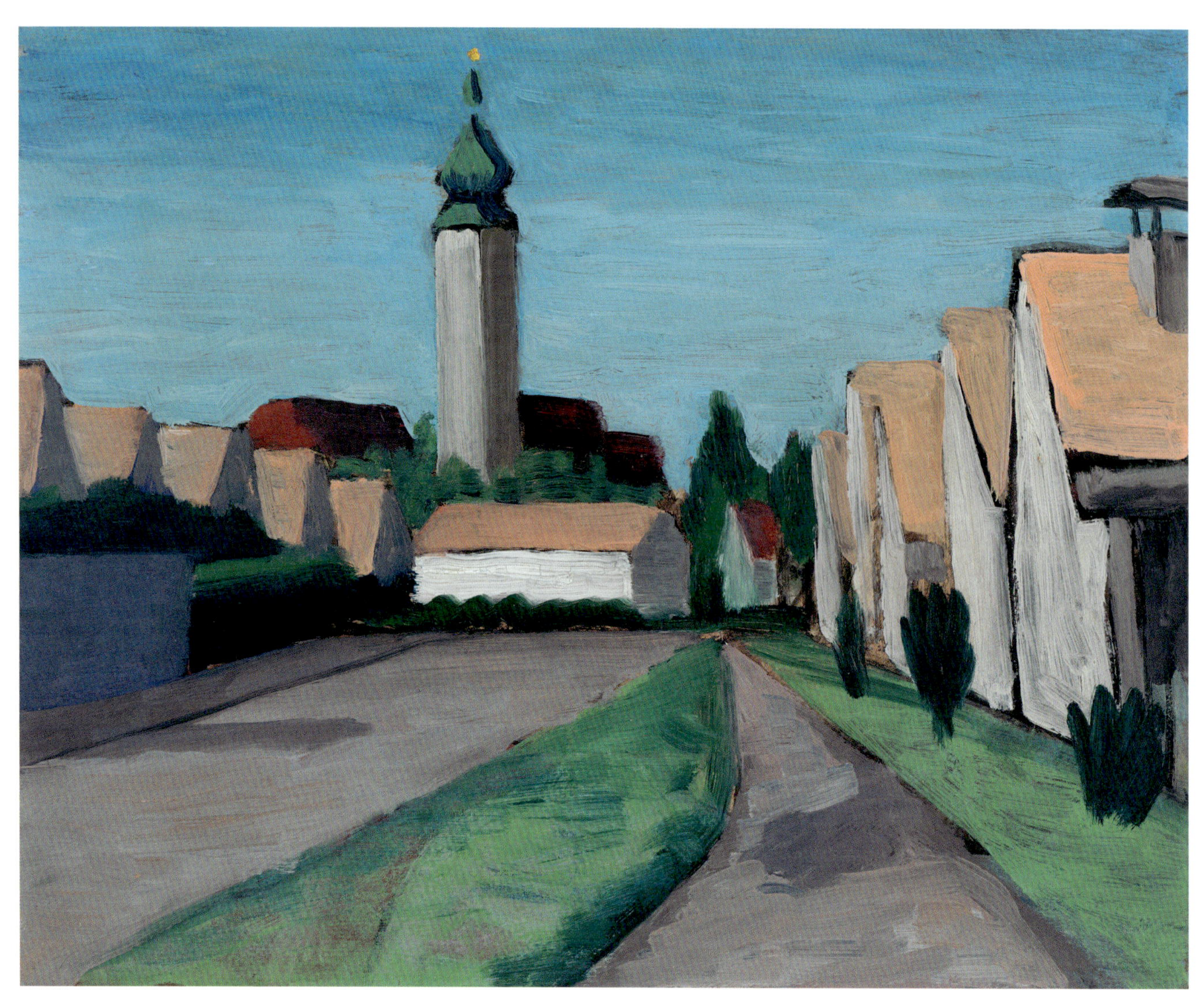

Cat. 77
Surburban Houses with Baroque Church (Ramersdorf: Scheubner-Richterstraße) [Vorstadthäuser mit Barockkirche (Ramersdorf. Scheubner-Richterstraße)], 1936
Oil on cardboard, 33 × 41 cm | Galerie Ludorff, Düsseldorf

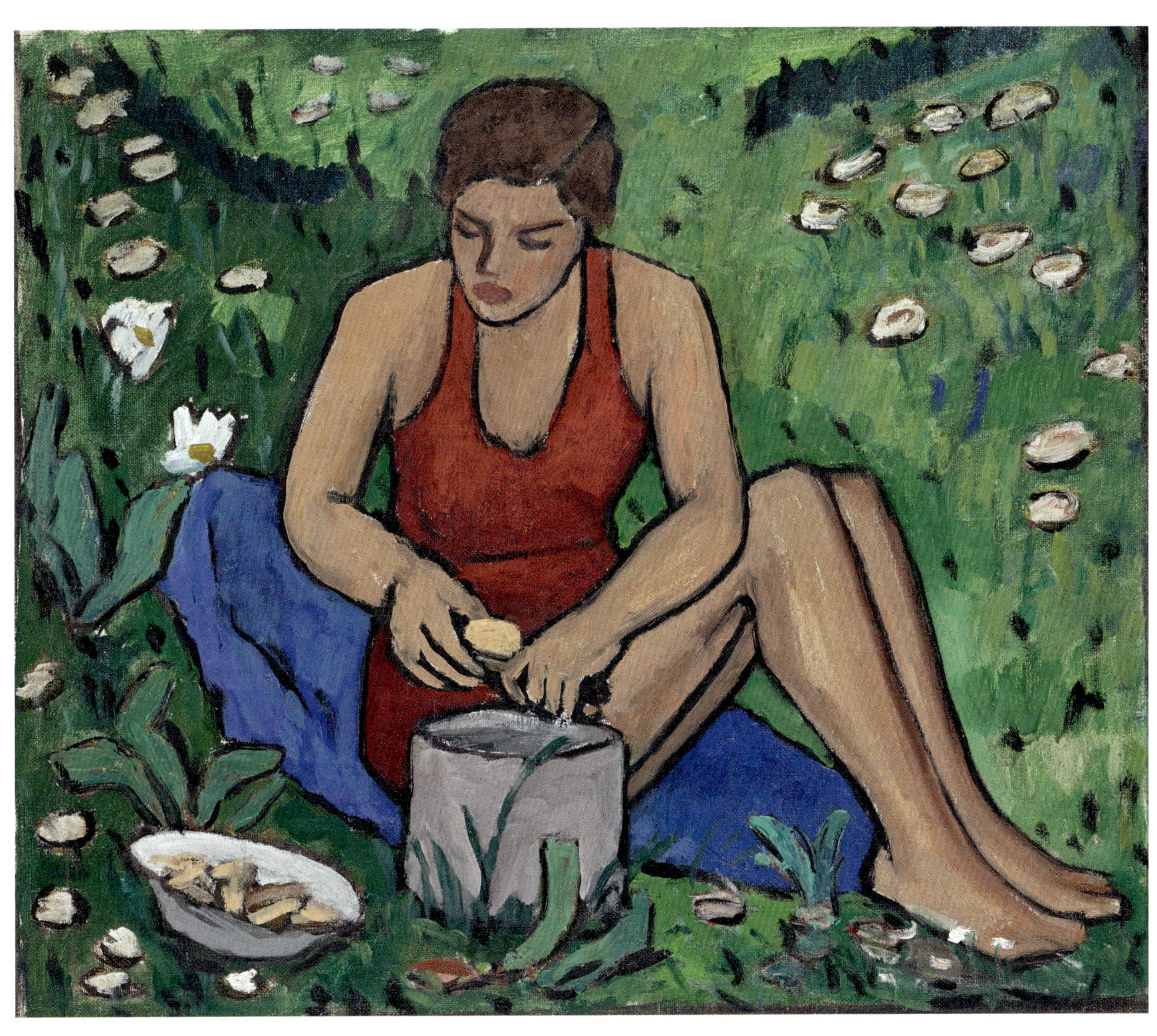

Cat. 78
Miss Ellen on the Grass
[Fräulein Ellen im Gras], 1934
Textile support, 47.5 × 65 cm |
Gabriele Münter- und Johannes Eichner-Stiftung, Munich, inv. no. V 96

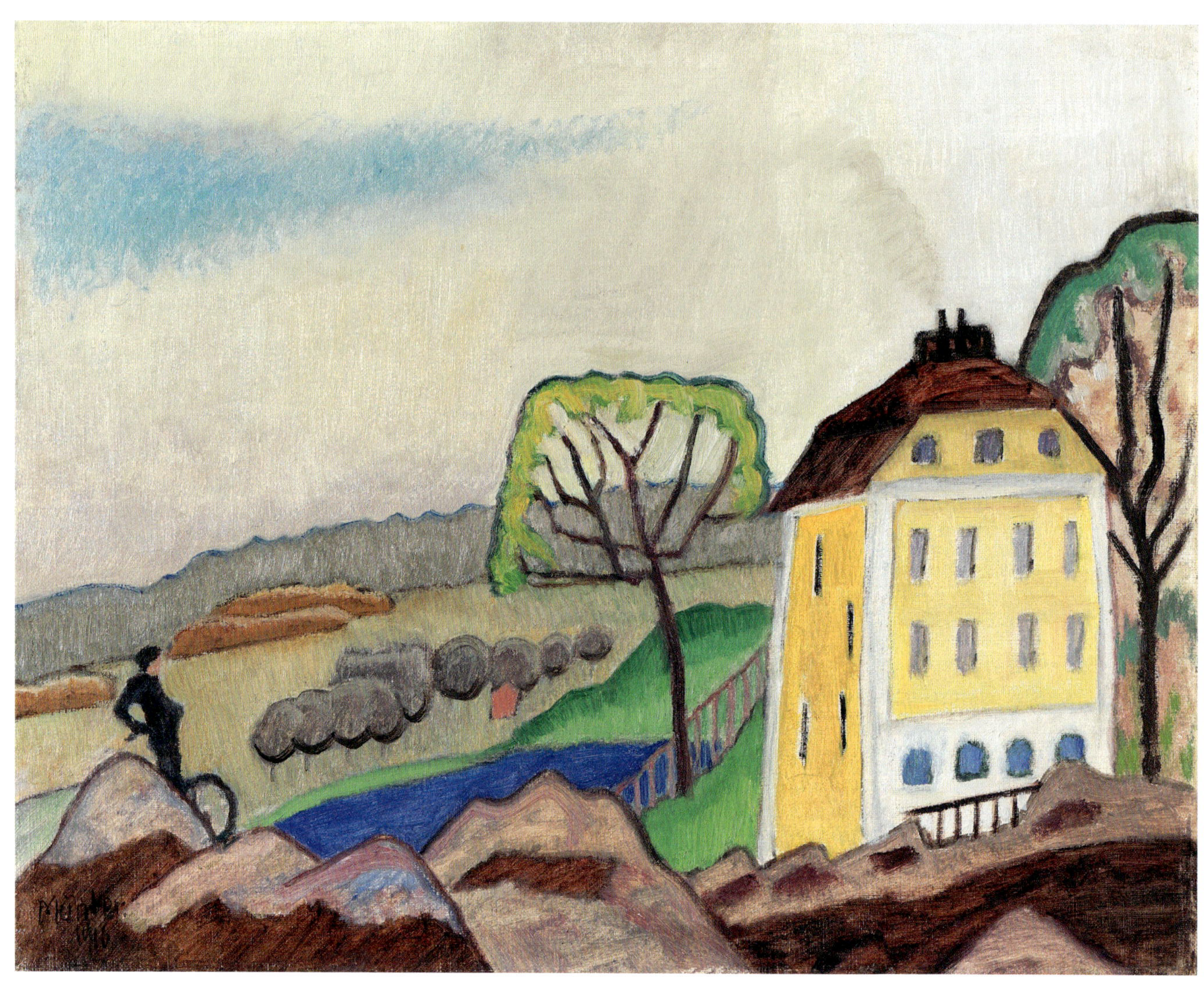

Cat. 79
Landscape with Yellow House [Landschaft mit gelbem Haus], 1916
Oil on canvas, 41.5 × 52.7 cm |
Private collection

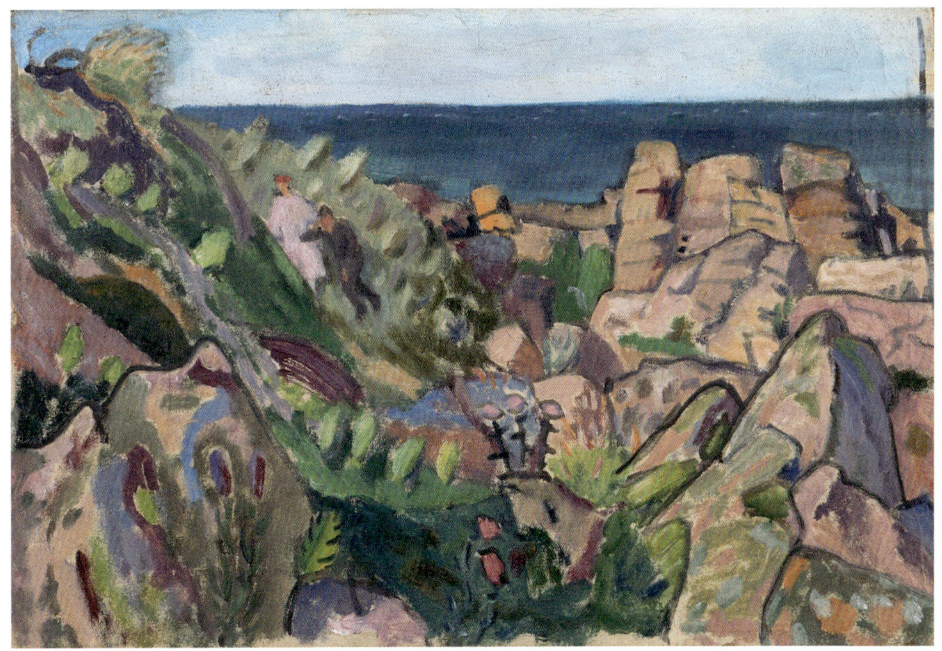

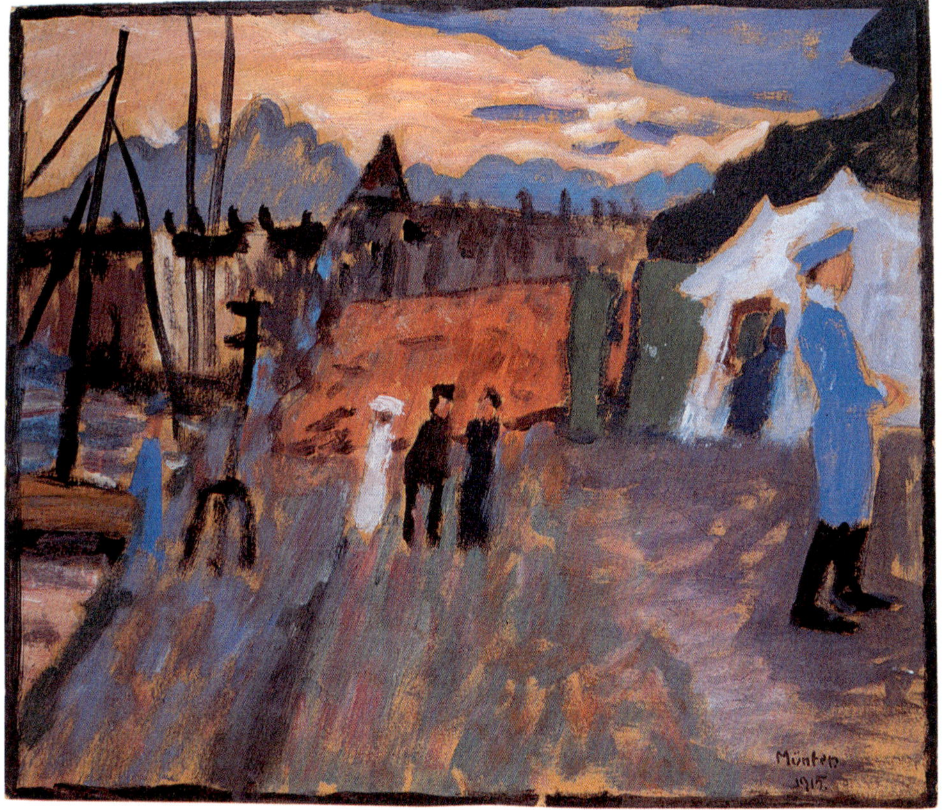

Cat. 80
Touring the Cliffs in Bornholm [Klippenpartie Bornholm], 1919
Textile support, 36.4 × 54.9 cm | Gabriele Münter- und Johannes Eichner-Stiftung, Munich, inv. no. L 342

Cat. 81
Från Djurgårdsbron, Stockholm, 1915
Oil on cardboard, 29.5 × 35 cm | Collett Prague/Munich

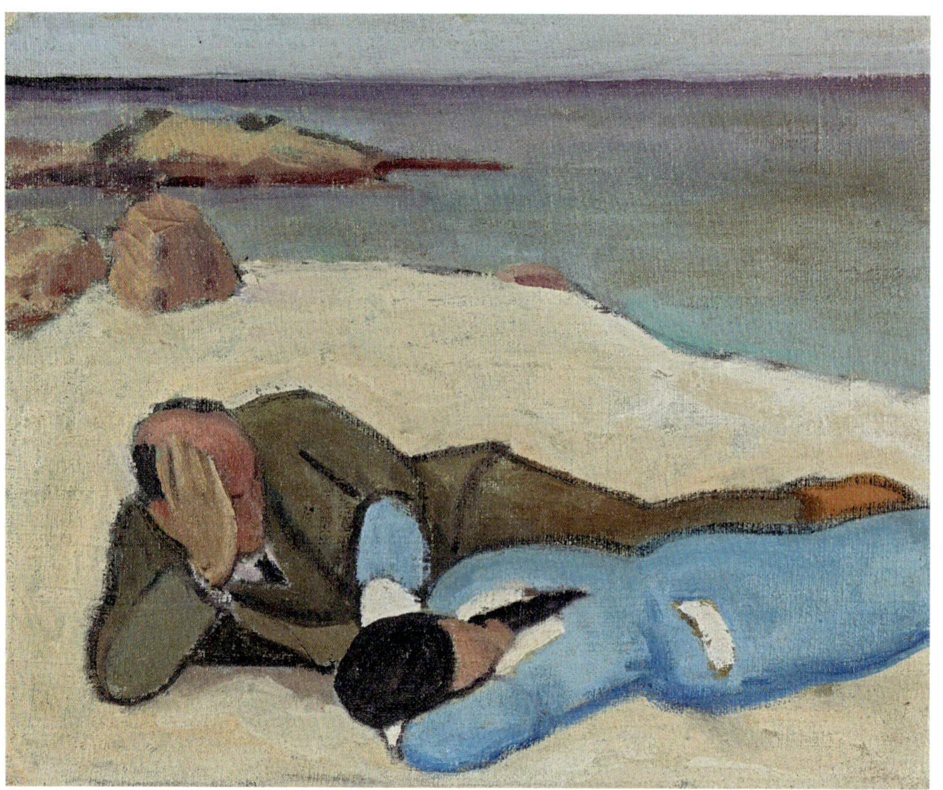

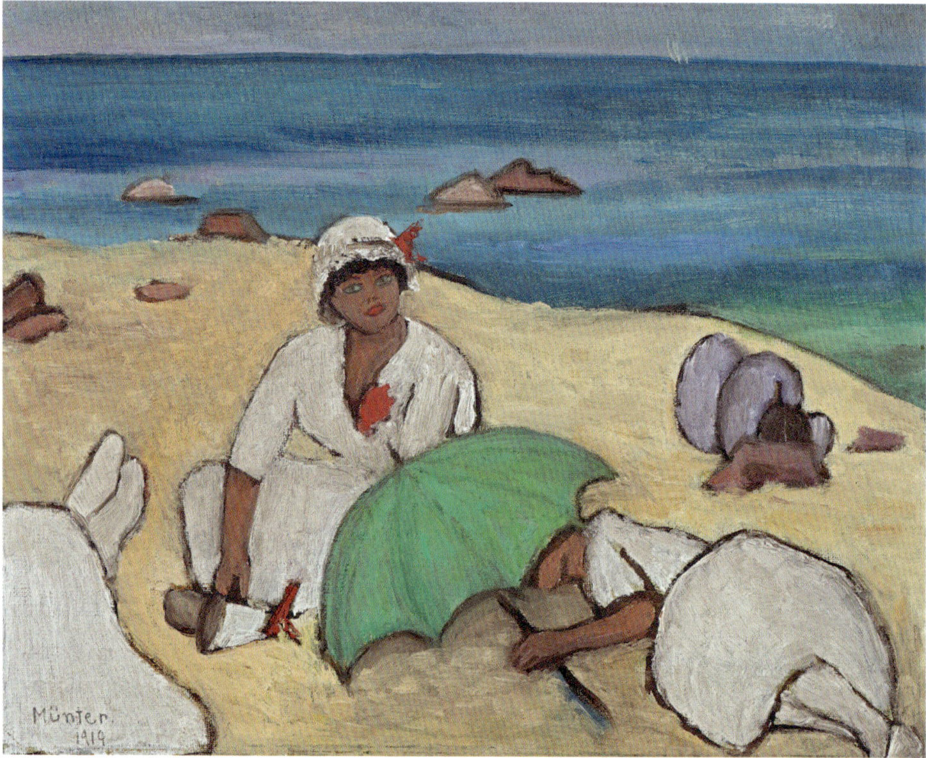

Cat. 82
Couple on the Beach [Paar am Strand], 1919
Textile support, 28.5 × 34.1 cm | Gabriele Münter- und Johannes Eichner-Stiftung, Munich, inv. no. V 98

Cat. 83
On the Beach [Am Strand], 1919
Textile support, 28 × 35.1 cm | Gabriele Münter- und Johannes Eichner-Stiftung, Munich, inv. no. V 99

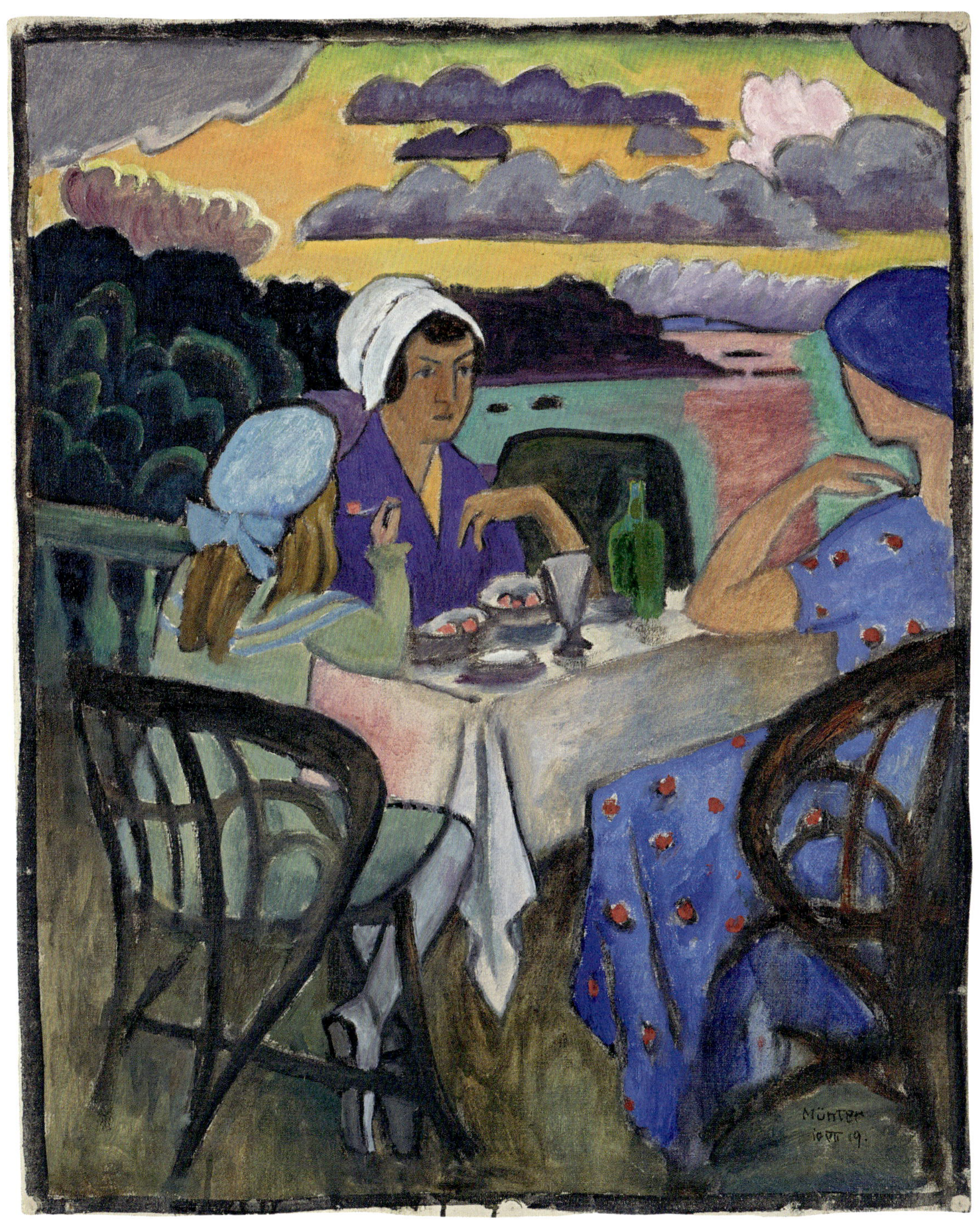

Cat. 84
During Strawberry Season [In der Erdbeerzeit], 1919
Textile support, 60.9 × 50.5 cm | Gabriele Münter- und Johannes Eichner-Stiftung, Munich, inv. no. V 97

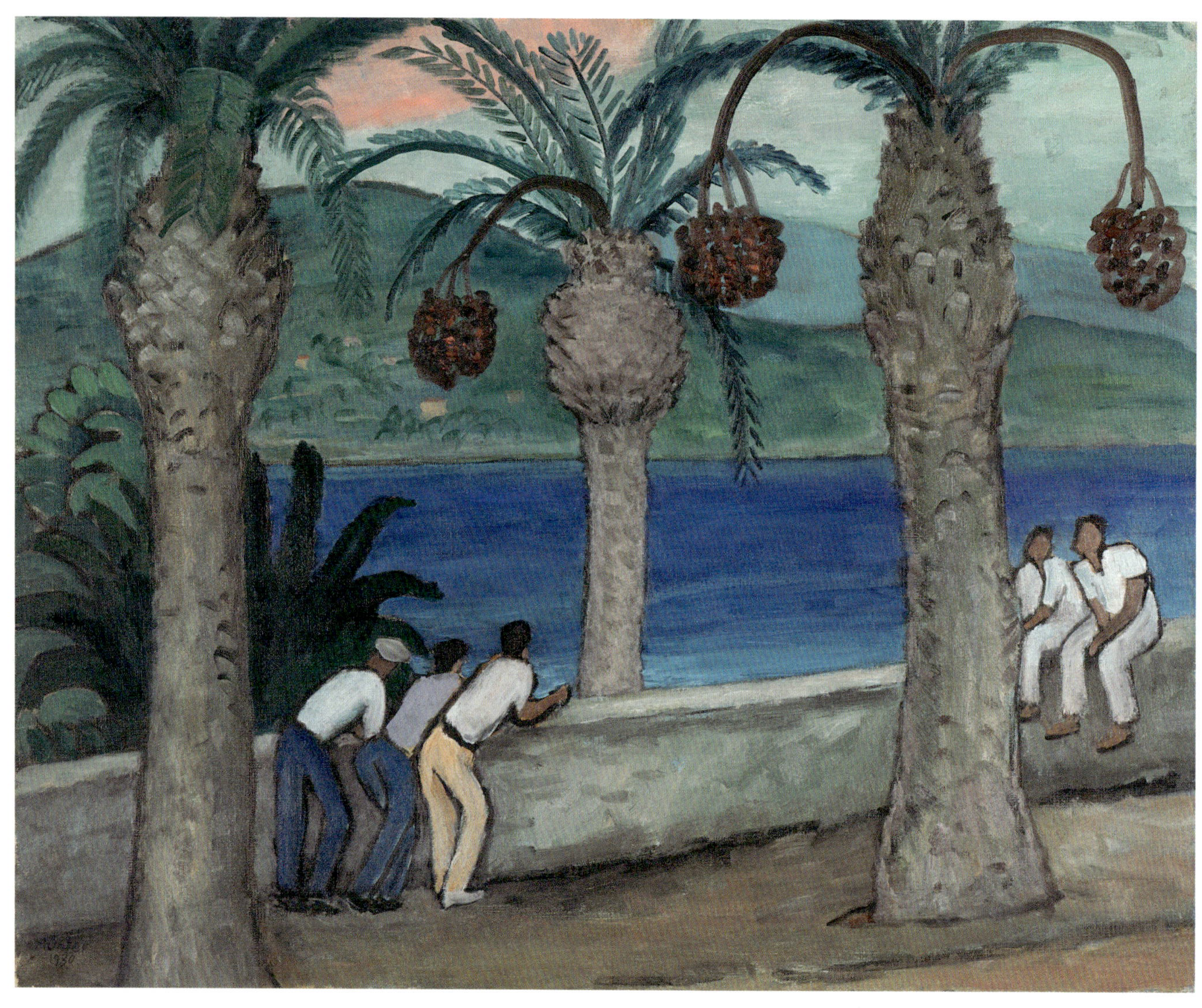

Cat. 85
At the Wall (Bandol)
[An der Mauer (Bandol)], 1930
Textile support, 65.2 × 81.4 cm |
Gabriele Münter- und Johannes Eichner-Stiftung, Munich, inv. no. L 491

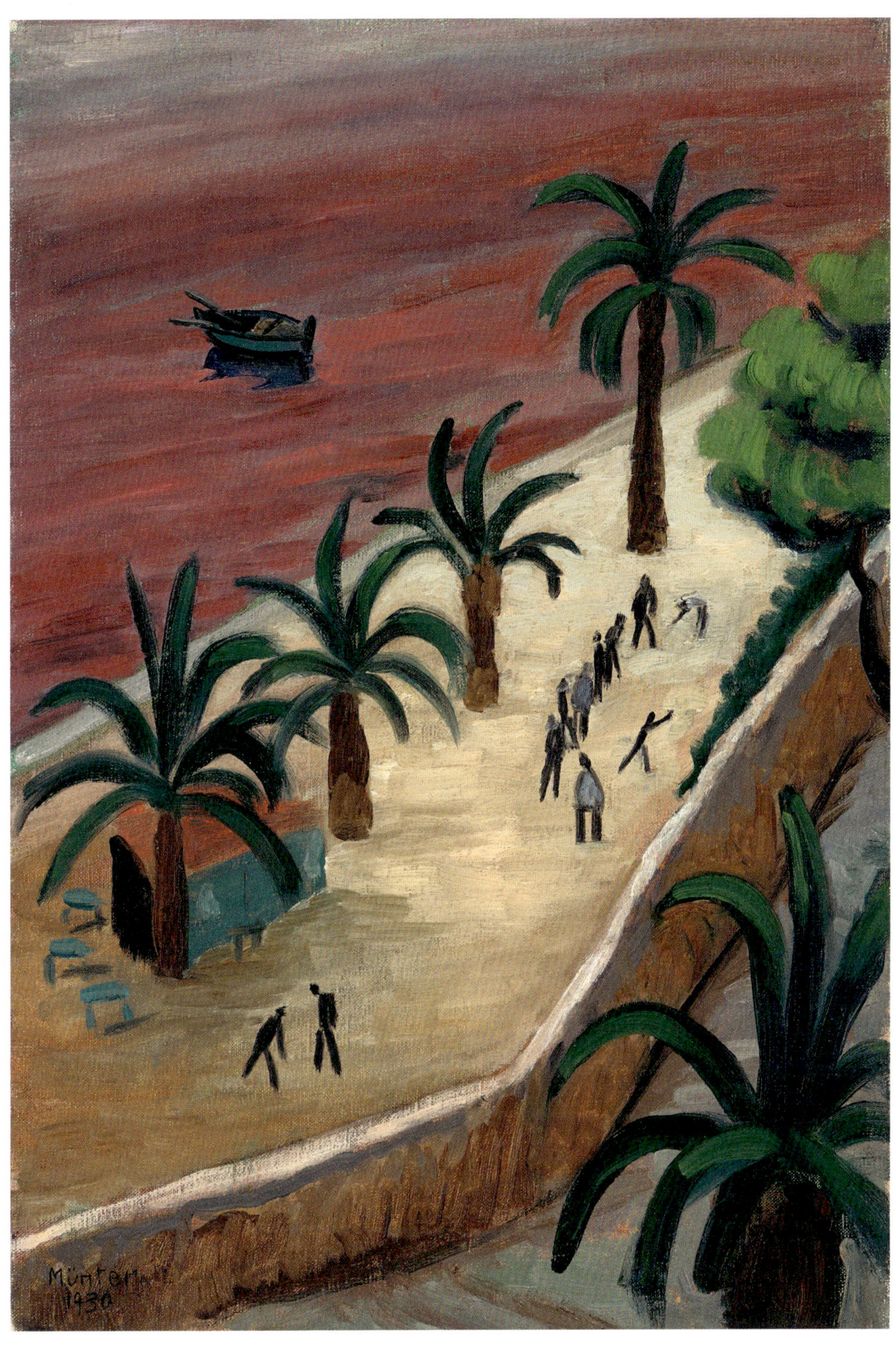

Cat. 86
Men Playing Boules [Kugelspieler], 1930
Textile support, 55.3 × 38.2 cm | Gabriele Münter- und Johannes Eichner-Stiftung, Munich, inv. no. L 82

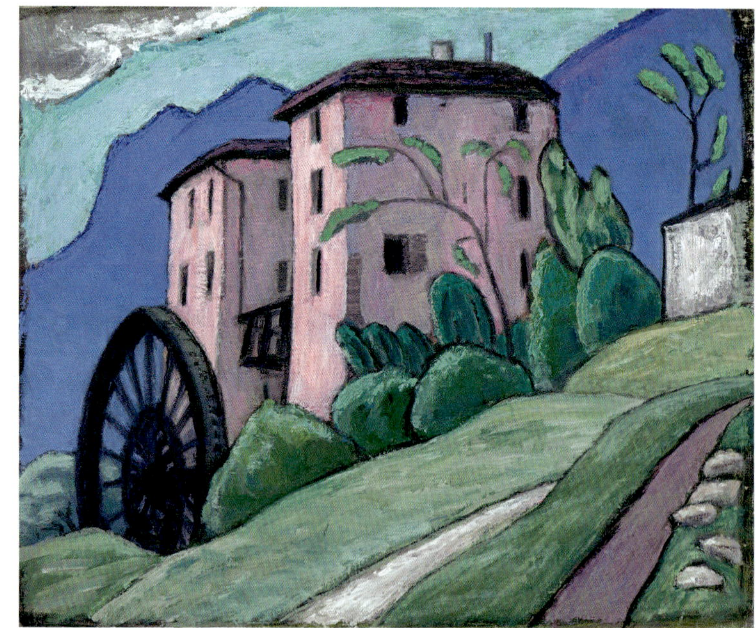

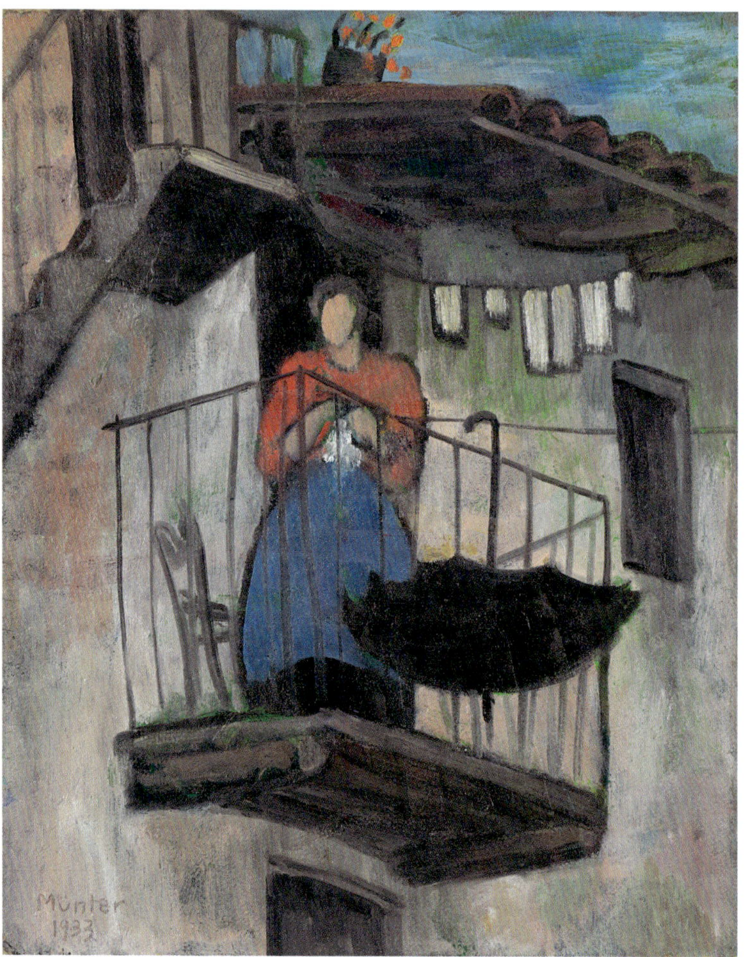

Cat. 87
Mill at Lake Iseo [Mühle am Iseosee], 1946
Textile support, 40.9 × 48.2 cm | Gabriele Münter- und Johannes Eichner-Stiftung, Munich, inv. no. L 667

Cat. 88
On the Balcony (Pisogne) [Auf dem Balkon (Pisogne)], 1933
Cardboard, 40.9 × 33 cm | Gabriele Münter- und Johannes Eichner-Stiftung, Munich, inv. no. V 50

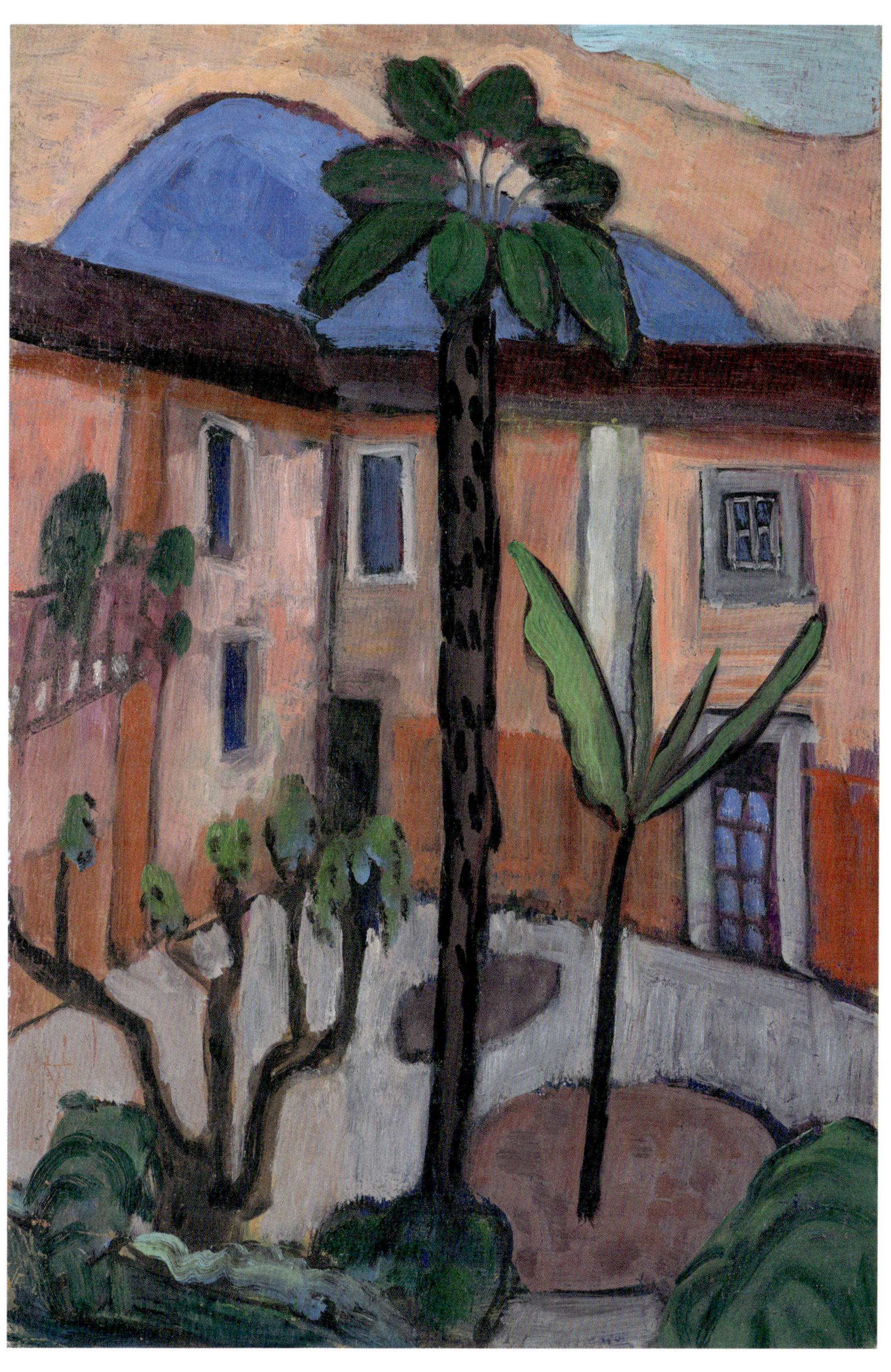

Cat. 89
Courtyard at Lake Iseo
[Hof am Iseosee], 1933
Cardboard, 50.8 × 34.5 cm |
Gabriele Münter- und Johannes Eichner-Stiftung, Munich, inv. no. L 48

“Portrait painting is the boldest and the most difficult, the most spiritual, the most extreme task for the artist.”[1]

Portraits

Portraits

Even as a child, Gabriele Münter loved to draw the people around her. She drew pictures of spa guests in the summer she was fourteen, later recalling that "the adults found my likenesses to be so accurate that they enjoyed stealing them from me."[2] While traveling in North America in the years 1898 to 1900, she immortalized her family members there in both photographs and drawings. Several years later, after turning to painting, the individual as a subject became important to her in this medium, too, whether in bust portraits or through the inclusion of figures in larger compositions, mostly of interiors.[3]

Münter produced some 250 portraits in the course of her career, around four-fifths of them of women. Our selection for the exhibition reflected this preponderance almost exactly. Portraits are quite rare in her painted oeuvre prior to 1907, although the earliest examples date from 1903. Those early works were painted from models in classes in Munich, Paris, and Berlin. Most of the portraits that Münter painted prior to World War I date from the years 1908 and 1909. Beginning in 1910, she focused more on still lifes, while also continuing her exploration of landscape.

The weeks that Münter spent painting alongside Kandinsky, Jawlensky, and Werefkin in the late summer of 1908 were crucial in enabling her to find her way to a fundamentally new style, which is also clearly in evidence in the portraits of 1908/09.[4] Bold colors applied fluidly to the support along with simplified forms, often circumscribed by dark outlining, are among the salient characteristics of this new style. Some of the representations of people produced just a few weeks earlier, among them the painting *Berlin Girl* of 1908, Fig. A evince an expressiveness that anticipates this change, although in portrait painting, as in other areas, Münter developed a style of many facets and pursued different ways of painting in parallel. For the 1913 portrait of her niece Annemarie Münter, for example, she used short brushstrokes and dispensed with outlining altogether. Fig. B Among the family members whose portraits Münter painted are her sister Emmy, her brother-in-law Georg Schroeter, her brother Carl, and her two nieces Annemarie Münter and Friedel Schroeter. She also produced likenesses of Kandinsky's mother. Otherwise, however, she seldom portrayed the people closest to her, preferring "genre portraits," by which she meant "genre-style portrait scenes set in domestic interiors."[5] Since the individuals in these works are shown in poses that are in some way typical of them, they seem more intimate than do the bust portraits, which, generally having to make do without any additional attributes, tend to look neutral by comparison. The dividing line between these two concepts of how to represent a human individual, the "pure" portrait and the "genre portrait," is of course a fluid one, as is evident in *Portrait of an Artist (Margret Cohen)*. Cat. 97

As far as we know, Münter never painted a portrait (in the narrow sense of the term) of Kandinsky, and with one notable exception, she did not paint the other artists belonging to the circle of the Blue Rider group either.[6] The exception is the now-famous *Portrait of Marianne von Werefkin*, which shows the Russian painter in front of the yellow basement of the Münter House in Murnau. Cat. 92 It is conceivable that Münter was inspired to produce this work by the painting *Femme au chapeau* (1905) by Henri Matisse (1869–1954), Fig. C which the American collector Leo Stein bought on the last day of the 1905 Salon d'Automne and hung in the apartment that he shared with his sister Gertrude on the rue de Fleurus in Paris.[7] Münter had been a guest at the Steins' home and hence would have had a chance to see Matisse's original—as opposed to the numerous reproductions of this supposedly "scandalous" painting that were circulating at the time. Werefkin's pose in Münter's portrait recalls Matisse's work, as do her large hat adorned with flowers and the colored shadow cast over her face. While the colors in Matisse's portrait are bolder, Münter took the synthesis of forms a stage further by presenting

1
Translated from Münter 1952a, n.p.

2
Ibid.

3
See the chapters "Interior Scenes," p. 114, and "Repetitions and Variations," pp. 185–86.

4
On this change of style, see the chapter "Primitivism," p. 142.

5
Translated from Reinhold Heller, "Innenräume: Erlebnis, Erinnerung und Synthese in der Kunst Gabriele Münters," in exh. cat. Munich/Frankfurt/Stockholm 1992/93, p. 63. See the chapter "Interior Scenes," p. 114.

6
Münter's paintings of Kandinsky belong to the category of "genre portraits." See the chapter "Interior Scenes," p. 116. There is a very fine linoleum cut portrait of Kandinsky by Münter dating from 1906; see exh. cat. Munich/Bonn/Murnau 2000/01, no. 6.

7
Exh. cat. *75 Years of Looking Forward*, ed. Janet Bishop, Corey Keller, and Sarah Roberts [San Francisco Museum of Modern Art, December 19, 2009–January 16, 2011], San Francisco 2009, n.p., text flanking fig. 19. Matisse's painting can be seen in a photograph of the Steins' home; see exh. cat. *The Steins Collect: Matisse, Picasso, and the Parisian Avant-Garde*, ed. Janet Bishop, Cécile Debray, and Rebecca Rabinow [San Francisco Museum of Modern Art, 2011; Paris, Grand Palais, Galeries nationales, 2011/12; New York, The Metropolitan Museum of Art, 2012], New Haven, CT 2011, pp. 362–63, 370–71.

8
See the chapter "Landscapes and Outdoor Scenes," p. 55.

9
Exh. cat. Munich/Frankfurt/Stockholm 1992/93, p. 17. There is a sketchbook dated 1917/18 containing a large number of portrait sketches; Städtische Galerie im Lenbachhaus und Kunstbau München, inv. no. GMS 1134.

Werefkin's body simply as a white triangle, delineated by a pink scarf. The simplification of forms coupled with a monotone background make this an instantly eye-catching work.

In July 1915 Münter left Germany and traveled to Scandinavia, where she remained until 1920.[8] From 1916, financial necessity drove her to accept portrait commissions from patrons in Sweden,[9] and she retained this source of revenue even after her return to Germany, especially after she had settled in Murnau in the 1930s. She also began portraying those in her immediate circle of friends and acquaintances, which she had scarcely done at all prior to 1914. Among those she painted were her teacher in Berlin, the artist Arthur Segal; friends like

A **Berlin Girl [Berliner Mädel], 1908**
Cardboard, 36.8 × 34.6 cm |
Gabriele Münter- und Johannes Eichner-Stiftung, Munich, inv. no. P 113

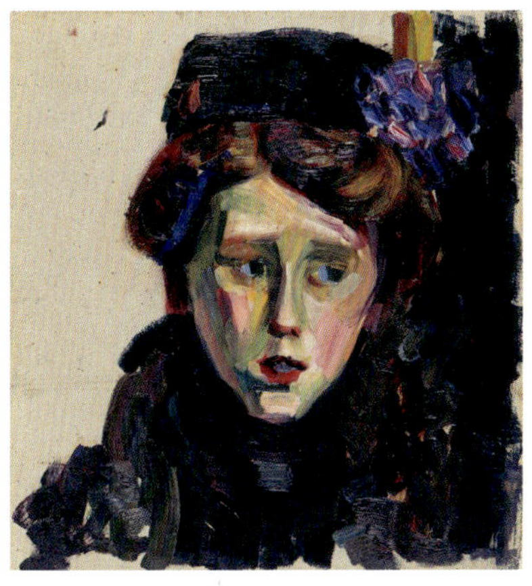

B **The Jolly Little Gnat (Annemarie Münter) [Das lustige Mückchen (Annemarie Münter)], 1913**
Oil on cardboard, 40 × 31.5 cm |
Private collection

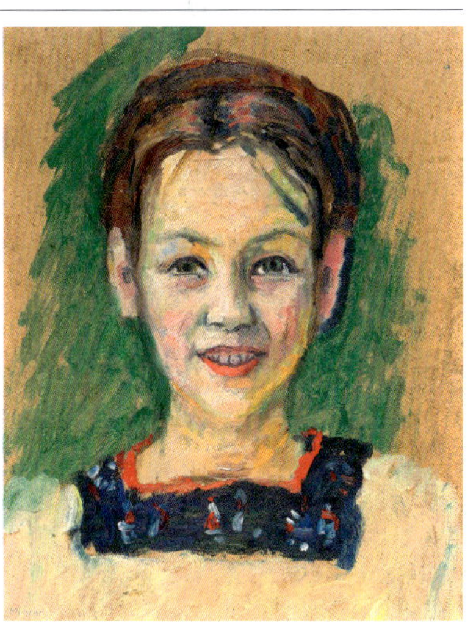

C **HENRI MATISSE**
Femme au chapeau (Woman with a Hat), 1905
Oil on canvas, 80.7 × 59.7 cm |
San Francisco Museum of Modern Art, Bequest of Elise S. Haas

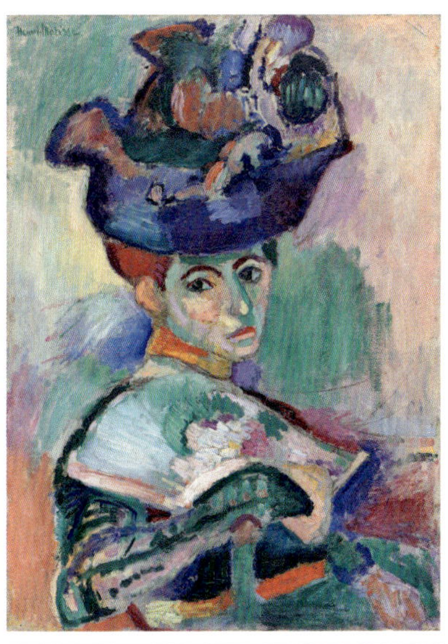

the painter Loulou Albert-Lazard (1885–1969); the art historian Hanna Stirnemann; her housekeeper in Murnau, Ellen Brischke; and her new life partner from 1928, Johannes Eichner—to name but a few examples. Fig. D

Münter showed less interest in painting portraits of herself. We know of sixteen painted self-portraits altogether, the only record of four of them being entries in Münter's logbooks. Paula Modersohn-Becker (1876–1907), in contrast, painted and drew herself fifty times in the course of her short life.[10] Münter's very first self-portrait dates from around 1909, in other words from the period when she settled in Bavaria. She bought her country house in Murnau in August of that year and moved into Kandinsky's apartment on Ainmillerstraße in Munich in October. As a painter, she had found her own distinctive idiom by then and was working alongside other artists, both male and female; together, as the Neue Künstlervereinigung München (New Artists' Association Munich), founded in 1909, they began staging exhibitions of their work.[11] She produced her last self-portrait in 1952, when she was seventy-five.[12]

Whereas prior to World War I Münter occasionally portrayed herself working at her easel, this pose seems not to have interested her later on.[13] A self-portrait of around 1908–09 showing a frontal view of the artist at her easel, clad in a broad-brimmed hat and white blouse with a large red pendant slung round her neck, forms a kind of compromise between two distinct tropes: the self-portrait as painter and as bourgeois lady. Cat. 93 The artist's gaze seems to be leveled directly at the viewer, although in fact she was looking in a mirror, which is why she portrayed herself with her palette in her right hand—a mirror image of herself, in other words. The large hat festooned with flowers recalls the *Portrait of Marianne von Werefkin*, even if the two paintings differ in both style and impact. Although we are dealing here with a self-portrait whose purpose was clearly to assert the subject's status as an artist, true to the tradition of the "official" artist's self-portrait, it is impossible not to notice that Münter denies herself the kind of self-assured aplomb that is typical of this genre;[14] instead, she looks at us with a scrutinizing gaze. Her *Self-Portrait at the Easel*, which she probably painted a few years later, exemplifies a very different kind of self-representation. Fig. E Standing in the foreground is a stool with a palette resting on it, while the painter herself lingers in the background, absorbed in her work.

Münter did not exhibit her self-portraits, apart from the portrait of herself in the hat decorated with flowers, which is thought to have been first shown in the double exhibition *Wassily Kandinsky, Gabriele Münter: Gabriele-Münter-Stiftung* at the Kunstverein Hamburg in 1958/59. That show was organized by the then director of the Städtische Galerie im Lenbachhaus, Hans Konrad Roethel, in recognition of Münter's gift of a large collection of works, presented to the Lenbachhaus the previous year. In addition to 123 works by Kandinsky, the exhibition included 50 paintings by Münter herself. She showed the same self-portrait again in 1960, this time as part of her first show in the United States, at the Dalzell Hatfield Galleries in Los Angeles.[15]

Portrait painting did not come easily to Münter: "I've often tried my hand at portraiture, but I must confess that many portraits of mine did not turn out well. Sometimes the result is a good painting, but not a real portrait; sometimes it is a real portrait, but not the desired painting. I often got stuck in the antechambers of art."[16] Perhaps these lines explain why she dedicated so little time and attention to portraiture between 1910 and 1914; while she created several impressive portraits in 1908/09, she seems not to have been able to make any further progress toward her goals in this genre in the years that followed. This changed only when she started accepting portrait commissions in Scandinavia and even more so from the 1920s when she produced a large number of portraits, albeit most of them on paper, since she painted very little during that decade.[17] The likenesses captured with just a few drawn outlines, some of which seem to reproduce

10
Exh. cat. *Paula Modersohn-Becker, 1876–1907: Retrospektive*, ed. Helmut Friedel [Städtische Galerie im Lenbachhaus und Kunstbau München, July 16–October 19, 1997], Munich 1997, n.p., introduction to the section on self-portraits.

11
Having enjoyed their painting vacation in Murnau in the late summer of 1908, Kandinsky, Münter, Jawlensky, and Werefkin decided to go public as a group. In January 1909, therefore, they got together with other artists and art lovers and launched the Neue Künstlervereinigung München (NKVM). Their first exhibition was held in Heinrich Thannhauser's Moderne Galerie in Munich in December 1909.

12
Since Münter repeatedly reworked and sometimes even overpainted her paintings, it is quite conceivable that she could have painted other self-portraits, of which no record has survived.

13
Since four self-portraits, of 1935, 1946, 1948, and 1952, are known to us only from written records, it is impossible to be categorical on this point.

14
One good example of this is the *Self-Portrait with Straw Hat* by Elisabeth Louise Vigée Le Brun, after 1782, oil on canvas, 97.8 × 70.5 cm, The National Gallery, London. Exh. cat. Milwaukee/Columbus/Richmond/San Antonio 1997–99, pp. 122–23.

15
Exh. cat. Los Angeles 1960, Dalzell Hatfield Galleries, unnumbered plate. According to the title, *Gabriele Münter: First American Exhibition with Seven Additional Major Paintings by Kandinsky*, the show was not, strictly speaking, a solo exhibition. There were thirteen paintings by Münter.

16
Translated from Münter 1952a, n.p.

17
On the reasons for the slump in her output of paintings in the 1920s, see the chapter "Landscapes and Outdoor Scenes," p. 54.

18
Translated from Gustav Friedrich Hartlaub, "Die Zeichnerin Gabriele Münter," in Hartlaub 1952, n.p.

19
Translated from Münter 1952a, n.p.

a certain type rather than an individual, attest to her magisterial command of line. Fig. F These are the works that moved the art historian Gustav Friedrich Hartlaub to describe Münter as "a secret master of the clean line, of pure outline."[18] Despite her self-doubt, she never abandoned portrait painting entirely, for "to abandon the task altogether merely on account of the risks would be too easy. Portrait painting is the boldest and the most difficult, the most spiritual, the most extreme task for the artist."[19]

D **Portrait Sketch of Loulou Albert-Lazard [Bildnisskizze Loulou Albert-Lazard], 1929**
Textile support, 55 × 33 cm | Gabriele Münter- und Johannes Eichner-Stiftung, Munich, inv. no. P 216

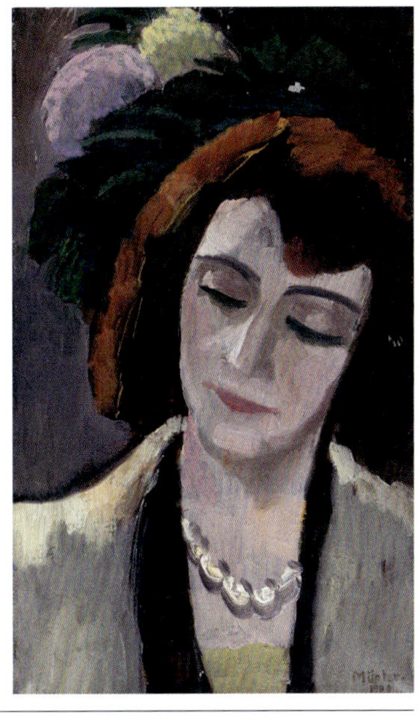

E **Self-Portrait at the Easel [Selbstbildnis an der Staffelei], ca. 1911**
Oil on cardboard, 37.5 × 30 cm | Private collection, Stuttgart

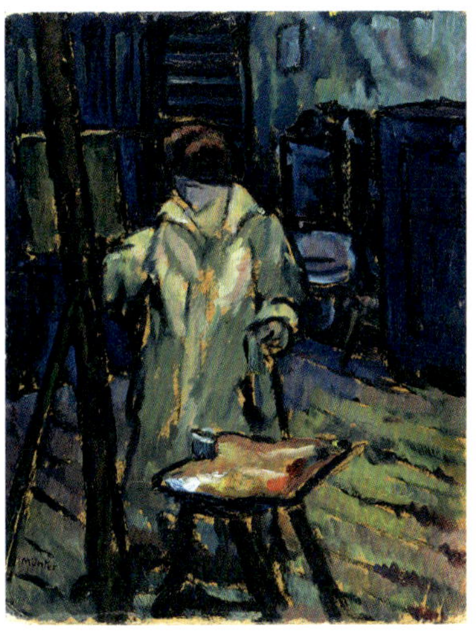

F **The Stylish One (The Poet G. v. B.) [Die Stilvolle (Die Dichterin G. v. B.)]**
Pencil on heavy paper, 18.4 × 13.3 cm | Gabriele Münter- und Johannes Eichner-Stiftung, Munich, inv. no. Kon. 29/62

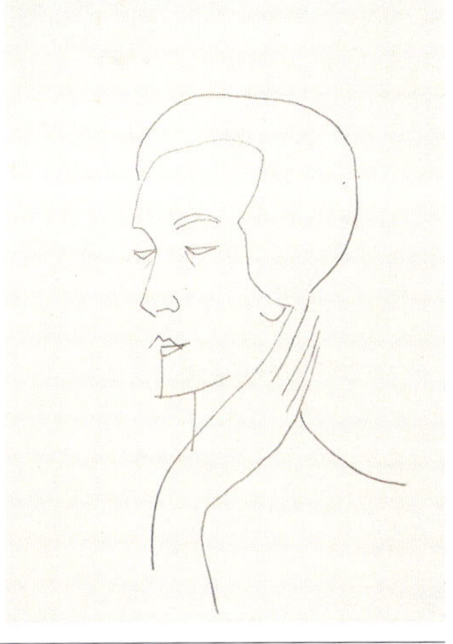

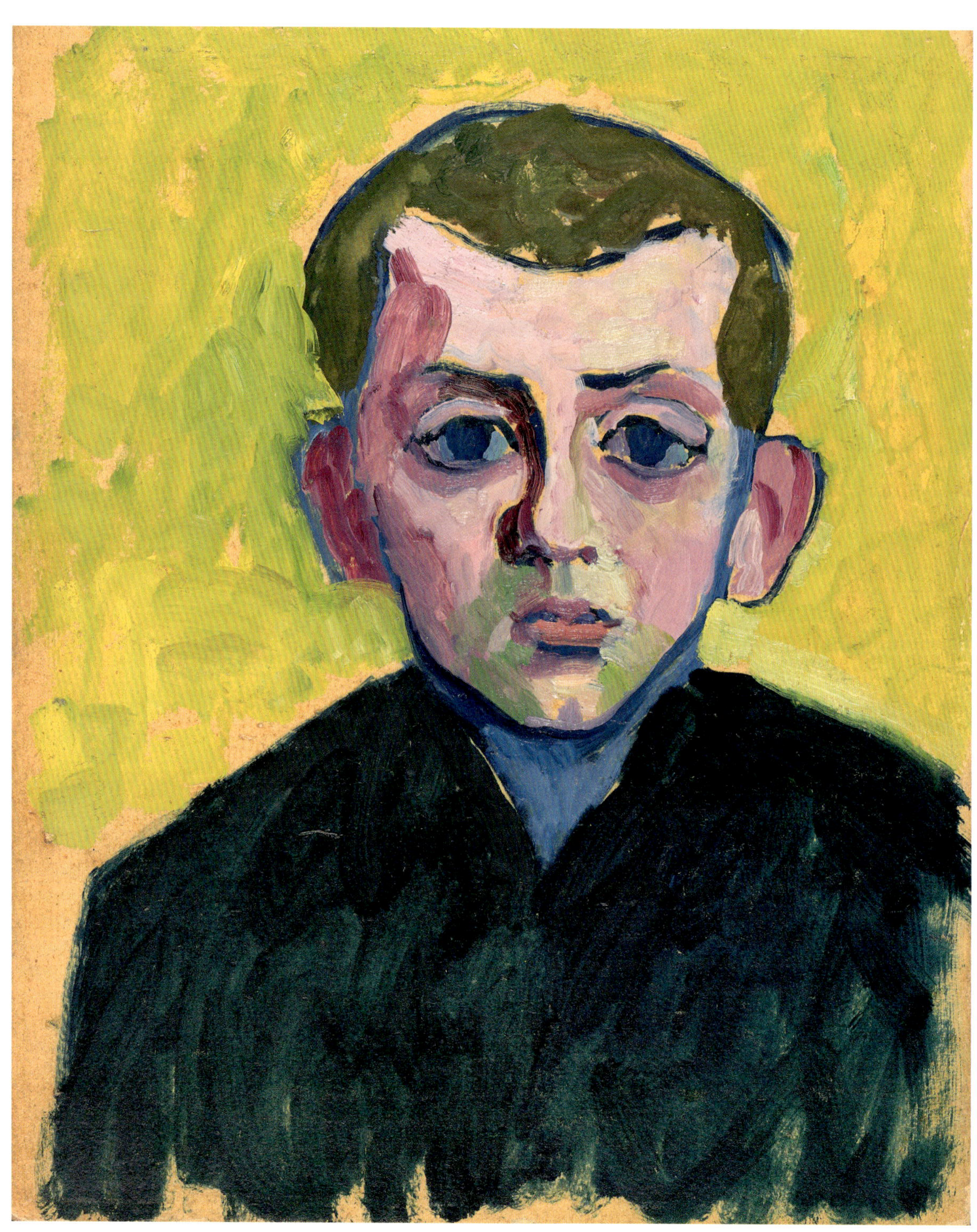

Cat. 90
Head of a Young Boy (Willi Blab) [Knabenkopf (Willi Blab)], 1908
Cardboard, 39.8 × 33.1 cm | Museum Ludwig, Cologne, inv. no. ML 10538

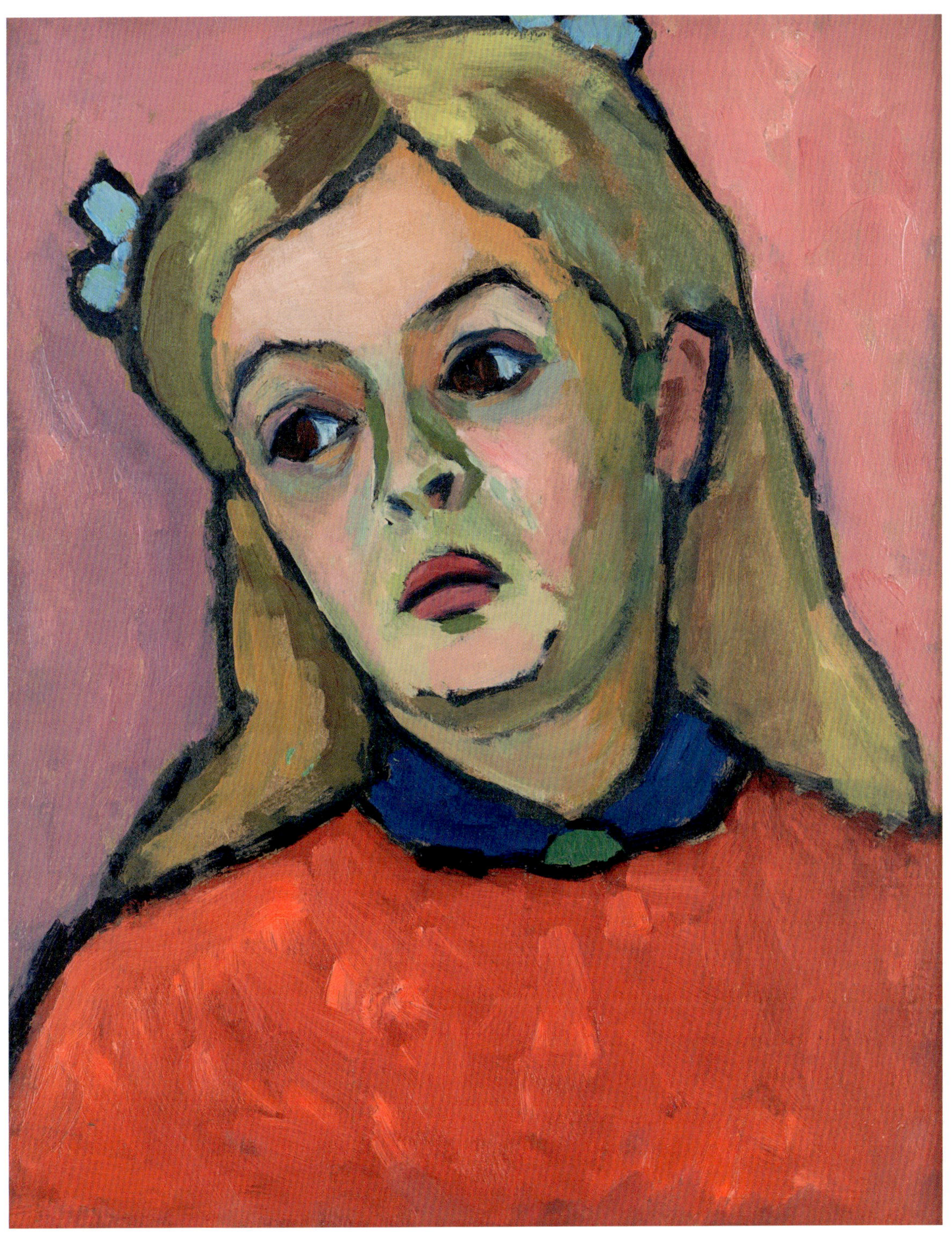

Cat. 91
Head of a Young Girl [Mädchenbildnis], 1908
Oil on board, 40.6 × 33 cm |
Des Moines Art Center, Iowa (USA).
Mildred M. Bohen Collection,
inv. no. 1983.11

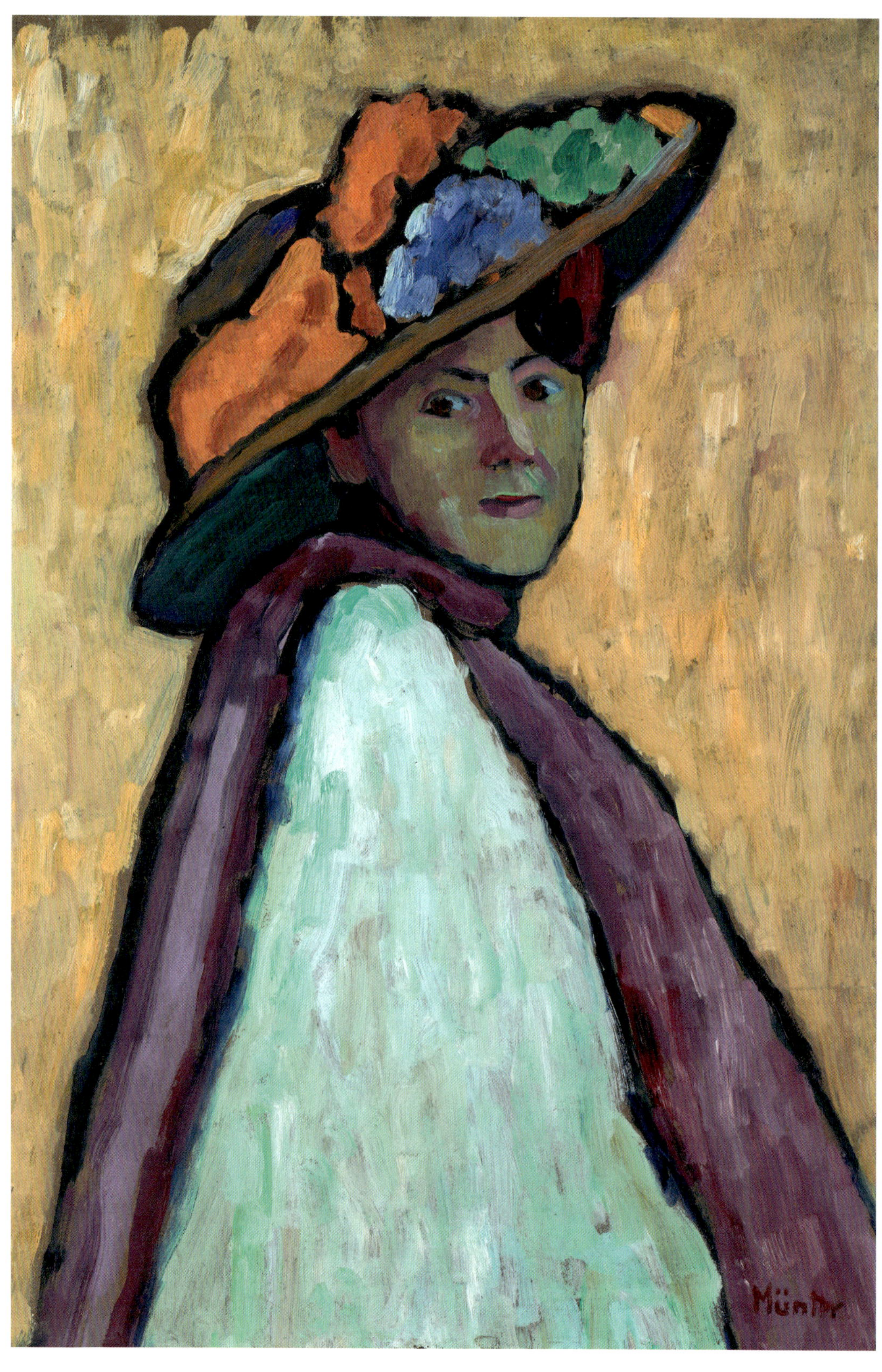

Cat. 92
Portrait of Marianne von Werefkin [Bildnis Marianne von Werefkin], 1909
Cardboard, 81 × 54.8 cm |
Städtische Galerie im Lenbachhaus und Kunstbau München, inv. no. GMS 656

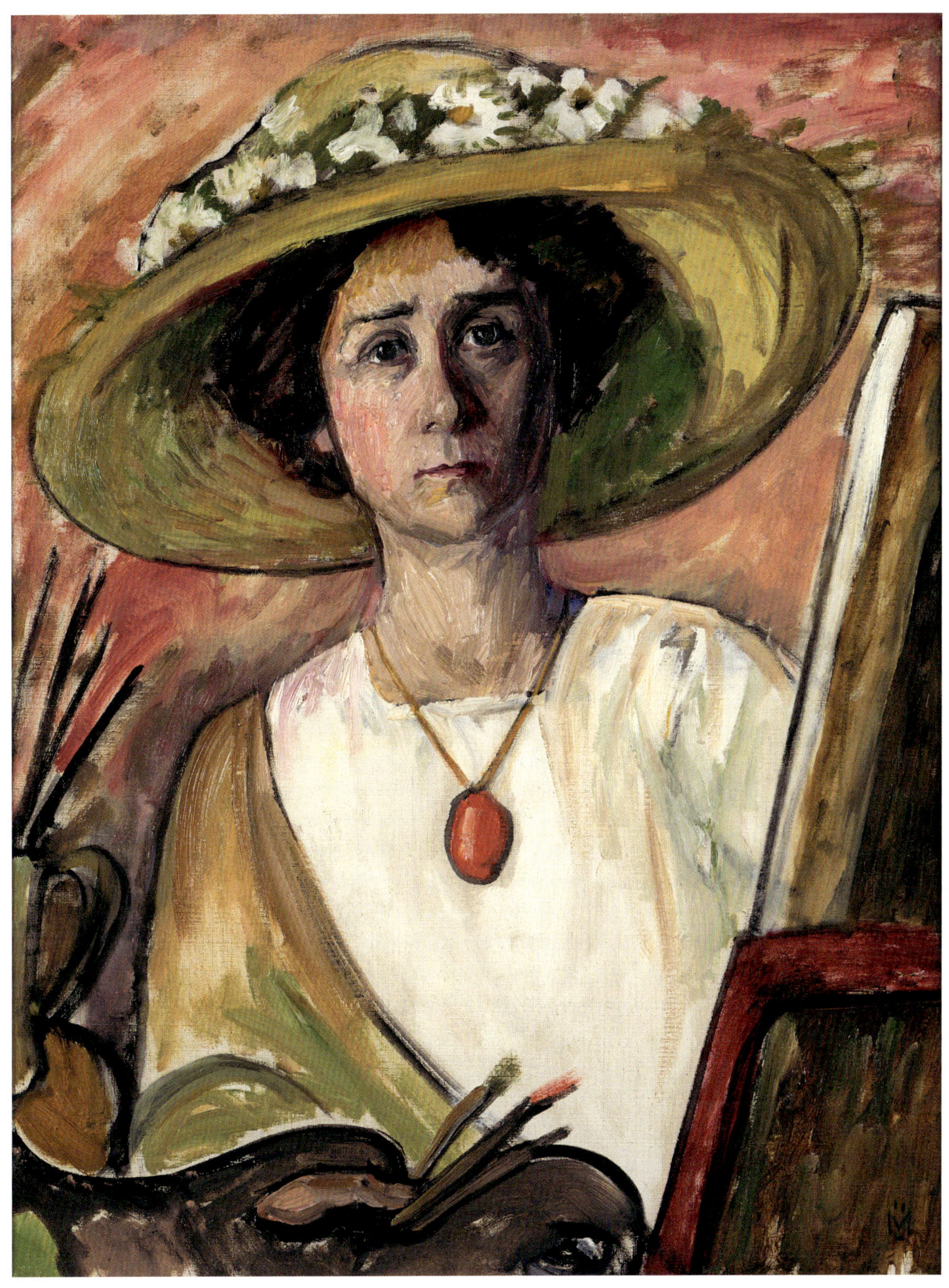

Cat. 93
Self-Portrait in Front of an Easel [Selbstbildnis vor der Staffelei], ca. 1908–09
Oil on canvas, 78 × 60.5 cm | Princeton University Art Museum. Gift of Frank E. Taplin Jr., Class of 1937, and Mrs. Taplin, inv. no. y1992-21

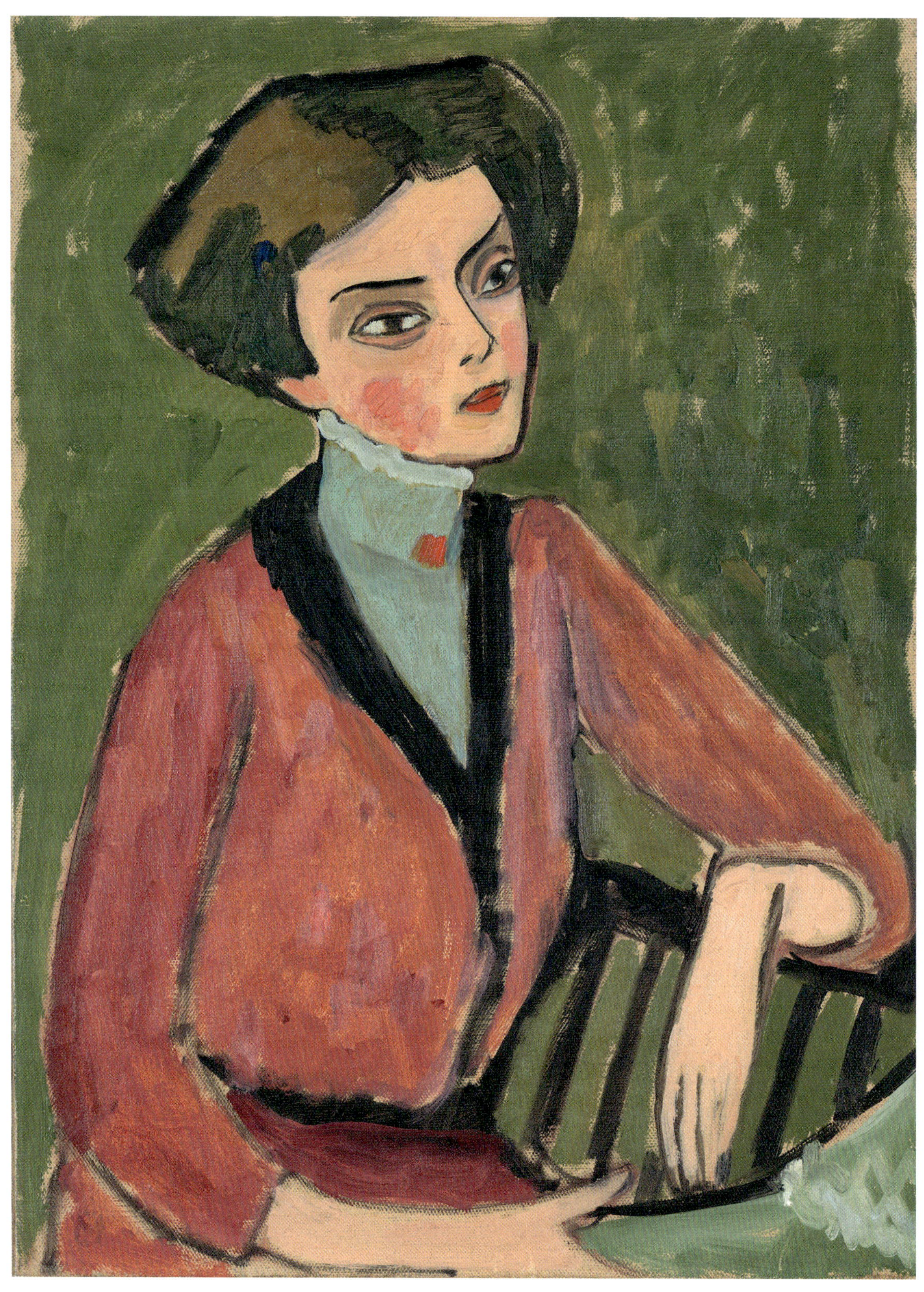

Cat. 94
Olga von Hartmann, ca. 1910
Textile support, 60.8 × 45.2 cm |
Gabriele Münter- und Johannes Eichner-Stiftung, Munich, inv. no. P 162

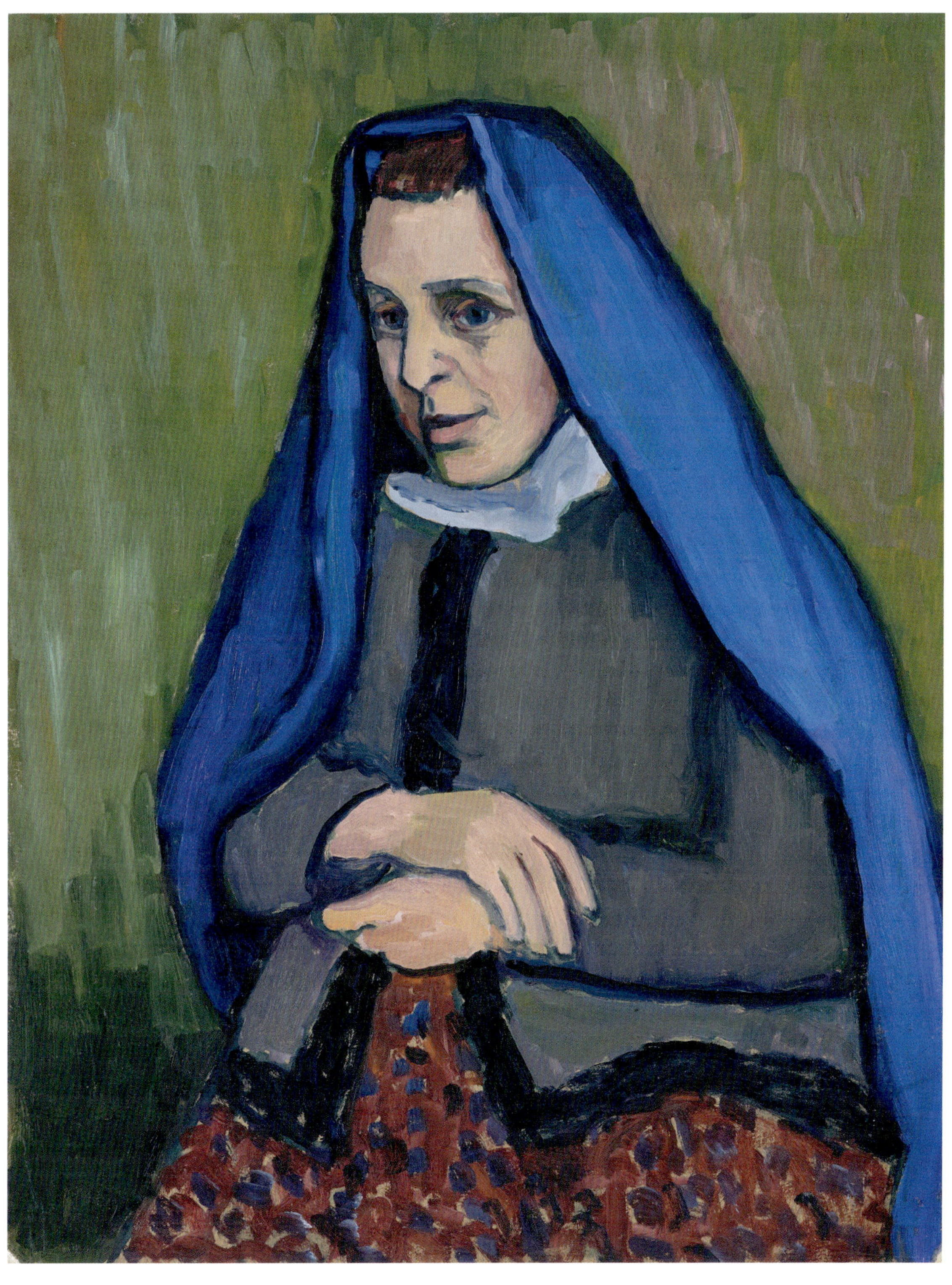

Cat. 95
Miss Mathilde Wearing a Blue Headscarf [Fräulein Mathilde mit blauem Kopftuch], 1909
Cardboard, 72 × 56.2 cm |
Gabriele Münter- und Johannes Eichner-Stiftung, Munich, inv. no. P 30

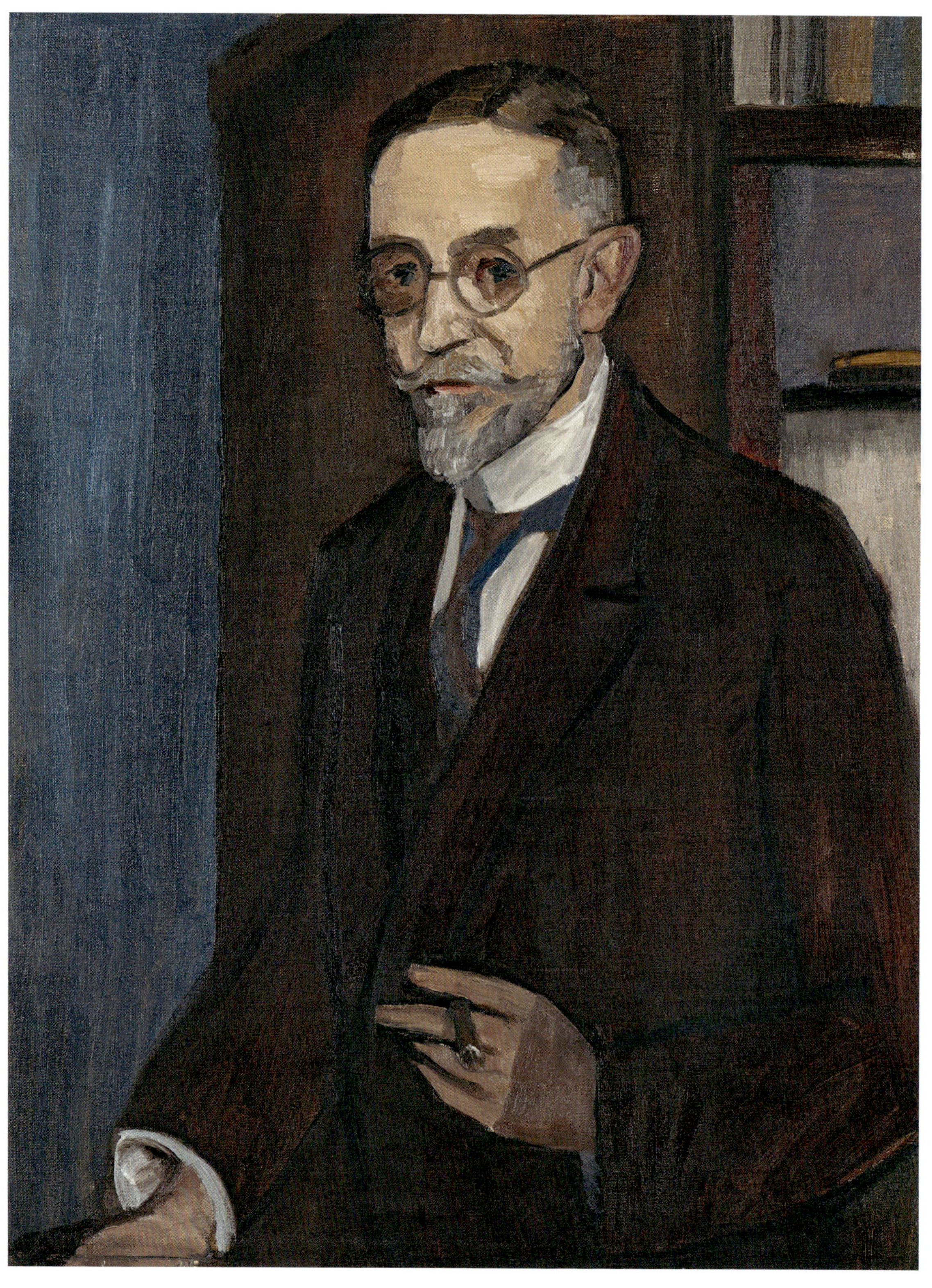

Cat. 96
Portrait of Georg Schroeter (Man with a Cigar) [Porträt Georg Schroeter (Mann mit Zigarre)], 1929
Textile support, 76.8 × 59.7 cm | Gabriele Münter- und Johannes Eichner-Stiftung, Munich, inv. no. P 221

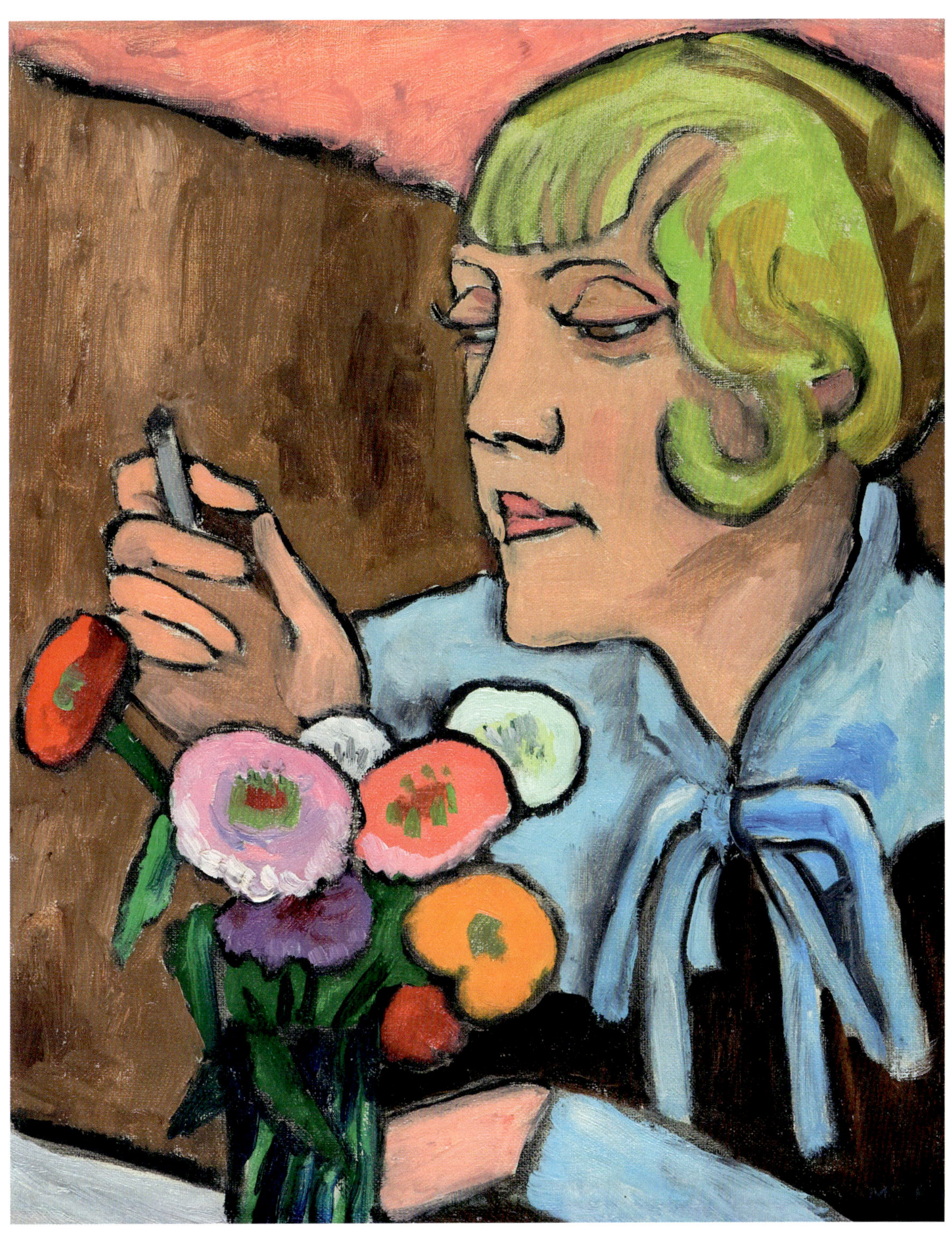

Cat. 97
Portrait of an Artist (Margret Cohen) [Bildnis einer Künstlerin (Margret Cohen)], 1932
Oil on canvas, 46.5 × 38.2 cm | Dreiländermuseum Lörrach, inv. no. CUV 103

“Lived spaces”[1]

Interior Scenes

Interior Scenes

After her stay in Murnau in the late summer of 1908, Gabriele Münter's painting changed in terms of both style and subject matter.[2] Whereas previously she had dedicated herself first and foremost to landscapes, in the second half of 1908 she began to take an interest in portraits and interiors, whether in the form of genre scenes, "genre portraits," or still lifes. This shift of focus from outside to inside coincided with the period in which she and Kandinsky were settling down together in Munich.[3]

For Münter, the "genre portrait," showing an individual in a domestic interior, constituted an alternative to the classical portrait. Genre scenes are something else again in that they show several people in an interior situation, sometimes just talking, sometimes engaged in a shared activity such as making music together. For both categories, the "genre portrait" and the genre scene, the interior itself is an essential part of the concept.[4]

Yet there are only two subjects dating from the period prior to World War I that can be categorized as genre scenes. The first shows Kandinsky and the painter Erma Bossi (1875–1952) engaged in conversation in the dining area of the Münter House. Cat. 172; 173 Four different versions of this scene were produced over a period of three years, with the earliest of these (ca. 1909/10) signaling the onset of Münter's preoccupation with genre scenes.[5] The second subject, *After Tea*, shows the art dealer Hans Goltz on a visit to Kandinsky and Münter at their home at Ainmillerstraße 36 in Schwabing and exists in two variants as well as an excerpt.[6] Figs. E; F, p. 186; Cat. 103 Both *Kandinsky and Erma Bossi at the Table* and *After Tea* are large-scale compositions that were preceded by numerous drawings, which is the exception rather than the rule in Münter's work.[7] While these paintings show people engaged in conversation, two other genre scenes which she painted in Stockholm in 1916, *Music (The Wallin Siblings of Stockholm)* and *At the Clockmaker's*, convey a calmer atmosphere. Figs. A; B The figures in these works are not directly connected to each other; each seems to be locked inside his or her own world, which lends

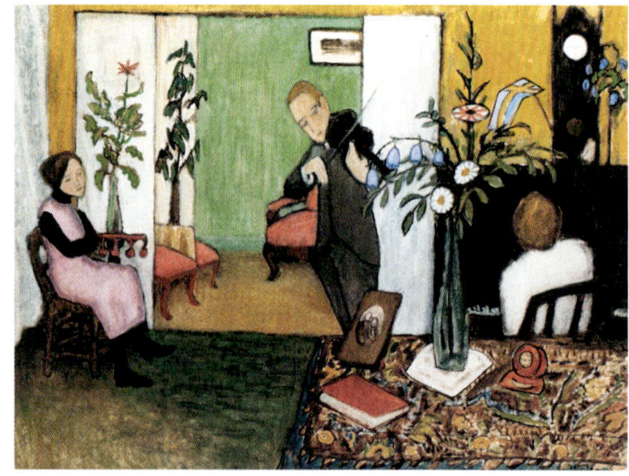

A **Music (The Wallin Siblings of Stockholm) [Musik (Geschwister Wallin Stockholm)], 1916**
Oil on canvas, 90 × 115 cm | Private collection

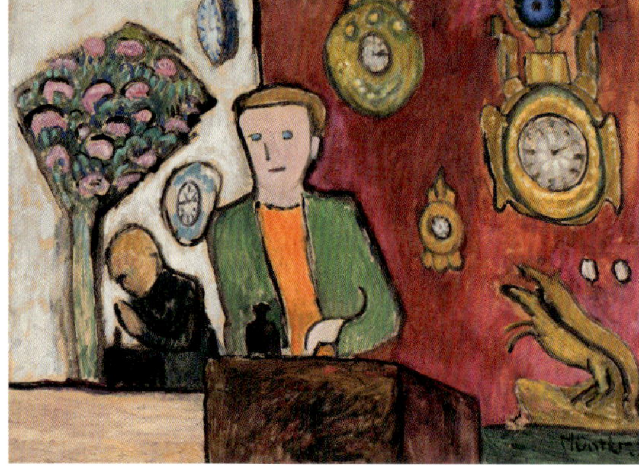

B **At the Clockmaker's [Im Uhrmacherladen], 1916**
Oil on canvas, 65.5 × 88 cm | Private collection, Switzerland

1
Translated from Griselda Pollock, "Die Räume der Weiblichkeit in der Moderne," in *Blick-Wechsel: Konstruktionen von Männlichkeit und Weiblichkeit in Kunst und Kunstgeschichte*, ed. Ines Lindner, Sigrid Schade, Silke Wenk, and Gabriele Werner, Berlin 1989, p. 317.

2
On the change in Münter's style while in Murnau, see the chapter "Landscapes and Outdoor Scenes," p. 54.

3
See the chapter "Portraits," p. 100.

4
On the concept of the "genre portrait" and portraits rendered as genre scenes in Münter's oeuvre, see Reinhold Heller, "Innenräume: Erlebnis, Erinnerung und Synthese in der Kunst Gabriele Münters," in exh. cat. Munich/Frankfurt/Stockholm 1992/93, pp. 47–66, here pp. 50–51.

5
See the chapter "Repetitions and Variations," pp. 185–86.

6
See ibid.

7
As note 4, pp. 47–66.

8
See the chapter "Primitivism," p. 139.

9
As note 4, pp. 57ff.

10
"It was not my intention to paint a portrait of Klee," she later wrote, "that's why I called the work 'Man in an Armchair.'" Translated from Münter 1952b, p. 53.

11
There is a second version of this work dated the same year: oil on canvas, 55 × 46 cm, whereabouts unknown.

the works an air of melancholy. In the former work, we see the eponymous Wallin siblings, who were close friends of Münter's, making music together, while a woman seated in the corner of the room listens. The painting *At the Clockmaker's* shows a work situation, even if the work itself is not readily identifiable at first. Standing at a desk in the foreground is the lady who presumably takes the customers' orders, while the clockmaker of the title is hunched over his workbench next to a stylized tree in the background. The tree is perplexing. Is it a tree out on the street reflected in the window? Or is it a bouquet of flowers that for compositional reasons Münter chose to depict as a tree? The ambiguity of the situation makes for a mysterious atmosphere. There is something almost theatrical about the three compositions *Kandinsky and Erma Bossi at the Table*, *After Tea*, and *Music (The Wallin Siblings of Stockholm)*. All three show people in a large room, much as if they were on stage. This is not true of the genre scenes that Münter produced in the 1930s, however, where the focus is on the individuals, and the room itself has almost no role to play at all. Clearly, we are dealing here with a different kind of image, one that is not unlike a snapshot photograph. Cat. 111

The majority of Münter's interior scenes, however, show only one person—usually a woman—absorbed in some solitary activity, be it reading, writing, sewing, or simply sitting next to a table. Cat. 107 Her representations of men include another variant: the man seated in an armchair. Cat. 110 The best-known example of this latter type is *Man in an Armchair*, the "genre portrait" of Paul Klee (1879–1940) that Münter painted when he came to visit her and Kandinsky at their home on Ainmillerstraße in 1913. Fig. C Standing in the middle of the composition is a little table with figures from Münter's collection of folk art. Klee is seated to the right of it, while hanging on the wall behind him are some folkish reverse-glass paintings. The painting *Still Life with Figure (Mrs. Simonovich)* Cat. 104 is similar in composition: the table full of objects and the wall hung with reverse-glass paintings again take pride of place and seem almost to be squeezing the Russian painter Simonovich out of the picture. Münter liked to rearrange the figures on the table before painting it.[8] This part of her study seems to have been especially important to her. According to Reinhold Heller, giving it such prominence in her "genre portraits" was a way of assuring herself of a presence in the composition.[9] The titles of these works, all of them Münter's own, tell us that to her mind, these paintings were not portraits at all.[10] In *Still Life with Figure (Mrs. Simonovich)* she even made the still life the centerpiece—both of the title and of the work itself.

After *Man in an Armchair*, Münter scarcely ever used her own home as a backdrop for her genre scenes. One of the rare exceptions is *Breakfast of the Birds* of 1934, which shows the artist herself, viewed from behind, seated at the breakfast table.[11] Cat. 112 In principle, the piece is not unlike Arnold Schoenberg's painting *Walking Self-Portrait*, which was included in the *First Exhibition of the "Blue Rider" Editorial Board* at the Galerie Thannhauser in Munich in 1911/12 as well as being reproduced in *The Blue Rider* almanac. Fig. D But the interior scene in

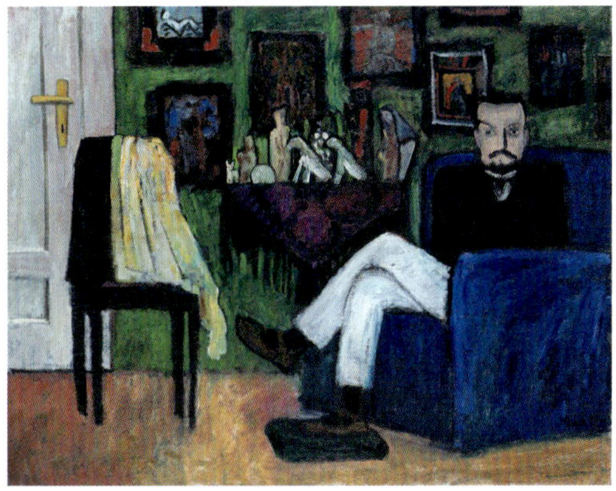

C **Man in an Armchair [Mann im Sessel], 1913**
Oil on canvas, 95 × 125.5 cm | Bayerische Staatsgemäldesammlungen, Munich, inv. no. 11227

Breakfast of the Birds does not occupy as important a place in Münter's oeuvre as *Man in an Armchair* or even *Still Life with Figure (Mrs. Simonovich)*.

Listening (Portrait of Jawlensky) and *Man at a Table (Kandinsky)* are two works of almost identical size—both painted on cardboard—which were produced within two years of each other and show two of Münter's most important companions. Cat. 100; 102 She herself titled the paintings simply *Listening* and *Sketch of a Man at the Table*. In her eyes, in other words, they were not portraits but rather representations of a certain situation and hence a hybrid of individual features and universal human characteristics. Both Jawlensky and Kandinsky are shown sitting at a table with a white tablecloth, but positioned firmly in either the left or the right half of the picture. The composition of *Listening* is dominated by a ceiling lamp and a wine glass, that of *Man at the Table* by a large plant. And there are narrative elements, too, in the form of a plate of sausages and a snail pastry on a plate. Yet neither work is without ambiguities. To the right of Kandinsky is a dark curtain that seems almost to be clamped between his elbow and body. Whether Kandinsky is in front of the curtain or behind it is not clear, and in any case the viewer is bound to ask why he is sitting so near to the curtain—which looks rather like a stage curtain being pulled closed. Kandinsky's serious bearing, moreover, makes for a stark contrast with the naïve painting style. The plant with its horizontal branches seems exceptionally unnatural and clumsily reproduced, while the patch of brown representing the artist's hands is similarly odd. Perhaps Münter had wanted to paint her partner in the attitude he typically adopted during conversation.

In *Listening*, Alexej von Jawlensky is shown listening to Kandinsky's latest theories on art. His expression is one of astonishment mingled with incomprehension—an effect accentuated by his raised eyebrows; his eyes, rendered as little blue dots; and the diagonal slant of his body, which echoes the line of the sausages on the plate in front of him. The painting verges on caricature.

Münter seems to have rated the two works very differently. Whereas *Man at the Table* was reproduced in *The Blue Rider* almanac and from 1913 was regularly included in exhibitions, *Listening* was not presented in public until after World War II.[12]

Kandinsky at Tea, by contrast, comes closer to traditional portraiture, even though the foreground is occupied by a still life rather than Kandinsky and the subject himself is not looking at the viewer, but has turned his head to the left. Cat. 101 His facial features, however, are reproduced with care, and the whole painting looks more official in character than does *Man at the Table (Kandinsky)*. It should also be remembered that Münter herself described *Man at the Table* as a sketch. "Sketch" could be a reference to the circumstances in which it was painted, since presumably it was done from life, unlike *Kandinsky at Tea*. One significant difference between *Kandinsky at Tea* and both *Man at the Table* and *Listening* is the way the figures in the latter two works are "juxtaposed with the objects on the table in a manner reminiscent of still-life painting."[13] Münter, in other words, placed the same importance on the still-life elements as on the figures—which is certainly not the case in *Kandinsky at Tea*.

What interested Münter in all these interiors was the relationship between room and figure, as she herself made clear when writing about *Man in an Armchair*: "He [Klee] was sitting in my big thinking chair and talking to Kandinsky, when suddenly I saw him in the room and the room with him in it as a picture."[14] Room and figure are here treated as equals. Yet the spatial situations in her works are not always easy to make out, which perhaps accounts for their almost secretive atmosphere. Nor is this true only of the interiors; it can also apply to the still lifes.[15] One of Münter's first interiors, *Christmas Still Life*, shows a Christmas tree on a table in the foreground. Cat. 99 Standing in the background, apparently in a different room, is a woman, looking back at the viewer. What we are really looking at, however, is a mirror reflecting the artist herself, busy painting. The painting *In the Salon*

12
The work's first recorded public appearance was at Münter's double exhibition with Paula Modersohn-Becker in Hannover in 1951; see appendix for details.

13
Friedel/Hoberg 2000, cat. no. 68.

14
Translated from Münter 1952b, p. 53.

15
Still Life with St. George (1911) is a good example of this. See the chapter "Primitivism," p. 139.

16
The same sketchbook contains sketches called *In the Salon* and *Man at the Table*, which Münter drew two days apart from each other. The sketch of *In the Salon*, pp. 2–3, is dated April 15, 1911; the sketch of *Man at the Table*, p. 5, April 17, 1911, sketchbook, inv. no. Kon. 46/39, MES.

is similarly enigmatic.[16] Cat. 105 Here we see two ladies in front of a patterned wallpaper with a mysterious large dark stain. In front of them, in the middle of the composition but cut off at the bottom, is the back of a girl's head. The cumulative effect of these elements is to obfuscate the composition, which in turn has the effect of firing the viewer's imagination and giving fantasy free rein. A much closer view of a single motif is that in the work *Still Life on the Tram (After Shopping)* of around 1912. Cat. 106 Shown here are the purchases that a woman has bought and is now cradling in her lap. It is the focus on these that makes this work a still life. The painting has the quality of a snapshot, and it is indeed possible that the idea for such a composition originally came from photography.

As we can see, the dividing line between interiors and still lifes was a fluid one for Gabriele Münter. Her *Still Life in Front of the Yellow House* (1953) shows that the boundary between still life and landscape was similarly blurred, although what this work illustrates most of all is just how playfully the painter handled space. Cat. 113 We think we are looking at a still life on a table in front of a window with a view of the houses beyond. Yet the table we are looking at is not, in fact, in front of a window at all; it is positioned in front of Münter's own painting *The Yellow House* of 1911. Fig. E

What all these examples tell us is that Münter's painting is not as easy to interpret as we might assume at first glance. Her playful handling of space, her painterly treatment of figures and their surroundings as motifs of equal importance, and the fluid boundaries between different genres all make for a conceptual complexity that leads to ambiguous creations. Viewers who want to better understand these works have no choice but to take their time with them—and not even then can all their mysteries be solved.

D **ARNOLD SCHOENBERG**
Walking Self-Portrait
[Gehendes Selbstportrait], 1911
Oil on cardboard, 49 × 44.9 cm | Arnold Schönberg Center, Vienna, inv. no. CR 18

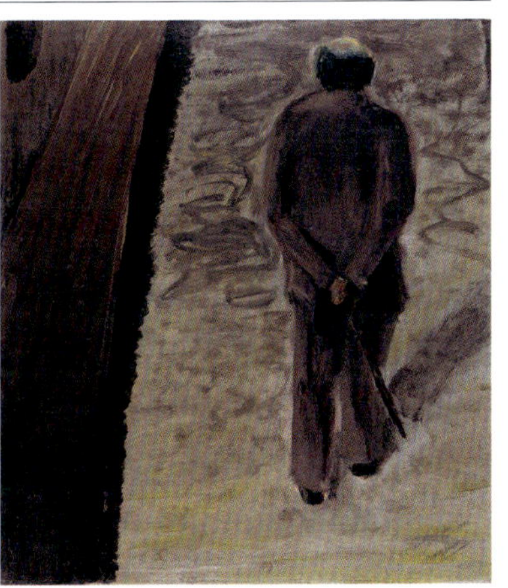

E **The Yellow House**
[Das gelbe Haus], 1911
Oil on cardboard, 51.8 × 75 cm | Bayerische Staatsgemäldesammlungen, Munich, inv. no. 12181

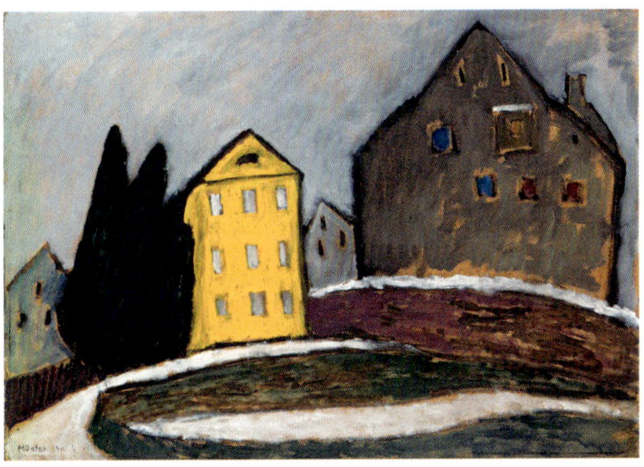

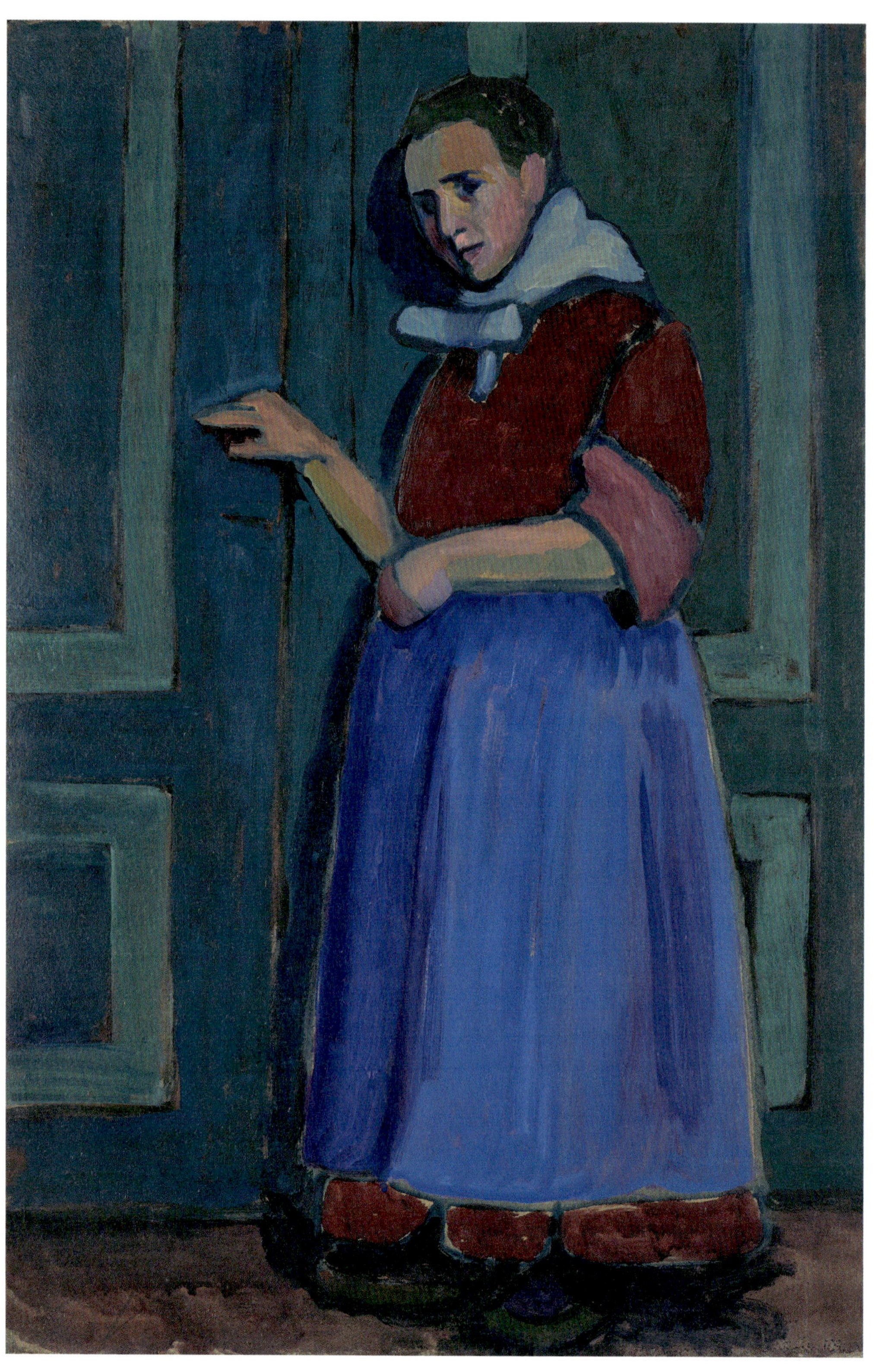

Cat. 98
Miss Mathilde
[Fräulein Mathilde], 1908/09
Cardboard, 75.6 × 51.1 cm |
Gabriele Münter- und Johannes Eichner-Stiftung, Munich, inv. no. P 26

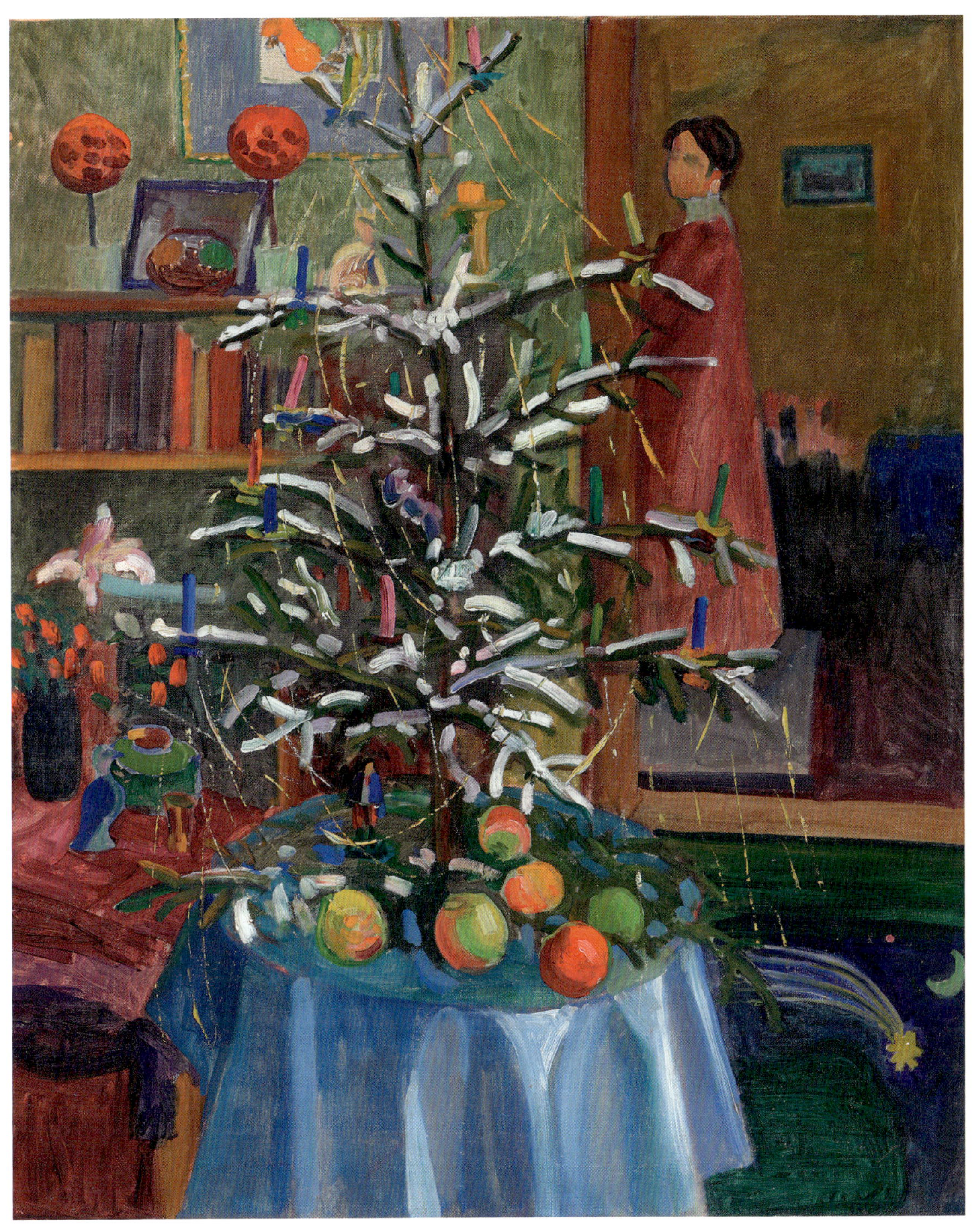

Cat. 99
Christmas Still Life [Weihnachtsstillleben], ca. 1908/09
Oil on canvas, lined painting, 88 × 72.5 cm | Kunstsammlung Nordrhein-Westfalen, Düsseldorf, inv. no. 0753

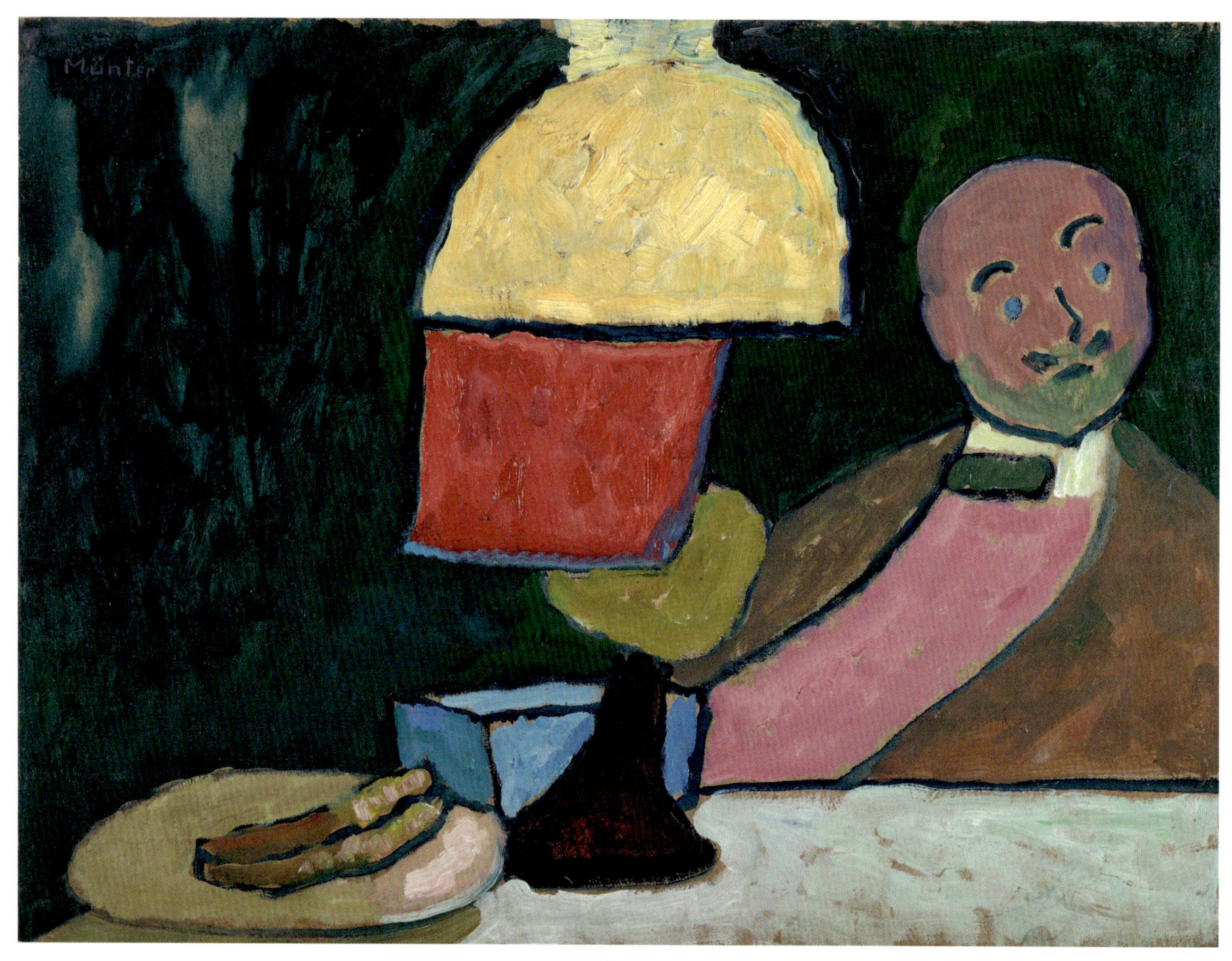

Cat. 100
Listening (Portrait of Jawlensky) [Zuhören (Bildnis Jawlensky)], 1909
Cardboard, 49.7 × 66.2 cm | Städtische Galerie im Lenbachhaus und Kunstbau München, inv. no. GMS 657

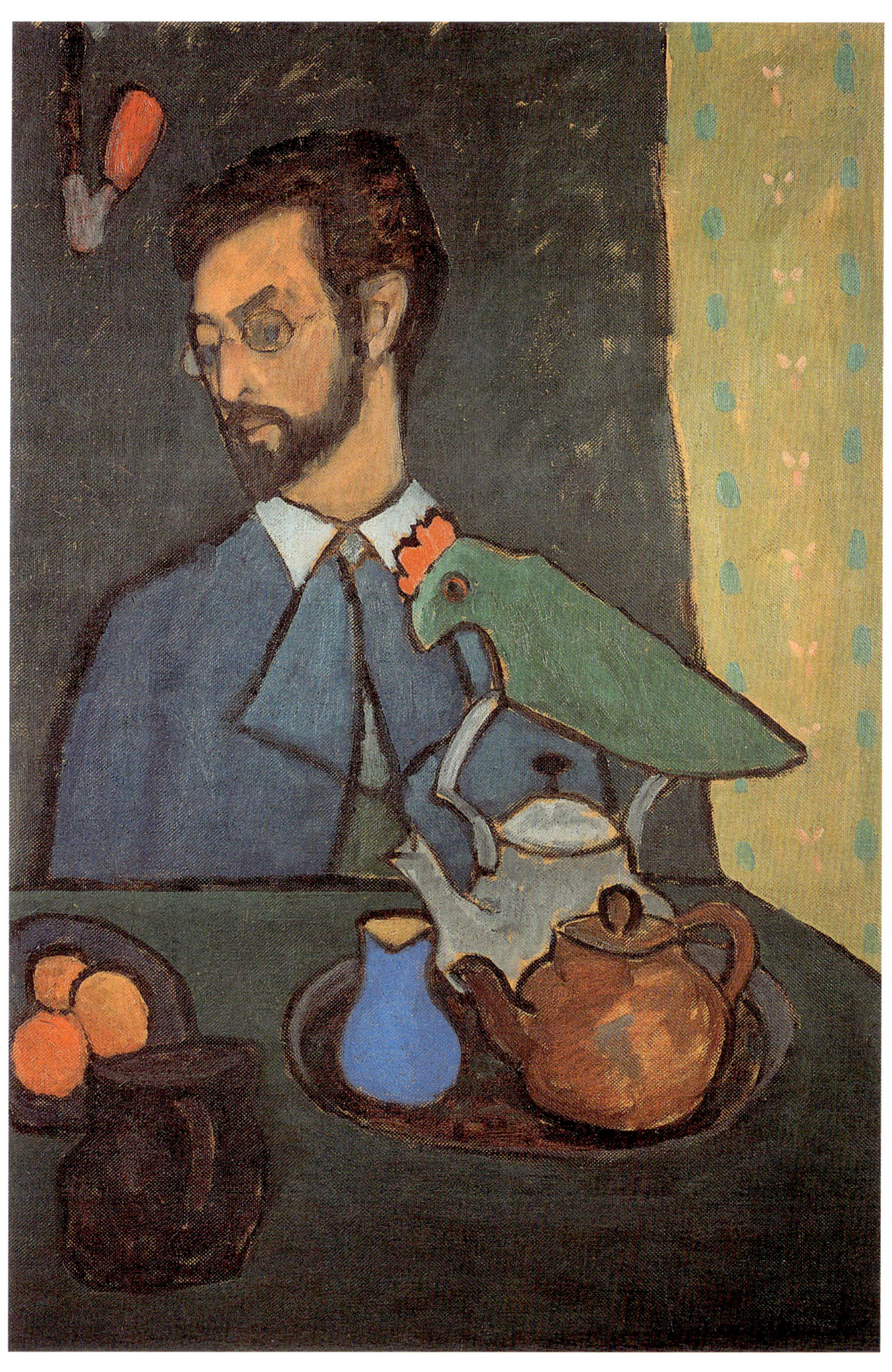

Cat. 101

Kandinsky at Tea [Kandinsky am Teetisch], ca. 1910

Oil on cardboard, 68 × 47 cm |
The Israel Museum, Jerusalem,
Gift of Billy Wilder, Los Angeles,
to American Friends of the Israel Museum,
inv. no. B 89.0078

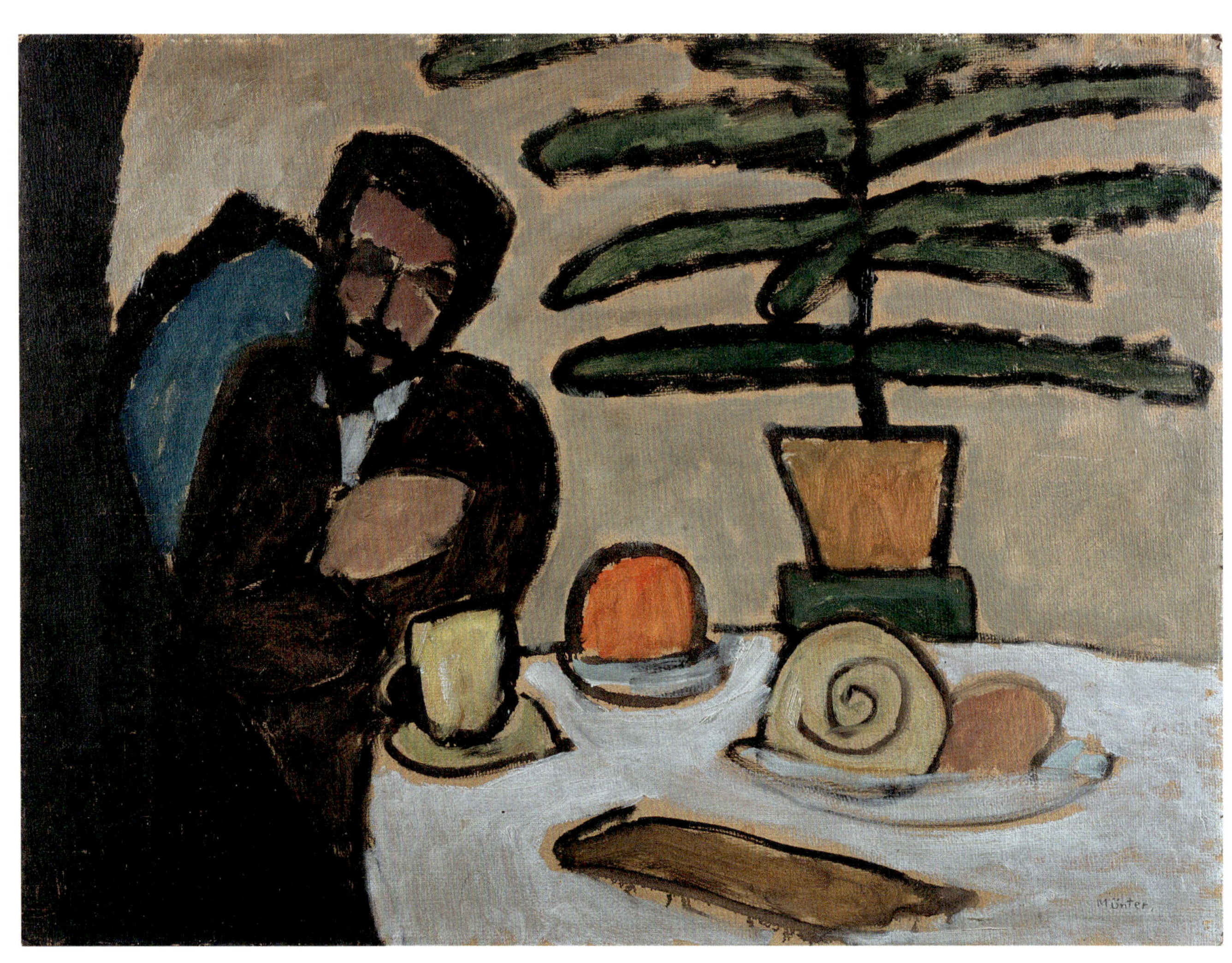

Cat. 102
Man at a Table (Kandinsky) [Mann am Tisch (Kandinsky)], 1911

Cardboard, 50.8 × 68.5 cm | Städtische Galerie im Lenbachhaus und Kunstbau München, inv. no. GMS 665

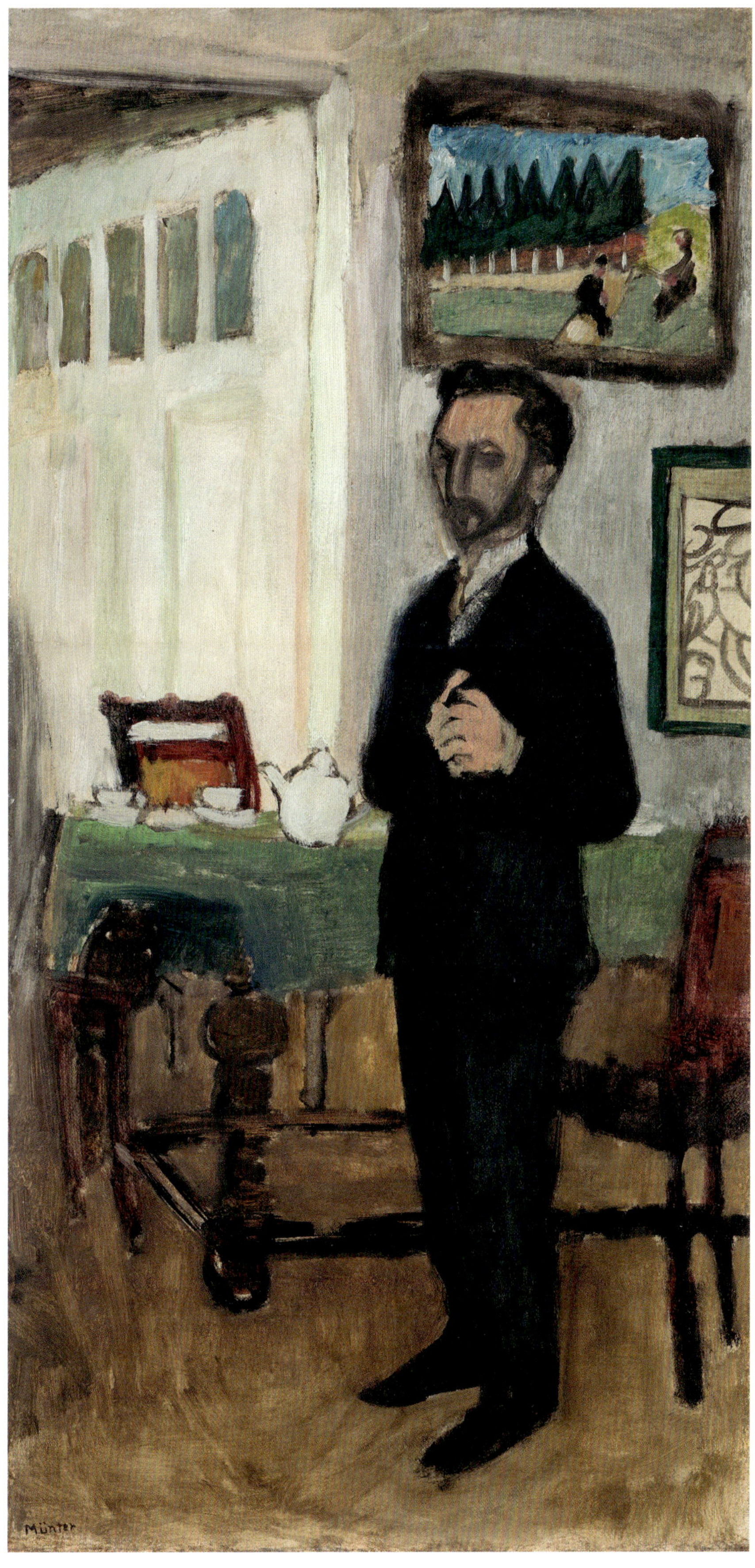

Cat. 103
Kandinsky in Interior [Kandinsky, stehend], 1912
Oil on canvas, 85.5 × 43.3 cm | Neue Galerie New York. This work is part of the collection of Estée Lauder and was made available through the generosity of Estée Lauder, inv. no. EL.123

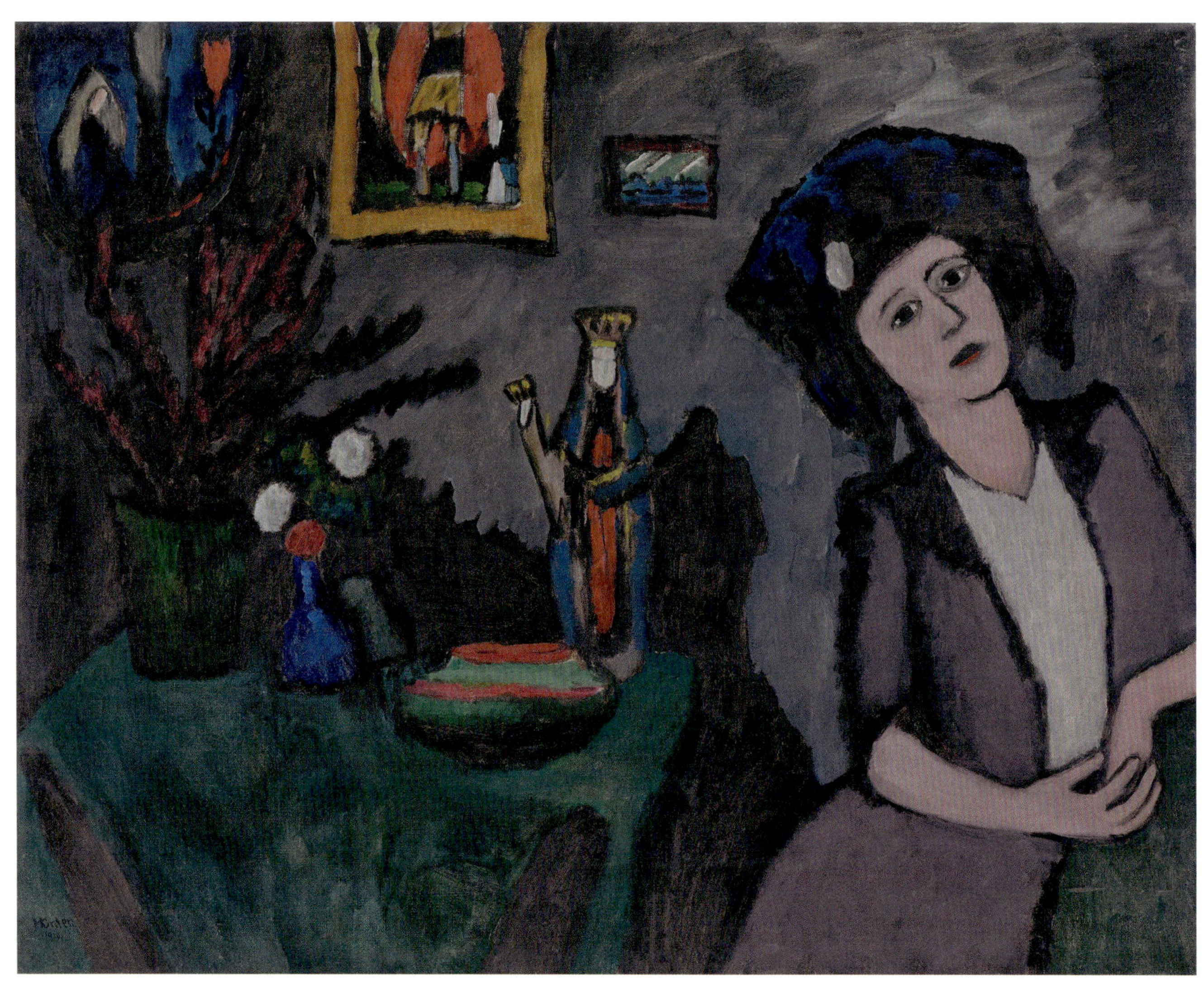

Cat. 104
Still Life with Figure (Mrs. Simonovich) [Stilleben mit Figur (Frau Simonowitsch)], 1910
Textile support, 78.5 × 100 cm | Gabriele Münter- und Johannes Eichner-Stiftung, Munich, inv. no. S 104

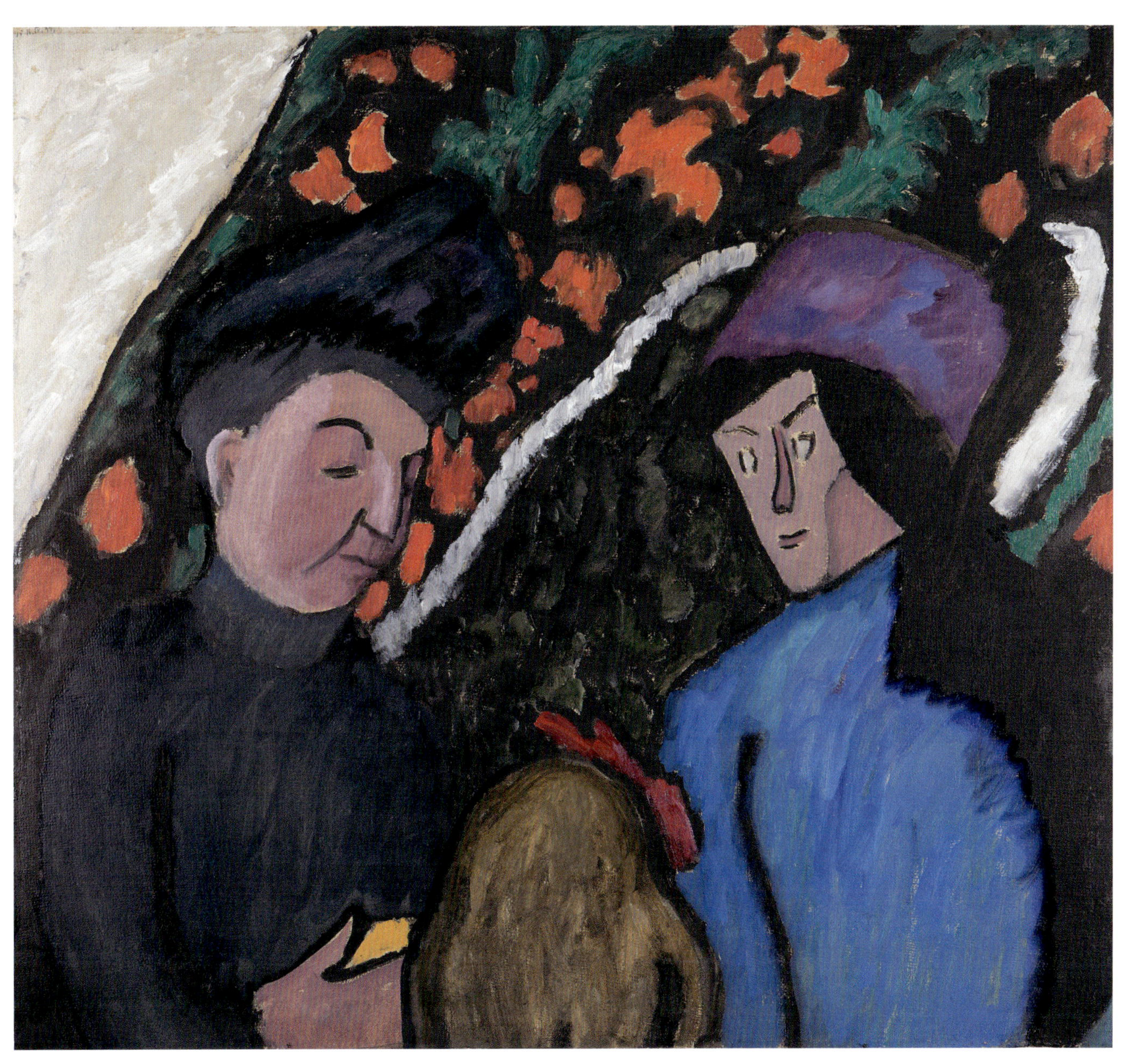

Cat. 105
In the Salon [Im Salon], 1911

Cardboard, 70.1 × 78.4 cm |
Gabriele Münter- und Johannes Eichner-Stiftung, Munich, inv. no. P 12

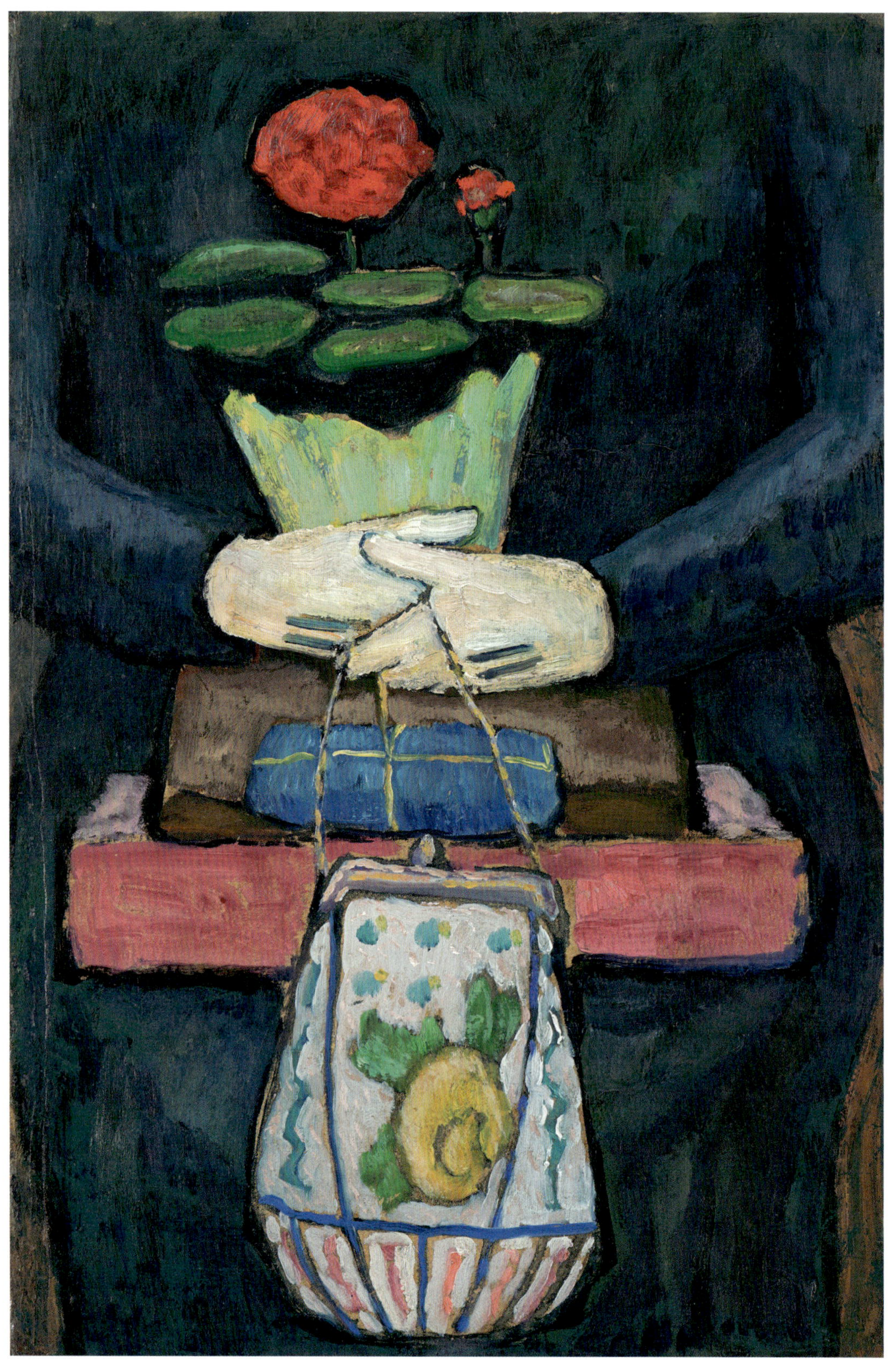

Cat. 106
Still Life on the Tram (After Shopping) [Stilleben in der Trambahn (Nach dem Einkauf)], ca. 1912
Cardboard, 50.2 × 34.3 cm | Gabriele Münter- und Johannes Eichner-Stiftung, Munich, inv. no. S 44

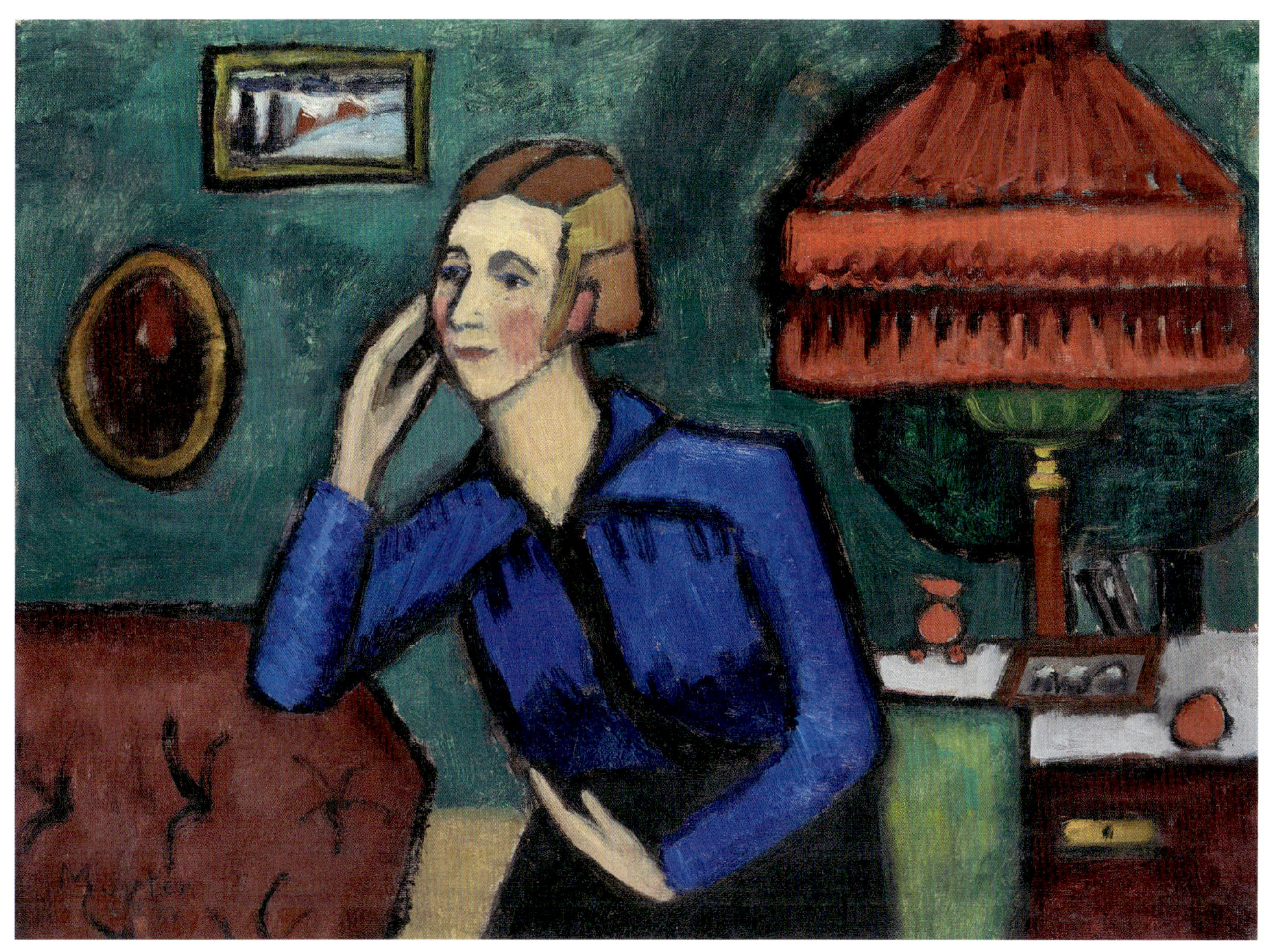

Cat. 107
The Blue Blouse (Mrs. Oscar Olson) [Die blaue Bluse (Frau Oscar Olson)], 1917
Textile support, 40.7 × 54.9 cm | Gabriele Münter- und Johannes Eichner-Stiftung, Munich, inv. no. P 182

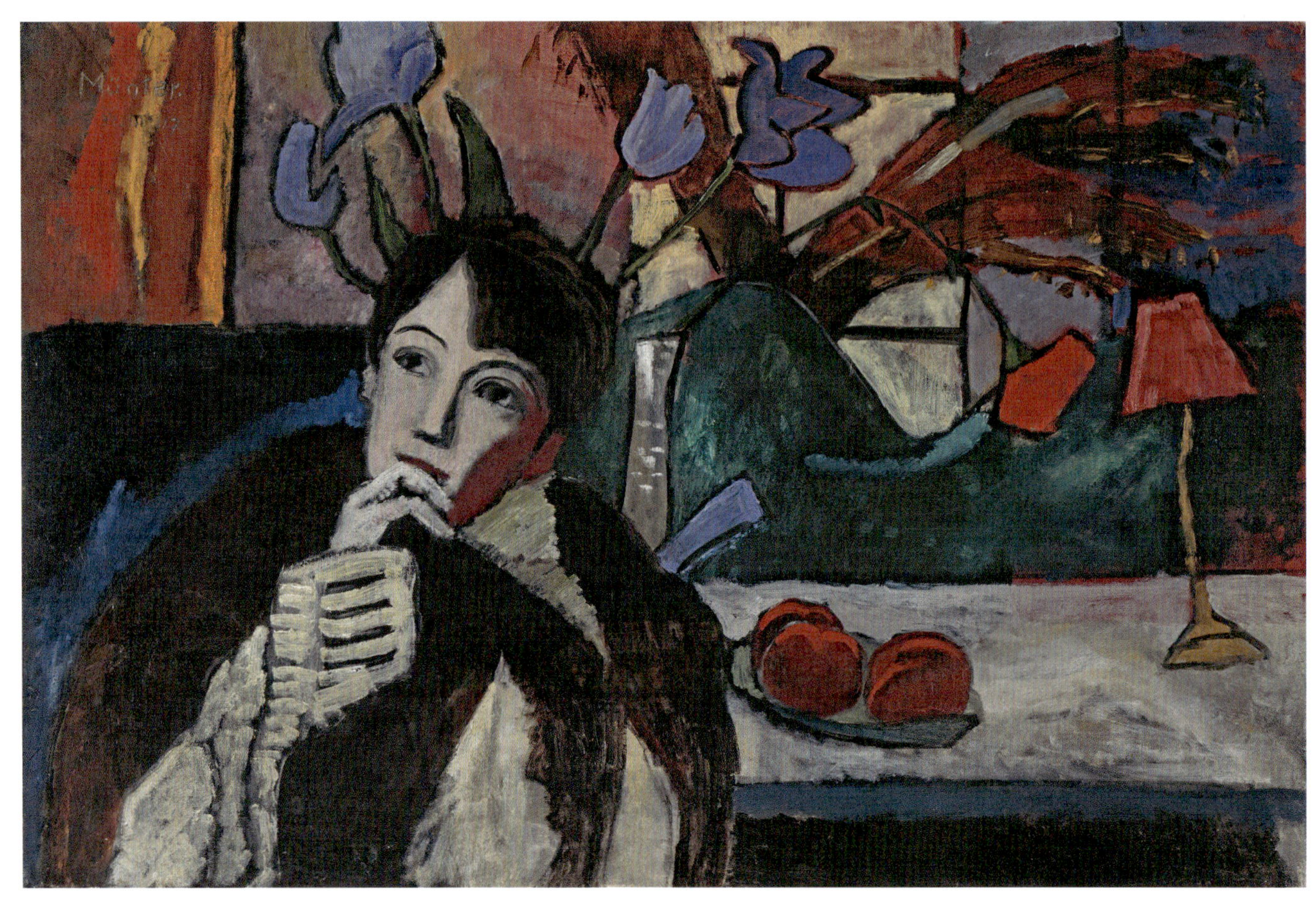

Cat. 108
Woman in Thought [Sinnende], 1917
Textile support, 66 × 99.5 cm | Städtische Galerie im Lenbachhaus und Kunstbau München, inv. no. GMS 646

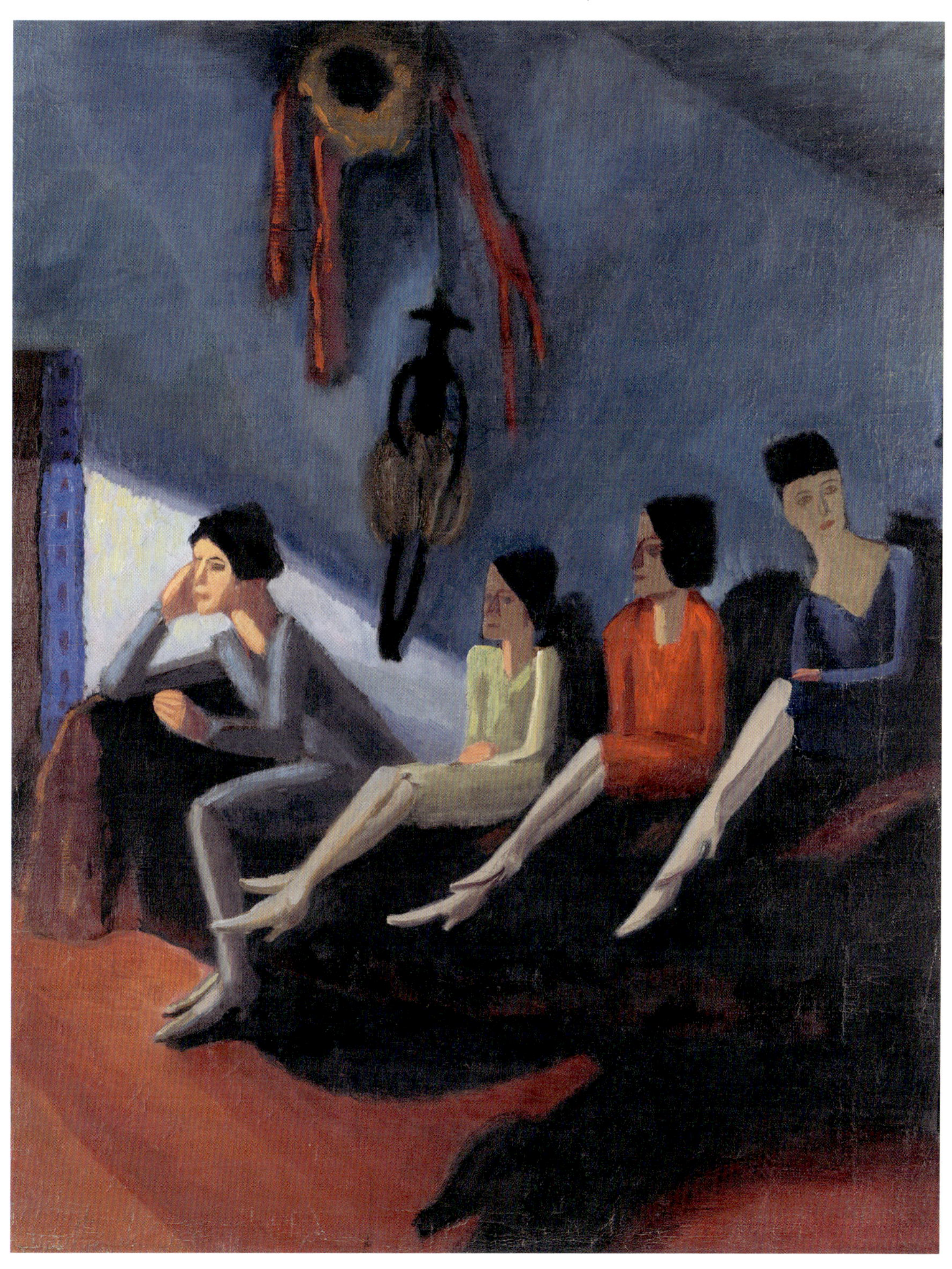

Cat. 109
Women Listening [Zuhörerinnen], ca. 1925–30
Textile support, 69.2 × 54 cm | Gabriele Münter- und Johannes Eichner-Stiftung, Munich, inv. no. P 223

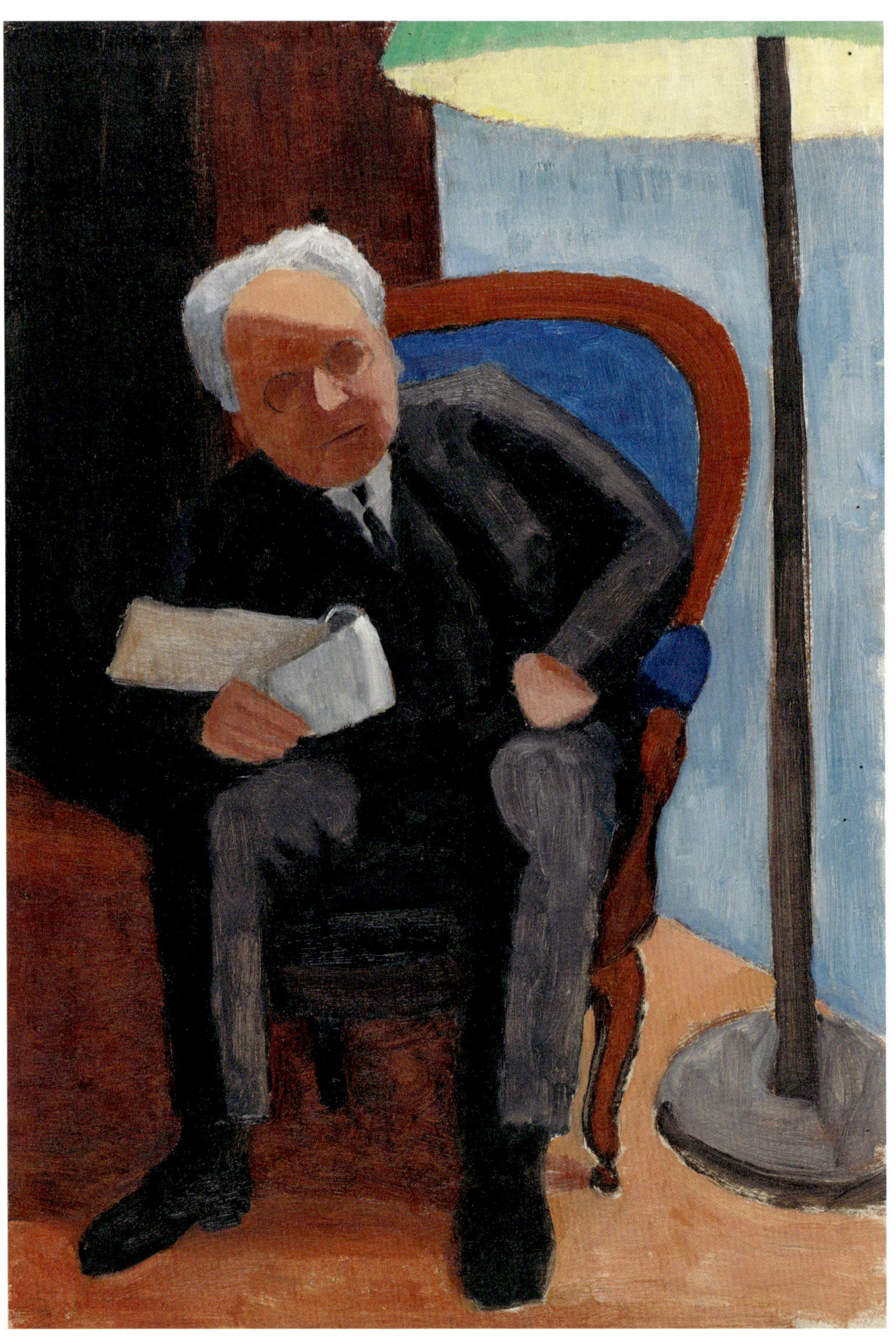

Cat. 110
Segal, Seated
[Segal, sitzend], 1928
Cardboard, 52.5 × 36 cm |
Gabriele Münter- und Johannes Eichner-Stiftung, Munich, inv. no. P 57

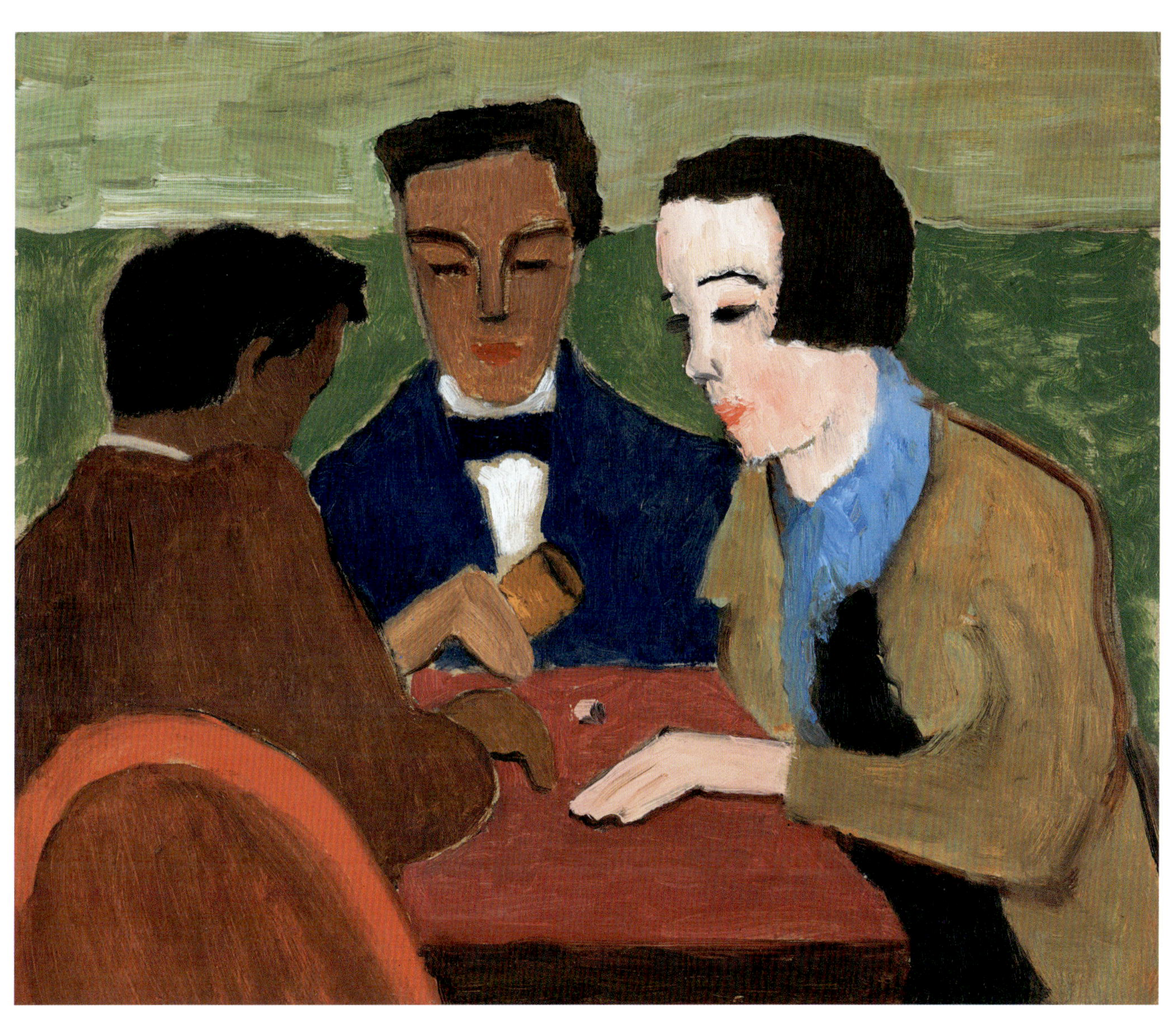

Cat. 111
Dice Players [Würfelspieler], 1930
Cardboard, 38 × 45.7 cm | Gabriele Münter- und Johannes Eichner-Stiftung, Munich, inv. no. P 127

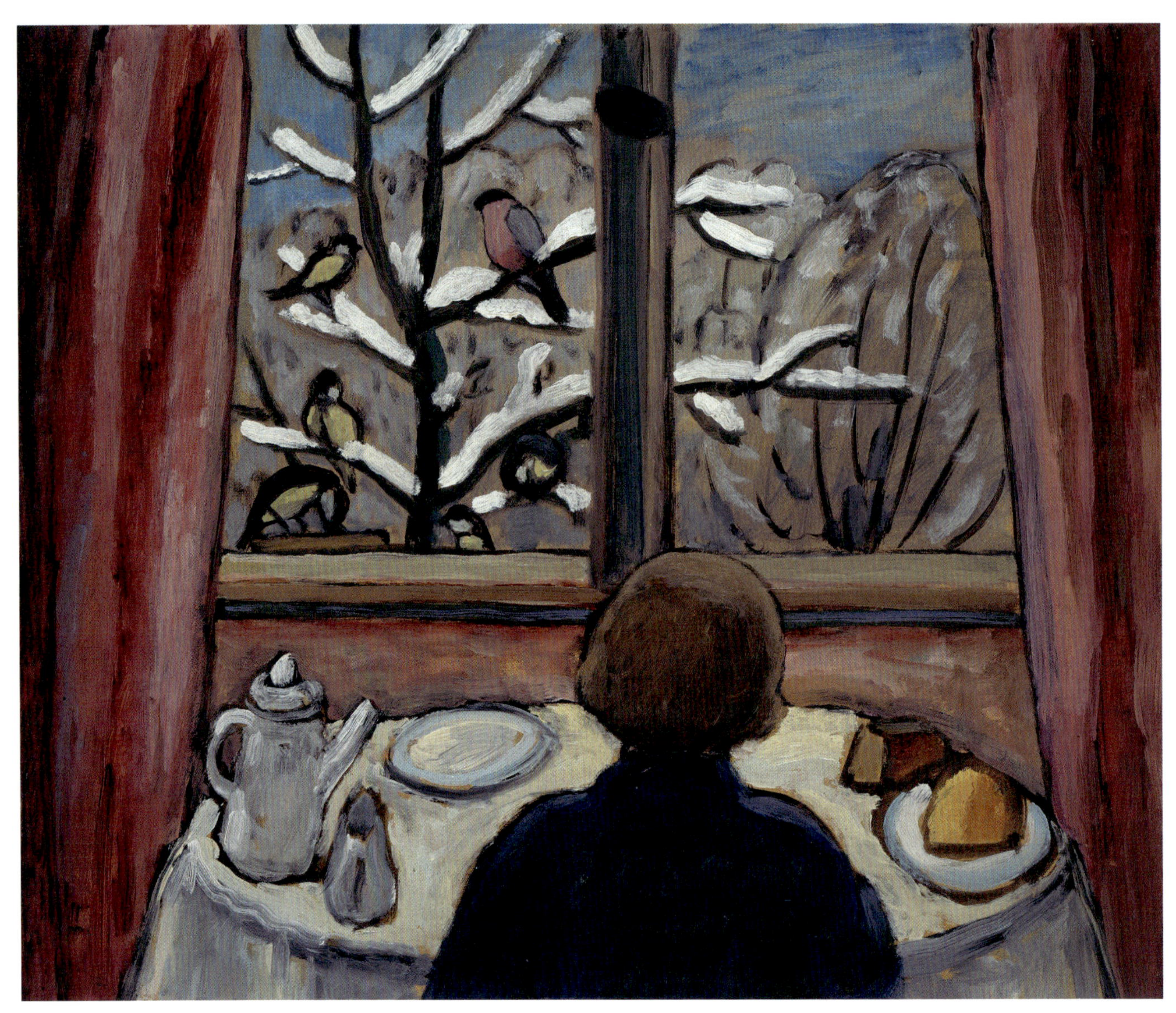

Cat. 112
Breakfast of the Birds
[Das Frühstück der Vögel], 1934
Oil on cardboard, 45.5 × 55 cm | Courtesy of the National Museum of Women in the Arts, Washington, D.C.
Gift of Wallace and Wilhelmina Holladay

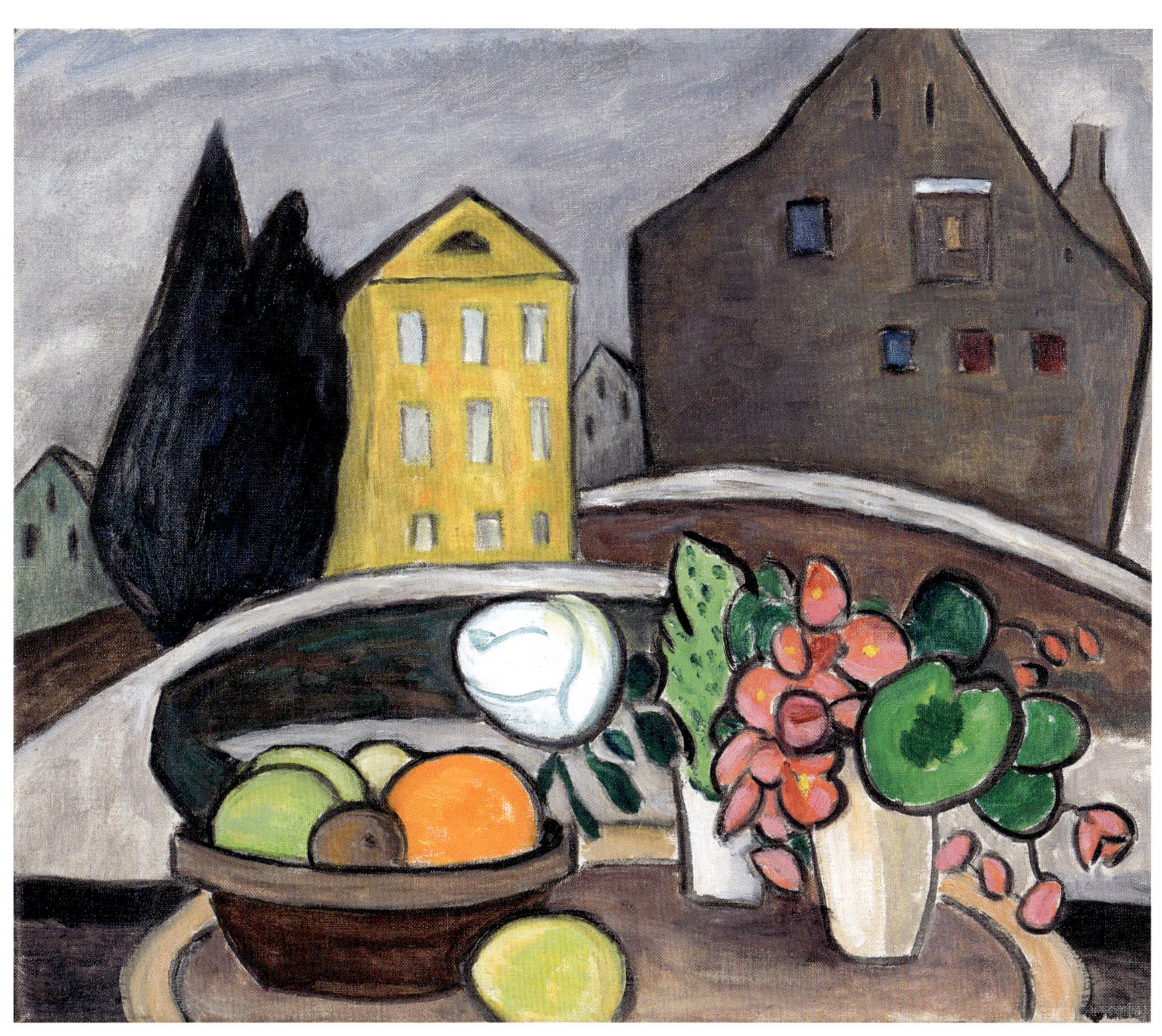

Cat. 113
Still Life in Front of the Yellow House [Stilleben vor dem gelben Haus], 1953
Textile support, 46.5 × 54.5 cm | Gabriele Münter- und Johannes Eichner-Stiftung, Munich, inv. no. S 19

“Searching for the roots of creativity”[1]

“Primitivism”

"Primitivism"

Gabriele Münter has often been described as a "primitive" artist, with her art characterized as *ursprünglich* (a German word which is difficult to translate in this context, best approximated by "authentic" or "genuine"). The Blue Rider artists were among the first to connect both the artist herself and her work with these qualities. Münter painted intuitively, they said, and her mode of expression was uncorrupted.[2] Kandinsky described Münter's paintings as the product of a "pure inner urge."[3] Interestingly, contemporary discourse adduced these same qualities, which tellingly exclude the involvement of the intellect in the creative process, to characterize women's creativity generally.[4] In the wider context of "primitivism," however, it quickly becomes apparent that Münter in fact drew on the same resources and wellsprings of inspiration as her male counterparts. The myth of the "primitive" female artist, and the notion of "untainted" creativity associated with it, was actually just an ideal projected onto her by fellow artists.[5] Authenticity, naturalness, instinct, and intuition were all qualities that the Blue Rider circle ascribed not just to Münter, as their friend and fellow painter, but also to non-Western cultures, folk artists, amateurs, and children.

Definitions and interpretations of "primitivism" as a concept are liable to generate controversy. Art historians have grappled with the theme over and over again.[6] In our postmodern, postcolonial present, both the concept itself and its history have become more problematic than ever, for what they signify is not just the erstwhile appreciation of original and authentic forms, but also the condescension, belittlement, and exploitation of other peoples, other cultures, and other concepts. Manuel J. Borja-Villel describes the situation as follows: "We have been surprisingly blind to the fact that, since the sixteenth century, the history of Europe has been inseparable from that of its colonies, and that modernity quite clearly does not exist without the center–periphery relationships that first arose with colonialism." And further: "In the current context the hypothesis of an advanced culture, endowed with technical and intellectual means superior to those of others, who are always one step behind, appears far-fetched."[7]

"Primitivism" as a principle is understood to mean the engagement of Western artists with works by peoples they view as "primitive." This raises the question of who or what in early twentieth-century Europe was considered "primitive"—and the answer to this is anything but straightforward. After all, "primitive" is not an inherent quality of a certain class of objects, "but rather a category of Western thinking that draws a distinction between the Self and the Other."[8] For the purposes of this discussion of Münter's engagement with the "art of the Other,"[9] however, we shall have to fall back on the objects and object worlds that inspired her. *The Blue Rider* almanac will also be referenced as a source that can help us understand the phenomenon of "primitivism" in her art.

Although it may sound disparaging to today's readers, the artists and scholars of the period around 1900 did not intend the adjective "primitive" to belittle anyone.[10] They used it rather to describe those works of art and artifacts that they regarded as the "original," "firsthand" testimonials of diverse cultural groups. Their concern was to find a way back to the origins of creativity, which they saw as uncorrupted by intellectual effort and hence all the more worthy of esteem. On the one hand, this view was very much of a piece with the prevailing evolutionism, according to which Western civilization was the highest developmental stage yet reached by humanity. But on the other hand, avant-garde artists regarded "primitive" artifacts as no less worthy of admiration than Western art.[11] The positioning of the "primitive" at the start of humanity's developmental timeline led to the most diverse products being classified as the expressions of people who had supposedly been left untouched by "civilization." Among them were works by children, folk artists, and people from non-European cultures. The only preconditions required for such a creative process were thought to be emotion, intuition,

1
Translated from Helmut Friedel and Josef Helfenstein, "Vorwort," in exh. cat. Munich/Bern 1995, pp. 10–12, here p. 11.

2
Sabine Windecker describes this tendentious reception of Münter and her art in greater detail in Windecker 1991, pp. 11–14, 17–42. Writing in 1957, Hans Konrad Roethel hailed Münter as "a genuine 'primitive,'" Röthel 1957, p. 8. That same year also saw the publication of *Kandinsky und Gabriele Münter: Von Ursprüngen moderner Kunst* by Johannes Eichner, Münter's partner, who in a chapter titled "Das Wesen Gabriele Münters" emphasized the "unsophisticated naturalness" of her art (pp. 28 and 32) and praised "the authenticity of her being" (p. 26).

3
Translated from Wassily Kandinsky, "Das Schicksal der Künstler, die wirklich Künstler sind . . ." (draft of an unprinted foreword that Kandinsky wrote for the catalogue of an exhibition of Münter's work shown at the Neuer Kunstsalon Dietzel, Munich, in 1913), in Kandinsky 2007, p. 494. In exh. cat. Milwaukee/Columbus/Richmond/San Antonio 1997–99, p. 58, Reinhold Heller describes how Münter and Eichner instrumentalized the notion of creativity driven by the individual's own innermost self to cast her work as wholly individual. Their aim was to prevent her being lumped together with the "degenerate" modernists so despised by the National Socialists.

4
According to Windecker 1991, p. 13, the qualities attributed to Münter by the other Blue Rider artists, which included intuition, instinct, and authenticity, were later reinterpreted as typically "feminine." In Obler 2014, pp. 96ff., Bibiana K. Obler argues that while Kandinsky emphasized the "feminine" aspects of Münter's art in an effort to establish it as different, but on a par with that of her male counterparts, he did so through recourse to stereotypical notions of "feminine" creativity, and therefore failed to do justice to what she had in fact accomplished.

5
On the male construct of "primitive" creativity in the Blue Rider circle, see Wienand 2015, p. 47.

6
Klaus H. Kiefer, "Primitivismus und Modernismus im Werk Carl Einsteins und in den europäischen Avantgarden," in *Carl Einstein und die europäische Avantgarde*, ed. Nicola Creighton and Andreas Kramer, Berlin 2012, pp. 186–209, here p. 193. I would like to thank Matthias Mühling for kindly providing this information. See also Michael F. Zimmermann, "Primitivismus," in *Lexikon Kunstwissenschaft: Hundert Begriffe*, ed. Stefan Jordan and Jürgen Müller, Stuttgart 2012, pp. 273–76.

and instinct, "which were assumed to have been both present and powerful at an early stage of human development, only to be suppressed and eventually supplanted by the cultural, scientific, and technical accomplishments of European civilization."[12] Projections like these at the same time reflected the yearnings of countless Western artists.

The term "primitive" is used several times in *The Blue Rider* almanac that Wassily Kandinsky and Franz Marc published in 1912,[13] though never in connection with any particular cultures or works. The idea of "authentic" art born of inner need or necessity nevertheless informs the whole book. There are reproductions of Bavarian and Russian folk art, non-European art, medieval art, and ancient art, as well as works by both children and amateurs. Kandinsky and Marc placed these alongside their own works and those of their peers, thus underscoring their equal worth. The common thread linking the works, in their view, was the honest, genuine approach of their creators. Kandinsky used the phrase "inner necessity" to express this,[14] while in his essay "Two Pictures," Franz Marc explained how "Genuine art can always be compared with genuine art, however different the expression may be."[15] And in a letter to August Macke, he describes lingering in the ethnological museum "to study the art of 'primitive peoples' (as Koehler and most of today's critics express it when seeking to characterize our efforts). I eventually came to the carvings of the Cameroons, which left me both awestruck and shaken, and which are perhaps surpassed only by the sublime works of the Incas. It seems so obvious to me that we should be searching for a rebirth of our artistic sensibility here in this cool dawn of artistic intelligence rather than in cultures that already have a thousand years of history behind them, like the Japanese or the Italians of the Renaissance."[16] That form was much less important was only logical: "Since form is only an expression of content, and content is different with different artists, it is clear that there may be *many different forms at the same time* that are *equally good*," wrote Kandinsky in his essay "On the Question of Form."[17] With theories like this, Kandinsky and Marc sought to distance themselves from an art that concentrated on reproducing visible reality. Not only had that particular mission been called into question by the invention of photography, but it was also tied to a positivist ideology which the Blue Rider artists rejected, and which had in any case reached its apogee in painting in the triumph of Impressionism.

The idea of creation based on "inner necessity" is also to be found in art historian Wilhelm Worringer's dissertation *Abstraction and Empathy: A Contribution to the Psychology of Style*, first published in German in 1907, with which both Kandinsky and Marc were familiar. What drove people to create, argued Worringer, was certainly not the motivation to reproduce reality: "At all times, art proper has satisfied a deep psychic need, but not the imitation impulse."[18]

Considerations on the beginnings and the development of art were sparked in part by Darwinism, in part by prehistoric finds, and in part by a growing interest in the art and artifacts of non-Western cultures, the latter factor being primarily a consequence of colonialism. All these reflections were manifested in the art publications of the day, where radically different forms of visual expression were reproduced side by side to invite comparisons and contrasts.[19] Kandinsky and Marc applied the same principle in *The Blue Rider* almanac, a work of unprecedented breadth, even if their objective was a different one.

Children were also becoming more and more a focus of attention in society. Unlike their adult counterparts, they were viewed as creatures who, being unaffected by prejudice and culturally determined habits of seeing, might still express themselves freely. Childhood therefore came to be regarded as a contemporary equivalent of the early, prehistoric stage of human history, which in turn led to parallels being drawn between works by children, prehistoric man, and artists belonging to non-Western cultures.[20]

7
Exh. cat. *The Potosí-Principle: How Can We Sing the Song of the Lord in an Alien Land?*, ed. Alice Creischer, Max Jorge Hinderer, and Andreas Siekmann [Haus der Kulturen der Welt], Berlin 2010, p. 2. On the ambivalent concept of "primitivism," see also Wienand 2015, pp. 37–49. In the absence of any more apposite term for this phenomenon, however, we decided to continue using it here.

8
Translated from Leeb 2013, p. 13. The idea that "primitivism" is an attitude rather than a clearly defined period or school was floated by Robert Goldwater as long ago as 1938: "Primitivism is not the name for a particular period or school in the history of painting, and consequently no description of a limited set of objective characteristics which will define it can be given. [. . .] Since primitivism [. . .] is an attitude productive of art, its results are bound to vary as the conditions upon which this attitude works also vary, although the variation of the second term need not be proportional to that of the first. But since the conditioning term is in reality a compound, whose different aspects can be picked out and combined in a multitude of ways, it can give rise to many artistic points of view." Robert Goldwater, *Primitivism in Modern Art*, enlarged ed., Cambridge/London 1986 (1st ed. 1938), p. XXIV.

9
This is the term used by Susanne Leeb to describe the art of non-European cultures, except that here its definition has been broadened in scope to include folk art and the art of amateurs, which for Münter were important sources of inspiration. Its use in the singular is significant, as both Münter and the other Blue Rider artists sought the same uncorrupted visual language in all three groups and drew no distinction between a reverse-glass painting from Bavaria and a mask from Africa. Leeb 2013, pp. 8 and 18. Cf. also Christoph Wagner, Ralph Melcher, eds., *Die "Brücke" und der Exotismus: Bilder des Anderen*, Berlin 2011.

10
It is important to understand the larger historical context here. Although the term "primitive," as it was used then, originated in a racist and colonialist mind-set, those who espoused it were almost certainly not aware of this.

11
Wienand 2015, pp. 38–39, 43. Wienand characterizes "this denial of difference and simultaneous emphasis on hierarchical distinctions [as] a characteristic of colonialist discourse." [Translated from the German.]

12
Translated from Windecker 1991, p. 45.

13
It is used in Franz Marc's essay "Two Pictures" and in August Macke's "Masks," in Lankheit 1974, pp. 65 and 88. The term does not appear in Kandinsky's essay "On the Question of Form," although he did use it in his book *Concerning the Spiritual in Art*, which was published in December 1911.

The Genevan draftsman Rodolphe Töpffer (1799–1846) had already compared the drawings of children with the works of so-called "savages" in the first half of the nineteenth century.[21] A few decades later, at the turn of the twentieth century, the theme became more popular still. Countless treatises were published in which a range of psychological, religious, and cultural explanations for the visual language manifested in the art and artifacts of different ages and different regions were propounded. Among those to follow this line of inquiry was the physiologist Max Verworn (1863–1921), whose 1908 text "Zur Psychologie der primitiven Kunst" (On the Psychology of Primitive Art) was an attempt to explain the differences between Paleolithic and Neolithic art on the basis of parallels with children's drawings, which he in turn compared to the art of the ancient Egyptians.[22] The magazine *Kind und Kunst* published an article with the revealing title "Primitive Kunst aus der Kindheit der Völker" (Primitive Art from the Childhood of the Nations).[23] The question of art's origins, however, was about more than just its chronological beginning; exactly what motivates man to produce art in the first place was also thought to merit investigation.[24] And so several different lines of inquiry were interwoven—which explains how "primitivism" came to be such a complex and wide-ranging subject.

We know from photographs of the interior of Kandinsky's and Münter's apartment on Ainmillerstraße in Munich that they had folk art hanging on their walls alongside children's drawings and works of non-European art. Fig. A Münter must have found this eclecticism very stimulating; her engagement with non-Western art, children's drawings, and the paintings of amateur and folk artists played an important role in her creative process from 1908 onward. That was the year in which she arrived at a new idiom, simplifying her forms and using much bolder colors that were in some cases far removed from reality.[25] This not only enhanced the expressiveness of her works, but also enabled her to venture beyond the dissemblance of reality and to articulate in paint the invisible sentiments lurking behind it. Münter herself spoke of "feeling the contents" and "giving an extract."[26]

Folk Art The reappraisal of folk art in the nineteenth century had led to the establishment of museums to house it. The Bayerisches Nationalmuseum on Maximilianstraße in Munich was founded on the initiative of King Maximilian II himself in 1855 and opened to the public in 1867.[27] The section dedicated to folk art opened in 1890.[28] The term "folk art" (*Volkskunst* in German), however, was not used until 1894, when the art historian Alois Riegl, in a booklet called *Volkskunst, Hausfleiß und Hausindustrie,* defined it as "the most primitive stage" in the development of art. Following the publication of Riegl's booklet, folk art began to

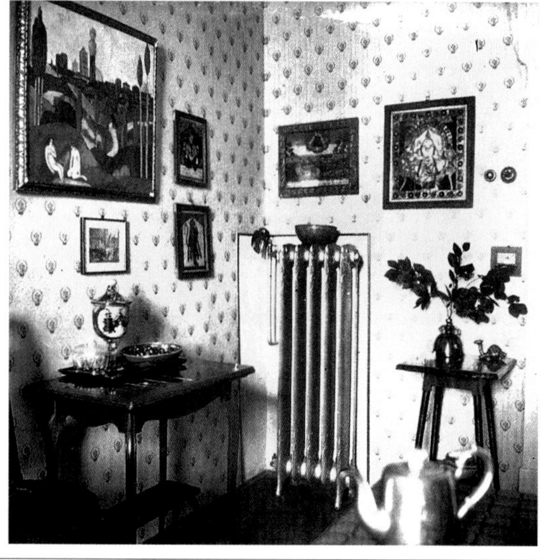

A **Corner of a room in Kandinsky's and Münter's apartment in Munich, Ainmillerstraße 36, ca. 1913**
Photograph by Gabriele Münter | Gabriele Münter- und Johannes Eichner-Stiftung, Munich, inv. no. 2189

14
Lankheit 1974, p. 153.

15
Ibid., p. 65.

16
The reference is to the Völkerkundemuseum in Berlin. Translated from a letter of January 14, 1911, in *August Macke, Franz Marc: Briefwechsel*, ed. Wolfgang Macke, Cologne 1964, p. 39.

17
Wassily Kandinsky, "On the Question of Form," in Lankheit 1974, p. 150.

18
Wilhelm Worringer, *Abstraction and Empathy: A Contribution to the Psychology of Style*, trans. Michael Bullock, Chicago 1997, p. 12. Worringer's idea of "artistic volition" follows Alois Riegl (1858–1905). On Worringer's theory, see Meike Hoffmann, "Urbild statt Vorbild: Die Künstlergruppe *Brücke* und der Exotismus – drei Missverständnisse," in *Die "Brücke" und der Exotismus* (see note 9), pp. 62ff.

19
Leeb notes the emergence in early twentieth-century art discourse of a "triad consisting of primitive man, child, and savage." Translated from Leeb 2013, pp. 12–13.

20
Exh. cat. Munich/Bern 1995, p. 23. See also Michael F. Zimmermann's entry on "Primitivismus" in *Lexikon Kunstwissenschaft: Hundert Begriffe*, p. 274 (see note 6): "Behind this was the notion, widespread since Johann Gottfried Herder, that the development of humanity was itself reflected in the developmental history of the individual."

21
Exh. cat. Munich/Bern 1995, p. 23. Rodolphe Töpffer, *Réflexions et menus propos d'un peintre genevois ou Essai sur le beau dans les arts*, Paris 1853, p. 252.

22
"Zur Psychologie der primitiven Kunst," a lecture by Max Verworn, Jena 1908. Note his comparison of schematic reproductions of two children's drawings with an Egyptian figure on p. 21.

23
Kind und Kunst, vol. 1, 1904/05, pp. 166–69. The article describes the creative development of the child and draws parallels with schematic drawings of various objects, including some from Peru: "The child naturally follows a development much like that which whole nations have undergone," p. 168.

play a role in aesthetic, political, and scientific discourse.[29] Riegl himself tied folk art to economic factors and used the term only for craft objects that were not mass-produced, industrial manufacture being ever more frequent from the mid-nineteenth century onward.

Münter and Kandinsky collected votive panels, popular prints, and carvings from Germany (mainly Bavaria), Russia, and other European and non-European countries. Since they acquired these works without giving much thought to their origins, their collection, strictly speaking, cannot count as folk art according to Riegl's definition.[30] They began collecting reverse-glass paintings in 1908, having first become acquainted with the technique in Murnau. Between them, Kandinsky and Münter amassed at least 130 objects, many of them purchased at Munich's Auer Dult flea market. Münter, especially, was fascinated by the technique. Besides being the driving force behind the collection, she was probably also the first of the artists in the Neue Künstlervereinigung München (New Artists' Association Munich) to take lessons in reverse-glass painting from the glass painter Heinrich Rambold (1872–1953). Although she began by copying existing works, most of them with religious motifs, she soon began inventing motifs of her own. Münter, Kandinsky, and the artists of the Blue Rider group and its wider circle saw these folk-art objects as expressive of an authentic inwardness of feeling that went hand in hand with an abstract way of seeing that accorded well with their own artistic aspirations.[31] Their fondness for folk art, however, developed at a time when it was already fast disappearing, mainly as a result of the spread of industrial production. This loss was often addressed by Münter's contemporaries.[32]

Gabriele Münter loved to paint her immediate surroundings her whole life long. That the objects in her folk-art collection inspired many an intimate still life, especially after 1910, is thus not surprising. She assembled the reverse-glass paintings of saints and carved figurines in diverse arrangements and then proceeded to paint them, as she explained in a letter to Kandinsky: "After breakfast did some painting—a new still life, again with my Madonna table. It is certainly more simply done than the previous one on a large canvas—but perhaps I'll try it again—simpler still—utterly simple for once—abstract, primitive. It will again be a very rewarding thing."[33] Fig. B

Alongside the still lifes in bright, bold colors, there are others in much darker hues that occupy a special place in her oeuvre. Here, the colors of the reverse-glass paintings appear to be glowing in the dark, while the carved figurines are often positioned in areas of shade; the surrounding space is not always clearly defined. In *Still Life with St. George*, for example, the reverse-glass painting bearing the eponymous saint seems almost to be floating in midair. Cat. 114 Münter also defamiliarized folk-art objects, leading to mysterious compositions such as her painting *Dragon Fight*, in which she transformed a little wooden sculpture from Russia into a bloody battle between a hydra-like dragon and Saint George.[34] Cat. 127; Fig. C

In these still lifes, Münter did more than just assemble assorted religious objects; she also conveyed something of their aura and so created new, very personal, self-contained picture worlds. She continued collecting folk-art objects even after 1914. The Staffordshire dog and wooden horse that she acquired in Sweden feature in several of her paintings of 1916 and thereafter; and in 1934, a white dove symbolizing the Holy Ghost inspired her to create an entire series on the theme of Pentecost in which she abstracted her folk-art motif to such a degree that it became unrecognizable and eventually looked more like a target. Cat. 120; 122–24 In 1940 Münter turned her attention to the *Maschkeragehen*, a Bavarian custom in which *Maschkera*—people wearing costumes and wooden masks—drive out the winter. This resulted in a painting called simply *Maschkera*, as well as various depictions of the masks on their own. Cat. 128 In her logbook the work is called *Mummenschanz* (i.e., mummery), with the subtitle "Three Indians." It was based on a drawing of "old folk masks" made at a 1937 exhibition.[35]

24
Leeb 2013, p. 15.

25
On the exact circumstances of Münter's change of style, see the chapter "Landscapes and Outdoor Scenes," p. 54.

26
Translated from a retrospective entry in her diary from May 1911, MES.

27
The building designed by Gabriel von Seidl on Prinzregentenstraße opened in 1900.

28
Köllner 1984, p. 93.

29
Gockerell 2000, p. 56.

30
Obler 2014, pp. 32–33.

31
Gockerell 2000, p. 5.

32
Henry van de Velde, for example, lamented the disappearance of folk art as a result of industrialization in an article called "Volkskunst (Aus Anlass der Internationalen Volkskunstausstellung des Lyceum-Klubs Berlin)" published in *Kunst und Künstler* 7, 1909, pp. 272–75, a copy of which Münter had in her library, MES. See also Gockerell 2000, p. 56.

33
Translated from a letter of November 7, 1910, about her work on the previous day, MES. On the importance to Münter of her "Madonna table," see the chapter "Interior Scenes," p. 139.

34
The sculpture is illustrated in *The Blue Rider* almanac, p. 14.

35
Süddeutsche Volkskunst was an exhibition of folk art from Southern Germany held at the Ausstellungspark in Munich from July 3 to October 17, 1937. Münter, accompanied by Johannes Eichner, went there twice: on August 12 and again on September 16, when she made drawings of the masks. Information gleaned from her diary, MES. The mention of *Three I.* is confusing. Perhaps the figures decorated with feathers reminded her of Native Americans.

The subject of masks had fascinated Münter ever since her days in the Blue Rider group. *Black Mask with Pink* (ca. 1912), for example, shows a mask lying next to a little bag that she had designed herself and embroidered with a peacock. Cat. 125; 126 Münter also possessed various folkish wooden toys, including a *Schepperdocke* (a hollowed-out wooden doll with little stones inside that rattled when shaken), a *Pfeifrössl* (a horse-shaped whistle), and a puppet theater, which she included as motifs in her still lifes. The puppet theater, for example, can be seen in the work *Pentecost Still Life* of 1934. Cat. 121; 122

The World of Children Münter was very interested in childhood and the world of children, and was certainly not alone in this around 1900. The subject became popular as a result of the change in attitudes to art education espoused by adherents of the Lebensreform movement. Parenting should take its cues from the child's needs, it was argued, just as children's behavior should be judged in light of their developmental stage.[36] Countless books were published, lectures given, and exhibitions of "children's art" organized. Nor was this a subject of interest only to educators; many art historians and artists also took an interest in children. One important contribution to the discourse was *Die Kunst in der Schule*, an 1887 book about the teaching of art in school by Alfred Lichtwark, director of the Hamburger Kunsthalle, who eleven years later co-curated an exhibition called *Das Kind als Künstler* (The Child as Artist) with the educator Carl Götze. Another major exhibi-

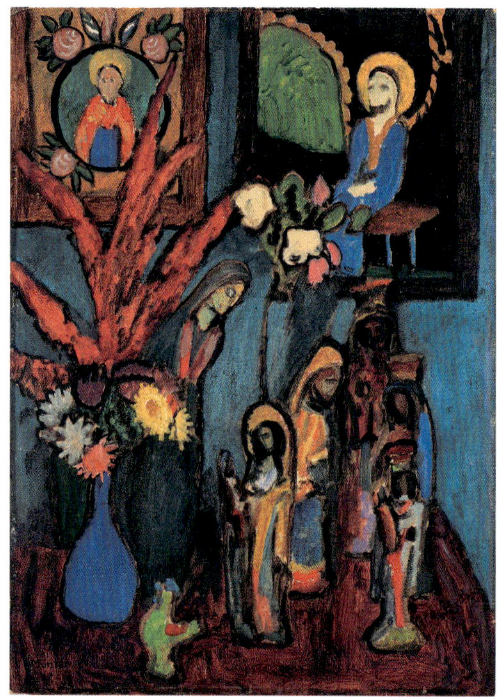

B **Still Life with Small Figures [Stilleben mit Figürchen], 1910**
Oil on cardboard, 69.5 × 51 cm | Saarlandmuseum Saarbrücken, Stiftung Saarländischer Kulturbesitz, inv. no. NI 3082

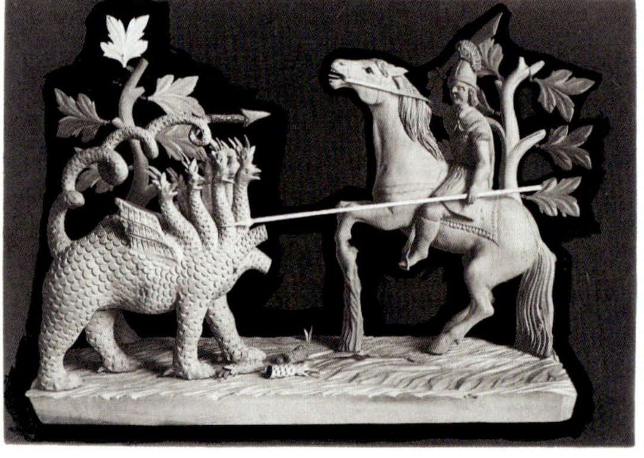

C **Saint George Battling the Dragon [Der Kampf des hl. Georg mit dem Drachen], sculpture, Russia, 19th century**
Photograph | Gabriele Münter- und Johannes Eichner-Stiftung, Munich

36
See exh. cat. Munich/Bern 1995, pp. 23–24; Reinhold Heller, "Expressionism's Ancients," in exh. cat. *Parallel Visions: Modern Artists and Outsider Art*, ed. Maurice Tuchman and Carol S. Eliel [Los Angeles, Los Angeles County Museum of Art, 1992/93; Madrid, Museo Nacional Reina Sofía, 1993; Basel, Kunsthalle Basel, 1993; Tokyo, Setagaya Art Museum, 1993], p. 82; Priebe 2010.

37
Priebe 2010, pp. 16–17.

38
Ibid., p. 12. The titles translate as "Children's Drawings Up to Age Fourteen: With Parallels from Prehistory, Cultural History, and Ethnography" and "How the Ability to Draw Develops."

39
Their library also contained the 1898 issues of the Vienna-based magazine *Ver Sacrum*, whose July 1898 issue featured an article called "Der Dilettantismus: Die Neue Volkskunst" describing Alfred Lichtwark's experiments in Hamburg. Priebe 2010, p. 14.

40
Volume 1 (1904/05) of the magazine *Kind und Kunst* included an appeal to readers to collect children's drawings. Its author, Karl Lamprecht, was collecting children's drawings from all over the world with the aim of using them to study the psychological development of the child, which he believed paralleled "those periods of human history that are described as prehistory and that are characterized by the same traits as are peculiar to the cultures of those people of nature who are at a lower developmental stage than us. The study of children, therefore, is in a position to supply material of great value to the comparative cultural history of the various races and to the history of humanity generally" (p. 360).

41
Exh. cat. Munich/Bern 1995, p. 10. "Children's drawings" is used here to mean both drawings and paintings. For a more detailed account of the techniques used, see Wörwag 1995, p. 177.

tion, *Die Kunst im Leben des Kindes* (Art in the Life of the Child), opened at the Altes Rathaus in Munich in the winter of 1901, followed by *Kinderkunst* (Children's Art) at the Kunstsalon Richter in Dresden in 1905. Münter happened to be in these places when the exhibitions were held and so would have had an opportunity to see the shows. The Munich exhibition was organized by a whole team of educators, publicists, and artists, including Max Liebermann and Walter Leistikow.[37]

In 1905 two books were published that in the course of time became classics in the field: *Kinderzeichnungen bis zum 14. Lebensjahr: Mit Parallelen aus der Urgeschichte, Kulturgeschichte und Völkerkunde* by Siegfried Levinstein and *Die Entwicklung der zeichnerischen Begabung* by Georg Kerschensteiner.[38] Many periodicals also devoted considerable space to the theme, whether they were art magazines or pedagogical journals such as *Kind und Kunst*, an illustrated monthly launched in 1904 containing works about and by children. Münter's and Kandinsky's library also contained several issues of *Der Kunstwart*, a magazine that first rolled off the press in 1897 and went on to play an important role in the drive to push through educational reforms.[39]

This was the larger context that turned children's drawings into collectibles and led to their being widely published and exhibited.[40] Münter and Kandinsky amassed nearly 300 children's drawings and thus probably had the largest collection of all their fellow artists.[41] Exactly when they began collecting, and on whose initiative, is not clear.[42] The literature generally cites 1908, that being the year when the two artists settled in Munich. But Münter had been given drawings by her nieces Elfriede (Friedel) Schroeter and Annemarie (Mückchen) Münter—and taken care to preserve them—even before that. The children's artwork in Münter's estate comprises some 250 loose-leaf drawings as well as two exercise books containing drawings by Friedel and Annemarie. The formats, the types of paper, and the techniques vary considerably: some are black and white, others in color; some are painted on the back of an envelope, others on thick cardboard in a larger format. Kandinsky and Münter collected drawings mainly from youngsters in their wider circle of friends and family, but occasionally also from children they did not know personally. Many of the drawings are dated and bear the child's name and age, usually in either Münter's or Kandinsky's hand. The drawings are by children of all ages and generally date from the years 1905 to 1916, although a few are dated as late as the 1920s and 1930s. Münter's interest in children's drawings, in other words, was an enduring one. A few paintings by amateur artists—among them Münter's sister Emmy—reproduced in *The Blue Rider* almanac and preserved in the artist's estate should also be mentioned in this context.[43]

The world of children was expressed in Münter's own works very early on, in her drawings and photographs from North America. These often included the children of family members, sometimes with their playthings. The world of children also occupied an important place in her work from 1908 onward, that being the year in which she produced a series of five colored linoleum cuts showing lively arrangements of the toy belonging to her niece Friedel. Cat. 134–38 The toy series was produced in the winter of 1907/08, when Kandinsky and Münter were living with Münter's sister and her family in Berlin, and the artist exhibited them in Paris, Cologne, and Bonn later in 1908.[44] In contrast, between 1907 and 1910 she also designed a picture book called *Friedels Bilderbuch* intended for Friedel's own private use only. It contained thirteen drawings by Münter and five more by Moissej Kogan (1879–1943), Alexander Sacharoff (1886–1963), Kandinsky, Wladimir Bechtejeff (1878–1971), and Werefkin.[45] For her other niece, Annemarie, she created four pictures for a dollhouse, all of them miniature versions of her own paintings.[46] Fig. D

In addition to toys, most of them folkish in style and origin, Münter also included children's drawings in some of her own paintings, as in the work called *In the Room*. Cat. 143 This shows ten-year-old Friedel sitting in her room and

42
Wörwag 1995, p. 173.

43
Emmy Schroeter, *Portrait Ella* [Gabriele] Münter, 1909 (?), cardboard, 40.5 × 32.5 cm; unknown creator, *Portrait of a Woman*, 1909 (?), cardboard, 40.5 × 32.5 cm; unknown creator, *Portrait of a Boy*, 1909 (?), cardboard, 40.5 × 32.8 cm. The three paintings are now in the collection of the Gabriele Münter- und Johannes Eichner-Stiftung. The whereabouts of the fourth painting is unknown. Illustrated in Kandinsky/Marc 1912, pp. 92–93, and in exh. cat. *Der Almanach "Der Blaue Reiter": Bilder und Bildwerke in Originalen* [Schlossmuseum Murnau], Murnau 1998, nos. I 1–I 3. The whereabouts of the children's drawings reproduced in the almanac are likewise unknown. Among the "amateurs" to contribute to the almanac were Henri Rousseau and Arnold Schoenberg.

44
Exh. cat. Munich/Bonn/Murnau 2000/01, nos. 32–36.

45
Described in Kleine 1997, pp. 11–21, 28–33, and 63–67.

46
End of the Village, 1910, oil on cardboard, 33 × 40.8 cm; *Garden Concert*, 1912, oil on cardboard, 32.7 × 40.9 cm; *The Blue Lake*, 1912. The whereabouts of these three paintings are unknown. We do not know of any large-format painting on which the fourth work might have been based.

reading a newspaper, while next to her on the floor, propped up against the furniture, are two paintings—a still life and a portrait—painted by Friedel with her aunt's help.[47] In 1914 Münter took her engagement with children's drawings a stage further when she produced five oil paintings after children's drawings. Four of these show a house; the fifth is a landscape with a stream.[48] Cat. 147; 148; 150; 151 Where the original was in color, Münter adopted the same palette. In a sketchbook of 1914/15, moreover, she drew a frieze consisting of two of these children's drawings, even though she modified one of the compositions by inserting human figures. Fig. E Unfortunately, we do not know exactly when in her creative development Münter produced this drawing. Whether it was before or after the five oil paintings is impossible to say, but the aim is clear: Through the process of copying, Münter hoped to appropriate, or at least approximate, the visual language of the child. The date of 1914 is nevertheless surprising; works such as these would have seemed more likely in 1908, the year that marked an important turning point in Münter's painting. By 1914 she had already produced many of the works that now count among the Blue Rider's great masterpieces. Yet she still seems to have felt the need to probe children's art even more intensively than before—forever "searching for the roots of creativity."[49]

Starting in the summer of 1908, we notice a certain naïveté, a simplified mode of expression, and a bolder palette taking hold in Münter's painting: all features that are characteristic of folk art and children's paintings. She must have hoped that her confrontation with works of that origin would point up solutions to the challenges that she as an artist was then facing. The crucial role played by Alexej von Jawlensky in this change in her visual language should not be forgotten, however. By the time Kandinsky, Jawlensky, Münter, and Werefkin came together to paint in Murnau in the late summer of 1908, he had already broken quite radically with nineteenth-century tradition. His study of the art of Paul Gauguin (1848–1903) and the Fauvists had enabled him to venture beyond Late Impressionism and to develop a more two-dimensional style of painting. Münter learned a lot from him—during those crucial weeks in Murnau she abandoned the impasto she had hitherto practiced in favor of colored shapes painted in fluid brushstrokes.

The "innocent" gaze of the child who, seeing many things for the first time, has an exceptional intensity of perception, fascinated Münter, as did the imaginary worlds of children's drawings.[50] Children, she noticed, do not distinguish between the outer and inner world and hence have no inhibitions about visualizing their feelings in pictures. This emotional idiom, which in both form and color concentrates on the essentials, accorded very well with Münter's desire to express what was "felt in the face of external impressions" in order to convey things unseen.[51] Presumably she also wished to create a universal visual language. Being timeless and easy to understand irrespective of cultural origin, children's drawings are an especially stimulating source for such a purpose.[52] Münter retained her interest in the world of children her whole life long. Some of the watercolors dating from her time in Scandinavia (1915 to 1920) evince a style that recalls children's book illustrations, as can be seen in *Swedish Farmhouse* and *At Midnight. Svolvær. Lofoten.* Cat. 141; 142 Also dating from this period is a series of watercolors illustrating the children's poem "Der süße Schura."[53] Cat. 139; 140 Among her most notable creations of the 1930s, which was a very prolific decade for Münter, is a series on the theme of mother and child and another that turns on the motif of a child with a cat and doll.[54] Cat. 149; Fig. F

Transcultural Inspiration Like many of her European contemporaries, Münter also sought inspiration in the artistic output of "other," as yet unfamiliar cultures. In these works, created outside Western traditions, Western artists believed they had found the unadulterated, expressive visual language that corresponded to their own notions of renewal and innovation. The idea of the "exotic" reflected

47
Wörwag 2001, p. 158.

48
The reference is to *Landscape with House (based on a child's drawing)*, cardboard, 32.9 × 37 cm, inv. no. Mü 1 (copy after a 1909 drawing by a child named Jakob, pencil on thin drawing board, 20 × 23.9 cm, inv. no. KIZ 115; this drawing, as well as KIZ 144, is illustrated in the plates section); *House (based on a child's drawing)*, cardboard, 40.5 × 32.8 cm, inv. no. Mü 2a (copy of a drawing by Rudi Schindler, colored chalk and pencil on drawing paper, 23.9 × 19.9 cm, inv. no. KIZ 121); *Landscape with Stream (based on a child's drawing)*, cardboard, 32.8 × 40.5 cm, inv. no. Mü 2b (copy of a drawing by Thomas Herrman, pencil on drawing paper, 20.1 × 24.1 cm, inv. no. KIZ 116); *Mill (based on a child's drawing)*, cardboard, 37.1 × 32.8 cm, inv. no. Mü 3 (copy of a drawing by Martin Musner, colored chalk and pencil on drawing paper, 23.9 × 20 cm, inv. no. KIZ 117); *House (based on a child's drawing)*, cardboard, 37.3 × 32.8 cm, inv. no. Mü 4 (copy of a drawing by a child named Robert, colored chalk and pencil on thin drawing board, 24 × 19.9 cm, inv. no. KIZ 144). All in the Gabriele Münter- und Johannes Eichner-Stiftung, Munich, some reproduced in exh. cat. Munich/Bern 1995, nos. 3. 49–3. 51. Since the children's drawings KIZ 115, 116, 117, 121, and 144 are identical in both format and paper, it seems likely that they were produced at school; I would like to thank Daniel Oggenfuss for kindly pointing this out.

49
As note 1.

50
Wörwag 2001, p. 149.

51
Translated from ibid., p. 160.

52
Ibid., p. 165.

53
Der süße Schura, 1918/19, inv. nos. Kon. 12/2 and Kon. 12/3 (marked on verso by Münter: "Children's poem by Mr. Meerson 1918 or 1919 in Saunte. Pension. Denmark") and three more sheets without inv. nos., various sizes, MES.

54
See the chapter "Repetitions and Variations," note 19.

their desire for an escape from their own civilization as well as a search for an unknown “primal” and “natural” essence, which had made the geopolitical and economic expansion of the colonial powers possible to begin with. It was fueled by novels, photographs, travel guides, exhibitions, and commercial spectacles such as the numerous “Völkerschauen” (ethnological expositions) in which people from colonized countries were degradingly exhibited to an attending public. The longings and projections held by these artists are presented to us today in the context of their time—their view of these cultures, with which they sincerely hoped to engage, was widespread and by no means impartial. In 1901, Münter took six photographs of such an ethnological exposition, which, through the visible confrontation between Europeans and people from other cultures put on display, are a testimony to these racist events.[55] Cat. 157–62 Ten years later, her work on *The Blue Rider* almanac included, among other things, collecting illustrations; to aid her memory, Münter drew two figures from the ethnological museum in Berlin.[56] Fig. G Among her works of 1916 and 1917, moreover, are some with “exotic”

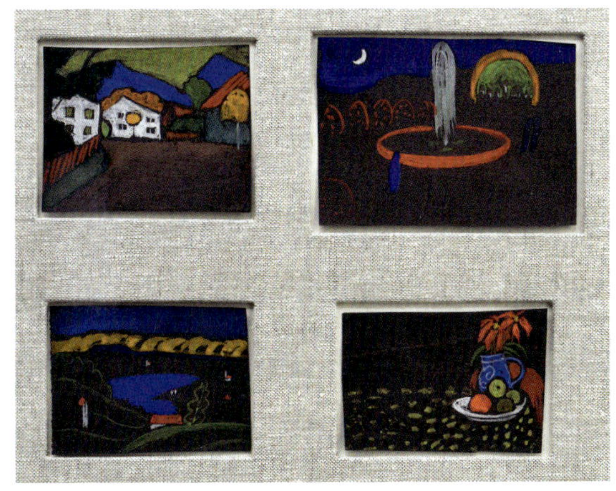

D **Dollhouse Pictures [Puppenstubenbilder], 1912**

Gouache on black cardboard, 6.2 × 8.8 cm / 7 × 9.1 cm / 6 × 8.9 cm / 7.8 × 11.2 cm | Franz Marc Museum, Kochel am See. Permanent loan from the ahlers collection

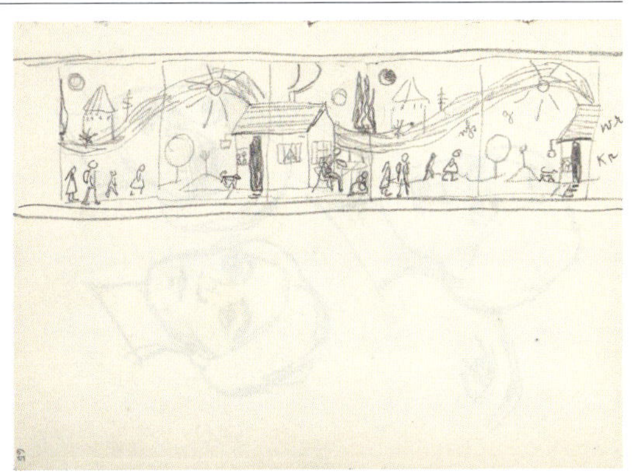

E **Frieze [Fries], 1914/15**

Pencil on paper, 15.3 × 11 cm | Gabriele Münter- und Johannes Eichner-Stiftung, Munich, sketchbook, inv. no. Kon. 46/43, p. 65

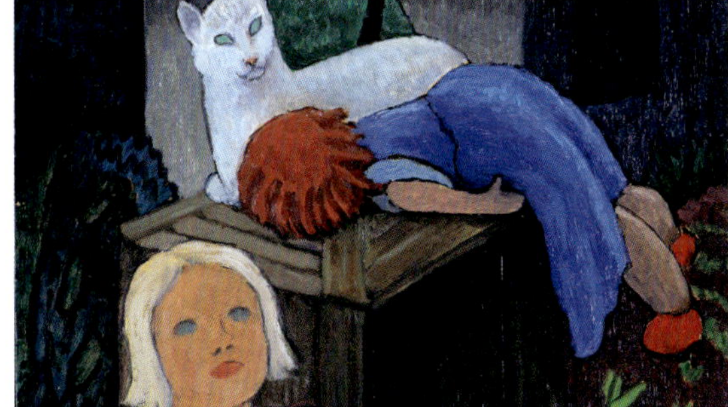

F **Doll, Cat, Child [Puppe, Katze, Kind], 1930**

Cardboard, 37.9 × 45.8 cm | Gabriele Münter- und Johannes Eichner-Stiftung, Munich, inv. no. V 34

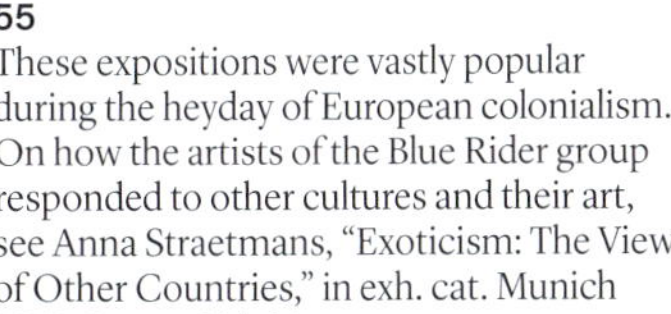

55
These expositions were vastly popular during the heyday of European colonialism. On how the artists of the Blue Rider group responded to other cultures and their art, see Anna Straetmans, “Exoticism: The View of Other Countries,” in exh. cat. Munich 2021–24, pp. 231–36.

56
Exh. cat. Murnau 2012, pp. 17–19.

motifs, including a drawing of artifacts from Alaska and a painting called *In India*. Fig. H; Cat. 166 Where the inspiration for these heterogeneous images came from is not known, although a Swedish memoir containing an account of hunting in Egypt in her library perhaps bespeaks a certain interest in non-European hunting scenes during that period.[57]

The sketch with objects from Alaska might have been made during a visit to a museum, whereas the painting *In India* looks more like a scene from a movie. An enthusiastic moviegoer, Münter was thrilled by the jungle sequences in Eduard von Borsody's 1938 film *Kautschuk*.[58]

The largest cluster of paintings with global cultural themes in Münter's oeuvre dates from the 1930s. Among them are four paintings of 1931 after works from Central Asia seen in the ethnological museum in Berlin.[59] Cat. 163–65; Fig. I *The Blue Demon*, for example, was painted after a pencil sketch made in situ on her first visit there on March 13. The three other works date from March 17, when she spent three hours painting from the originals.

The landscapes of Tripoli and its environs—at least three of them—painted in November 1939 are attributable to very different circumstances.[60] Fig. J The inspiration in this case came from sketches made by Johannes Eichner on a journey from Italy to Libya in early June 1939.[61] Her partner's comments and works were quite often a stimulus for Münter during the period of the

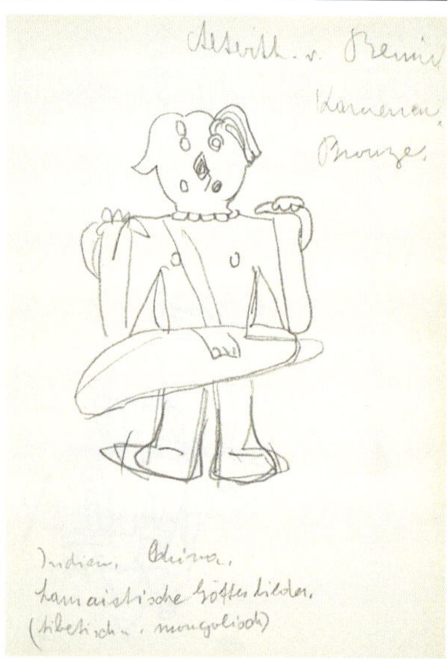

G **Human Figure with the Head of a Catfish [Menschliche Figur mit dem Kopf eines Welses], 1911**

Pencil on paper, 20.1 × 13.2 cm | Gabriele Münter- und Johannes Eichner-Stiftung, Munich, sketchbook, inv. no. Kon. 46/40, p. 13

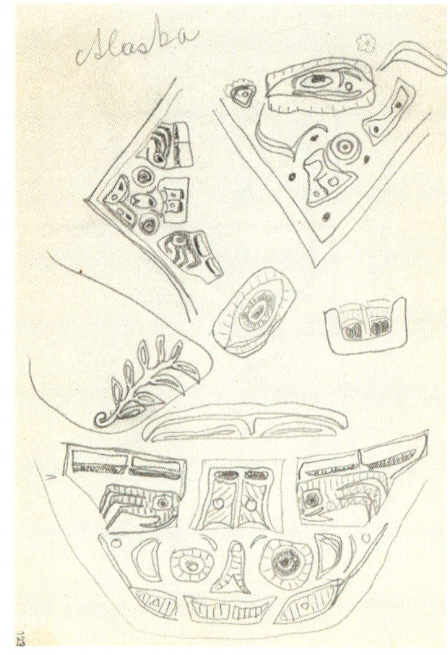

H **Artifacts from Alaska, 1916/17**

Pencil on paper, 16 × 10.2 cm | Gabriele Münter- und Johannes Eichner-Stiftung, Munich, sketchbook, inv. no. Kon. 46/47, p. 123

57
John Gustaf Wibom, *Jaktminnen från Nilen och Giraff-Floden*, Stockholm 1914. Inscribed by Münter on the first page: "Monday. 18. VI. 17. G. Münter."

58
Diary entry of March 10, 1939, MES.

59
She noted the name of the museum on the verso.

60
Including *Sea at Tripoli*, cardboard, 50 × 35 cm; *From Tripoli*, cardboard, 67.6 × 48.6 cm. Whereabouts of both unknown.

61
This can be inferred from her logbook of 1939 and her diary entries of November 18 and 19 of that year. Eichner's travel sketchbook has unfortunately been lost.

62
See the chapter "Repetitions and Variations," pp. 188–89.

63
Hermann Leicht, *Indianische Kunst und Kultur: Ein Jahrtausend im Reiche der Chimu*, Zurich 1944.

1930s.[62] Similarly, Hermann Leicht's book *Indianische Kunst und Kultur: Ein Jahrtausend im Reiche der Chimu* inspired a drawing in 1953.[63] Fig. K That Münter only occasionally took an interest in "exotic" motifs seems nonetheless consistent with her creative development. Bearing in mind how fond she was of depicting her immediate surroundings, it is hardly surprising that she painted such faraway places and motifs only sporadically.

Münter's wide-ranging interests, which extended from folk art and the artwork of children and amateurs to those with global cultural themes, attest to her intellectual open-mindedness. Such excursions into far-off worlds—which could be quite immersive—were not exceptional at the time; what is unusual is that they were not limited to any one period but instead were spread throughout her career. It seems that for Münter they had a deeper meaning than for most other

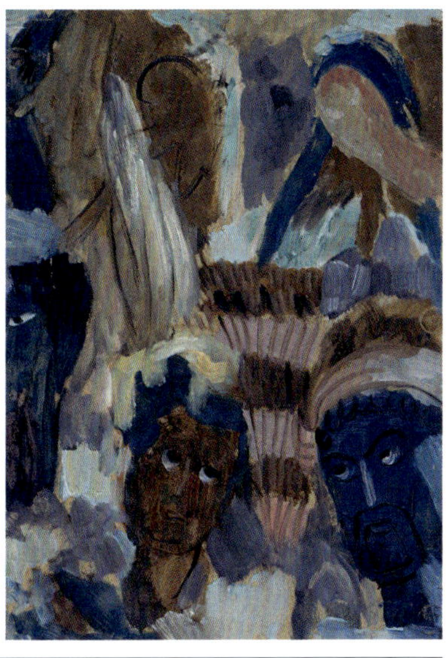

I **Study from the Ethnological Museum, Berlin, Turkestan [Studie aus dem Völkerkundemuseum Berlin, Turkestan], 1931**

Cardboard, 46.2 × 32.9 cm | Gabriele Münter- und Johannes Eichner-Stiftung, Munich, inv. no. V 125

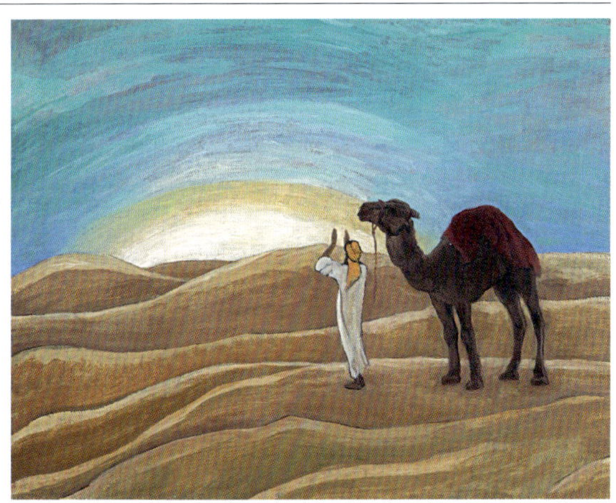

J **In the Desert [In der Wüste], 1939**

Textile support, 50.4 × 65.2 cm | Gabriele Münter- und Johannes Eichner-Stiftung, Munich, inv. no. L 38

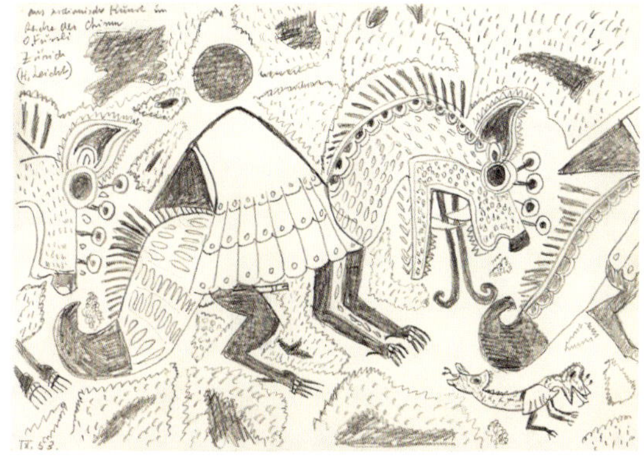

K **Balcony ornament from Hermann Leicht's "Indianische Kunst und Kultur: Ein Jahrtausend im Reiche der Chimu," 1953**

Pencil on paper, 18.4 × 13.3 cm | Gabriele Münter- und Johannes Eichner-Stiftung, Munich

artists. Her need to seek inspiration in cultures distant from her own and to flee the materialistic society of which she was a part developed in parallel to her interest in the occult, theosophy, and psychoanalysis—three preoccupations that were widespread at the time. Münter herself began reading occultist books early on; she also took part in spiritualist séances and was interested in psychoanalysis.[64] Kandinsky described this contemporary phenomenon in his book *Concerning the Spiritual in Art*: "On the other hand, the number is increasing of those men who put no trust in the methods of materialistic science when it deals with those questions which have to do with 'non-matter,' or matter which is not accessible to our minds. Just as art is looking for help from the primitives, so these men are turning to half-forgotten times in order to get help from their half-forgotten methods. However, these very methods are still alive and in use among nations whom we, from the height of our knowledge, have been accustomed to regard with pity and scorn."[65]

Inspired by those themes that shaped the prevailing zeitgeist on the eve of World War I, Gabriele Münter created some very personal and distinctive works, even long after 1914. Here, again, we can observe just how important the principle of continuity was to her output as an artist.

64
Eichner 1957, p. 30. Her library contained numerous occultist publications, and we know from an entry in her pocket diary of November 19, 1918, that she attended a lecture on psychoanalysis while in Copenhagen.

65
Wassily Kandinsky, *Concerning the Spiritual in Art*, trans. and with introduction by M. T. H. Sadler, New York 1997, p. 13.

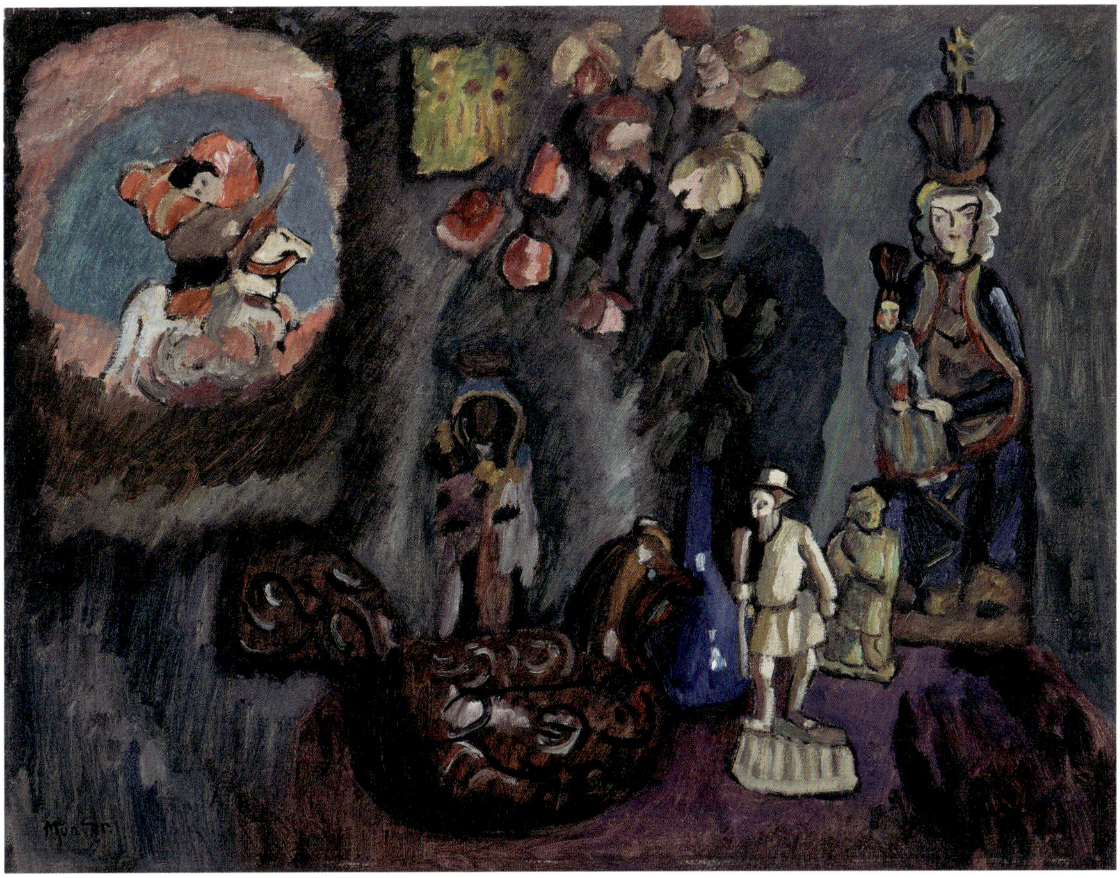

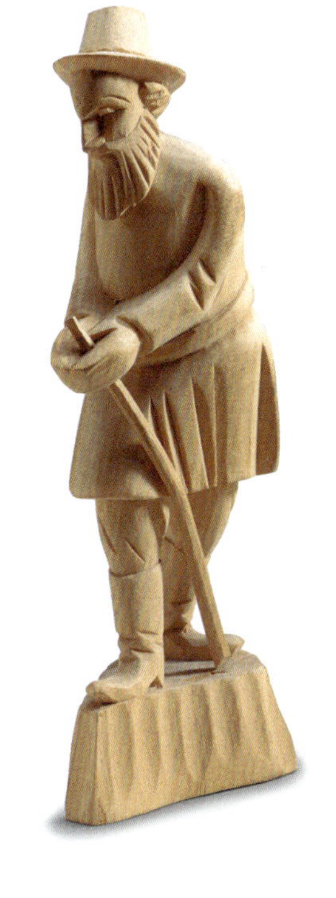

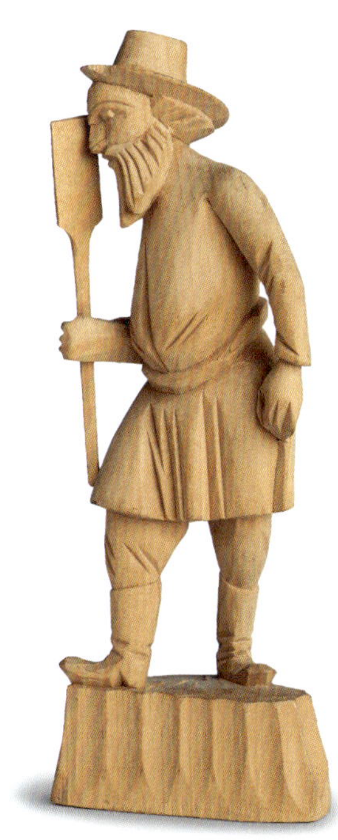

Cat. 114
Still Life with St. George [Stilleben mit Heiligem Georg], 1911
Cardboard, 51.2 × 68 cm | Städtische Galerie im Lenbachhaus und Kunstbau München, inv. no. GMS 666

Cat. 115
Carved figurine (man walking), Sergiyev Posad, ca. 1900
From Münter's and Kandinsky's collection Wood, H: 16 cm | Gabriele Münter- und Johannes Eichner-Stiftung, Munich, inv. no. HP 26

Cat. 116
Carved figurine (man standing), Sergiyev Posad, ca. 1900
From Münter's and Kandinsky's collection Wood, H: 16 cm | Gabriele Münter- und Johannes Eichner-Stiftung, Munich, inv. no. HP 27

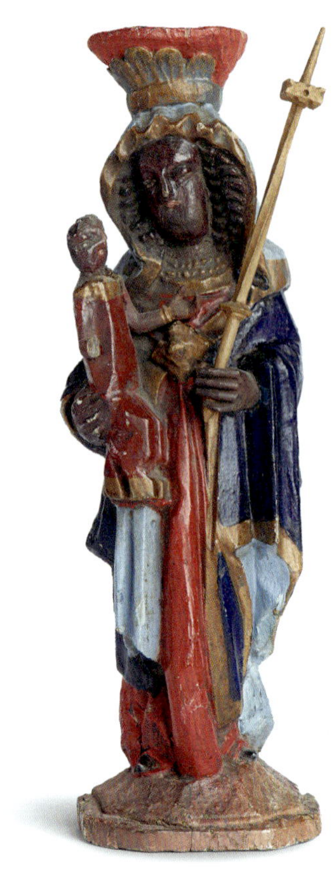

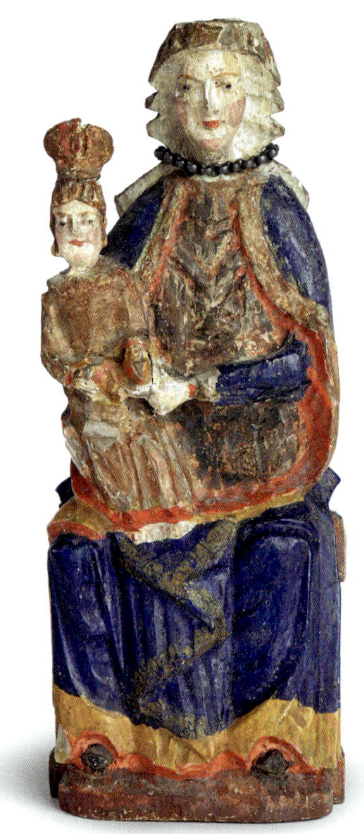

Cat. 117
Miraculous Image from Mariazell
From Münter's and Kandinsky's collection
Wood, colored, H: 25 cm, W: 9.5 cm, D: 4.8 cm | Gabriele Münter- und Johannes Eichner-Stiftung, Munich, inv. no. HP 7

Cat. 118
Copy of the Miraculous Image of the Virgin Mary from Altötting, mid-19th century
From Münter's and Kandinsky's collection
Wood, colored, H: 29.5 cm, W: 9 cm | Gabriele Münter- und Johannes Eichner-Stiftung, Munich, inv. no. HP 6

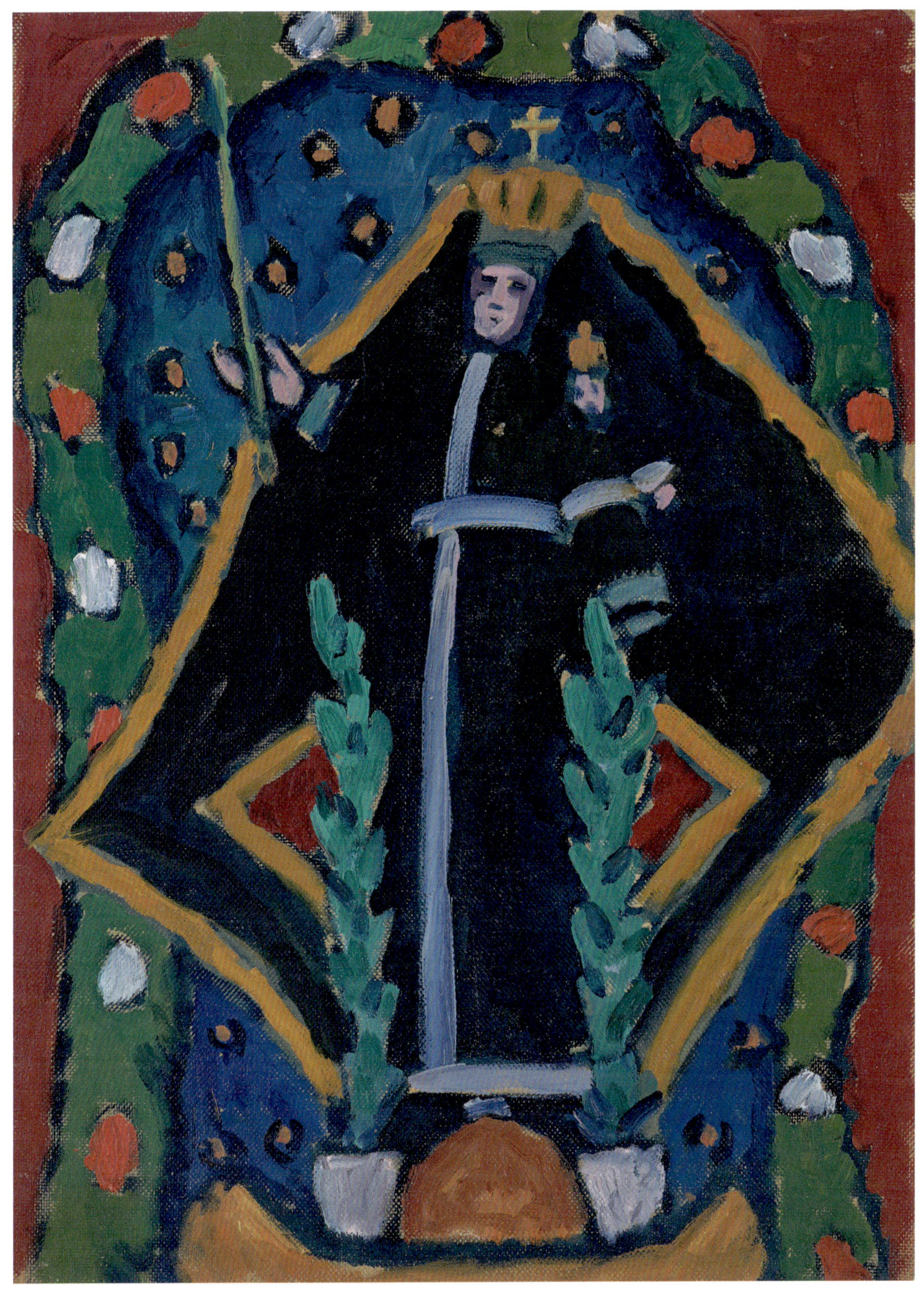

Cat. 119
Still Life with Madonna [Stilleben mit Madonnenfigur], 1910
Cardboard, 44.8 × 33 cm | Gabriele Münter- und Johannes Eichner-Stiftung, Munich, inv. no. S 72

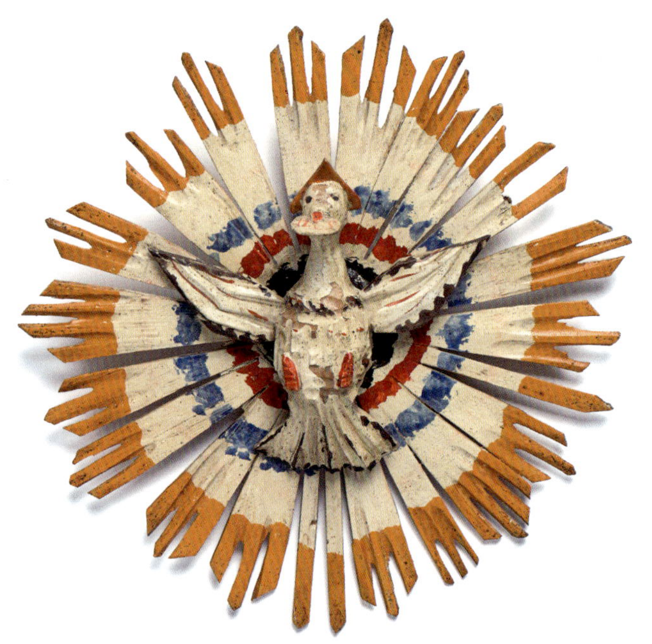

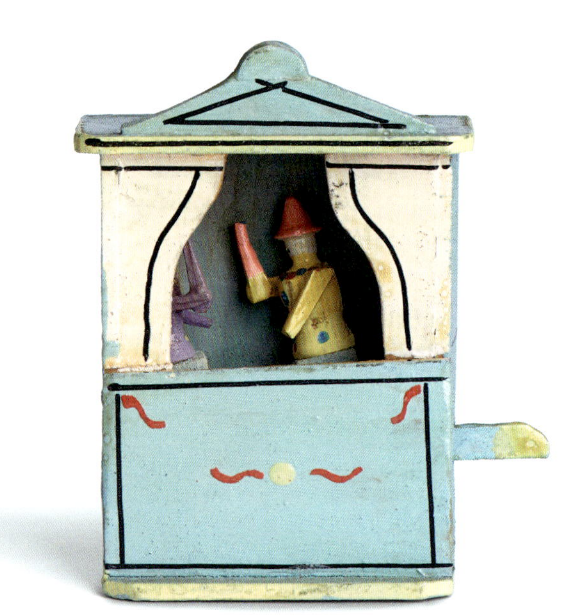

Cat. 120
Holy Spirit as Dove, Southern Germany, mid-19th century
From Münter's and Kandinsky's collection
Softwood, colored, diameter: max. 36 cm, D: 8 cm | Gabriele Münter- und Johannes Eichner-Stiftung, Munich, inv. no. D 19

Cat. 121
"Kasperltheater" (puppet theater) from the Erzgebirge region, ca. 1900
From Münter's and Kandinsky's collection
Softwood, colored, H: 9 cm, W: 7.9 cm, D: 3.2 cm | Gabriele Münter- und Johannes Eichner-Stiftung, Munich, inv. no. HP 45

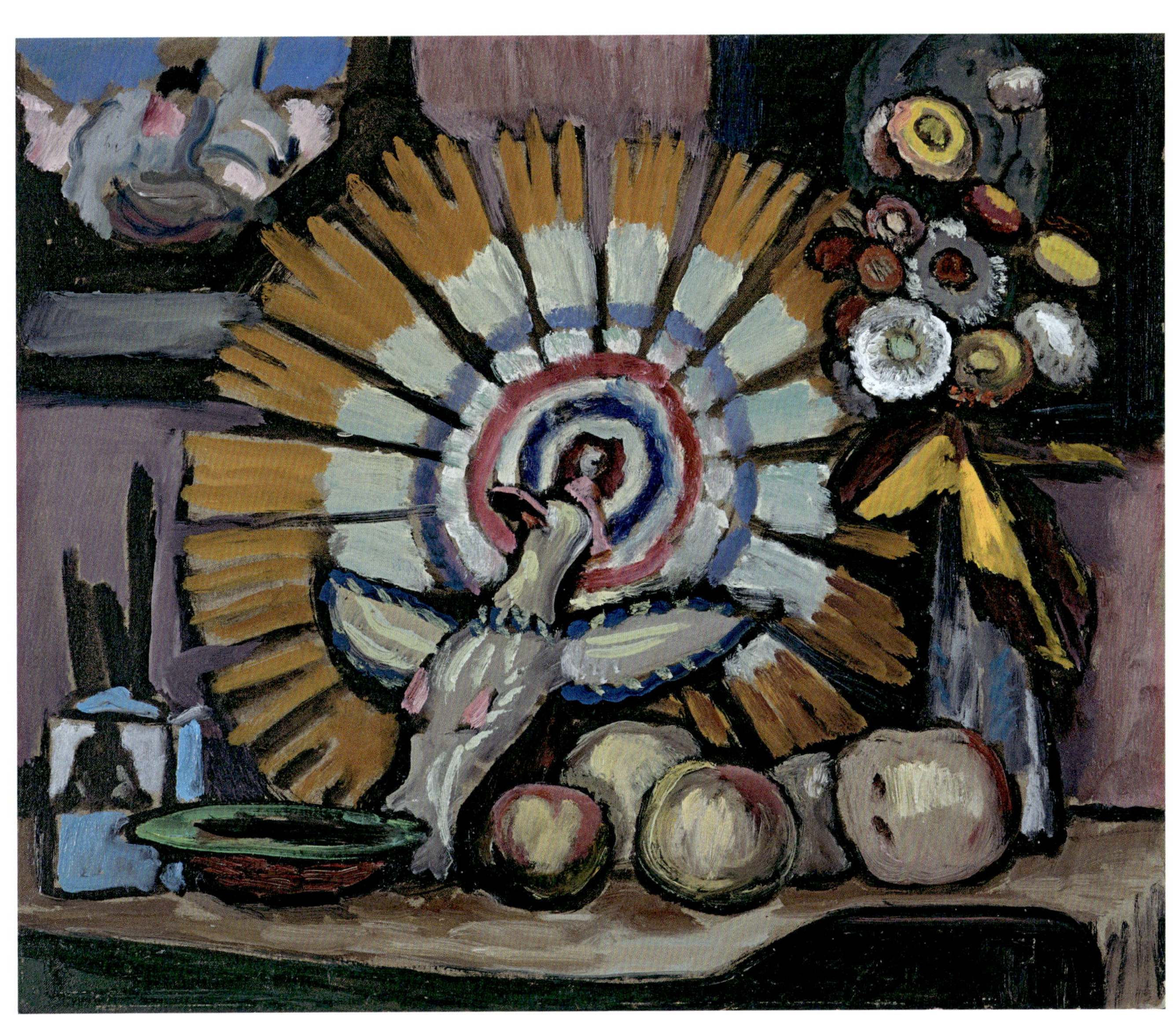

Cat. 122
Pentecost Still Life
[Stillleben Pfingsten], 1934
Cardboard, 38.1 × 46.2 cm |
Gabriele Münter- und Johannes Eichner-Stiftung, Munich, inv. no. S 50

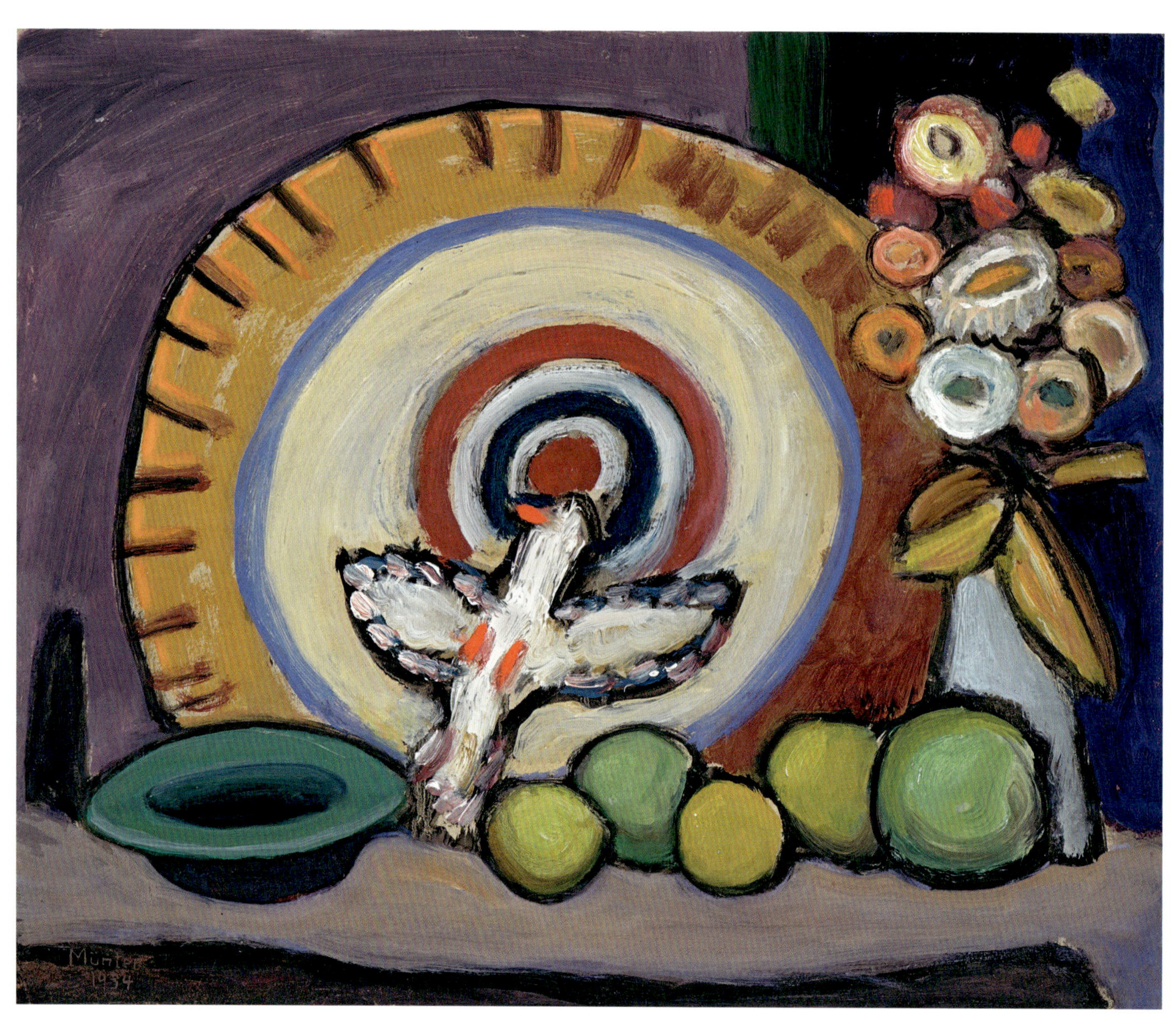

Cat. 123
Pentecost Still Life II [Stillleben Pfingsten II], 1934
Cardboard, 38.4 × 46.2 cm |
Gabriele Münter- und Johannes Eichner-Stiftung, Munich, inv. no. S 58

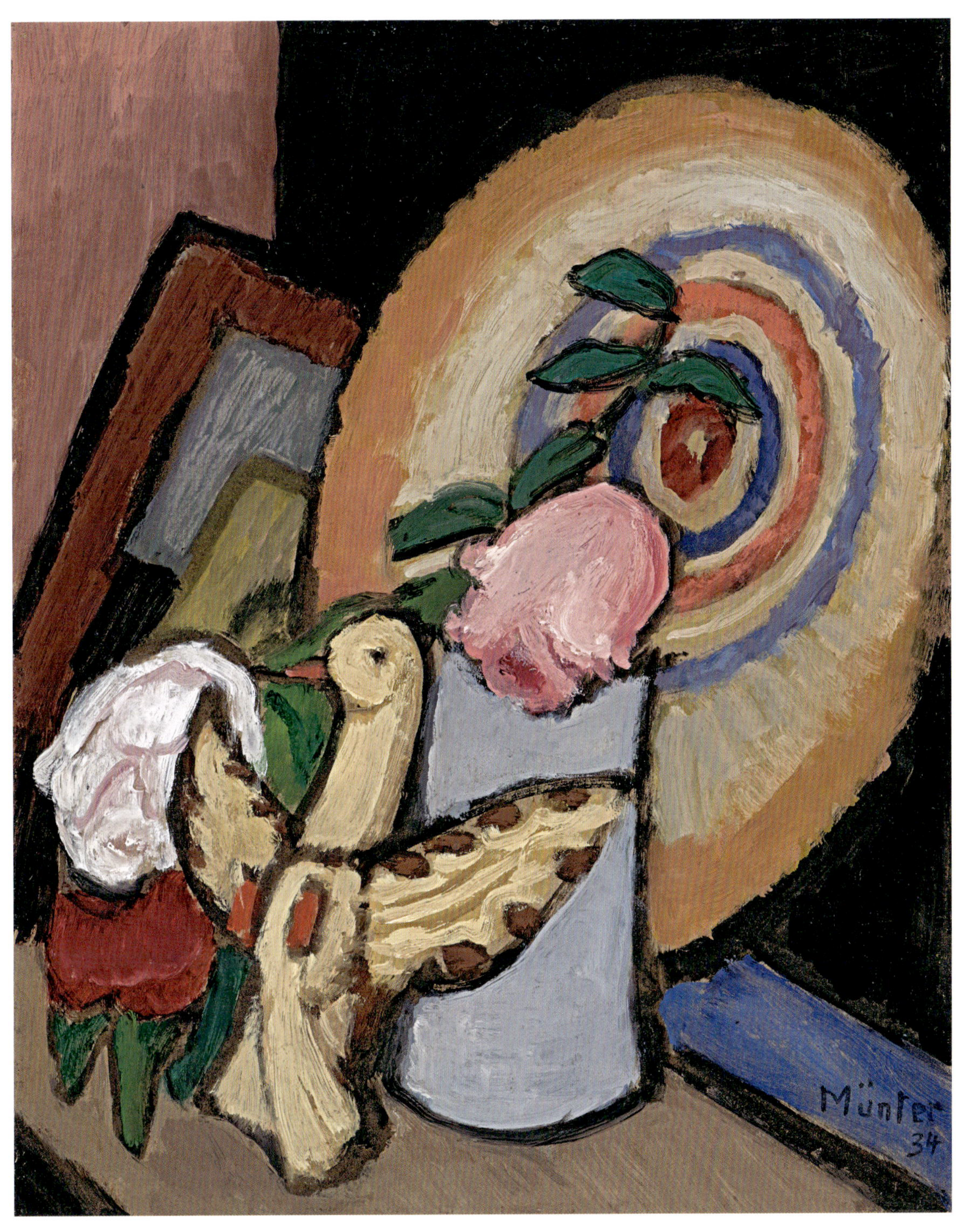

Cat. 124
Still Life from Tyrol
[Tiroler Stilleben], 1934
Cardboard, 41.3 × 33.2 cm |
Gabriele Münter- und Johannes Eichner-Stiftung, Munich, inv. no. S 71

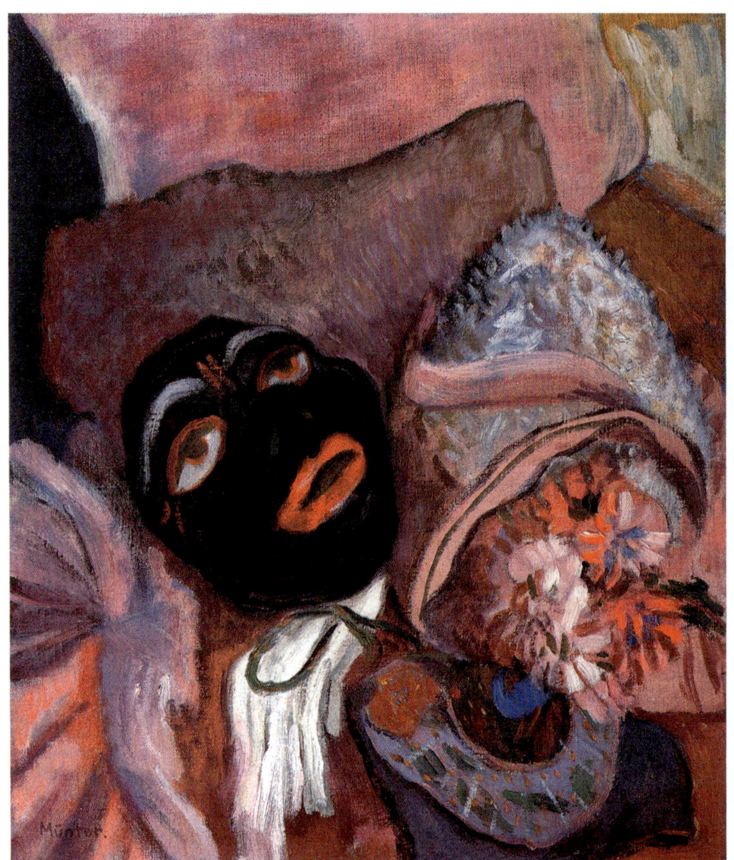

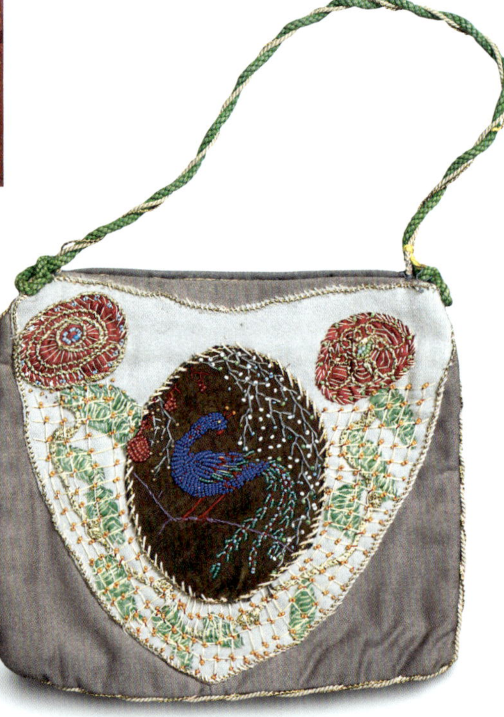

Cat. 125
Black Mask with Pink [Schwarze Maske mit Rosa], ca. 1912
Oil on canvas, 56.7 × 49.2 cm |
Private collection, Southern Germany

Cat. 126
Small gray handbag: peacock in a medallion bordered with stylized flowers, ca. 1911–13
Appliqué, beadwork, 18.5 × 21 cm |
Gabriele Münter- und Johannes Eichner-Stiftung, Munich, inv. no. D 45

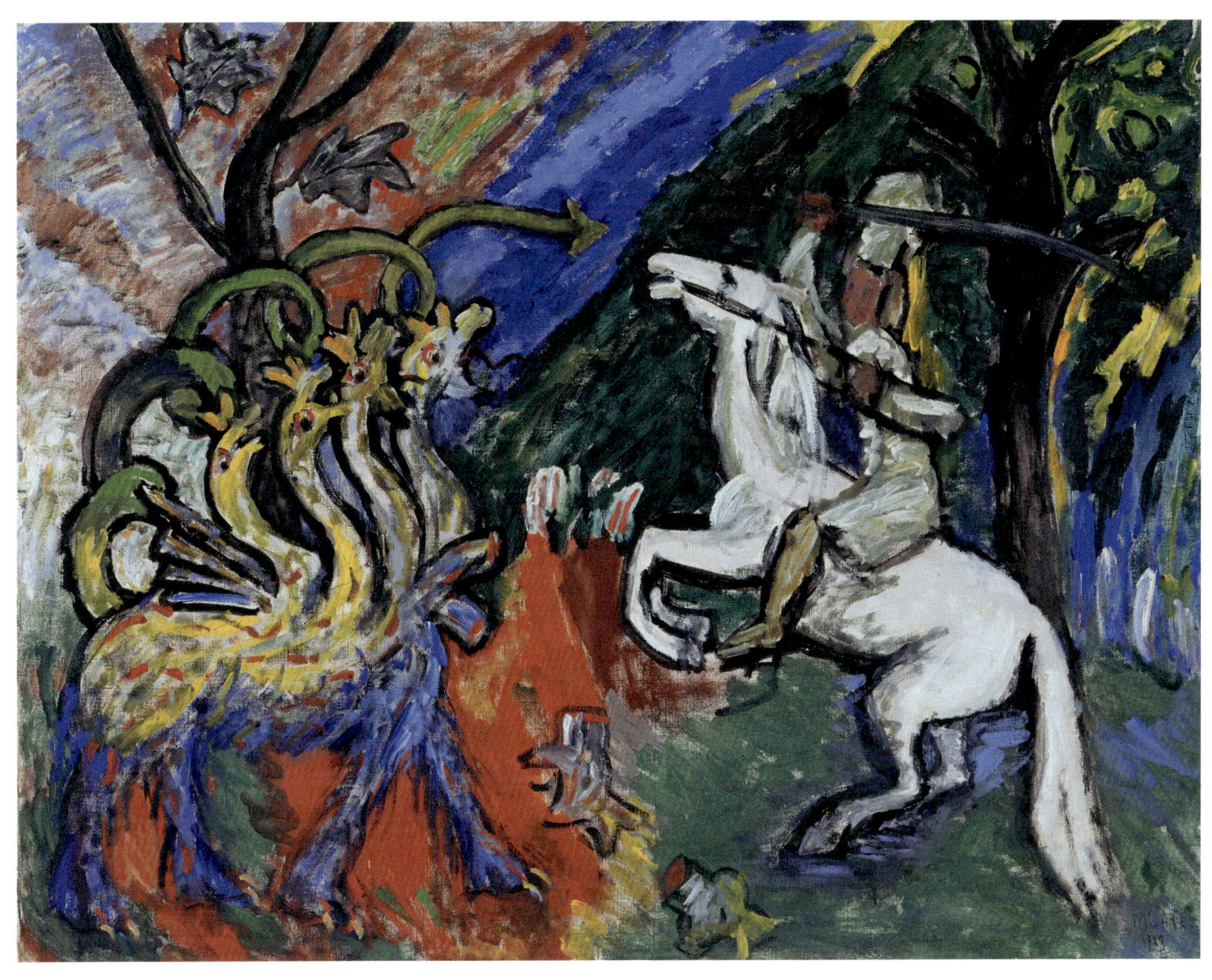

Cat. 127
Dragon Fight
[Drachenkampf], 1913
Oil on canvas, 78 × 100 cm | Centre Pompidou, Paris. Musée national d'art moderne – Centre de création industrielle, donated by the Société Kandinsky, 2015, inv. no. AM 2015-152

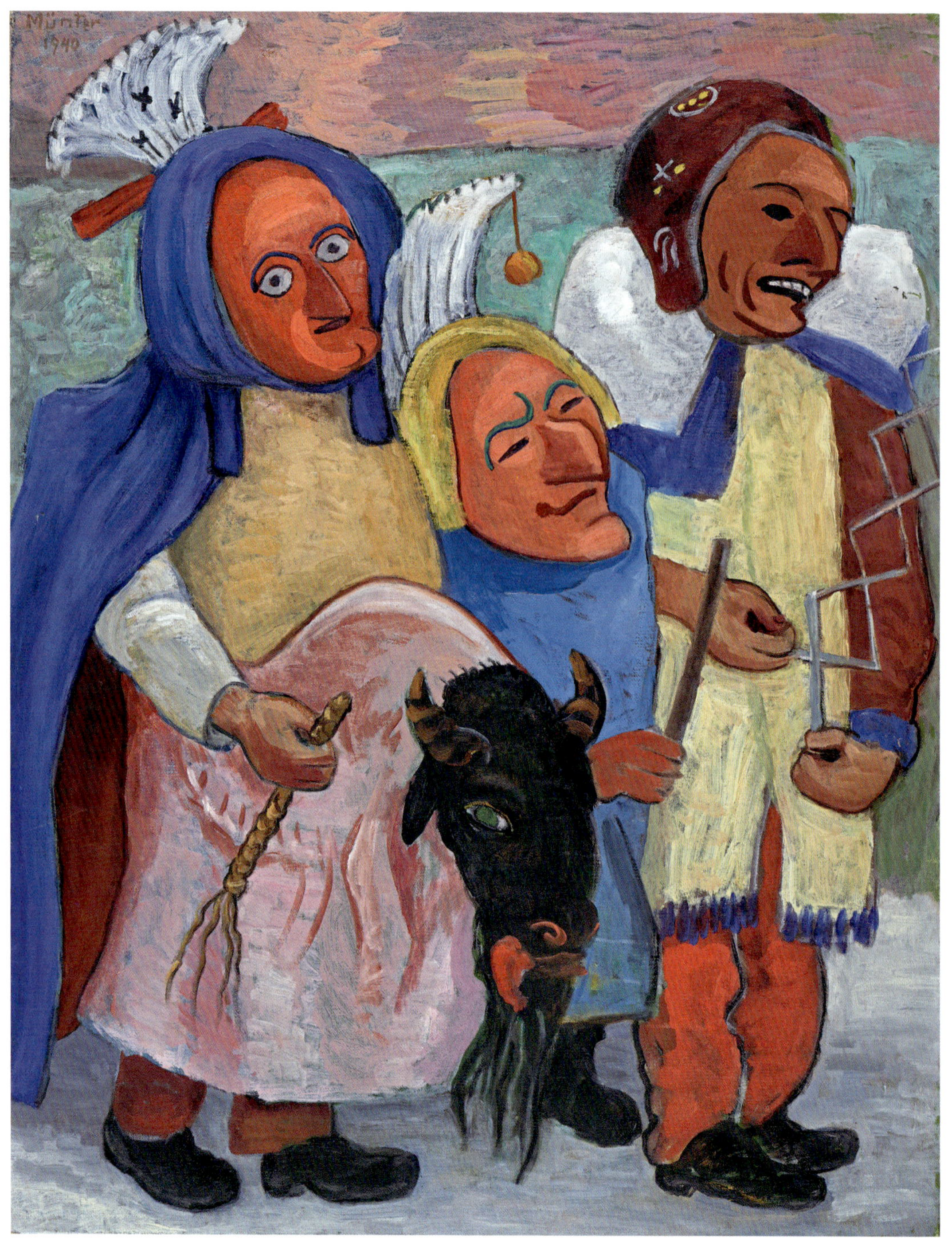

Cat. 128
Maschkera, 1940
Textile support, 100.2 × 78.4 cm |
Gabriele Münter- und Johannes Eichner-Stiftung, Munich, inv. no. V 116

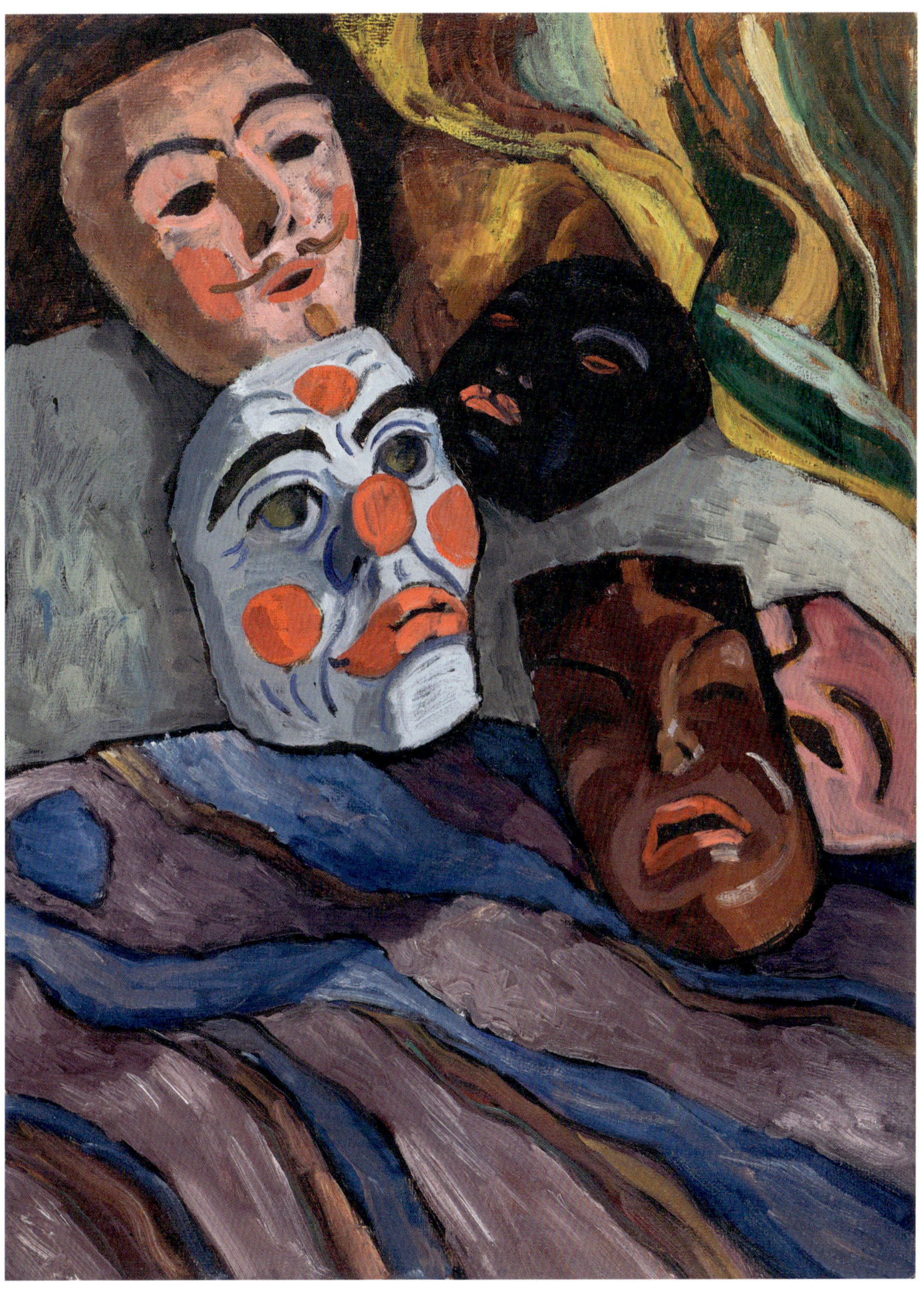

Cat. 129
Mask Still Life [Masken-stilleben], 1940
Cardboard, 68.5 × 50.7 cm |
Gabriele Münter- und Johannes Eichner-Stiftung, Munich, inv. no. V 4

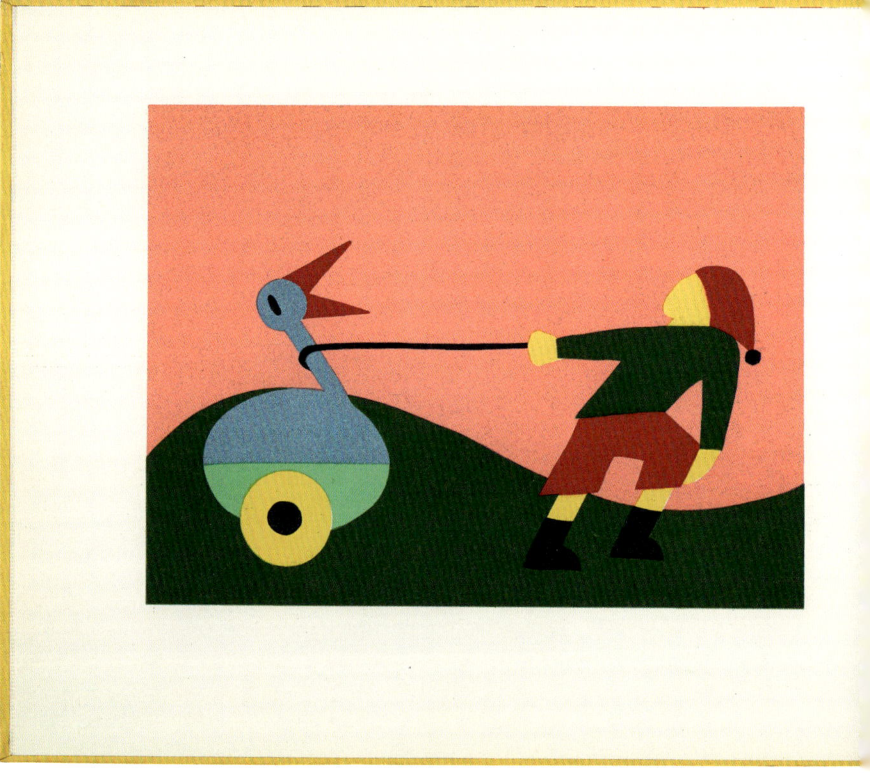

Cat. 130
LILY HILDEBRANDT
Klein-Rainers Weltreise
[Little Rainer's Trip around the World]
Munich 1918, children's book
Gabriele Münter- und Johannes Eichner-Stiftung, Munich

Klein-Rainers Weltreise

von

Lily Hildebrandt

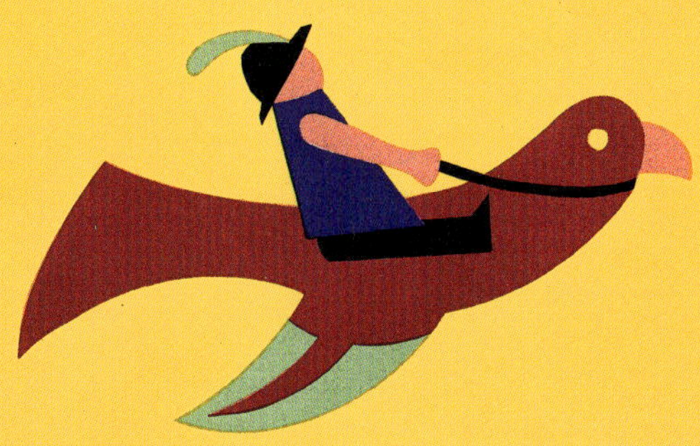

Bei Georg W. Dietrich / Hofverleger
München

Freund Schnabellang setzt ihn in Gras.
Ei, was ist das?
Ente mit grünen und blauen Federn
Rollt über die Wiese auf gelben Rädern.
Klein-Rainer fängt mit dem Stock sie ein
Und läßt sie quaken und zeterschrein.

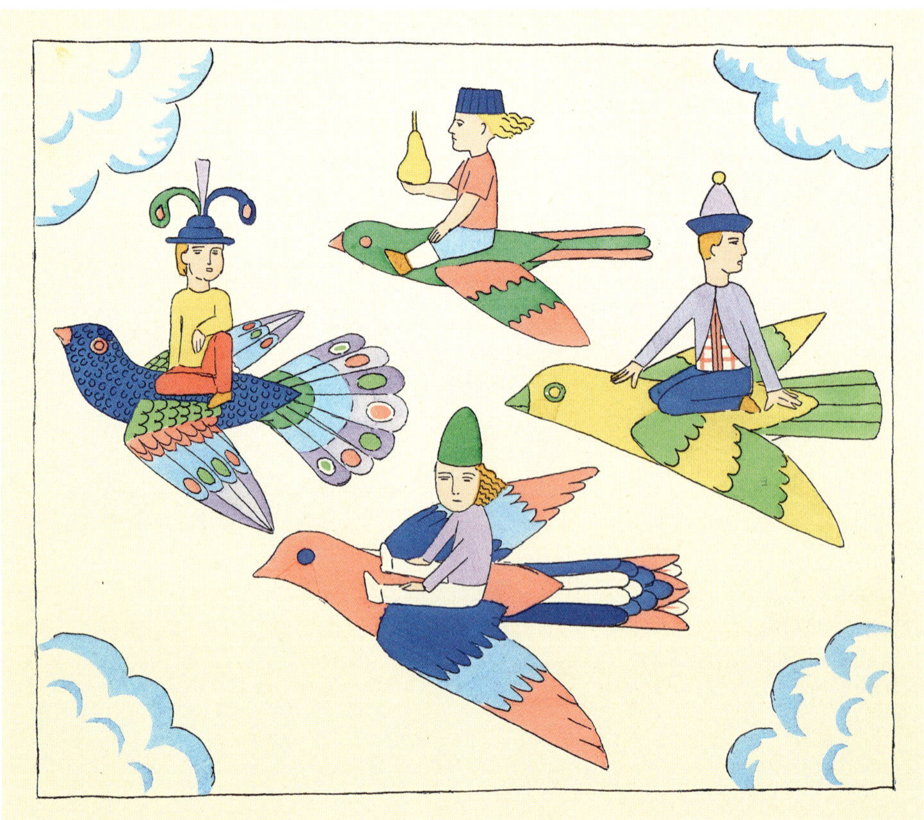

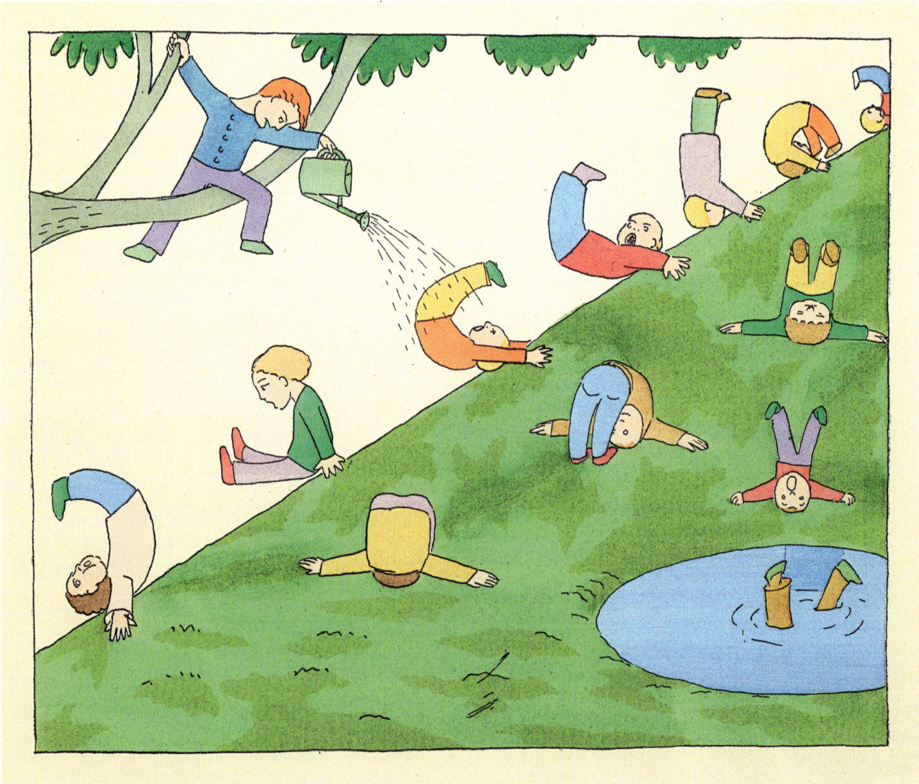

Cat. 131
KONRAD F. VON FREYHOLD
Sport und Spiel [Sports and Games]
Cologne 1906, children's book
Gabriele Münter- und Johannes Eichner-Stiftung, Munich

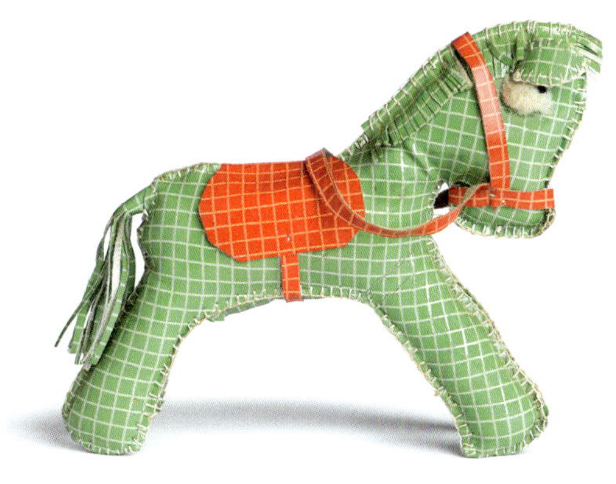

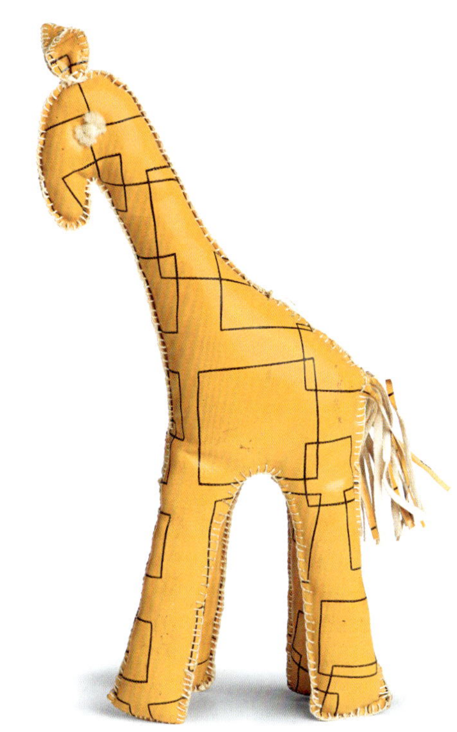

Cat. 132
Horse (toy)
Plastic-coated, printed fabric, padding material, H: 11.8 cm, W: 15 cm, D: 3.4 cm | Gabriele Münter- und Johannes Eichner-Stiftung, Munich

Cat. 133
Giraffe (toy)
Plastic-coated, printed fabric, padding material, H: 24 cm, W: 13.5 cm, D: 3 cm | Gabriele Münter- und Johannes Eichner-Stiftung, Munich

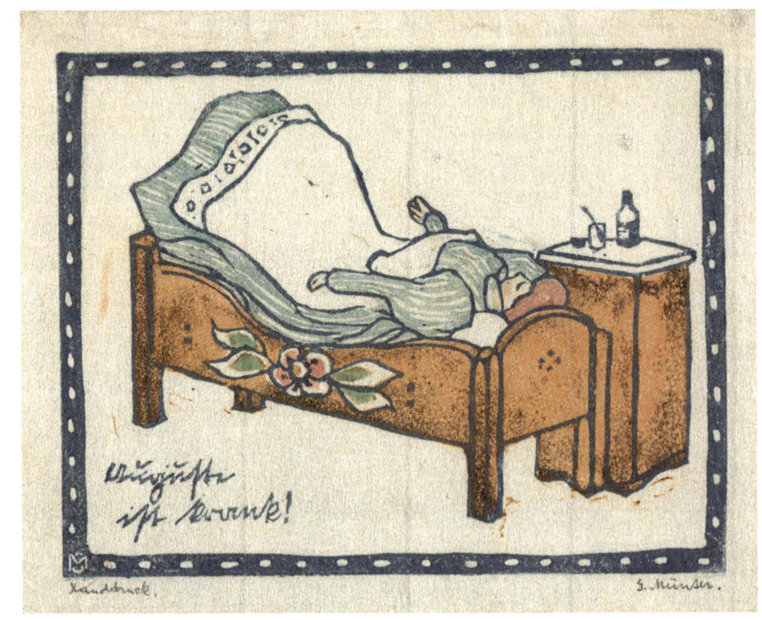

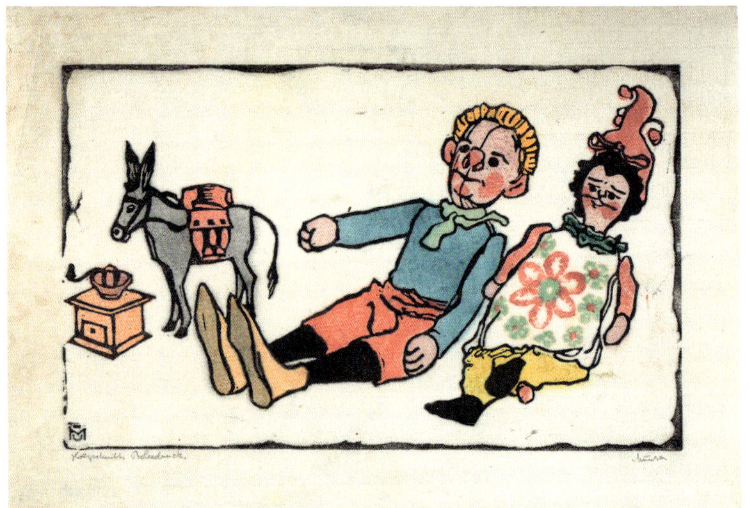

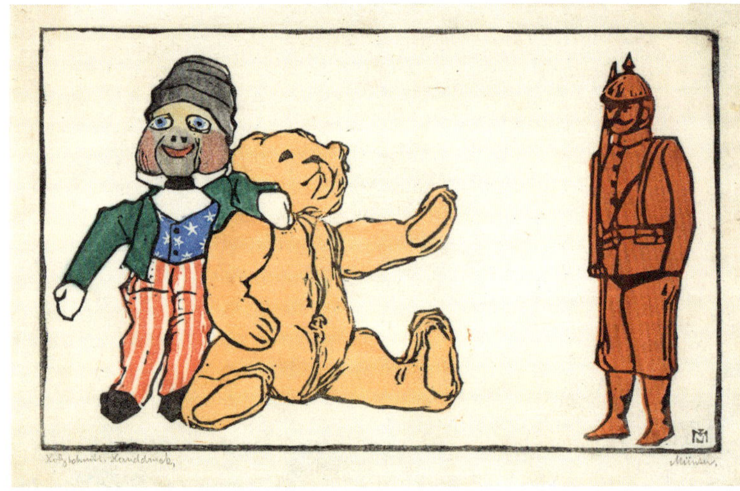

Cat. 134
Auguste Is Sick (toy no. 1) [Auguste ist krank (Spielzeug Nr. 1)], 1908
Colored linoleum cut on Japan paper, mounted on gray cardboard (original), 11 × 13.9 cm | Städtische Galerie im Lenbachhaus und Kunstbau München, inv. no. GMS 874

Cat. 135
Tünnes and Companions (toy no. 2) [Tünnes und Gesellschaft (Spielzeug Nr. 2)], 1908
Colored linoleum cut on Japan paper, 17.5 × 26.1 cm | Städtische Galerie im Lenbachhaus und Kunstbau München, inv. no. GMS 875

Cat. 136
Uncle Sam and Companions (toy no. 3) [Onkel Sam und Gesellschaft (Spielzeug Nr. 3)], 1908
Colored linoleum cut on Japan paper, 15.5 × 24 cm | Städtische Galerie im Lenbachhaus und Kunstbau München, inv. no. GMS 879

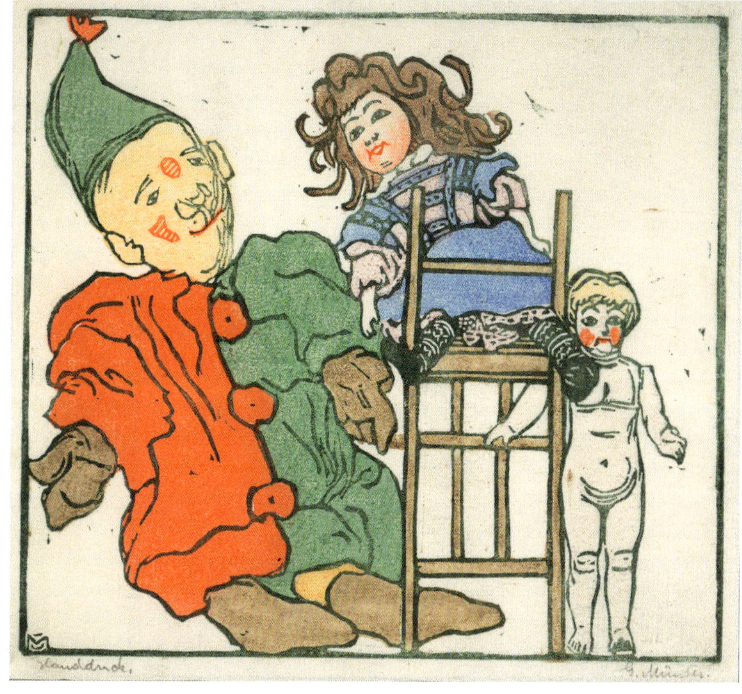

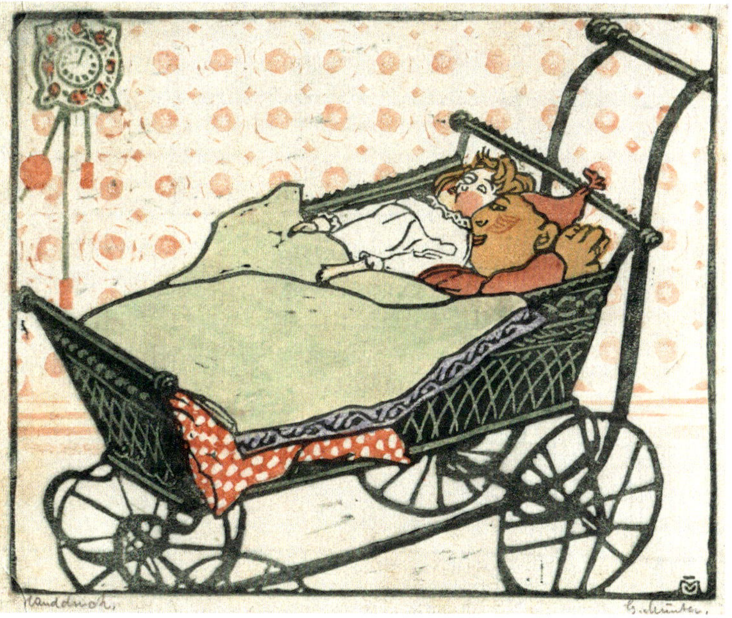

Cat. 137
Talking (toy no. 4) [Im Gespräch (Spielzeug Nr. 4)], 1908
Colored linoleum cut on Japan paper, mounted on gray cardboard (original), 18 × 19.6 cm | Städtische Galerie im Lenbachhaus und Kunstbau München, inv. no. GMS 882

Cat. 138
Good Night (toy no. 5) [Gute Nacht (Spielzeug Nr. 5)], 1908
Colored linoleum cut on Japan paper, mounted on gray cardboard (original), 16.8 × 20.6 cm | Städtische Galerie im Lenbachhaus und Kunstbau München, inv. no. GMS 883

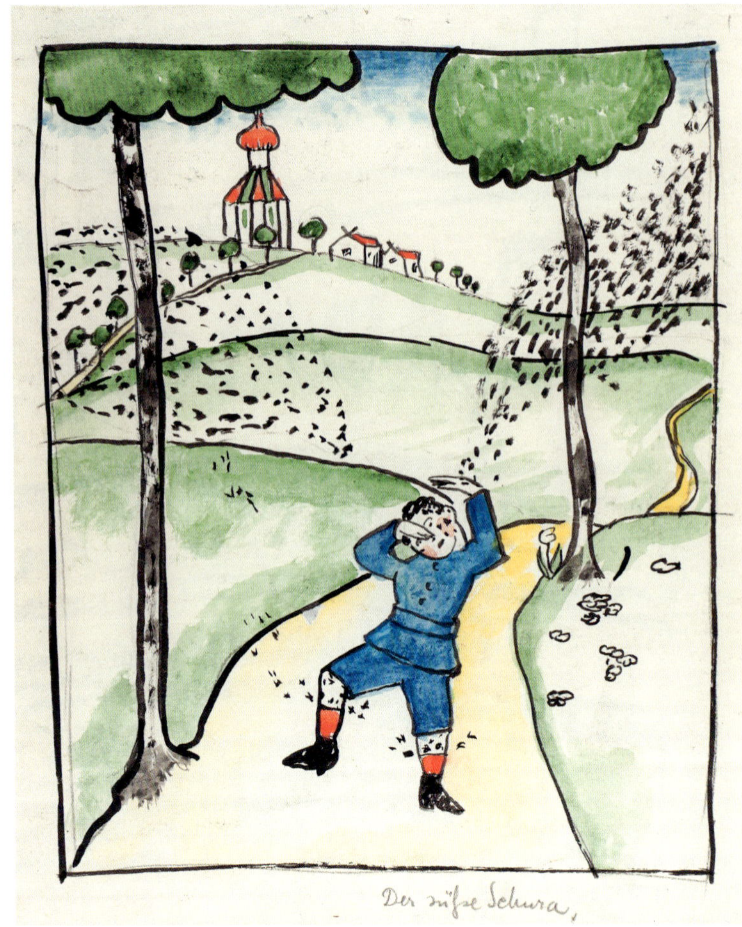

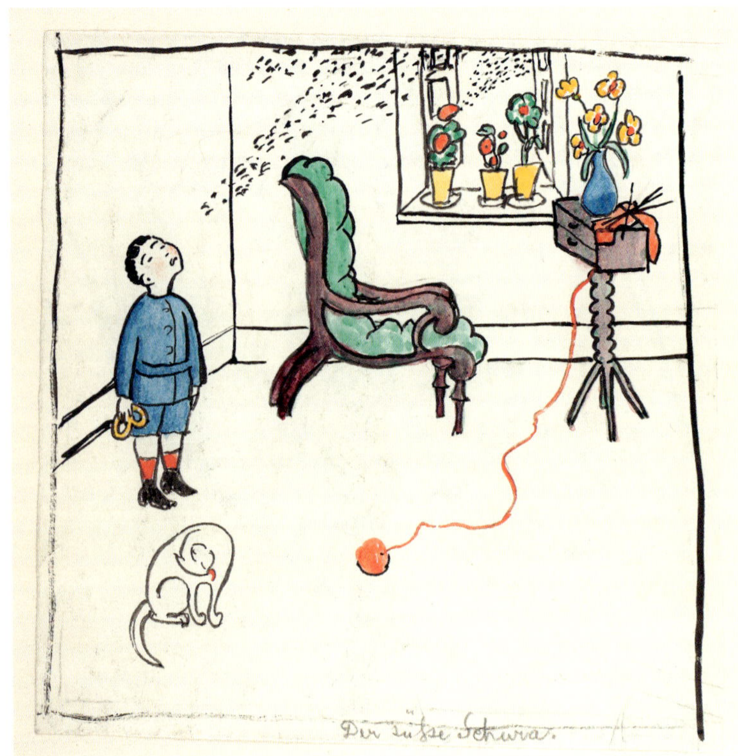

Cat. 139
Sweet Schura on a Walk [Der süße Schura auf einem Spaziergang], 1918/19
Pencil, ink, and watercolor on machine-smooth paper, 23.1 × 16 cm | Gabriele Münter- und Johannes Eichner-Stiftung, Munich, inv. no. Kon. 12/2

Cat. 140
Sweet Schura [Der süße Schura], 1918/19
Pencil, ink, and watercolor on machine-smooth paper, mounted on thin cardboard, 16.1 × 16.1 cm | Gabriele Münter- und Johannes Eichner-Stiftung, Munich, inv. no. Kon. 12/3

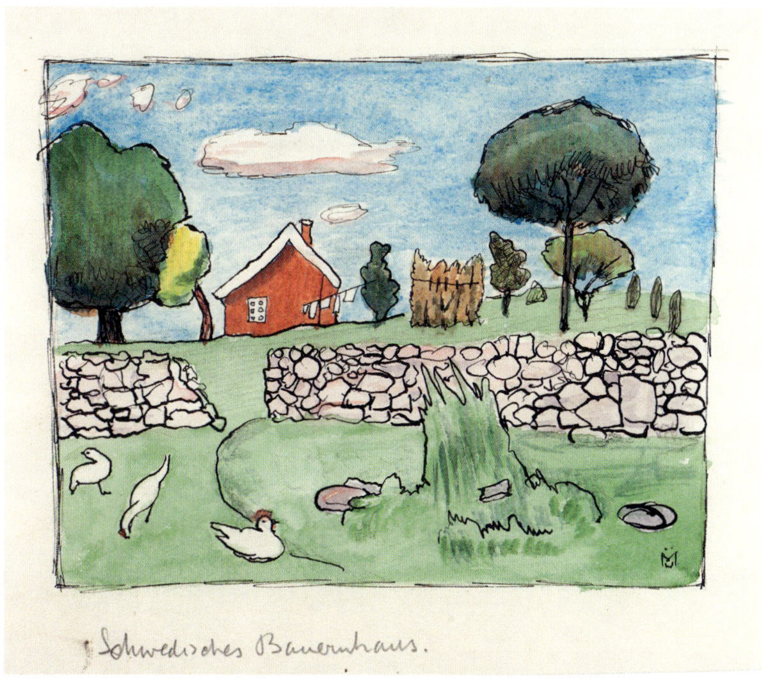

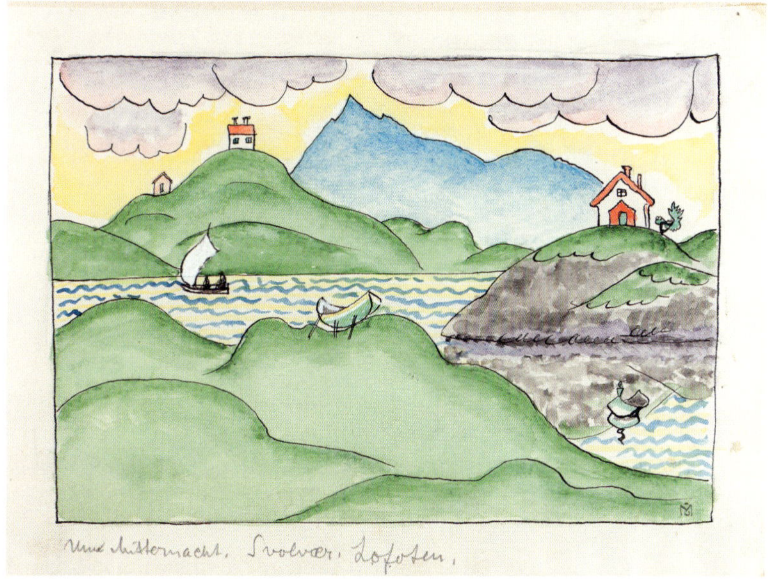

Cat. 141
Swedish Farmhouse [Schwedisches Bauernhaus], 1916
Pencil, ink, and watercolor on drawing paper, 16.1 × 19.9 cm | Gabriele Münter- und Johannes Eichner-Stiftung, Munich, inv. no. Kon. 34/25

Cat. 142
At Midnight. Svolvær. Lofoten [Um Mitternacht. Svolvær. Lofoten], 1916
Pencil, ink, and watercolor on drawing paper, glued to cardboard, 16.4 × 22.6 cm | Gabriele Münter- und Johannes Eichner-Stiftung, Munich, inv. no. Kon. 34/21

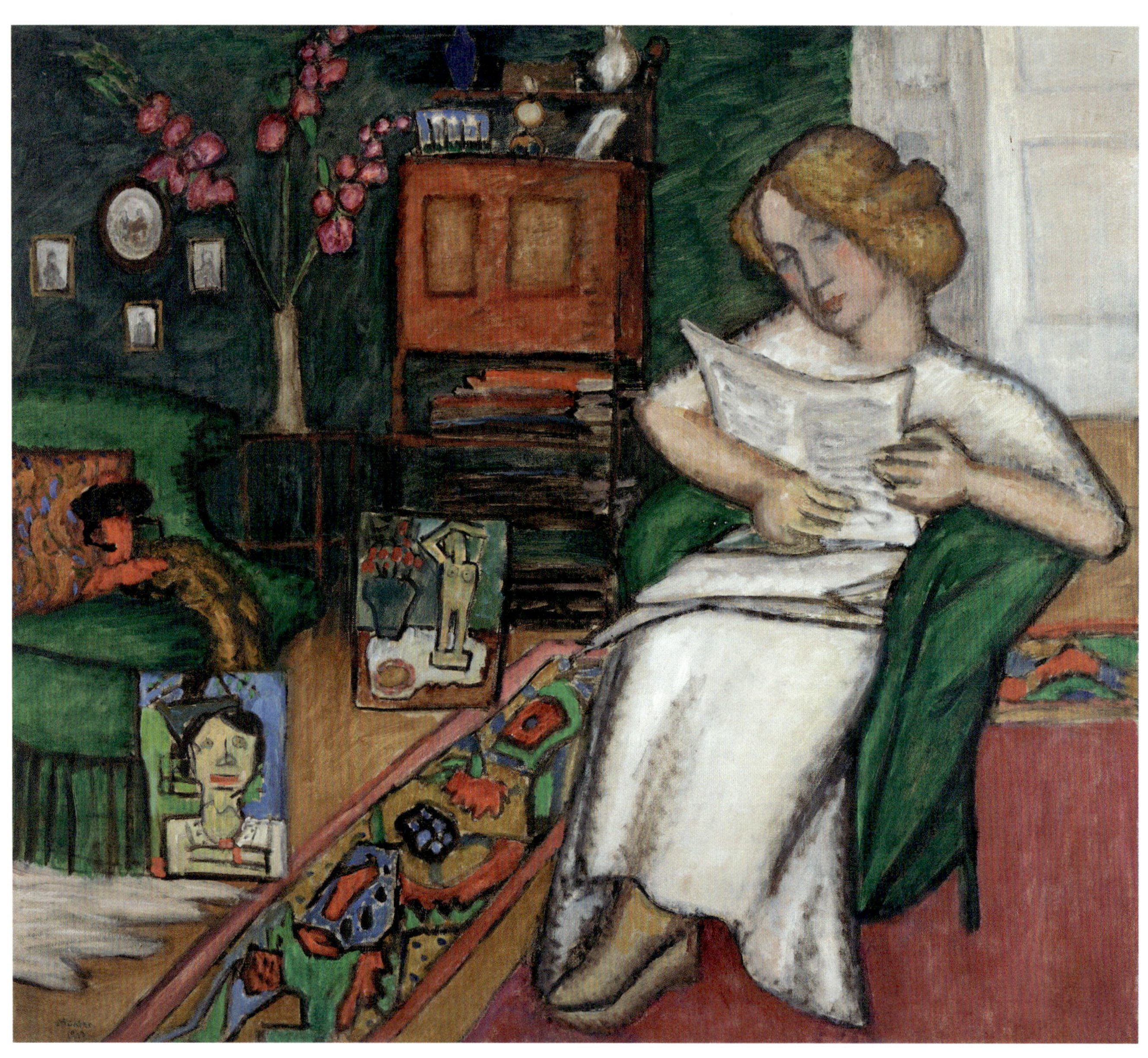

Cat. 143
In the Room [Im Zimmer], 1913
Textile support, 88.1 × 99.8 cm |
Städtische Galerie im Lenbachhaus und
Kunstbau München, inv. no. G 18729

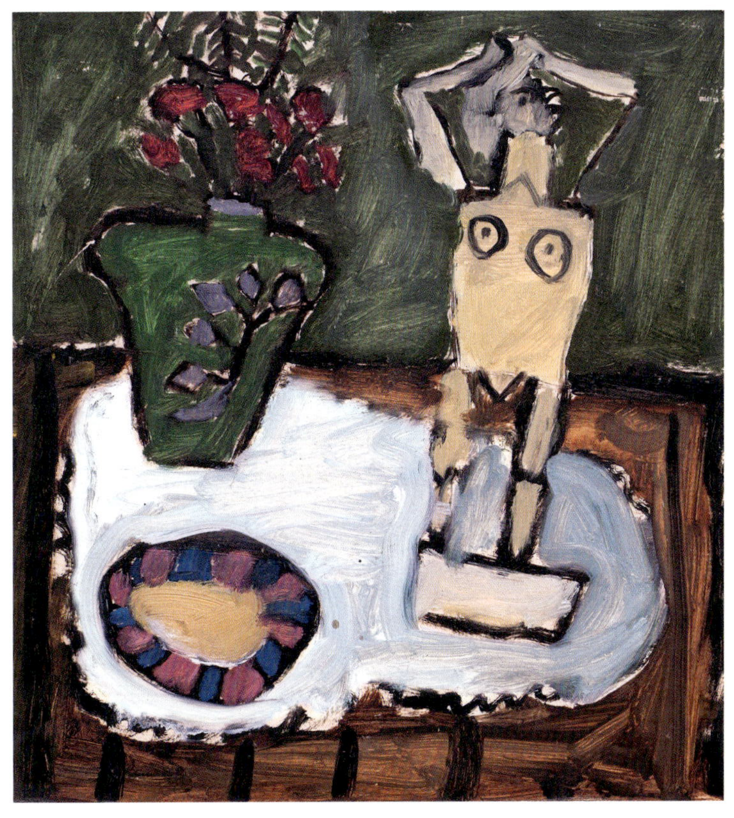

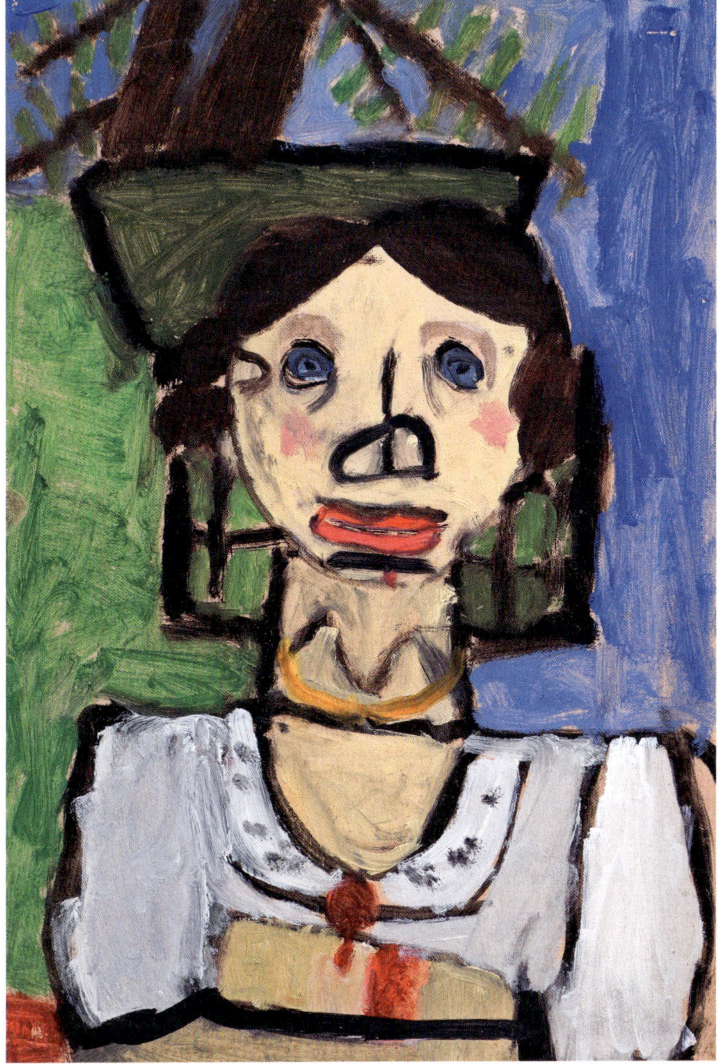

Cat. 144
ELFRIEDE SCHROETER
Still Life [Stillleben] (child's painting), ca. 1913
Cardboard, 35.7 × 33.4 cm | Gabriele Münter- und Johannes Eichner-Stiftung, Munich, inv. no. KIZ 185

Cat. 145
ELFRIEDE SCHROETER
Feminine Portrait [Weibliches Porträt] (child's painting), ca. 1913
Cardboard, 47.5 × 32.8 cm | Gabriele Münter- und Johannes Eichner-Stiftung, Munich, inv. no. KIZ 180

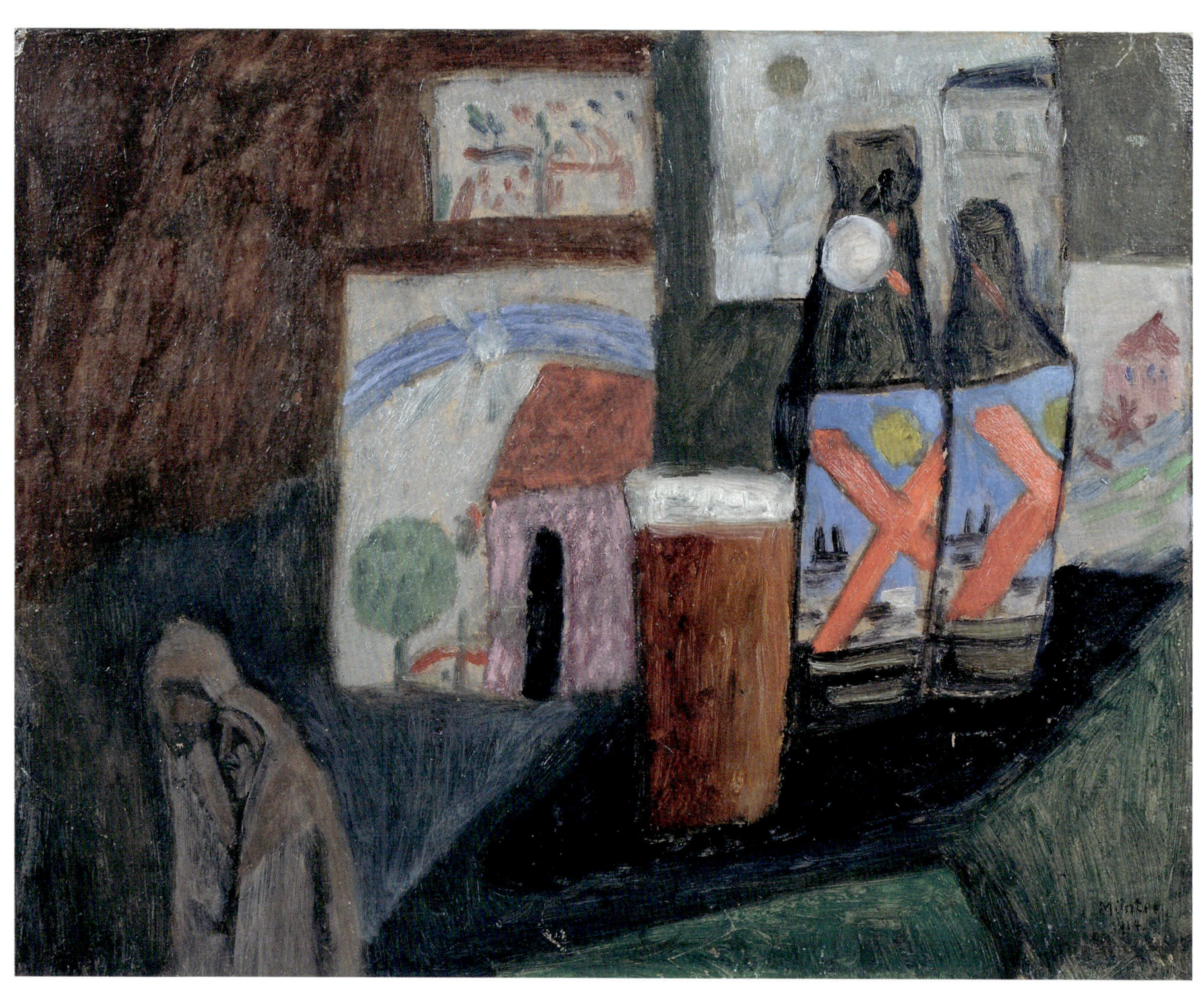

Cat. 146
Still Life with X Beer
[Stillleben mit X-Bier], 1914
Oil on cardboard, 33 × 41.3 cm |
Private collection, Munich

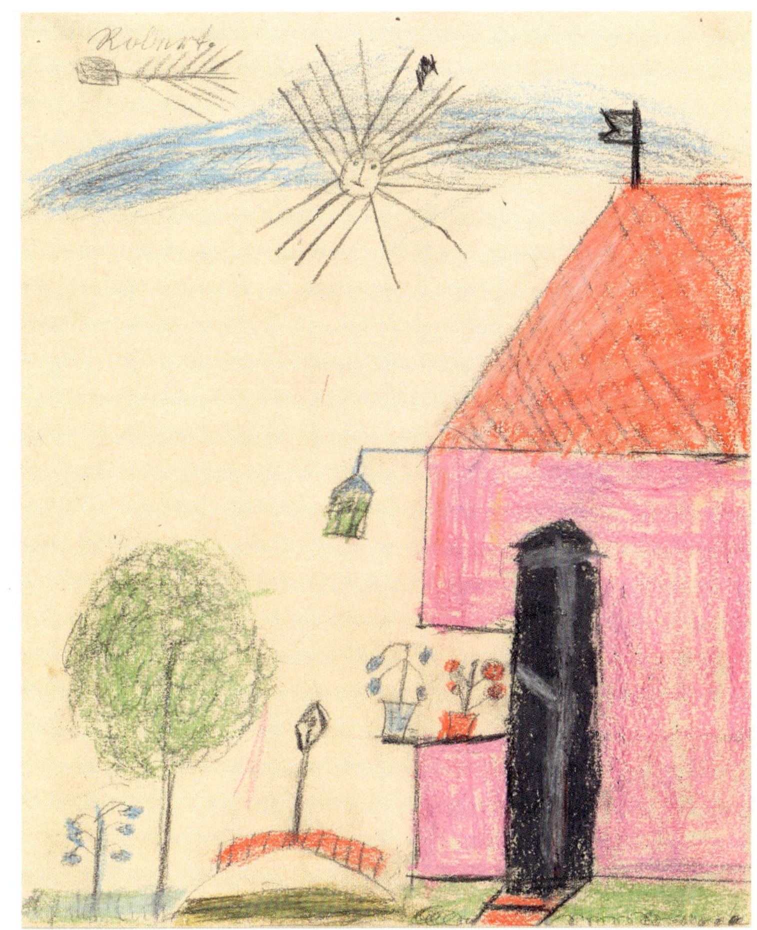

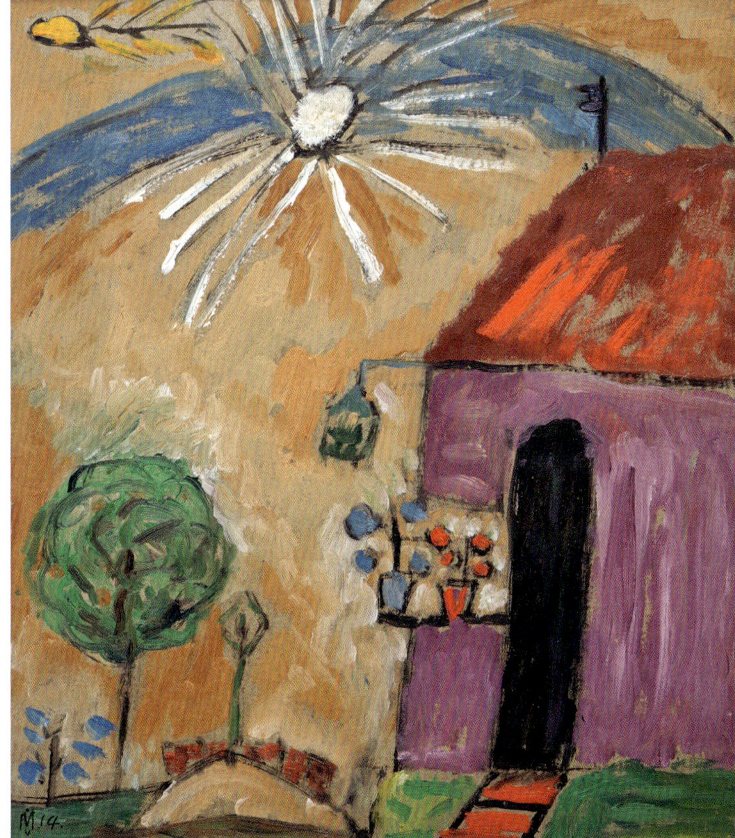

Cat. 147
Child's drawing (Robert), basis for Münter's painting "House"
Pencil and colored chalk on thin drawing board, 24 × 19.9 cm | Gabriele Münter- und Johannes Eichner-Stiftung, Munich, inv. no. KIZ 144

Cat. 148
House [Haus] (based on a child's drawing), 1914
Cardboard, 37.3 × 32.8 cm | Gabriele Münter- und Johannes Eichner-Stiftung, Munich, inv. no. Mü 4

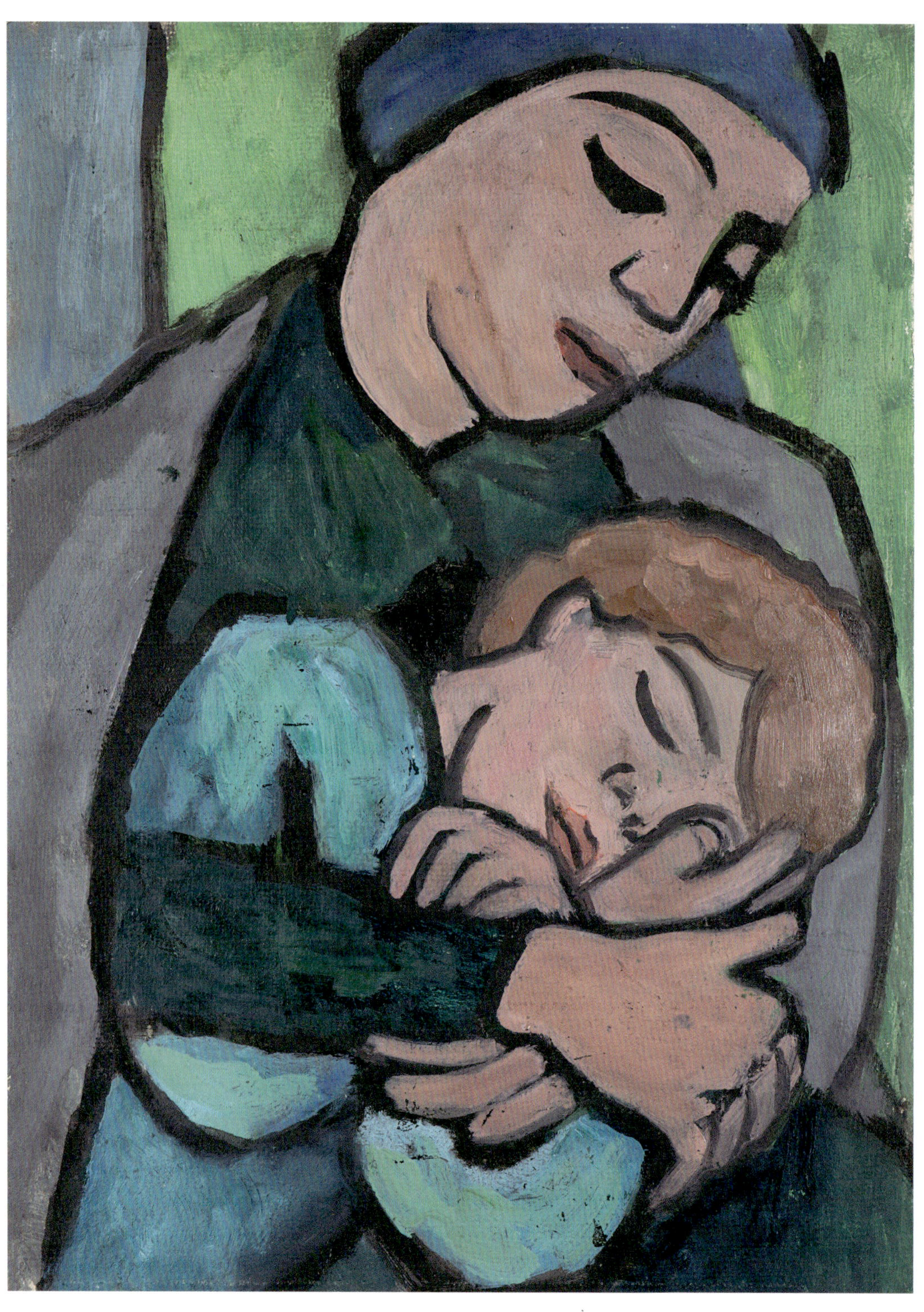

Cat. 149
Mother and Sleeping Child [Mutter mit schlafendem Kind], 1934
Cardboard, 44.6 × 33 cm | Gabriele Münter- und Johannes Eichner-Stiftung, Munich, inv. no. P 40

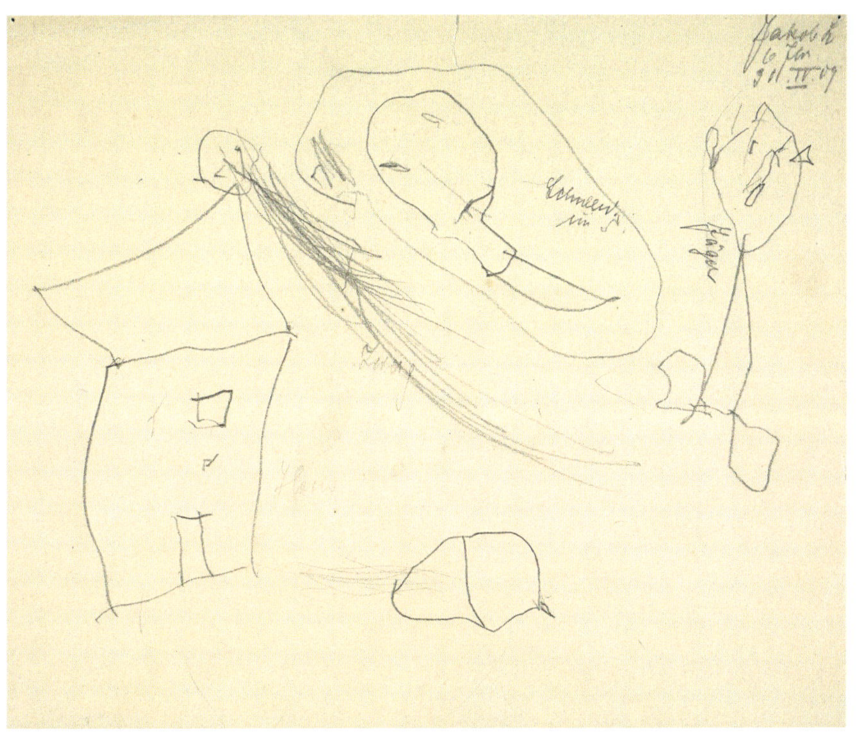

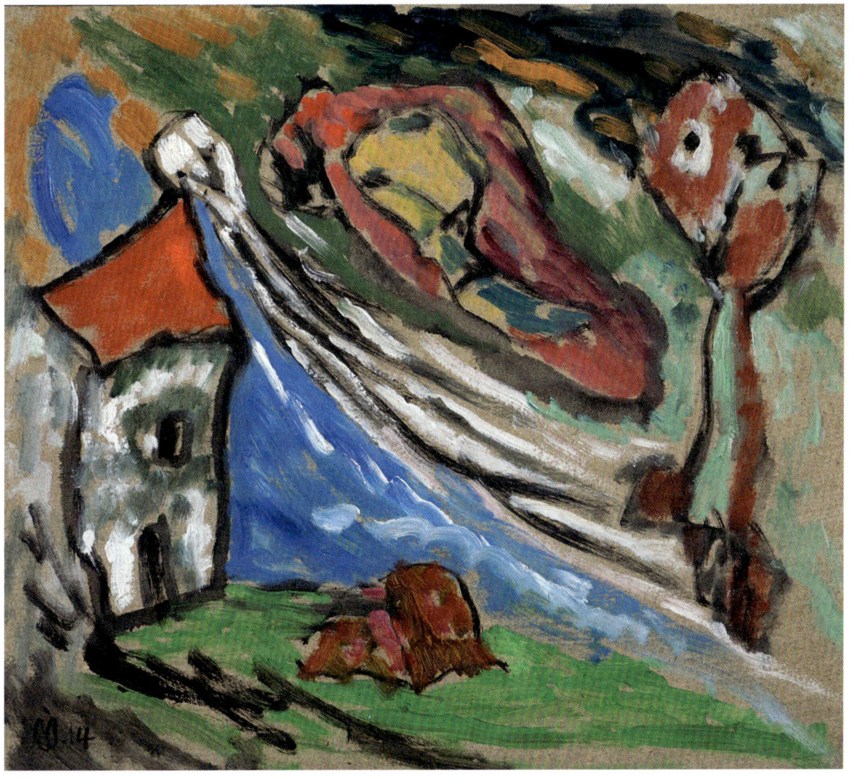

Cat. 150
Child's drawing (Jakob), basis for Münter's painting "Landscape with House"
Pencil on thin drawing board, 20 × 23.9 cm | Gabriele Münter- und Johannes Eichner-Stiftung, Munich, inv. no. KIZ 115

Cat. 151
Landscape with House [Landschaft mit Haus] (based on a child's drawing), 1914
Cardboard, 32.9 × 37 cm | Gabriele Münter- und Johannes Eichner-Stiftung, Munich, inv. no. Mü 1

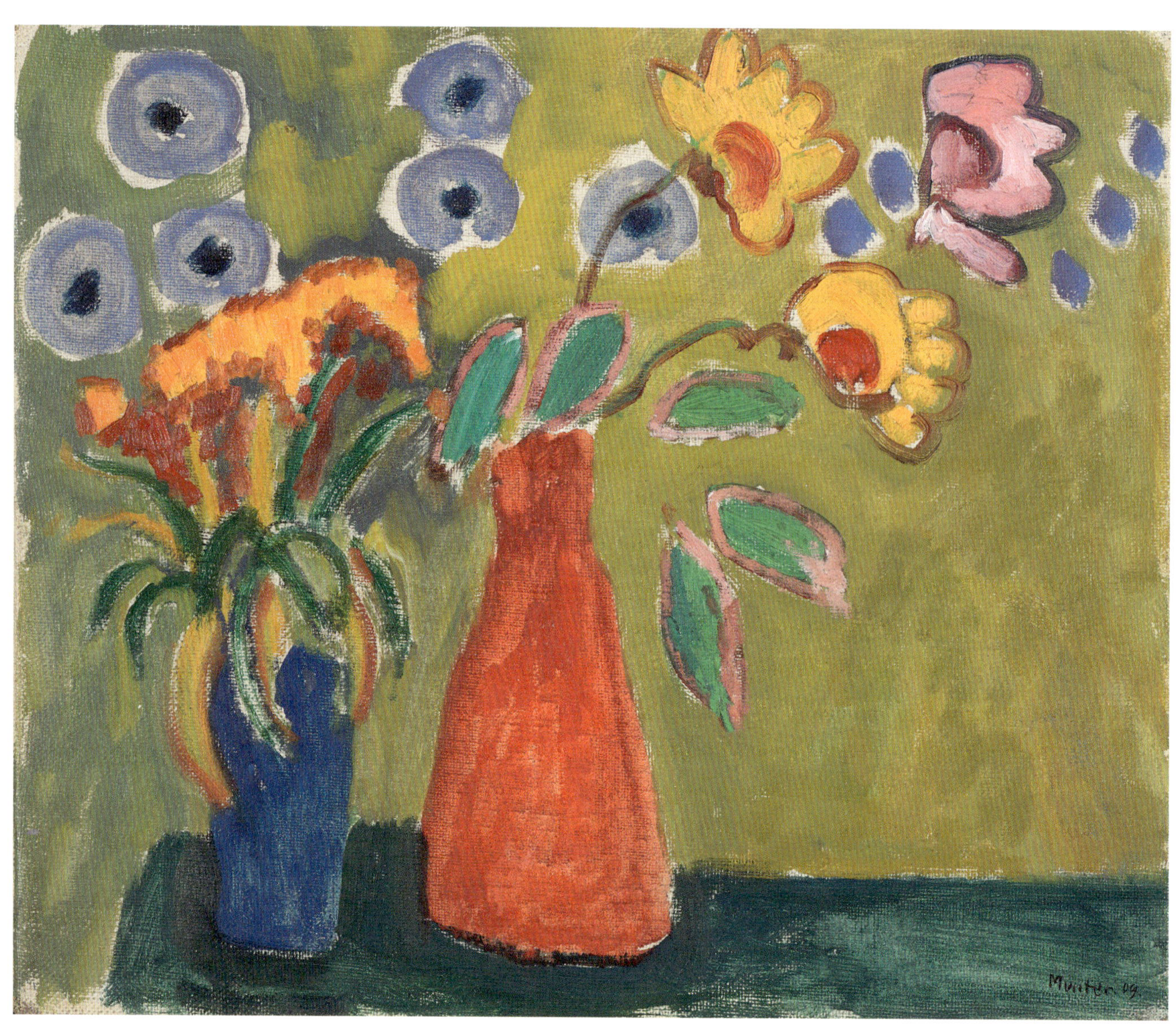

Cat. 152
Vase rouge, 1909
Textile support, 38.2 × 45.5 cm |
Gabriele Münter- und Johannes Eichner-Stiftung, Munich, inv. no. B 308

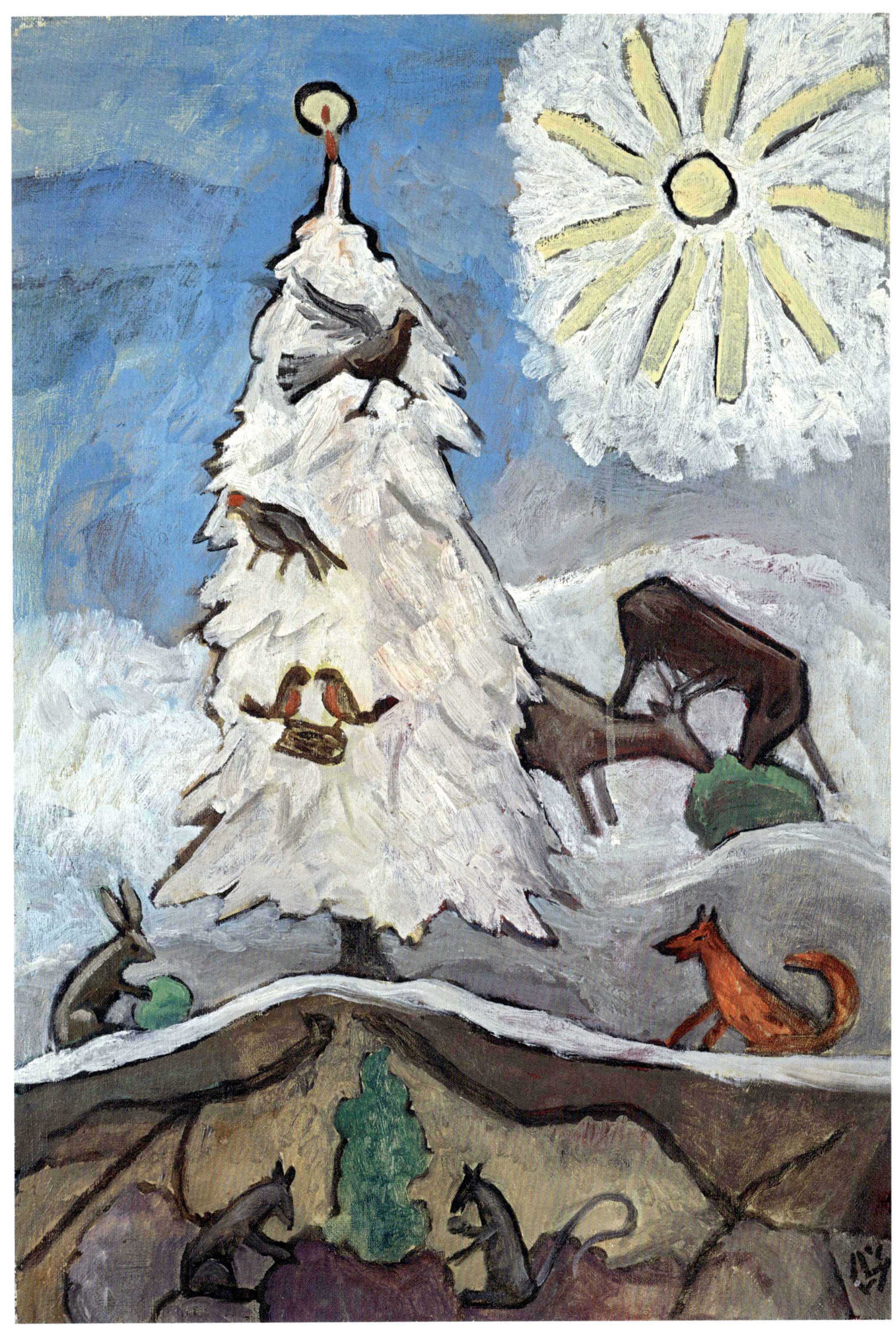

Cat. 153
Animals' Christmas Tree [Weihnachtsbaum der Tiere], 1951
Textile support, 55.4 × 38.5 cm | Gabriele Münter- und Johannes Eichner-Stiftung, Munich, inv. no. V 12

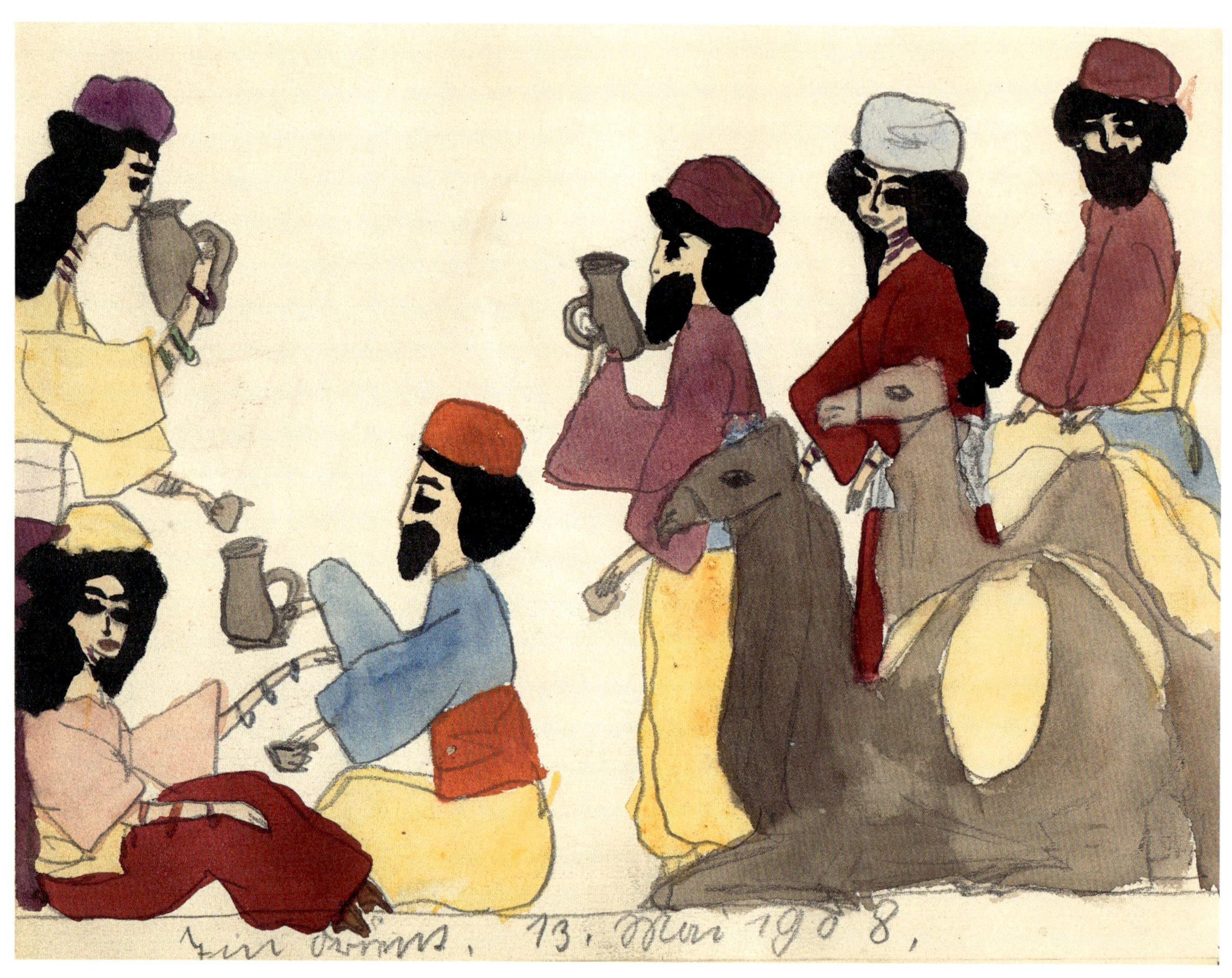

Cat. 154
LYDIA WIEBER
In the Orient [Im Orient] (child's painting), May 13, 1908
Pencil and watercolor on paper, 15.7 × 21 cm | Gabriele Münter- und Johannes Eichner-Stiftung, Munich, inv. no. KIZ 254-6

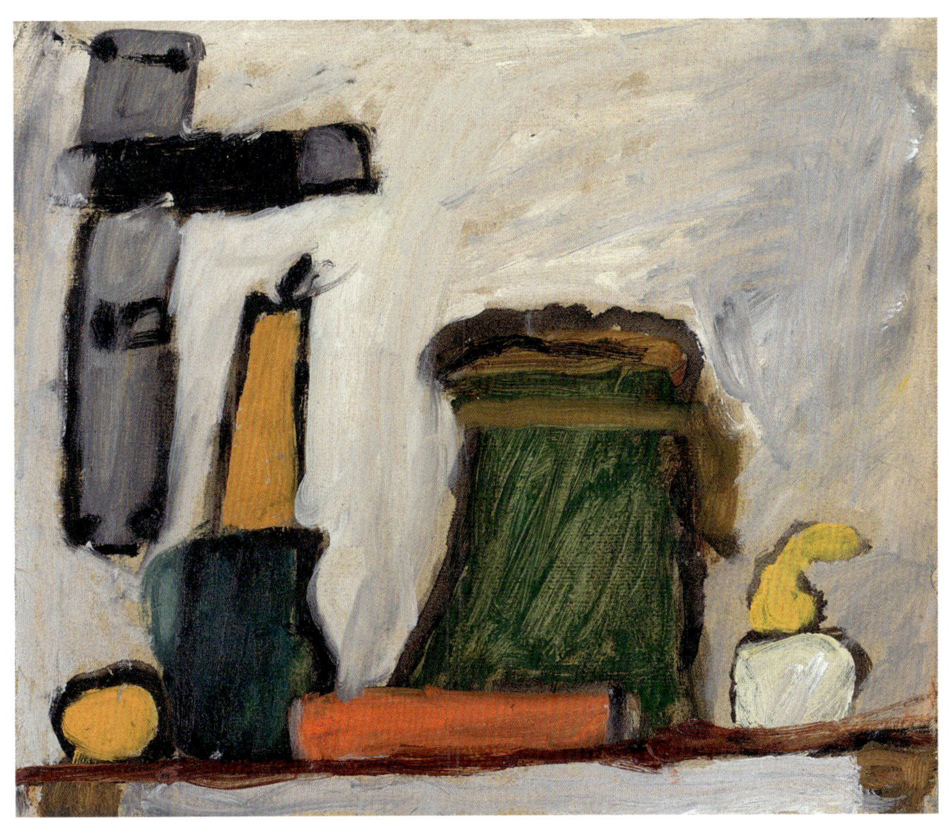

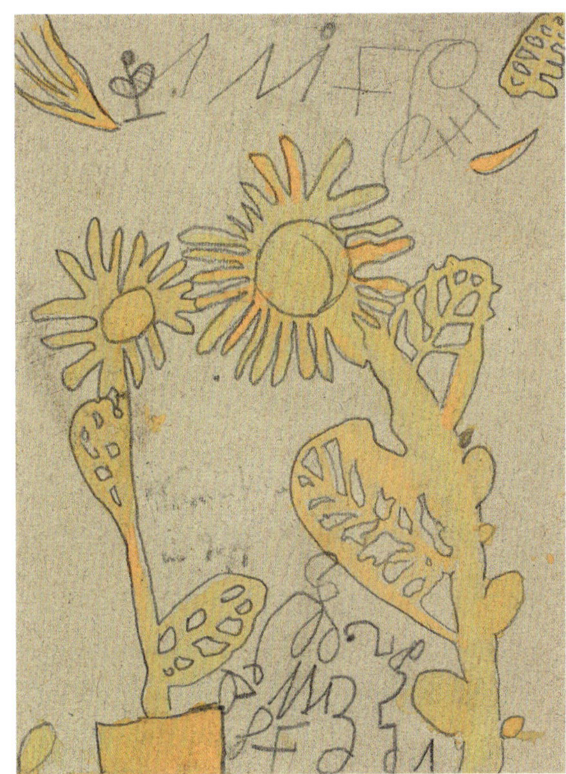

Cat. 155
ELFRIEDE SCHROETER
Untitled (Still life with candle, red book, green bag, and door handle) (child's painting), 1913
Cardboard, 25.1 × 30 cm | Gabriele Münter- und Johannes Eichner-Stiftung, Munich, inv. no. KIZ 181

Cat. 156
Presumably KÄTHE BUSSE
Sunflowers in a Pot [Sonnenblumen im Topf]
Pencil over watercolor on toned tan paper, 15.7 × 11.8 cm | Gabriele Münter- und Johannes Eichner-Stiftung, Munich, inv. no. KIZ 73

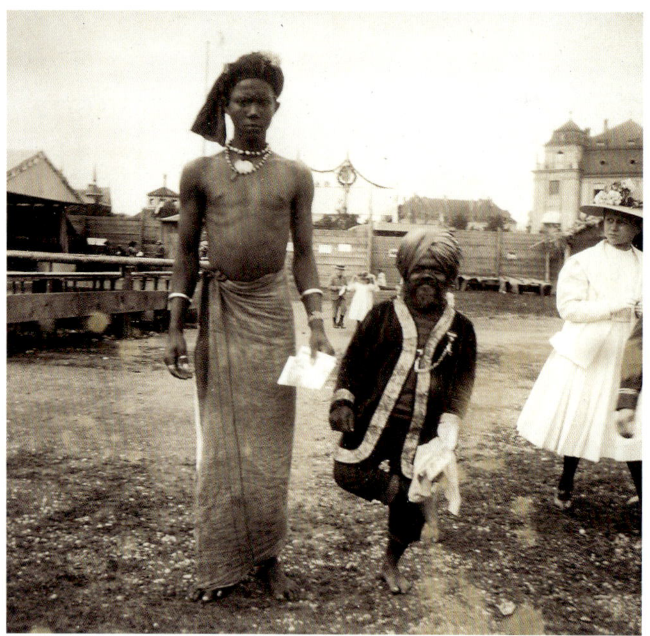

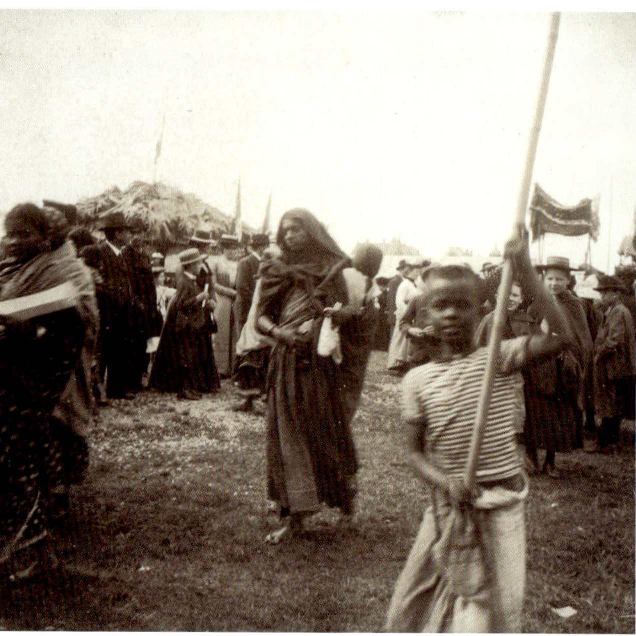

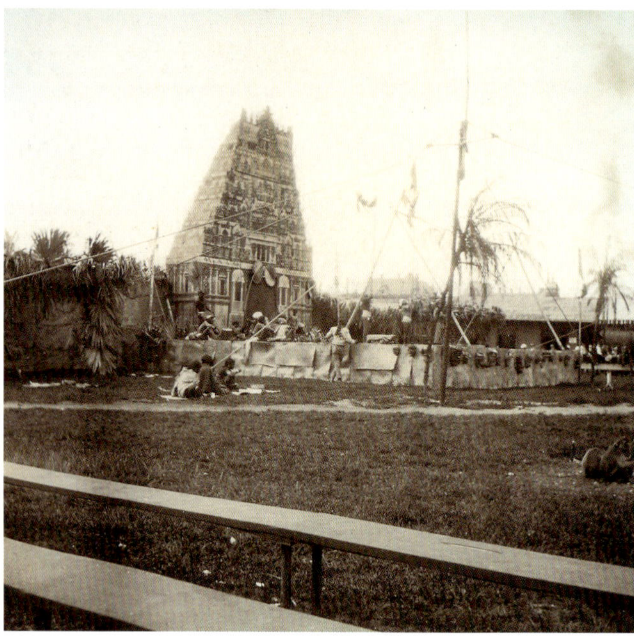

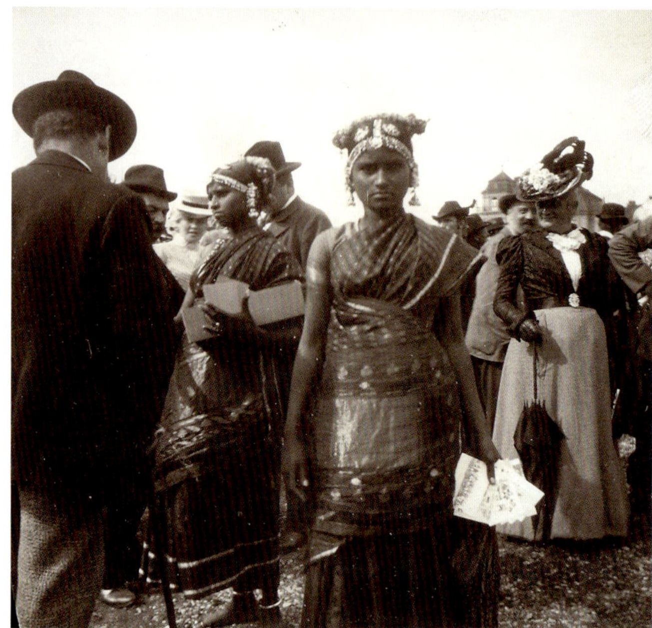

Cat. 157, 158, 159, 160, 161, and 162
Ethnological exposition ["Völkerschau"], Munich, 1901
Six photographs by Gabriele Münter, printing out paper, 8.9 × 8.9 cm | Gabriele Münter- und Johannes Eichner-Stiftung, Munich, inv. no. 3000-3005

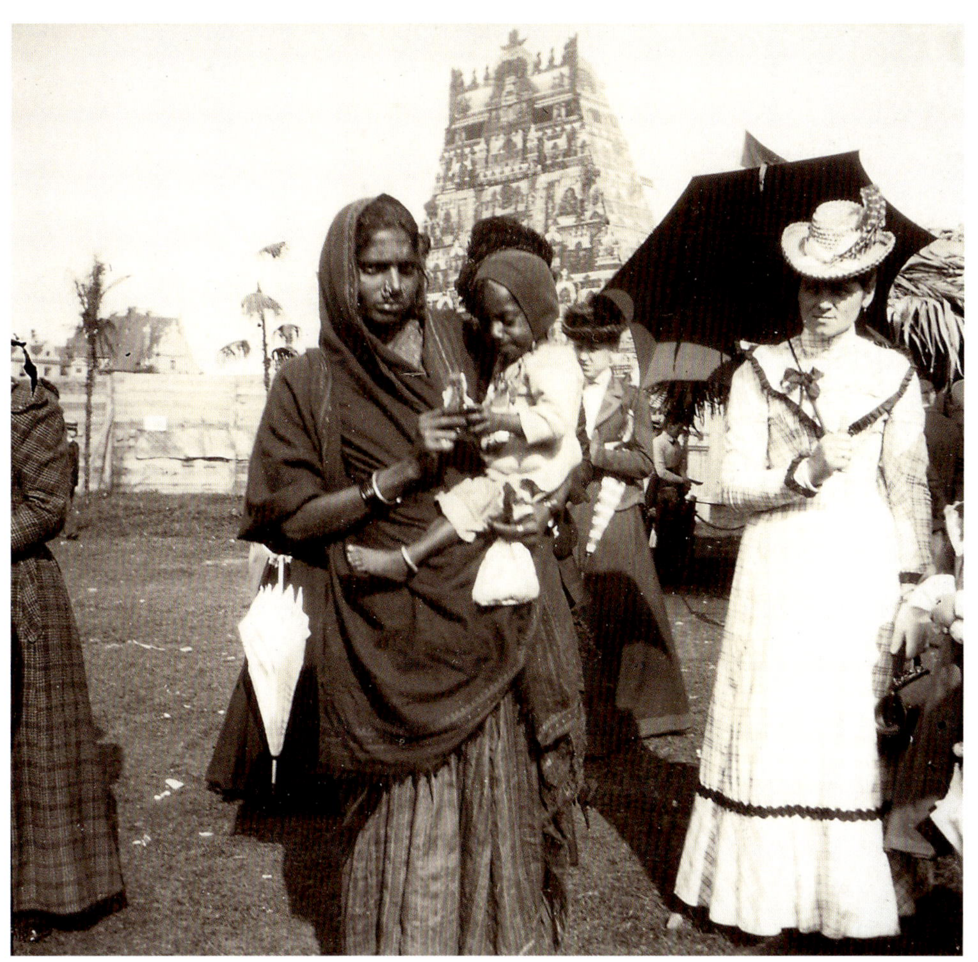

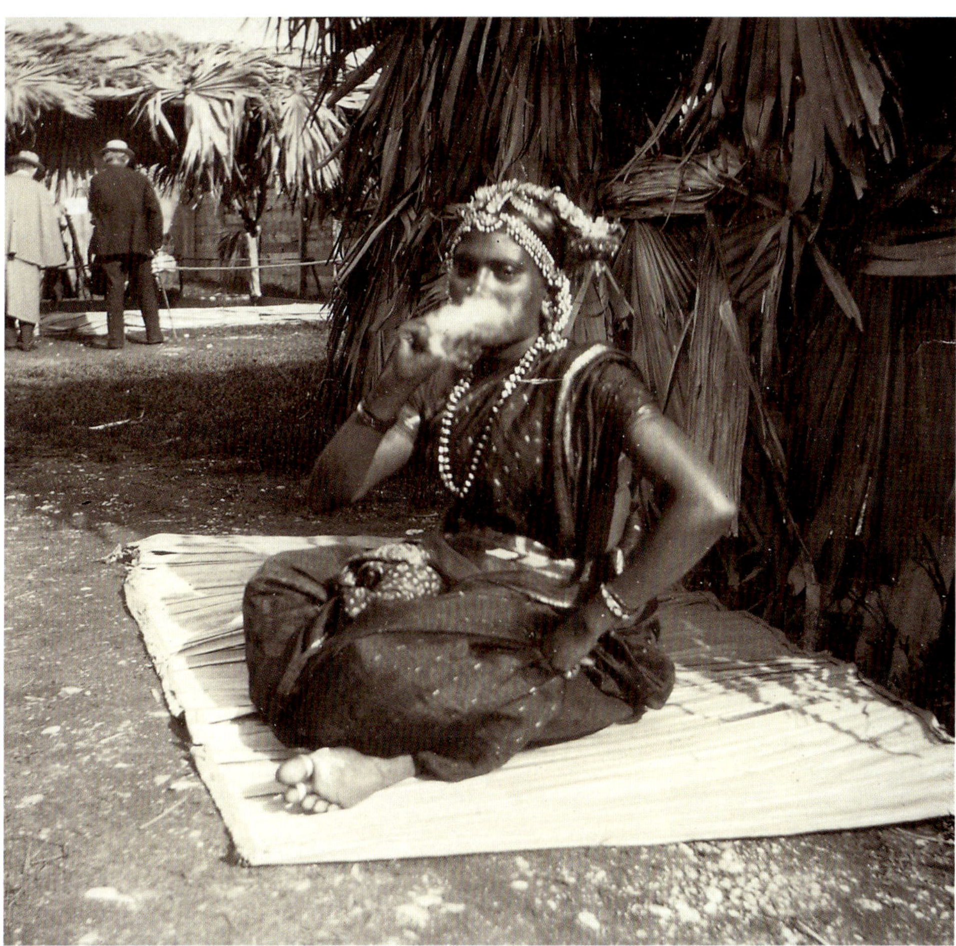

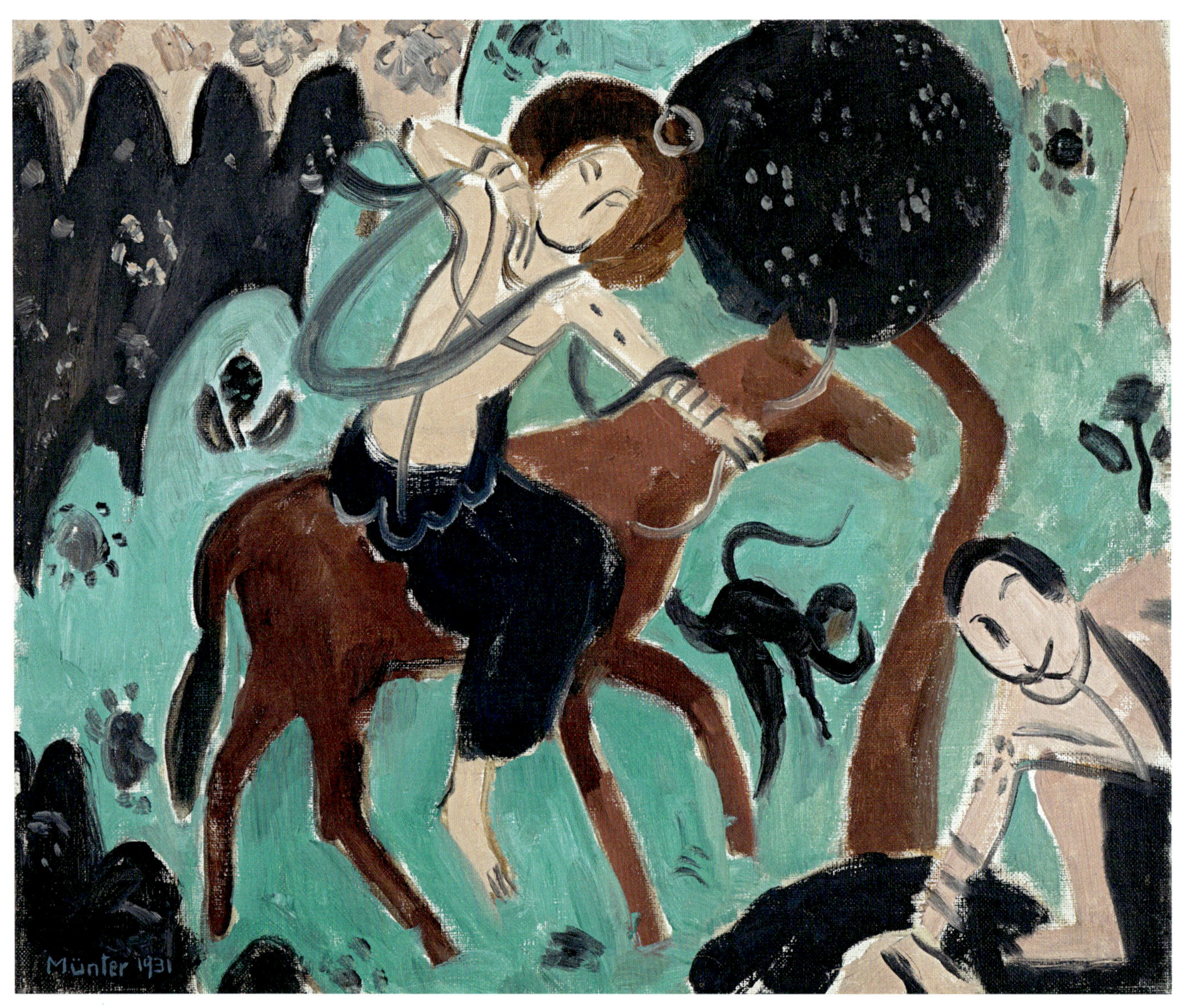

Cat. 163
Buddha Legend (Turkestan) [Buddha-Legende (Turkestan)], 1931
Textile support, 38.4 × 46.5 cm | Gabriele Münter- und Johannes Eichner-Stiftung, Munich, inv. no. V 5

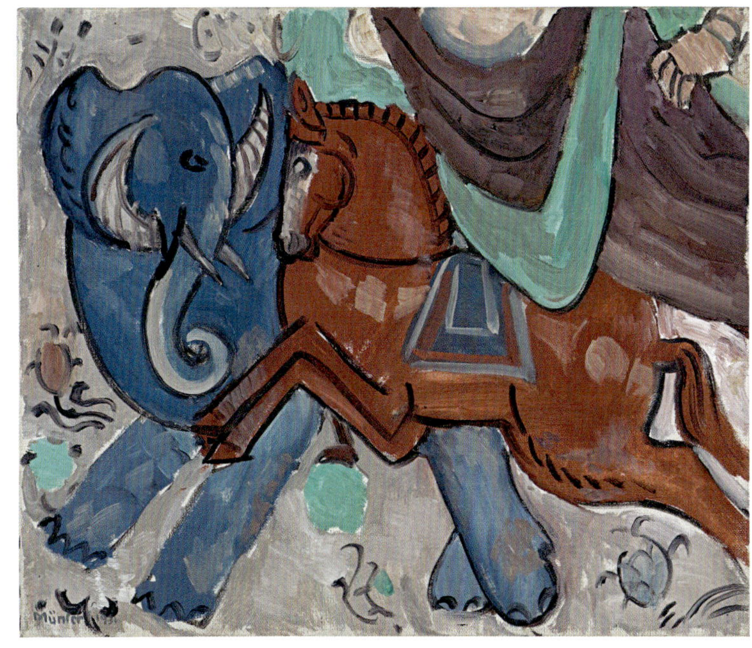

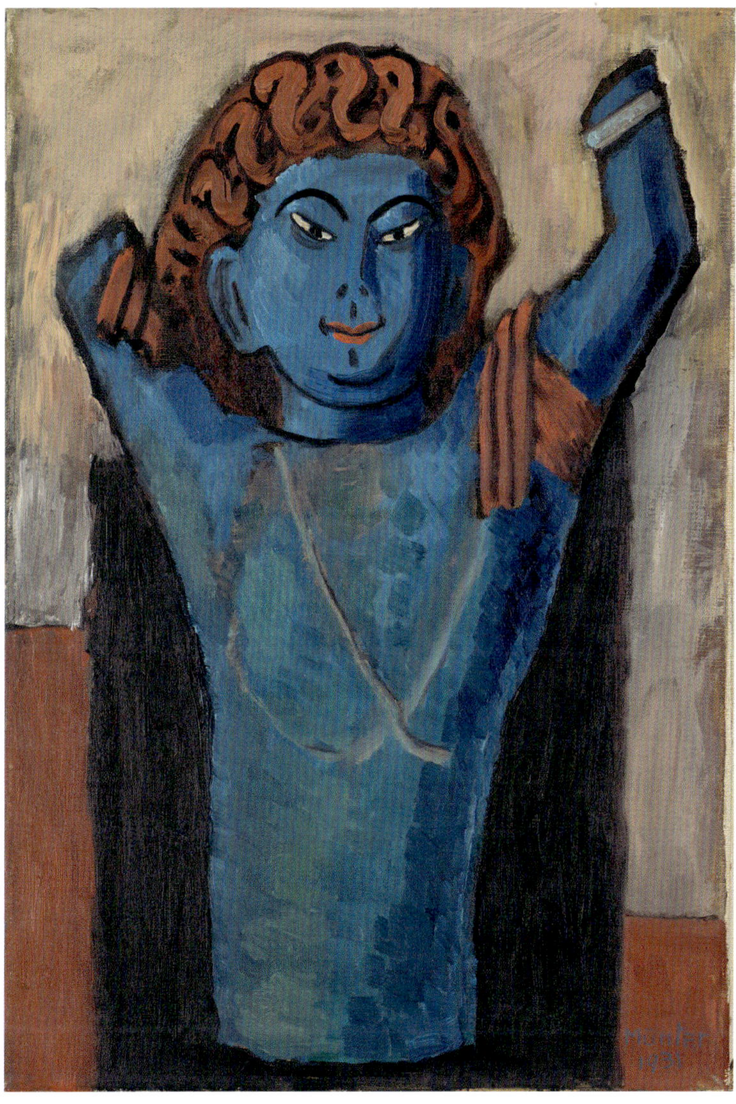

Cat. 164
Turkestanish (Elephant and Horse) [Turkestanisch (Elefant und Pferd)], 1931
Textile support, 38.8 × 46.2 cm | Gabriele Münter- und Johannes Eichner-Stiftung, Munich, inv. no. S 15

Cat. 165
The Blue Demon [Der blaue Dämon], 1931
Textile support, 55.5 × 38.5 cm | Gabriele Münter- und Johannes Eichner-Stiftung, Munich, inv. no. V 6

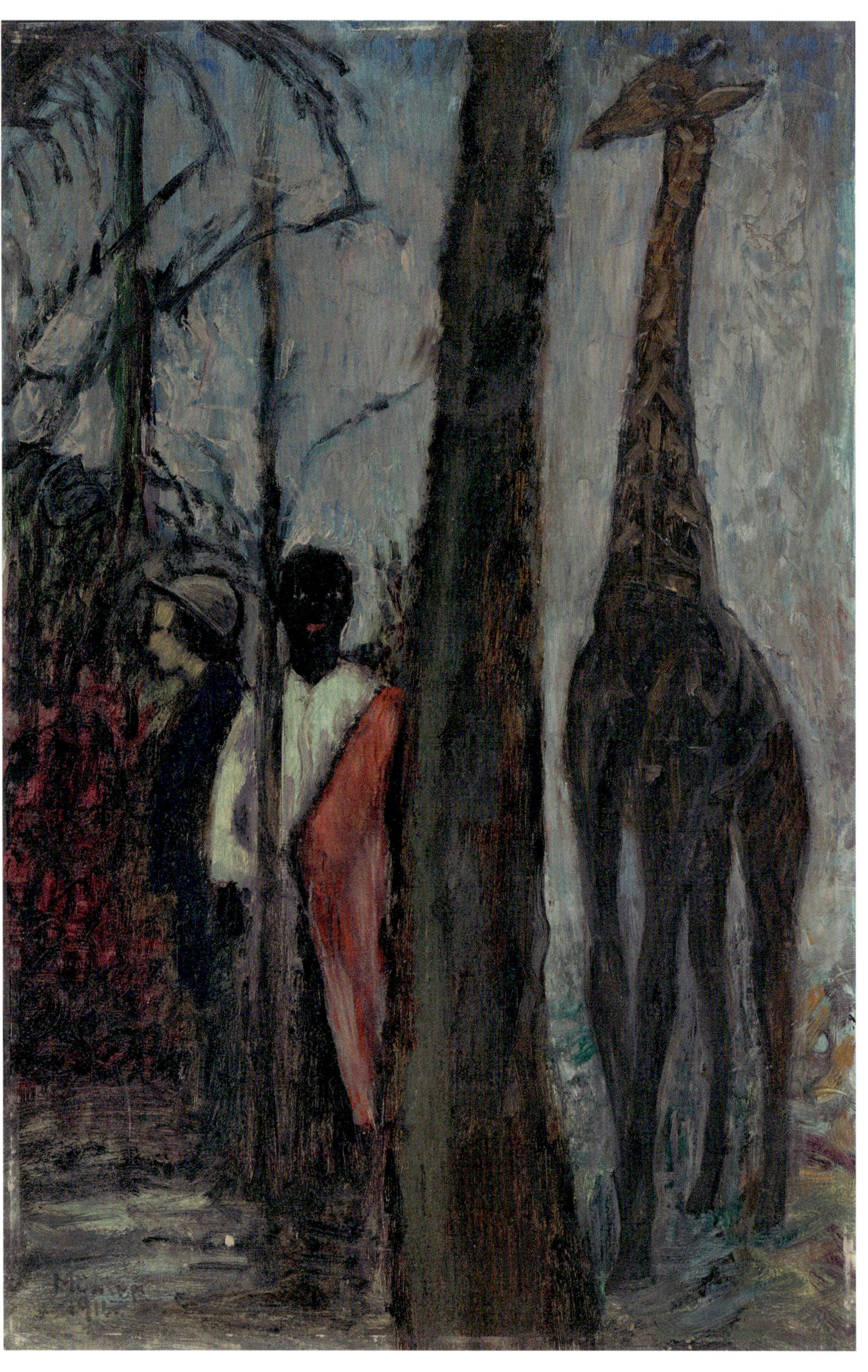

Cat. 166
In India [In Indien], 1916
Cardboard, 46.6 × 30.9 cm |
Gabriele Münter- und Johannes Eichner-Stiftung, Munich, inv. no. V 92

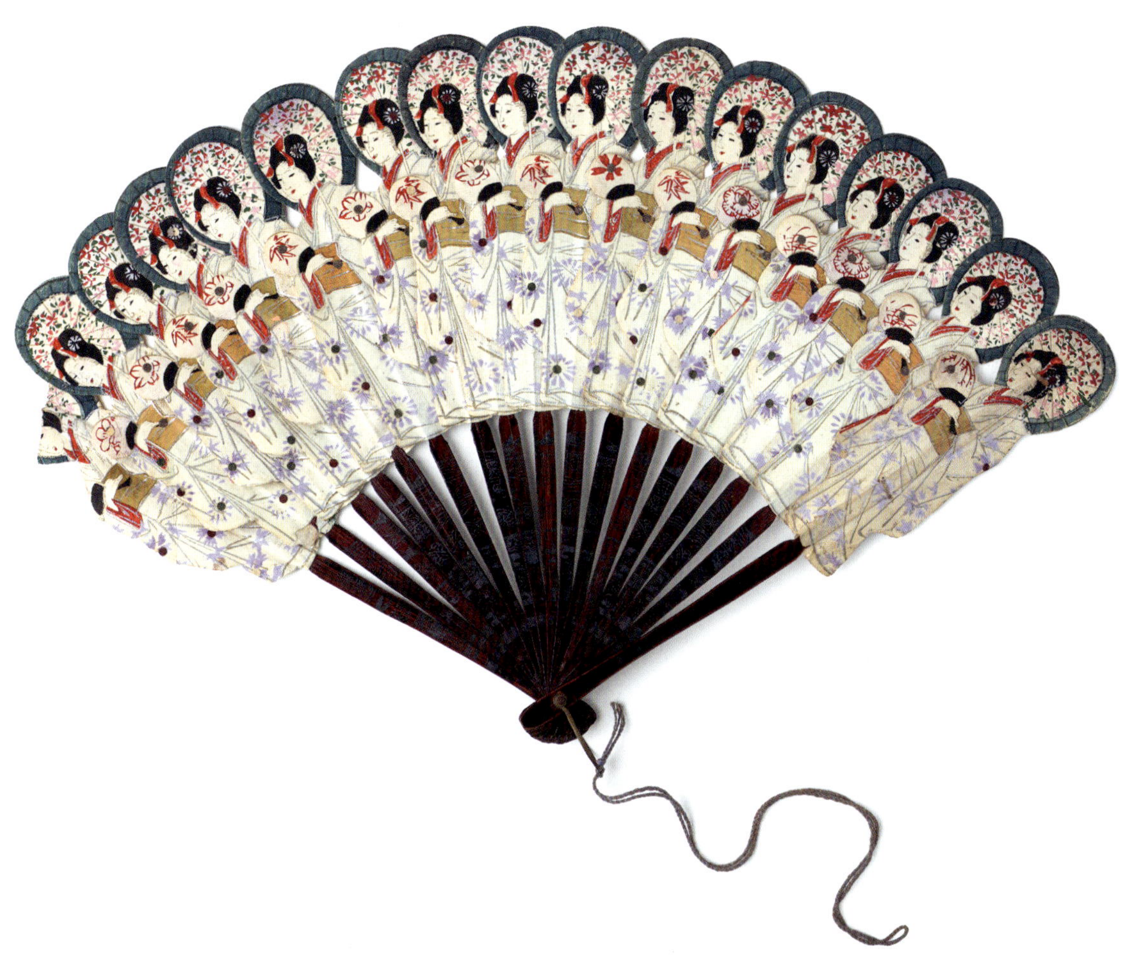

Cat. 167
Japanese fan
From Münter's belongings
Lacquered and printed wooden sticks with brass hinges and colored threads. Japan paper printed in multiple colors, with applied colored paper dots. Reverse: Glossy varnish, "speckled" | Gabriele Münter- und Johannes Eichner-Stiftung, Munich

“Now the time has come to experiment.”[1]

Repetitions and Variations

Repetitions and Variations

The exact repetition or variation of original pictorial ideas is a phenomenon that emerged in Münter's painting quite early on and persisted into the last years of her career. Replications and variations of certain motifs were produced either in close succession or over periods of years and even decades. Münter later described this working method in the following words: "Sometimes I do preliminary sketches or paint a picture over and over again (as many as 7 times) until I am satisfied with the outcome or until I simply can't go on. So it was with the Blue Lake in 1913. I painted the subject 7 × –."[2] Four versions of this motif are known to us today, the latest of which dates from 1958.[3] Cat. 74

Particularly noteworthy is the fact that this creative process, which includes the practices of repetition and variation, clearly contradicts the prevailing image of Gabriele Münter as a naïve artist who worked intuitively. In her case, self-repetition usually went hand in hand with work on an artistic problem, which reflects a tendency toward self-criticism and self-correction. The term "self-repetition," referring to the repetition of one's own creations, cannot be reduced to a simple definition. It encompasses various aspects of the creative process: "There is the replica as a repetition of a work by its creator, as opposed to a copy made by another artist. A replica differs from a variation, which, although it recognizably bears a close resemblance to an existing work, clearly deviates from it in certain ways. And then there is the version, in which the underlying idea of a work is reformulated while the original visual context and compositional scheme are retained."[4] It is a highly productive practice that is "deliberately employed in modern art."[5]

As early as 1904/05, during her stay in Tunis, Münter painted some motifs multiple times; among these were her *Landscape with a Blue Mountain (Tunis)*, of which two variations exist.[6] In 1906, the artist painted two variations of the view of the bay in Rapallo, Figs. A; B where she spent the winter with Kandinsky. Both works are painted on textile supports, which Münter probably mounted on cardboard herself. The dimensions are nearly identical (17 × 25.1 centimeters and 18.5 × 27 centimeters), as are motif and composition. The only difference is that the distance from the subject—the boardwalk with the cabins and the boats in the water—is slightly greater in one of the works. Münter presumably painted both

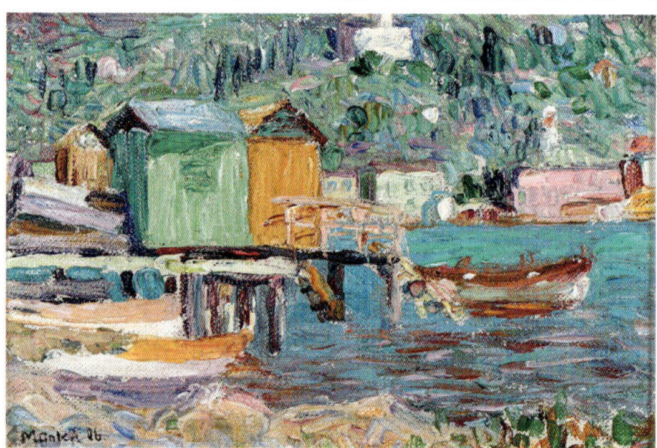

A **Bagni Louisa, Rapallo, 1906**
Oil on canvas, mounted on cardboard, 18.5 × 27 cm | THE EKARD COLLECTION

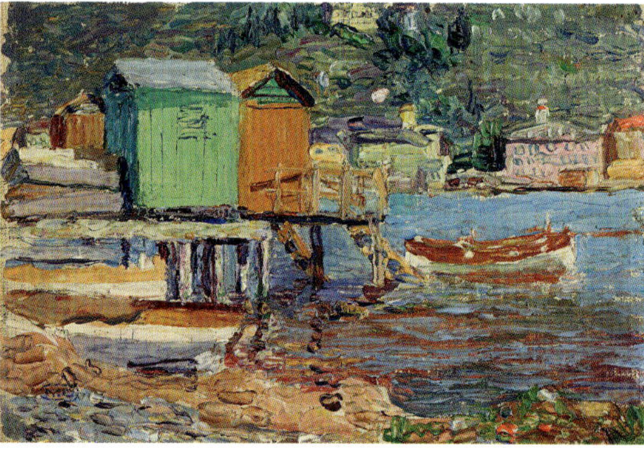

B **At the Beach in Rapallo (Bagni Louisa) [Am Strand von Rapallo (Bagni Louisa)], 1906**
Oil on canvas, mounted on cardboard, 17 × 25.1 cm | Private collection, Southern Germany

1
Translated from diary entry of February 14, 1940, MES.

2
Translated from undated note, MES.

3
Oil on canvas, 49.5 × 64.5 cm, Museum für Kommunikation, Frankfurt am Main. Two other versions, whose whereabouts are unknown, were completed before 1914.

4
Translated from the introduction to *'wiederholungstäter': die selbstwiederholung als künstlerische praxis in der moderne,* ed. Verena Krieger and Sophia Stang, Cologne, Weimar, Vienna 2017, p. 8. The concept of self-repetition was popularized at the conference of the same title, which took place at the Staatsgalerie Stuttgart in conjunction with the exhibition *Giorgio de Chirico: Magie der Moderne* from April 21 to 23, 2016.

5
Ibid.

6
Tunis Landscape, oil on canvas, mounted and glued on cardboard, 16.7 × 25.2 cm, private collection. *Landscape with a Blue Mountain*, 25 × 37 cm, oil on canvas, private collection; color plate in exh. cat. Munich 1977, p. 50.

7
See the chapter "Pre-Painting: Münter's Early Work," p. 16.

8
Sketchbook, inv. no. Kon. 37/12, MES. Reinhold Heller provides a detailed analysis of this figure composition in his essay "Innenräume: Erlebnis, Erinnerung und Synthese in der Kunst Gabriele Münters," sin exh. cat. Munich/Frankfurt/Stockholm 1992/93, pp. 47–49 and 59–62.

9
Translated from letter of March 3, 1904, MES.

10
Translated from Reinhold Heller, "Innenräume," in exh. cat. Munich/Frankfurt/Stockholm 1992/93, note 25, p. 65.

works outdoors at the same time. She had already experimented with this method of depicting a given motif both close up and from a distance in some of the photographs from her travels in the United States.[7]

She began employing the principle of self-repetition regularly in 1909. One famous example is the scene showing Kandinsky and Erma Bossi at a table. The two are seated in the dining corner in the living room of the house in Murnau purchased by Münter in August 1909. They are immersed in conversation. Münter realized four nearly identical variations of this scene between 1909/10 and 1912. Cat. 172; 173; Figs. C; D The only discernible differences are in minor details, such as individual objects on the wall and along the top of the wood paneling and the design of the tablecloth and dishware.

Another figure composition also dates from 1912: *After Tea I* and *After Tea II*, for which Münter did numerous preparatory pencil sketches. Figs. E; F The work recalls a visit by the art dealer Hans Goltz in Kandinsky's and Münter's apartment on Ainmillerstraße in Munich. A sketchbook contains ten loose sheets and three pages featuring sketches of the individual figures, different perspective views of the room, the entire composition of *After Tea II*, and pictorial conceptions in which elements of *After Tea I* and *II* are mixed.[8] In contrast to *Kandinsky and Erma Bossi at the Table*, the two versions of this work were executed in the same year, are the same size, were painted on cardboard, and exhibit significant differences in composition. Most importantly, the sketches offer clear evidence of the intensity with which Münter devoted herself to this subject and her quest for a satisfactory solution. She wrote Kandinsky in 1904, saying, "perhaps my horrid mood was merely [an expression of] my longing for you. But it was initially a product of my reluctance to work and the fact that I wanted to paint without a drawing—which isn't possible—you can't paint what you can't draw."[9] According to Reinhold Heller, her elaborate preliminary studies enabled her "to fix the scene in her mind, so that she could then realize a 'spontaneous' painting."[10] Heller states that Münter adopted this method from Kandinsky. This assessment of Münter's working method requires some qualification, however. These figure compositions were the first ones Münter had ever painted, which would explain her uncertainty and her need

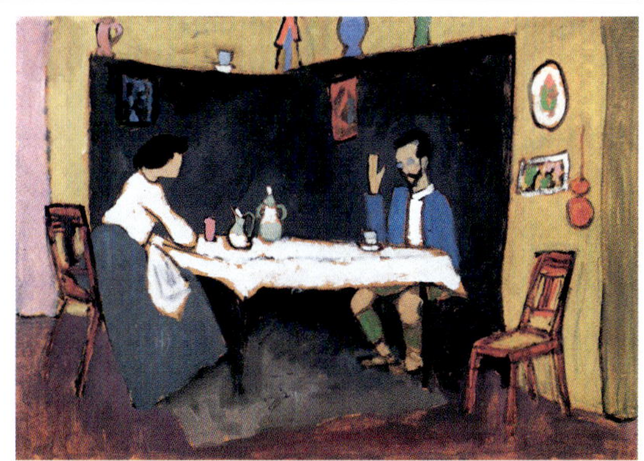

C **After the Meal (Kandinsky and Erma Bossi) [Nach Tisch (Kandinsky und Erma Bossi)], 1909/10**
Oil on cardboard, 44.5 × 65.2 cm | Private collection

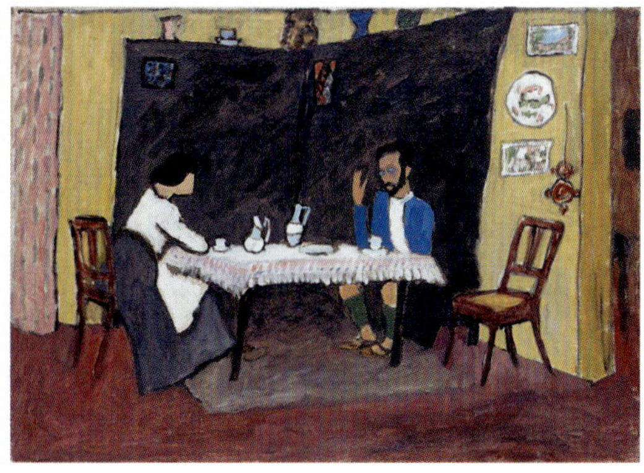

D **Kandinsky and Erma Bossi at the Table [Kandinsky und Erma Bossi am Tisch], ca. 1910**
Oil on canvas, 49.3 × 70 cm | Schloßmuseum Murnau, inv. no. 7370

to experiment with the motif in numerous sketches.[11] In addition, they are exceptions within the context of Münter's creative process, since she usually did only one preliminary sketch (at most) for a single painting.

Münter presumably painted a third, larger version of the scene from *After Tea*, of which only one part—showing *Kandinsky in Interior*—has survived. Cat. 103 This piece is a section of the right half of *After Tea II*. Kandinsky is shown standing in front of a table with his hands folded in a posture he typically assumed in conversation. Recognizable on the wall is a painting by Henri Rousseau, *The Painter and His Model*.[12] However, the painting hanging below it is not the same one shown in *After Tea II*, which is a colored work, whereas the scene that appears in *Kandinsky in Interior* is black and white. It is quite possible that Münter was not satisfied with this version, which was 34 centimeters higher than *After Tea II*, and that she cut it to size herself.[13] She appears to have regarded the resulting fragment as a finished painting, as her signature in the lower left corner indicates.

We find another example of self-repetition in the motif of Kocheler Landstraße. Münter depicted the road in two paintings titled *Straight Road* in 1910. Figs. G; H The idea for the painting is based on a photograph she took in 1902.[14] She explained her reason for painting a replica of the work in a letter to Kandinsky dated November 7, 1910: "Since I consider the Kocheler straight road study very good, I definitely want to send it to Moscow. But because I can't do it better, I've copied it in an even larger version—as precisely as possible—although the sm[all] study is better."[15] Kandinsky was in Moscow at the time, organizing the submission of works by members of the Neue Künstlervereinigung München (New Artists' Association Munich) for the exhibition presented by the Bubnovy Valet (Jack of Diamonds) group.[16] Thus Münter painted a reproduction of *Straight Road* for that show, although she was not happy with the outcome. Whereas she had allowed the cardboard to show through in the first painting, she covered it completely with paint in the other variation, producing a stiff impression. As a result, the second work looks a bit like a painting exercise. The painting lost its vitality in the attempt

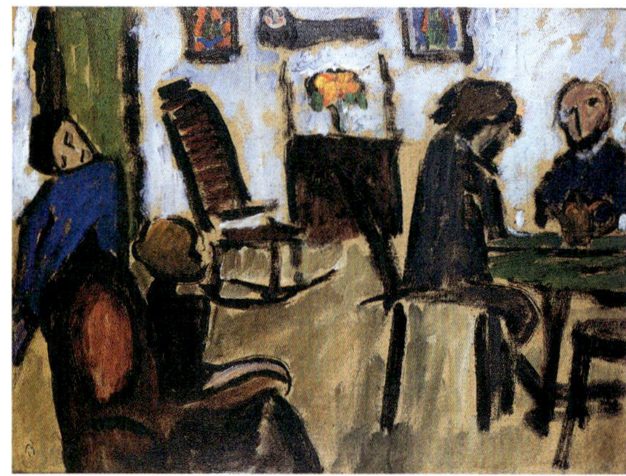

E **After Tea I [Nach dem Tee I], 1912**
Oil on cardboard, 51.5 × 68.5 cm | Toyota Sogo Co., Ltd., Toyota-shi

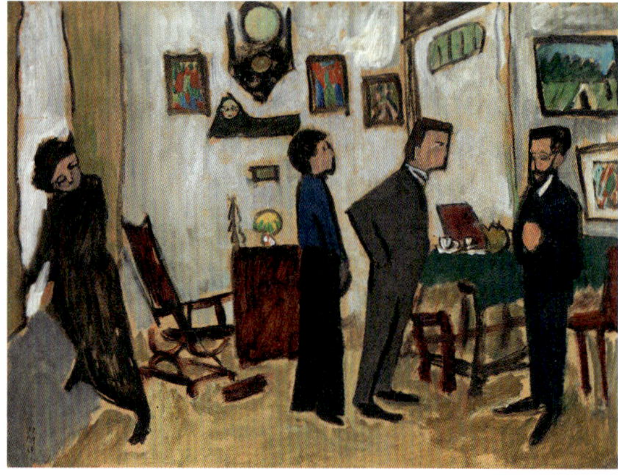

F **After Tea II [Nach dem Tee II], 1912**
Oil on cardboard, 51.1 × 68.3 cm | Private collection

11
See the chapter "Interior Scenes," p. 114.

12
Le peintre et son modèle, 1900–1905, oil on canvas, 46.5 × 55.5 cm, Musée national d'art moderne – Centre Pompidou, Paris. Legs Mme Nina Kandinsky 1981, inv. no. AM 81-65-861.

13
The painting is from the artist's estate and is listed as cut apart in the estate inventory book. Since the back of the painting is covered with an aluminum plate today, the edges of the canvas are no longer visible. Consequently, it is impossible to determine whether Münter painted the canvas in the present format or whether she cut it apart after painting it.

14
Exh. cat. Munich 2007, plate 9.

15
Translated from letter of November 7, 1910, MES.

16
Moscow, December 1910–January 1911. On the Neue Künstlervereinigung München, see the chapter "Portraits," p. 102.

17
Self-repetition inevitably leads to the development of groups of works or series. In most cases, the series appear to play no conceptual role in Münter's oeuvre. They were simply the result of her intense work with a given motif. The series devoted to the theme of sleep may represent an exception, however. The eight paintings were realized in just a few days between January 26 and February 2, 1934, and Münter documented their production meticulously.

18
Entry in the artist's logbook. Sketchbook, inv. no. Kon. 37/17 (1930/31), pp. 25, 27, 31, MES. Johannes Eichner wrote that the motif was inspired by a young girl seen tossing and turning on the train out of sheer boredom; Eichner 1957, p. 187.

to copy it. How important the first variation was to her is clearly indicated by the frequency with which she exhibited it.

Numerous series were produced in the particularly productive decade of the 1930s.[17] Münter painted several variations on the subject of sleep in 1934. In a few days in January/February 1934 she realized eight pictures, each depicting the upper body of a sleeping young girl. Cat. 177; 178 She is shown lying on her back in some cases, on her side with her arm bent over her face in others. The artist was inspired in this case by sketches she had made during a stay in France in 1929/30.[18] We note a tendency toward an abstract painting style in these works. Although the first version is quite realistic, Münter made use of a simplified formal language and dark contours in the last version. Fig. I; Cat. 178 Typical of Münter's

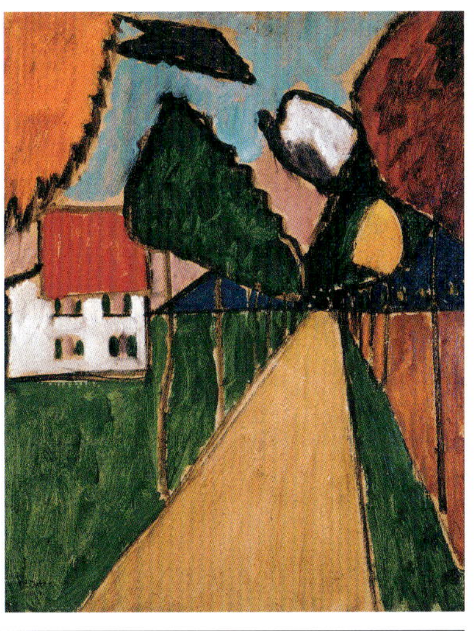

G **Straight Road [Gerade Straße], 1910**
Oil on cardboard, 40.5 × 32.9 cm | Kunstmuseum Ravensburg / Loan from the Peter und Gudrun Selinka-Stiftung, Ravensburg, inv. no. SEL 2012/0009

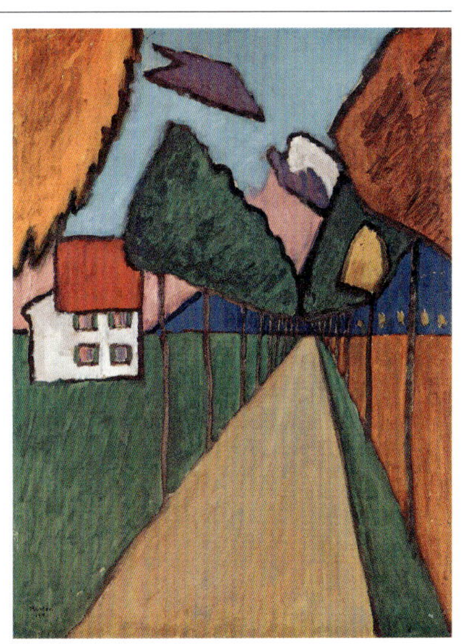

H **Straight Road [Gerade Straße], 1910**
Oil on cardboard, 67.5 × 49.5 cm | Private collection

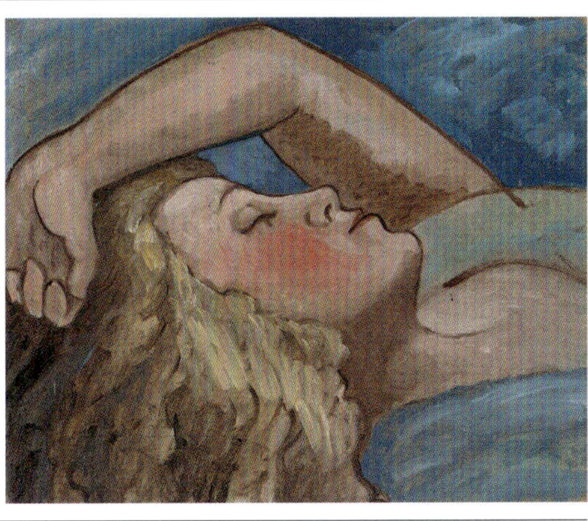

I **Sleeping Girl, Blonde [Schlafendes Mädchen, blond), 1934**
Cardboard, 40.8 × 32.8 cm | Gabriele Münter- und Johannes Eichner-Stiftung, Munich, inv. no. P 105

self-repetition process in the 1930s and later years is the large number of paintings within a group of works. This clearly reflects both her love of experimentation and the demanding standards she set with respect to the results.[19]

Johannes Eichner, Münter's life partner from 1928, played an occasional role in her pictorial development process, as is recognizable in her *Evening Landscape with White Moon*. Presumably working outdoors, the artist did a small oil sketch featuring the motif in 1938. She then realized a larger painting based on her sketch.[20] Two years later, she painted an even larger version in a sober style very close to that of New Objectivity. Fig. J She mentioned it in her diary on February 14, 1940: "The beginning of the painting was dark, delicately colored, very

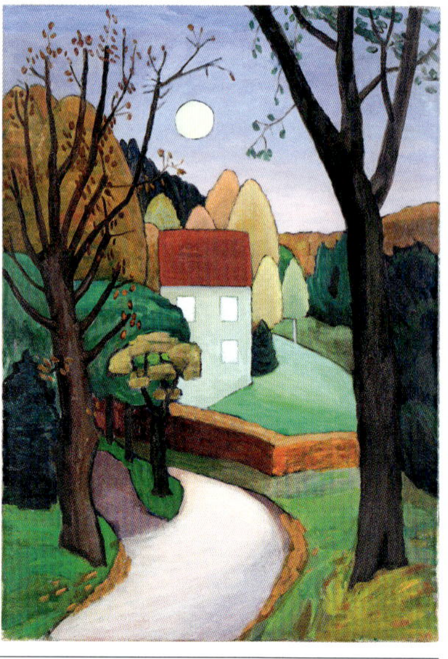

J **Evening Landscape with White Moon (Rising Moon) [Abendlandschaft mit weißem Mond (Aufgehender Mond)], 1940**
Oil on canvas, 85.4 × 60.5 cm | Museum Wiesbaden, gift from M. and W. Rick 2013

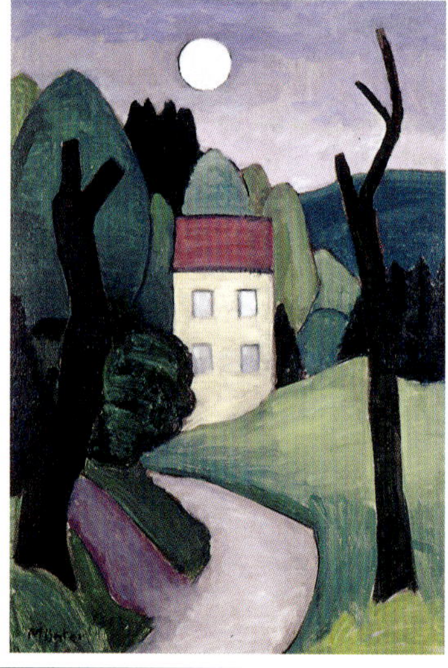

K **Evening Landscape with White Moon (House in the Country) [Abendlandschaft mit weißem Mond (Haus im Grünen)], 1940**
Oil on cardboard, 66 × 46.5 cm | Kunstsammlungen Chemnitz, inv. no. L210, permanent loan from the Sammlung Claus Hüppe

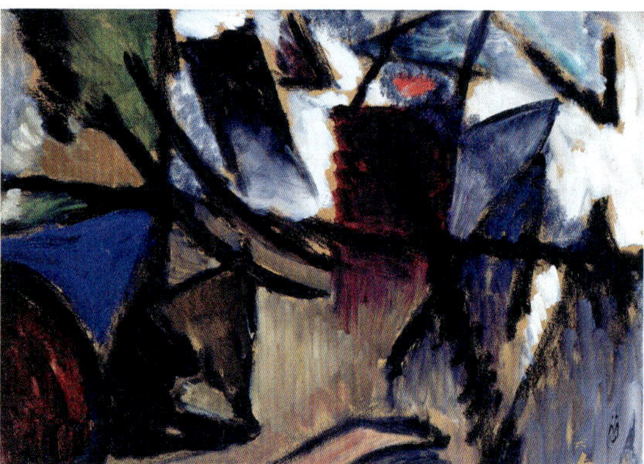

L **Abstraction [Abstraktion], 1912**
Oil on cardboard, 50 × 71 cm | Staatliche Museen zu Berlin, Nationalgalerie. Permanent loan from the State of Berlin, inv. no. B 72/20

19
Doll, Cat, Child is another motif which she painted at least seven times, using different techniques, between 1930 and 1950. One version is reproduced in this catalogue, p. 143.

20
Landscape with a Full Moon, 1938, oil on cardboard, 14 × 9.9 cm, private collection; *Evening Landscape with a White Moon*, 1938, oil on canvas, 65.1 × 50 cm, current whereabouts unknown.

21
Diary, MES.

22
Kleine 1994, p. 550.

23
For other tour venues see the appendix, p. 264. On Eichner's role in the process of popularizing Münter's art, see the chapter "Promoting the Art of Gabriele Münter," p. 245.

24
One of the best-known examples is the motif of the Vilsgasse in Kallmünz, which she photographed, sketched, painted, and depicted in a print. See exh. cat. Munich/Bonn/Murnau 2000/01, no. 2, and Isabelle Jansen, "Fotografieren oder Malen? Das Wechselspiel zwischen Fotografie und Malerei im Frühwerk von Gabriele Münter," in exh. cat. Kochel am See 2015, pp. 150–51.

25
Reinhold Heller, "Innenräume," in exh. cat. Munich/Frankfurt/Stockholm 1992/93, p. 48; Eichner 1957, pp. 154–55.

26
See the chapters "Pre-Painting: Münter's Early Work," p. 16, and "Primitivism," p. 146.

harmonious—[afternoon] overpainted in brighter tones, with a very different effect—there's still a lot to be done there. Interesting, wonderful work. Ei[chner] came over around noon with lot [*sic*] of wishes and suggestions. Now the time has come to experiment." The next day she wrote, "finished the branches—it's become an 'autumn landscape' with yellow trees. I think Ei[chner] talked me into too much."[21] The next day she proceeded to paint yet another version based on a drawing by Eichner and his instructions: "I drew the moon picture again from Ei[chner]'s drawing and then asked him to dictate the next steps. We worked together until noon. Cool, bright. Not a Münter, more like an Eichner." Fig. K After completing his studies in philosophy, Eichner had studied art history under Heinrich Wölfflin in Berlin.[22] He actively promoted Münter's art by writing articles about it and above all by organizing exhibitions of her work, such as the touring exhibition entitled *Gabriele Münter: "50 Gemälde aus 25 Jahren" (1908–1933)*, which opened at the Paula Modersohn-Becker-Haus in Bremen in April 1933 and spent the following two years on tour.[23] Eichner's book *Kandinsky und Gabriele Münter: Von Ursprüngen moderner Kunst*, based in part on Münter's own recollections, was published in 1957. Yet his commitment went much further and even involved the painter's creative process. She appears to have regarded his behavior as a form of support rather than interference in her freedom as an artist. Her interest in Eichner's comments, some of which prompted her to do new paintings, is a sign of openness and, to some extent, of a certain sense of humility. She, the artist who had accumulated a wealth of experience over a period of decades, was willing to accept tips offered by a theorist, or at least to try them out.

The examples of self-repetition discussed in this chapter are limited to the replicas and variations of motifs in Münter's paintings. We also know, however, that the artist often depicted or repeated a given subject using different techniques.[24] Uncertainty, the desire to process experiences, her love of experimentation, and more practical considerations, such as the need for a copy for an exhibition, offered ample opportunities for multiple repetitions of a pictorial idea. Self-repetition also served as a principle of organization, as a means of resolving aesthetic issues. When Münter came to a standstill with a composition, she is said to have sometimes fled into abstraction.[25] One example is the painting *Abstraction*, which is an abstract variation of *After Tea*. Fig. L

In any event, Münter's frequent reliance on the practice of self-repetition clearly shows that her creative process was anything but consistent. Since the artist did not develop a systematic working method, she was always free to create something new. It is also an indication of the intensity with which Münter worked on some of her pictorial creations. This repetitive concern with a given work not only contradicts the popular idea that Münter painted thoughtlessly but may be understood as the expression of a certain continuity that was also a fundamental principle of her creative process.[26]

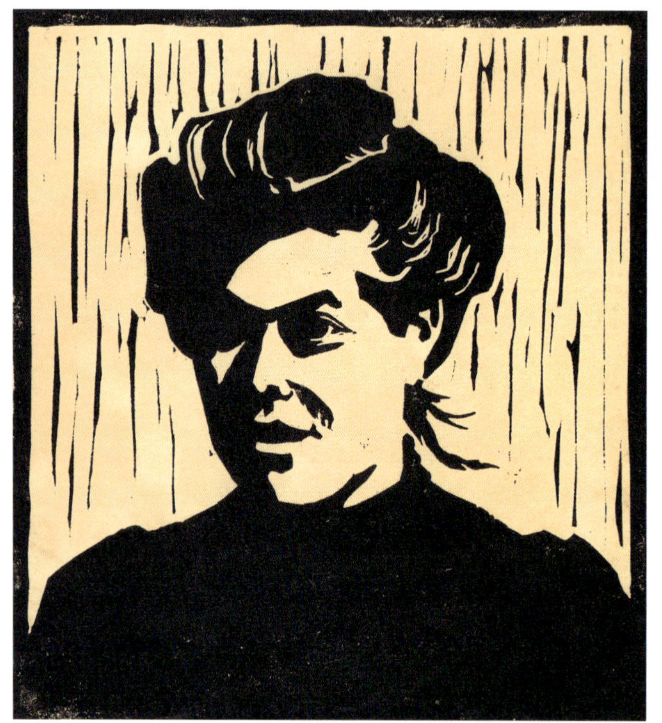

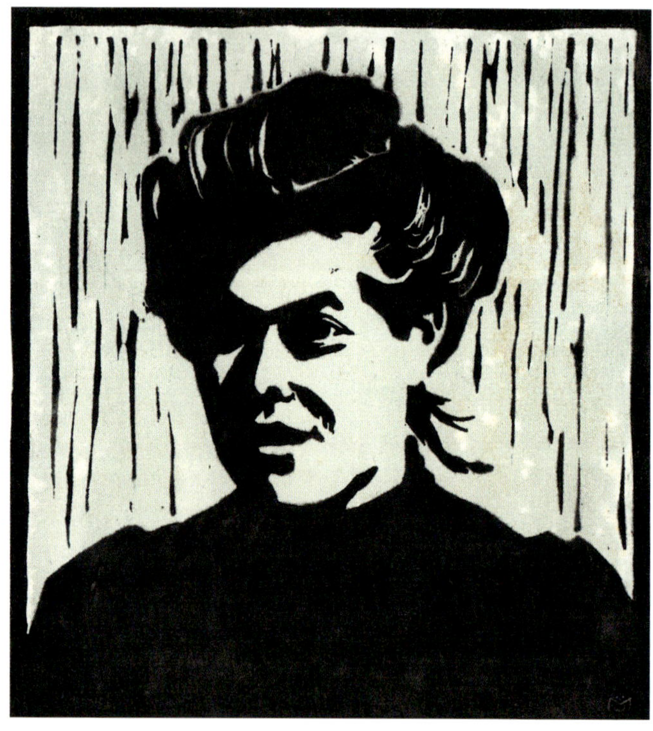

Cat. 168, 169, 170, and 171
Aurélie, 1906
1 linoleum cut on machine paper, 19 × 17.9 cm, inv. no. GMS 791
3 colored linoleum cuts on Japan paper, inv. no. GMS 792: 21 × 18.9 cm, inv. no. GMS 793: 18.7 × 17 cm, inv. no. GMS 794: 18.7 × 17 cm | Städtische Galerie im Lenbachhaus und Kunstbau München

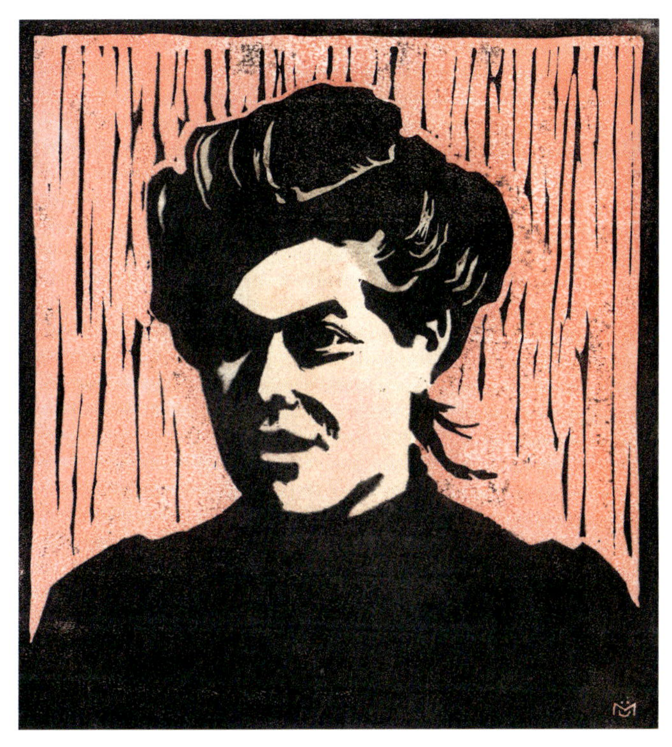

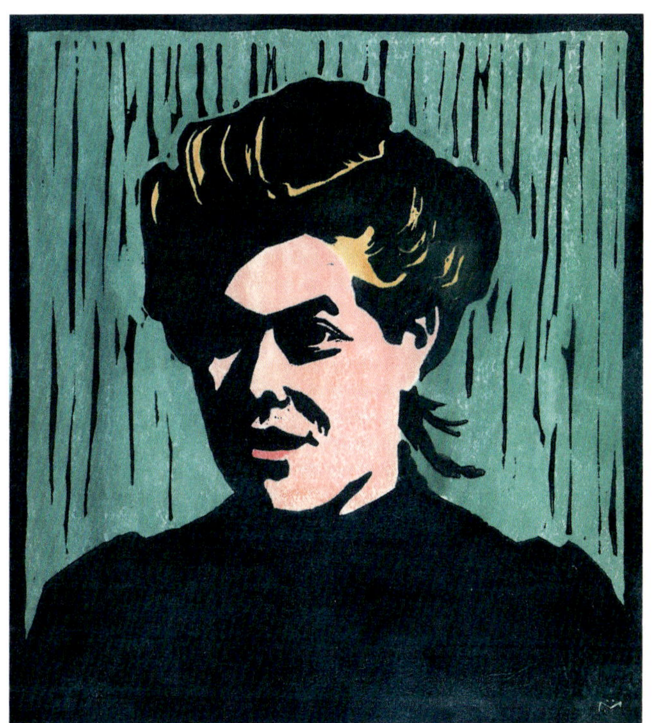

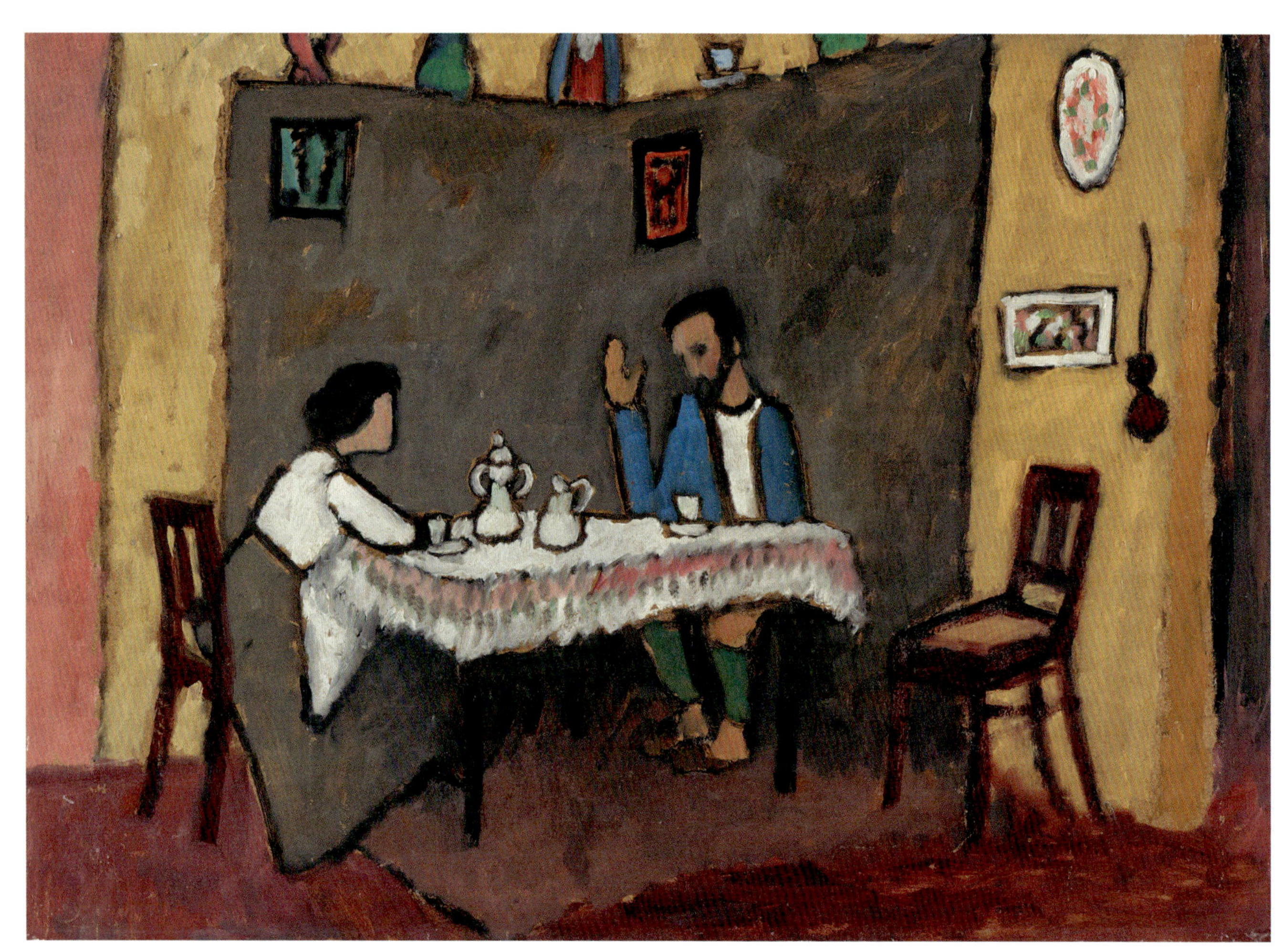

Cat. 172
Kandinsky and Erma Bossi [Kandinsky und Erma Bossi], ca. 1910
Oil on cardboard, 48.9 × 70.5 cm | Princeton University Art Museum. In loving memory of Frank and Peggy Taplin, inv. no. 2012-21

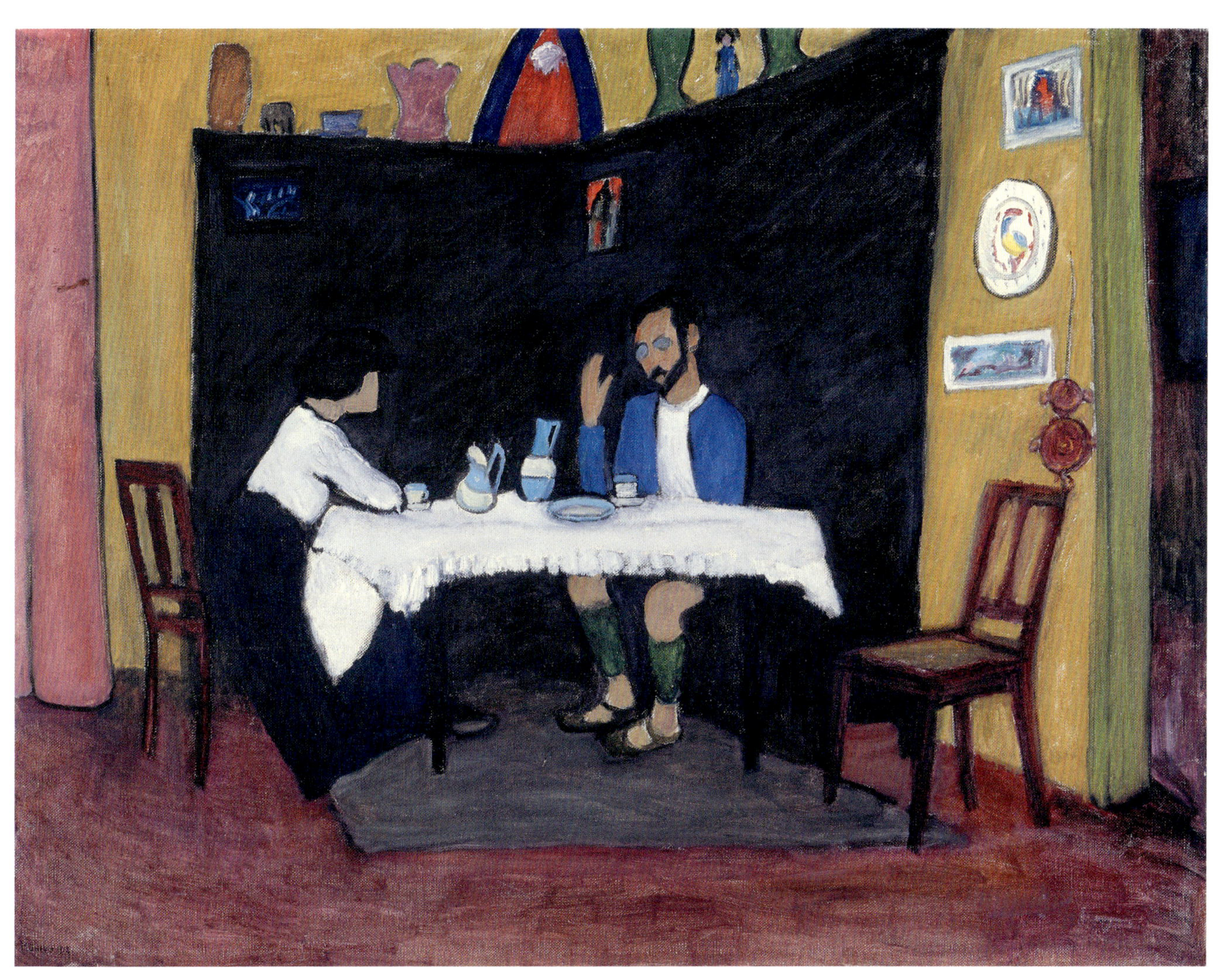

Cat. 173

Kandinsky and Erma Bossi at the Table (After the Meal) [Kandinsky und Erma Bossi am Tisch (Nach Tisch)], 1912

Textile support, 94.6 × 125 cm | Städtische Galerie im Lenbachhaus und Kunstbau München, inv. no. GMS 780

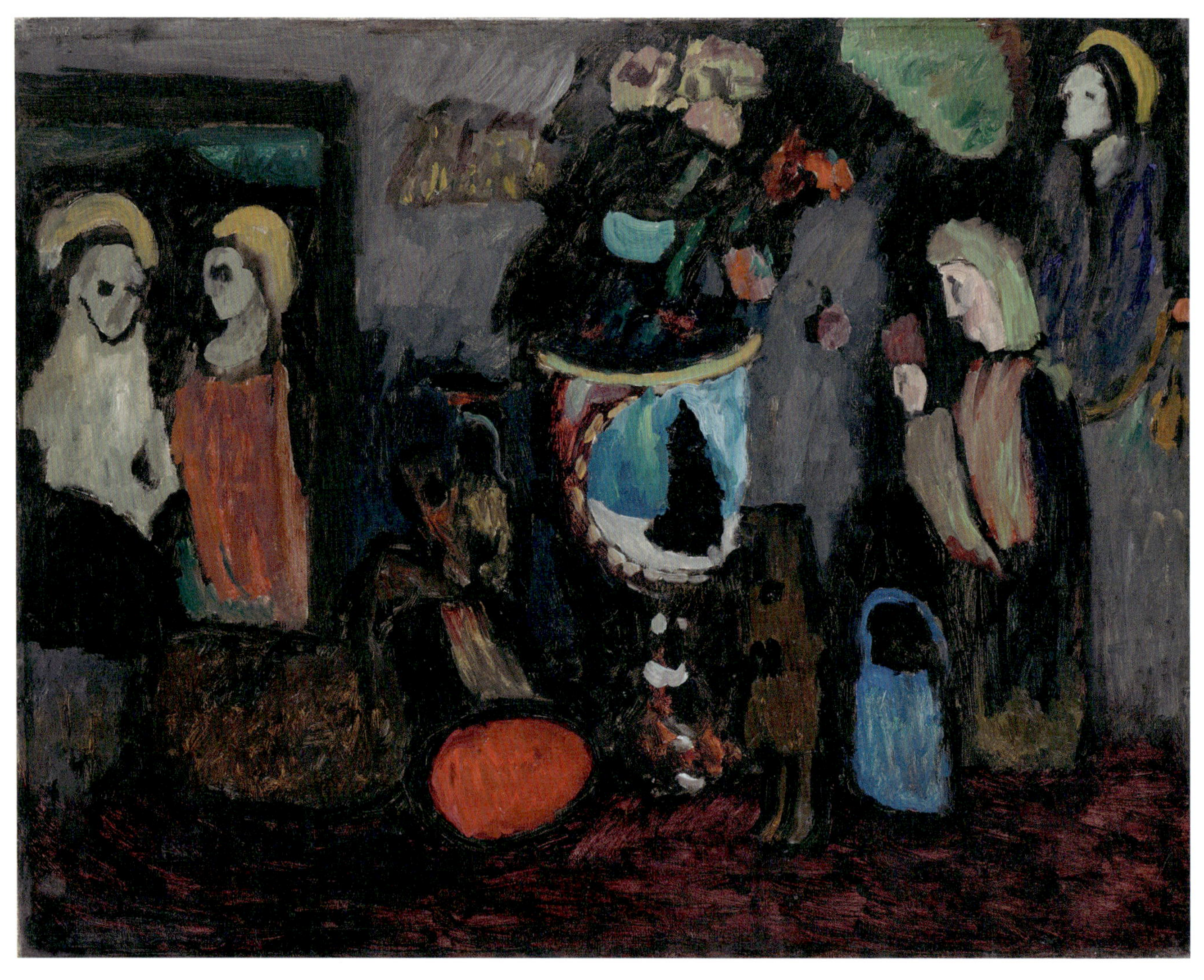

Cat. 174
Dark Still Life (Mystery) [Dunkles Stilleben (Geheimnis)], 1911
Textile support, 78.1 × 100.6 cm | Gabriele Münter- und Johannes Eichner-Stiftung, Munich, inv. no. S 152

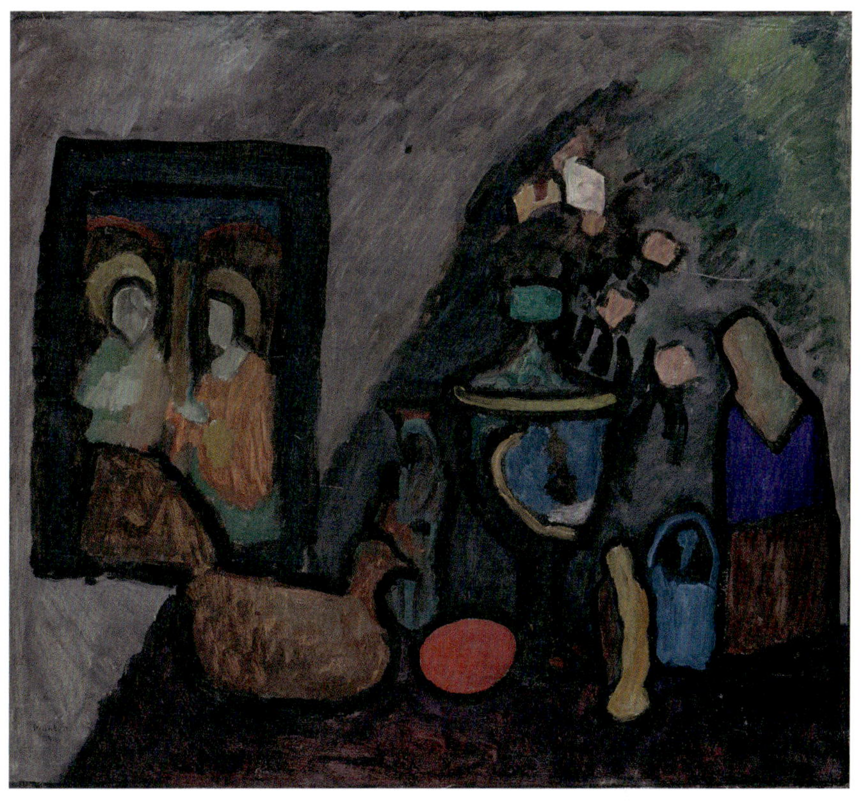

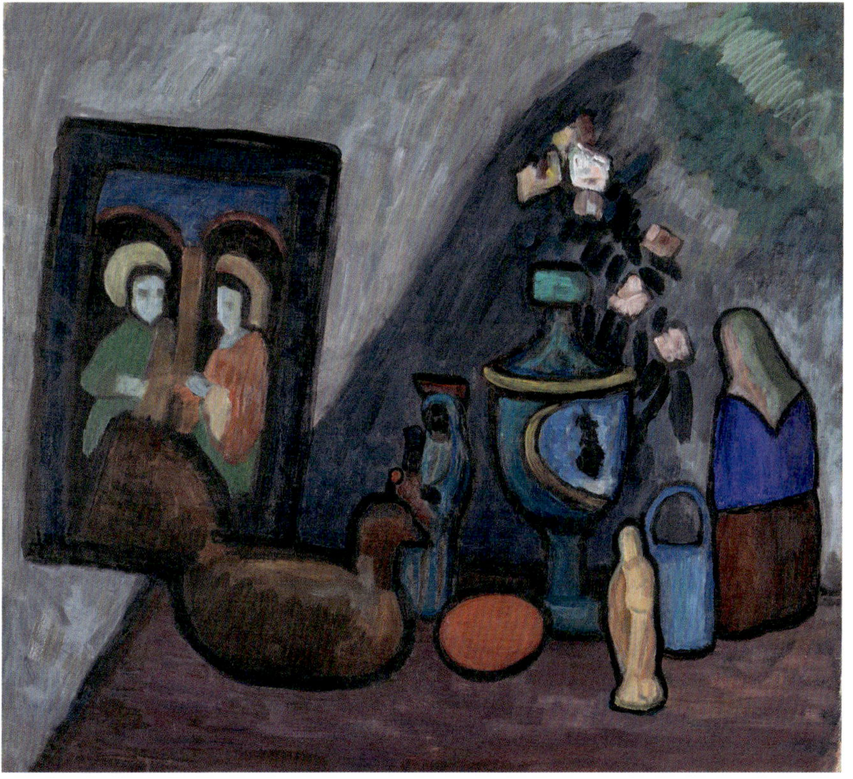

Cat. 175
Still Life Lament [Stilleben Klage], 1911
Cardboard on wood, 70.3 × 78.7 cm | Gabriele Münter- und Johannes Eichner-Stiftung, Munich, inv. no. S 106

Cat. 176
Still Life Mystery [Stilleben Geheimnis], 1912
Textile support, 70.8 × 78.4 cm | Gabriele Münter- und Johannes Eichner-Stiftung, Munich, inv. no. S 4

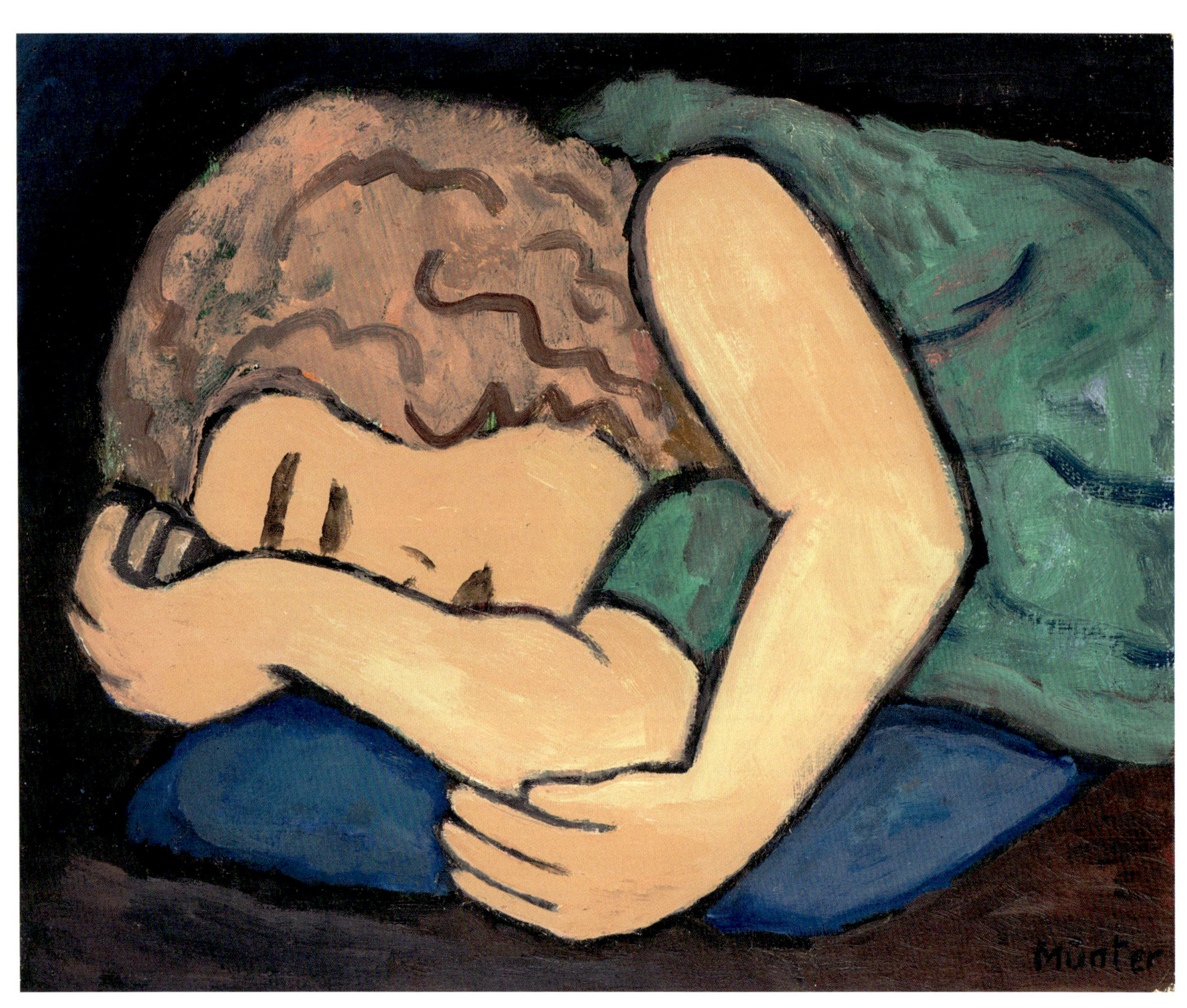

Cat. 177

Sleeping Child (Green on Black) [Schlafendes Kind (grün auf schwarz)], 1934

Cardboard, 33 × 40.8 cm | Gabriele Münter- und Johannes Eichner-Stiftung, Munich, inv. no. V 52

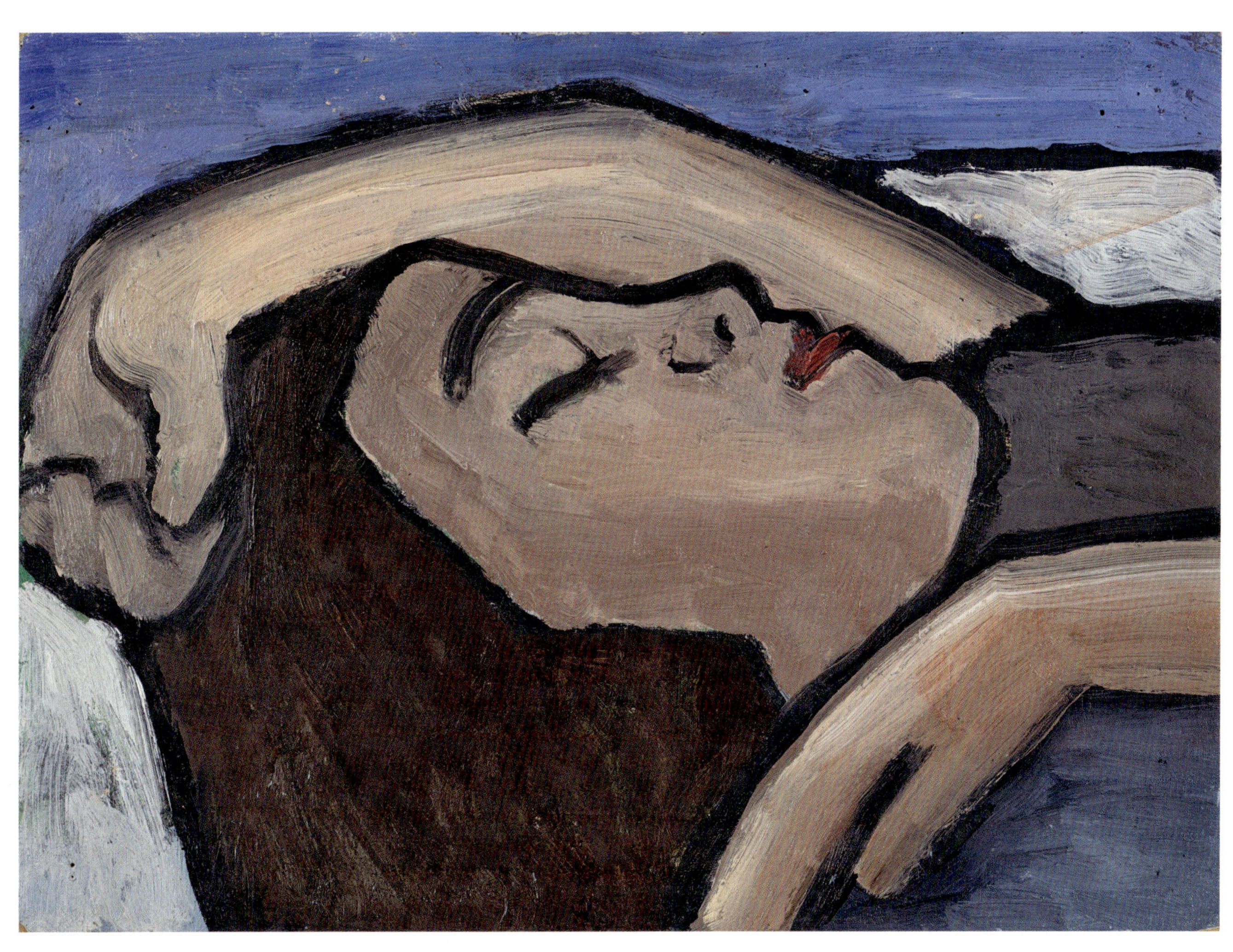

Cat. 178
Sleeping Girl (Brown, Blue) [Schlafendes Mädchen (braun, blau)], 1934
Cardboard, 24.1 × 33 cm | Gabriele Münter- und Johannes Eichner-Stiftung, Munich, inv. no. V 63

A New Way of Seeing?

Gabriele Münter and the New Representational Painting of the 1920s

Gabriele Münter and the New Representational Painting of the 1920s

European painting experienced a change of direction after World War I. Many artists turned away from abstraction and other avant-garde currents that reflected a lack of interest in an accurate representation of the visible world, such as Expressionism and Futurism, and resorted instead to a concept of reality "that demands new artistic as well as sociopolitical solutions. Dissolution is opposed by insistence, decomposition by a stable order of things, and that in a political sense as well."[1] In painting, these tendencies found expression in a new form of objectivity that relied above all on a puristic visual language. It gave rise to a wide range of stylistic currents, such as Pittura Metafisica in Italy and the Neue Sachlichkeit (New Objectivity) in Germany during the era of the Weimar Republic.[2] Gabriele Münter traveled extensively during this time; she spoke five languages, maintained a far-reaching network of contacts, and concerned herself with these new developments in art.

In February 1920 Münter returned to Germany after a five-year absence.[3] She stayed in Berlin until May, after which she lived primarily in Munich and Murnau, making frequent visits to Schloss Elmau, until late 1924. From December 1924 to May 1925 she spent most of her time in Cologne. She then stayed in Murnau for several months before moving to Berlin in October 1925, where she remained until June 1929. She went to France in October 1929 and spent a year there, staying first in Paris and then, from September 1930, in the south of the country. During this checkered phase of her life, Münter visited numerous exhibitions and met with many fellow artists. A consistently curious observer wherever she happened to be—in Berlin, Munich, or Paris—she was always well informed about the most recent trends in art. However, she did relatively little painting herself during this decade. Roughly 120 paintings have been identified from the period.[4] Yet a change in her painting style is evident in one group of pictures. The essential features of this new style are an unpretentious formal language, clearly outlined motifs, and the reduction—in some cases the total elimination—of the traces of the painting process. This sharp, sober painting style imbues these works with an emotionless atmosphere, and some scenes look strikingly artificial. These paintings were primarily executed between 1926 and 1930—the years during which the artist lived in Berlin and Paris—alongside works reflecting various other styles.

The first dated works featuring this new visual style were created in Berlin in 1926. The new language is evident in portraits as well as still lifes and interiors. Figs. A; B *Woman in Thought II*, a prominent example of this painting style from 1928, shows a woman sitting in a nondescript room. Cat. 180 Because of the woman's pose, with her head supported by one hand, part of her face is concealed, which intensifies the mysterious mood conveyed by the painting. The subtle color gradations may have been inspired by works painted by Münter's teacher Arthur Segal, whose courses she attended in 1926 and later years. The most remarkable feature is the way in which Münter geometricizes the woman's body. The cylinder-like forms whose surfaces reflect vibrant light are reminiscent of the Cubist works of Fernand Léger (1881–1955). Fig. C Léger was not unknown to Gabriele Münter. Herwarth Walden had invited him to the *Erster Deutscher Herbstsalon* (First German Autumn Salon) in Berlin in September 1913, where Münter was also prominently represented by six paintings.[5] From that point on, the French artist not only exhibited repeatedly at Walden's gallery, Der Sturm, but also regularly took part in other German exhibitions. In 1928—the year in which *Woman in Thought II* was completed—Alfred Flechtheim organized Léger's most comprehensive exhibition to date at his gallery in Berlin.[6] Thus Münter had ample opportunity to view Léger's most recent paintings before embarking on her extended stay in Paris.

The majority of the paintings Münter executed in this style with its close affinities to New Objectivity were done during her stay in Paris from 1929 to

1
Translated from Olaf Peters, "Ästhetik der Neuen Sachlichkeit," in exh. cat. *Das Auge der Welt: Otto Dix und die Neue Sachlichkeit*, Kunstmuseum Stuttgart, ed. Ilka Voermann [Kunstmuseum Stuttgart, 2012/13], Ostfildern 2012, p. 33. Information kindly provided by Karin Althaus.

2
On the international character and diversity of New Objectivity, see Peters 2012 (as note 1).

3
See the chapter "Landscapes and Outdoor Scenes," p. 55.

4
This figure is based on work on the catalogue raisonné of Gabriele Münter's paintings, which is currently being prepared at the Gabriele Münter- und Johannes Eichner-Stiftung. On the reasons for this low level of productivity, see the chapter "Landscapes and Outdoor Scenes," p. 54.

5
On Herwarth Walden, see the chapter "Work and Technology," p. 214.

6
The exhibition at the Galerie Alfred Flechtheim took place from February 6 to March 2, 1928. On this exhibition and the critical reception of Fernand Léger's oeuvre in Germany, see Martin Schieder, "Fernand Légers Ausstellung bei Alfred Flechtheim 1928 in Berlin," in *Distanz und Aneignung: Kunstbeziehungen zwischen Deutschland und Frankreich 1870–1945*, ed. Alexandre Kostka and Françoise Lucbert, Berlin 2004, pp. 139–58. In his article Schieder notes that the influence of Léger's painting on the works of the German artists of Expressionism, the Bauhaus, and New Objectivity deserves further study, p. 142.

7
Diary entry of November 28, 1929, MES. On Münter's participation in the drawing course at the Académie de la Grande Chaumière in 1906, see Isabelle Jansen, "Gabriele Münter in Paris 1906 bis 1907," in exh. cat. Munich/Bonn/Murnau 2000/01, p. 40.

8
See the chapter "Portraits," pp. 102–3.

1930. The artist arrived in the city on October 26, 1929, initially staying at the Hôtel d'Odessa in Montparnasse. Two days later she visited the Académie de la Grande Chaumière, where she had attended a drawing course in 1906.[7] Between December 1929 and April 1930, she repeatedly took advantage of the academy's offer of drawing. Münter encountered a number of fellow artists from Germany in Paris, among them the painter Loulou Albert-Lazard (1885–1969), whom she had first met in Berlin and who had been living in the French capital since 1928.[8] The two women spent a great deal of time together during Münter's first two months in the city. Münter also met frequently with her friend Constanze Schwedeler (1876–1962), a painter from Munich. Although her first impressions of the city were not entirely positive, she apparently found Paris inspiring and invigorating, much as she had during her stay from 1906 to 1907. She visited museums, galleries, and

A **Röschen, 1926**
Oil on cardboard, 33 × 44.7 cm | Hubertus Melsheimer, Ascona

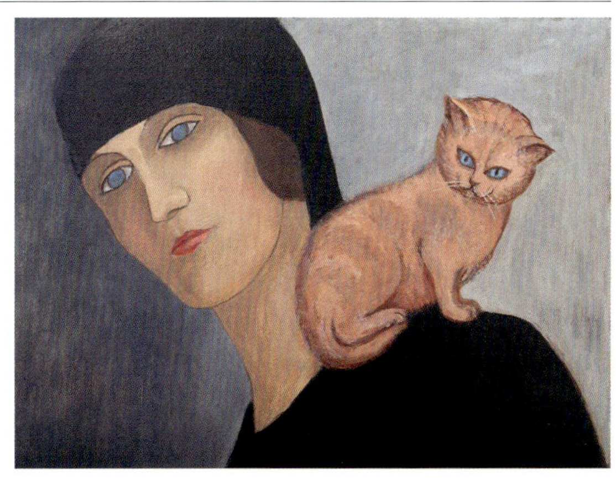

B **Red Cactus Blossoms on a Blue Background [Rote Kakteenblüten auf blauem Grund], 1926**
Oil on cardboard, 45 × 33.3 cm | Private collection

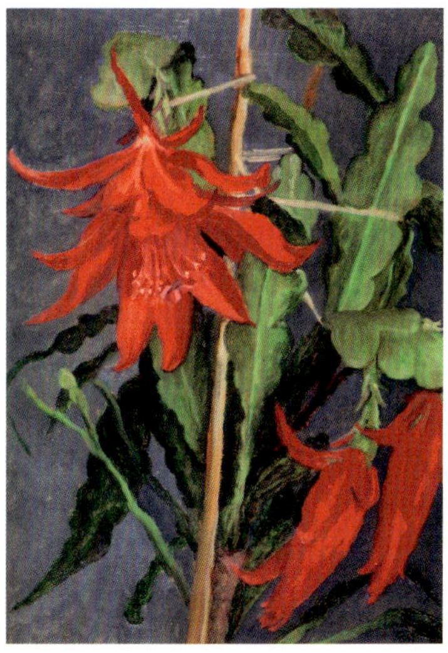

C **FERNAND LÉGER**
Les Femmes au Bouquet, 1921
Oil on canvas, 73.2 × 92 cm | Musée national Fernand Léger, Biot, Donation Nadia Léger et Georges Bauquier (Biot), 1969, inv. no. MNFL 97029

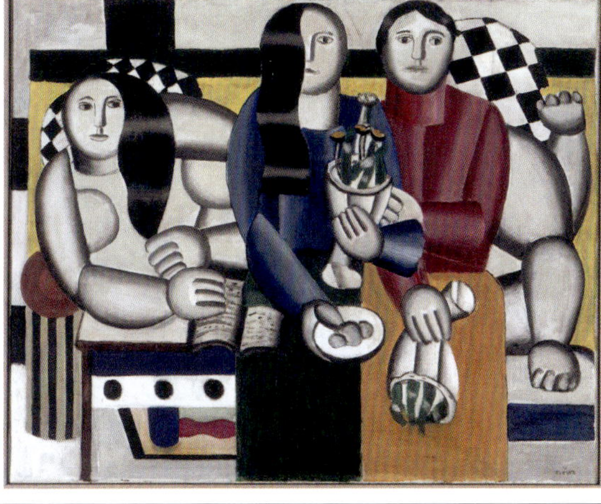

cafés (including the famous La Rotonde, La Coupole, and Le Dôme cafés), enjoyed the French cuisine, attended concerts, and went to movies. She made an effort to forge new contacts and exhibit her work—and met, among others, the gallery owner Wilhelm Uhde. She became a member of the Fédération des Artistes in April. And once again, she began to paint more. Two-thirds of the nearly twenty paintings she completed in 1929 were done in Paris. She realized seventy-five works in 1930, making it her most productive year in painting since 1911. All in all, she painted some sixty pictures in France. In December 1929 she executed *Lady in an Armchair, Writing (Stenography: Swiss Woman in Pyjamas)*, Cat. 179 whose composition—a seated woman in a nondescript room—is similar to that of the earlier work *Woman in Thought II*. Although this is also an unpretentious, clearly composed work, it has a more intimate, personal effect by virtue of the absence of geometric forms.

Still Life with Red Salad Servers Cat. 186 exhibits a sober style that is also typical of this group of paintings. In its simplicity and its focus on the bowl, which has been torn from its familiar surroundings, the painting calls to mind a photographic close-up. Münter was inspired to paint this motif while clearing the table after an evening meal.[9]

This simple formal language is also at work in a small series of scenes from Paris and its environs. Cat. 183–85 The subject of construction work in the painting *Scaffolding* was not new for Münter; she had created a woodcut called *Construction Work* in 1912.[10] The painting done in Paris was executed in March 1930 from a pencil sketch drawn in the rue du Cherche-Midi in Montparnasse on January 18 of the same year.[11] The construction workers and the scaffolding are particularly remarkable; both are rendered as silhouettes, and the workers appear only as stick figures. Münter's drawing talent is demonstrated in impressive fashion in this work.

Münter realized a number of individual works in this lucid style in subsequent years. *Suburban Houses with Baroque Church (Ramersdorf: Scheubner-Richterstraße)* of 1936 evokes a cool atmosphere that is achieved not by means of sharply outlined objects but rather in the motif of a street devoid of people and cars and in the absence of all details, such as windows and doors on the houses.[12] Cat. 77 The painting is based on a pencil sketch Münter drew on August 16. Fig. D It is interesting to note that the sketch is highly detailed; thanks to the depiction of shrubs and branches, it looks more idyllic and less ghostly than the oil painting. Münter noted not only the date, but also the exact address in the upper right-hand corner of the sketch: "Scheubner Richterstr. 31." This street was located in the Ramersdorf district of Munich, a model estate that was built and opened in 1934 in conjunction with the *Deutsche Siedlungsausstellung* (German Settlement Exhibition), along with an exhibition on the fairgrounds and a garden show. Relevant to our topic is the fact that Juliane and Franz Roh lived on this street.[13] The art historian Franz Roh introduced the term "magic realism" in his book *Nachexpressionismus: Magischer Realismus, Probleme der neuesten europäischen Malerei* (Post-Expressionism: Magic Realism, Problems of the Newest European Painting) in 1925. He sought to describe the new representational trend in painting with this term. At about the same time, Gustav Friedrich Hartlaub presented his 1925 exhibition *Neue Sachlichkeit: Deutsche Malerei seit dem Expressionismus* (New Objectivity: German Painting since Expressionism) at the Kunsthalle Mannheim; it was Hartlaub's term that eventually found widespread acceptance as the name of this style. Münter had been acquainted with Roh since at least 1924, as an entry in her diary indicates, and she visited the couple quite often in Ramersdorf, a district she described as "picturesque."[14] She saw the Rohs' "pretty little house" for the first time on March 29, 1936, and mentioned in her diary that she liked it very much. Thus *Suburban Houses with Baroque Church* was based on an impression gained during a visit to the Rohs. Yet the motif of the National Socialist model

9
"Yesterday evening I wanted to write cards and l[ette]rs, as I had been planning to do for some time—there were also things to sew—but I painted a still life instead, something I saw while clearing the table. The red salad servers in a white bowl+(and lemon)+with a shadow." Translated from letter to Eichner dated February 13, 1930, MES.

10
See the chapter "Work and Technology," pp. 214–15.

11
In sketchbook, inv. no. Kon. 46/69, p. 57, MES.

12
On this painting and other works that exhibit affinities with New Objectivity, see Windecker 1991, pp. 185ff. and 191ff.

13
Information kindly provided by Ursula Henn on January 7, 2015.

14
Translated from diary entry of January 13, 1939, MES.

15
She noted the date of origin in her logbook, MES. On this question, see the chapter "Work and Technology," pp. 216–18.

16
Hille 2012, color illustration, p. 204.

estate and the date of origin, August 21, 1936—shortly before the opening of the exhibition *Die Strassen Adolf Hitlers in der Kunst* (The Streets of Adolf Hitler in Art), in which Münter took part—raise the question of whether the work may be seen as an attempt by the artist to reconcile herself with an issue that was close to the hearts of National Socialist cultural policymakers.[15]

The 1938 still life *Two Kinds* Fig. E is another example from the 1930s of this cool visual language. The sharpness of the objects in this composition culminates in the shadow of the table on the bare wall. A painting of flowers with yellow blossoms done in 1951 shows that Münter sometimes resorted to this simple mode of representation even many years later.[16]

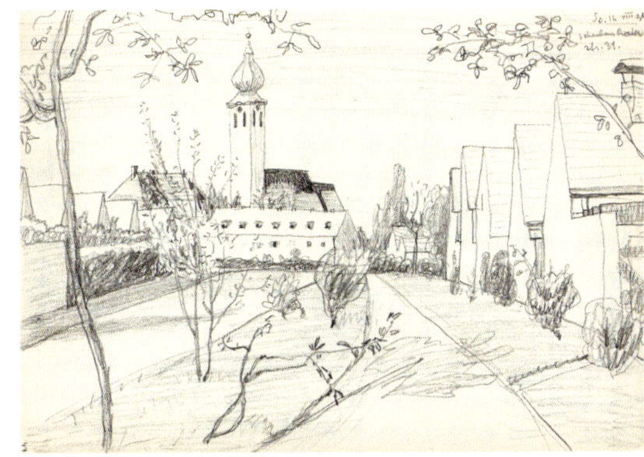

D **Sketch for the painting entitled Suburban Houses with Baroque Church [Skizze zu dem Gemälde Vorstadthäuser mit Barockkirche], 1936**
Pencil on paper, 15.2 × 22.1 cm | Gabriele Münter- und Johannes Eichner-Stiftung, Munich, sketchbook, inv. no. Kon. 37/20, p. 47

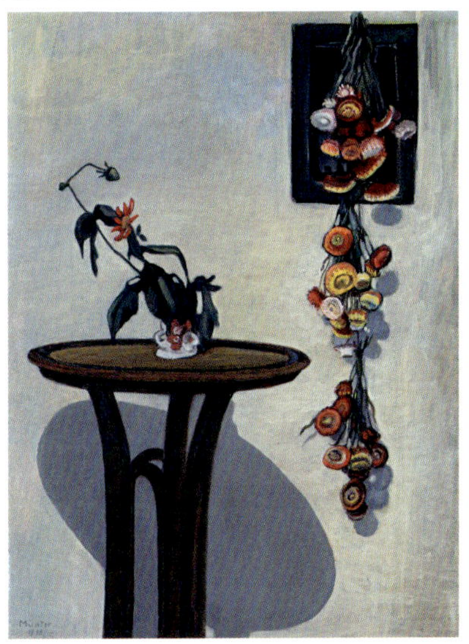

E **Two Kinds [Zweierlei], 1938**
Textile support, 88.5 × 66.4 cm | Gabriele Münter- und Johannes Eichner-Stiftung, Munich, inv. no. S 108

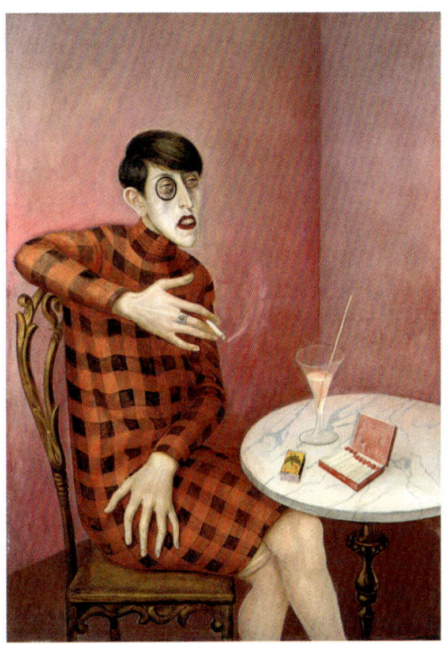

F **OTTO DIX**
Portrait of the Journalist Sylvia von Harden [Bildnis der Journalistin Sylvia von Harden], 1926
Oil on wood, 121 × 89 cm | Centre Pompidou, Paris. Musée national d'art moderne – Centre de création industrielle, inv. no. AM 3899 P

The new objective aesthetic is evident in Münter's paintings from 1926 (when she was in Berlin) onward. She had plenty of opportunities in Berlin to familiarize herself with the most recent developments in art. She frequented the Romanisches Café—an important gathering point for artists and intellectuals—where she met the writer and actress Eleonore Kalkowska (1883–1937).[17] She was also acquainted with the journalist Sylvia von Harden (1894–1963), whom Otto Dix (1891–1969) had portrayed in 1926 in a painting that later acquired the status of an icon of New Objectivity. Fig. F Münter drew multiple portraits of the journalist around 1928.[18] She also maintained ties with the painter Elli Heimann, who worked in the style of New Objectivity.[19] She had presumably met the art historian Hartlaub at Schloss Elmau in the summer of 1923. As mentioned above, it was he who organized the exhibition from which the new movement took its name.[20] All of this serves as evidence that Münter was a familiar figure within the circles of artists associated with New Objectivity. However, her own painting style did not undergo a significant change until 1929/30, when she was in Paris. There, she became as productive as she had been eighteen years earlier, and it was there that she realized a number of paintings in a "new objective" style. Yet her affinities with this stylistic current were purely formal. Her repertoire of motifs did not change at all, nor did she address critical social issues, as the Verist wing of the movement was wont to do. Her inclination in favor of this stylistic movement may be interpreted simply as a reaction to her environment. It is a sign of her love of experimentation and her openness to new developments in art.

17
Diary entry of March 26, 1926, MES.

18
The Incomparable (The Poet Sylvia von Harden), 1928, pencil, 28.7 × 22 cm, Städtische Galerie im Lenbachhaus und Kunstbau München, inv. no. GMS 1073, illustrated in exh. cat. Munich/Frankfurt/Stockholm 1992/93, no. 179; *The Incomparable* and *Seated Woman with Cigarette,* both ca. 1928, Centre Pompidou, Paris. Musée national d'art moderne – Centre de création industrielle, inv. nos. AM 2019-622 and AM 2019-623; *On the Sofa,* (two sheets), both ca. 1928, MES inv. nos. Kon. 29/56 and 29/57. According to a diary entry, Münter met Von Harden on March 19, 1928.

19
Exh. cat. Munich/Frankfurt/Stockholm 1992/93, text for no. 180, p. 284.

20
She did his portrait in a sketchbook from 1923/24. The inscription on the drawing reads as follows: "Dr. G. Hartlaub 30 VIII," inv. no. Kon. 46/57, p. 41, MES.

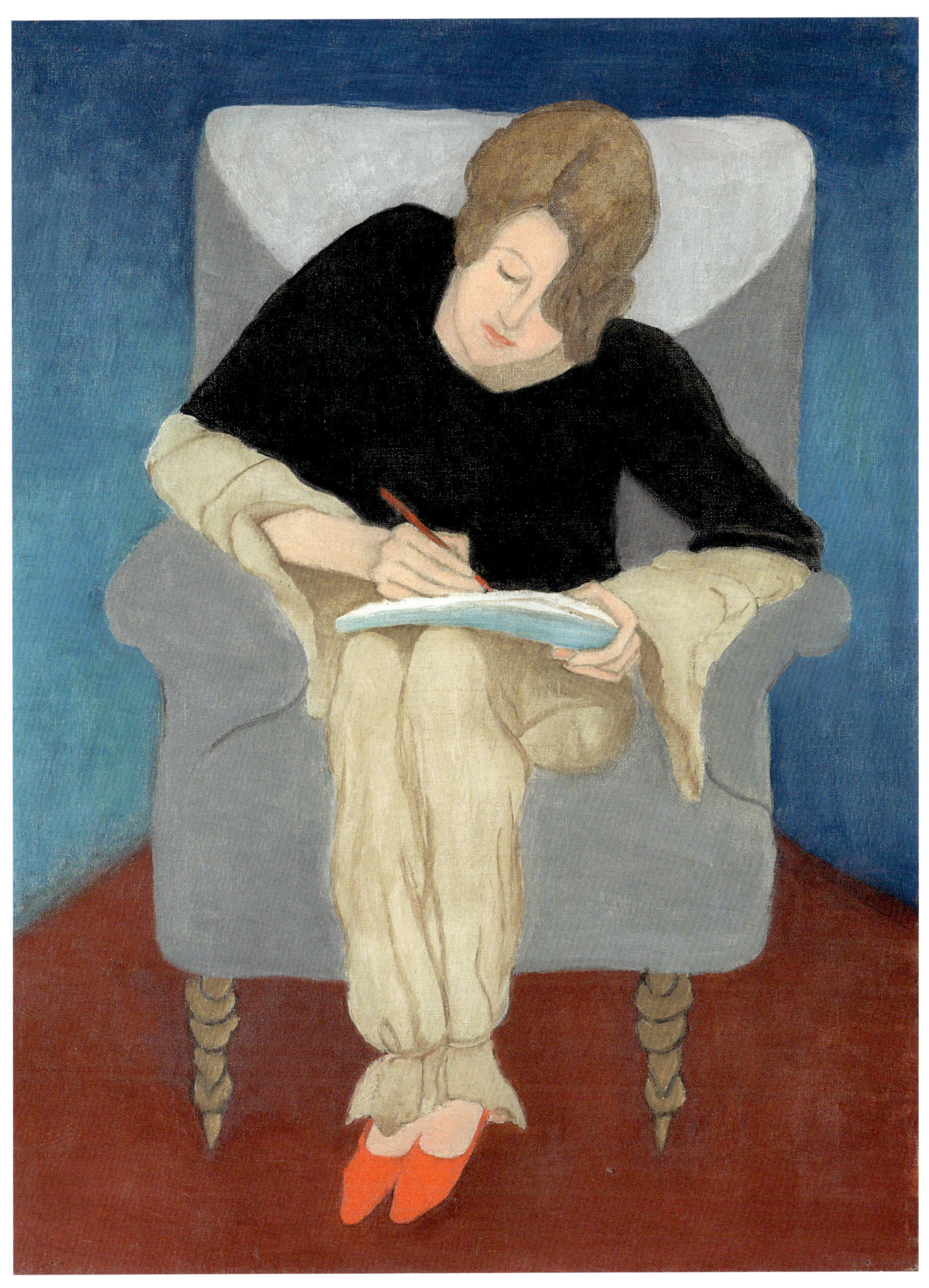

Cat. 179

Lady in an Armchair, Writing (Stenography: Swiss Woman in Pyjamas) [Dame im Sessel, schreibend (Stenographie. Schweizerin in Pyjama)], 1929

Textile support, 61.5 × 46.2 cm | Gabriele Münter- und Johannes Eichner-Stiftung, Munich, inv. no. P 39

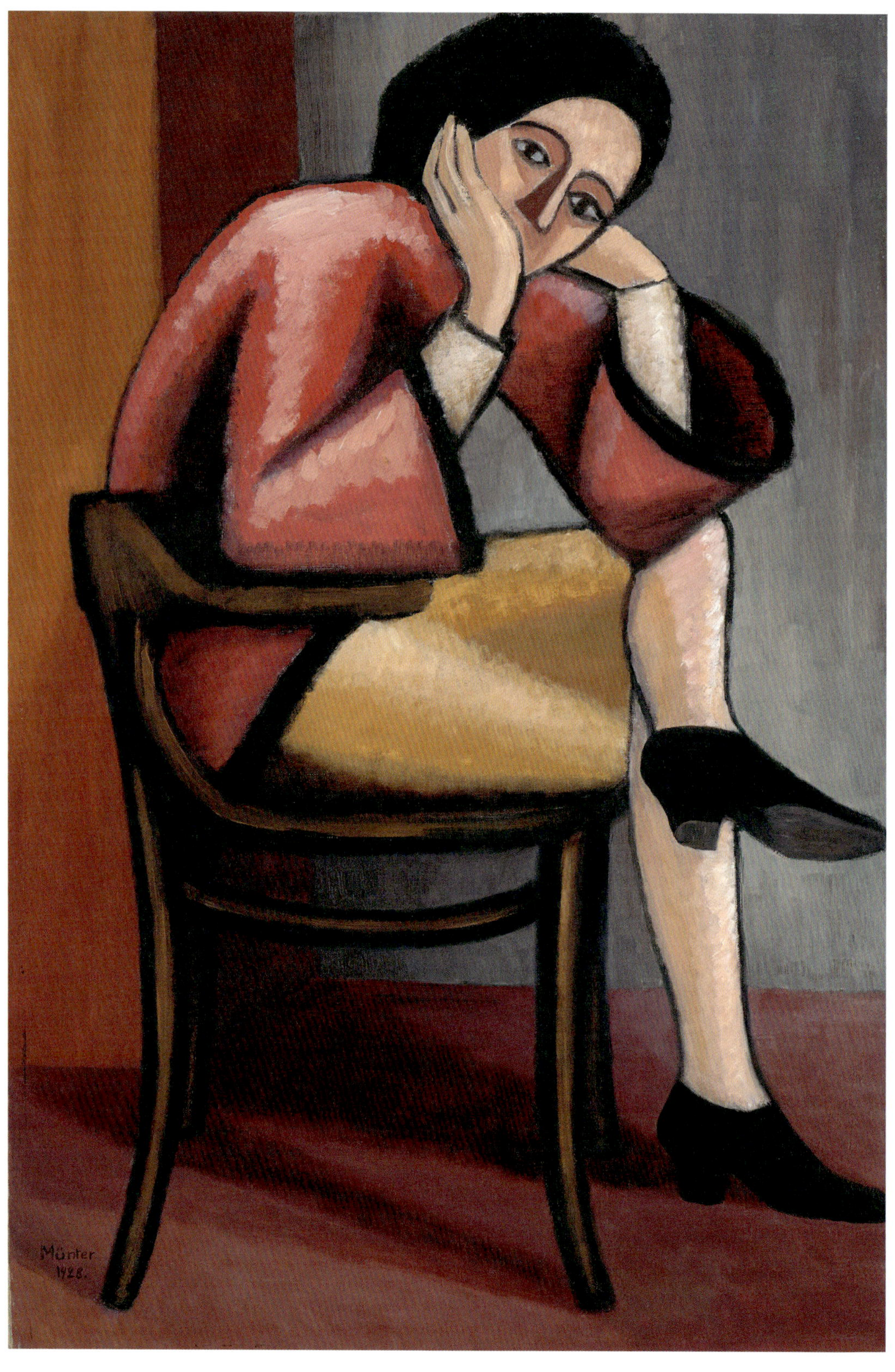

Cat. 180
Woman in Thought II [Sinnende II], 1928
Textile support, 95 × 65 cm |
The Museum of Modern Art, New York, promised gift of Marie-Josée and Henry R. Kravis, inv. no. PG136.2019

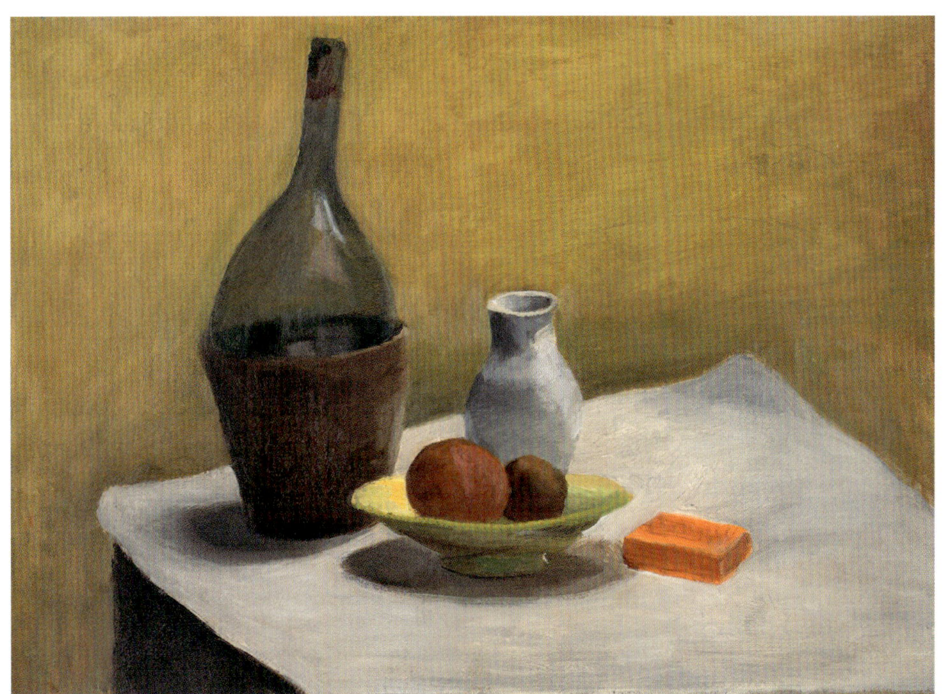

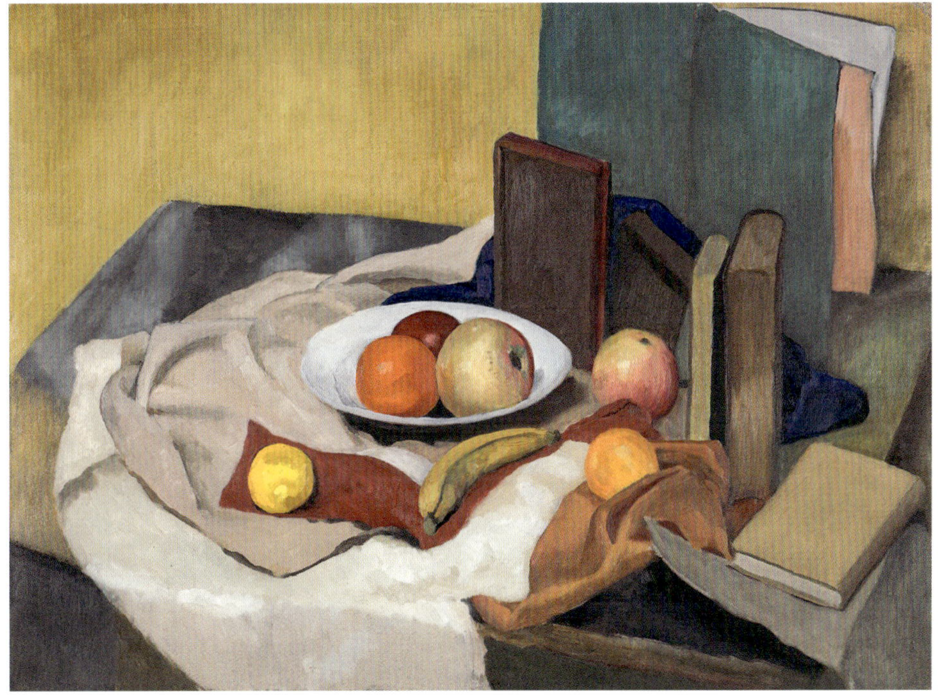

Cat. 181
Still Life on a White Tablecloth [Stillleben auf weißem Tisch-tuch], ca. 1926–30
Cardboard, 50 × 70 cm | Gabriele Münter- und Johannes Eichner-Stiftung, Munich, inv. no. S 8

Cat. 182
Still Life with Books and Fruit [Stillleben mit Büchern und Früchten], ca. 1926–30
Cardboard, 51.2 × 70 cm | Gabriele Münter- und Johannes Eichner-Stiftung, Munich, inv. no. S 7

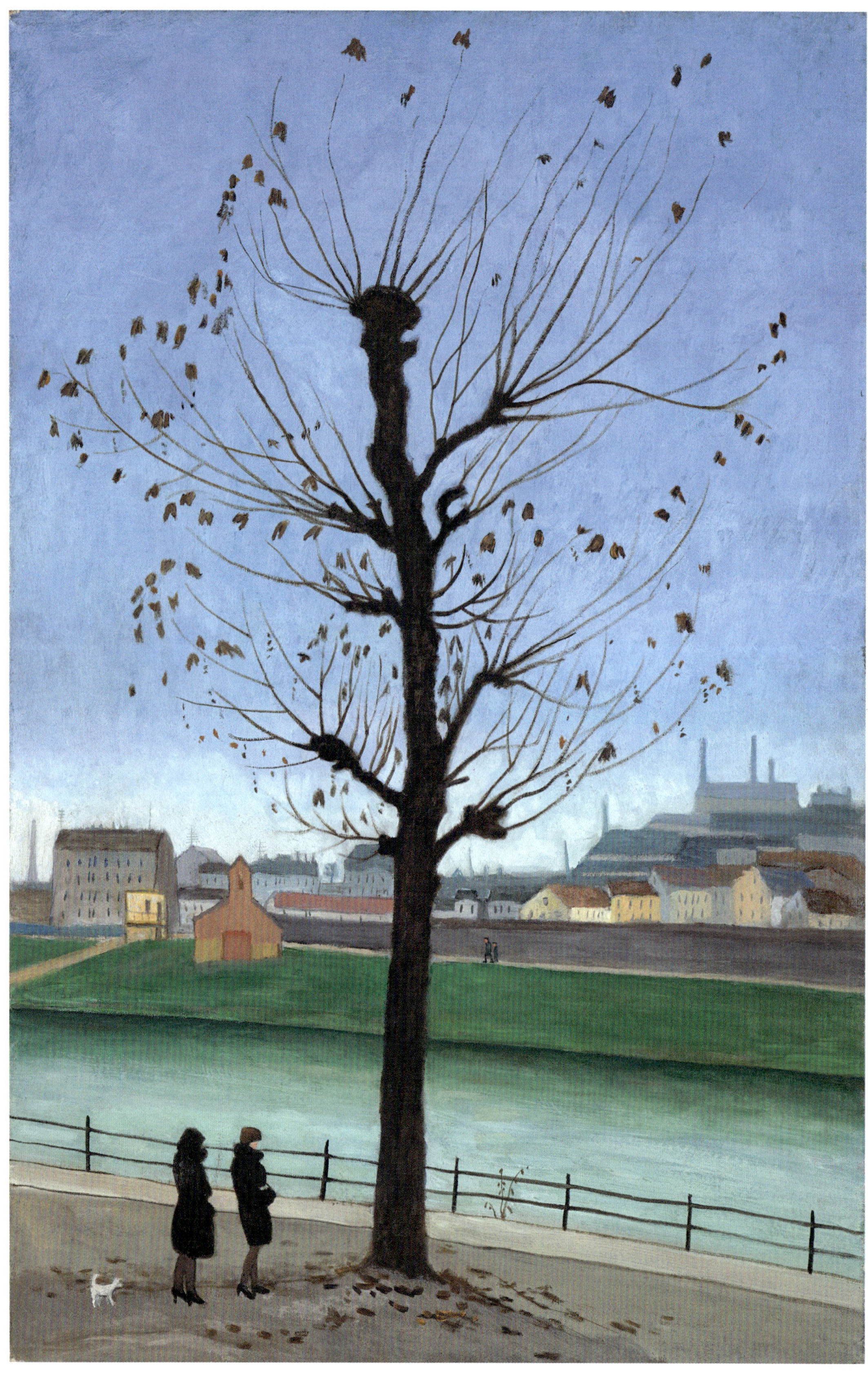

Cat. 183
Tree on the Bank of the Seine [Baum an der Seine], 1930
Textile support, 92 × 60 cm | Gabriele Münter- und Johannes Eichner-Stiftung, Munich, inv. no. L 10

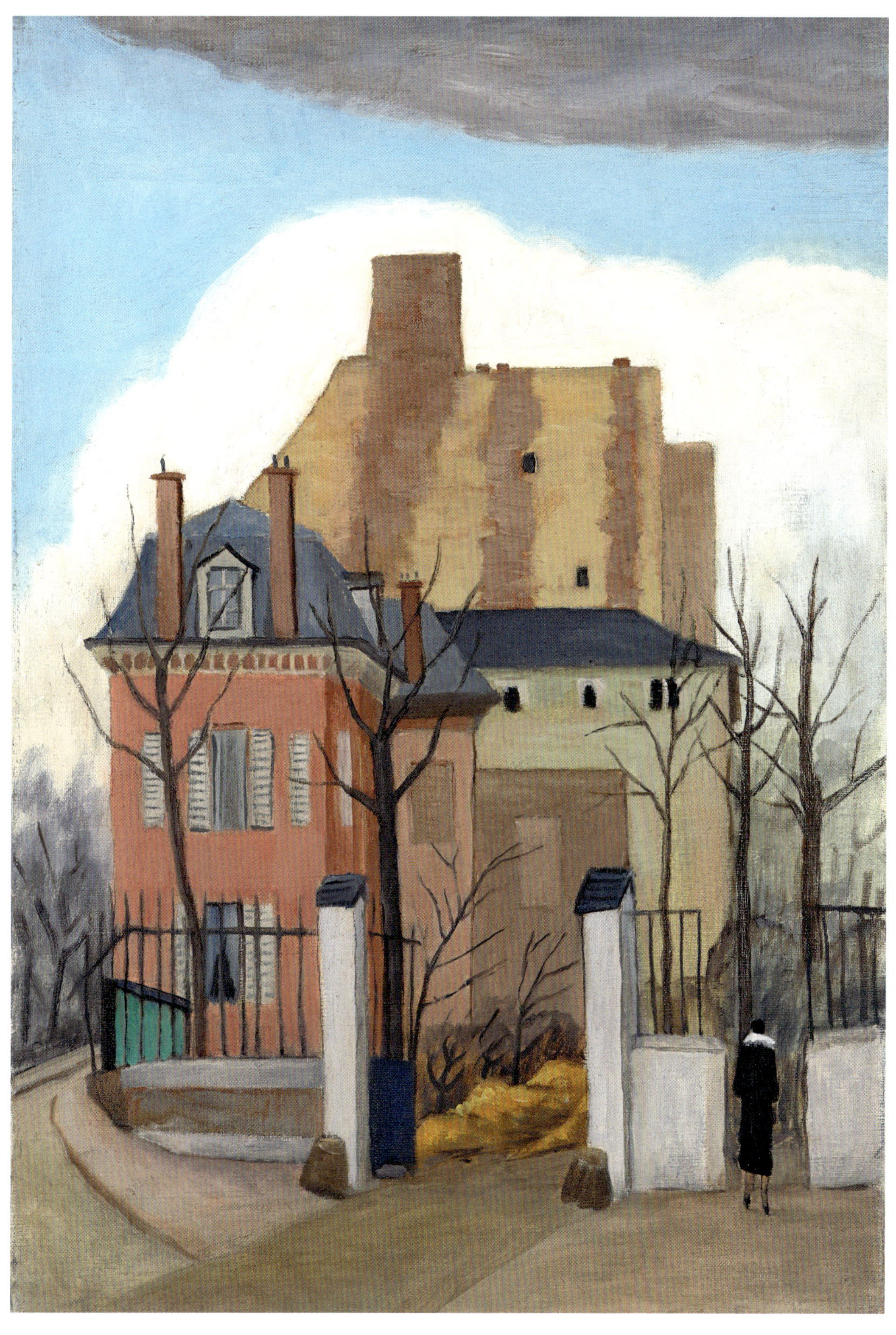

Cat. 184
Paris, Villa les Fleurettes, 1930
Textile support, 55.4 × 38.4 cm |
Gabriele Münter- und Johannes Eichner-Stiftung, Munich, inv. no. L 53

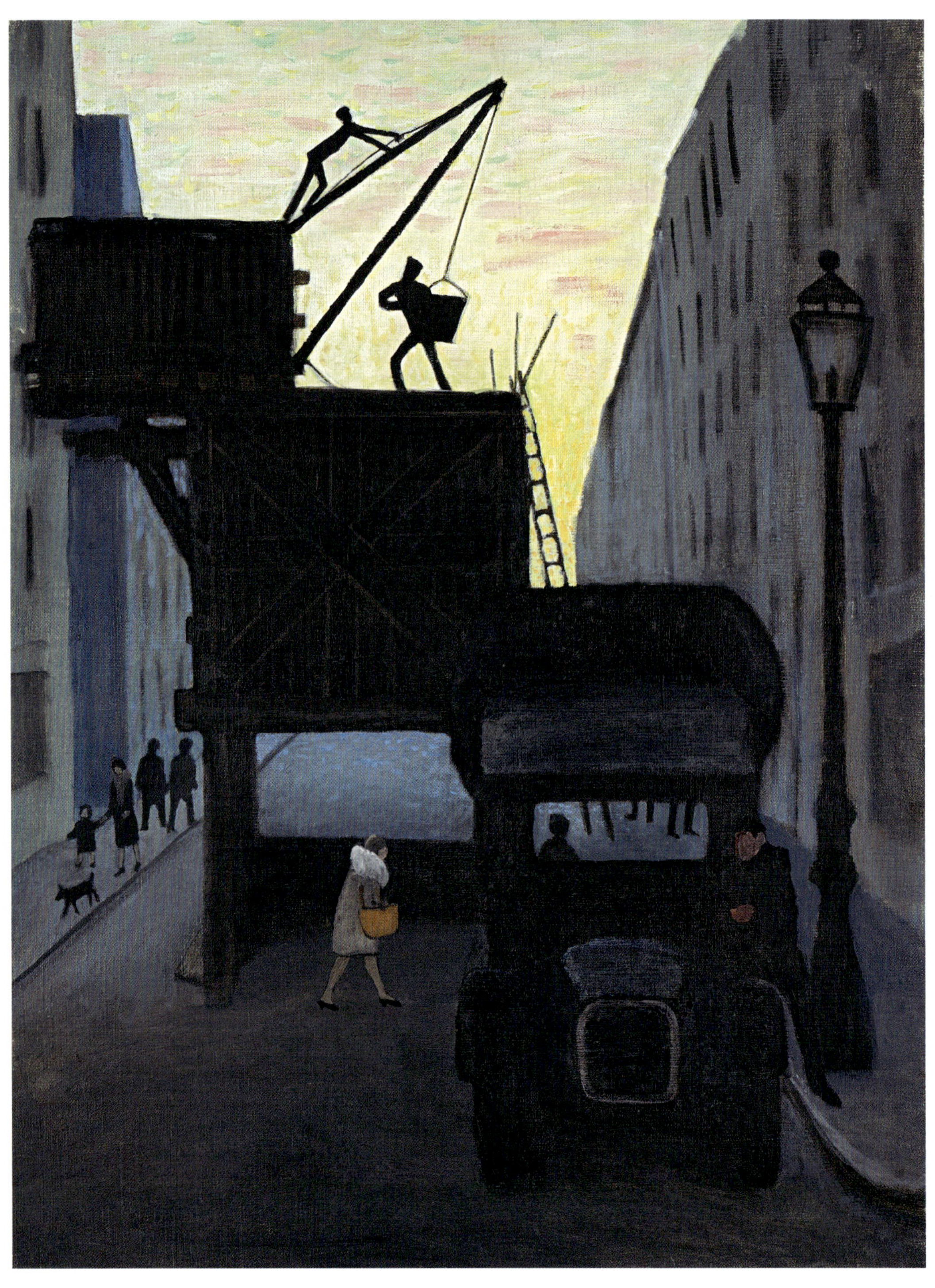

Cat. 185
Scaffolding [Baugerüst], 1930
Textile support, 61.2 × 46.6 cm |
Gabriele Münter- und Johannes Eichner-Stiftung, Munich, inv. no. V 8

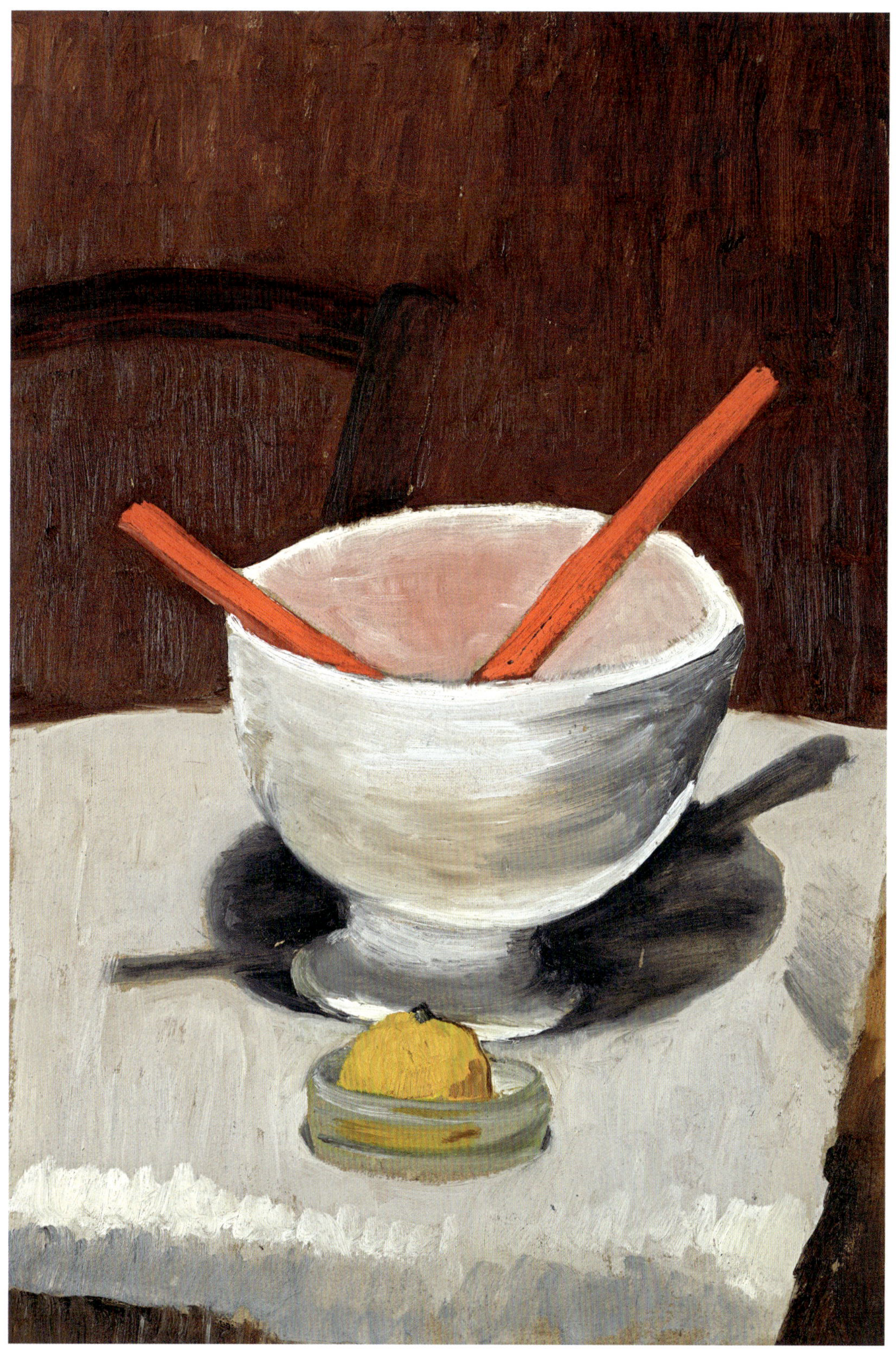

Cat. 186
Still Life with Red Salad Servers [Stilleben mit rotem Besteck], 1930
Cardboard, 55 × 38.1 cm |
Gabriele Münter- und Johannes Eichner-Stiftung, Munich, inv. no. S 31

“The monster devours everything and spits it out.”[1]

Work and Technology

Work and Technology

Although Gabriele Münter addressed the subjects of work and technology early and often over the course of her career, they have been given little critical attention to date.[2] She dealt with these themes as early as 1898 to 1900, during her travels in the United States—drawing and photographing her relatives at work in the fields and standing in front of roller mills (for wood-processing) managed by her cousin John Schreiber in Moorefield, Arkansas.[3] Fig. A; Cat. 19; 20 She also photographed steamboats on the Mississippi, as well as railroad structures and locomotives. Münter recognized the space-shaping potential of technical objects and employed ropes and lines as elements of composition in her photographs. Cat. 23; 24; 21 Her first paintings featuring work-related motifs were realized in 1911 and include such works as *From the Ruhr Region II* and *Street in Murnau with an Ox-Drawn Cart*.[4] Figs. B; C *From the Ruhr Region II* depicts an industrial landscape, while *Street in Murnau with an Ox-Drawn Cart* features a scene of farm life in Murnau.

Construction scenes were Münter's favorite motif in the context of work and technology, and she focused intensely on such images during two different phases of her life—in 1912 and again from 1935 to 1937. While only a single painting (*Construction Work* Cat. 187) was realized in 1912, an entire series of drawings was inspired by construction sites during that same year. They show horse-drawn wagons and road construction workers unloading rubble.[5] Münter also produced a woodcut with a simplified version of the subject which appeared on the cover of the magazine *Der Sturm* in November.[6] Fig. D The painting entitled *Construction Work* is a highly atmospheric piece featuring a cement mixer and a pile of dirt in the foreground. Visible in the background is a laborer at a workbench. The appeal of this scene consists above all in the rendering of the light. The scene is set on a cold winter's day, and the objects appear orange and purple in the light of the setting sun.

In the years following World War I, most of Münter's paintings concerned with the theme of work were realized in the 1930s. She painted a construction crane in Paris, workers at the harbor of Cassis in southern France, and a hay harvest at the Riegsee Lake near Murnau, to name only a few examples.[7] Cat. 185; 188 Yet it was not until 1935 that she once again turned her attention to the theme of technology in multiple works. She found source material right outside her door in Murnau: the construction of a second track on the Murnau–Garmisch-Partenkirchen railroad line and the construction project for the road to Garmisch-Partenkirchen, known as Olympiastraße, both of which were carried out in preparation for the 1936 Winter Olympics. Cat. 191–99 Alone or accompanied by her partner, Johannes Eichner, Münter visited the "excavation site" (by which she meant the Olympiastraße construction site) quite often—sometimes daily—to draw, paint, and converse with the laborers. She entered the following note in her diary on August 26, 1935: "with Ei[chner] to the excavation site after 11. Especially interesting and beautiful today. [Stayed] there until after 1." She was particularly fascinated by the excavator as a powerful machine. It became the focal point of most of her works relating to these construction projects. She saw it as a "monster [that] devours [everything] a[nd] spits [it] out."[8] In early August 1935 she produced two versions of a brown backhoe. One version was done in the presence of the motif, Cat. 194 the other from a drawing in her studio. Cat. 195 Although Münter continued to make regular visits to the "excavation site" through the month of August and into September, she produced no more paintings of it from August 7 to September 17. The blue excavator appeared in her repertoire in October, and she worked on the large-scale painting *The Blue Excavator (Construction Site on Olympiastraße to Garmisch)* from November 19 to 23, 1935. She overpainted or repainted the work in May 1936, during a time in which she realized numerous works on paper featuring the construction site motif.[9] Cat. 199 In the same month she also revised another painting, *Smoking Excavator in the Landscape (Construction Site on Olympiastraße)*, by incorporating figures into the composition. Cat. 198

1
Translated from diary entry of August 2, 1935, MES.

2
One exception is Reinhold Heller, who mentions the subject in exh. cat. Milwaukee/Columbus/Richmond/San Antonio 1997–99, p. 151.

3
Annegret Hoberg, "Gabriele Münter in Amerika," in exh. cat. Munich 2006/07, p. 19.

4
There are two known versions of *From the Ruhr Region*: *From the Ruhr Region I*, 32.9 × 40.7 cm, and *From the Ruhr Region II*, 32.8 × 44.8 cm, both 1911, cardboard, MES; sketches in sketchbook, inv. no. Kon. 46/38, pp. 13–17, and sketchbook, inv. no. Kon. 46/40, pp. 32–33, MES. Study entitled *Horse-Drawn Wagon with Sun – Drawing No. 4, Herford*, ca. 1911/12, watercolor and ink, 21.2 × 16.4 cm, Städtische Galerie im Lenbachhaus und Kunstbau München, inv. no. GMS 1076, illustrated in exh. cat. *"The Blue Rider": Watercolours, Drawings and Prints from the Lenbachhaus, A Dance in Colour*, ed. Helmut Friedel and Annegret Hoberg [Munich, Städtische Galerie im Lenbachhaus und Kunstbau München, 2010; Vienna, Albertina, 2011] Munich 2010, no. 244.

5
Illustrated in exh. cat. Munich/Bonn/Murnau 2000/01, under no. 41, and in exh. cat. *"The Blue Rider": Watercolours, Drawings and Prints from the Lenbachhaus* (see note 4), nos. 238–40.

6
Herwarth Walden, editor of *Der Sturm* (which he founded in 1910) and director of the Sturm gallery (which he opened in 1912), presented a solo exhibition featuring works by Gabriele Münter in January/February 1913, with subsequent presentations in other cities, including Munich, Frankfurt am Main, and Dresden—see the list of solo exhibitions in the appendix to this catalogue, p. 264. In conjunction with the exhibition, he published woodcuts by the artist in his magazine from November 1912 to May 1913.

7
At the Riegsee Lake, 1931, oil on cardboard, 33 × 40.5 cm, Kunsthalle Emden. Permanent loan from a private collection. Color illustration in exh. cat. Bietigheim-Bissingen 1999, p. 150.

8
As note 1.

9
According to entries in her logbook, she revised the painting again in January 1937 and overpainted it the following month.

A **Roller Mills in Moorefield [Roller Mills in Moorefield], 1899**

Pencil on paper, 17.3 × 21.3 cm | Gabriele Münter- und Johannes Eichner-Stiftung, Munich, sketchbook, inv. no. Kon. 36/2, p. 33

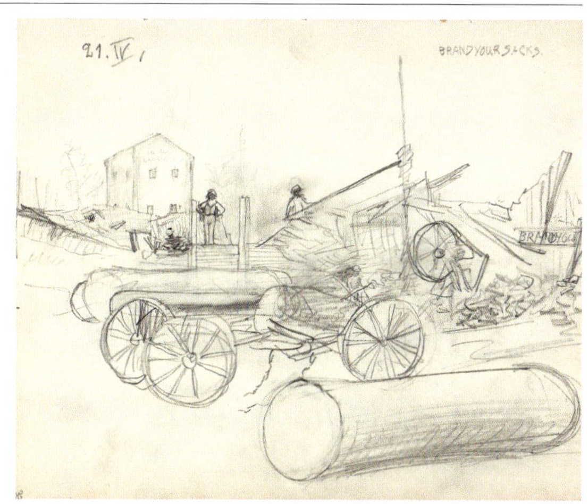

B **From the Ruhr Region II [Aus dem Ruhrgebiet II], 1911**

Cardboard, 32.8 × 44.8 cm | Gabriele Münter- und Johannes Eichner-Stiftung, Munich, inv. no. L 391

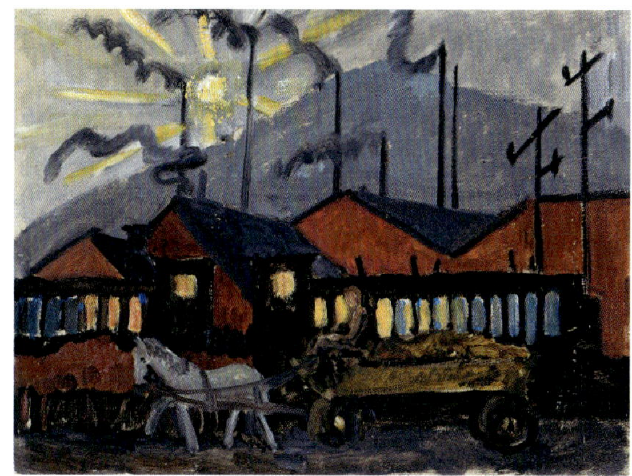

C **Street in Murnau with an Ox-Drawn Cart [Murnauer Straße mit Ochsengespann], 1911**

Oil on cardboard, 49.5 × 66 cm | Private collection, Southern Germany

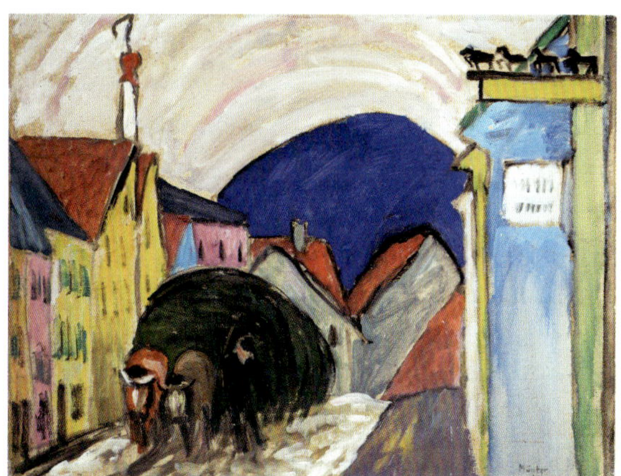

D **Construction Work [Bauarbeit], 1912**

Woodcut on Japan paper, 16.9 × 29.2 cm | Städtische Galerie im Lenbachhaus und Kunstbau München, inv. no. GMS 893

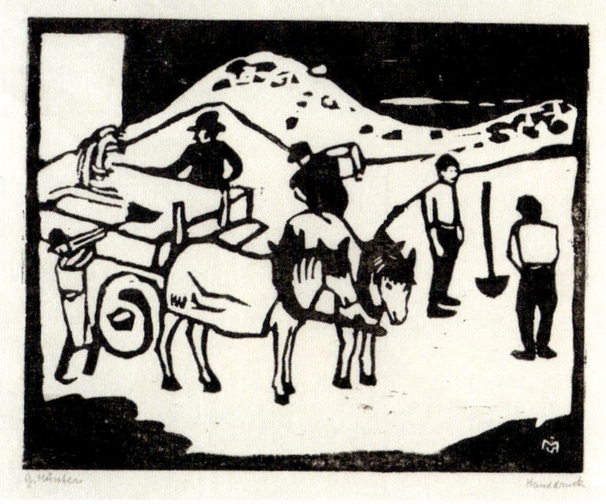

Her preliminary work for *The Blue Excavator (Construction Site on Olympiastraße to Garmisch)* and her subsequent revisions were particularly time-consuming; they extended the creative process from 1935 to 1937. This way of working was by no means unusual for Münter; she employed it in other works, such as *Doll, Cat, Child*, as well.[10] In January 1937 she removed the figure of a man carrying a heavy burden[11] in response to Eichner's wishes, before completely overpainting the work in February. Eichner quite often exerted influence on her painting process.[12] *The Blue Excavator (Construction Site on Olympiastraße to Garmisch)* is the only large-scale painting (it measures 60.5 × 92.5 centimeters) in the series devoted to the Olympiastraße construction site. The other works are much smaller (33 × 41/45 centimeters).[13] It is also the only painting executed with such precision, as the others look more spontaneous. Münter wrote the following remark in her diary in January 1937: "The excavator painting is more naturalistic than the others." As noted above, Eichner had intervened in the creative process. Thus it is entirely possible that he provided the inspiration for this different style.

Although they present a quite consistent visual impression, these "'work' pictures," as Münter referred to them,[14] were produced in different ways. She painted some of them in the presence of the subject, others from drawings or oil studies, and still others from photographs. In her diary for 1935 she wrote that she had gone to the "excavation site" with her friend Elly Ehren, who owned a Kodak camera, to take three pictures of the excavator. A sketchbook featuring a detailed sketch for *The Blue Excavator (Construction Site on Olympiastraße to Garmisch)* contains a small collection of materials that served as a basis for this work that she considered very important. It includes several sketches on separate sheets; two photographs of an excavator; Fig. E and a newspaper article from the *Münchner Neueste Nachrichten* of March 18, 1936, in which the construction project for the transformation of the Kleinhesseloher Lake in the English Garden in Munich is described.[15] The article is illustrated with two photographs showing excavators at work.

The series of works relating to the construction site on Olympiastraße raises the question of what might have motivated the artist to take up this subject, which was of particular interest within the context of National Socialist cultural policy. In terms of composition and style, these pictures are not compatible with the art policies propagated by the regime. Münter made no attempt to portray the road construction workers in a heroic light; they look more like toy figures in her scenes.[16] This is also true of another work, *Harvest in Upper Bavaria*, which she painted in 1942. Cat. 190

Yet even more problematic than Münter's presumed attempt to adapt her subject to the policies of the National Socialist government is her exhibition activity. In 1936 she showed two paintings in the exhibition *Die Strassen Adolf Hitlers in der Kunst* (The Streets of Adolf Hitler in Art) in Munich.[17] They are listed in the catalogue under numbers 302 and 303 with the rather vague titles "Excavator (Oil)" and "Blue Excavator (Oil)." We can identify the paintings today on the basis of the catalogue numbers, which were noted on the backs of the paintings. The works in question are *Excavator* and *The Blue Excavator (Study)*.[18] Cat. 194; 196 In 1957 Johannes Eichner described the circumstances under which these two works came to be shown in *Die Strassen Adolf Hitlers in der Kunst* in the following words: "And finally, Erna Hanfstaengl, an influential lady who had already distanced herself from the dictatorial system, introduced a satyr play out of pure malice by smuggling two sketches by Gabriele Münter into the exhibition 'Die Strassen Adolf Hitlers' in Munich and Berlin—free, small works (33 × 41 cm) that appeared in this setting as a mockery of National Socialist principles, yet were found acceptable under the authority of the exhibition. They had nothing to do with autobahns; they simply depicted excavators in the landscape, and they beat the whole wall full of great paintings to death with their picturesque approach."[19]

10
See the chapter "Repetitions and Variations," p. 188, note 19.

11
Diary entry of January 27, MES.

12
See the chapter "Repetitions and Variations," pp. 188–89.

13
Exceptions include *Construction Site on Olympiastraße (Cement Mixer, Rising Moon)*, 1935, textile support, 46.2 × 55 cm, inv. no. V 11, and *Construction Site on Olympiastraße (Smoking Excavator in the Landscape)*, 1935, 50.2 × 65 cm, textile support, inv. no. L 39, both MES.

14
Translated from diary entry of September 17, 1935, MES.

15
Sketchbook, inv. no. Kon. 36/13, MES. Although the two photographs cannot be identified with certainty as the pictures of the "excavation site" taken by Münter and Elly Ehren, it is quite probable that they are.

16
Kleine 1994, p. 612.

17
Exhibition park at Theresienhöhe, September 16 to mid-October 1936. Other venues: Berlin; Breslau, Schlesisches Museum der bildenden Künste, December 1936–January 1937; Stuttgart; Ulm.

18
Up till now, scholars have wrongly asserted that *The Blue Excavator (Construction Site on Olympiastraße to Garmisch)* was shown at the exhibition: exh. cat. Munich/Frankfurt/Stockholm 1992/93, no. 223, and Ickerott-Bilgic 2012 (see note 16), p. 42.

19
Translated from Eichner 1957, p. 189.

Thus, according to Eichner, the series of pictures of construction works from 1935/36 was not an attempt to fit in, since they differed from the other exhibited paintings by virtue of their small size, their motifs, and their style. Furthermore, Eichner appears to suggest that Münter was unaware of her participation in the exhibition. It seems that he was trying to rehabilitate the artist with this statement made in 1957, just as he had attempted to emphasize the "naïve and folkloric" character of her works during the National Socialist years in order to set her apart from the circle of the Blue Rider and thus to protect her. However, Münter maintained close contact with the art dealer Erna Hanfstaengl after 1936, and Hanfstaengl had been friends with Hitler since 1923.[20] The relationship with Hanfstaengl was particularly important to Münter, as the dealer was willing to promote the sale of her works. Hanfstaengl first visited Münter in Munich on February 29, 1936: "Frl. Erna Hanfstängl [*sic*] was here from half past 9 until 10—looked at works quickly. Was very impressed with them. Spoke of Americ. friends and concerning the road construction pictures of Todt—and the journal 'Vogue.' we [*sic*] got along well a[nd] I was very happy," noted Münter in her diary. On March 24, 1936, she wrote to Eichner, who had remained in Murnau to supervise renovation work at their house: "Dr. Willemoes photographed man[y] of my pictures, including the road construction sketches—if they are good, we could perhaps give them to E. Hanfstängl [*sic*] for Todt." Fritz Todt, the inspector general for the German roads department, was in charge of the construction of the German autobahns and was the patron of the exhibition *Die Strassen Adolf Hitlers in der Kunst*.[21] Münter visited Erna Hanfstaengl again on August 18. According to a note in the artist's diary, the art dealer and her managing director "demand[ed]" that she take part in the "road exhib[ition]."[22]

Münter had more to say in an undated letter to Eichner: "To stay here for the opening of the exhibition—wouldn't that be a rather costly pleasure? Spoke with Frl. Hanfstängl [*sic*] personally on the matter—she isn't going to go, as [it would be] a 'waste of time.' Showed me a l[ette]r from Frau Rose (different name).[23] [Said] the jury was long since over and they were already in the midst of the hanging process—Rose had been delighted to see Münter's works and hoped he could still hang something. In any event, the exhibition will move on to Berlin, and he thinks he will surely be able to get something accepted there." She mentions in a diary entry of September 12, 1936, that Erna Hanfstaengl showed her the letter from Frau Rose. Thus her undated letter to Eichner can be attributed to the same day. Up to that point, then, it was apparently uncertain whether Münter's paintings would be shown in Munich. As we read in her diary entry of September 16, 1936, Münter ultimately attended the opening ceremony for the exhibition and discovered that "2 excavator studies" of hers were being shown. And as she wrote several weeks later, on November 27, 1936, "Ei[chner] is dictating a l[ette]r to the road exhibition in Berlin—prices for paintings." It follows that both Münter and Eichner were aware of the presentation of the two paintings featuring the excavator motif in the exhibition *Die Strassen Adolf Hitlers in der Kunst* in Munich and Berlin, and

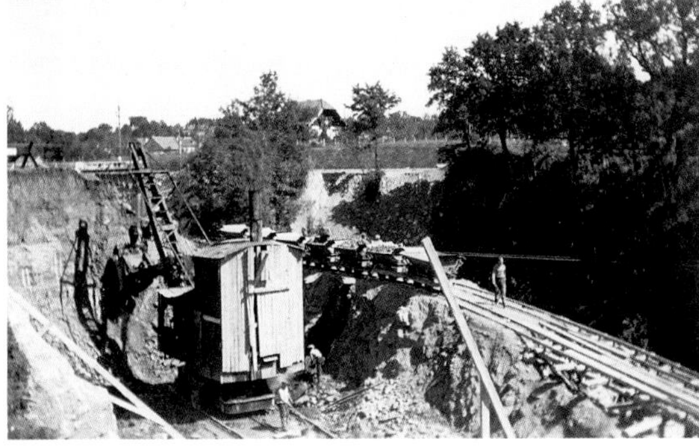

E **Excavator at a construction site in Murnau, 1935**
Photograph |
Gabriele Münter- und Johannes Eichner-Stiftung, Munich

20
Kleine 1994, p. 615. According to an entry in the artist's diary dated February 17, 1936, she was introduced to Erna Hanfstaengl by the gallerist Günther Franke.

21
Kleine 1994, p. 616.

22
"Tram before 11 with works on paper to Frl Hanfstängl [*sic*]. also Managing Director Herr Schmidt—both demand that I submit [works] for the road exhib."

23
What Münter means here is that the wife of the artist Rose went by a different surname than he did.

that they were not opposed to it. However, the initiative for Münter's participation in the exhibition had been taken by the art dealer Hanfstaengl, who, according to the aforementioned entry in Münter's diary, may have exerted a certain amount of pressure on the artist. Thus Münter may not have been able to refuse if she wanted Hanfstaengl to continue representing her.

Later, Münter wrote the following comments with regard to those years: "The dictatorship that had forced me to conceal my existence as an artist since 1937 and the war put the finishing touches on my life in seclusion, but without hindering or distorting my work."[24] Her last major public appearance during the National Socialist dictatorship seems to have taken place after 1937, however—namely, at an exhibition with the artist Lena Gierl (1880–1970) of Murnau at the local Wiegelmann bookshop in 1939. In May 1942, she participated in the art exhibition held during the Weilheim *Kreistag* (District Assembly) of the National Socialist Party with the painting *Comfrey and Small Pinks Before the Window*. She had wanted to show *Harvest in Upper Bavaria (Field Work near Dettendorf)*, Cat. 190 but Eichner did not agree with the choice, so they decided upon the still life.[25]

Münter shared her interest in work and technology with many other avant-garde artists. She lived in an age of major upheavals, during which technology played an increasingly important role in society. Given her open-mindedness and her broad range of interests, it comes as no surprise that she wanted to express her fondness for such subjects in her art. Thus when the huge Olympiastraße construction project was launched practically outside her door, it was perfectly natural for her to incorporate it into her art. Still, the decision to devote herself with such intensity to the Olympiastraße construction site was surely motivated by certain practical considerations as well. The subject was acceptable to the regime, which meant that she not only caused no trouble for herself but could even hope to exhibit her work—which she actually did. Yet neither the style nor the composition of the paintings in question offers evidence of an artistic compromise—in contrast with her decisions regarding participation in exhibitions during this period.

24
Translated from "Gabriele Münter über sich selbst," in *Das Kunstwerk*, no. 7, 1948, p. 25.

25
Entries in her diary from 1942 on April 30, May 1, and May 10, MES. *Comfrey and Small Pinks Before the Window,* 1935, textile support, 60 × 50 cm, inv. no. B 17, MES. The exhibition was held in the boys' schoolhouse of Weilheim from May 13 to 17. See also Kleine 1994, p. 639.

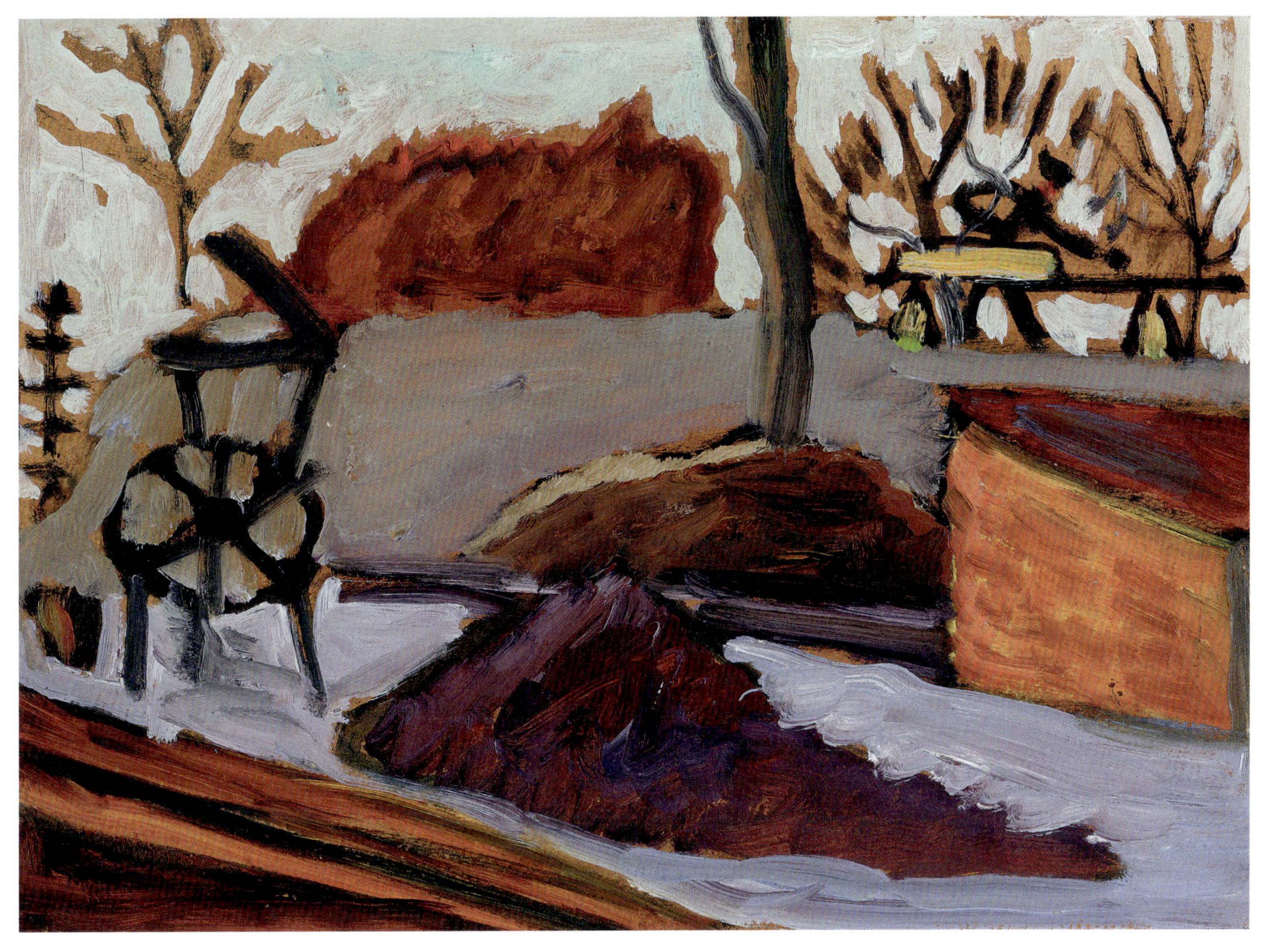

Cat. 187
Construction Work [Bauarbeit], 1912
Oil on cardboard, 33 × 45 cm |
Private collection

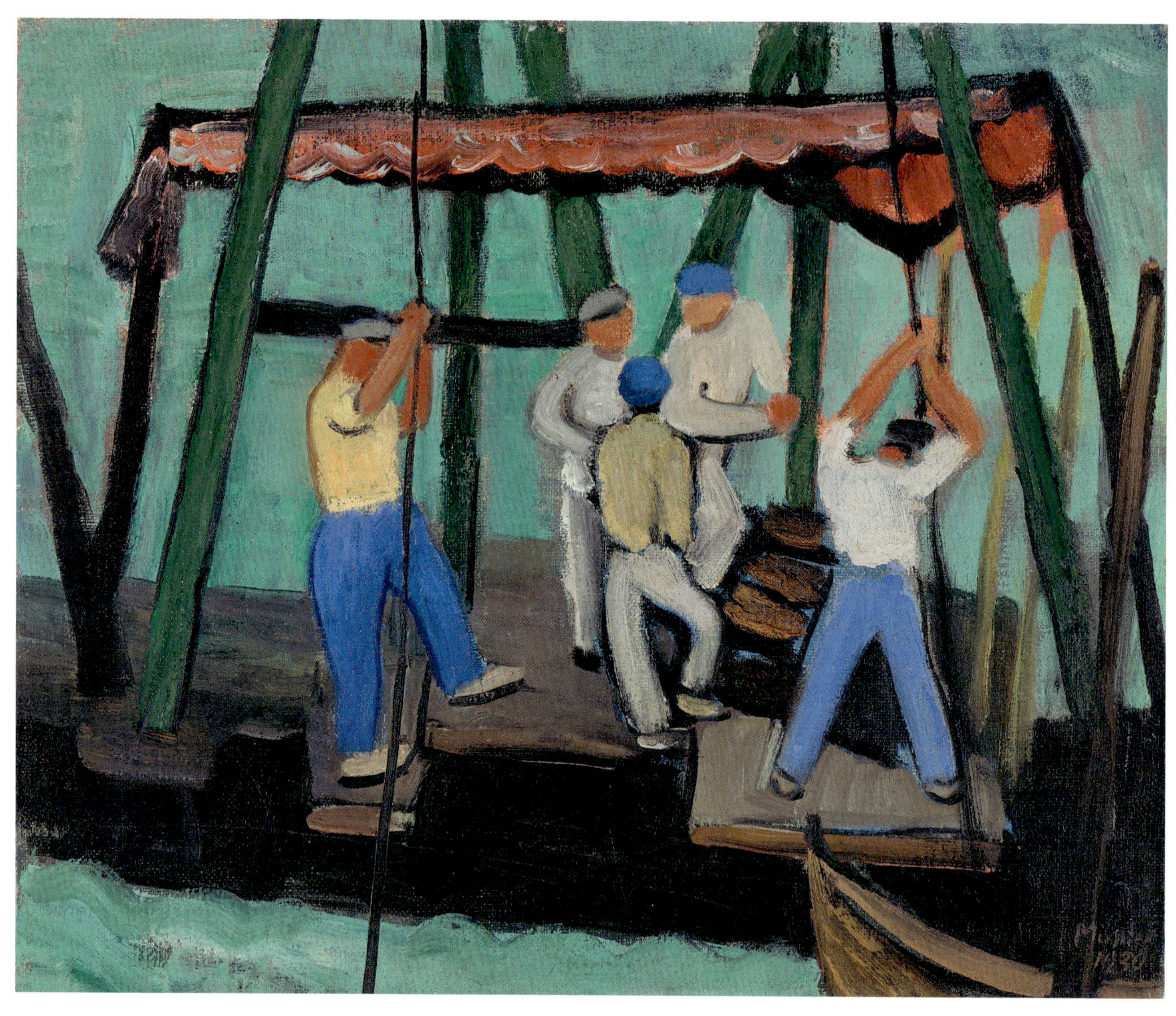

Cat. 188
Harbor Work in Cassis [Hafenarbeit in Cassis], 1930
Textile support, 38 × 46 cm |
Gabriele Münter- und Johannes Eichner-Stiftung, Munich, inv. no. V 87

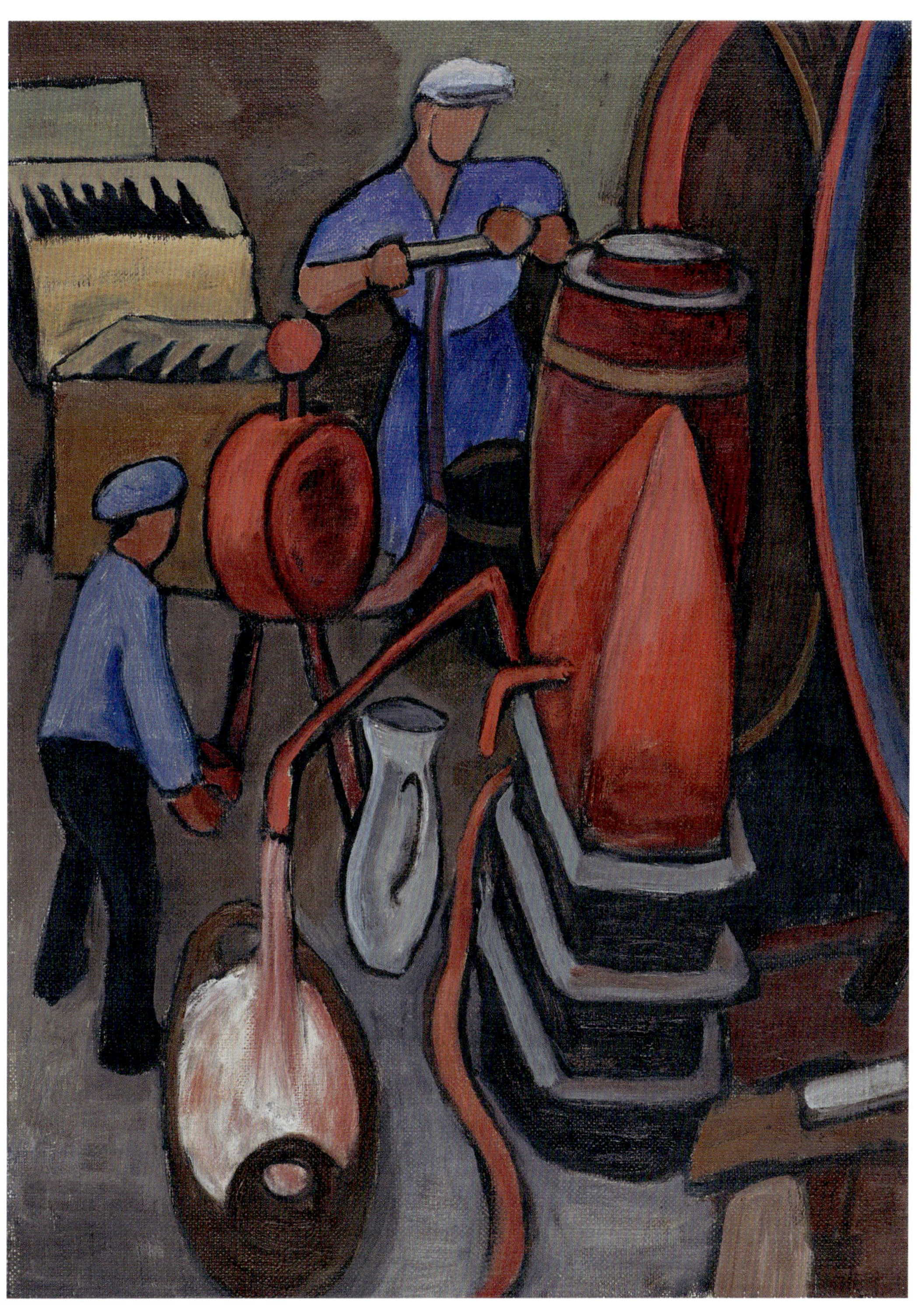

Cat. 189
Working in the Wine Cellar [Arbeit im Weinkeller], 1937
Textile support, 45 × 33.5 cm | Gabriele Münter- und Johannes Eichner-Stiftung, Munich, inv. no. V 135

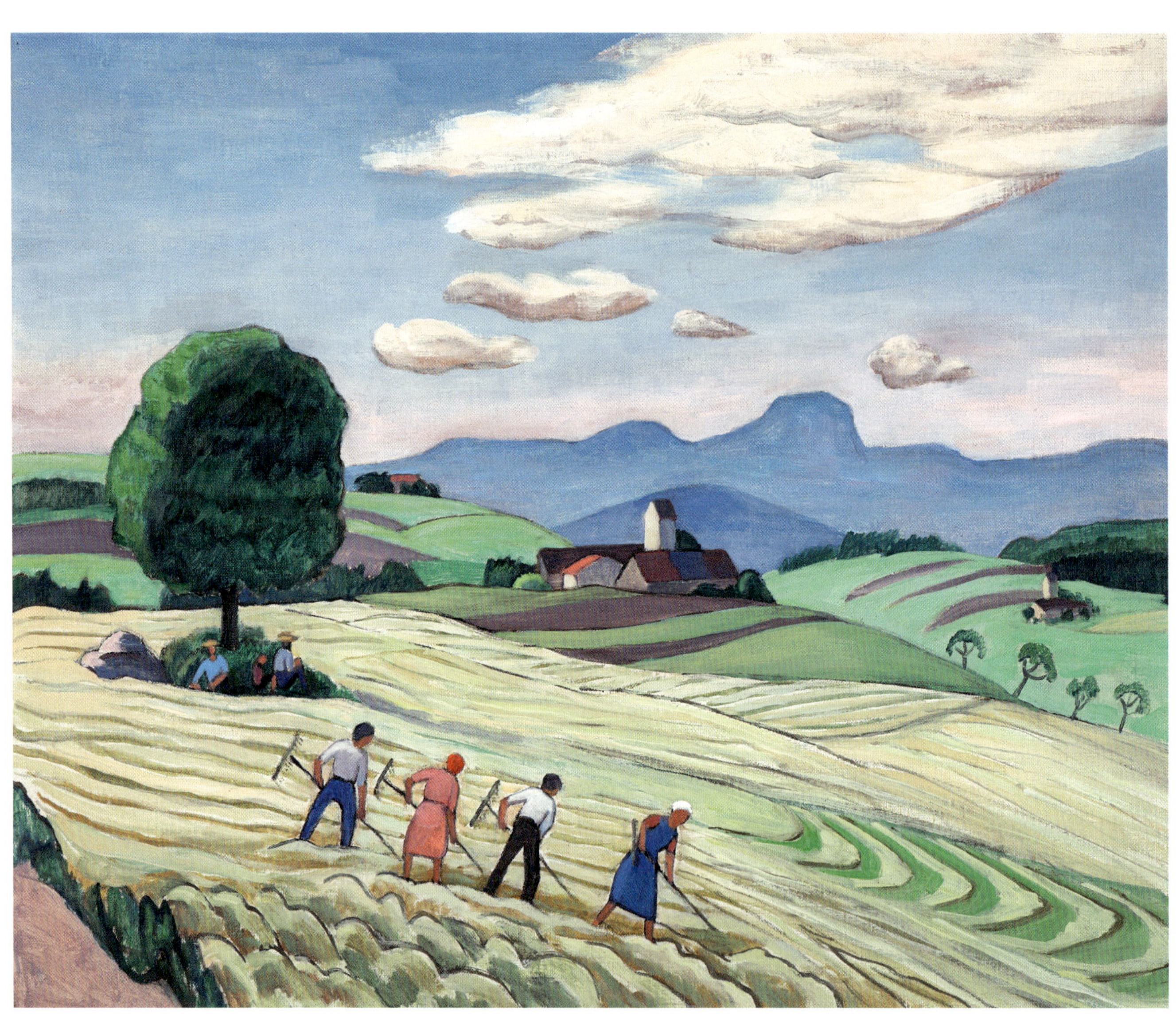

Cat. 190

Harvest in Upper Bavaria (Field Work near Dettendorf) [Ernte in Oberbayern (Feldarbeit bei Dettendorf)], 1942

Textile support, 60.3 × 73.5 cm | Gabriele Münter- und Johannes Eichner-Stiftung, Munich, inv. no. L 19

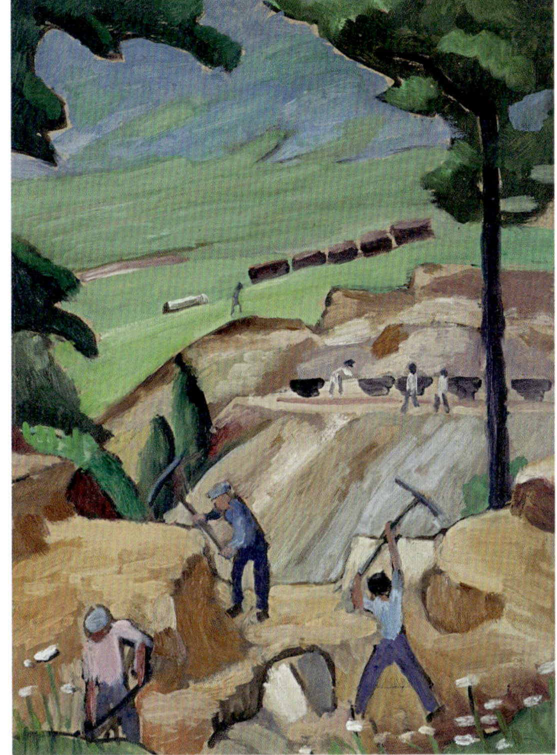

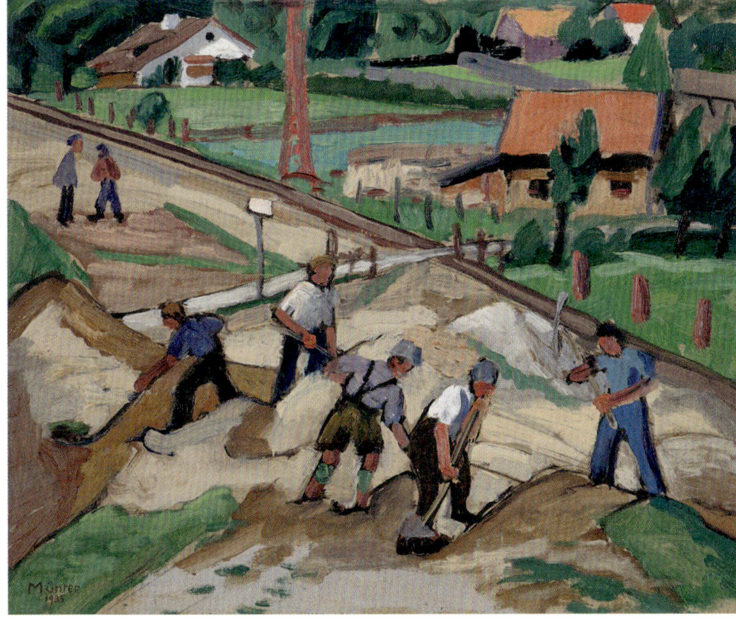

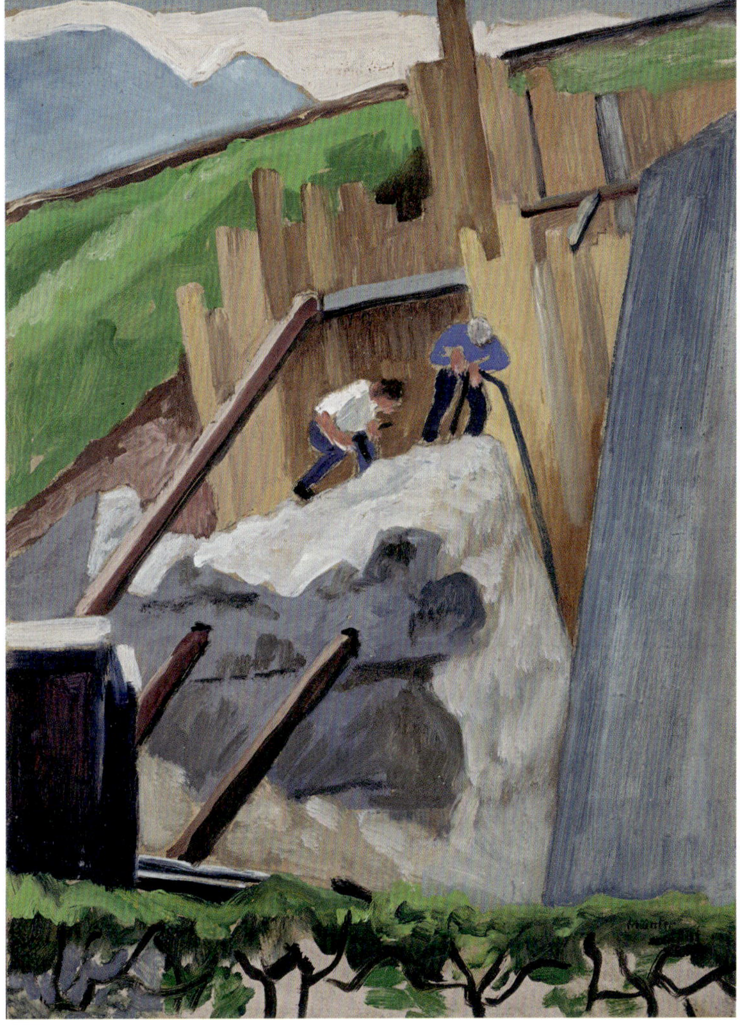

Cat. 191
Study with Three Laborers (Road Workers II) [Studie mit drei Arbeitern (Straßenarbeiter II)], 1935
Cardboard, 45.1 × 33.1 cm | Gabriele Münter- und Johannes Eichner-Stiftung, Munich, inv. no. L 321

Cat. 192
Excavation Work [Erdarbeiten], 1935
Cardboard, 33.1 × 41.1 cm | Gabriele Münter- und Johannes Eichner-Stiftung, Munich, inv. no. V 32

Cat. 193
Wall Breakers [Mauerbrecher], 1935
Cardboard, 45.1 × 33.1 cm | Gabriele Münter- und Johannes Eichner-Stiftung, Munich, inv. no. L 299

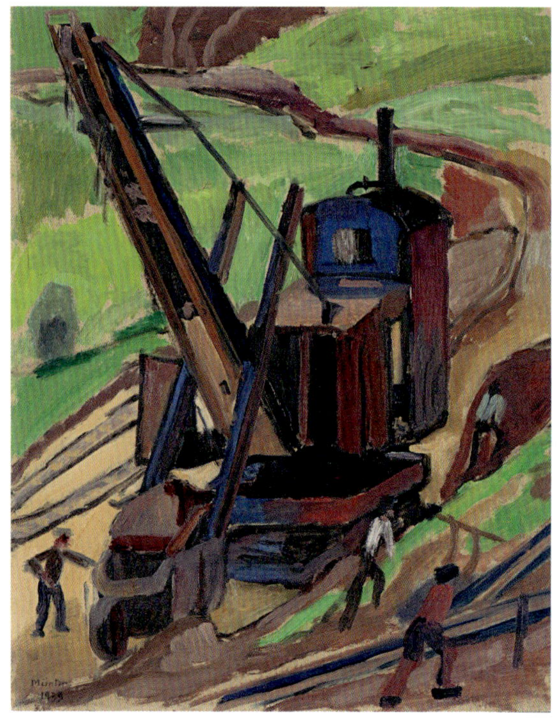

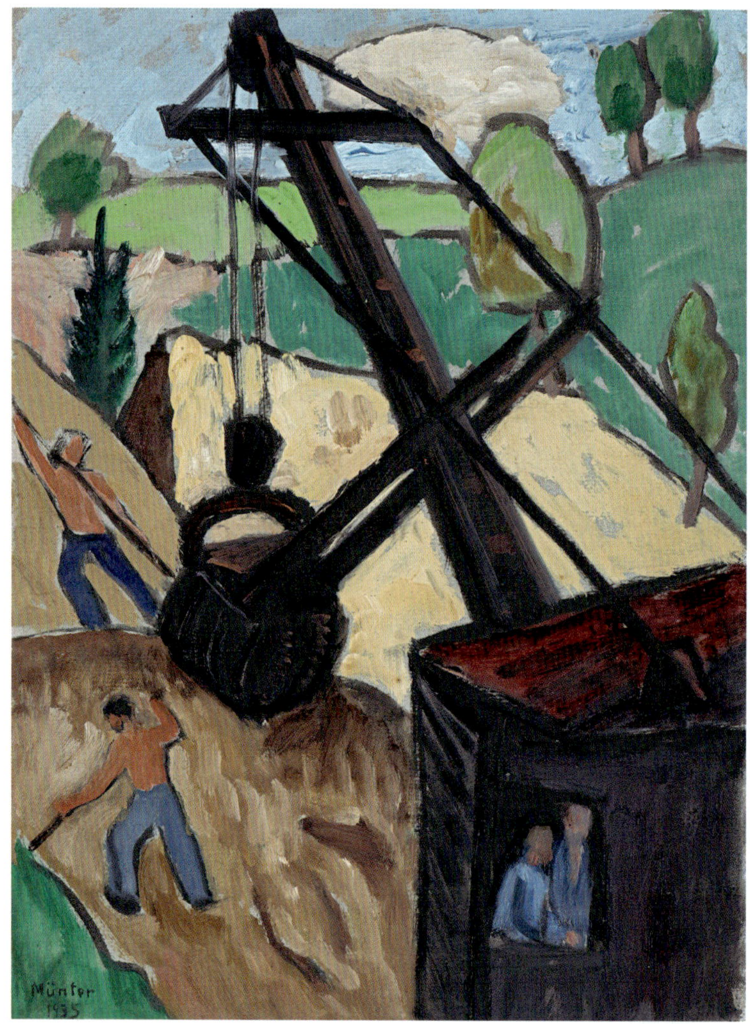

Cat. 194
Excavator [Löffelbagger], 1935
Cardboard, 41.1 × 33.1 cm |
Gabriele Münter- und Johannes Eichner-Stiftung, Munich, inv. no. V 51

Cat. 195
Excavator Shovel [Baggerlöffel], 1935
Cardboard, 44.8 × 33.2 cm | Gabriele Münter- und Johannes Eichner-Stiftung, Munich, inv. no. V 42

Cat. 196
The Blue Excavator (Study) [Der blaue Bagger (Studie)], 1935
Cardboard, 32.9 × 41.1 cm |
Gabriele Münter- und Johannes Eichner-Stiftung, Munich, inv. no. L 331

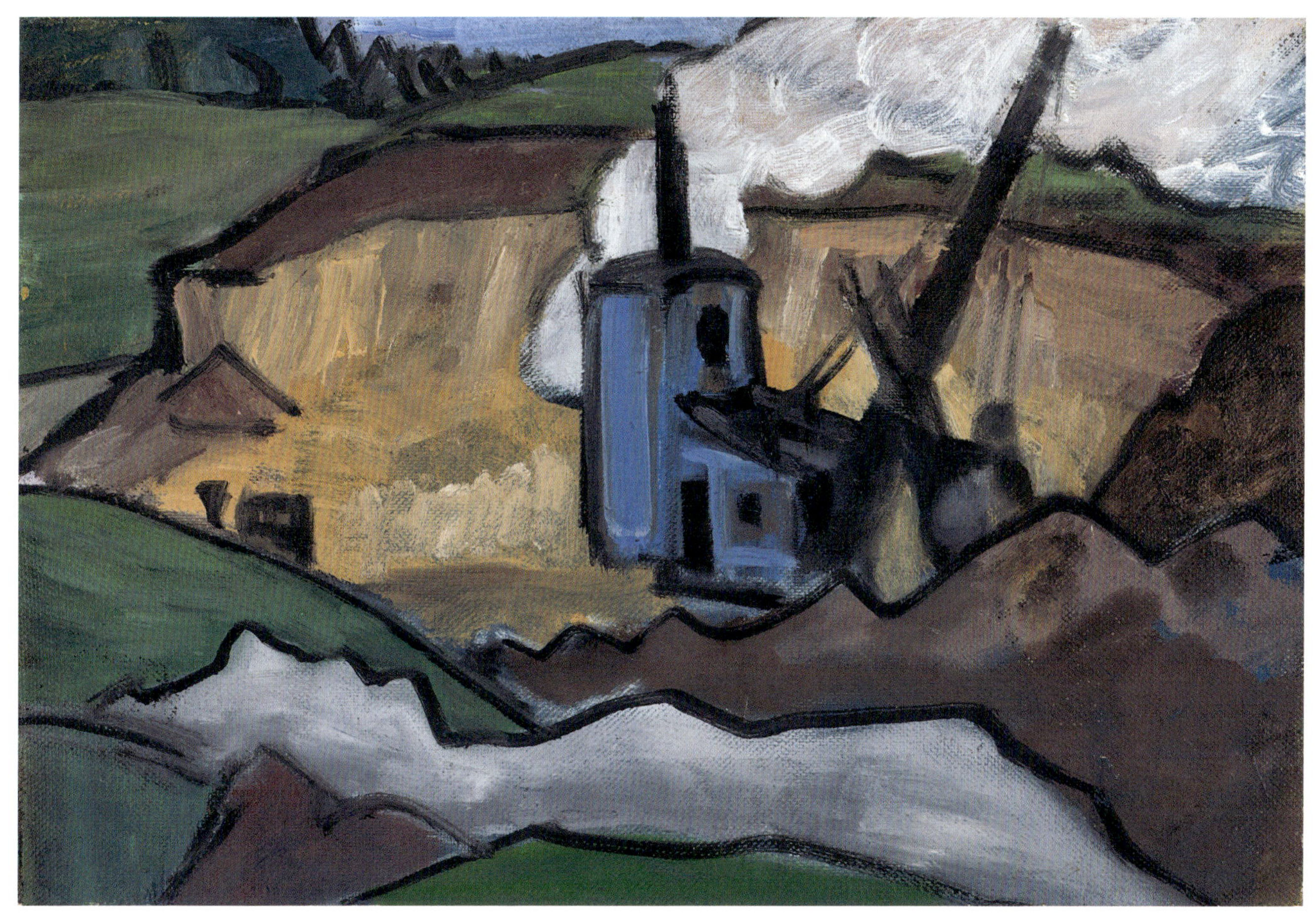

Cat. 197
Blue Excavator
[Blauer Bagger], 1935
Cardboard, 27.2 × 40.6 cm |
Gabriele Münter- und Johannes Eichner-Stiftung, Munich, inv. no. L 435

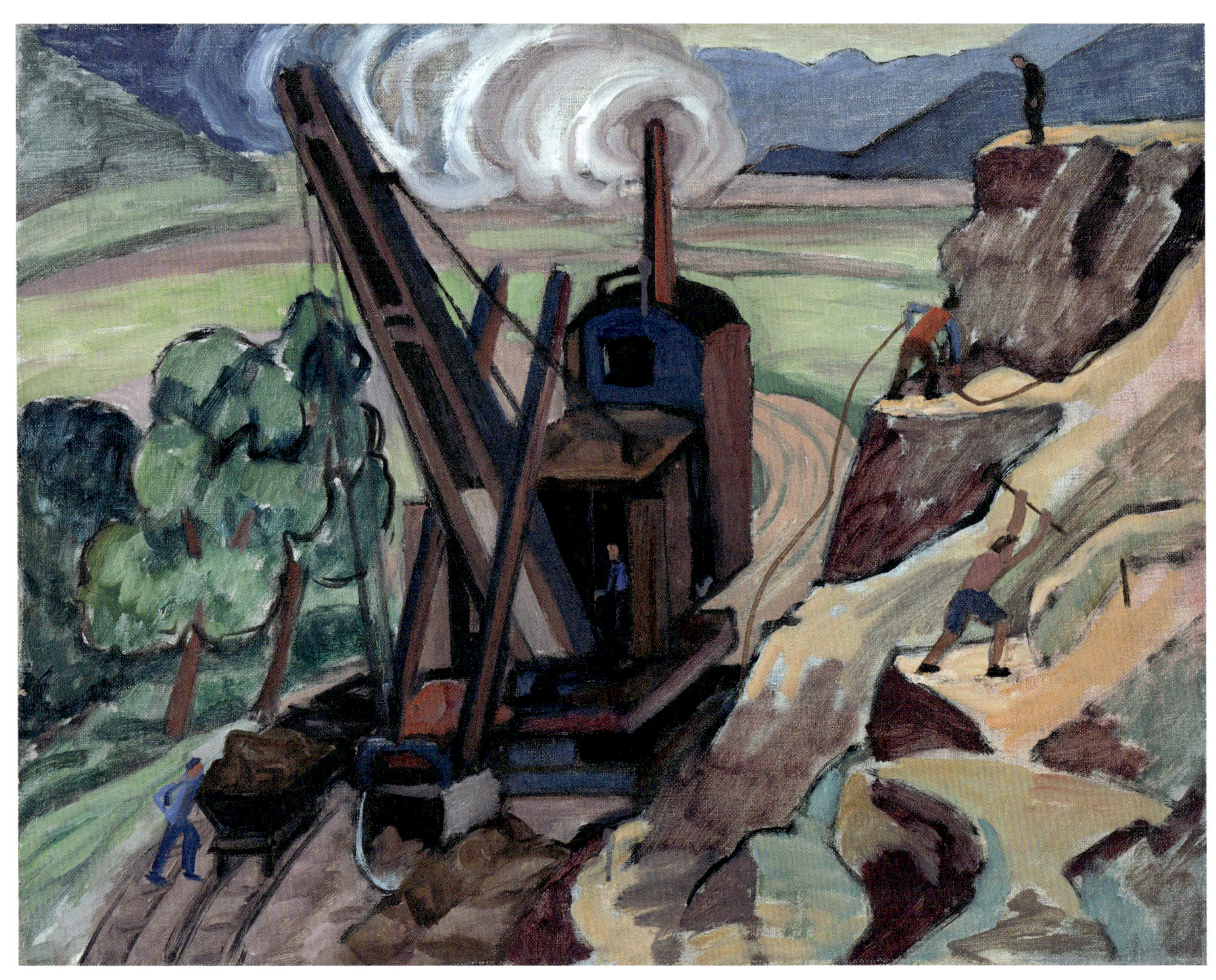

Cat. 198

Smoking Excavator in the Landscape (Construction Site on Olympiastraße) [Rauchender Bagger in der Landschaft (Baustelle an der Olympiastraße)], 1935

Textile support, 50.5 × 65.4 cm | Gabriele Münter- und Johannes Eichner-Stiftung, Munich, inv. no. L 39

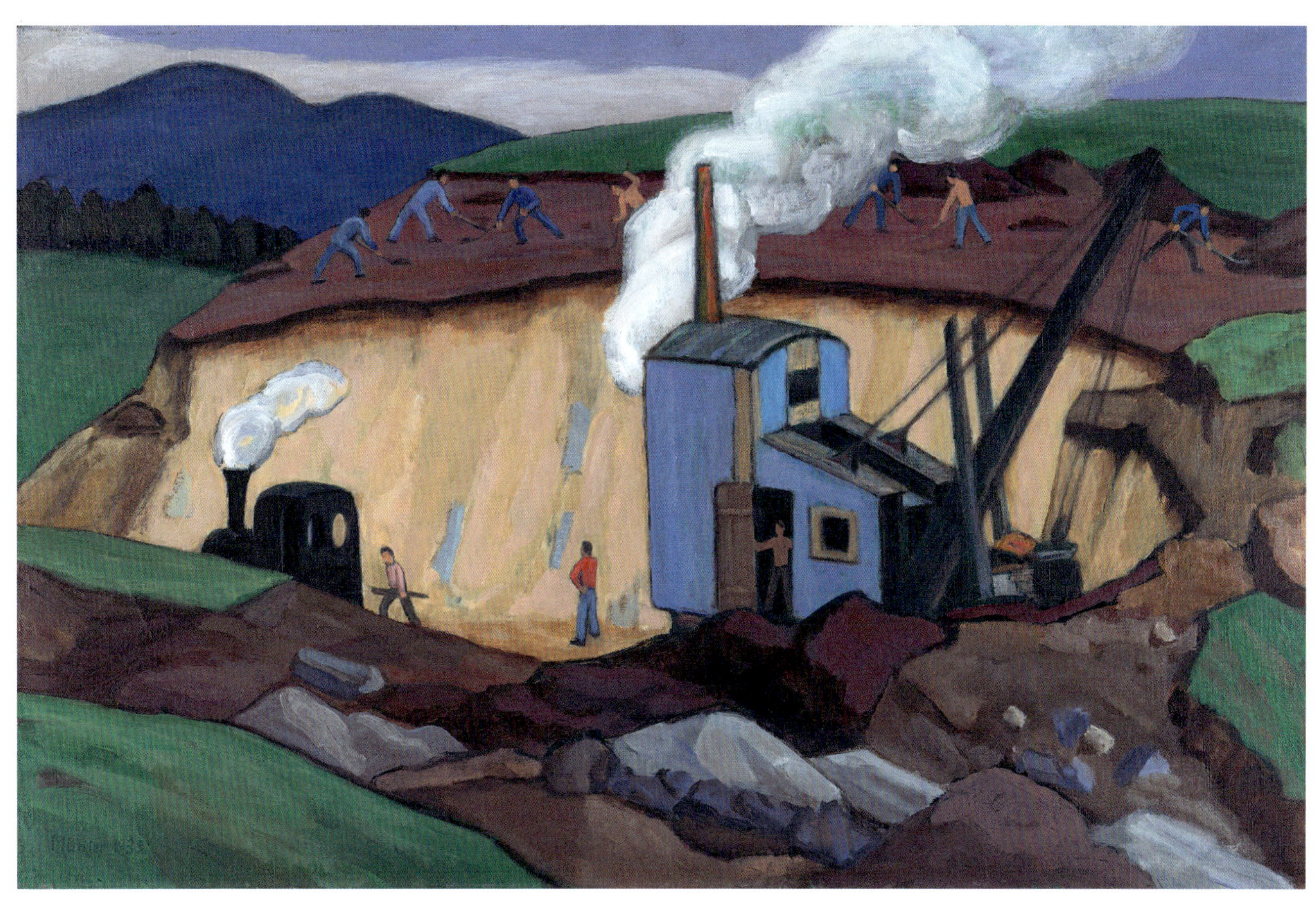

Cat. 199
The Blue Excavator (Construction Site on Olympiastraße to Garmisch) [Der blaue Bagger (Baustelle an der Olympiastraße nach Garmisch)], 1935–37
Textile support, 60.5 × 92.5 cm | Gabriele Münter- und Johannes Eichner-Stiftung, Munich, inv. no. L 12

“One is freer and less encumbered in the ‘nonobjective’ mode”[1]

Working with Abstraction

Working with Abstraction

"I did not paint abstractly because my eyes constantly provided me with motifs from nature."[2] This quote from a letter written by Gabriele Münter to the American art historian Kenneth Lindsay in 1956 is somewhat surprising, since Münter did indeed paint in an abstract style and had focused her attention on abstraction once again at that particular time. Although her oeuvre contains relatively few abstract paintings, two distinct phases of her career as a painter stand out: the years 1914 to 1915 and the 1950s. Moreover, the numerous drawings in her sketchbooks from 1914/15 and the list of paintings in her logbook from 1952/53 that she identified as "abstract" bear witness to her intense interest in the possibilities offered by abstraction at certain times in her life. Thus one wonders why Münter denied having such an interest in the aforementioned letter. Did she do so in order to distance herself from Kandinsky? Or was it because she could not identify with this part of her oeuvre? Her attempt to steer the critical reception of her own art in a specific direction is reminiscent of her efforts to propagate the equally spurious myth of the spontaneously creative artist.[3] Like most of her male colleagues in the field of modern art, Münter was consciously concerned with defining her place in art history.

We can identify not only two abstract phases in Münter's oeuvre but two types of abstraction as well. The first traces its source to a figurative motif, as in the *After Tea* paintings, for example.[4] The creative process involved here is one of abstracting. The other form of abstraction is nonobjective painting that has no basis in reality. Most of the works produced during the first phase (1914/15) are of the first type. *At the Café* is a fascinating example of Münter's practice of transforming figurative compositions into an abstract painting. Cat. 200–202 The scene is set in a coffee house, with the artist seated at a table; the back of her head is visible in the foreground. Thus the viewer can observe what is happening in the room from the same perspective as the artist herself. Münter used a similar composition scheme in other works as well.[5] Using this café scene as a point of departure, Münter created a series of three paintings, all of which were presumably produced in 1914.[6] Two of these works are figurative and of different sizes. The smaller variation, more sketch-like than the larger one, is based on a pencil drawing.[7] The third painting, *Abstract Interior*, looks abstract at first glance. Yet a close comparison with the other two works reveals the blue and green coloration of the back of the artist's head, the pink arm, the chairs, and the waitresses. It is particularly interesting to note that Münter made two sketches of this abstract composition, in two different sketchbooks, somewhat later. One sheet is dated March 19, 1915, the other March 28, 1915. Figs. A; B These sketches are accompanied by other abstract composition studies. When viewing the eight sketches on the sheet dated March 28, one has the impression that the café scene served as the point of departure for what appears in the left half of most of the studies. The scene was reworked and altered in part, almost to the point of unrecognizability, however. The right halves of most of the sketches call to mind other abstract paintings by Münter, such as her *Abstract Study*. Fig. C This sketchbook sheet is a fine example of the extent to which Münter repeatedly used the same motif from the café scene and combined it with other abstract images to produce new pictorial creations.

Another example of Münter's process of abstraction can be found in the 1914 painting titled *Abstract*. The painter drew the subject from her *Still Life with Birds*, a work completed in the same year. Figs. D; E The two birds are still essentially recognizable in the foreground of the abstract composition—the red-and-green one on the left and the yellow one on the right.

Münter turned her attention to abstraction again forty years later. This time, her investigations took place primarily in her works on paper. The highlight of this phase of her career as a painter can be dated to the year 1954. It was then that the other form of abstraction—nonobjective painting—gained the upper

1
Translated from exh. cat. Munich/Frankfurt/Stockholm 1992/93, introduction to the chapter " Die vierziger und fünfziger Jahre: Konzentration und Rückbesinnung."

2
Quoted in exh. cat. Milwaukee/Columbus/Richmond/San Antonio 1997–99, p. 169.

3
See the chapters "Primitivism," p. 136, and "Pre-Painting: Münter's Early Work," p. 17, as well as exh. cat. Milwaukee/Columbus/Richmond/San Antonio 1997–99, p. 58.

4
See the chapter "Repetitions and Variations," pp. 188–89. Another example is the following series of three paintings: *Still Life in Circle*, 1911, oil on cardboard, 84.7 × 70 cm, private collection, Berlin; *Still Life with Toy Bird*, ca. 1912, cardboard, 68.8 × 51 cm, inv. no. S 9, MES; *Abstract: Study with White Spots*, 1912, cardboard, 38.6 × 25.6 cm, Städtische Galerie im Lenbachhaus und Kunstbau München, inv. no. GMS 667. Illustrated in exh. cat. Milwaukee/Columbus/Richmond/San Antonio 1997–99, pp. 96–97.

5
For example in *Breakfast of the Birds*, Cat. 112.

6
Only the small variation on *At the Café* is not dated. The larger is dated "1914?" on the reverse, and *Abstract Interior* is dated 1914.

7
In sketchbook, inv. no. Kon. 46/43 (1914/15), p. 15, MES.

8
Eichner 1957, pp. 190ff.

hand. Her palette is comparable to that of the paintings from her first abstract phase. In terms of style, however, the paintings differ by virtue of the artist's use of clearly defined forms. Cat. 207 According to Johannes Eichner, this renewal of interest in abstract painting was triggered by a purely practical matter. After a fall in 1951, Münter suffered from physical balance problems and left her house less often. Exposed to fewer stimuli from the outside world, she relied increasingly on an abstract visual language, as Eichner explains.[8] While that may be one explanation for her interest in abstraction, it is certainly not the whole story. After the end of the National Socialist dictatorship, during which avant-garde movements were brought to an abrupt halt and only figurative art was tolerated, a tendency in favor of nonobjective painting emerged. Münter expressed the following thoughts about her recent abstract works in 1952: "During the past few years in which the epidemic of nature-free painting has emerged, I have joined the parade and taken frequent 'nonobjective walks.' I have filled folders full of free form and

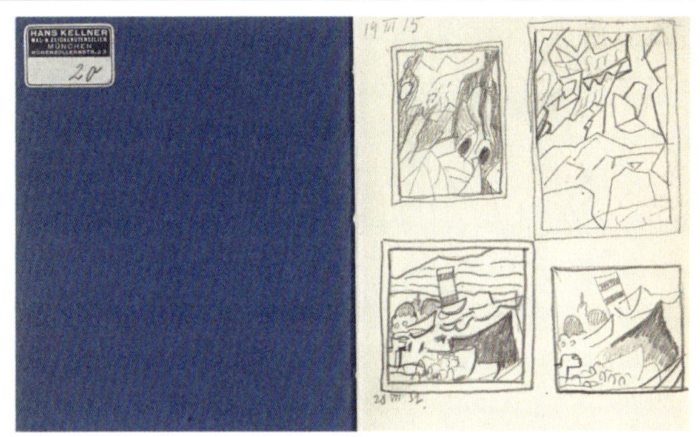

A **Sketchbook page with four draft compositions [Skizzenheftblatt mit vier Kompositionsentwürfen], 1915**
Pencil on paper, 14.6 × 11 cm |
Städtische Galerie im Lenbachhaus und Kunstbau München, inv. no. GMS 1132, p. 1

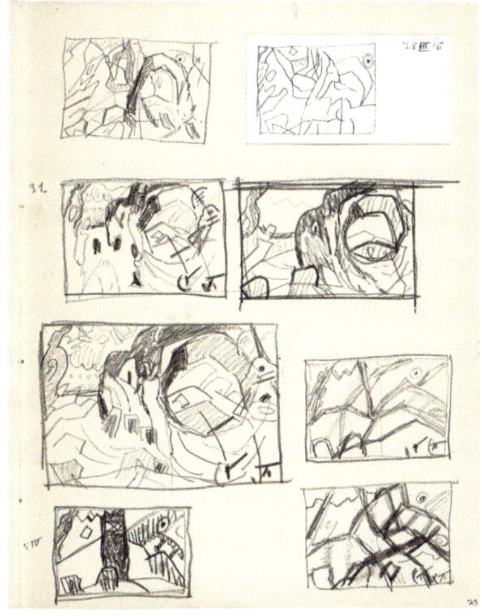

B **Sketchbook page with eight draft compositions [Skizzenbuchblatt mit acht Kompositionsentwürfen], 1915**
Pencil on paper, 21.1 × 16.6 cm |
Gabriele Münter- und Johannes Eichner-Stiftung, Munich, inv. no. Kon. 36/11, p. 21

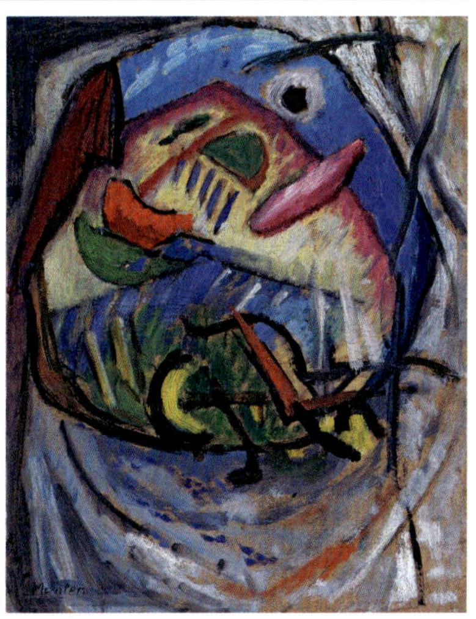

C **Abstract Study [Abstrakte Studie], 1915**
Cardboard, 41.1 × 33 cm |
Gabriele Münter- und Johannes Eichner-Stiftung, Munich, inv. no. V 113

color studies, and the possibilities appear virtually inexhaustible. Yet I prefer to dispense with large formats. One no longer feels responsible for the natural source image—one is freer and less encumbered in the 'nonobjective' mode."[9] Münter maintained close ties with the Munich gallerists Otto and Etta Stangl, whose exhibition program was heavily weighted toward abstract art.[10] They organized an exhibition of Münter's abstract works on paper under the title *Improvisationen* in the spring of 1955.[11] The artist wrote to the art educator Irene von Schaller in advance of the exhibition: "Stangl is planning an exhibition of my nonobjective improvisations—what do you suppose people will think about that!?"[12] At least one painting was shown among the works on paper, namely *With Two White Arrows*.[13] Cat. 206 Kandinsky had used the term "improvisations" for a group of his works as early as 1909. He regarded them as "chiefly unconscious, for the most part suddenly arising expressions of events of an inner character, [. . .] impressions of 'internal nature.'"[14] Münter used a different term, also borrowed from Kandinsky's oeuvre, for her own abstract works: "bagatelles."[15] The word referred to her small, quickly executed abstract works on paper. Her use of terms from Kandinsky's world with reference to her later abstract works is all the more remarkable in view of the fact that Kandinsky did not apply those terms exclusively to his abstract compositions.

The two abstract phases of Münter's career as an artist differ not only with respect to style but also in terms of the significance the painter attached to them. Although she had written in 1952 that she did not intend to realize larger paintings in this formal language, her abstract paintings from the 1950s are larger, for the most part, than the works produced in 1914/15. This somewhat paradoxical statement actually related to the works on paper, which are smaller and much more numerous. Her choices of works for exhibitions are another indication of how little she thought of her abstract works from the 1950s. While she presented

D **Abstract [Abstrakt], 1914**
Cardboard, 33.5 × 41 cm | Gabriele Münter- und Johannes Eichner-Stiftung, Munich, inv. no. V 13

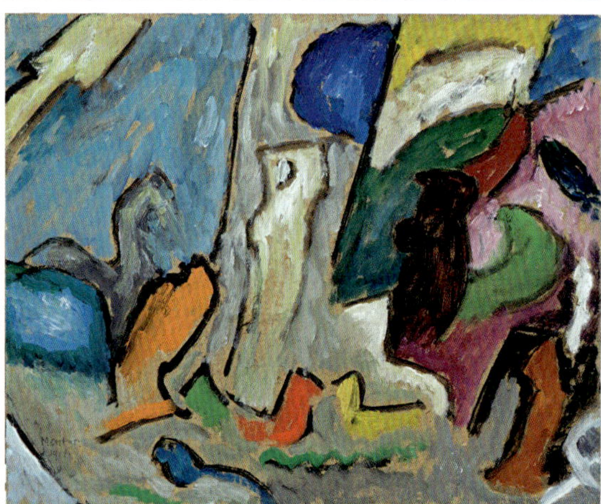

E **Still Life with Birds [Stilleben mit Vögeln], 1914**
Oil on canvas, 60.5 × 78 cm | Private collection

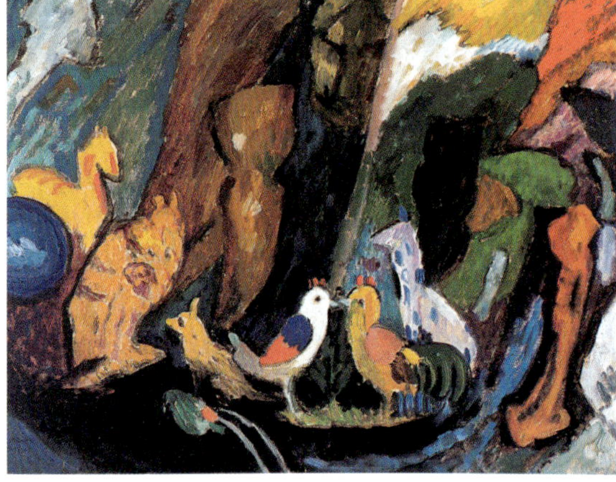

9
As note 1.

10
Clelia Segieth, *Etta und Otto Stangl: Galeristen, Sammler, Museumsgründer*, Cologne 2000, p. 34.

11
February to March 1955, Kunstkabinett Otto Stangl.

12
Letter dated December 31, 1954, MES.

13
It is visible in a photograph of the exhibition, MES.

14
Quoted in Friedel/Hoberg 2000, text accompanying plate 12, Wassily Kandinsky, *Study for Improvisation 2 (Funeral March)*, 1909.

15
See the chapter "Primitivism," pp. 143–44.

16
Gabriele Münter, Der Sturm, 35th exhibition, Berlin [opening: October 24, 1915]; *Gabriele Münter-Kandinsky: Oljemalninger, Glastavler, Grafik*, Den Frie Udstilling, Copenhagen, March 7–13, 1918; *Maleriudstilling Gabriele Münter-Kandinsky*, Københavns Ny Kunstsal, Copenhagen, October 4–20, 1919. Münter showed a few abstract paintings from the second phase in commercial art galleries. She exhibited her abstract works on paper from the 1950s, however.

17
Katarina Borgh Bertorp, "Sigrid Hjertén, Erbin Matisses aus dem Hohen Norden," and Annegret Hoberg, "Sigrid Hjertén und Gabriele Münter," in exh. cat. *Sigrid Hjertén: Wegbereiterin des schwedischen Expressionismus*, ed. Katarina Borgh Bertorp [Munich, Städtische Galerie im Lenbachhaus, 1999; Berlin, Käthe-Kollwitz-Museum, 1999; Borås, Borås Konstmuseum, 1999–2000], Stockholm 1999, pp. 15, 43ff., and 49ff.

18
See the chapter "Landscapes and Outdoor Scenes," p. 55.

19
This idea was also the fundamental principle adopted by the artists of the Blue Rider.

20
Translated from undated note on a slip of paper, MES.

21
Translated from note on a slip of paper, dated February 21, 1951, MES.

her early abstract paintings in major solo exhibitions shortly after completing them, she hardly ever exhibited the later ones.[16]

The first phase is characterized by a more thorough investigation into the phenomenon of abstraction. As is evident in her drawings and paintings, Münter was seriously interested in this form of expression. These were not occasional works, but rather the products of her search for new artistic possibilities. She was not satisfied with the results, however, which is why she turned away from this particular visual language in 1915—the year in which she also moved to Stockholm. There she came in contact with artists who had studied under Henri Matisse in Paris.[17] Abstract painting was irrelevant for Matisse, the leading exponent of Fauvism. Thus Münter suddenly found herself in a milieu populated by painters who were pursuing very different goals, which may explain her waning interest in an abstract style of painting. She looked for new points of orientation. The paintings she realized in Scandinavia actually do bear witness to a shift in terms of both style and content. Her colors grew increasingly restrained, and the image of the human being assumed a position of central importance in her art.[18]

Münter was already more than seventy years old by the time she again turned her attention to abstract art and developed a visual language that was new to her in the 1950s. It is astonishing to realize how creative and open to experimentation the artist was throughout her life. Unfortunately, that has been overlooked or deliberately ignored all too often, since her work has been considered primarily with reference to her biography and her relationship with Kandinsky. This approach to interpretation has resulted in a one-sided reception of her art, one that is by no means justified by the facts. Although Münter preferred working in her immediate surroundings, she did not merely process her personal life in her works. Her oeuvre is both multifaceted and atypical, for its manifold character is manifested simultaneously and not in phases. This may have contributed to further confusion. In Münter's view, the most important aspect of a work of art was its expression and not its form.[19] That is why she was able to employ more than one visual language at a time. As she wrote herself, "Everyone sees things formalistically, externally—only very few people grasp the inner, living nature of art and give precedence to expression as opposed to form. That has always been a disadvantage for me, and it remains so today."[20] Yet that had no effect on her firm belief in the value of her art, as she pointed out in 1951: "One thing became clear to me after my visit to the museum: if there is such a thing as comprehension of art, then my works will eventually hang in all of the world's great museums."[21]

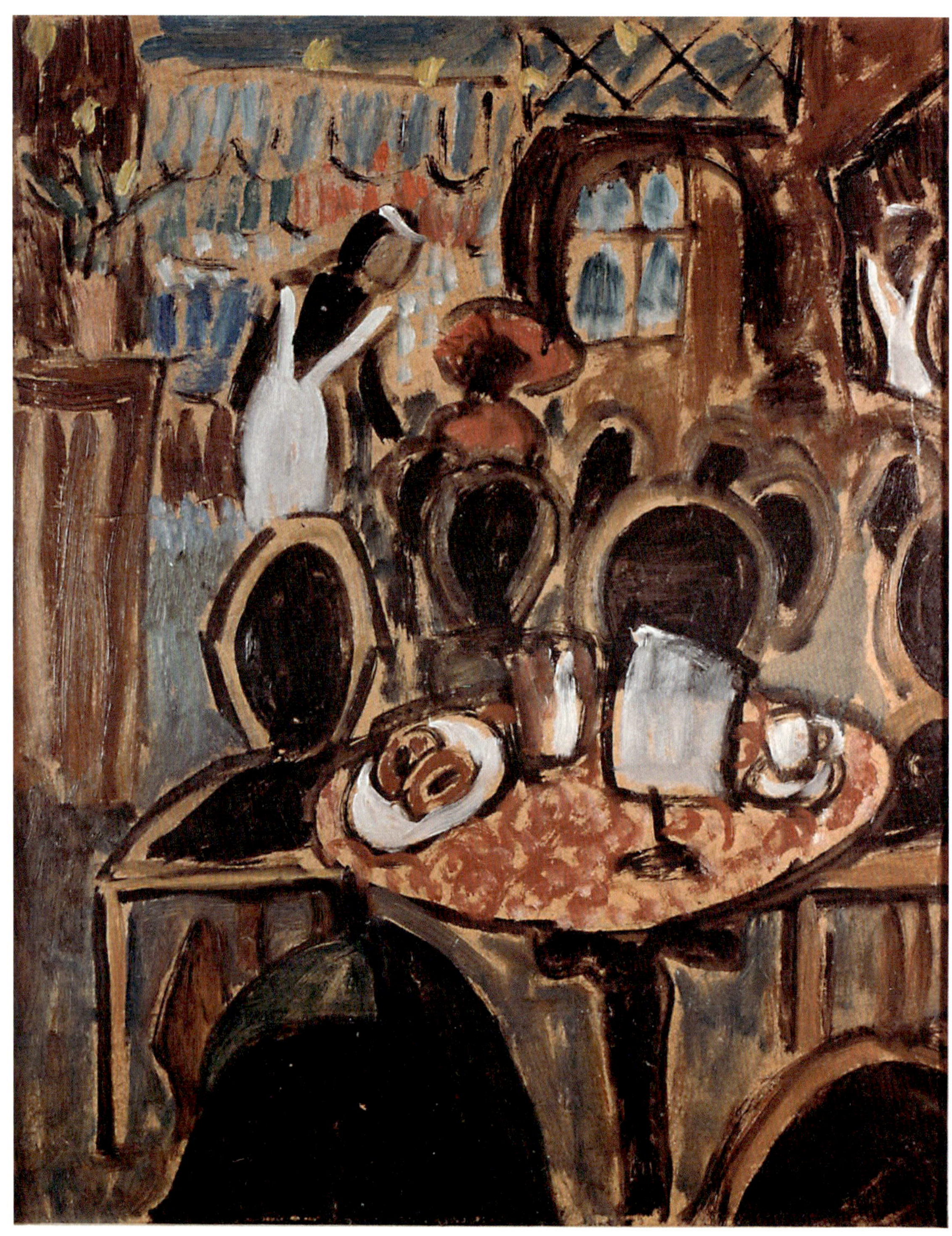

Cat. 200
At the Café [Im Café], 1914
Oil on cardboard, 40.3 × 32.5 cm |
Private collection

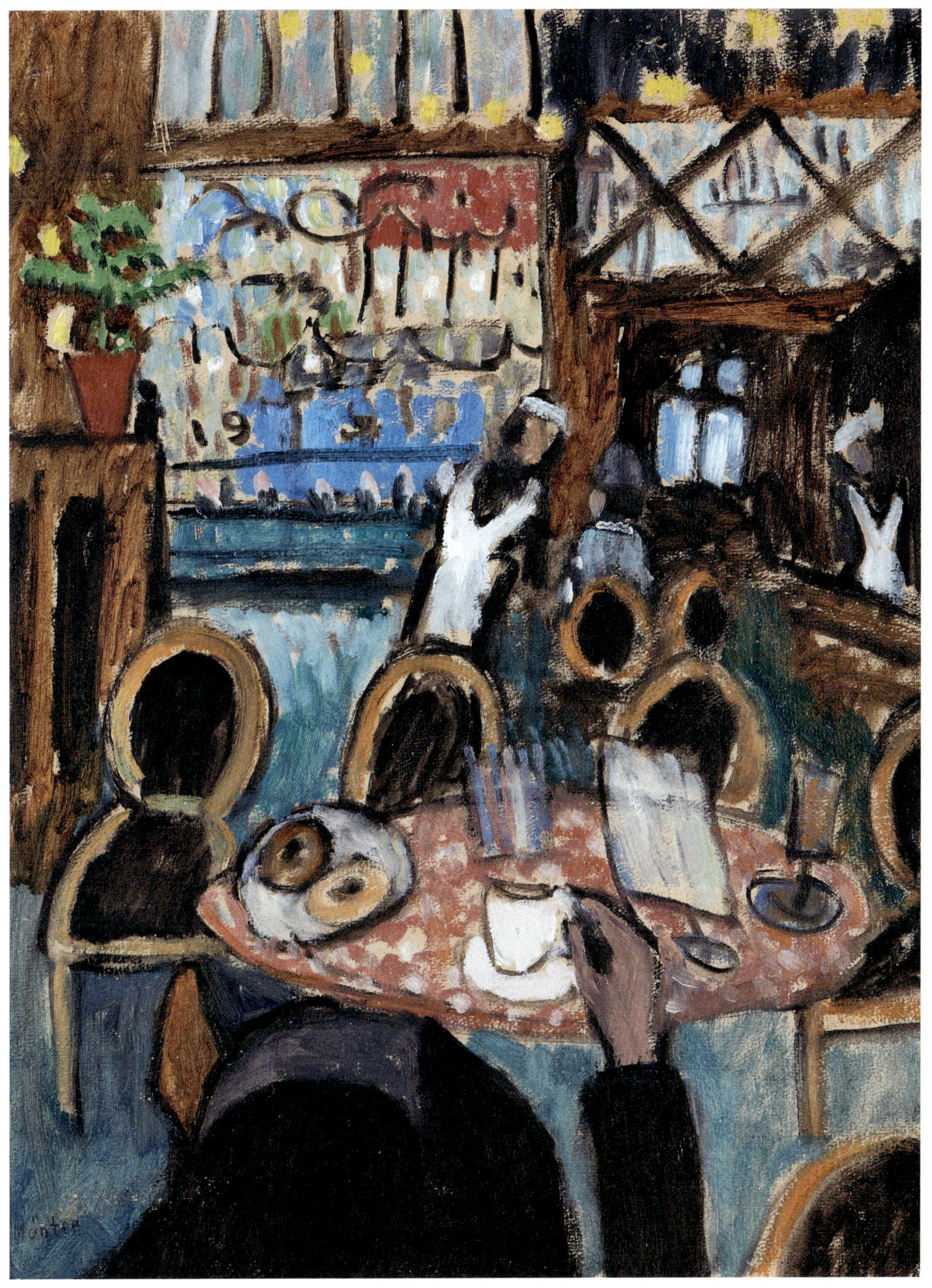

Cat. 201
At the Café [Im Café], 1914
Oil on cardboard, 61 × 46.5 cm |
Family collection, Dortmund

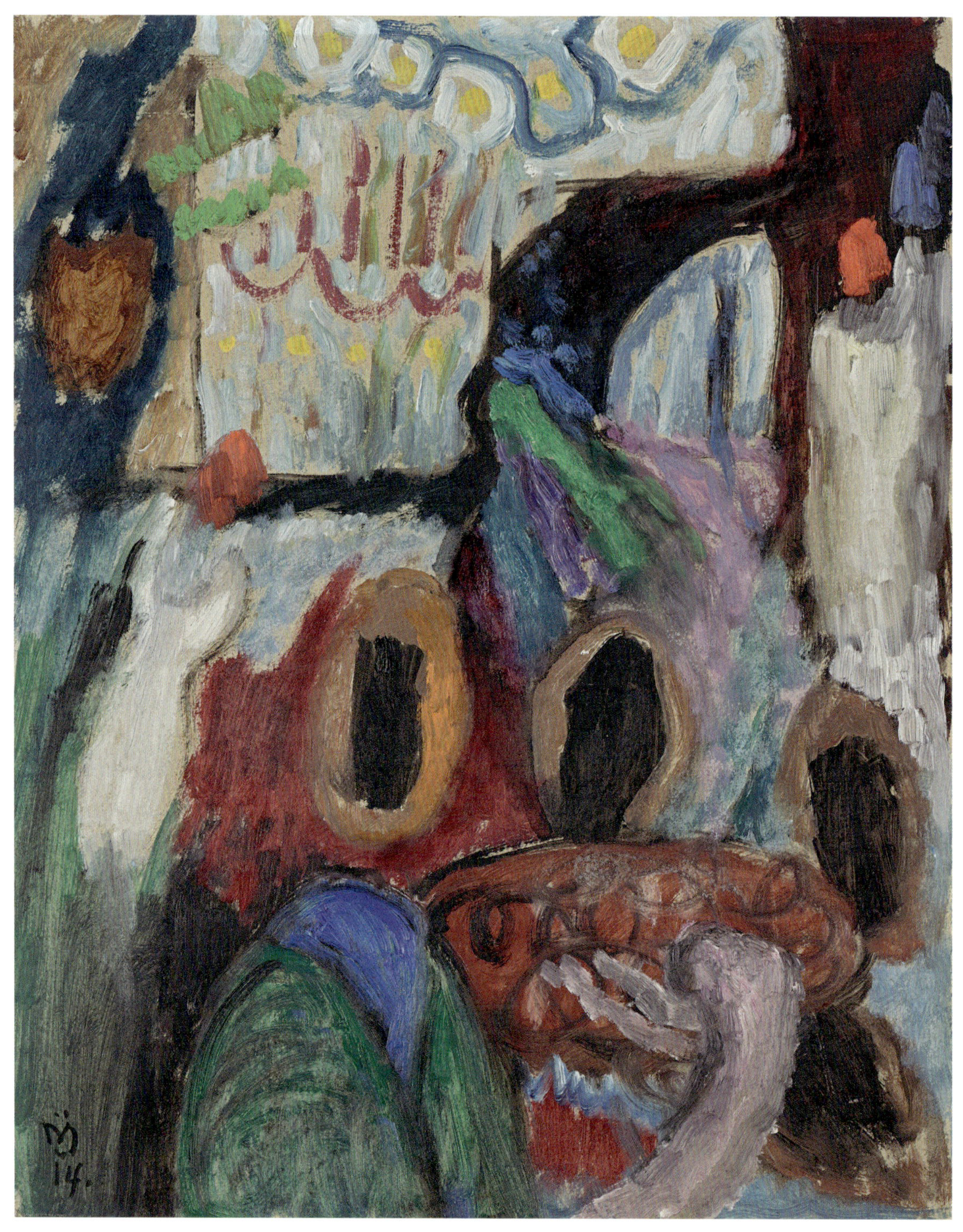

Cat. 202
Abstract Interior
[Abstraktes Interieur], 1914
Cardboard, 41 × 33 cm | Gabriele Münter- und Johannes Eichner-Stiftung, Munich, inv. no. V 14

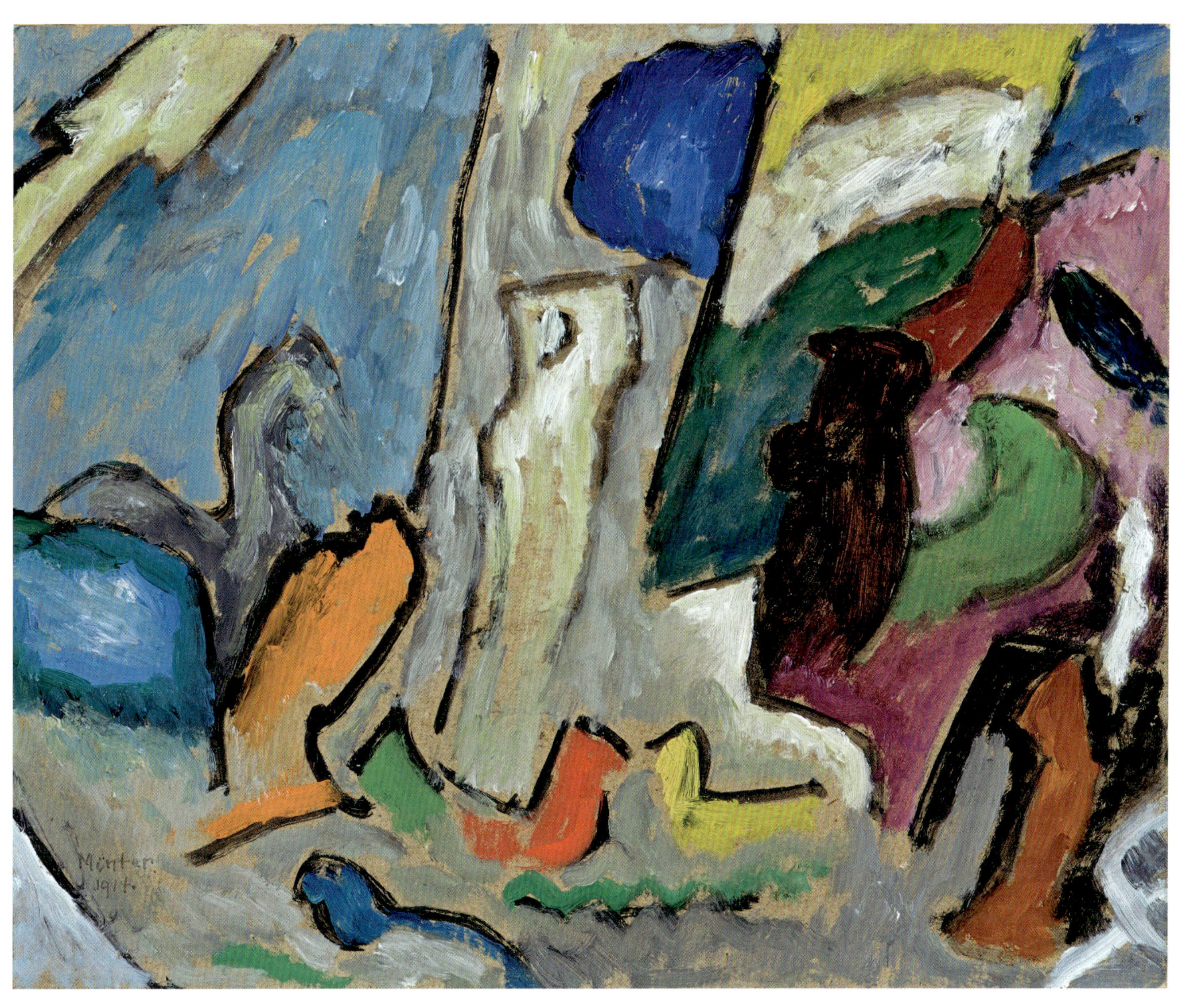

Cat. 203
Abstract [Abstrakt], 1914
Cardboard, 33.5 × 41 cm | Gabriele Münter- und Johannes Eichner-Stiftung, Munich, inv. no. V 13

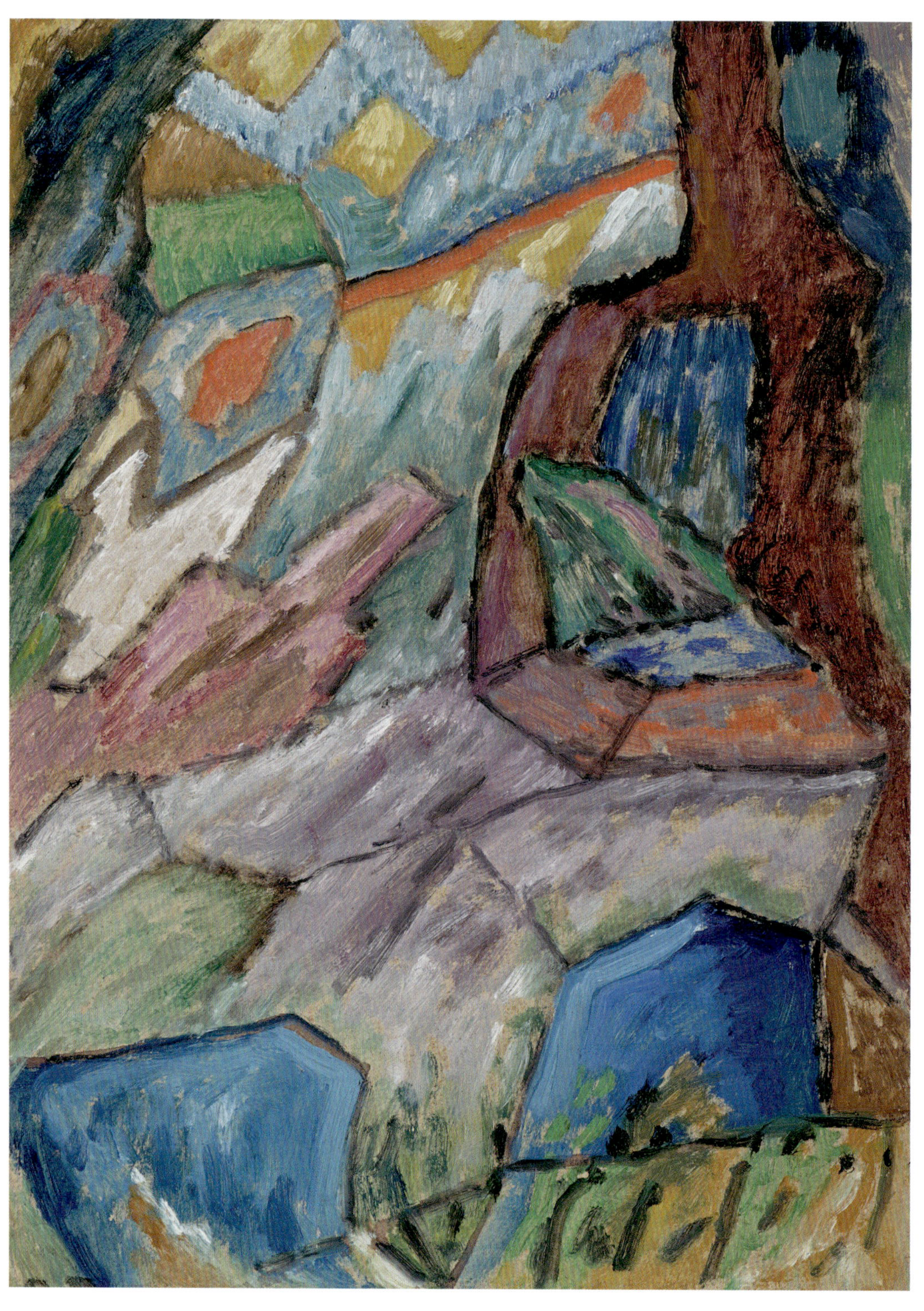

Cat. 204
Abstract Study No. 6
[Abstrakte Studie Nr. 6], 1915
Cardboard, 44.9 × 32.9 cm |
Gabriele Münter- und Johannes Eichner-Stiftung, Munich, inv. no. V 39

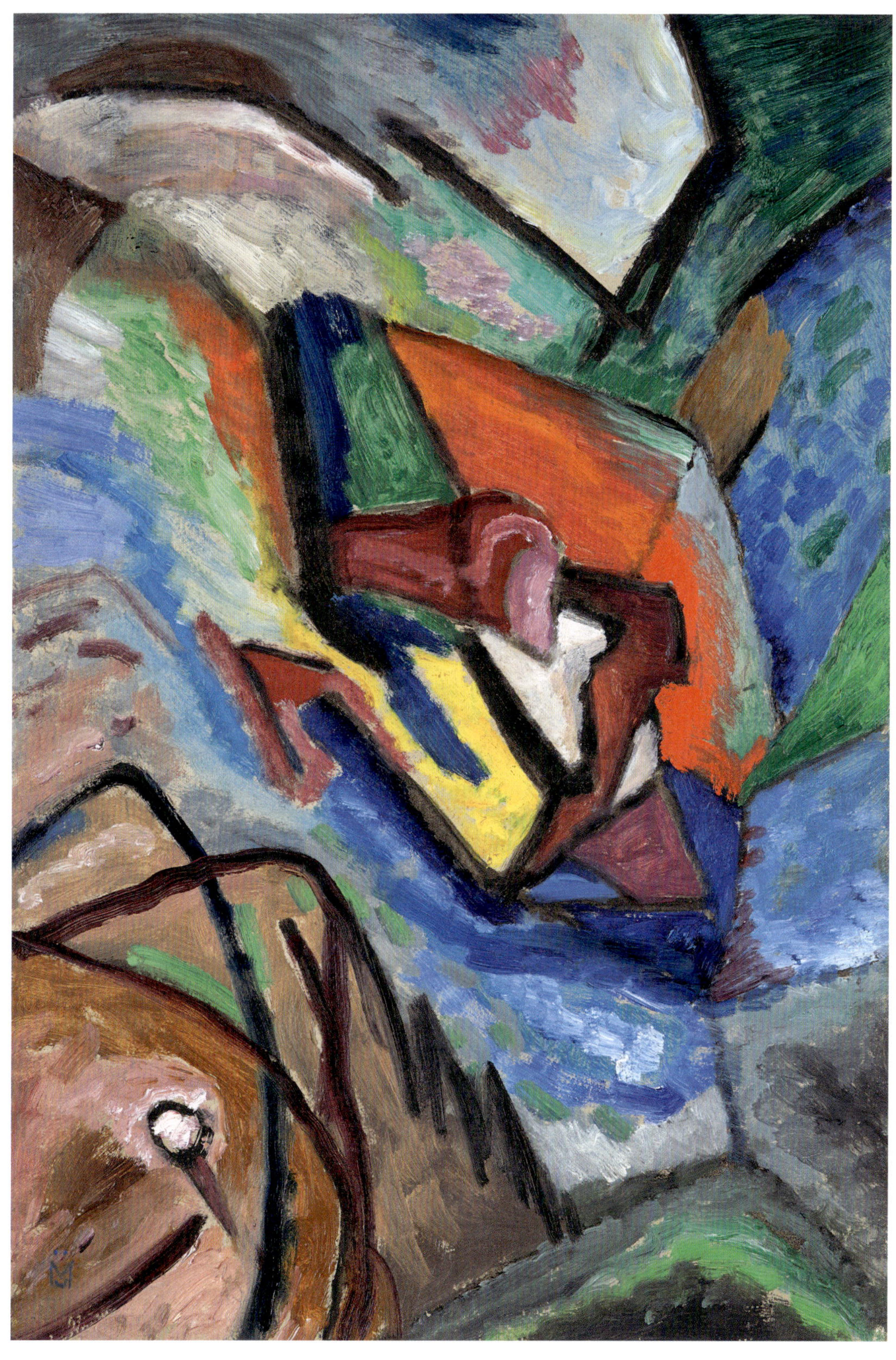

Cat. 205
Abstract (study)
[Abstrakt (Studie)], 1918
Cardboard, 49.2 × 33.7 cm | Gabriele Münter- und Johannes Eichner-Stiftung, Munich, inv. no. V 18

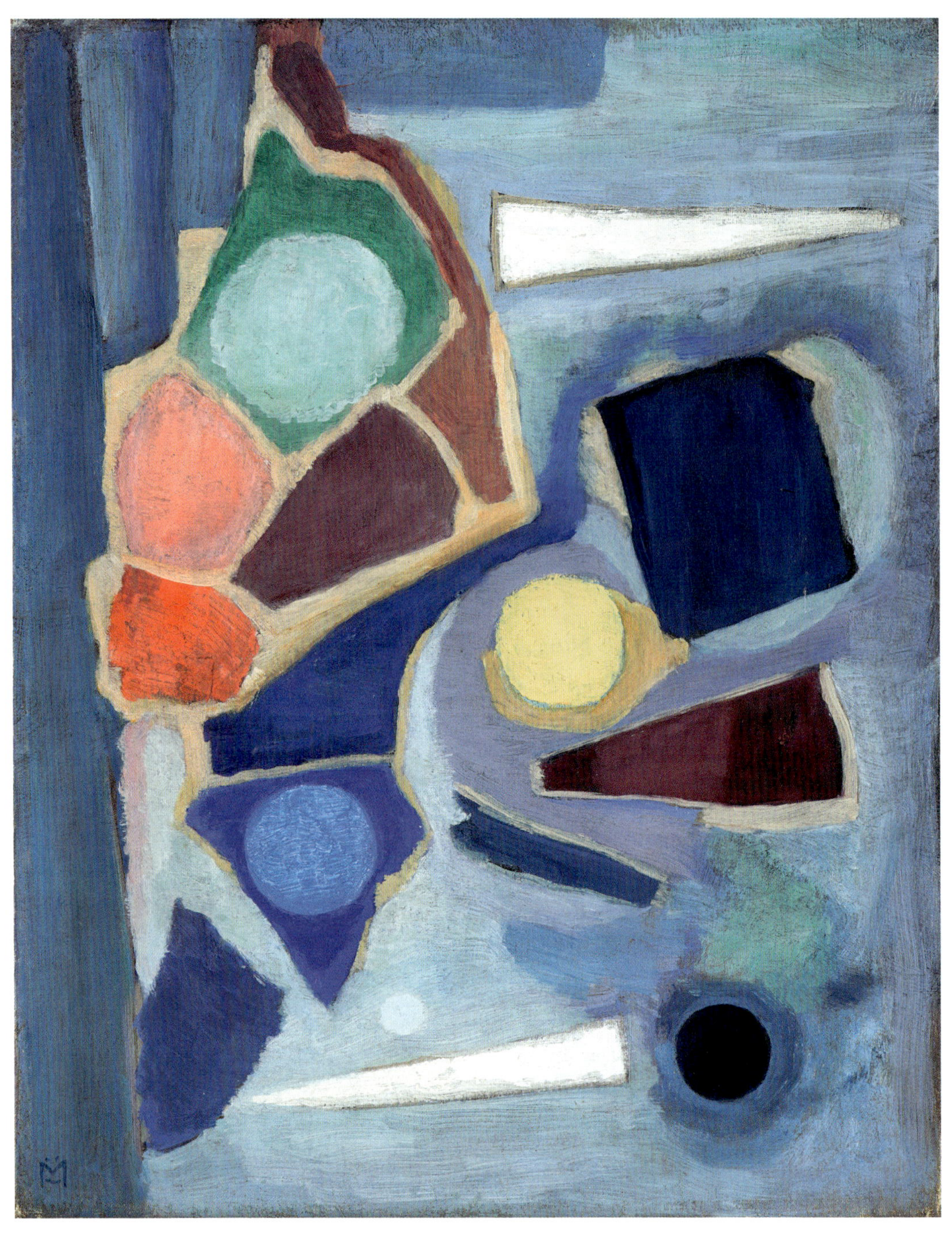

Cat. 206
With Two White Arrows
[Mit zwei weißen Pfeilen], 1952
Textile support, 41.6 × 33.5 cm |
Gabriele Münter- und Johannes Eichner-Stiftung, Munich, inv. no. V 121

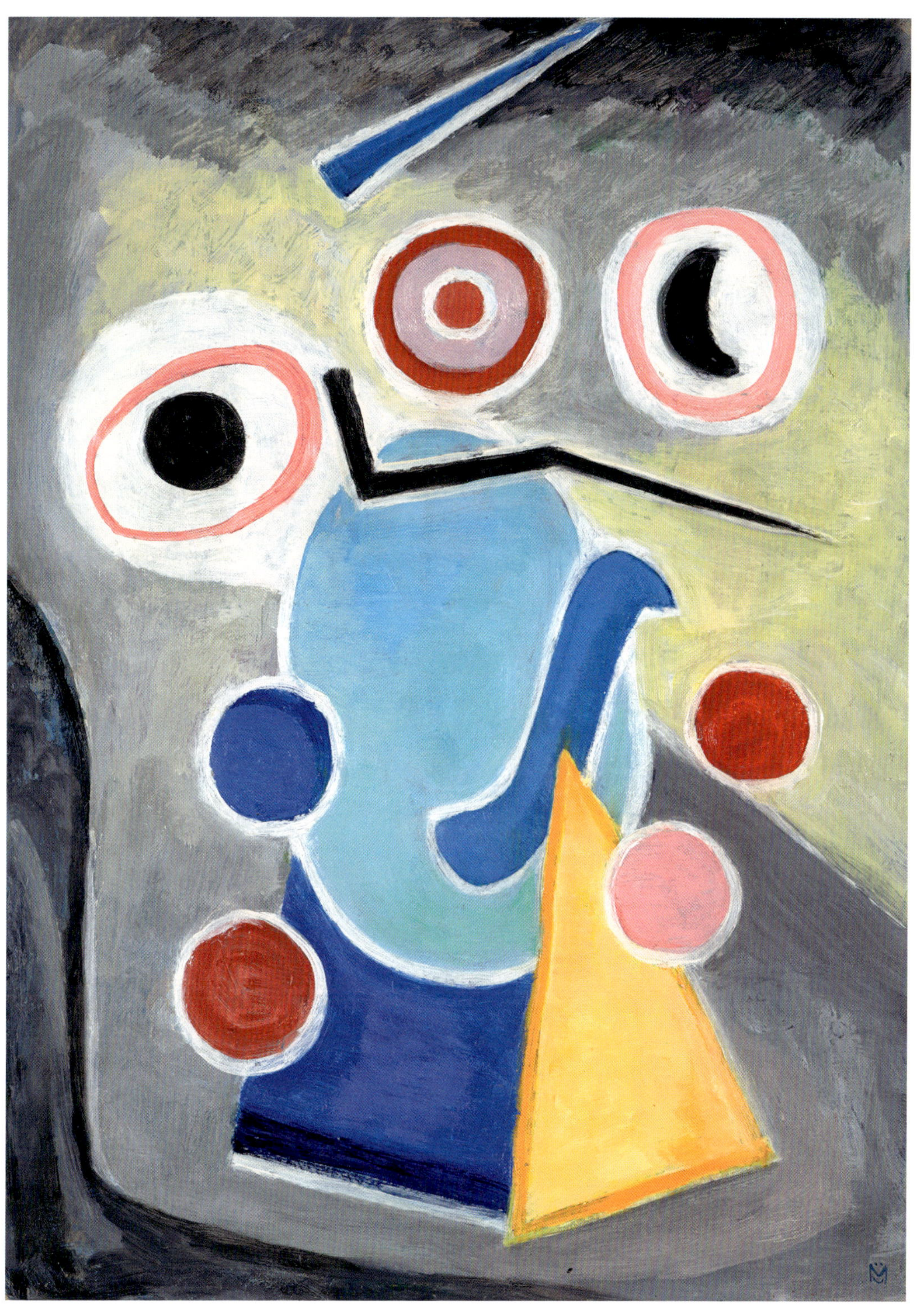

Cat. 207
Abstract (Middle Light Blue, Oval) [Abstrakt (Mitte hellblau, oval)], 1954
Cardboard, 44.9 × 32.9 cm | Gabriele Münter- und Johannes Eichner-Stiftung, Munich, inv. no. V 20

“I earned a name again, a[nd] numerous works have remained in museums.”[1]

Promoting the Art of Gabriele Münter

Promoting the Art of Gabriele Münter

Gabriele Münter established her status as a successful artist during her lifetime. She made her first public appearance as an artist in Paris in 1907, when she exhibited six paintings featuring views of Sèvres, Bellevue, and the park of Saint-Cloud at the Salon des Indépendants from March until June. That fall she showed a selection of her woodcuts at the Salon d'Automne. And just a few months later, in January 1908, she presented her first solo exhibition at the Kunstsalon Lenobel in Cologne, where she exhibited fifty-seven paintings, most of which featured motifs from her stay in France, although the group included several works from Tunisia and Rapallo as well. The critical response was positive, with reviewers praising the "elegant colorfulness" of her paintings.[2] The subsequent presentation of the exhibition at the Kaiser Wilhelm Museum in Krefeld was an extraordinary sign of success for Münter. Kandinsky was the intermediary for the showing in Krefeld, as can be gathered from a letter Friedrich Deneken, the museum's founding director, sent to the Russian artist: "You wouldn't believe the number of inquiries I receive from ladies who paint. So I am always very cautious in such cases. But I had Lenobel send me two paintings by Miss G. Münter on a trial basis and was very happy to discover that a lady had achieved something good in this case. So I asked Lenobel to send the collection here for an exhibition. I assume that it will arrive within the next few days. Of course there is no way of knowing in advance whether the venture will bring financial success for the lady."[3] The derogatory tone of the letter ("ladies who paint") was typical of the time, but Deneken was nevertheless clear-sighted enough to recognize this unknown artist's gifts as a painter and to agree to exhibit her works. Deneken was a progressive museum director who dedicated himself fervently to the task of promoting modern art. In fact, he was one of the first representatives of his profession who exhibited (and in some cases purchased) works by such masters of modern French art as Cézanne, Signac, Van Gogh, Gauguin, Monet, and Rodin.[4] Münter was barely thirty-one years old when this first museum exhibition took place. It is worth noting by way of comparison that Franz Marc, who was only three years younger than Münter, was never honored with an exclusive museum exhibition during his lifetime.[5]

After the presentation in Krefeld, the extensive body of works by the artist moved on—in occasionally modified form—to Düren, Hamburg, Breslau, Karlsruhe, and Stuttgart.[6] This tour may reasonably be regarded as the prelude to a successful series of exhibitions over a period of many years. In May 1908, the Kunstsalon Lenobel presented a second solo exhibition devoted to the artist's printed graphic oeuvre which was subsequently shown at the Kunstbuchhandlung Friedrich Cohen in Bonn.

Münter's remarkably fruitful collaboration with the Berlin gallerist Herwarth Walden began five years later. Her next solo exhibition took place at his gallery Der Sturm in 1913. On Walden's initiative, the show was also presented on a smaller scale at the opening of Max Dietzel's Neuer Kunstsalon in Munich.[7] Walden represented Münter and showed her works in solo and group exhibitions both in Germany and abroad until the early 1920s. Thus he played a key role in the promotion of her art.[8] Thanks to Walden's efforts as an agent, in 1918 Münter was able to present the largest exclusive exhibition of her works to date, featuring one hundred oil paintings, twenty reverse-glass paintings, seven etchings, and numerous drawings, in the rooms of the artists' association known as Den Frie Udstilling in Copenhagen. Fig. A Just one year later, she was honored with another major solo exhibition at the Ny Kunstsal in the Danish capital.[9] These exhibitions brought Münter's reception in Scandinavia to its highest point. The artist was recognized by critics and within the Scandinavian art scene as an international representative of the avant-garde.[10]

After returning to Germany in 1920 following her five-year stay in Scandinavia, Münter had to regain a foothold in her homeland. Since she no longer

1
Translated from letter to Dr. Gerhard Budde dated October 31, 1953, private collection. Gerhard Budde was a member of the board of directors of the Herforder Heimatverein. He and Johanna Ahlers initiated the founding of the Kunstverein (local art society), for which he served as chairman from 1955 to 1965.

2
Translated from "Kunst und Wissenschaft: Ausstellung im Kunstsalon Lenobel," *Rheinische Zeitung*, January 7, 1908.

3
Translated from letter dated January 31, 1908, MES. Kandinsky himself had exhibited at the Kaiser Wilhelm Museum in 1906. Vivian Endicott Barnett, *Kandinsky: Drawings. Catalogue Raisonné. Volume One, Individual Drawings*, London 2006, p. 558.

4
Rainer Stamm, "Aufbruch in die Moderne: Das Kaiser Wilhelm Museum unter seinem ersten Direktor Friedrich Deneken (1897–1922)," in exh. cat. *Farbwelten: Von Monet bis Yves Klein, Werke der klassischen Moderne aus den Kunstmuseen Krefeld*, ed. Rainer Stamm [Bremen, Kunstsammlungen Böttcherstraße, Paula-Modersohn-Becker-Museum, 2009/10; Erfurt, Kunsthalle Erfurt, 2010; Würzburg, Museum im Kulturspeicher, 2010; Cottbus, Museum Dieselkraftwerk, 2010; Freiburg, Museum für Neue Kunst, 2010/11; Rotterdam, Chabot Museum, 2011], Bremen 2009, pp. 9–19.

5
Annegret Hoberg and Isabelle Jansen, *Franz Marc: The Complete Works, Volume I, The Oil Paintings*, Munich 2004, pp. 301–2.

6
For further information about the exhibition, see appendix, p. 264.

7
Annegret Hoberg, "Gabriele Münter in München und Murnau 1901–1914," in exh. cat. Munich/Frankfurt/Stockholm 1992/93, p. 41.

8
Annegret Hoberg, "Gabriele Münter: STURM Artist in Munich, Berlin and Scandinavia," in exh. cat. Frankfurt am Main 2015/16, pp. 376–77, with additional references to literature on Gabriele Münter and Herwarth Walden. See also *Wassily Kandinsky, Gabriele Münter, Herwarth Walden: Briefe und Schriften 1912–1914*, ed. Karla Bilang, with a foreword by Jelena Hahl-Fontaine, Bern 2012.

9
For details about this exhibition, see appendix, p. 264.

10
Hille 2012, p. 227.

belonged to a circle of artists as she had during the years of the Blue Rider or during certain periods of her stay in Scandinavia, she was forced to find her own way for the first time in her life. The process of forging new ties demanded a great deal of time and energy, but the effort proved successful, as evidenced by her touring exhibition of 1925/26, which was presented in seven cities.[11]

With her participation in the *International Exhibition of Modern Art* organized by the Société Anonyme in New York in 1926/27, Münter accomplished the leap across the Atlantic. And her encounter with Johannes Eichner on New Year's Eve in 1927 in Berlin marked a turning point in both her personal life and her professional career. The art historian Eichner became Münter's agent; he organized major touring exhibitions and arranged for invitations to participate in numerous group exhibitions. Fig. B The exhibition *Gabriele Münter: "50 Gemälde aus 25 Jahren" (1908–1933)* was presented in seven German cities from 1933 to 1935. Eichner also wrote articles about her work. This gave Münter the freedom to once again devote herself entirely to her art, as can be seen from the extensive body of paintings she produced during the 1930s. In 1940 she resolved to withdraw from the public eye. Nevertheless, in 1942 she took part in the art exhibition held during the Weilheim *Kreistag* (District Assembly) of the National Socialist Party.[12]

A major Blue Rider exhibition was presented at the Haus der Kunst in Munich in 1949. The show was organized by Ludwig Grote (1893–1974), who later served as the first director of the Germanisches Nationalmuseum in Nuremberg, on behalf of the Museums, Fine Arts and Cultural Materials Exchange Section Cultural Affairs Branch E. R. Divisions-HQ OMGB, the Bayerische Staatsgemäldesammlungen, and the Städtische Galerie im Lenbachhaus. It was one of the most important exhibition events of the postwar era in Munich. Münter was elected to the *Ehrenausschuss* (Honors Committee) in 1948 and presented nine paintings at the exhibition.[13] She firmly believed that the event marked the beginning of her "rediscovery."[14] That assessment was not entirely correct, however, as Münter was regarded from that point on as a fringe figure associated with the Blue Rider and no longer as an autonomous painter.

A **View of a room in Münter's solo exhibition at the artists' association Den Frie Udstilling, Copenhagen, 1918**
Photograph |
Gabriele Münter- und Johannes Eichner-Stiftung, Munich

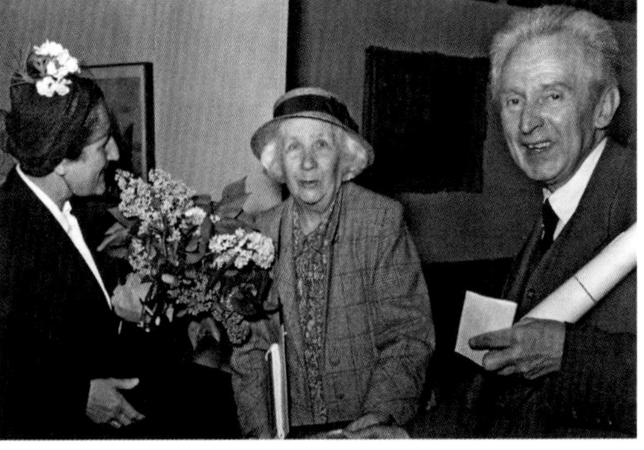

B **Münter and Eichner with Flora Scherer at an exhibition opening, ca. 1955**
Photograph |
Gabriele Münter- und Johannes Eichner-Stiftung, Munich, inv. no. 3499

11
For further details about this exhibition, see appendix, p. 264.

12
See the chapter "Work and Technology," pp. 216–18.

13
Exh. cat. Munich/Frankfurt/Stockholm 1992/93, p. 23; exh. cat. *Der Blaue Reiter: München und die Kunst des 20. Jahrhunderts, 1908–1914*, Bayerische Staatsgemäldesammlungen and Städtische Galerie, Munich [Munich, Haus der Kunst, September–October 1949], Munich 1949.

14
Only nine of her works were exhibited, whereas her fellow artists Kandinsky, Marc, and Macke were represented with more than forty works each. Hille 2012, p. 206 and footnote 201, p. 250.

Beginning in the 1950s, three other individuals played significant roles in promoting Münter's art: the Munich gallerists Etta Stangl (1913–1990) and Otto Stangl (1915–1990) and the art historian Hans Konrad Roethel (1909–1982). Otto Stangl had opened the Moderne Galerie Otto Stangl in Munich with his wife Etta in 1948. The gallerists met Münter that same year and accepted works by the artist on commission in 1952 at the latest. To this day it is not clear how the relationship actually came about. The Stangls' circle of acquaintances included such figures as Ludwig Grote, Maria Marc, and Franz and Juliane Roh, who were all acquainted with Münter and who may have recommended her to the art dealers. Otto Stangl committed himself to the goal of making her work better known. He supported Münter and Eichner in organizing exhibitions, arranged new shows, and sold works to private collectors. Of key importance was his role as her agent in negotiations with museums. On his recommendation, *The Yellow House* (1911) was donated to the Bayerische Staatsgemäldesammlungen in December 1954; the museum had already acquired her *Man in an Armchair* (1913) in 1950. Fig. E, p. 117; Fig. C, p. 115 It was also thanks to Stangl's initiative that Münter was invited to exhibit a painting at the first documenta in Kassel in 1955. Stangl wrote to Eichner on May 14, 1955: "I have some good news for you. I have reached an agreement with the director of the Documenta, the major exhibition which will take place in Kassel for two months, to have Gabriele Münter's painting 'Still Life in Gray,' which is currently being shown in our exhibition 'Unknown Works,' displayed there. I am very pleased to know that Gabriele Münter will be represented in this significant show—which gives an extensive overview of the art of the first half of the XXth century."[15] Figs. C; D Only seven of the 147 participating artists were women.[16] Münter had already taken part in another important international exhibition in 1950, namely the twenty-fifth Venice Biennale.[17] Fig. E

Johannes Eichner met Hans Konrad Roethel, then chief conservator at the Bayerische Staatsgemäldesammlungen, in 1952. The two became close friends over the years, and Roethel was invited to Murnau. In December 1956, Münter and Eichner took him into their basement, in which hundreds of paintings

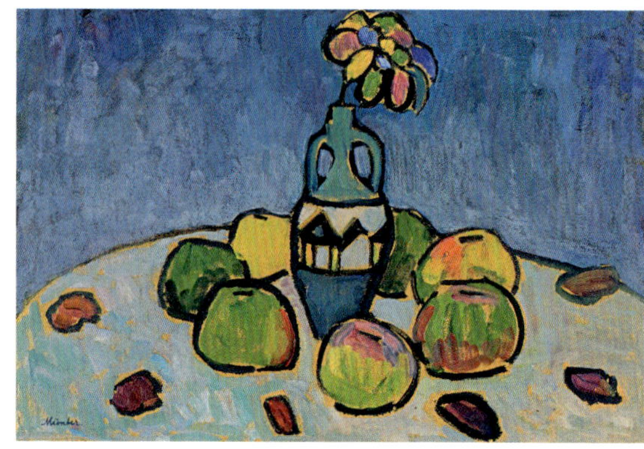

C **Still Life in Gray [Stillleben grau], 1909**
Cardboard, 34.5 × 50.4 cm | Städtische Galerie im Lenbachhaus und Kunstbau München, inv. no. GMS 662

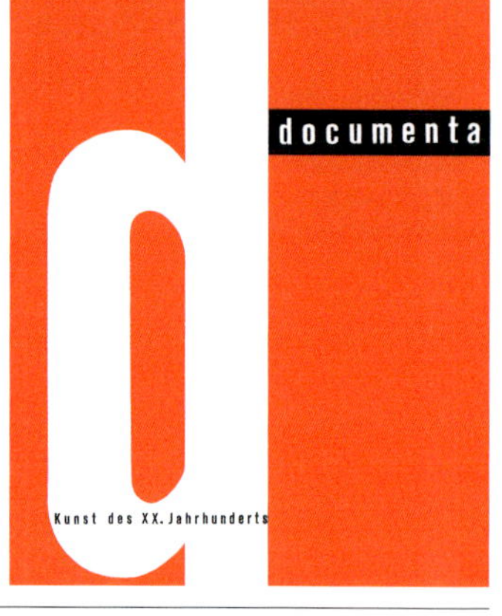

D **Catalogue for the first documenta exhibition, 1955**
Front of dust jacket

15
Translated from letter in the MES. Exh. cat. Kassel 1955, no. 470. Presumably thanks to Stangl's initiative, Münter also showed a second painting that is listed under no. 469 in the catalogue as follows: *Evening Sun*, 1908, oil, Dr. Bernhard Sprengel, Hannover. Current whereabouts unknown.

16
Hille 2012, p. 217.

17
She exhibited three paintings: *Landscape with White Wall*, 1910, oil on canvas, 50 × 65 cm, Osthaus Museum Hagen, inv. no. K 1506, cat. no. 49; *Man in an Armchair*, 1913, oil on canvas, 95 × 125.5 cm, Bayerische Staatsgemäldesammlungen, Munich, inv. no. 11227, cat. no. 50; *Still Life with Easter Eggs*, 1914, cardboard, 48.8 × 55.6 cm, Städtische Galerie im Lenbachhaus und Kunstbau München, inv. no. GMS 668, cat. no. 470.

18
Although Etta and Otto Stangl were also invited to Murnau on a number of occasions, they never got to see the hidden "treasure." Clelia Segieth describes the history of the relationships between Eichner, Münter, and the Stangls in her book *Etta und Otto Stangl: Galeristen, Sammler, Museumsgründer*, Cologne 2000, pp. 156–61.

19
The mission of the foundation is to promote the art of Gabriele Münter. It administers the artist's estate, which includes (among other things) the Münter House in Murnau, now a museum commemorating the art and lives of Münter and Kandinsky, as Münter desired.

by Münter and her fellow Blue Rider painters were stored. When Kandinsky had to flee Germany virtually overnight in 1914, he was compelled to leave his belongings, including his art collection, behind in Munich. He attempted to recover his property after the war; an extended legal dispute between Kandinsky and Münter lasted until 1926. In the end, several paintings were returned to Kandinsky, but the majority of his surviving works remained in Münter's possession. The collection was initially stored in a shipping warehouse in Munich. Faced with the increasing threat of persecution by the National Socialists, Münter hid all of the works in her house in Murnau and thus prevented their seizure. On the occasion of her eightieth birthday in 1957, she donated significant parts of this collection to the Städtische Galerie im Lenbachhaus, where Roethel had since been appointed director. The news of Münter's donation to the Lenbachhaus was all the more surprising to Otto Stangl since he had not been informed of it in advance. The incident put an end to their relationship.[18]

The bonds of trust shared by Roethel, Münter, and Eichner remained intact as long as the artist lived, however. Thus the Gabriele Münter- und Johannes Eichner-Stiftung, which was established on the basis of the couple's will and recognized as a legal entity in 1966, found a home at the Städtische Galerie im Lenbachhaus.[19] Fig. F

Official recognition of Münter's activities was also expressed in the form of awards. In 1956 she received the Kunstpreis der Stadt München für Malerei (Art Prize of the City of Munich for Painting), and in February 1957, on the occasion of her eightieth birthday, she was awarded the Goldene Ehrenmünze der Landeshauptstadt München (Golden Medal of Honor of the State Capital

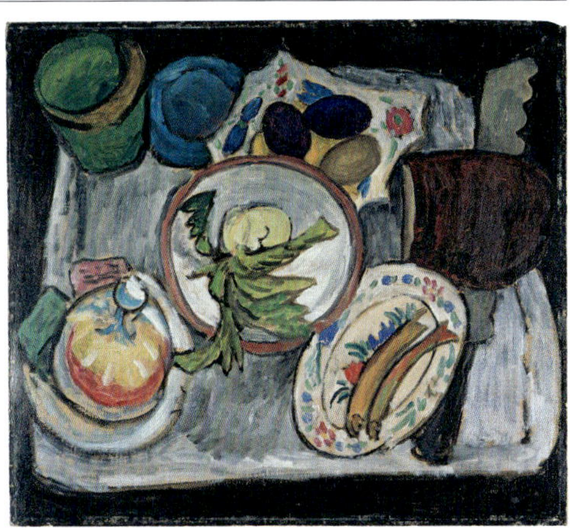

E **Still Life with Easter Eggs [Stilleben mit Ostereiern], 1914**

Cardboard, 48.8 × 55.6 cm | Städtische Galerie im Lenbachhaus und Kunstbau München, inv. no. GMS 668

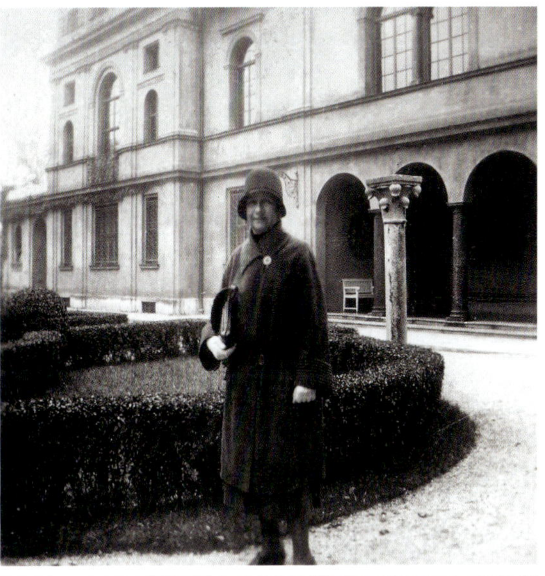

F **Münter in the garden of the Städtische Galerie im Lenbachhaus, 1934**

Photograph | Gabriele Münter- und Johannes Eichner-Stiftung, Munich, inv. no. 3326

of Munich) and the Grosse Verdienstkreuz des Verdienstordens der Bundesrepublik Deutschland (Grand Cross of the Order of Merit of the Federal Republic of Germany).

Münter was very pleased with her own success. After the end of *Wanderausstellung Gabriele Münter: Werke aus fünf Jahrzehnten*, the touring exhibition that was presented in twenty-two cities between 1949 and 1953, she wrote a letter to Gerhard Budde, cofounder of the Herforder Kunstverein, who had lobbied for his native city of Herford as an exhibition venue: "The success was gratifying everywhere. I earned a name again, a[nd] numerous works have remained in museums."[20] Most of the museums that hold paintings by Münter today are in Germany and the United States. The efforts of Roethel, who maintained privileged relationships with gallerists Leonard Hutton in New York and Dalzell Hatfield in Los Angeles, played a key role in the distribution of Münter's art in the United States. Interest in Münter's works has since grown progressively—most notably during the past thirty years. The Musée national d'art moderne in the Centre Pompidou in Paris has owned two of the artist's paintings since 2015, for example: the large composition *Dragon Fight* (1913) and *Garden Gate in Sèvres, Petite rue des Binelles* (ca. 1906).[21] Cat. 127 These are the first paintings by Münter to be acquired by a French museum.

This brief sketch shows that contrary to the prevailing assumption, Münter began exhibiting alone early on and did so very often during her career. Karoline Hille has published an illuminating description of the radical changes in the critical reception of Münter's art over the course of seventy years.[22] Whereas the artist's creative talent was the focus of attention in 1916, it gave way to her biography after World War II. Münter was perceived merely as the pupil of a genius, as an artist who had produced an interesting oeuvre, but only as long as she lived and worked at Kandinsky's side. This view was reinforced by her donation to the Lenbachhaus in 1957. From that point on, Münter was regarded above all as the woman who rescued Kandinsky's early works. Moreover, the role played by Eichner and Roethel in promoting her art is ambiguous. On the one hand, they presented her as often as possible in public; yet on the other hand, they portrayed her in their articles in exhibition catalogues as a naïve artist who relied primarily on her intuition, entirely in keeping with the prevailing preconceptions about "women's art."[23]

In an attempt to counteract this one-dimensional, superficial view, we have not presented Münter's works in chronological order but rather in a number of different thematic sections. Thus, instead of focusing on her biography and her Blue Rider phase, the exhibition emphasizes her creative process and her efforts to come to grips with artistic issues. This shift in perspective reveals a more nuanced picture of the artist Gabriele Münter and of her art.

20
Exh. cat. Touring Exhibition 1949–52. A new version of the catalogue authored by Johannes Eichner, with a slightly revised list of works, was issued for the years 1952 to 1953: exh. cat. Touring Exhibition 1952–53; for more detailed information, see appendix, p. 264. Translated from letter to Dr. Gerhard Budde dated October 31, 1953, private collection.

21
Garden Gate in Sèvres, Petite rue des Binelles, ca. 1906, oil on canvas, mounted on cardboard, 34.4 × 45 cm, Centre Pompidou, Paris. Musée national d'art moderne/Centre de création industrielle – Don de la Société Kandinsky, 2015, inv. no. AM 2015-151.

22
Karoline Hille, "Gabriele Münter und ihr Publikum: Nachwort," in Hille 2012, pp. 226–32.

23
See the chapter "Primitivism," p. 136.

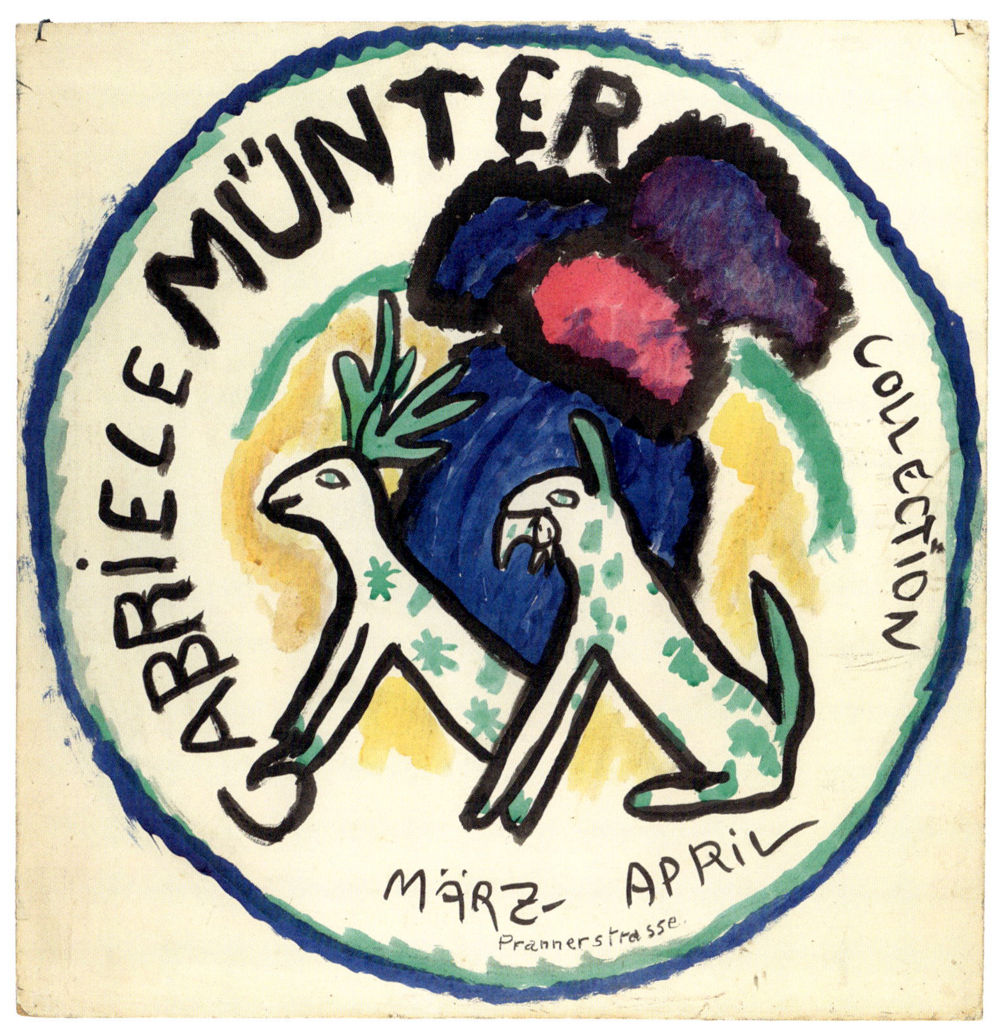

Cat. 208
Design for a poster for the 1913 Gabriele Münter exhibition in the Neuer Kunstsalon Max Dietzel, Munich, 1913
Watercolor on cardboard, 49.5 × 49.8 cm | Gabriele Münter- und Johannes Eichner-Stiftung, Munich, inv. no. V 88

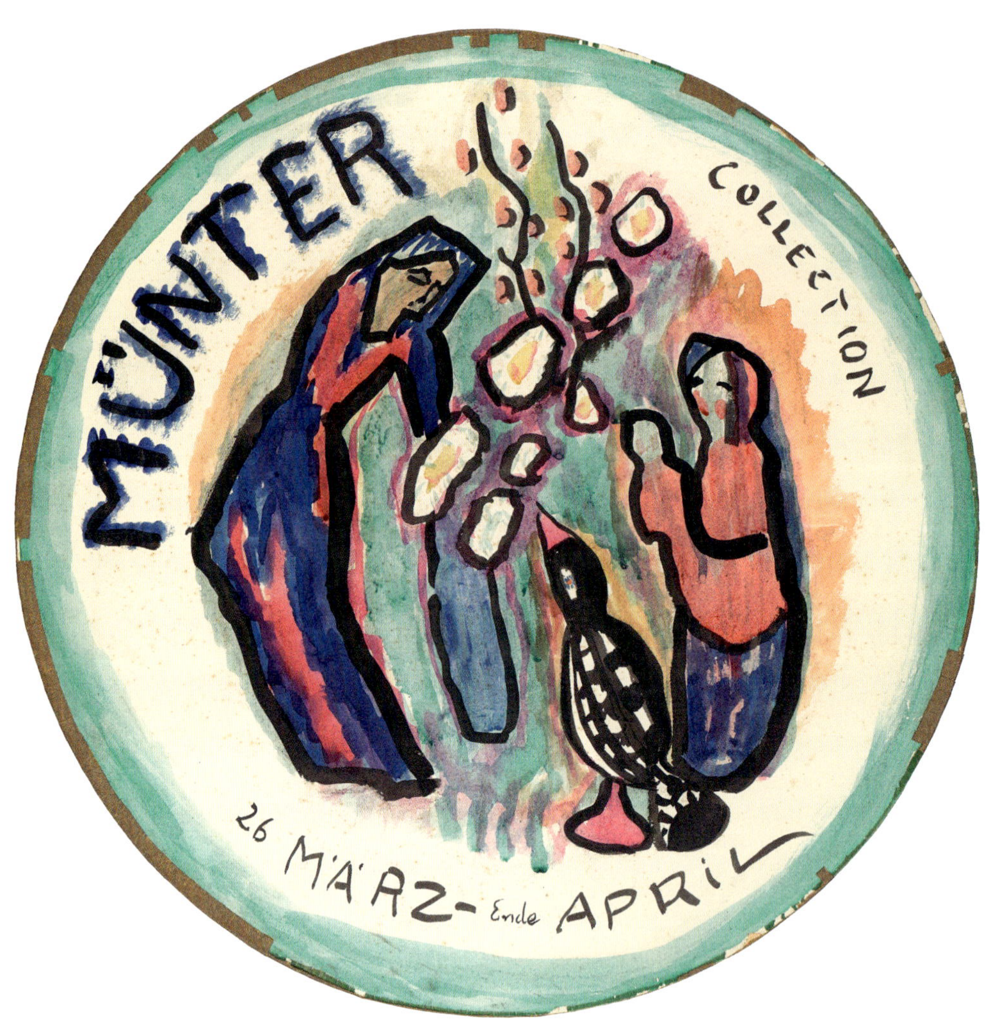

Cat. 209
Design for a poster for the 1913 Gabriele Münter exhibition in the Neuer Kunstsalon Max Dietzel, Munich, 1913
Watercolor on cardboard, diameter: 47.5 cm | Gabriele Münter- und Johannes Eichner-Stiftung, Munich, inv. no. V 89

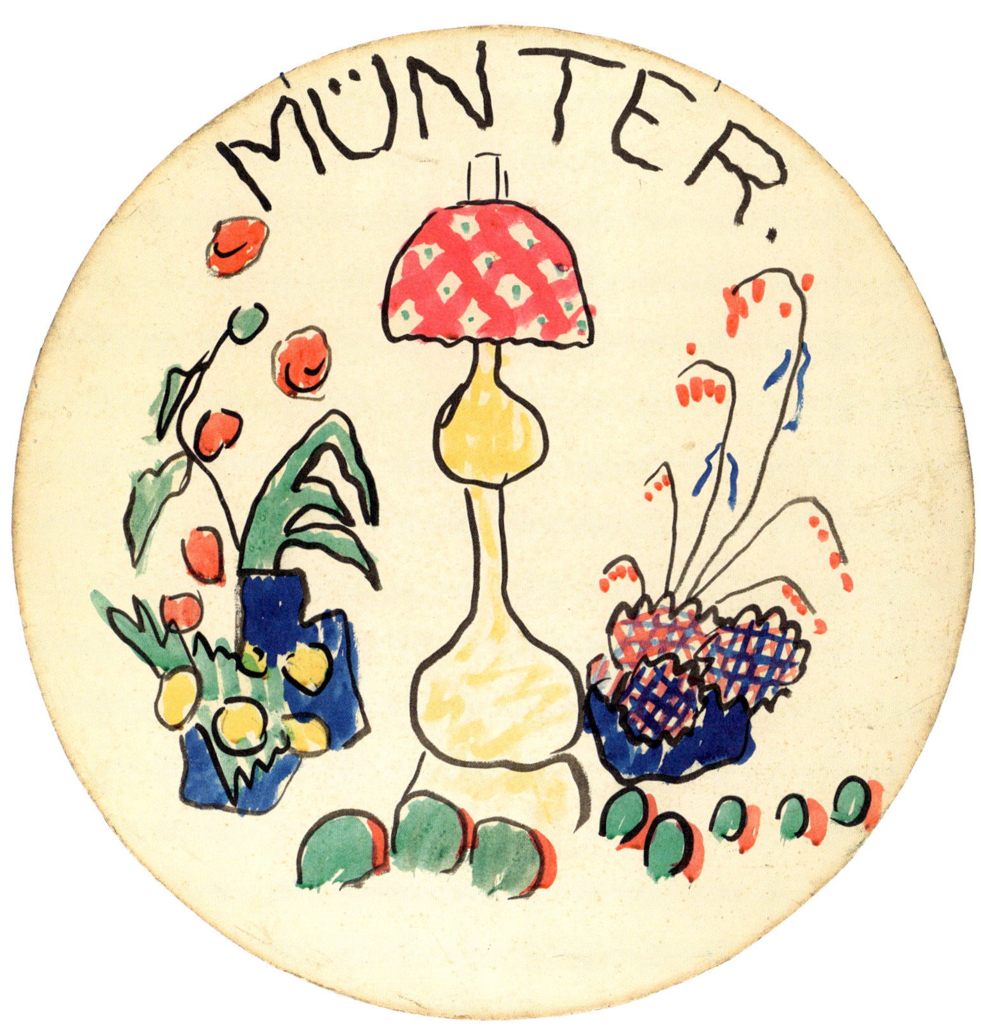

Cat. 210
Design for a poster for the 1913 Gabriele Münter exhibition in the Neuer Kunstsalon Max Dietzel, Munich, 1913
Watercolor on cardboard, diameter: 47.4 cm | Gabriele Münter- und Johannes Eichner-Stiftung, Munich, inv. no. V 90

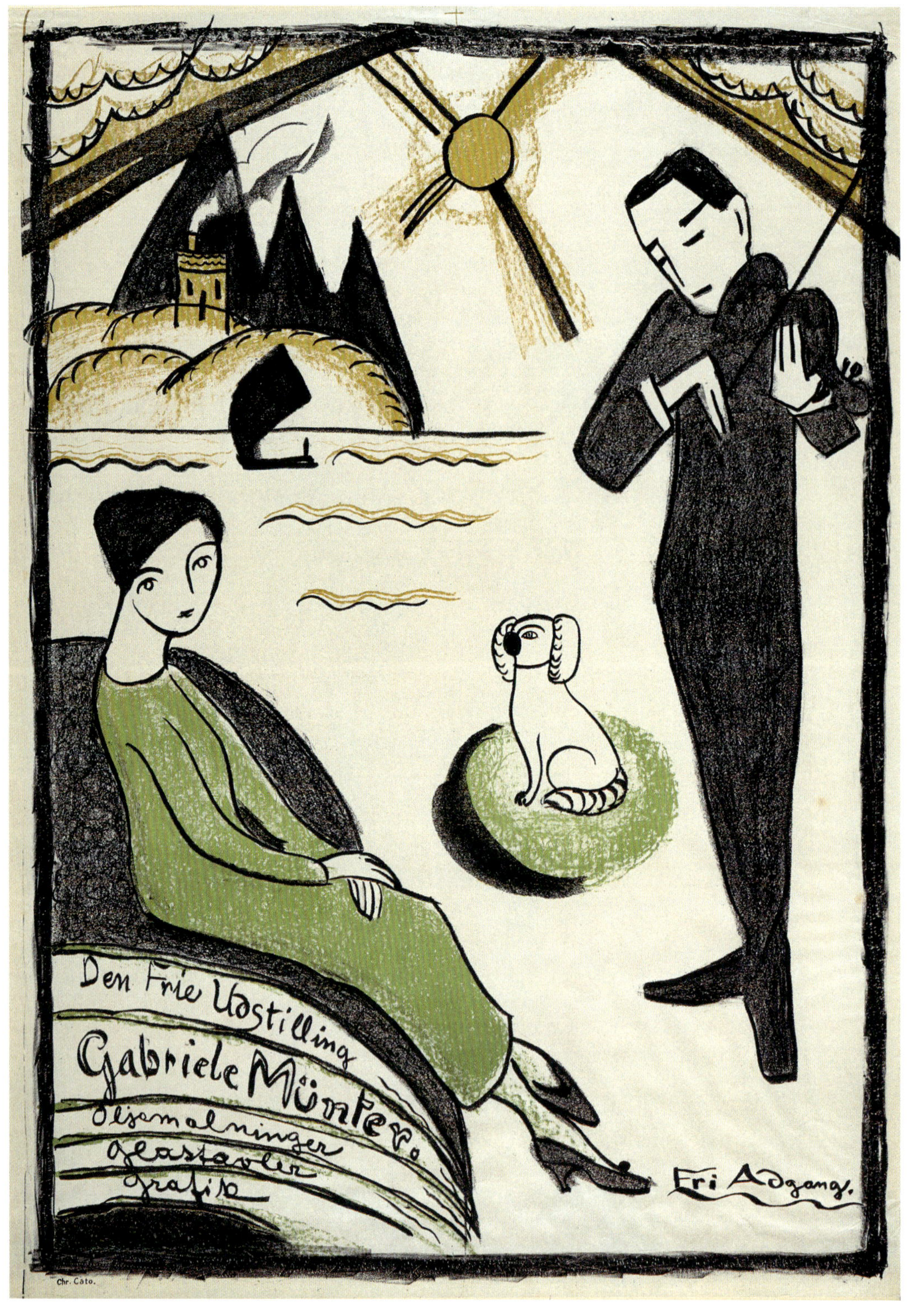

Cat. 211

Poster for the Gabriele Münter exhibition in Copenhagen, 1918

Color lithograph on machine paper, 90 × 64 cm | Städtische Galerie im Lenbachhaus und Kunstbau München, inv. no. GMS 930

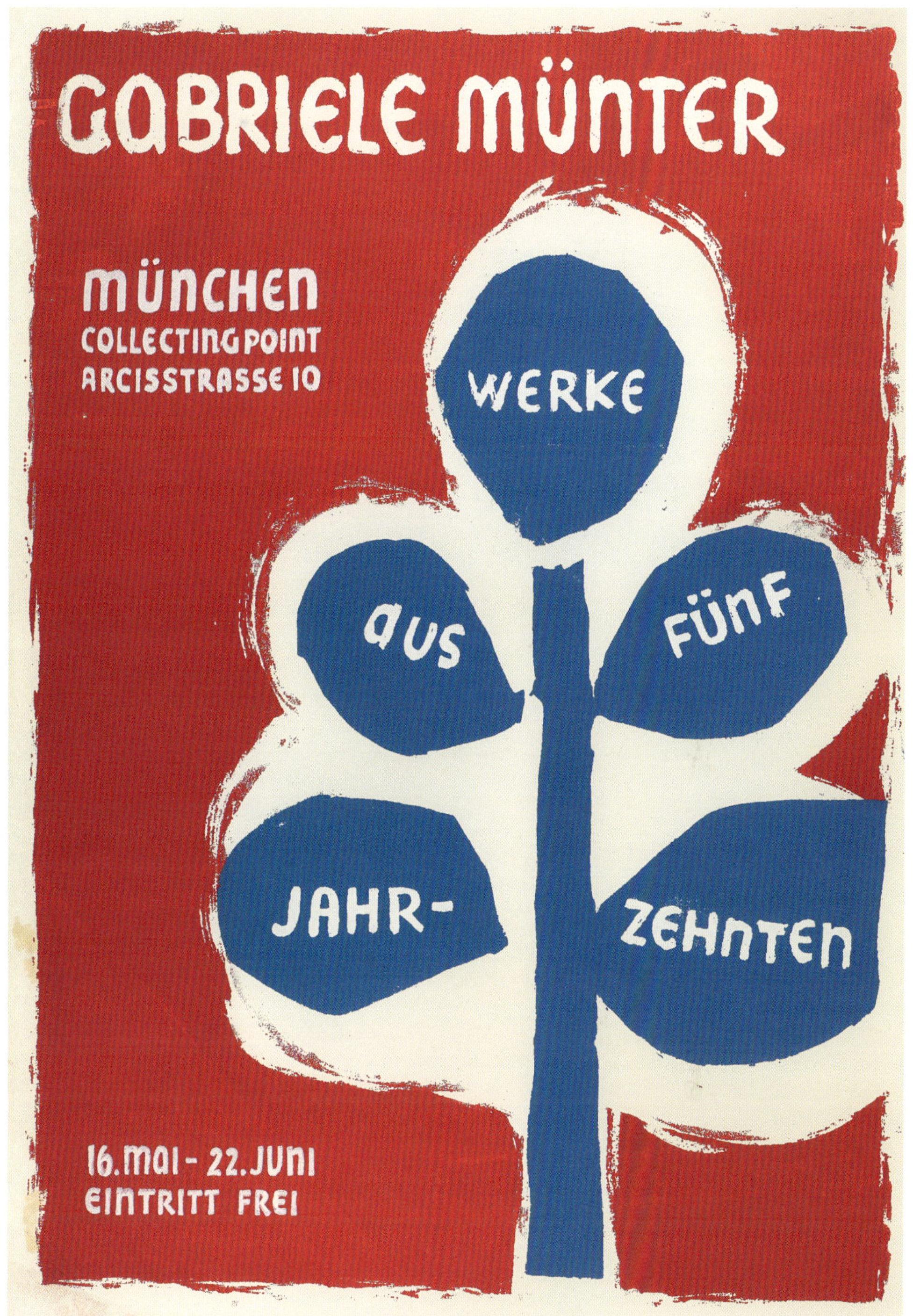

Cat. 212
Poster for the Munich presentation of the Gabriele Münter touring exhibition, 1949–53
Linoleum cut from three printing blocks in blue, red, and white, 60 × 42 cm | Gabriele Münter- und Johannes Eichner-Stiftung, Munich

Note on Terms Used in the Description of Gabriele Münter's Painting Technique

Information on Gabriele Münter's painting technique is limited to painting supports in this catalogue. The terms "cardboard" and "textile support" stand for various types of painting cardboard and canvas. The decision in favor of this approach was based on the recognition that the recent extensive research on techniques employed by artists has not only shed new light on the discussion regarding materials and their correct designations but has raised new questions as well. Paint systems that look like oil paint but contain hardly any oil, on the one hand, and aqueous binder systems containing high concentrations of oil, on the other hand, show the complexity of the paint systems used by modern artists.

However, the phrase "oil on canvas" has remained the standard classification among artists, as it ultimately represents a simplified description of a diverse range of painting techniques while referring at the same time to the material value of the work of art. Specific clues to Münter's paint systems can be found in a few sources.

For example, Wassily Kandinsky recommended Behrendt's oil paint to Münter in her early years: "Ehrmann's paints are called Behrendt's Oil Paints and can be purchased either from Schmid, the frame-maker, at Leopoldstr. 41 in Munich, or directly from Behrendt at the factory (Fr. Behrendt, art painter) Wildenroth and Grafrath. The paints are quite good and extremely cheap. . . ."[1]

The logbooks Münter kept from 1929 on also contain information about her painting technique, such as "on a piece of hard canvas" (1950), as well as references to binding agents, such as her use of "fig milk" in several works.

Oil has frequently been detected in recent analyses of binding agents used in selected works.[2] However, since detailed binding-agent and fiber analyses are not available for all the exhibited works, the phrases "oil on canvas" and "oil on cardboard" have deliberately not been used in connection with the paintings from the Gabriele Münter- und Johannes Eichner-Stiftung and the Städtische Galerie im Lenbachhaus München.

Iris Winkelmeyer

1
Translated from letter of June 17, 1903, MES.

2
From 2012 to 2014 the Städtische Galerie im Lenbachhaus, the Doerner Institut of the Bayerische Staatsgemäldesammlungen (Bavarian State Painting Collections), Munich, and the Gabriele Münter- und Johnannes Eichner-Stiftung carried out a project on Münter's painting technique. Nine paintings and a palette from the Lenbachhaus and the Münter-Eichner-Stiftung were examined. Unpublished report by the Doerner Institut.

Appendix

Stations in the Life of Gabriele Münter

1877 Gabriele Münter is born in Berlin on February 19.

Her father, Carl Friedrich Münter, had emigrated to North America as a young man. Her mother, Wilhelmine Münter, née Scheuber, had lived in the United States since childhood. The two married in Savannah, Tennessee, in 1857 and returned to Germany in 1864.

Münter has three older siblings: August (b. 1865), Carl Theodor (b. 1866), and Emmy (b. 1869).

1878 The family moves to Herford in Westphalia, the hometown of Münter's father.
→1

1884 The family moves to Koblenz.
→2

1886 Münter's father dies.

1887 Her brother August dies.

1897 June–mid-October

Münter takes drawing lessons at the private Ladies Art School in Düsseldorf. Her mother dies.

1898 Late September 1898–October 1900: United States

Münter and her sister, Emmy, stay with relatives on her mother's side in various places in North America.
→3

1900 October 22, 1900–late April 1901: Bonn

1901 April 30: Münter moves to Munich.

She attends the so-called Ladies' Academy of the Künstlerinnen-Verein (Association of Women Artists), first taking a beginners' class taught by Maximilian Dasio (1865–1954) and then a life drawing class under Angelo Jank (1868–1940).
→4

1902 Münter takes a woodcut course at the Wolff-Neumann School.

At the Phalanx School, she takes a sculpture course taught by Wilhelm Hüsgen which includes painting instruction under Wassily Kandinsky.

June 24–August 22:
She stays in Kochel with Kandinsky's painting class from the Phalanx School.

August 25–October 7:
Münter spends most of her time in Bonn.

December 1:
She returns to Kandinsky's Phalanx class.
→5

1903 May–early June:
Herford

June 19–August 18:
She spends part of the summer in Kallmünz with Kandinsky's painting class from the Phalanx School.

Late August–late September:
She stays with her sister, Emmy Schroeter, and her family in Bonn.

1904 April 1–May 11:
She again stays with Emmy Schroeter and her family in Bonn.

May 23, 1904–early June 1908: Münter lives in various cities and countries.

May 23–June 22:
She travels with Kandinsky to Holland.

June 22–early December:
Münter lives in Bonn, mainly with the Schroeters; from the end of July until early September she stays with her brother, Carl, also in Bonn.

December 6:
She travels with Kandinsky to Tunis via Strasbourg, Basel, Lyon, and Marseille.

December 25:
They arrive in Tunis.

1905 Until April 5:
Tunis (with excursions to Carthage, Kairouan, and Sousse)

Until April 15:
Return trip to Germany via Palermo, Naples, Florence, Bologna, and Verona

April 15–May 23:
Munich

May 24–June 1:
Bicycle tour with Kandinsky through Saxony

June 1–August 15:
Dresden with Kandinsky

August 17–November:
Bonn (initially at the home of Carl Münter and later with Emmy Schroeter)

November 18:
She travels with Kandinsky to Rapallo via Liège, Brussels, Milan, Sestri Levante, and Genoa; they arrive during the Christmas holidays.

1906 Until May 1:
Rapallo; she travels with Kandinsky to Paris via Genoa, Milan, Lucerne, and Basel.

May 22, 1906–June 10, 1907:
Paris, Sèvres

June 28, 1906:
The couple moves into an apartment on the ground floor of a villa in Sèvres, a suburb of Paris.

November 17, 1906–March 1907:
Münter rents a room in Paris; Kandinsky remains in Sèvres.

1907 From June 10:
Bonn

August:
She travels with Kandinsky through Switzerland.

September 8, 1907–late April 1908:
Berlin with Kandinsky

1908 January:
Münter presents her first solo exhibition at the Kunstsalon Lenobel in Cologne.

Late April–early June:
She travels to South Tyrol with Kandinsky.

Early June 1908–early August 1914: Munich

June:
Münter visits the Upper Bavarian town of Murnau am Staffelsee for the first time.

Mid-August–late September:
She stays at the Gasthof Griesbräu in Murnau with Kandinsky, Alexej von Jawlensky, and Marianne von Werefkin.

1909 February 22–March 9:
Kochel with Kandinsky and Olga and Thomas von Hartmann

Mid-June–mid-September:
Murnau

August 21:
Münter buys the house on Kottmüllerallee in Murnau.

Early October:
She moves in with Kandinsky in Schwabing, Ainmillerstraße 36.

December 1–after December 15:
The first exhibition of the Neue Künstler-vereinigung München (New Artists' Association Munich) is held at the Moderne Galerie Heinrich Thannhauser.
→6

1910 September 1–14:
A second exhibition of the Neue Künstler-vereinigung München is held at the Moderne Galerie Heinrich Thannhauser.

1911 Late June–mid-August:
Münter stays in Berlin with the Schroeters, in Herford, and in Bonn with her brother Carl and his family.

December 18, 1911–January 1, 1912:
The "First Exhibition of the 'Blue Rider' Editorial Board" is held at the Moderne Galerie Heinrich Thannhauser in Munich.
→7

1912 February 12–March 18:
The Second Exhibition organized by the editorial board of the Blue Rider, *Black and White*, is held in the art showroom of Hans Goltz in Munich.
→8

1913 September 20–November 1:
The *Erster Deutscher Herbstsalon* (First German Autumn Salon) is presented at Herwarth Walden's gallery Der Sturm in Berlin.

1914 **August 6, 1914–January 16, 1915: Switzerland**

August 6–November 16:
Kandinsky flees Germany following the outbreak of war. He and Münter travel to Mariahalden near Goldach in Switzerland via Lindau.

November 16, 1914:
Travels to Zurich with Kandinsky

November 25:
Kandinsky returns to Moscow.

December 17, 1914–January 5, 1915:
Solothurn, Oschwand, Bern, Weggis

January 5, 1915:
Returns to Zurich

1915 **January 16–July 3, 1915: Munich, Berlin**

June 3–July 3, 1915:
Berlin

July 3, 1915–February 1920: Scandinavia

July 3–17, 1915:
Copenhagen

July 17, 1915–late fall 1917:
Sweden, primarily Stockholm (with trips to Lapland and Norway in the summer of 1916)

December 23, 1915–March 16, 1916:
Kandinsky visits Stockholm.
The two artists meet for the last time.
→9 →10

1917 Late fall 1917–February 1920:
Denmark, primarily Copenhagen

1918 March 7–13:
An exhibition is held at Den Frie Udstilling in Copenhagen; it is Münter's largest show to date.

1920 **February 28–May 12, 1920: Berlin**

May 12, 1920–early December 1924: Munich, Murnau, and Elmau
→11

1922 January:
Münter attends an evening course in life drawing in Munich.

1924 **December 9, 1924–May 1925: Cologne**

1925 February 1925–late October 1926:
A touring exhibition travels to seven venues in Germany.

May 15–October 1925: Munich and Murnau

October 29, 1925–June 1929: Berlin

1926 August 12–September 30:
Münter stays at Burg Lauenstein, near the border between Franconia and Thuringia.

From November:
She attends a course at Arthur Segal's painting school in Berlin.

1927 Early July–late August:
Münter travels to Ticino, Switzerland, and visits Marianne von Werefkin in Ascona.

August 25–October 16:
Elmau

From November:
She attends another course at Segal's painting school.

December 31:
Münter meets Johannes Eichner for the first time at a New Year's Eve party at the home of the painter and art historian Hermann Konnerth (1881–1966) in Berlin.
→12

1928 January, April, and June:
Segal School

August 3–November 20:
Murnau and Munich

1929 April:
Segal School

June 4–October 3, 1929: Murnau

October 3–25, 1929: Munich

October 26, 1929–late October 1930: France

1930 Until September 1, 1930:
Paris; from March 1930 with Eichner

September 1–15:
She travels with Eichner to Sanary-sur-Mer via Chamonix, Avignon, and Marseille.

September 15–October 29:
Sanary

October 29:
They return to Berlin via Paris.

November 1, 1930–March 31, 1931: Berlin

1931 **April 1: Münter settles in Murnau.**

1933 April 1933–June 1935:
A touring exhibition travels to seven venues in Germany.

May 16–July 3, 1933:
She travels with Eichner to the lake district of northern Italy.
→13

1934 December 29, 1934–March 23, 1935:
Munich

1935 December 17, 1935–April 3, 1936:
Münter looks for an apartment in Munich.
→14

1936 July 27–September 16:
She stays in Munich during the renovation of her house in Murnau.

1949 July 1949–September 1953:
A touring exhibition travels to twenty-two venues in Germany.

September–October 1949:
An exhibition entitled *Der Blaue Reiter: München und die Kunst des 20. Jahrhunderts, 1908–1914* is held at the Haus der Kunst in Munich, featuring nine paintings by Münter.
→15 →16

1950 Münter exhibits three paintings at the 25th Venice Biennale.
→17

1955 Münter presents two paintings at the first documenta in Kassel.
→18

1956 Münter is awarded the Kunstpreis der Stadt München für Malerei (Art Prize of the City of Munich for Painting).

1957 She receives the Goldene Ehrenmünze der Landeshauptstadt München (Golden Medal of Honor of the State Capital of Munich) and the Grosse Verdienstkreuz des Verdienstordens der Bundesrepublik Deutschland (Grand Cross of the Order of Merit of the Federal Republic of Germany).

On the occasion of her eightieth birthday, Münter donates numerous works by members of the Blue Rider and associated artists to the Städtische Galerie im Lenbachhaus, thereby establishing the international reputation of the Lenbachhaus. The donated works form the core of the current Blue Rider collection at the Lenbachhaus.

1958 Eichner dies on February 11.

1960 June 20–July 30:
The first solo exhibition of Münter's art in the United States is held at the Dalzell Hatfield Galleries in Los Angeles.

1962 Münter dies at her home in Murnau on May 19.
→19

1966 The Gabriele Münter- und Johannes Eichner-Stiftung is established in accordance with a testamentary behest of Münter and Eichner. Based in the Städtische Galerie im Lenbachhaus in Munich, the foundation administers Münter's estate, including the Münter House in Murnau.

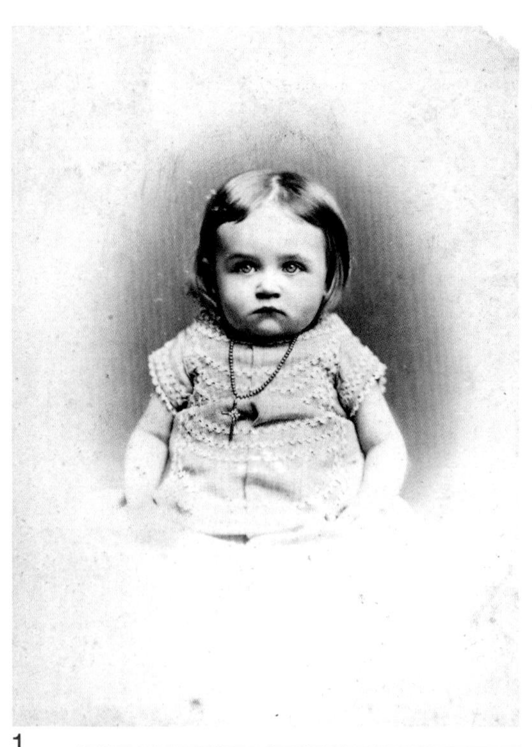

1

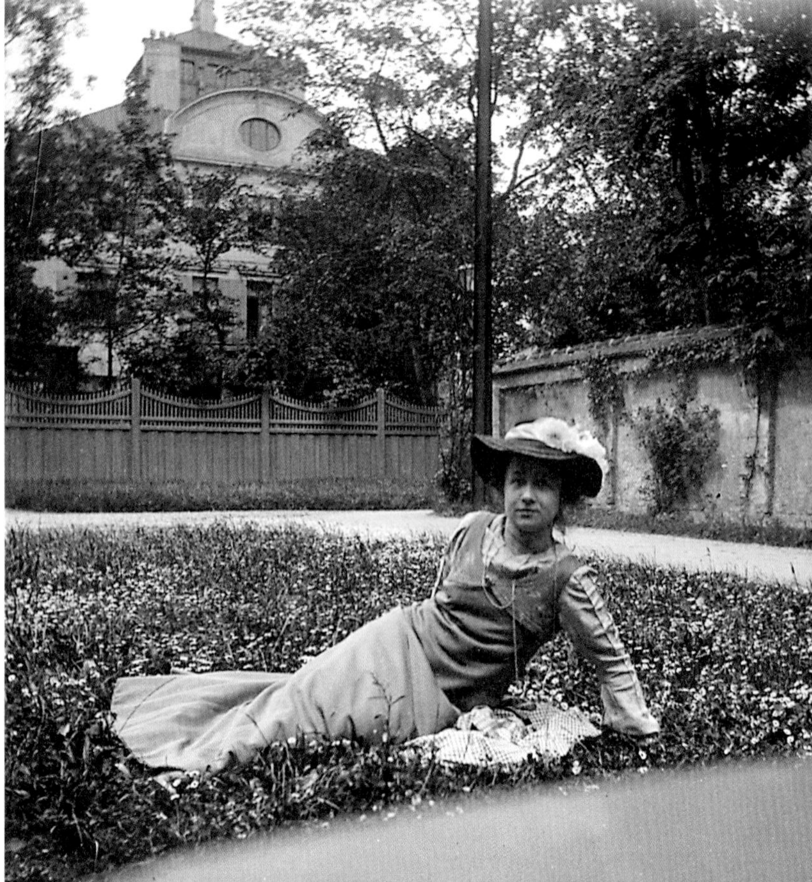

4

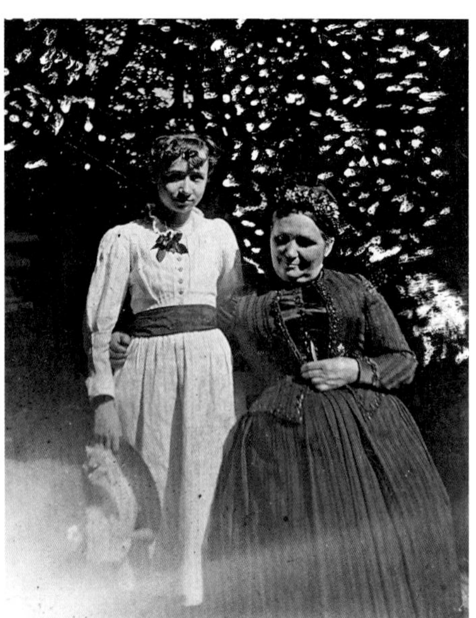

2

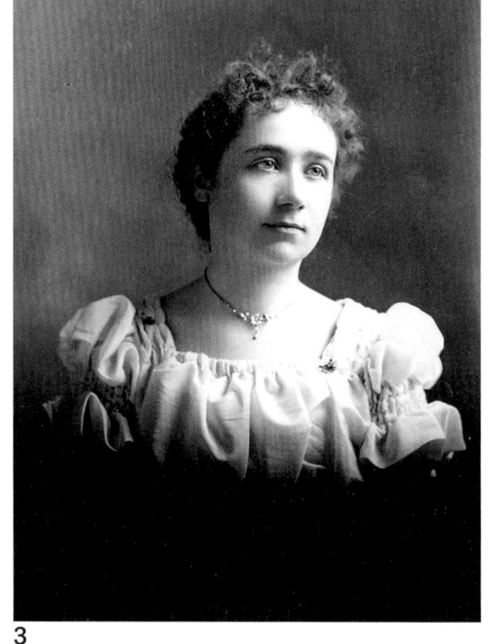

3

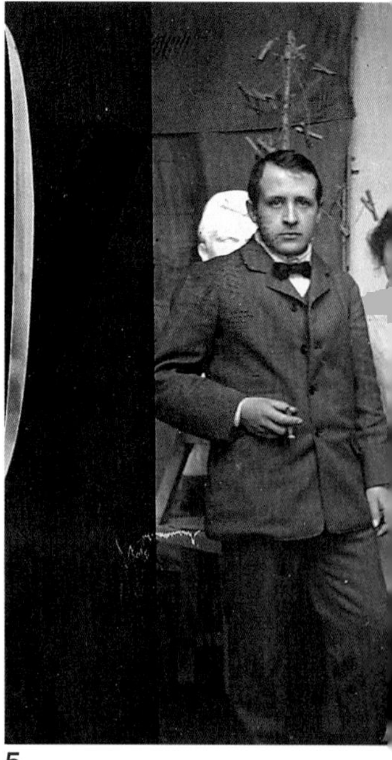

5

1 “Ella Münter in her first year,” ca. 1877, inv. no. 2951

2 Gabriele Münter with her mother in Koblenz, ca. 1891, inv. no. 2963

3 Gabriele Münter, 1899, photo: Murillo photo studio, Saint Louis, Missouri, USA, inv. no. 2962

4 Gabriele Münter in the front garden of the Künstlerinnen-Verein (Association of Women Artists), Munich, 1901, inv. no. 2137

5 Wilhelm Hüsgen’s sculpture class at the Phalanx School, May 1902. Left: Wilhelm Hüsgen, Gabriele Münter, inv. no. 2087

6

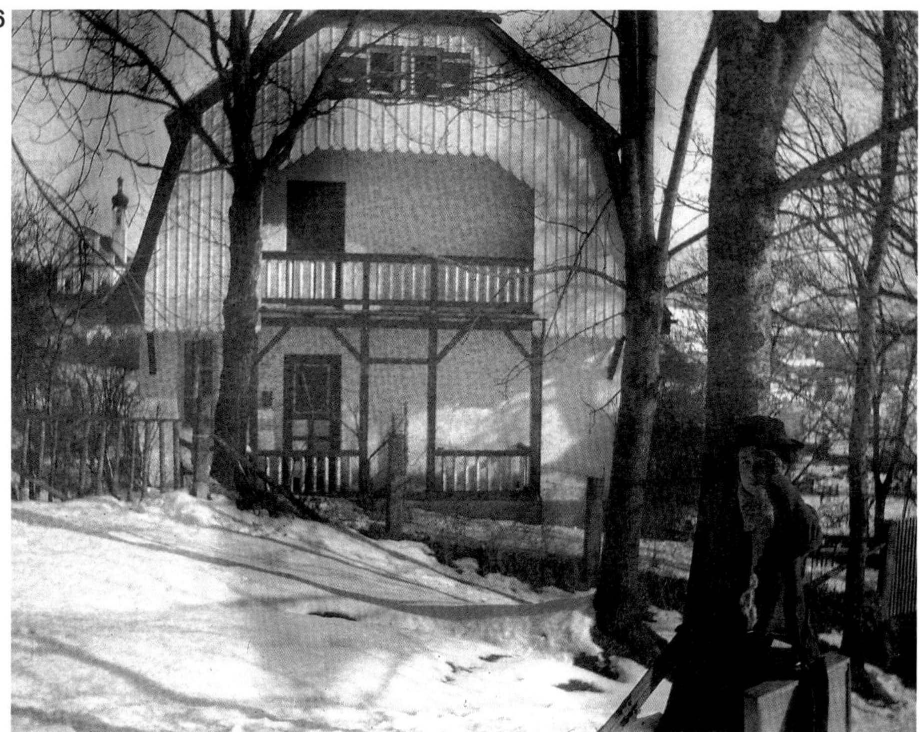

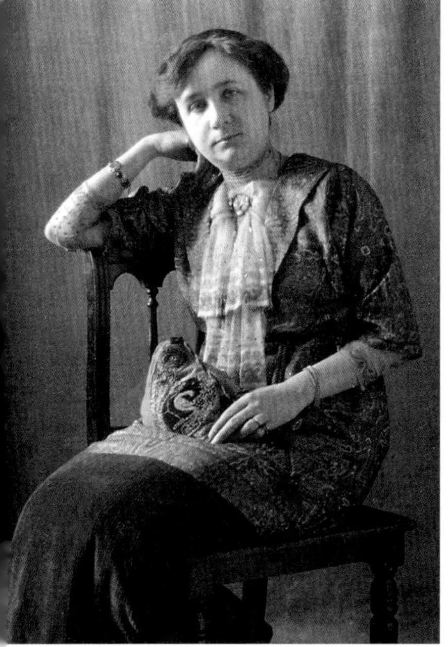

8

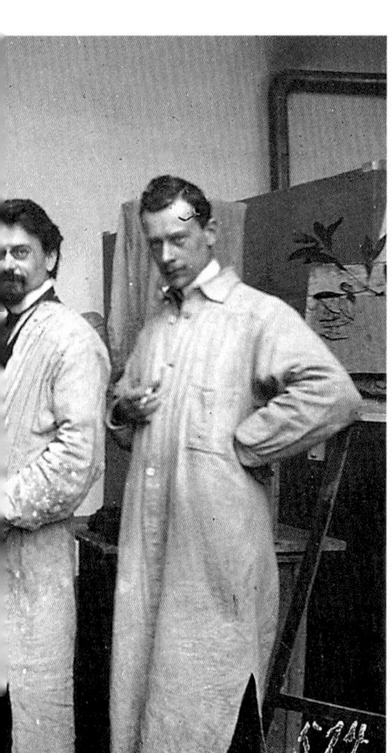

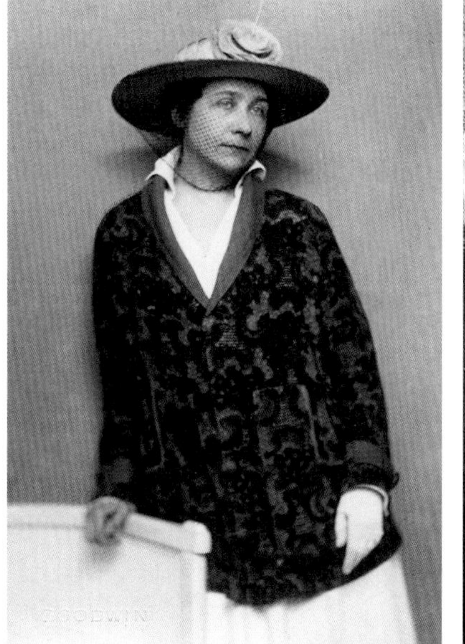

10

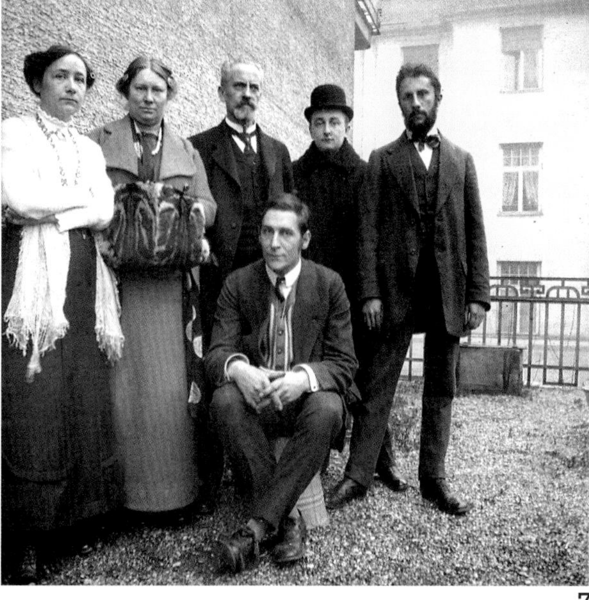

7

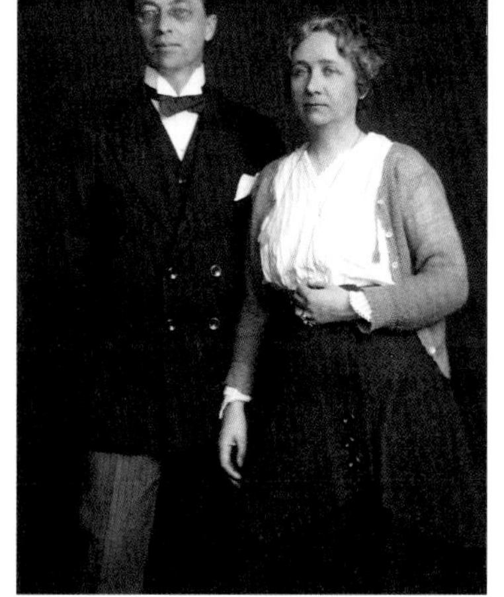

9

6 Gabriele Münter with painting materials in front of her house in Murnau, February 1910; photo: Wassily Kandinsky, inv. no. 2253

7 Members of the Blue Rider on the balcony at Ainmillerstraße 36, Munich, 1911. Left: Gabriele Münter; photo: Wassily Kandinsky, inv. no. 2204

8 Gabriele Münter holding a handbag of her own design with a peacock motif, Munich, ca. 1912, inv. no. 2183

9 Gabriele Münter and Wassily Kandinsky in Stockholm, Sweden, 1916, inv. no. 2900

10 Gabriele Münter, 1917, Stockholm, Sweden; photo: Henry Goodwin, inv. no. 3286

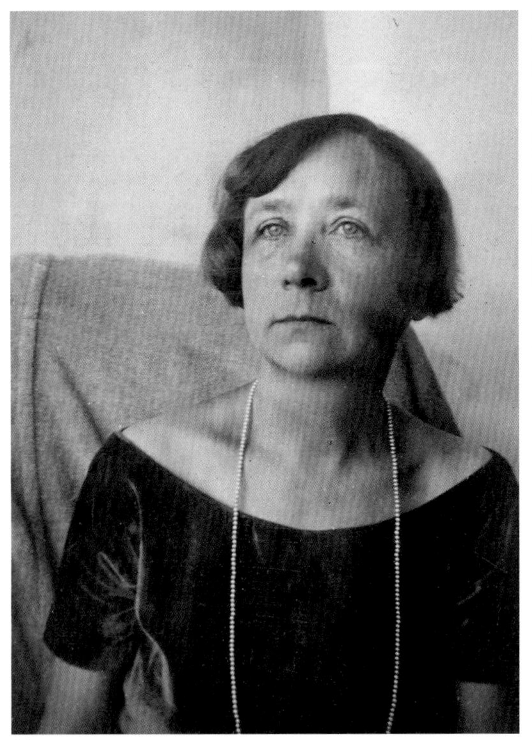

11

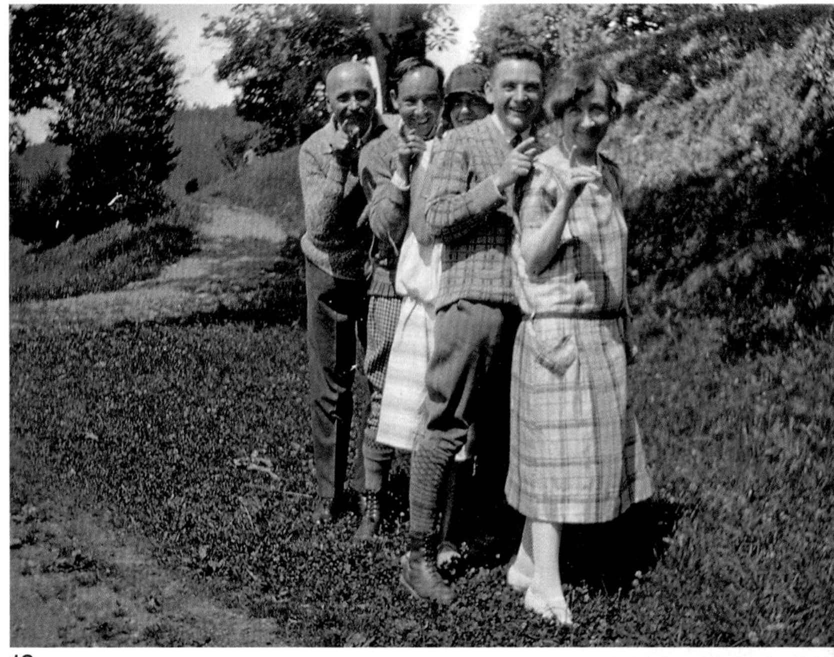

12

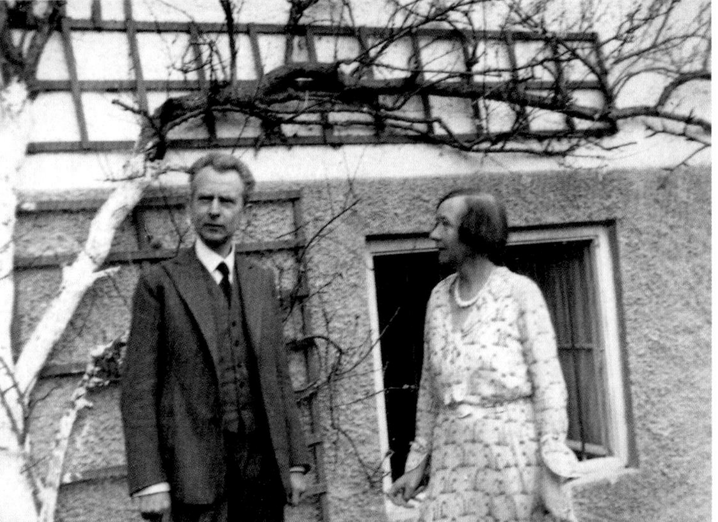

13

14

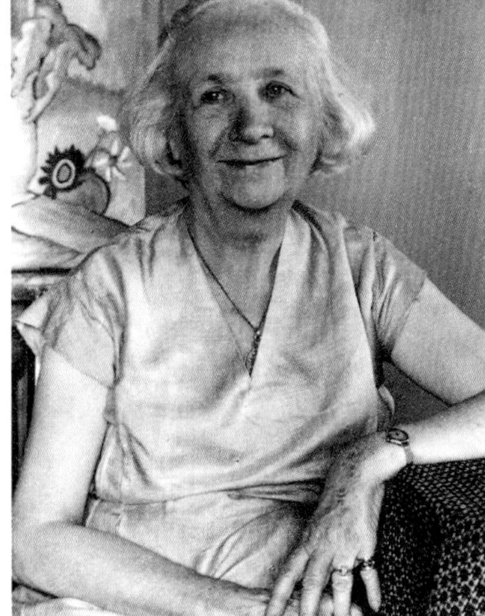

15

11 Gabriele Münter, ca. 1921, inv. no. 3301

12 Gabriele Münter with friends in Cademario, Ticino, Switzerland, 1927, inv. no. 3310

13 Johannes Eichner and Gabriele Münter standing in front of the house in Murnau, spring 1933; photo: Gertrud Haff, inv. no. 3317

14 Gabriele Münter, ca. 1935, inv. no. 3339

15 Gabriele Münter, ca. 1945; photo: Kaethe Augenstein, Bonn, inv. no. 3363

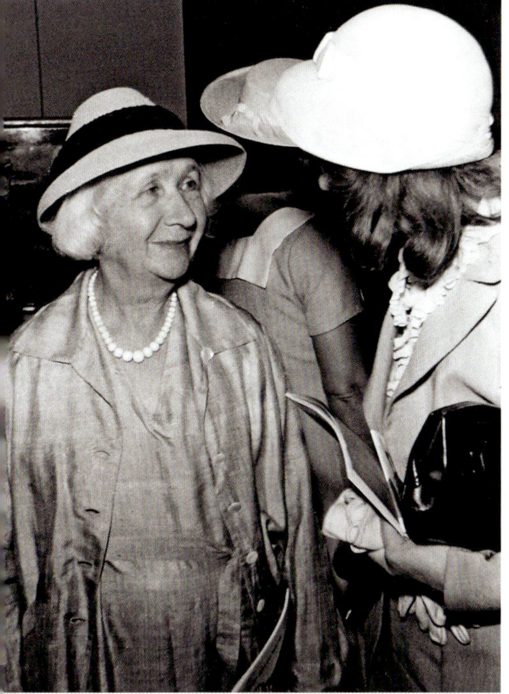

16

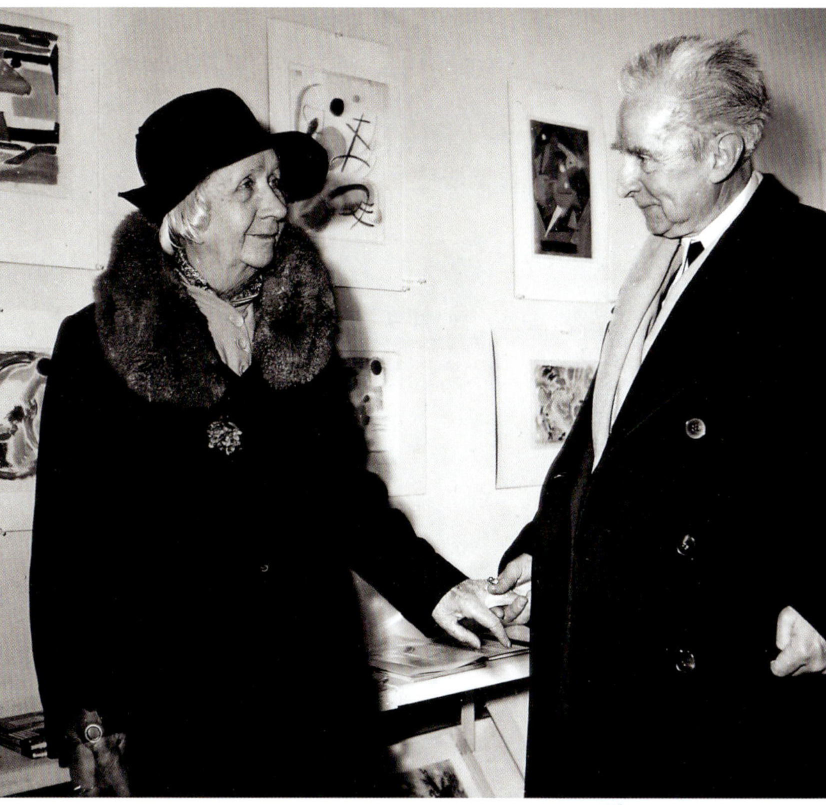

18

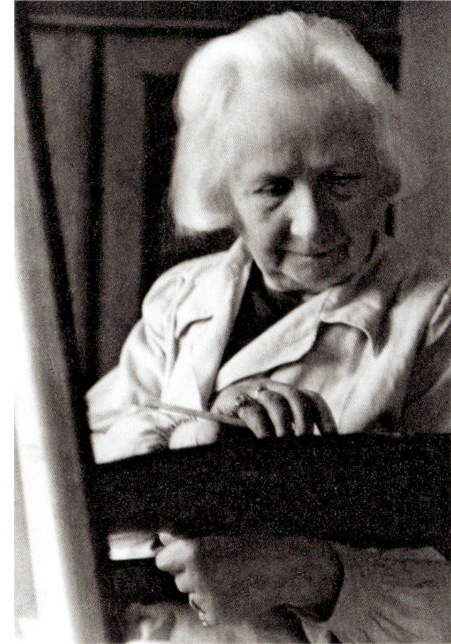

17

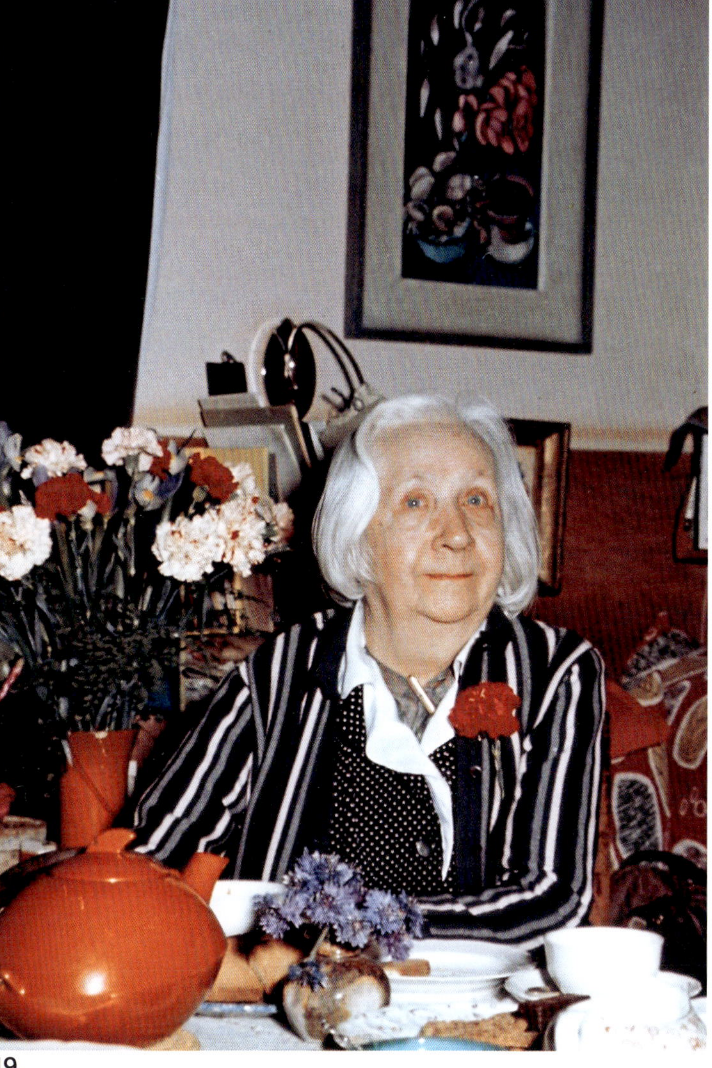

19

16 Gabriele Münter at the opening of the exhibition *Der Blaue Reiter* at the Haus der Kunst, Munich, 1949; photo: Felbermeyer, Munich, inv. no. 3490

17 Gabriele Münter painting, Murnau, 1952; photo: Sigrid Bühring, inv. no. 3385

18 Gabriele Münter and Johannes Eichner at the Kunstkabinett Otto Stangl, Munich, 1955, inv. no. 3496

19 Gabriele Münter, 1959; photo: Dalzell Hatfield, inv. no. 3474

"The cinema is so much more enjoyable than the theater!"

Gabriele Münter's Passion for Film

After spending the evening at the movie theater in Murnau, where she watched *Es war eine rauschende Ballnacht* (released in English as *It Was a Gay Ballnight*) starring Zarah Leander, Gabriele Münter wrote the following comment in her diary on November 9, 1939: "I never cease to be astonished at what has become of the 'cinematograph' of 1899—when I laughed myself silly over those rascals in Cologne. . . . The cinema is so much more enjoyable than the theater!"

Münter was an enthusiastic moviegoer as long as she lived. From her first experience of the cinema—which most likely took place around 1900, as she was still in the United States in 1899 and did not return to Germany until October 1900—until her death, film played an important role in her everyday life. She wrote the following about her life in Murnau in a letter to the art educator Irene von Schaller in 1955: "I haven't been to the city for three years. I am content with my work and lots of (current) reading and daily walks and a visit to the cinema now and then."[1] Her life partners, first Wassily Kandinsky and from 1928 on Johannes Eichner, shared her passion. Eichner even published articles about film, as well as movie reviews.[2]

In view of the fact that Münter began her career in art as a photographer, it comes as no surprise that she developed a strong interest in the new medium of film. She appears to have found the opportunity to view the world through the filter of a mechanical device especially appealing. This underscores both her modernity and her open-minded approach to life. The young media of photography and film had a lasting impact on her visual mindset. Thus a selection of films the artist is known to have seen was incorporated into the exhibition.

Beginning in the 1920s, she frequently noted the titles of films she had seen in her diaries. These notes form the basis for the following list of films, to which we have added the names of the directors and actors in leading roles. Striking is the large number of films the artist saw from 1940 onward, which might be explained by the lack of other forms of entertainment. Just as Münter rarely commented on the visual arts, she had very little to say about her visits to the cinema. As a result, we seldom know her assessment of the films she saw.

1
Translated from letter to Irene von Schaller dated June 22, 1955, MES. The "city" to which she refers is Munich.

2
Kleine 1994, pp. 557–58.

Films Seen by Gabriele Münter, in the Order in Which She Saw Them (Selection)

1914 *Karl der Große: Bilder aus der deutschen Geschichte* (Germany, 1911)
Director: Franz Porten
Starring: Gerhard Dammann

1919 *Der Rattenfänger von Hameln* (Germany, 1918)
Director: Paul Wegener
Starring: Paul Wegener

1921 *Sumurun* (Germany, 1920)
Director: Ernst Lubitsch
Featuring: Jenny Hasselqvist, Pola Negri, Ernst Lubitsch, Paul Wegener, Carl Clewing, Harry Liedtke, et al.

Der Mann ohne Namen III (Germany, 1921)
Director: Georg Jacoby
Starring: Harry Liedtke

1922 *Seefahrt ist not!* (Germany, 1921)
Director: Rudolf Biebrach
Featuring: Rudolf Biebrach, Lucie Höflich, Albert Kunze, Hugo Döblin, Ilka Güning, et al.

1925 *Das große weiße Schweigen* (Germany, 1924)
[documentary with footage from Robert Falcon Scott's English expedition to the South Pole (Terra Nova Expedition), 1912]

Zapfenstreich (Germany, 1925)
Director: Conrad Wiene
Featuring: Owen Gorin, Claire Lotto, Bernhard Goetzke, et al.

Charleys Tante (*Charley's Aunt*, USA, 1925)
Director: Scott Sidney
Starring: Sydney Chaplin

Peter Pan (USA, 1924)
Director: Herbert Brenon
Starring: Betty Bronson

1926 *Bismarck 1862–1898*, Part 1 (Germany, 1926)
Director: Curt Blachnitzky
Starring: Franz Ludwig

Der Dieb von Bagdad (*The Thief of Bagdad*, USA, 1924)
Director: Raoul Walsh
Starring: Douglas Fairbanks

Manon Lescaut (Germany, 1926)
Director: Arthur Robison
Starring: Lya de Putti

Mensch und Tier im Urwald (Germany, 1924)
Director: Hans Schomburgk
Camera: Paul Lieberenz

Goldrausch (*Gold Rush*, USA, 1925)
Director: Charlie Chaplin
Starring: Charlie Chaplin

Der Geiger von Florenz (Germany, 1926)
Director: Paul Czinner
Starring: Elisabeth Bergner

Wehe, wenn sie losgelassen (Germany, 1926)
Director: Carl Froelich
Featuring: Henny Porten, Bruno Kastner, Curt Bois, et al.

Menschen untereinander (Germany, 1926)
Director: Gerhard Lamprecht
Featuring: Alfred Abel, Aud Egede-Nissen, Erika Glässner, Olga Limburg, et al.

Die Biene Maja und ihre Abenteuer (Germany, 1926)
Directors: Waldemar Bonsels and Wolfram Junghans

Die Abenteuer des Prinzen Achmed (Germany, 1926)
Director: Lotte Reiniger

1927 *Schaffende Hände: Die Maler* (Germany, 1926)
Producer: Hans Cürlis

Schaffende Hände: Die Bildhauer (Germany, 1926)
Producer: Hans Cürlis

Laster der Menschheit (Germany, 1926/27)
Director: Rudolf Meinert
Starring: Asta Nielsen and Alfred Abel

Moana: A Romance of the Golden Age (USA, 1926)
Director: Robert J. Flaherty
[documentary about the people of Samoa]

Das edle Blut (Germany, 1926/27)
Director: Carl Boese
Featuring: Hanna Ralph, Harry Hardt, Wolfgang Zilzer, et al.

Liebe (Germany, 1926)
Director: Paul Czinner
Starring: Elisabeth Bergner

Der General (*The General*, USA, 1926)
Director: Buster Keaton
Starring: Buster Keaton

Wunderland Bali (1926/27)
Director: Lola Kreutzberg

Der Tänzer meiner Frau (Germany, 1925)
Director: Alexander Korda
Starring: Maria Korda, Willy Fritsch, and Michael Varkonyi

Die Dritte Eskadron (Austria/Germany, 1926)
Director: Carl Wilhelm
Featuring: Clair Rommer, Fritz Spira, Eugen Burg, et al.

Der Musterschüler (*College*, USA, 1927)
Director: James W. Horne
Starring: Buster Keaton

Chang (USA/Siam, 1927)
Directors: Merian C. Cooper and Ernest B. Schoedsack

Schwere Jungs, leichte Mädchen (Germany, 1927)
Director: Carl Boese
Featuring: Lissy Arna, Gustav Fröhlich, Eugen Burg, et al.

1928 *Die Sandgräfin* (Germany, 1927)
Director: Hans Steinhoff
Featuring: Christa Tordy, Käthe von Nagy, Jack Trevor, et al.

Madame Pompadour (Great Britain, 1927)
Director: Herbert Wilcox
Starring: Dorothy Gish

Matrosenliebchen (*God Gave Me Twenty Cents*, USA, 1926)
Director: Herbert Brenon
Featuring: Lois Moran, Lya de Putti, Jack Mulhall, et al.

Der Zirkus (*The Circus*, USA, 1928)
Director: Charlie Chaplin
Starring: Charlie Chaplin

Schwarzwaldmädel (Germany, 1920)
Director: Arthur Wellin
Starring: Uschi Elleot

Titanic (*East Side, West Side*, USA, 1927)
Director: Allan Dwan
Starring: George O'Brien, Virginia Valli, and June Collyer

Chicago (USA, 1927)
Director: Frank Urson
Starring: Phyllis Haver

Leichte Kavallerie / Verrat (Germany, 1927)
Director: Rolf Randolf
Featuring: Alphons Fryland, André Mattoni, et al.

Der Untergang der "Hesperus" (*The Wreck of the Hesperus*, USA, 1927)
Directors: Elmer Clifton and John Mescall
Featuring: Virginia Bradford, Frank Marion, Alan Hale, et al.

Der Florentiner Hut (*Un Chapeau de Paille d'Italie*, France, 1928)
Director: René Clair
Featuring: Albert Préjean, Maryse Maia, Olga Tschechowa, et al.

Petronella (Germany/Switzerland, 1927)
Director: Hanns Schwarz
Starring: Maly Delschaft, Wilhelm Dieterle, and Oskar Homolka

Vom Täter fehlt jede Spur (Germany, 1928)
Director: Constantin J. David
Featuring: Hanni Weisse, Gritta Ley, Kurt Gerron, et al.

Der vierte Musketier (*The Three Musketeers*, USA, 1921)
Director: Fred Niblo
Starring: Douglas Fairbanks

1929 *Mönche, Tänzer und Soldaten* (Germany, 1924)
Director: Wilhelm Filchner

Der Patriot (*The Patriot*, USA, 1928)
Director: Ernst Lubitsch
Starring: Emil Jannings

Fräulein Else (Germany, 1928/29)
Director: Paul Czinner
Starring: Elisabeth Bergner

Doktor Dolittle und seine Tiere (Germany, 1928)
Director: Lotte Reiniger

Der König der Gaukler (*The Best Bad Man*, USA, 1925)
Director: J. G. Blystone
Starring: Tom Mix

1930 *Le Mystère de la Villa rose* (France, 1929)
Directors: René Hervil and Louis Mercanton
Featuring: Léon Mathot, Simone Vaudry, Louis Baron fils, et al.

Napoléon (France, 1927)
Director: Abel Gance
Starring: Albert Dieudonné

L'Instinct (France, 1929)
Directors: André Liabel and Léon Mathot
Featuring: Léon Mathot, Madeleine Carroll, André Marnay, et al.

Mon Gosse de Père (France, 1930)
Director: Jean de Limur
Starring: Adolphe Menjou, Alice Cocéa, and Roger Tréville

La Tendresse (France, 1930)
Director: André Hugon
Starring: Marcelle Chantal, Jean Toulout, and José Noguéro

Muche (France, 1927)
Director: Robert Péguy
Featuring: Nicolas Koline, Elmire Vautier, Madeleine Guitty, Jean Aymé, et al.

Le Ruisseau (France, 1929)
Director: René Hervil
Featuring: Louise Lagrange, Lucien Dalsace, Olga Day, et al.

L'Homme qui ne ment pas (*George Washington Cohen*, USA, 1928)
Director: George Archainbaud
Starring: George Jessel

Tempête sur l'Asie (*Potomok Chingiskhana*, USSR, 1928)
Director: Vsevolod Pudovkin
Starring: Valéry Inkijinoff

La Nuit est à nous (France, 1929)
Director: Roger Lion
Featuring: Marie Bell, Henry Roussell, Jean Murat, et al.

Arabesques (France, 1929)
Director: Germaine Dulac

Disque 957 (France, 1928)
Director: Germaine Dulac

Thèmes et Variations (France, 1928)
Director: Germaine Dulac

1931 *Urwaldsymphonie* (Germany, 1930/31)
Director: Pola Bauer-Adamara

Der unsterbliche Lump (Germany, 1929/30)
Director: Gustav Ucicky
Starring: Liane Haid and Gustav Fröhlich

Die Drei von der Tankstelle (Germany, 1930)
Director: Wilhelm Thiele
Starring: Lilian Harvey, Willy Fritsch, Oskar Karlweis, and Heinz Rühmann

Stürme über dem Mont Blanc (Germany, 1930)
Director: Arnold Fanck
Starring: Leni Riefenstahl

1932 *Douaumont: Die Hölle von Verdun* (Germany, 1931)
Director: Heinz Paul

1934 *Flowers and Trees, Mickey's Review* (USA, 1932)
A Walt Disney production

Ein Mann will nach Deutschland (Germany, 1934)
Director: Paul Wegener
Starring: Karl Ludwig Diehl, Brigitte Horney, and Hermann Speelmans

1935 *Triumph des Willens* (Germany, 1935)
Director: Leni Riefenstahl

Kirschen in Nachbars Garten (Germany, 1935)
Director: Erich Engels
Featuring: Liesl Karlstadt, Karl Valentin, et al.

1936 *Nanga Parbat: Ein Kampfbericht der deutschen Himalaya-Expedition 1934* (Germany, 1934/35)
Director: Frank Leberecht

Der Kaiser von Kalifornien (Germany, 1935/36)
Director: Luis Trenker
Starring: Luis Trenker

1937 *Moskau – Shanghai* (Germany, 1936)
Director: Paul Wegener
Starring: Pola Negri, Gustav Diessl, and Wolfgang Keppler

Die Tochter des Samurai (Germany/Japan, 1937)
Director: Arnold Fanck
Featuring: Isamu Kusogi, Setsuko Hara, Ruth Eweler, et al.

Ramona (USA, 1936)
Director: Henry King
Starring: Loretta Young

Mutterschaft (*Maternité*, France, 1935)
Director: Jean Choux
Starring: Françoise Rosay and Félix Oudart

1939 *Der Schritt vom Wege* (Germany, 1938/39)
Director: Gustaf Gründgens
Starring: Marianne Hoppe

Lauter Lügen (Germany, 1938)
Director: Heinz Rühmann
Starring: Hertha Feiler, Albert Matterstock, Fita Benkhoff, and Hilde Weissner

Kautschuk (Germany, 1938)
Director: Eduard von Borsody
Starring: René Deltgen, Vera von Langen, and Gustav Diessl

Der Florentiner Hut (Germany, 1939)
Director: Wolfgang Liebeneiner
Starring: Heinz Rühmann

Manege (Germany, 1937)
Director: Carmine Gallone
Starring: Albert Matterstock, Attila Hörbiger, and Anneliese Uhlig

Zigeunerprinzessin (*Wings of the Morning*, Great Britain, 1937)
Director: Harold D. Schuster
Starring: Annabella, Henry Fonda, and Leslie Banks

Napoleon ist an allem schuld (Germany, 1938)
Director: Curt Goetz
Featuring: Curt Goetz, Valérie von Martens, Else von Möllendorff, et al.

Hallo Janine (Germany, 1939)
Director: Carl Boese
Featuring: Marika Rökk, Johannes Heesters, Rudi Godden, Else Elster, et al.

Konzert in Tirol (Austria, 1938)
Director: Karlheinz Martin
Featuring: Heli Finkenzeller, Ferdinand Mayerhofer, Hans Holt, et al.

Dreizehn Mann und eine Kanone (Germany, 1938)
Director: Johannes Meyer
Featuring: Alexander Golling, Otto Wernicke, Herbert Hübner, Erich Ponto, et al.

Robert Koch, der Bekämpfer des Todes (Germany, 1939)
Director: Hans Steinhoff
Starring: Emil Jannings and Werner Krauß

Es war eine rauschende Ballnacht (Germany, 1939)
Director: Carl Froelich
Starring: Zarah Leander, Hans Stüwe, and Marika Rökk

Burgtheater (Austria, 1936)
Director: Willi Forst
Featuring: Werner Krauß, Carl Esmond, Hortense Raky, Olga Tschechowa, et al.

1940 *Maria Ilona* (Germany, 1939)
Director: Géza von Bolváry
Starring: Paula Wessely and Willy Birgel

Das Lied der Wüste (Germany, 1939)
Director: Paul Martin
Starring: Zarah Leander and Gustav Knuth

Der Postmeister (Germany 1940)
Director: Gustav Ucicky
Starring: Heinrich George, Hilde Krahl

Ein Mann auf Abwegen (Germany 1940)
Director: Herbert Selpin
Starring: Hans Albers, Charlotte Thiele

Streit um den Knaben Jo (Germany 1937)
Director: Erich Waschneck
Starring: Lil Dagover, Willy Fritsch

Donauschiffer (Germany 1940)
Director: Robert A. Stemmle
Starring: Attila Hörbiger, Hilde Krahl

Bal paré (Germany 1940)
Director: Karl Ritter
Starring: Ilse Werner, Hannes Stelzer

Die 3 Codonas (Germany 1940)
Director: Arthur Maria Rabenalt
Starring: René Deltgen, Ernst von Klipstein

Eine kleine Nachtmusik (Germany 1939)
Director: Leopold Hainisch
Starring: Hannes Stelzer, Christl Mardayn

Der Herrscher (Germany 1937)
Director: Veit Harlan
Starring: Emil Jannings, Marianne Hoppe

Achtung! Feind hört mit! (Germany 1940)
Director: Arthur Maria Rabenalt
Starring: René Deltgen, Kirsten Heiberg

Das Herz der Königin (Germany 1940)
Director: Carl Froelich
Starring: Zarah Leander, Walther Suessenguth

Jud Süß (Germany 1940)
Director: Veit Harlan
Starring: Ferdinand Marian, Werner Krauß, Heinrich George

1941 *Aus der Geschichte des Fähnleins Florian Geyer* (Germany 1940)
Director: Eduard Wieser, Adam Eckart Schneider
[short documentary]

Das Fräulein von Barnhelm (Germany 1940)
Director: Hans Schweikart
Starring: Käthe Gold, Ewald Balser

Kora Terry (Germany 1940)
Director: Georg Jacoby
Starring: Marika Rökk, Will Quadflieg

Das Wunschkonzert (Germany 1940)
Director: Eduard von Borsody
Starring: Ilse Werner, Carl Raddatz

Der ewige Jude (Germany 1940)
Director: Fritz Hippler
Starring: Harry Giese

Operette (Germany 1940)
Director: Willi Forst
Starring: Willi Forst, Maria Holst

Kampfgeschwader Lützow (Germany 1941)
Director: Hans Bertram
Starring: Christian Kayßler, Heinz Welzel

Über alles in der Welt (Germany 1941)
Director: Karl Ritter
Starring: Paul Hartmann, Hannes Stelzer

Carl Peters (Germany 1941)
Director: Herbert Selpin
Starring: Hans Albers, Karl Dannemann

Ohm Krüger (Germany 1941)
Director: Hans Steinhoff, Karl Anton, Herbert Maisch
Starring: Emil Jannings, Lucie Höflich

Kopf hoch, Johannes! (Germany 1941)
Director: Viktor de Kowa
Starring: Klaus Detlef Sierck, Albrecht Schoenhals

Der Weg ins Freie (Germany 1941)
Director: Rolf Hansen
Starring: Zarah Leander, Hans Stüwe

Das leichte Mädchen (Germany 1940)
Director: Fritz Peter Buch
Starring: Willy Fritsch, Friedl Czepa

Friedemann Bach (Germany 1941)
Director: Traugott Müller
Starring: Gustav Gründgens, Eugen Klöpfer

Die Goldschläger von Schwabach (Germany 1934/35)
Director: Günther L. Arko

Artisten (Germany 1935)
Director: Harry Piel
Starring: Harry Piel, Hilde Hildebrand

Jungens (Germany 1941)
Director: Robert A. Stemmle
Starring: Albert Hehn, Hilde Sessak, Eduard Wandrey

Komödianten (Germany 1941)
Director: G. W. Pabst
Starring: Käthe Dorsch, Hilde Krahl, Henny Porten

Annelie (Germany 1941)
Director: Josef von Báky
Starring: Luise Ullrich, Karl Ludwig Diehl

Variété (*Variétés*, Germany/France 1935)
Director: Nicolas Farkas
Starring: Annabella, Hans Albers, Attila Hörbiger

Der ahnungslose Engel (Germany 1935/36)
Director: Franz Seitz Sr.
Starring: Lucie Englisch, Joe Stöckel

Clarissa (Germany 1941)
Director: Gerhard Lamprecht
Starring: Sybille Schmitz, Gustav Fröhlich

1942 *Kadetten* (Germany 1941)
Director: Karl Ritter
Starring: Mathias Wieman, Carsta Löck

Alarmstufe V (Germany 1941)
Director: Alois J. Lippl
Starring: Heli Finkenzeller, Ernst von Klipstein

Tanz der Farben (Germany 1938/39)
Director: Hans Fischinger

Zwei in einer großen Stadt (Germany 1942)
Director: Volker von Collande
Starring: Claude Farell, Karl John

Zwischen Himmel und Erde (Germany 1942)
Director: Harald Braun
Starring: Werner Krauß, Wolfgang Lukschy

Mann für Mann (Germany 1939)
Director: Robert A. Stemmle
Starring: Gustav Knuth, Viktoria von Ballasko

Maja zwischen zwei Ehen (Germany 1938)
Director: Fritz Kirchhoff
Starring: Lil Dagover, Peter Petersen

Liselotte von der Pfalz (Germany 1935)
Director: Carl Froelich
Starring: Renate Müller, Hans Stüwe

Krach um Jolanthe (Germany 1934)
Director: Carl Froelich
Starring: Wilhelm P. Krüger, Marianne Hoppe

Wiener Blut (Germany 1942)
Director: Willi Forst
Starring: Fred Liewehr, Willy Fritsch

Traumulus (Germany 1936)
Director: Carl Froelich
Starring: Emil Jannings, Hilde Weissner

Der Schützenkönig (Germany 1932)
Director: Franz Seitz Sr.
Starring: Weiß Ferdl, Max Adalbert

Geheimakte W. B. 1 (Germany 1942)
Director: Herbert Selpin
Starring: Alexander Golling, Eva Immermann

Frauen sind doch bessere Diplomaten (Germany 1941)
Director: Georg Jacoby
Starring: Marika Rökk, Willy Fritsch

Die große Liebe (Germany 1942)
Director: Rolf Hansen
Starring: Zarah Leander, Viktor Staal

Hochzeit auf Bärenhof (Germany 1942)
Director: Carl Froelich
Starring: Heinrich George, Lina Carstens, Paul Wegener

Ein Windstoß (Germany 1942)
Director: Walter Felsenstein
Starring: Paul Kemp, Margit Debar

So endete eine Liebe (Germany 1934)
Director: Karl Hartl
Starring: Paula Wessely, Willi Forst

Die große und die kleine Welt (Germany 1935/36)
Director: Johannes Riemann
Starring: Ludwig Schmitz, Adele Sandrock, Heinrich George

Mutterlied (Germany/Italy 1937)
Director: Carmine Gallone
Starring: Beniamino Gigli, Maria Cebotari

Andreas Schlüter (Germany 1942)
Director: Herbert Maisch
Starring: Heinrich George, Mila Kopp

Diesel (Germany 1942)
Director: Gerhard Lamprecht
Starring: Willy Birgel, Hilde Weissner, Paul Wegener

1955 *Rampenlicht* (*Limelight*, USA 1952)
Director: Charlie Chaplin
Starring: Charlie Chaplin, Claire Bloom

Uli der Knecht (Switzerland 1954)
Director: Franz Schnyder
Starring: Liselotte Pulver, Hannes Schmidhauser

Die Wüste lebt (*The Living Desert*, USA 1953)
Starring: James Algar
[documentary]

Ludwig II. – Glanz und Ende eines Königs (Germany 1955)
Director: Helmut Käutner
Starring: O. W. Fischer, Ruth Leuwerick

Im Tal der Biber (*In Beaver Valley*, USA 1950)
Director: James Algar
[short documentary]

Lili (USA 1953)
Director: Charles Walters
Starring: Leslie Caron, Mel Ferrer

Das Lied von Kaprun (*Das Lied der Hohen Tauern*, Germany/Austria 1955)
Director: Anton Kutter
Starring: Albert Lieven, Waltraut Haas

1957 *Im Schatten des Karakorum* (Germany/Austria, 1955)
Director: Eugen Schuhmacher

Solo Exhibitions

The term "paintings" refers to pictures on textile, cardboard, or wooden supports.

Cologne 1908, Kunstsalon Lenobel (paintings)
Gabriele Münter: Gemälde, Cologne, Kunstsalon Lenobel, January 1908 (57 paintings); subsequent venues: Krefeld, Kaiser Wilhelm Museum, February 1908 (57 paintings); Düren, April 1908; Hamburg, Bock und Sohn, May 1908; Breslau, Galerie Lichtenberg, June–July 1908 (43 paintings); Karlsruhe, Badischer Kunstverein, September 1908; Stuttgart, Württembergischer Kunstverein, October 1908.

Cologne 1908, Kunstsalon Lenobel
Gabriele Münter: Farbige Druckgraphik, Cologne, Kunstsalon Lenobel, May 1908 (24 color prints); subsequent venue: Bonn, Kunstbuchhandlung Friedrich Cohen, joint presentation with Karl Jozsa, 1908.

Berlin 1913, Der Sturm
11. Ausstellung Der Sturm: Gabriele Münter, Berlin, Der Sturm, January 6–February 1913 (84 paintings); subsequent venues (featuring different selections of works): Munich, Der Neue Kunstsalon Max Dietzel (see the following entry); Frankfurt am Main, Kunstsalon des Warenhauses Wronker & Co., May 15 (opening)–June 25, 1913 (53 paintings); Dresden, Kunstsalon Emil Richter, July 9–ca. 25, 1913; Stuttgart, Neuer Kunstsalon am Neckartor, October 1913; Fürth, Kunstverein, January 1914; Erlangen, Kunstverein, February 1914; Wiesbaden, March 1914.

Munich 1913, Der Neue Kunstsalon Max Dietzel
Gabriele Münter (1904–1913): Kollektiv-Ausstellung, Munich, Der Neue Kunstsalon Max Dietzel, March 26–April 30, 1913 (67 paintings). On April 8, 19 paintings were removed for the Sturm exhibition in Copenhagen and replaced with different works.

Copenhagen 1913, Der Sturm
[Gabriele Münter], Copenhagen, Københavns Kunstsalon, May 1 (opening)–end of May 1913 (35 paintings).

Berlin 1915, Der Sturm
Der Sturm: Fünfunddreißigste Ausstellung, Gabriele Münter, Berlin, Der Sturm, opening: October 24, 1915 (53 paintings).

Stockholm 1916, Gummesons Konsthandel
Der Sturms konstutställning, Kollektiv utställning Münter, Oljemålning och grafik, Stockholm, Carl Gummesons Konsthandel, March 1–14, 1916 (28 paintings).

Copenhagen 1918, Den Frie Udstilling
Gabriele Münter-Kandinsky: Oljemalninger, Glastavler, Grafik, Copenhagen, Den Frie Udstilling, March 7–13, 1918 (100 paintings, 20 reverse-glass paintings, 7 etchings, one wall of drawings).

Copenhagen 1919, Ny Kunstsal
Maleriudstilling Gabriele Münter-Kandinsky, Copenhagen, Københavns Ny Kunstsal, October 4–20, 1919 (93 paintings, 18 reverse-glass paintings).

München 1920, Galerie Thannhauser
Gabriele Münter: Gemälde und Zeichnungen, Munich, Moderne Galerie Heinrich Thannhauser, December 1920

Touring Exhibition 1925/26
Gabriele Münter-Kandinsky, Cologne, Kunstverein, February 1–15, 1925 (56 paintings, as well as drawings); Essen, Baedeker, March 1–31 (49 paintings); Krefeld, Kaiser Wilhelm Museum, July 1–30 (49 paintings); as a special exhibition with several changes in the 5th Jahrtausend-Ausstellung organized by the city of Duisburg, *Neuere rheinische Kunst*, Duisburg, Duisburger Museums-Verein, August 1–30 (66 paintings); Hagen, October 1–31; Elberfeld, February 1–28, 1926; Dresden, Galerie Baumbach, summer 1926; under the title *Gabriele Münter* in Braunschweig, Gesellschaft der Freunde junger Kunst, Schloß, 1st exhibition 1926/27, until October 31, 1926 (56 paintings, 19 drawings, 14 watercolors, 6 etchings, 6 lithographs).

Murnau 1928, Buchhandlung Wiegelmann
Gabriele Münter, Murnau, Buchhandlung Wiegelmann, September 1928.

Berlin 1930, Galerie Wiltschek
Kollektiv-Ausstellung Gabriele Münter, Berlin, Galerie Rudolf Wiltschek, November 15–December 5, 1930 (21 paintings).

Murnau 1931, Buchhandlung Wiegelmann
Gabriele Münter, Murnau, Buchhandlung Wiegelmann, September 1931.

Murnau 1932, Buchhandlung Wiegelmann
[Gabriele Münter], Murnau, Buchhandlung Wiegelmann, July 1932.

Augsburg 1932, Kunstverein
[Gabriele Münter], Augsburg, Kunstverein, October–November 1932.

Touring Exhibition 1933–35
Gabriele Münter: "50 Gemälde aus 25 Jahren" (1908–1933), touring exhibition, Bremen, Paula Modersohn-Becker-Haus, April/May 1933 (8 weeks); Barmen, Barmer Kunstverein, Ruhmeshalle, August 1933; Bochum, Städtische Gemäldegalerie, 1933; Jena, Prinzessinnenschlößchen, January 14, 1934; Eisenach, Schloss, February 16/17–mid-March 1934; Altenburg in Thüringen, Museum, 1935; Stuttgart, Kunsthaus Valentien im Königsbau, May/June 1935.

Munich 1937, Kunstverein
Gabriele Münter, with Paul Roloff and Hans Reinhold Lichtenberger, Munich, Kunstverein, March 19–April 4, 1937 (37 paintings). The exhibition subsequently moved on to the Galerie Valentien in Stuttgart (37 paintings), where it was presented along with works by August Macke and Oskar Schlemmer.

Herford/Heilbronn 1937/38
Gabriele Münter, Herford, exhibition organized by the Herforder Verein für Heimatkunde in the new exhibition hall of the Städtisches Museum, December 15, 1937–January 18, 1938 (more than 50 works); Heilbronn, 1938.

Touring Exhibition 1949–52
Wanderausstellung Gabriele Münter: Werke aus 5 Jahrzehnten, Braunschweig, Kunstverein, Haus "Salve Hospes," July 17–August 7, 1949 (58 paintings, approx. 30 sketchbook sheets, 2 colored woodcuts); Bremen, Kunsthalle Bremen, January 22–February 19, 1950 (60 paintings, 40 sketches and prints); Düsseldorf, Galerie Vömel / Kunstsalon Vömel Trojanski, March/April 1950 (60 oil paintings); Aachen, Suermont-Museum, April 28–May 31, 1950; Krefeld, Kaiser Wilhelm Museum, July 6/7–30, 1950; Witten, Märkisches Museum, 1950 (along with works by Ida Kerkovius, Willibald Kramm, Anton Rovers, and Hilde Broer); Marburg (Lahn), Universitäts-Museum (Jubiläumsbau, Biegenstraße), 1950 (along with works by Robert Budzinski); Frankfurt am Main, Kunstverein, March 4–April 1, 1951 (63 paintings, sketches, color woodcuts); Karlsruhe, Kunstverein, 1951 (along with woodcuts by Gertrud Sentke); Freiburg im Breisgau, Kunstverein, in the rooms of the casino, 1951 (55 oil paintings, sketches, 2 handmade prints); Essen, Museum Folkwang, opening: August 12, 1951 (approx. 60 paintings); Hannover, Kestner-Gesellschaft, 1951 (50 works by Münter and 65 works by Paula Modersohn-Becker; a separate catalogue entitled *Paula Modersohn-Becker. Gabriele Münter*, featuring a foreword by Alfred Hentzen, was published for this venue); Bochum, Städtischer Ausstellungsraum, opening: December 2, 1951 (70 paintings and prints); Oberhausen, Städtische Galerie Schloß Oberhausen, March 1952 (90 works).

Touring Exhibition 1952/53
Wanderausstellung Gabriele Münter: Werke aus fünf Jahrzehnten, Munich, Central Collecting Point, May 1952 (63 paintings, 2 color woodcuts, approx. 30 sketchbook sheets, along with works by Max Peiffer-Watenphul); Gießen, Oberhessisches Museum, in the Liebig-Realgymnasium, July 9–[?] 1952 (paintings, drawings, woodcuts); Bielefeld, Städtisches Kunsthaus, November 9–30/December 7, 1952 (paintings, drawings); Hagen in Westphalia, Karl Ernst Osthaus-Museum, opening: February 14, 1953 (nearly 70 paintings, few drawings); Münster, Westfälischer Kunstverein im Landesmuseum Münster, March 15–April 12, 1953; Leverkusen, Schloß Morsbroich, April 15–May 3, 1953 (63 works); Wuppertal, Kunst- und Museumsverein, May–June 7, 1953 (paintings, graphic works); Herford, Heimatmuseum, exhibition organized by the Herforder Kunstverein, August 30–September 22, 1953 (43 paintings, drawings, smaller works).

Itzehoe 1952, Itzehoer Künstlerverein
[Gabriele Münter], Itzehoe, Itzehoer Künstlerverein in the exhibition hall of the Kunstgewerbehaus Otto (25 items: oil paintings, drawings).

Munich 1955, Kunstkabinett Otto Stangl
Gabriele Münter: Improvisationen, 1952 bis 1954, Munich, Kunstkabinett Otto Stangl, February–March 1955.

Remscheid 1955
[Gabriele Münter], Remscheid, Heimatmuseum (35 paintings).

Berlin 1955, Galerie Gerd Rosen
Gabriele Münter, Berlin, Galerie Gerd Rosen, ca. September 30–ca. November 15, 1955 (17 paintings).

Düsseldorf 1957, Galerie Alex Vömel
Gabriele Münter: Oelbilder, Düsseldorf, Galerie Alex Vömel, February 6–March 5, 1957.

Berlin 1957
Gabriele Münter: Gemälde, Graphik, Berlin, Haus am Lützowplatz, December 1–21, 1957 (81 paintings, 16 drawings, 8 woodcuts).

Los Angeles 1960, Dalzell Hatfield Galleries
Gabriele Münter: First American Exhibition with Seven Additional Major Paintings by Kandinsky, Los Angeles, Dalzell Hatfield Galleries, June 20–July 30, 1960 (13 paintings).

San Francisco 1960, Dalzell Hatfield Galleries
Münter, San Francisco, California Palace of the Legion of Honor, in collaboration with the Dalzell Hatfield Galleries (Los Angeles), August 13–September 11, 1960 (40 paintings, 20 colored works on paper, 5 paintings by Kandinsky).

London 1960, Marlborough Fine Art Ltd.
Gabriele Münter: Oil Paintings 1903–1937, London, Marlborough Fine Art Ltd., September–October 1960 (50 paintings).

Cologne 1960/61, Galerie Änne Abels
Gemälde von Gabriele Münter, Cologne, Galerie Änne Abels, December 10, 1960–January 28, 1961.

Mannheim 1961
Gabriele Münter, Mannheim, Kunsthalle Mannheim, September 30–October 29, 1961 (59 paintings).

New York 1961, Leonard Hutton Galleries
Gabriele Münter: Murnau to Stockholm (1908–1917), New York, Leonard Hutton Galleries, November 22–December 30, 1961 (44 paintings).

Munich 1962
Gabriele Münter: 1877–1962, Munich, Städtische Galerie im Lenbachhaus, October 13–December 2, 1962 (126 paintings, 20 prints, 8 handcrafted items, 5 watercolors, drawings).

Los Angeles 1963, Dalzell Hatfield Galleries
Gabriele Münter: 1877–1962, Memorial Exhibition, Los Angeles, Dalzell Hatfield Galleries, May 1–25, 1963 (9 paintings).

Böblingen 1963, Firma Eisenmann KG
Gabriele Münter, Böblingen, Firma Eisenmann KG, October 19–27, 1963 (30 works). The exhibition was presented in conjunction with an exhibition of works by employees of Eisenmann KG.

Zurich 1965, Galerie Daniel Keel
Gabriele Münter, Zurich, Galerie Daniel Keel, June 3–August 7, 1965 (29 paintings).

New York 1966, Leonard Hutton Galleries
Gabriele Münter, 1877 to 1962: Fifty Years of Her Art: Paintings, 1906–1956, New York, Leonard Hutton Galleries, March/April 1966 (66 paintings).

New York 1966/67, Leonard Hutton Galleries
An Exhibition of Unknown Work by Gabriele Münter, 1877–1962: Hinterglasmalerei (Painting on Glass), Woodcuts in Color, Etchings, Collages, New York, Leonard Hutton Galleries, December 1966–January 1967 (43 reverse-glass paintings, 32 color woodcuts, 12 etchings, 8 woodcuts, 6 lithographs, 6 collages).

Munich 1967
Gabriele Münter: Das druckgraphische Werk, Munich, Städtische Galerie im Lenbachhaus, March 10–April 23, 1967.

Heidelberg/Stuttgart/Münster 1967/68
Gabriele Münter: Gedächtnisausstellung zum 90. Geburtstag, Heidelberg, Heidelberger Kunstverein, July 2–August 13, 1967 (54 paintings, 13 reverse-glass paintings, 4 works in oil on paper, 2 watercolors); Stuttgart, Württembergischer Kunstverein, August 24–October 1, 1967; Münster, Westfälischer Kunstverein, January 7–February 11, 1968.

Düsseldorf 1968, Galerie Alex Vömel
Münter, Düsseldorf, Galerie Alex Vömel, January 8–February 3, 1968 (25 paintings).

Bremen 1969, Kunsthandlung Voigt
Gabriele Münter: Gemälde, Graphik, Bremen, Graphisches Kabinett, Kunsthandlung U. Voigt KG, February 7–April 26, 1969 (12 paintings, 12 prints, 1 gouache).

Munich 1969/70, Galerie Gunzenhauser
Gabriele Münter: Ölbilder und Graphik, Munich, Galerie Gunzenhauser, November 12, 1969–January 31, 1970 (43 prints, 21 paintings, 1 gouache).

Munich 1971, Galerie Gunzenhauser
Münter: Frühe Ölbilder, Munich, Galerie Gunzenhauser, until April 30, 1971 (30 paintings).

Bremen 1972/73
Gabriele Münter: Aquarelle und Handzeichnungen, Bremen, Kunsthalle Bremen, December 10, 1972–January 21, 1973.

Düsseldorf 1973, Galerie Wilhelm Grosshennig
Sonderausstellung Gabriele Münter, Düsseldorf, Galerie Wilhelm Grosshennig, August 15–October 15, 1973 (21 paintings).

Frankfurt am Main 1974, Kunstkabinett Hanna Bekker vom Rath
Gabriele Münter, 1877–1962: 30 Gemälde aus den Jahren 1906 bis 1959, Frankfurt am Main, Frankfurter Kunstkabinett Hanna Bekker vom Rath, January 25–March 23, 1974 (31 paintings).

Düsseldorf 1974, Galerie Vömel
Ölbilder von Gabriele Münter, Düsseldorf, Galerie Vömel (in cooperation with the Galerie Gunzenhauser, Munich), November 25–December 1974 (30 paintings).

Herford 1975, Herforder Kunstverein
Gabriele Münter: Graphik aus dem Lenbachhaus München, Herford, Herforder Kunstverein, November 23–December 14, 1975.

Garbsen (near Hannover) 1976, Schloß Ricklingen
Gabriele Münter, Garbsen, Schloß Ricklingen, Auktionshaus, 1976 (12 paintings).

Munich 1977
Gabriele Münter, 1877–1962: Gemälde, Zeichnungen, Hinterglasbilder und Volkskunst aus ihrem Besitz, Munich, Städtische Galerie im Lenbachhaus, April 22–July 3, 1977 (81 paintings, 34 drawings, 30 reverse-glass paintings, 8 colored works on paper, 3 pieces of embroidery, 1 sculpture, 54 objects of folk art).

Munich 1977, Galerie Gunzenhauser
Gabriele Münter: Aus Anlaß ihres 100. Geburtstages. Ölbilder, Holzschnitte, Munich, Galerie Gunzenhauser, May 5 (opening)–July 15, 1977.

Herford 1977, Herforder Kunstverein
Gabriele Münter, Herford, Herforder Kunstverein im Daniel Pöppelmann-Haus, September 17–October 16, 1977 (41 paintings, 24 drawings).

Stuttgart 1977, Galerie Maercklin
Gabriele Münter: Gemälde, Stuttgart, Galerie Maercklin, October 21–December 3, 1977.

Laguna Beach 1978
Gabriele Münter (1877–1962), Laguna Beach, CA, Laguna Beach Museum of Art, January 10–February 28, 1978 (40 paintings, 19 prints, 1 work on paper).

Munich 1978/79, Galerie Gunzenhauser
Gabriele Münter: 50 unbekannte Aquarelle, Handzeichnungen und ausgewählte Handdrucke, Munich, Galerie Gunzenhauser, November 2, 1978 (opening)–January 31, 1979 (30 drawings, 14 prints, 10 watercolors, 1 gouache, 1 oil and egg tempera painting).

Cambridge/Princeton 1980/81
Gabriele Münter: Between Munich and Murnau, Cambridge, MA, Busch-Reisinger-Museum, September 25–November 8, 1980; Princeton, NJ, Princeton University Art Museum, November 22, 1980–January 18, 1981 (36 paintings, 17 drawings, 10 linoleum cuts, 1 woodcut, 6 colored works on paper, 1 lithograph, 1 trial proof for a 1918 exhibition poster).

Cologne 1981, Galerie Orangerie-Reinz
Gabriele Münter, 1877–1962, Cologne, Galerie Orangerie-Reinz, 1981 (24 paintings, 21 drawings, 7 colored works on paper, 5 prints, 1 reverse-glass painting).

Munich 1985
Gabriele Münter: Zeichnungen und Aquarelle, Munich, Städtische Galerie im Lenbachhaus, July 17–November 3, 1985 (70 drawings, 13 watercolors, 3 gouaches; accompanying publication: Pfeiffer-Belli 1979).

Bad Säckingen 1986, Kunstverein Hochrhein
Gabriele Münter: Ölbilder, Aquarelle, Zeichnungen, Bad Säckingen, Kunstverein Hochrhein e.V., Villa Berberich, September 7–October 5, 1986 (41 paintings, 12 drawings, 10 colored works on paper, 4 prints).

Hamburg/Darmstadt/Aichtal-Aich 1988
Gabriele Münter, Hamburg, Kunstverein, April 9–May 29, 1988; Darmstadt, Hessisches Landesmuseum, June 29–August 21, 1988; Aichtal-Aich, Eisenmann KG, September 3–25, 1988 (83 paintings, 40 drawings, 13 prints, 8 colored works on paper).

Munich/Frankfurt/Stockholm 1992/93
Gabriele Münter, 1877–1962: Retrospektive, Munich, Städtische Galerie im Lenbachhaus, July 29–November 1, 1992; Frankfurt am Main, Schirn Kunsthalle, November 29, 1992–February 10, 1993; Stockholm, Liljevalchs Konsthall, April 4–May 31, 1993; presentation in Berlin, Staatliche Kunsthalle, July 3–August 22, 1993 (157 paintings, 41 drawings, 28 prints, 24 colored works on paper).

Munich 1994/95, Galerie Thomas
Gabriele Münter: Gemälde und Aquarelle, Munich, Galerie Thomas, November 22, 1994–January 28, 1995.

Murnau/Bonn 1996/97
Gabriele Münter malt Murnau: Gemälde 1908–1960 der Künstlerin des "Blauen Reiters," Murnau, Schloßmuseum Murnau, July 26–November 3, 1996; Bonn, Verein August Macke Haus, November 10, 1996–February 16, 1997 (43 paintings, 10 watercolors, 2 reverse-glass paintings, 1 woodcut, 1 drawing).

Munich 1996/97
Hinterglasbilder aus der Sammlung Gabriele Münter, Munich, Städtische Galerie im Lenbachhaus, November 26, 1996–June 8, 1997.

Milwaukee/Columbus/Richmond/San Antonio 1997–99
Gabriele Münter: The Years of Expressionism, 1903–1920, Milwaukee, WI, Milwaukee Art Museum, December 5, 1997–March 1, 1998; Columbus, OH, Columbus Museum of Art, April 18–June 21, 1998; Richmond, VA, Virginia Museum of Fine Arts, July 13–September 20, 1998; San Antonio, TX, Marion Koogler McNay Art Museum, November 3, 1998–January 3, 1999 (59 paintings, 16 prints, 7 drawings).

Bietigheim-Bissingen 1999
Gabriele Münter, Bietigheim-Bissingen, Städtische Galerie, July 3–September 19, 1999 (76 paintings, 24 prints, 20 drawings).

Munich 1999, Galerie Gunzenhauser
Kabinettausstellung "Gabriele Münter," Munich, Galerie Gunzenhauser, September 10–November 3, 1999 (9 paintings, 6 prints, 2 drawings, 1 exhibition poster).

Munich/Bonn/Murnau 2000/01
Gabriele Münter: Das druckgraphische Werk, Munich, Städtische Galerie im Lenbachhaus, December 16, 2000–April 16, 2001; Bonn, August Macke Haus, April 29–July 8, 2001; Murnau, Schloßmuseum Murnau, July 20–November 4, 2001 (88 prints).

Munich 2001, Galerie Thomas
Gabriele Münter: Gemälde, Munich, Galerie Thomas, October 11–December 31, 2001 (10 paintings, 1 work on paper).

Mannheim 2002
Gabriele Münter zum 125. Geburtstag: Das druckgraphische Werk, Mannheim, Städtische Kunsthalle Mannheim, July 13–September 22, 2002 (approx. 50 prints, 4 paintings).

Bordeaux 2004/05
Gabriele Münter, une artiste du Cavalier Bleu, Bordeaux, Musée des Beaux-Arts, October 25, 2004–January 23, 2005 (accompanying publication: Hoberg 2003, in French).

Munich 2004/05, Galerie Gunzenhauser
Gabriele Münter: Ölbilder, anläßlich des 40-jährigen Jubiläums der Galerie Gunzenhauser, Munich, Galerie Gunzenhauser, November 5, 2004–January 2005 (5 paintings, 5 works in oil on cardboard, 1 colored work on paper).

London 2005
Gabriele Münter: The Search for Expression 1906–1917, London, Courtauld Institute of Art Gallery, June 23–September 11, 2005 (21 paintings).

Munich 2006, Galerie Gunzenhauser
Gabriele Münter (1877–1962): Ausgewählte Arbeiten, Galerie Gunzenhauser, Munich, 2006.

Munich 2006/07
Gabriele Münter: Die Reise nach Amerika. Photographien 1899–1900, Munich, Städtische Galerie im Lenbachhaus, September 30, 2006–January 14, 2007 (130 photographs).

Munich 2006/07, Galerie Gunzenhauser
Gabriele Münter (1877–1962), Munich, Galerie Gunzenhauser, November 9, 2006–January 10, 2007 (5 paintings, 1 work on paper).

Munich 2007
Gabriele Münter: Die Jahre mit Kandinsky. Photographien 1902–1914, Munich, Städtische Galerie im Lenbachhaus, February 10–June 3, 2007 (225 photographs).

Bad Homburg 2007
Gabriele Münter – "Verwandlung der Wirklichkeit": Druckgraphiken aus der Sammlung des Lenbachhauses, München, Bad Homburg, Sinclair-Haus, November 30, 2007–February 10, 2008 (88 prints, 6 drawings, 4 paintings, 2 watercolors, 1 gouache).

Chemnitz 2008
Gabriele Münter: Gemälde, Hinterglasmalerei, Arbeiten auf Papier, Chemnitz, Kunstsammlungen Chemnitz, Museum Gunzenhauser, November 2, 2008–April 19, 2009 (42 prints, 11 paintings, 1 watercolor, 1 reverse-glass painting).

Würzburg 2009
Gabriele Münter: Zwischen Paris und Murnau. Druckgraphik aus dem Lenbachhaus München, Würzburg, Museum im Kulturspeicher, November 13, 2008–March 1, 2009 (89 prints, 6 drawings, 1 watercolor).

Murnau 2012
Gabriele Münter: Die Zeit nach Kandinsky in Murnau, Murnau, Schloßmuseum Murnau, July 26–November 4, 2012 (37 paintings, 15 drawings, 9 colored works on paper, 2 lithographs).

Hannover 2015/16
Kontur, Farbe, Licht: Das Wesentliche zeigen. Gabriele Münter 1877–1962, Hannover, Stiftung Ahlers Pro Arte / Kestner Pro Arte, September 11, 2015–January 10, 2016.

Berlin 2017
Gabriele Münter Preis 2017, Berlin, Akademie der Künste, March 14–April 17, 2017 (6 paintings, 2 works on paper, 9 photographs).

Murnau/Oberammergau 2017
Gabriele Münter und die Volkskunst: "Aber Glasbilder, scheint mir, lernten wir erst hier kennen," Murnau, Schloßmuseum Murnau; Oberammergau, Oberammergau Museum, July 27–November 12, 2017 (18 paintings, 18 prints, 10 reverse-glass paintings, 4 pen-and-ink drawings, 3 hand-painted objects, 1 watercolor).

Munich/Humlebæk/Cologne 2017–19
Gabriele Münter: Malen ohne Umschweife/ Gabriele Münter: Painting to the Point, Munich, Städtische Galerie im Lenbachhaus und Kunstbau München, October 31, 2017–April 8, 2018; Humlebæk, Louisiana Museum of Modern Art, May 3–August 19, 2018; Cologne, Museum Ludwig, September 15, 2018–January 13, 2019 (133 paintings, 38 photographs, 2 drawings, 7 colored works on paper, 11 prints, 6 objects of folk art, 1 piece of embroidery)

Munich 2017/18, Galerie Thomas
Gabriele Münter, Munich, Galerie Thomas, November 10, 2017–February 10, 2018 (23 paintings, 2 colored works on paper)

Murnau 2019–23
Zu Gast bei Gabriele Münter: Das Münter-Haus als Ort der Begegnungen, Murnau, Münter-Haus, September 2019–2023 (13 paintings, 9 photographs) (booklet)

Murnau 2021/22
Schneefarben: Winterbilder von Gabriele Münter, Murnau, Schloßmuseum Murnau, December 7, 2021–March 27, 2022 (10 paintings, 2 colored works on paper) (no catalogue)

Bern 2022
Gabriele Münter: Pionierin der Moderne, Bern, Zentrum Paul Klee, January 29–May 8, 2022 (85 paintings, 49 photographs, 7 drawings, 2 colored works on paper, 15 prints, 6 objects of folk art, 5 pieces of embroidery) (no catalogue)

Hamburg 2023
Gabriele Münter: Menschenbilder, Hamburg, Bucerius Kunst Forum, February 11–May 21, 2023

Selected Bibliography

Articles by the Artist Herself

Münter 1948
Gabriele Münter, "Gabriele Münter über sich selbst," in: *Das Kunstwerk*, 2/7 (1948), p. 25

Münter 1952a
Gabriele Münter, "Bekenntnisse und Erinnerungen," in: Hartlaub 1952, n.p.

Münter 1952b
Gabriele Münter, "Gabriele Münter: Mein Bild 'Mann im Sessel,'" in: *Die Kunst und das schöne Heim*, 51/2 (1952), p. 53

Monographs

Busch/Hanfstaengl et al. 1952
Der Malerin Gabriele Münter zum 75. Geburtstag, am 19. Februar 1952: 23 Stimmen zu ihrer Würdigung, birthday address by G. Busch, E. Hanfstaengl, W. Passarge, C. G. Heise, L. Grote, P. F. Schmidt, M. Unold, K. Hofer, and others. Bochum 1952

Hartlaub 1952
Gustav Friedrich Hartlaub, *Gabriele Münter: Menschenbilder in Zeichnungen*. With recollections from the artist. Berlin 1952

Eichner 1952
Johannes Eichner, "Ein Nachklang aus dem 'Blauen Reiter': Gabriele Münter," in: *Die Kunst und das schöne Heim*, special print, vol. 49 (1951), pp. 282–85

Eichner 1957
Johannes Eichner, *Kandinsky und Gabriele Münter: Von Ursprüngen moderner Kunst*. Munich 1957

Eichner 1957/58
Johannes Eichner, "Gabriele Münter, die Achtzigjährige," special print from the periodical *Westfalen*, 35/3 (1957/58), pp. 131–45

Röthel 1957
Hans Konrad Röthel, *Gabriele Münter*. Munich 1957

Helms 1967
Gabriele Münter: Das druckgraphische Werk, ed. Sabine Helms, collection catalogue, Städtische Galerie im Lenbachhaus München. Munich 1967

Lahnstein 1971
Peter Lahnstein, *Münter*. Ettal 1971

Pfeiffer-Belli 1979
Erich Pfeiffer-Belli, *Gabriele Münter: Zeichnungen und Aquarelle*, with a catalogue by Sabine Helms. Berlin 1979

Gollek 1981
Rosel Gollek, *Gabriele Münter: Hinterglasbilder*. Munich/Zurich 1981

Kleine 1990
Gisela Kleine, *Gabriele Münter und Wassily Kandinsky: Biographie eines Paares*. Frankfurt am Main 1990 (new editions 1991, 1992, 1993, 1994, 1998, 2008, 2009)

Windecker 1991
Sabine Windecker, *Gabriele Münter: Eine Künstlerin aus dem Kreis des "Blauen Reiter."* Berlin 1991

Hoberg 1994
Wassily Kandinsky and Gabriele Münter: Letters and Reminiscences, 1902–1914, ed. Annegret Hoberg, trans. Ian Robson. Munich et al. 1994 (new edition 2005)

Kleine 1997
Gisela Kleine, *Gabriele Münter und die Kinderwelt*. Frankfurt am Main/Leipzig 1997

Gockerell 2000
Nina Gockerell, *Hinterglasbilder, Schnitzereien und Holzspielzeug von Gabriele Münter gesammelt, kopiert und in ihren Werken dargestellt*. Munich et al. 2000

Hoberg 2003
Annegret Hoberg, *Gabriele Münter*. Munich et al. 2003

Hille 2012
Karoline Hille, *Gabriele Münter: Die Künstlerin mit der Zauberhand*. Cologne 2012

Schury 2012
Gudrun Schury, *Ich Weltkind: Gabriele Münter, Die Biographie*. Berlin 2012

Hoberg 2016
Annegret Hoberg, *Gabriele Münter*. Junge Kunst, vol. 22. Munich 2016

Hoberg 2017
Annegret Hoberg, *Gabriele Münter*. Wienands kleine Reihe der Künstlerbiografien. Cologne 2017

Brauchitsch 2017
Boris von Brauchitsch, *Gabriele Münter: Eine Biografie*. Berlin 2017

Group Exhibitions
(for solo exhibitions, see pp. 265–67)

Munich 1909/10, Neue Künstlervereinigung München
Neue Künstlervereinigung München e.V. [1. Ausstellung]. Turnus 1909–1910, Neue Künstlervereinigung München e.V. [Munich, Moderne Galerie Heinrich Thannhauser, December 1–15, 1909; subsequently: Brünn, Elberfeld, Barmen, Hamburg, Düsseldorf, Wiesbaden, Schwerin, Frankfurt am Main. Munich 1909

Munich 1910/11, Neue Künstlervereinigung München
Neue Künstlervereinigung München e.V. [2. Ausstellung]. Turnus 1910/11, Neue Künstlervereinigung München e.V. [Munich, Moderne Galerie Heinrich Thannhauser, September 1–14, 1910; subsequently: Karlsruhe, Mannheim, Hagen, Berlin, Leipzig, Dresden, Weimar]. Munich 1910

Odessa 1910/11, Salon Isdebsky
Салон 2. Международная Художесвенная Выставка. Устроитель В. А. Издебский [Salon of the 2nd International Art Exhibition. B. A. Isdebsky; Odessa, Salon Isdebsky, December 1910]. Odessa 1910

Moscow 1910/11, Bubnovy Valet
Каталог выставки "Бубновый Валет": Москва [catalogue accompanying the exhibition *Bubnovy Valet* (Jack of Diamonds), Moscow, Levisson Trading House, December 10, 1910–January 16, 1911 (November 27, 1910–January 3, 1911)]. Moscow 1910

Munich 1911, Der Blaue Reiter
Die erste Ausstellung der Redaktion Der Blaue Reiter. 1911–12, ed. Wassily Kandinsky and Franz Marc [Munich, Galerie Thannhauser, December 18, 1911–January 1, 1912]. Munich 1911

Moscow 1912, Bubnovy Valet
Каталог Выставки Картин Общества Художников "Бубновый Валет": Москва. 1912 год. [catalogue accompanying the exhibition of paintings by the artists' association "Bubnovy Valet" (Jack of Diamonds), Moscow, January 1912]. Moscow 1912

Munich 1912, Der Blaue Reiter
Die zweite Ausstellung der Redaktion Der Blaue Reiter. Schwarz-Weiss, Kunsthandlung Hans Goltz [Munich, Kunsthandlung Hans Goltz, February 12–March 18, 1912]. Munich 1912

Berlin 1912, Der Sturm
Der Sturm: Erste Ausstellung, Der Blaue Reiter; Franz Flaum; Oskar Kokoschka; Expressionisten, ed. Herwarth Walden [Berlin, Tiergartenstraße 34a, March 12–May 10, 1912]. Berlin 1912

Zurich 1912, Moderner Bund
Kunsthaus Zürich: Ausstellung, Zürcher Kunstgesellschaft [Zurich, Kunsthaus Zürich, July 7–31, 1912]. Zurich 1912

Munich 1912, Neue Kunst Hans Goltz
Neue Kunst Hans Goltz München Odeonsplatz: Erste Gesamt-Ausstellung [Munich, Neue Kunst Hans Goltz, October 1912]. Munich [1912]

Budapest 1913
Katalogus a Müvészaház nemzetközi postimpresszionista kiállításához (Catalogue of the International Post-Impressionist Exhibition at the Artists' House) [Budapest, Müvészház (Artists' House), May 1913]. Budapest 1913

Berlin 1913, Der Sturm
Erster Deutscher Herbstsalon: Berlin 1913, Der Sturm, ed. Herwarth Walden [Berlin, Potsdamerstraße 75, September 20–November 1, 1913]. Berlin 1913

Dresden 1914, Galerie Ernst Arnold
Expressionistische Ausstellung: Die neue Malerei, Galerie Ernst Arnold, foreword by Richard Reiche-Barmen [Dresden, Galerie Ernst Arnold, January 1914]. Dresden 1914

Leipzig 1914, Leipziger Sezession
Juryfreie Ausstellung Leipziger Sezession 1914: Offizieller Katalog, Leipziger Sezession [Leipzig, Leipziger Sezession, February–April 1914]. Leipzig 1914

Helsinki/Trondheim/Göteborg 1914, Der Sturm
Der Sturm: Der Blaue Reiter, ed. Herwarth Walden, foreword by Franz Marc [Helsinki, February–March 1914; Trondheim, April–May 1914; Göteborg, June–July 1914]. Berlin [1913]

The Hague 1916, Der Sturm
Der Sturm: Zweite Ausstellung, Den Haag/ Holland, Expressionisten, Kubisten, ed. Herwarth Walden [The Hague, Kunstzalen d'Audretsch, March 17–April 16, 1916]. Berlin 1916

Christiania (Oslo) 1916, Der Sturm
Der Sturm: Zweite Ausstellung, Christiania, Kandinsky, Gabriele Münter, ed. Herwarth Walden [Christiania, Permanent Kunstutstilling, C. W. Blomquist, 1916]. Berlin [1916]

Stockholm 1917
Föreningen Svenska Konstnärinnor, Vereinigung Bildende Künstlerinnen Österreichs, Liljevalchs Konsthall: Katalog No 5 [Stockholm, Liljevalchs Konsthall, January–February 1917]. Stockholm 1917

Berlin 1917, Der Sturm
Einblick in die Kunst: Expressionismus, Futurismus, Kubismus, ed. Herwarth Walden, publication accompanying the 50th Sturm exhibition [Berlin, Der Sturm, March 1917]. Berlin 1917

Helsingborg 1917
Föreningen Svenska Konstnärinnor och Vereinigung Bildende Künstlerinnen Österreichs, Katalog för Konst-Utställningen i Hälsingborg [Helsingborg, April–May 1917]. Helsingborg 1917

Stockholm 1917, Nya Konstgalleriet Ciacelli
Utställning av Georg Pauli och Gabriele Münter, Nya Konstgalleriet Ciacelli [Stockholm, Nya Konstgalleriet Ciacelli, May 3–14, 1917]. Stockholm 1917

Berlin 1917, Der Sturm
Der Sturm: Achtundfünfzigste Ausstellung, Gösta Adrian-Nilsson, Paul Klee, Gabriele Münter, Gemälde und Aquarelle, Zeichnungen, ed. Herwarth Walden [Berlin, Der Sturm, December 1917]. Berlin 1917

Munich 1924, Neue Secession
Münchener Neue Secession: X. Ausstellung, Münchener Neue Secession [Munich, Glaspalast, 1924]. Munich 1924

New York 1926/27
International Exhibition of Modern Art, assembled by the Société Anonyme, introduction by Katherine S. Dreier [New York, Brooklyn Museum, November 19, 1926–January 1, 1927]. New York 1926

Berlin 1927, Galerie Johannes Hinrichsen im Künstlerhaus
Ausstellung: Die schaffende Frau in der bildenden Kunst, Johannes Hinrichsen im Künstlerhaus [Berlin, Galerie Johannes Hinrichsen im Künstlerhaus, 1927]. Berlin 1927

Berlin 1927, Verein der Künstlerinnen zu Berlin
Verein der Künstlerinnen zu Berlin: Herbst-Ausstellung, Verein der Künstlerinnen zu Berlin [Berlin, November/December 1927]. Berlin 1927

Berlin 1928
Grosse Berliner Kunstausstellung 1928, Kartell der Vereinigten Verbände bildender Künstler Berlins e.V. [Berlin, Landesausstellungsgebäude, May 9–end of July, 1928]. Berlin 1928

Chicago 1931/32
The Arthur Jerome Eddy Collection of Modern Paintings and Sculpture, Art Institute of Chicago [Chicago, Art Institute of Chicago, December 22, 1931–January 17, 1932]. Chicago 1931

Munich 1936
Ausstellung: Die Strassen Adolf Hitlers in der Kunst 1936, Ausstellungsleitung München e. V. im Auftrage des Generalinspektors für das deutsche Strassenwesen [Munich, 1936]. Munich 1936

Weilheim 1942
Kunstausstellung des Weilheimer Kreistages der NSDAP, May 13–17, 1942

Munich 1949
Der Blaue Reiter: München und die Kunst des 20. Jahrhunderts, 1908–1914, Bayerische Staatsgemäldesammlungen and the Städtische Lenbach-Galerie, introduction by Ludwig Grote, ed. Leonie v. Wilckens [Munich, Haus der Kunst, September–October 1949]. Munich 1949

Basel 1950
Der Blaue Reiter 1908–14: Wegbereiter und Zeitgenossen, Kunsthalle Basel, introduction by Ludwig Grote [Basel, Kunsthalle Basel, spring 1950]. Basel 1950

Venice 1950
XXV Biennale di Venezia: Catalogo, "La Biennale di Venezia," foreword by Giovanni Ponti, Presidente della XXV Biennale [Venice, XXV Esposizione Biennale Internazionale d'Arte bandita dall'Ente Autonomo "La Biennale di Venezia," June 8–October 15, 1950]. Venice 1950

New York 1954, Curt Valentin Gallery
Der Blaue Reiter, Curt Valentin Gallery [New York, Curt Valentin Gallery, December 7, 1954–January 8, 1955]. New York 1954

Munich 1954/55, Moderne Galerie Otto Stangl
Kandinsky, Marc, Münter: Unbekannte Werke, Moderne Galerie Otto Stangl, introduction by Hans Konrad Röthel [Munich, Moderne Galerie Otto Stangl, October–November 1954; Essen, Folkwang Museum, January–February 1955; Bremen, Kunsthalle Bremen, May 15–June 12, 1955; Bern, Galerie Gutekunst und Klipstein]. Munich 1954

Cambridge, MA 1955
Artists of the Blaue Reiter: Exhibition of Painting and Graphic Works, Busch-Reisinger Museum, Harvard University [Cambridge, MA, Busch-Reisinger Museum, Harvard University, January 21–February 24, 1955]. Cambridge, MA 1955

Witten 1955
Gabriele Münter – Hans Brasch, Märkisches Museum Witten [Witten, Märkisches Museum, February 20–March 20, 1955]. Witten 1955

Kassel 1955
documenta: Kunst des XX. Jahrhunderts, Internationale Ausstellung im Museum Fridericianum in Kassel, ed. Arnold Bode, introduction by Werner Haftmann [Kassel, Museum Fridericianum, July 15–September 18, 1955]. Munich 1955

Düsseldorf 1956, Deutscher Künstlerbund
Deutscher Künstlerbund. 6. Ausstellung, Deutscher Künstlerbund [Düsseldorf, Ausstellungshallen, May 2–June 8, 1956]. Düsseldorf 1956

Munich/Herford 1957
Kandinsky, Gabriele-Münter-Stiftung und Gabriele Münter: Werke aus fünf Jahrzehnten, ed. Hans Konrad Röthel [Munich, Städtische Galerie im Lenbachhaus, February 19–March 31, 1957; Herford, Herforder Kunstverein, September 1957]. Munich 1957

Hamburg 1958/59
Wassily Kandinsky, Gabriele Münter: Gabriele-Münter-Stiftung, ed. Hans Konrad Röthel [Hamburg, Kunstverein, November 22, 1958–January 11, 1959]. Hamburg 1958

London 1960
The Blue Rider Group, Arts Council of Great Britain, ed. Hans Konrad Röthel [London, Tate Gallery, September 30–October 30, 1960]. London 1960

Munich 1960, Deutscher Künstlerbund
Deutscher Künstlerbund: Zehnte Ausstellung, mit Sonderausstellung "Das frühe Bild – Malerei und Plastik," Deutscher Künstlerbund [Munich, Haus der Kunst, October 18–December 11, 1960]. Munich 1960

Baden-Baden 1960
Alfred Lörcher, Gabriele Münter, Emy Roeder, Staatliche Kunsthalle Baden-Baden [Staatliche Kunsthalle Baden-Baden, December 4–31, 1960]. Baden-Baden 1960

Edinburgh 1960
The Blue Rider Group: An Exhibition Sponsored by the Edinburgh Festival Society and Arranged Jointly with the Royal Scottish Academy and the Arts Council of Great Britain, Royal Scottish Academy, texts by Hans Konrad Röthel [Edinburgh, Royal Scottish Academy, 1960]. Edinburgh 1960

Paris 1961, Club International Féminin
Club International Féminin: 6e exposition, Peintures, Sculptures, Tapisseries, Catalogue, Club International Féminin [Paris, Musée d'Art moderne de la Ville de Paris, April 12–30, 1961]. Paris 1961

Winterthur 1961
Der Blaue Reiter und sein Kreis: Ausstellung im Kunstmuseum Winterthur, Kunstmuseum Winterthur [Kunstmuseum Winterthur, April 23–June 11, 1961]. Winterthur 1961

Berlin 1961
Der Sturm: Herwarth Walden und die europäische Avantgarde Berlin, 1912–1932, Nationalgalerie, Berlin, West, foreword by Leopold Reidemeister [Berlin, Orangerie des Schlosses Charlottenburg, September 24–November 19, 1961]. Berlin 1961

Bergen/Stavanger/Trondheim/Oslo 1962
Ekspresjonisme: Tysk maleri fra 1900 til 1915, Expressionismus, Deutsche Malerei von 1900 bis 1915, Landesmuseum für Kunst und Kulturgeschichte Münster/Westfalen, ed. Carl Bäufer and Herbert Rickmann [Kunstforeningene Bergen; Stavanger; Trondheim; Oslo, 1962]. Münster 1962

New York 1963, Leonard Hutton Galleries
Exhibition "Der Blaue Reiter," Leonard Hutton Galleries, foreword by Will Grohmann [New York, Leonard Hutton Galleries, February 19–March 30, 1963]. New York 1963

Florence 1964
L'espressionismo: Pittura, scultura, architettura, ed. Marisa Volpi Orlandini and Giovanni Klaus König [Florence, Palazzo Strozzi, May–June 1964]. Florence 1964

Marseille 1965
Expressionnisme allemand: 1900–1920, ed. Marielle Latour and Simone Collin [Marseille, Musée Cantini, May 17–August 15, 1965]. Marseille 1965

Paris/Munich 1966
Le Fauvisme français et les débuts de l'Expressionnisme allemand / Der französische Fauvismus und der deutsche Frühexpressionismus, ed. Michel Hoog and Leopold Reidemeister [Paris, Musée national d'art moderne, January 15–March 6, 1966; Munich, Haus der Kunst, March 26–May 15, 1966]. Munich 1966

London 1966, Marlborough Fine Art Ltd.
Kandinsky and His Friends: Centenary Exhibition, Marlborough Fine Art Ltd. [London, Marlborough Fine Art Ltd., November–December 1966]. London 1966

New York 1968, Leonard Hutton Galleries
Fauves and Expressionists, Leonard Hutton Galleries [New York, Leonard Hutton Galleries, April 18–June 12, 1968]. New York 1968

Los Angeles 1968, Dalzell Hatfield Galleries
Creators and Masters of German Expressionist Art, Dalzell Hatfield Galleries and Artorama VIII [Los Angeles, Dalzell Hatfield Galleries, August 30–September 26, 1968]. Los Angeles [1968]

Tokyo 1971
Der deutsche Expressionismus, ed. Horst Keller [exhibition organized by the National Museum of Western Art, Tokyo, with support from the Foreign Office of the Federal Republic of Germany; Tokyo, Kokuritsu Seiyō Bijutsukan, January 15–March 14, 1971]. Tokyo 1971

Turin 1971
Il Cavaliere Azzurro: Der Blaue Reiter, ed. Luigi Carluccio and Luigi Mallé [Turin, Galleria Civica d'Arte Moderna, March 18–May 16, 1971]. Turin 1971

Vienna 1971
Der Blaue Reiter, Städtische Galerie im Lenbachhaus München, ed. Johannes Segieth, introduction by Erika Hanfstaengl [Vienna, special exhibition at the Städtische Galerie München on the occasion of the "München in Wien" weeks, Secession, October 8–24, 1971]. Munich 1971

New York 1972/73, Leonard Hutton Galleries
German Expressionist Paintings, Drawings, Watercolors, Sculpture, Leonard Hutton Galleries [New York, Leonard Hutton Galleries, November 1972–February 1973]. New York 1972

Pasadena 1974
German Expressionist Painting and Sculpture from California Collections, Norton Simon Museum [Pasadena, Museum of Modern Art, April 16–June 2, 1974]. Pasadena 1974

Villingen-Schwenningen 1975
Der Blaue Reiter und sein Kreis: Der Blaue Reiter und die Neue Künstlervereinigung München, Gemälde, Aquarelle, Zeichnungen, Graphik, 24. Kunstausstellung Villingen-Schwenningen, ed. Margarete Willmann [Stadtbezirk Schwenningen, Beethovenhaus, April 26–May 19, 1975]. Villingen-Schwenningen 1975

Belgrade 1976
Plavi Jahač: Der Blaue Reiter, ed. Wolf-Dieter Dube [Belgrade, Muzej savremene umetnosti, March 4–April 4, 1976]. Belgrade 1976

Los Angeles/Austin/Pittsburgh/New York 1976/77
Women Artists: 1550–1950, ed. Ann Sutherland Harris and Linda Nochlin [Los Angeles, Los Angeles County Museum of Art, December 21, 1976–March 13, 1977; Austin, University Art Museum, April 12–June 12, 1977; Pittsburgh, Museum of Art, July 14–September 4, 1977; New York, Brooklyn Museum, October 8–November 27, 1977]. New York 1976

New York 1977, Leonard Hutton Galleries
Der Blaue Reiter und sein Kreis, Leonard Hutton Galleries [New York, Leonard Hutton Galleries, March 18–May 1977]. New York 1977

Sapporo 1977
Münchner Malerei 1892–1914: Von der Sezession zum Blauen Reiter, ed. Liselotte Camp and Wolf-Dieter Dube [Sapporo, Hokkaidōritsu Kindai Bijutsukan, July 21–August 21, 1977]. Sapporo 1977

Chicago 1978
German and Austrian Expressionism: Art in a Turbulent Era, ed. Peter Selz [Chicago, Museum of Contemporary Art, March 10–April 30, 1978]. Chicago 1978

Paris 1978
Paris–Berlin, 1900–1933: Rapports et Contrastes France – Allemagne 1900–1933. Art, Architecture, Graphisme, Littérature, Objets industriels, Cinéma, Théâtre, Musique, ed. Marie-Laure Besnard-Bernadac and Günter Metken [Paris, Centre national d'art et de culture Georges Pompidou, July 12–November 6, 1978]. Paris 1979

New York 1980, Leonard Hutton Galleries
Jawlensky & Major German Expressionists, Leonard Hutton Galleries [New York, Leonard Hutton Galleries, opening: October 17, 1980]. New York 1980

Munich 1982
Kandinsky und München: Begegnungen und Wandlungen, 1896–1914, ed. Armin Zweite [Munich, Städtische Galerie im Lenbachhaus, January 22–March 21, 1982]. Munich 1982

New York 1982
Kandinsky in Munich: 1896–1914, ed. Peg Weiss [New York, The Solomon R. Guggenheim Museum, 1982]. New York 1982

Chicago 1983
Naive and Outsider Painting from Germany and Paintings by Gabriele Münter, ed. John Hallmark Neff, Mary Jane Jacob, and Carol Schreiber [Chicago, Museum of Contemporary Art, March 26–May 29, 1983]. Chicago 1983

Florence 1986
Capolavori dell'espressionismo tedesco: Dipinti, 1905–1920, ed. Erich Steingräber and Annegret Hoberg [Florence, Palazzo Medici Riccardi, September 20–November 30, 1986]. Milan 1986

Bern 1986/87
Der Blaue Reiter, ed. Hans Christoph von Tavel [Bern, Kunstmuseum Bern, November 21, 1986–February 15, 1987]. Bern 1986

Munich 1988, Galerie Gunzenhauser
Jawlensky, Münter, Kandinsky und der Blaue Reiter, Galerie Gunzenhauser [Munich, Galerie Gunzenhauser, April 12–May 31, 1988]. Munich 1988

Essen 1990, Galerie Neher
Gabriele Münter und ihre Zeit: Malerei der Klassischen Moderne in Deutschland, ed. Marion Agthe [Essen, Galerie Neher, November 10–December 18, 1990]. Essen 1990

Paris 1992/93
Figures du Moderne: L'Expressionnisme en Allemagne, 1905–1914: Dresde, Munich, Berlin, ed. Suzanne Pagé [Paris, Musée d'Art moderne de la Ville de Paris, November 18, 1992–March 14, 1993]. Paris 1992

Munich/Basel 1993, Galerie Thomas
Künstler des Blauen Reiter: Gemälde, Aquarelle, Zeichnungen, Graphiken, ed. Gabriele Karpf, Giannina Spargnapani, and Silke Thomas [Munich, Galerie Thomas, June 16–September 30, 1993; Basel, ART Basel 24'93, June 16–21, 1993]. Munich 1993

Touring Exhibition 1993, Sammlung Firmengruppe Ahlers
Expressionistische Bilder: Sammlung Firmengruppe Ahlers, Adolf Ahlers AG, ed. Jutta Hülsewig-Johnen [Berlin, Käthe-Kollwitz-Museum; Munich, Städtische Galerie im Lenbachhaus; Duisburg, Wilhelm-Lehmbruck-Museum; Frankfurt am Main, Schirn Kunsthalle; Emden, Kunsthalle in Emden, Stiftung Henri Nannen; Bielefeld, Kunsthalle Bielefeld]. Stuttgart 1993

Bietigheim-Bissingen 1994/95
Von Gabriele Münter bis Georg Baselitz: Die Geschichte des Linolschnitts, Beispiele aus der Sammlung der Städtischen Galerie Bietigheim-Bissingen, ed. Herbert Eichhorn [Bietigheim-Bissingen, Städtische Galerie, November 26, 1994–January 22, 1995]. Bietigheim-Bissingen 1994

Munich/Bern 1995
Jonathan Fineberg, *Mit dem Auge des Kindes: Kinderzeichnung und moderne Kunst*, ed. Helmut Friedel and Josef Helfenstein [Munich, Städtische Galerie im Lenbachhaus und Kunstbau München, May 31–August 20, 1995; Bern, Kunstmuseum Bern, September 7–November 26, 1995]. Ostfildern 1995

Dortmund 1996
Von der Brücke zum Blauen Reiter: Farbe, Form und Ausdruck in der deutschen Kunst von 1905 bis 1914, ed. Tayfun Belgin [Dortmund, Museum am Ostwall, September 15–December 15, 1996]. Heidelberg 1996

Sendai/Tokyo/Nagoya/Sapporo 1996/97
Wassily Kandinsky – Gabriele Münter: 1901–1917, Miyagi Museum of Art et al. [Sendai, Miyagi-ken-Bijutsukan, October 26–December 8, 1996; Tokyo, Sezon-Bijutsukan, December 14, 1996–February 2, 1997; Nagoya, Aichi-ken-Bijutsukan, February 8–March 16, 1997; Sapporo, Geijutsu-no-Mori-Bijutsukan, April 5–May 25, 1997]. Tokyo 1996

Hannover/Wuppertal 1996/97
Garten der Frauen: Wegbereiterinnen der Moderne in Deutschland, 1900–1914, ed. Ulrich Krempel and Susanne Meyer-Büser [Hannover, Sprengel Museum, November 17, 1996–February 9, 1997; Wuppertal, Von der Heydt-Museum, March 2–April 27, 1997]. Hannover 1996

Murnau 1998
Der Almanach "Der Blaue Reiter": Bilder und Bildwerke in Originalen, ed. Brigitte Salmen [Murnau, Schloßmuseum Murnau, 1998]. Murnau 1998

Berlin/Tübingen 1998/99
Der Blaue Reiter und seine Künstler, ed. Magdalena M. Moeller [Berlin, Brücke-Museum, October 3, 1998–January 3, 1999; Tübingen, Kunsthalle Tübingen, January 16–March 28, 1999]. Munich 1998

Munich 1999
Der Blaue Reiter und das Neue Bild: Von der "Neuen Künstlervereinigung München" zum "Blauen Reiter," ed. Annegret Hoberg and Helmut Friedel [Munich, Städtische Galerie im Lenbachhaus München, July 2–October 3, 1999]. Munich et al. 1999

Paris 1999/2000
Le fauvisme ou "l'epreuve du feu": Éruption de la modernité en Europe, ed. Suzanne Pagé and Juliette Laffon [Paris, Musée d'Art moderne de la Ville de Paris, October 29, 1999–February 27, 2000]. Paris 1999

Bremen 2000
Der Blaue Reiter, ed. Christine Hopfengart [Bremen, Kunsthalle Bremen, March 25–June 12, 2000]. Cologne 2000

Munich 2001
Mattis-Teutsch und Der Blaue Reiter, Haus der Kunst [Munich, Haus der Kunst, July 6–October 7, 2001]. Munich 2001

Bietigheim-Bissingen 2001
KinderBlicke: Kindheit und Moderne von Klee bis Boltanski, Kultur- und Sportamt der Stadt Bietigheim-Bissingen, Städtische Galerie, ed. Herbert Eichhorn and Isabell Schenk [Bietigheim-Bissingen, Städtische Galerie, July 7–September 16, 2001]. Ostfildern-Ruit 2001

Ibaraki 2002
Deutscher Expressionismus: Werke von 1905–1930, ed. Kunio Motoe [Ibaraki, Museum of Modern Art, 2002]. Tokyo 2002

Bielefeld 2003/04
Der Blaue Reiter: Avantgarde und Volkskunst, Sammlung Hertha Koenig, ed. Jutta Hülsewig-Johnen [Bielefeld, Kunsthalle Bielefeld, October 5, 2003–January 11, 2004]. Bielefeld 2003

Ludwigshafen 2003/04
Der Blaue Reiter: Die Befreiung der Farbe, ed. Richard W. Gassen [Ludwigshafen, Wilhelm-Hack-Museum, November 11, 2003–February 29, 2004]. Ostfildern-Ruit 2003

Saint-Tropez 2006
Le Cavalier Bleu: Der Blaue Reiter, ed. Jean-Paul Monery [Saint-Tropez, Musée de l'Annonciade, July 1–October 16, 2006]. Saint-Tropez 2006

Murnau 2006
Maler des "Blauen Reiter," Paul Klee, Deutsche Expressionisten: Eine Privatsammlung, ed. Brigitte Salmen [Murnau, Schloßmuseum Murnau, July 20–November 5, 2006]. Murnau 2006

Vienna 2006/07
Deutsche Expressionisten: Mit Meisterwerken aus der Sammlung Thyssen-Bornemisza, ed. Rudolf Leopold and Michael Fuhr [Vienna, Leopold Museum, September 28, 2006–January 10, 2007]. Vienna 2006

Murnau 2008
1908–2008, vor 100 Jahren: Kandinsky, Münter, Jawlensky, Werefkin in Murnau, ed. Brigitte Salmen [Murnau, Schloßmuseum Murnau, July 11–November 9, 2008]. Murnau 2008

Kochel am See 2009
Der Große Widerspruch: Franz Marc zwischen Delaunay und Rousseau, ed. Cathrin Klingsöhr-Leroy, Franz-Marc-Museumsgesellschaft [Kochel am See, Franz Marc Museum, June 21–September 13, 2009]. Berlin/Munich 2009

Paris 2009/10
Fauves et expressionnistes: De Van Dongen à Otto Dix, Chefs-d'œuvre du Musée Von der Heydt / Fauves and Expressionists: From Van Dongen to Otto Dix, Masterpieces from the Von der Heydt-Museum, Musée Marmottan, ed. Christine Poullain [Paris, Musée Marmottan, October 28, 2009–February 20, 2010]. Paris 2009

Murnau 2010/11
Gabriele Münter und Wassily Kandinsky: Perlenstickereien und Textilarbeiten, ed. Helmut Friedel, Gabriele Münter- und Johannes Eichner-Stiftung, Isabelle Jansen [Murnau, Münter-Haus, October 19, 2010–April 15, 2011]. Munich 2010

Wiesbaden 2010/11
The Spiritual in Art: From the Blue Rider to Abstract Expressionism, ed. Volker Rattemeyer [Wiesbaden, Museum Wiesbaden, October 31, 2010–February 27, 2011]. Wiesbaden 2010

Paris 2011/12
Expressionismus & Expressionismi: Der Blaue Reiter vs Brücke, Berlin-Munich, 1905–1920, ed. Marc Restellini [Paris, Pinacothèque de Paris, October 13, 2011–March 11, 2012]. Paris 2011

Murnau 2012/13
"Die blaue Reiterei stürmt voran": Bildquellen für den Almanach Der Blaue Reiter, Die Sammlung von Wassily Kandinsky und Gabriele Münter, ed. Helmut Friedel and Isabelle Jansen, Gabriele Münter- und Johannes Eichner-Stiftung [Murnau, Münter-Haus, May 10, 2012–December 1, 2013]. Munich 2013

Innsbruck 2014
Tirol – München: Begegnungen von 1880 bis heute, ed. Wolfgang Meighörner [Innsbruck, Tiroler Landesmuseum Ferdinandeum, April 11–August 24, 2014]. Innsbruck 2014

Munich 2014/15
Ab nach München! Künstlerinnen um 1900, ed. Antonia Voit [Munich, Münchner Stadtmuseum, September 12, 2014–February 8, 2015]. Munich 2014

Kochel am See 2015
Schöne Aussichten: Der Blaue Reiter und der Impressionismus, Franz-Marc-Museumsgesellschaft, Cathrin Klingsöhr-Leroy [Kochel am See, Franz Marc Museum, March 22–July 19, 2015]. Munich 2015

Frankfurt am Main 2015/16
Sturm-Frauen: Künstlerinnen der Avantgarde in Berlin, 1910–1932 / Women Artists of the Avant-Garde in Berlin, 1910–1932, ed. Ingrid Pfeiffer and Max Hollein [Frankfurt am Main, Schirn Kunsthalle, October 30, 2015–February 7, 2016]. Cologne 2015

Turin 2017
L'Emozione dei Colori nell'Arte, ed. Carolyn Christov-Bakargiev, Marcella Beccaria, and Elif Kamisli [Turin, Galleria Civica d'Arte Moderna e Contemporanea, GAM, March 14–July 23, 2017]. Milan 2017

Kochel am See 2018
Lektüre: Bilder vom Lesen – vom Lesen der Bilder, ed. Franz-Marc-Museumsgesellschaft by Cathrin Klingsöhr-Leroy [Kochel am See, Franz Marc Museum, June 17–September 23, 2018]. Munich 2018

Metz/London 2018/19
Couples modernes 1900–1950, ed. Emma Lavigne with Elia Biezunski and Cloé Pitiot, with the collaboration of Pauline Créteur [Metz, Centre Pompidou-Metz, April 28–August 20, 2018]. Paris 2018; *Modern Couples: Art, Intimacy and the Avant-Garde*, ed. Jane Alison and Coralie Malissard [London, Barbican Art Gallery, October 10, 2018–January 27, 2019]. Munich/London/New York 2018

New York/Paris 2018/19
Franz Marc and August Macke, 1909–1914, ed. Vivian Endicott Barnett [New York, Neue Galerie New York, October 4, 2018–January 21, 2019]. Munich/London/New York 2018; *Franz Marc, August Macke: L'aventure du Cavalier bleu*, ed. Musées d'Orsay et de l'Orangerie Paris [Paris, Musée de l'Orangerie, March 6–June 17, 2019]. Paris 2019

Munich 2018/19
Phantastisch! Alfred Kubin und der Blaue Reiter, ed. Annegret Hoberg and Matthias Mühling [Munich, Städtische Galerie im Lenbachhaus und Kunstbau München, October 9, 2018–February 17, 2019]. Cologne 2018

Halle (Saale) 2019
Die schaffende Galatea: Frauen sehen Frauen, ed. Matthias Rataiczyk [Halle (Saale), Kunsthalle "Talstrasse," July 13–October 13, 2019]. Halle (Saale) 2019

Berlin 2019
Straying from the Line, Berlin, Schinkel Pavillon e. V., April 13–July 28, 2019

Krefeld 2019/20
Folklore & Avantgarde: Die Rezeption volkstümlicher Traditionen im Zeitalter der Moderne, ed. Katia Baudin and Elina Knorpp [Krefeld, Kunstmuseen Krefeld, Kaiser Wilhelm Museum, November 10, 2019–February 23, 2020]. Munich 2020

Munich/Wiesbaden/Ascona 2019/20
Lebensmenschen – Alexej von Jawlensky und Marianne von Werefkin/Compagni di vita – Alexej Jawlensky e Marianne Werefkin, ed. Roman Zieglgänsberger, Annegret Hoberg, and Matthias Mühling [Munich, Städtische Galerie im Lenbachhaus und Kunstbau München, October 22, 2019–February 16, 2020; Wiesbaden, Museum Wiesbaden, Hessisches Landesmuseum für Kunst und Natur, March 13–July 12, 2020; Ascona, Museo Comunale d'Arte Moderna Ascona, August 2–November 8, 2020]. Munich 2019

Bonn 2020
Mit Stich und Faden: Expressionistische und zeitgenössische Kunst im Gegenüber, ed. Klara Drenker-Nagels and Ina Ewers-Schultz [Bonn, Museum August Macke Haus, March 6–November 1, 2020]. Bonn 2020

Würzburg/Zwickau/Bonn 2020/21
Italiensehnsucht! Auf den Spuren deutscher Künstlerinnen und Künstler 1905 bis 1933, ed. Martina Padberg, Klara Drenker-Nagels, Henrike Holsing, and Petra Lewey [Würzburg, Museum im Kulturspeicher Würzburg, November 14, 2020–March 7, 2021; Zwickau, Kunstsammlungen Zwickau Max-Pechstein-Museum, March 27–May 30, 2021; Bonn, Museum August Macke Haus, June 18–September 19, 2021]. Cologne 2020

Marseille/Metz 2020/21
Folklore: Artistes et folkloristes, une histoire croisée, ed. Jean-Marie Gallais and Marie-Charlotte Calafat [Metz, Centre Pompidou-Metz, March 21–October 4, 2020; Marseille, Musée des civilisations de l'Europe et de la Méditerranée, scheduled dates: November 4, 2020–February 22, 2021 – could not open due to the COVID-19 pandemic]. Paris/Marseille/Metz 2020

Munich 2020/21
Mehr Moderne für das Lenbachhaus: Die Neuerwerbungen in der Sammlung Blauer Reiter, Munich, Städtische Galerie im Lenbachhaus und Kunstbau München, October 13, 2020–February 7, 2021 (booklet)

Kochel am See 2021
Ich bin mein Stil: Künstlerbildnisse im Kreis von Brücke und Blauem Reiter, ed. Franz-Marc-Museumsgesellschaft by Cathrin Klingsöhr-Leroy [Kochel am See, Franz Marc Museum, June 20–October 3, 2021]. Munich 2021

Murnau 2021
Punkt, Linie, Fläche: Die Kinderzeichnung und der Expressionismus, ed. Sandra Uhrig [Murnau, Schloßmuseum Murnau, July 29–November 7, 2021]. Munich 2021

Munich 2021–24
Group Dynamics: The Blue Rider, ed. Matthias Mühling, Annegret Hoberg, and Anna Straetmans [Munich, Städtische Galerie im Lenbachhaus und Kunstbau München, March 23, 2021–February 2024]. Berlin 2021

Madrid/Marseille/Roubaix 2021/22
Alexéi von Jawlensky: El paisaje del rostro/Jawlensky: La promesse du visage, ed. Fundación MAPFRE [Madrid, Fundación MAPFRE, February 11–May 9, 2021; Marseille, Musée Cantini, June 11–September 26, 2021; Roubaix, La Piscine, Musée d'art et d'industrie André Diligent, November 6, 2021–February 6, 2022]. Madrid/Paris 2021

Wuppertal/Chemnitz/Bernried 2021/22
Brücke und Blauer Reiter, ed. Frédéric Bussmann, Roland Mönig, Daniel J. Schreiber [Wuppertal, Von der Heydt-Museum, November 21, 2021–February 27, 2022; Chemnitz, Kunstsammlungen Chemnitz, March 27–June 26, 2022; Bernried am Starnberger See, Buchheim Museum der Phantasie, July 16–November 13, 2022]. Cologne 2021

Munich 2020–22
Unter freiem Himmel: Unterwegs mit Wassily Kandinsky und Gabriele Münter, ed. Sarah Louisa Henn and Matthias Mühling [Munich, Städtische Galerie im Lenbachhaus und Kunstbau München, October 13, 2020–January 30, 2022]. Munich 2020

Dortmund 2022
Flowers! Blumen in der Kunst des 20. und 21. Jahrhunderts, ed. Regina Selter and Stefanie Weißhorn-Ponert [Dortmund, Museum Ostwall im Dortmunder U, April 30–September 25, 2022]. Munich 2022

Murnau 2022
"Und morgen nach Murnau!": Meisterwerke von Gabriele Münter und Wassily Kandinsky aus Privatsammlungen, ed. Schloßmuseum des Marktes Murnau [Murnau, Schloßmuseum Murnau, July 6–October 9, 2022]. Munich 2022

Munich 2022/23
Was von 100 Tagen übrig blieb... Die documenta und das Lenbachhaus, Munich, Städtische Galerie im Lenbachhaus und Kunstbau München, July 19, 2022–June 11, 2023

Essen 2022/23
Expressionisten am Folkwang: Entdeckt-Verfemt-Gefeiert, ed. Museum Folkwang [Essen, Museum Folkwang, August 20, 2022–January 8, 2023]. Essen 2022

Speyer 2022/23
Künstlerpaare der Moderne: Hans Purrmann und Mathilde Vollmoeller-Purrmann im Diskurs, Speyer, Museum Purrmann-Haus, September 25, 2022–March 26, 2023. Accompanying publication for the conference series, ed. Felix Billeter, Hans Purrmann Archiv München, and Maria Leitmeyer, Purrmann-Haus Speyer. Berlin 2021

Munich 2022/23
Kunst und Leben 1918 bis 1955, ed. Karin Althaus, Sarah Bock, Lisa Kern, Matthias Mühling, Melanie Wittchow – Städtische Galerie im Lenbachhaus und Kunstbau München [Munich, Städtische Galerie im Lenbachhaus und Kunstbau München, October 15, 2022–April 16, 2023]. Berlin 2022

Munich 2022/23
Etel Adnan, ed. Sébastien Delot with Matthias Mühling for the Lenbachhaus and with Susanne Gaensheimer for the Kunstsammlung Nordrhein-Westfalen [Munich, Städtische Galerie im Lenbachhaus und Kunstbau München, October 25, 2022–February 26, 2023; Düsseldorf, Kunstsammlung Nordrhein-Westfalen, April 1–July 16, 2023]. Munich 2022

London 2022/23
Making Modernism. Paula Modersohn-Becker, Käthe Kollwitz, Gabriele Münter and Marianne Werefkin, ed. Royal Academy of Arts [London, Royal Academy of Arts, November 12, 2022–February 12, 2023]. London 2022

Solo Exhibition Catalogues Cited in the Texts

Touring Exhibition 1949–52
Johannes Eichner, *Gabriele Münter: Werke aus 5 Jahrzehnten* [for locations and durations, see the list of solo exhibitions in the present catalogue, p. 264]. Braunschweig 1949

Touring Exhibition 1952–53
Johannes Eichner, *Gabriele Münter: Werke aus fünf Jahrzehnten* [for locations and durations, see the list of solo exhibitions in the present catalogue, p. 264]. Munich 1952

Los Angeles 1960, Dalzell Hatfield Galleries
Gabriele Münter: First American Exhibition with Seven Additional Major Paintings by Kandinsky, Dalzell Hatfield Galleries [Los Angeles, Dalzell Hatfield Galleries, June 20–July 30, 1960]. Los Angeles [1960]

Munich 1977
Gabriele Münter 1877–1962: Gemälde, Zeichnungen, Hinterglasbilder und Volkskunst aus ihrem Besitz, Städtische Galerie im Lenbachhaus, ed. Rosel Gollek [Munich, Städtische Galerie im Lenbachhaus, April 22–July 3, 1977]. Munich 1977

Cambridge/Princeton 1980/81
Gabriele Münter: Between Munich and Murnau, ed. Anne Mochon [Cambridge, MA, Busch-Reisinger-Museum, September 25–November 8, 1980; Princeton, NJ, Princeton University Art Museum, November 22, 1980–January 18, 1981]. Cambridge, MA 1980

Munich/Frankfurt/Stockholm 1992/93
Gabriele Münter 1877–1962: Retrospektive, ed. Annegret Hoberg and Helmut Friedel [Munich, Städtische Galerie im Lenbachhaus, July 29–November 1, 1992; Frankfurt am Main, Schirn Kunsthalle, November 29, 1992–February 10, 1993; Stockholm, Liljevalchs Konsthall, April 4–May 31, 1993; Station in Berlin, Staatliche Kunsthalle, July 3–August 22, 1993]. Munich et al. 1992

Milwaukee/Columbus/Richmond/San Antonio 1997–99
Gabriele Münter: The Years of Expressionism, 1903–1920, ed. Reinhold Heller [Milwaukee, Wisconsin, Milwaukee Art Museum, December 5, 1997–March 1, 1998; Columbus, Ohio, Columbus Museum of Art, April 18–June 21, 1998; Richmond, Virginia, Virginia Museum of Fine Arts, July 13–September 20, 1998; San Antonio, Texas, Marion Koogler McNay Art Museum, November 3, 1998–January 3, 1999]. Munich et al. 1997

Bietigheim-Bissingen 1999
Gabriele Münter, Städtische Galerie Bietigheim-Bissingen, ed. Herbert Eichhorn and Barbara Wörwag [Bietigheim-Bissingen, Städtische Galerie, July 3–September 19, 1999]. Ostfildern-Ruit 1999

Munich/Bonn/Murnau 2000/01
Gabriele Münter: Das druckgraphische Werk, ed. Helmut Friedel [Munich, Städtische Galerie im Lenbachhaus, December 16, 2000–April 16, 2001; Bonn, August Macke Haus, April 29–July 8, 2001; Murnau, Schloßmuseum Murnau, July 20–November 4, 2001]. Munich 2000

Munich 2006/07
Gabriele Münter: Die Reise nach Amerika, Photographien 1899–1900, ed. Helmut Friedel, Gabriele Münter- und Johannes Eichner-Stiftung [Munich, Städtische Galerie im Lenbachhaus, September 30, 2006–January 14, 2007]. Munich 2006

Munich 2007
Gabriele Münter: Die Jahre mit Kandinsky, Photographien 1902–1914, ed. Helmut Friedel, Gabriele Münter- und Johannes Eichner-Stiftung [Munich, Städtische Galerie im Lenbachhaus, February 10–June 3, 2007]. Munich 2007

Murnau 2012
Gabriele Münter: Die Zeit nach Kandinsky in Murnau, Schloßmuseum des Marktes Murnau, ed. Sandra Uhrig [Murnau, Schloßmuseum Murnau, July 26–November 4, 2012]. Murnau 2012

Further Cited Literature

Friedel/Hoberg 2000
Helmut Friedel and Annegret Hoberg, *The Blue Rider in the Lenbachhaus, Munich*. Munich et al. 2000

Kandinsky/Marc 1912
Wassily Kandinsky and Franz Marc (eds.), *Der Blaue Reiter*. Munich 1912

Kandinsky 2007
Wassily Kandinsky: Gesammelte Schriften, 1889–1916. Farbensprache, Kompositionslehre und andere unveröffentlichte Texte, ed. Helmut Friedel, with essays by Boris P. Chichlo, Barbara Mackert-Riedel, Jean-Claude Marcadé, Reinhard Richardi, Friedrich-Christian Schroeder, Felix Thürlemann, and Peter Vergo. Munich et al. 2007

Köllner 1984
Sigrid Köllner, *Der Blaue Reiter und die "Vergleichende Kunstgeschichte,"* diss. Universität Karlsruhe 1984

Lankheit 1974
The Blaue Reiter Almanac, ed. Wassily Kandinsky and Franz Marc, new documentary edition ed. and with introduction by Klaus Lankheit, trans. Henning Falkenstein with the assistance of Manug Terzian and Gertrude Hinderlie, The Documents of Twentieth-Century Art. New York 1974

Lankheit 1983
Wassily Kandinsky, Franz Marc: Briefwechsel, ed. and with introduction and commentary by Klaus Lankheit. Munich/Zurich 1983

Leeb 2013
Susanne Leeb, *Die Kunst der Anderen: "Weltkunst" und die anthropologische Konfiguration der Moderne*, diss. Europa-Universität Viadrina Frankfurt an der Oder 2006, published online in 2013 [URL: https://opus4.kobv.de/opus4-euv/frontdoor/index/index/docId/69] [URN: urn:nbn:de:kobv:521-opus-807] (revised book version: Berlin 2015)

Macke/Marc 1964
August Macke, Franz Marc: Briefwechsel, ed. Wolfgang Macke. Cologne 1964

Mühling/Jansen 2014
Matthias Mühling and Isabelle Jansen (eds.), *The Münter House in Murnau*. Munich 2014

Obler 2014
Bibiana K. Obler, *Intimate Collaborations: Kandinsky & Münter, Arp & Taeuber*. New Haven, CT, et al. 2014

Priebe 2010
Evelin Priebe, *Kandinsky und die Kunsterziehungsbewegung*. Göttingen 2010

Roditi 1960
Edouard Roditi, *Dialogues on Art*. London 1960

Wienand 2015
Kea Wienand, *Nach dem Primitivismus? Künstlerische Verhandlungen kultureller Differenz in der Bundesrepublik Deutschland, 1960–1990: Eine postkoloniale Relektüre*. Bielefeld 2015

Wörwag 1995
Barbara Wörwag, "Es ist eine unbewußte enorme Kraft im Kinde: Zur Bedeutung der Kinderzeichnung bei Wassily Kandinsky und Gabriele Münter," in: *Kinderzeichnung und die Kunst des 20. Jahrhunderts*, ed. Jonathan Fineberg. Ostfildern-Ruit 1995, p. 172

Wörwag 2001
Barbara Wörwag, "Wirklichkeit 'mit ungewohnten Augen' schauen. Die Künstler des Blauen Reiters und die Kinderzeichnung," in: exh. cat. *Kinder-Blicke: Kindheit und Moderne von Klee bis Boltanski*, Städtische Galerie Bietigheim-Bissingen. Ostfildern-Ruit 2001, p. 146

This catalogue was first published in conjunction with the exhibition
Gabriele Münter (1877–1962): Painting to the Point

An exhibition of the Gabriele Münter- und Johannes Eichner-Stiftung, Munich, and the Städtische Galerie im Lenbachhaus und Kunstbau München, in cooperation with the Louisiana Museum of Modern Art, Humlebæk, and the Museum Ludwig, Cologne.

Städtische Galerie im Lenbachhaus und Kunstbau München:
October 31, 2017 – April 8, 2018

Louisiana Museum of Modern Art, Humlebæk, Denmark:
May 3 – August 19, 2018

Museum Ludwig, Cologne:
September 15, 2018 – January 13, 2019

Editors
Isabelle Jansen
for the Gabriele Münter- und Johannes Eichner-Stiftung, Munich
Matthias Mühling
for the Städtische Galerie im Lenbachhaus und Kunstbau München
Concept for the Exhibition and Catalogue
Isabelle Jansen
Assistant
Marta Koscielniak
Texts
Isabelle Jansen
Editing
Isabelle Jansen and Marta Koscielniak
Additional Editing
Karin Althaus, Elisabeth Giers, Ursula Keltz: Städtische Galerie im Lenbachhaus und Kunstbau München. Marta Koscielniak: Gabriele Münter- und Johannes Eichner-Stiftung, Munich.
Front Cover:
Lady in an Armchair, Writing (Stenography: Swiss Woman in Pyjamas) [*Dame im Sessel, schreibend (Stenographie. Schweizerin in Pyjama)*], 1929, textile support, 61.5 × 46.2 cm, Gabriele Münter- und Johannes Eichner-Stiftung, Munich

2nd, revised and updated English edition 2023

Editors for the 2nd English edition:
Isabelle Jansen and Carmen Kühnert

A CIP catalogue record for this book is available from the British Library.

Luisenstraße 33
80333 Munich
www.muenter-stiftung.de

The Münter House in Murnau

Kottmüllerallee 6
82418 Murnau
Tel. + 49 88 41 62 88 80
Fax + 49 88 41 62 88 81

Opening hours:
daily except for Mondays, 2–5 p.m.
Visits outside the opening hours by arrangement
No parking in front of the Münter House
Hourly train connection between Munich and Murnau

Städtische Galerie im Lenbachhaus und Kunstbau München

Städtische Galerie im Lenbachhaus und Kunstbau München
Luisenstraße 33
80333 Munich
Tel. + 49 89 233 969-33
Fax + 49 89 233 320-03
www.lenbachhaus.de

Project Coordination, Prestel
Anja Besserer, with support from Laura Ilse
Copyediting
Rita Forbes, Germering; José Enrique Macián, Valencia (2nd edition)
Translation from the German
Bronwen Saunders, Basel ("Visual Delight," "Landscapes and Outdoor Scenes," "Portraits," "Interior Scenes," "Primitivism"); José Enrique Macián, Valencia (Preface to the New Edition); John Southard, Groß-Umstadt (all other texts)
Layout and Design
Hug & Eberlein, Leipzig-Basel
Typesetting
Vornehm Mediengestaltung, Munich
Production
Cilly Klotz
Origination
Reproline Mediateam, Munich
Printing and Binding
Alföldi AG, Debrecen
Typeface
Lyon Display
Theinhardt

Paper
135 g/m² Magno matt

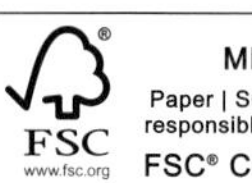

Penguin Random House Verlagsgruppe FSC® N001967

ISBN 978-3-7913-7984-5
(English edition)
ISBN 978-3-7913-7983-8
(German edition)

Printed in Hungary

Image Credits

(2nd edition)

Ascona, Hubertus Melsheimer, Ascona / photo: Börries Brakebusch, Düsseldorf, p. 201
Augsburg, Collectio Artium / photo: Simone Gänsheimer, Ernst Jank, Städtische Galerie im Lenbachhaus und Kunstbau München / © VG Bild-Kunst, Bonn 2023, p. 67 top and middle
Berlin, © Fotostudio Bartsch, Karen Bartsch, p. 91 bottom
bpk | Bayerische Staatsgemäldesammlungen, pp. 115, 117
bpk | CNAC-MNAM / Georges Meguerditchian, p. 155
bpk | CNAC-MNAM / Jean-Claude Planchet / © VG Bild-Kunst, Bonn 2023, p. 203
bpk | Kunstsammlung Nordrhein-Westfalen, Düsseldorf / Achim Kukulies, p. 119
bpk | Nationalgalerie, SMB / Jörg P. Anders, p. 188 bottom
bpk | RMN – Grand Palais / Gérard Blot / © VG Bild-Kunst, Bonn 2023, p. 201 bottom
bpk | Saarbrücken, Saarlandmuseum Saarbrücken, Stiftung Saarländischer Kulturbesitz / Tom Gundelwein; p. 140 top
Chemnitz, Kunstsammlungen Chemnitz – Museum Gunzenhauser / PUNCTUM/Bertram Kober, pp. 68, 76, 188
Cologne, Museum Ludwig © Rheinisches Bildarchiv Köln, rba_d048547, p. 104
Des Moines Art Center, Iowa (USA) / photo: Rich Sanders, Des Moines, Iowa, p. 105
Dortmund, photo: Jürgen Spiler, p. 235
Düsseldorf, Galerie Ludorff / photo: Achim Kukulies, p. 88
Frankfurt am Main, Sammlung Deutsche Bank / photo: Haydar Koyupinar, Munich, p. 65
Hannover, ahlers collection / photo: Thomas Ganzenmüller, Hannover, p. 143 top
Jerusalem, The Israel Museum / photo: David Harris, p. 121
Linz, LENTOS Kunstmuseum Linz / photo: Reinhard Haider, p. 86 top
Lörrach, Dreiländermuseum Lörrach, p. 111
Milwaukee, Milwaukee Art Museum / photo: Efraim Lev-er, © Artists Rights Society (ARS), New York / ADAGP, Paris, p. 80
Milwaukee, Milwaukee Art Museum / photo: P. Richard Eells, © Artists Rights Society (ARS), New York / VG Bild-Kunst, Bonn, p. 82
Munich, photo: Christian Mitko, p. 55 bottom
Munich, Gabriele Münter- und Johannes Eichner-Stiftung, pp. 9, 17, 18 middle, 20–45, 53 middle, 138, 140 bottom, 245, 247 bottom, 258–61 / photo: Gunther Adler, Ernst Jank, Städtische Galerie im Lenbachhaus und Kunstbau München, p. 147 middle / photo: Simone Gänsheimer, Ernst Jank, Städtische Galerie im Lenbachhaus und Kunstbau München, pp. 46–49, 58, 60–64, 67 bottom, 70, 74, 83, 84, 89, 91 top, 92–97, 101 top, 103 top and bottom, 108–10, 118, 124–27, 129–31, 133, 143 middle and bottom, 144, 145, 147 bottom, 148, 149, 150–53, 154 right, 156, 157–161, 164, 165, 167, 169–81, 187 bottom, 194–97, 203 top and middle, 205, 207–11, 215 top and middle, 217, 220–27, 231 middle and bottom, 232 top, 236–41, 249–51, 253
Munich, Karl & Faber Kunstauktionen GmbH, p. 87
Munich, Städtische Galerie im Lenbachhaus und Kunstbau München / photo: Simone Gänsheimer, Ernst Jank, pp. 18 top, 53 top, 66, 69, 75, 78, 85 bottom, 106, 120, 128, 147 top, 162, 163, 166, 190, 191, 193, 215 bottom, 231 top, 246 top, 247 top, 252
Murnau, Schloßmuseum, photo: Städtische Galerie im Lenbachhaus und Kunstbau München, p. 59; © Bildarchiv, Schloßmuseum Murnau, p. 185 bottom
New York, Neue Galerie New York / photo: Hulya Kolabas, pp. 81, 123
New York, © 2023. The Museum of Modern Art, New York/Scala, Florence, p. 206
Princeton, © 2023. Princeton University Art Museum/Art Resource NY/ Scala, Florence, pp. 107, 192
Ravensburg, Kunstmuseum Ravensburg / photo: Thomas Weiss, p. 187
San Francisco, San Francisco Museum of Modern Art / © Succession H. Matisse / VG Bild-Kunst, Bonn 2023 / photo: Ben Blackwell, p. 101 bottom
Vienna, Arnold Schönberg Center / © Belmont Music Publishers, p. 117 top
Washington, DC, National Museum of Women in the Arts / photo: Lee Stalsworth, p. 132

It has not always been possible to discover the owners of the rights to the images. Justified claims in this regard will of course be recompensed according to the usual agreements.